Law in History: Histories of Law and Society
Volume I

The International Library of Essays in Law and Legal Theory
Series Editor: Tom D. Campbell

Schools

Natural Law, Vols I & II *John Finnis*
Justice *Thomas Morawetz*
Law and Economics, Vols I & II *Jules Coleman and Jeffrey Lange*
Critical Legal Studies *James Boyle*
Marxian Legal Theory *Csaba Varga*
Legal Reasoning, Vols I & II *Aulis Aarnio and D. Neil MacCormick*
Legal Positivism *Mario Jori*
American Legal Theory *Robert Samuel Summers*
Postmodernism and Law *Dennis Patterson*
Law in History, Vols I & II *David Sugarman*
Law and Language *Fred Schauer*
Sociological Theories of Law *Kahei Rokumoto*
Rights *Carlos Nino*
Law and Psychology *Martin Lyon Levine*
Feminist Legal Theory, Vols I & II *Frances Olsen*
Law and Society *Roger Cotterrell*
Contemporary Criminological Theory *Francis T. Cullen and Velmer S. Burton Jr.*

Areas

Criminal Law *Thomas Morawetz*
Tort Law *Ernest J. Weinrib*
Contract Law, Vols I & II *Larry Alexander*
Anti-Discrimination Law *Christopher McCrudden*
Consumer Law *Iain Ramsay*
International Law *Martti Koskenniemi*
Property Law, Vols I & II *Elizabeth Mensch and Alan Freeman*
Constitutional Law *Mark V. Tushnet*
Procedure *D.J. Galligan*
Evidence and Proof *William Twining and Alex Stein*
Company Law *Sally Wheeler*
Privacy, Vols I & II *Raymond Wacks*
Lawyers' Ethics *David J. Luban*
Administrative Law *D.J. Galligan*
Child Law *Harry D. Krause*
Family Law, Vols I & II *Harry D. Krause*
Welfare Law *Peter Robson*
Medicine and the Law *Bernard M. Dickens*
Commercial Law *Ross Cranston*
Environmental Law *Michael C. Blumm*
Conflict of Laws *Richard Fentiman*
Law and Religion *Wojciech Sadurski*
Human Rights Law *Philip Alston*
European Community Law, Vols I & II *Francis Snyder*
Tax Law, Vols I & II *Patricia D. White*
Media Law *Eric Barendt*
Labour Law *David L. Gregory*
Alternative Dispute Resolution *Michael D.A. Freeman*

Legal Cultures

Comparative Legal Cultures *Csaba Varga*
Law and Anthropology *Peter Sack*
Hindu Law and Legal Theory *Ved Nanda*
Islamic Law and Legal Theory *Ian Edge*
Chinese Law and Legal Theory *Michael Palmer*
Russian Legal Theory *W. Butler*
Common Law *Michael Arnheim*
Japanese Law and Legal Theory *Koichiro Fujikura*
Law and Development *Anthony Carty*
Jewish Law and Legal Theory *Martin P. Golding*
Legal Education *Martin Lyon Levine*
Civil Law *Ralf Rogowski*
African Law and Legal Theory *Gordon Woodman and Akintunde Obilade*

Future Volume
Cumulative index

Law in History: Histories of Law and Society Volume I

Edited by

David Sugarman

Professor of Law,
University of Lancaster

NEW YORK UNIVERSITY PRESS
REFERENCE COLLECTION

First published in the USA in 1996 by
NEW YORK UNIVERSITY PRESS
Washington Square
New York NY 10003

Library of Congress Cataloging-in-Publication Data
Law in history / edited by David Sugarman.
p. cm. – (International library of essays in law and legal theory. Schools ; 17)
"New York University Press reference collection."
Includes bibliographical references.
Contents: v. 1. Between history and law — v. 2. Law and society.
ISBN 0-8147-8025-3 (set). — ISBN 0-8147-8032-6 (v. 1). — ISBN 0-8147-8033-4 (v. 2)
1. Law—Great Britain—History. 2. Law—United States—History. 3. Law—History. I. Sugarman, David. II. Series.
K160.L39 1996
340'.09–dc20 95-52778
CIP

For Leonie, Erica and Clare

Contents

PART III THE NEW HISTORY OF CRIMINAL JUSTICE

PART IV WRITING 'LAW AND SOCIETY' HISTORIES: NEW DIRECTIONS

Acknowledgements

The editor and publishers wish to thank the following for permission to use copyright material.

Blackwell Publishers for the essays: David Sugarman (1980), 'Review Essays: By M.J. Horowitz, The Transformation of American Law, 1780–1860', *British Journal of Law and Society*, **7**, pp. 297–310; Douglas Hay (1984), 'The Criminal Prosecution in England and its Historians', *Modern Law Review*, **47**, pp. 1–29; David Sugarman (1992), 'Review Article: Writing "Law and Society" Histories', *Modern Law Review*, **55**, pp. 292–308.

Frank Cass Publishers for the essay: Reiner Schulze (1992), 'European Legal History – A New Field of Research in Germany', *Journal of Legal History*, **13**, pp. 270–95. Reprinted by permission of Frank Cass Co. Ltd, London.

Peter Charles Hoffer (1993), 'Text, Translation, Context, Conversation: Preliminary Notes for Decoding the Deliberations of the Advisory Committee that Wrote the Federal Rules of Civil Procedure', *American Journal of Legal History*, **37**, pp. 409–39. Copyright © Peter Charles Hoffer.

Georgetown University Law Center for the essay: Robert W. Gordon (1994), 'Tribute: E.P. Thompson's Legacies', *Georgetown Law Journal*, **82**, pp. 2005–11.

Law and Society Association for the essays: Robert W. Gordon (1975), 'Introduction: J. Willard Hurst and the Common Law Tradition in American Legal Historiography', *Law and Society Review*, **10**, pp. 9–55; Aviam Soifer (1988), 'Beyond Mirrors: Lawrence Friedman's Moving Pictures', *Law and Society Review*, **22**, pp. 995–1016; Lawrence M. Friedman (1990), 'Opening the Time Capsule: A Progress Report on Studies of Courts Over Time', *Law and Society Review*, **24**, pp. 229–40.

Longman Group UK Ltd for the essay: P. Vinogradoff (1907), 'Frederic William Maitland', *English Historical Review*, April, pp. 280–89. Permission given by the Review Editor of the English Historical Review.

Manchester University Press for the essay: Joanna Innes and John Styles (1986), 'The Crime Wave: Recent Writing on Crime and Criminal Justice in Eighteenth-Century England', in Adrian Wilson (ed.), *Rethinking Social History: English Society 1570–1920 and its Interpretation*, pp. 201–65.

New York University Law Review for the essay: Peter Linebaugh (1985), '(Marxist) Social History and (Conservative) Legal History: A Reply to Professor Langbein', *New York University Law Review*, **60**, pp. 212–43.

Oxford University Press for the essay: John H. Langbein (1983), 'Albion's Fatal Flaws', *Past and Present*, **98**, pp. 96–120.

Barry Rose Law Periodicals for the essay: Steve Hedley (1989), '"Superior Knowledge or Revelation": An Approach to Modern Legal History', *Anglo-American Law Review*, **18**, pp. 177–200.

Routledge for the essays: L.R. Poos and Lloyd Bonfield (1986), 'Law and Individualism in Medieval England', *Social History*, **11**, pp. 287–301; Christopher Tomlins (1995), 'How Who Rides Whom. Recent "New" Histories of American Labour Law and What They May Signify', *Social History*, **20**, pp. 1–21.

Triangle Journals Ltd for the essay: Shani D'Cruze (1993), 'Approaching the History of Rape and Sexual Violence: Notes Towards Research', *Women's History Review*, **1**, pp. 377–96.

The University of Chicago Press for the essay: Donald R. Kelley (1983), 'Hermes, Clio, Themis: Historical Interpretation and Legal Hermeneutics', *Journal of Modern History*, **55**, pp. 350–68.

The University of Illinois Press for the essays: Robert W. Gordon (1988), 'Review Essay: An Exchange on Critical Legal Studies between Robert W. Gordon and William Nelson: Letter to William Nelson from Robert W. Gordon and Gordon's Response to Nelson', *Law and History Review*, **6**, pp. 139–56, 169–83. Copyright © 1988 by the Board of Trustees of the University of Illinois. Used with the permission of the author and of the University of Illinois Press. William Nelson (1988), 'William Nelson Replies to Robert Gordon and Nelson's Second Reply to Gordon', *Law and History Review*, **6**, pp. 157–68, 184–6. Copyright © 1988 by the Board of Trustees of the University of Illinois. Used with the permission of the author and of the University of Illinois Press. Saul Cornell (1994), 'Moving Beyond the Canon of Traditional Constitutional History: Anti-Federalists, the Bill of Rights, and the Promise of Post-Modern Historiography', *Law and History Review*, **12**, pp. 1–28. Copyright © 1994 by the Board of Trustees of the University of Illinois. Used with permission of the author and of the University of Illinois Press.

The Yale Law Journal Company and Fred B. Rothman & Company for the essays: S.F.C. Milsom (1975), 'An Old Play in Modern Dress', *Yale Law Journal*, **84**, pp. 1585–90; Daniel R. Ernst (1993), 'Review Essays: The Critical Tradition in the Writing of American Legal History', *Yale Law Journal*, **102**, pp. 1019–76.

Zeitschrift für Neuere Rechtsgeschichte for the essay: John H. Baker (1986), 'Two Decades of English Legal History', *Zeitschrift für Neuere Rechtsgeschichte*, **8**, pp. 43–53.

Every effort has been made to trace all the copyright holders but if any have been inadvertently overlooked, the publishers will be pleased to make the necessary arrangement at the first opportunity.

Series Preface

The International Library of Law and Legal Theory is designed to provide important research materials in an accessible form. Each volume contains essays of central theoretical importance in its subject area. The series as a whole makes available an extensive range of valuable material which will be of considerable interest to those involved in the research, teaching and study of law.

The series has been divided into three sections. The Schools section is intended to represent the main distinctive approaches and topics of special concern to groups of scholars. The Areas section takes in the main branches of law with an emphasis on essays which present analytical and theoretical insights of broad application. The section on Legal Cultures makes available the distinctive legal theories of different legal traditions and takes up topics of general comparative and developmental concern.

I have been delighted and impressed by the way in which the editors of the individual volumes have set about the difficult task of selecting, ordering and presenting essays from the immense quantity of academic legal writing published in journals throughout the world. Editors were asked to pick out those essays from law, philosophy and social science journals which they consider to be fundamental for the understanding of law, as seen from the perspective of a particular approach or sphere of legal interest. This is not an easy task and many difficult decisions have had to be made in order to ensure that a representative sample of the best journal essays available takes account of the scope of each topic or school.

I should like to express my thanks to all the volume editors for their willing participation and scholarly judgement. The interest and enthusiasm which the project has generated is well illustrated by the fact that an original projection of 12 volumes drawn up in 1989 has now become a list of some 60 volumes. I must also acknowledge the vision, persistence and constant cheerfulness of John Irwin and the marvellous work done by Mrs Margaret O'Reilly and Sonia Hubbard.

TOM D. CAMPBELL
Series Editor
The Faculty of Law
The Australian National University

Introduction:
Histories of Law and Society

As we approach the end of the millenium, the rule of law, the constitution and the role of law in society have once more assumed centre stage in the political life of many countries east and west of the former 'Iron Curtain'. At almost every turn – from the operation of democracy, government, the monarchy, the judiciary, constitutional politics, federalism, human rights and citizenship, to religion, the press and allied media, trade unions, political parties and transnational organizations – the legal order continues to be a central vehicle for shaping and reshaping the political and economic certainties of the post-war era. While some seek more legal regulation, others press for deregulation and privatization. As ever, the debate revolves around different interpretations of the role of law in society and its libertarian (or otherwise) past.

However, these contemporary resonances provide just one of the inspirations for the present collection. It is difficult to conceive of a historical subject with broader significance than that of law and society. For example, many of the core languages that helped to define national identity – the constitution, liberty, citizenship, property and justice – were grounded in and policed by the legal system.[1] The English common law provided a crucial framework for the development of the world's first industrial nation and the expansion of a vast empire whose colonies were signally shaped by their common law inheritance.[2] The importance of law within historical research is heightened because legal records are often the fullest and most extensive evidence available for reconstructing society in past times.[3]

Here then is a subject-matter sufficiently important to warrant a distinctive contribution to the *International Library of Essays in Law and Legal Theory*. What makes this contribution timely is that during the last three decades the writing of histories of law has changed significantly. The extent of this change is such as to entitle us to speak of a 'new legal history'.[4] This metamorphosis reflects and has sustained changes in the disciplines of law and history, as law and legal institutions have come to occupy a central position in history writing and as history has come to play a more important role in legal education and research.

II

This anthology brings together a wide range of insightful, representative and seminal essays to illuminate the history of law and society and some of the major contemporary approaches to the writing of those histories. In other words, it provides a map (albeit a partial one), enabling the reader to explore the inter-disciplinary twilight zone at the intersection of 'Law' and 'History'. The anthology illustrates some of the new and important sets of topics and questions, and the melting pot of influences, that increasingly characterize this contested territory. It brings together substantive and methodological work in order to convey a sense of the richness, the complexity, the tensions, the passions and the unfulfilled promise of this inter-disciplinary field of studies. With respect to those working on or interested in the history of law and society, I hope that the collection will enhance their appreciation of the choices in subject-matter and methodology that are at their disposal. I also hope that it will demonstrate the potential of the history of law and society to enrich more traditional legal history, the increasing sub-fields within the discipline of history as well as cognate areas such as law, socio-legal studies, law and economics and sociology.

My brief was to select articles which were of 'theoretical interest' and 'predominantly within the Anglo-American tradition'. Given the breadth of this field of studies and the explosion of work during the last 30 years, selecting the contents of this 'rough guide' has involved hard choices. Restrictions of space have inevitably precluded the inclusion of some important work. The guidelines for this series have also limited the scope of the collection. The anthology is restricted to material in English-language journals. Extracts from articles, books and chapters of books are also excluded (although I have managed to include one revised article now published in a book).

I have opted for a relatively catholic coverage of different nations, rather than a deeper treatment of England and the United States, although I am aware that chauvinism would have been an alternative resolution of the dilemma posed by an embarrassment of riches. Several chapters enable the reader to investigate how the law touched the lives of assorted segments of society: ruling elites, middling sorts, plebeian masses and 'outsiders' such as women, homosexuals and 'colonials'. I have been particularly concerned to include diverse points of view and salient contributions that are not easily available or widely known.[5]

Each volume in this two-volume set is organized under several broad sub-headings which address major debates, approaches and topics. Volume I is arranged in the following sections:

- law and society histories of pre-industrial England;
- theory and politics in American legal history;
- the new history of criminal justice; and
- new directions in the writing of 'law and society' histories.

Volume II is framed thus:

- law, history and the construction of national identity;
- lawyers, courts and the cultural significance of legal institutions;
- law and popular culture;
- gender and the law; and
- law and society.

The 47 essays that comprise this anthology were originally published between 1909 and 1995. Because the last three decades have witnessed a major resurgence of interest in history writing on law and society the majority of papers chosen were published in the 1980s and 1990s. As regards the geographical and chronological sweep of the collection, three chapters focus on medieval England; many concern Europe *circa* 1600–1800; and a significant number relate to Britain and her Empire, Canada, the United States and Continental

Europe since 1800. Several were chosen in part because they cast received periodization to the wind.

As befits a collection devoted to historical perspectives on law and society, the topics explored are diverse, stimulating and occasionally exotic: from pig keeping and custom in New York to the peculiarities of the German state; from wife beating, women's independence and male sexuality to the epistemic absurdities of the common law; from the impact of the British empire on the emergence of policing to lawyers and early modern culture; from the negotiation of subjectivity in Ontario defamation trials to the 'moral economy' of the English crowd. In contrast with the traditional concentration on constitutional history and central (national) courts, this collection seeks to redress the balance by illuminating the manifold dimensions of criminal and civil law, legislation, custom, Roman law, Church law, the legal profession, the culture and rituals of the courtroom, and the nature of legal thought. Under this wider optic, law was (amongst other things) a practical knowledge and an arcane 'science', a facilitator of private lawmaking, a source of coercion, a legitimator of violence, and a constitutor of meaning, identity and personhood.

As regards issues of theory and method, the rich menu on offer includes an assessment of leading figures such as Maitland, Macfarlane, Hurst, Thompson, Friedman, Langbein, Horwitz and Hay. It also comprises historiographical reviews of the new history of criminal justice, studies of courts over time, new histories of American labour law, the history of rape and sexual violence, law and political thought in early modern Europe, the supposed 'insularity' of the common law, and the overlapping worlds of lawyers, business and politics. The collection demonstrates the diversity of perspectives at work in this field – contextualist, critical, Foucauldian,[6] gender-centred and post-modern – as well as other approaches to writing law and society histories. This heterogeneity, and the 'epistemological hypochondria' that has accompanied it, can be seen as either a blessing or a curse. Inevitably, perhaps, some of these new intellectual resources are controversial, with opinion within the historical fraternity remaining deeply divided as to their utility. The anthology demonstrates that, while the new approaches have enriched the traditional concerns of historians by enlarging the frontiers of historical explanation, they have by no means displaced those concerns.

In the remainder of this Introduction, I shall briefly indicate the larger context of the selected essays and make reference to important works not included in the anthology.

III

The history of law and society is a hybrid enterprise, situated on the borderlines of law, history and the human sciences. It is at once a sub-field of the disciplines of law and history, and a discrete and foreign territory. Its ambiguous postion on the margins of law and history illuminates the indeterminate nature of the boundaries separating law from history.

Law and history have always been closely intertwined. History grew out of law, and the development of legal and historical argument and proof were intimately connected.[7] Both worked in tandem (alongside religion) to construct and reconstruct the 'imagined community' of national identity[8] and both were leading players in the construction and transmission of the 'meta-narratives' of evolution, liberty and progress.[9]

Moreover, the common law and history share similar epistemologies. Both are hybrid forms of knowledge, connecting past and present, myth and memory. They involve the interpretation of evidence from an earlier era in the light of present concerns and sensibilities. In practice, they tend to be empirical, fact-centred, particularistic and pragmatic rather than abstract systems of thought. Both privilege description and experience. From this perspective, history and law are 'found' rather than 'made'. Both embrace an uneasy mixture of explanatory, descriptive, political and normative concerns, and may range into realms such as philosophy, medicine, etc.

History and law straddle a contradictory field of discourses. A tendency to recognize the complex interplay between history and law, the linguistic character of knowledge, the narrative, rhetorical and interpretative dimensions of their practices, the complex interdependence between content (the story) and form (how it's told) have coexisted with an indifference to these matters and a conscious and (more often) unconscious attempt to suppress them. A tendency towards universalism (notably, the ideas of continuity and the continuous progress of the human race) has been yoked to a commitment to particularism (history and law as singular, particular, discontinuous, different; as something to be understood in its own terms and in context). A highly rationalistic and positivistic conception of law and history has coexisted alongside one which treated them as the customary practices observed for some time by a particular caste (lawyers, historians etc.).

The legal community have employed history in diverse ways that are crucial to their common identity, work, status and power. The quest for previous decisions binding on the court (precedent) and the process of legislative and constitutional interpretation have been shaped by particular conceptions of history, custom and tradition.[10] Indeed, it is a commonplace that judges, lawyers and jurists have frequently had a confused or simply wrong understanding of the past. The pseudo-historical tradition of the common law is famously exemplified by the opinions of Sir Edward Coke.[11] Similarly, it has recently been demonstrated that the notion that the governance and property regimes of pre-Crusade Europe were 'feudal' is a myth invented by lawyers from the 12th century onwards.[12] Yet courts of law are in a unique position. They are the only institutions that have '... the power to *declare* history: that is, to articulate some understanding of the past and then compel the rest of society to conform its behaviour to that understanding ...'.[13]

While history and law were interdependent and close cousins, they were also rivals and adversaries. Thus Coke asserted that the common law was 'existent outside history and beyond memory as the intimate knowledge of a chosen profession'.[14] The on-going battle to ensure that historians and lawyers had something to keep to themselves can only be understood in relation to the jurisdictional warfare that each waged against the other and with those other competitors who sought to control their work. For example, the first generation of full-time university teachers of history and law in late 19th century England were concerned to create a distinctive professional identity. They thus selectively invoked the conventions of their respective communities, of liberalism and of science, as a way of seeking to control what was permitted to count as 'legal' and 'historical' scholarship.[15]

IV

The history of law and society has a long and distinguished pedigree. Broadly speaking, during the last 200 years or so, the dominant form of writing law and society histories has concerned the manner and the extent to which specific legal rules and institutions reflected or influenced particular types of society (such as feudalism, capitalism, the welfare state) or the relative power of particular interest groups (such as the landed elite, the middle classes, entrepreneurs, trade unions and workers).

During the Enlightenment the most exciting strain of legal science was a body of work which built upon and extended the jurisprudence of legal humanists such as Bodin, and the natural law's comparative 'laws of nations' orientation. This stressed that law was the product of time and historical development, and that it should be studied comparatively and, therefore, sociologically. The leading lights of this movement included Scotland's Kames, Smith, Robertson and Millar; England's Gibbon; the German historical school of Hugo and Savigny; and its most influential practitioner, France's Montesquieu.[16] In this way the study of law and its history became a principal way of studying society. For example, Montesquieu stressed the contingency of the law, the diverse causes that fashion distinctive nation states, the need for culturally specific approaches to the study of law, and the material and cultural forces that delimit all law makers. He also recognized the distinctive character of 'commercial society'. It was Montesquieu's Scottish and French disciples, notably Kames and Smith, Hume, and Tocqueville, who further developed a historical sociology of law and society, as did other subsequent writers in the late 19th and early 20th century, most notably, perhaps, Max Weber.

Weber's sociology of law is the most thorough and historically informed analysis of the role of law in economy and society. Capitalism, argued Weber, required not only changes in production and technology, but also a calculable (i.e. predictable) legal system. Formally rational law (i.e. legalism) was the most calculable type of law and therefore best suited to the needs of capitalism. Irrational law and substantively rational law were incapable of satisfying capitalism's need for '... the legal system to operate like a technically rationale machine'. Weber argued that the factors which made Europe uniquely conducive to capitalism were its highly formalistic and rationalistic forms of law and state.[17]

Juxtaposed alongside this tradition is that of 'lawyers' legal history', with its dominant focus on the evolution of legal doctrine. From this perspective, the primary job of legal history was to trace the rise of the fundamental principles and concepts of the common law: where did they come from and how did they grow? It was therefore primarily concerned with origins, and also with the law developed by the higher courts. The emergence of law and legal institutions was explained largely by reference to legal arguments, institutions and procedures.[18] While the formal analysis of law is undoubtedly important, it has tended to be overly preoccupied with the coherence and abstraction of the law devoting relatively little attention to the world of practice. The relationship between law and socioeconomic change, the larger political and cultural significance of law and lawyers and the transmission and diffusion of the common law to far-off continents, affecting countless millions, were often neglected or marginalized. Nonetheless, it has provided an indispensable source for understanding the internal world of the law and therefore the crucial role that law and legal institutions might play in the history of society.

The last three decades have witnessed a remarkable renaissance of the history of law, legal institutions and the relationship between law and society. While remaining distinct fields of inquiry, a degree of convergence has taken place. More and more historians are recognizing that the history of law in society is too important to be left to lawyers. The traditional boundaries separating legal histories from other varieties of history (social, political, intellectual, economic, cultural, gender, business, etc.) have been challenged by a 'new legal history'. Increasingly, law is treated not as some dry, functionally dependent variable or superstructure, separate from and marginal to 'society' and 'economy', but as one of the major constitutors of society and economy. From this perspective, law, society and economy were (and are) inextricably mixed. As E.P. Thompson emphasized, law was not confined to one field or level, but was almost everywhere. It defined property rights and productive relations, it constituted identities (families, women, men, children, masters, servants, employers, employees, corporations, companies, the public, the private, criminals, aliens, community, personhood, etc., etc.); it was an important element in philosophy and a major political language in its own right; and it was also an arena for struggle within which alternative notions of law were fought out.[19]

This burgeoning interest in the history of law and society has been a cosmopolitan and inter-disciplinary labour, involving many lawyers, historians and legal sociologists working and publishing in several countries. Several leading figures in the history of the social, the cultural, the political and gender relations – such as John Burrow, Stephan Collini, Natalie Zeman Davis, Donald Kelley, Alan Macfarlane, J.G.A. Pocock, Barbara Shapiro, Lawrence Stone, E.P. Thompson and Martin Wiener – have recently published major studies illustrative of this 'legal turn' within the discipline of history.[20] In law schools, too, the quantity and range of work being undertaken on law in history have never been greater.

In the last two decades, some of the work in this field has paralleled a larger tendency within the human sciences, namely, the so-called 'cultural turn' and 'linguistic turn'; that is, the shift from treating ideas and conduct as largely the reflection or manifestation of particular forms of society or interest groups to regarding them as cultural and discursive systems, connected in complex ways to other cultural and discursive systems (e.g., religion, political economy, ideologies, academic 'disciplines', popular constitutionalism). For some time now, a central issue in the human sciences has been the social construction of reality; that is, the idea that the most basic ways in which people conceive of the world, the most elementary categories that people use to organize their everyday life and understand reality – the public and the private, the market, the family, the individual – are manufactured by people through language, at a particular place and time. Thus, increasing attention is paid to how a specific social reality is constructed, how people conceive of that socially constructed reality, and how they interpret it to others.[21] Whilst these developments are concerned with behaviour and social structure, they lavish most attention on the creation and diffusion of meaning, symbols and language. From this perspective, then, social life is conceived as the construction, interpretation and negotiation of systems of meaning. The 'natural order of things' is not natural or given after all, but culturally and linguistically constructed. Furthermore, the social constructs and discourses of everyday life are necessarily value-laden. This is because they privilege some aspects of life or social interests over others, and therefore always give rise to questions of power and domination.[22]

Several of the papers in this anthology explain the context within which this new work, its significant antecedents and its diverse methodologies have emerged, and examine the controversies that it has engendered.[23] Although the bulk of the new legal history has concerned the history of crime and punishment, path breaking work has also emerged on the legal profession and on legal theory and doctrine (notably in the much neglected areas of private law, Church law and gender),[24] litigation, and legislation. Increasingly, work in this field attends to the role of law in the construction of meaning as well as an instrumentality of economic and political change. It explores the ways in which law and legal institutions are both culturally constituted and culturally constitutive. These new histories of the culture and languages of law, and their larger cultural and political significance, share the methodologies and concerns of many scholars in history, the law and society movement, feminist legal studies and critical legal studies.[25]

As historians of diverse specialisms and orientations have begun to take law and lawyers seriously, they have revitalized their old histories of interests, ideologies and organizations with new histories of law in society that are attentive to the coercive, instrumental, cultural and linguistic role of law in the construction, reconstruction and deconstruction of nations, subjects, political identities and traditions. It is, for instance, no longer possible simply to read the history of crime, punishment and policing as the reflection of the forward marching interests of various social classes. It is not just that historians have acknowledged the large use made of the criminal law by working-class prosecutors as well as the force of working-class toryism and middle-class radicalism, but that they now recognize that the languages and institutions of the law were themselves elastic, protean and multi-vocal, capable of being used in many contradictory ways.

The extent to which the penal sanctions of the law and the panoply of powers and facilities created by the law (contracts, wills, marriage, trusts, business arrangements, etc.) were shared equally across society remains a central concern. But it is increasingly recognized that, in several major domains, the law and its facilities were resorted to by a larger cross-section of society than has often been assumed, and that the law could be empowering as well as brutalizing. Thus, the history of law and society has become an important site within which historians and social theorists rethink the nature of power, identity and agency through attention to the language, forms and practices of the law. It has also played an important role in the assault on Whiggish chronologies and notions of historical change and the recovery of alternative conceptions of ordering and organization.

V

While the present anthology is testimony to the achievements of law and society histories and the larger possibilities that they hold, more might be done to fulfil its broader potential. Firstly, and in response to the restricted topics and agenda of much earlier history writing, the new history of law and society has been characterized by the multiplication of new fields of inquiry and sub-disciplines which have been reinforced by specialist seminars, conferences and journals. While this broader agenda has created space for subjects previously neglected and marginalized – topics that were 'hidden from history' –[26] it has had the unintended effect of reinforcing the compartmentalization and division of labour within the human sciences. Rather than contributing towards an integrated history of law and society, we have produced an ever-expanding list of subject areas. While many of these topics overlap in practice, there is relatively little effort devoted to the task of exploring their interconnections.[27] One underlying cause of this Balkanization is that the writing of law and society histories has tended to be conditioned by legal definitions of the phenomena that it has investigated: private law, public law, contract law, constitutional law, criminal law, etc. Perhaps the increasing fragmentation of the field will be mitigated if more historians follow the lead of legal anthropologists who have 'moved from a focus on dispute-processing [and other distinctively 'legal' phenomena] to an attempt to understand situations where legal forms and legal understandings are called into existence'.[28]

Secondly, much law and society history has ignored the state without which it is difficult to make sense of the relative stability of power in society. The fact that state-centred notions of power are unsatisfactory does not mean that the state and its interpenetration of and by legal institutions and other aspects of 'civil society' should be neglected. Thirdly, there is a tendency not directly to confront change over time, especially in the medium term and *longue durée*, let alone the more general issues raised by temporality, narrative and history.[29] Fourthly, some of the new legal history challenges long-standing, artificial notions of periodization and, therefore, simplistic models of 'medieval', 'pre-industrial', 'early modern' and 'modern' society. It is hoped that this work will gather impetus, and that the constraints imposed through arbitrary pigeonholing by period can be mitigated.[30]

Finally, much of the field remains parochial in its failure to connect the local to the national and international. Insular legal systems were not isolated systems; interaction was abundant, shaping and preserving legal identities at home and abroad. Given our increasing historical knowledge of international communities, colonialism, empire-building and globalization, we need to explore the changing form, content and role of law and legal institutions within the complex interface between the nation state and its international context and concerns.[31]

VI

In conclusion, the field of law and society histories echoes many of the strengths, weaknesses and uncertainties of the new domains within history, feminist legal studies, the law and society movement and critical legal studies. In its current form it is young and in a state of flux. It has only begun to change some of the accepted questions of the disciplines of law and history, making this collection very much an interim statement, a report on work in progress.

The new histories of law and society have played an important role in demonstrating the intersection between law, power and meaning and the fact that they can be understood only in relation to each other. 'If there is dissonance as well as counterpoint (and sometimes harmony) in the composition, it must be hoped that such a result is inseparable from the nature of the subject.'[32]

Notes

1 See, for example, Burns, J.H., and with the assistance of Mark Goldie, ed., *The Cambridge History of Political Thought 1450–1700*, (Cambridge: Cambridge University Press, 1991); Hont, Istvan, and Michael Ignatieff, eds, *Wealth and Virtue: The Shaping of Political Economy in the Scottish Enlightenment*, (Cambridge: Cambridge University Press, 1981); Pagden, Anthony, ed., *The Languages of Political Theory in Early Modern Europe*, (Cambridge: Cambridge University Press, 1987); Lacey, Michael J., and Knud Haakonssen, ed., *A Culture of Rights: The Bill of Rights in Philosophy, Politics and Law – 1791 and 1991*, (Cambridge: Cambridge University Press, 1991); Winch, Donald, *Riches and Poverty: An Intellectual History of Political Economy*

in Britain, 1750–1834, (Cambridge: Cambridge University Press, 1996); Kammen, Michael, *A Machine That Would Go Itself: The Constitution in American Culture*, (New York: Alfred A. Knopf, Inc., 1986).

2 See, for example, Pocock, J.G.A., ed., *The Varieties of British Political Thought, 1500–1800*, (Cambridge, Cambridge University Press, 1993); Cain, P.J. and A.G. Hopkins, *British Imperialism*, 2 vols, (London: Longman, 1993); Howell, P.A., *The Judicial Committee of the Privy Council 1833–1876*, (Cambridge: Cambridge University Press, 1979); McLaren, John P.S., 'The Burdens of Empire and the Legalization of White Supremacy in Canada, 1860–1910', *Legal History in the Making: Proceedings of the Ninth British Legal History Conference, Glasgow 1989*, ed. W.M. Gordon, and T.D. Fergus. (London: Hambledon Press, 1991) 187; Mendelsohn, Oliver, 'The Pathology of the Indian Legal System', *Modern Asian Studies* **15** (1981): 823; Washbrook, D.A., 'Law, State and Agrarian Society in Colonial India', *Modern Asian Studies* **15** (1981): 649; Palmer, S.H., *Police and Protest in England and Ireland, 1780–1850*, (Cambridge: Cambridge University Press, 1988); Fitzpatrick, Peter, *The Mythology of Modern Law*, (London: Routledge, 1992); Knafla, Louis A., and Susan W.S. Binnie, eds, *Law, Society and the State: Essays in Modern Legal History*, (Toronto: University of Toronto Press, 1995).

3 Maitland, Sir F. Pollock and F.W., *The History of English Law: Before the Time of Edward I*, 2nd edn, (Cambridge: Cambridge University Press, 1898); Macfarlane, Alan, Sarah Harrison and Charles Jardine, *Reconstructing Historical Communities*, (Cambridge: Cambridge University Press, 1977); Ladurie, Le Roy, *Montaillou*, (Harmondsworth: Penguin Books, 1975); Ginzburg, Carlo, *The Cheese and the Worms: the Cosmos of a Sixteenth-Century Miller*, (London: Routledge, 1980); Stone, L., *Road to Divorce in England 1530–1987*, (Oxford: Oxford University Press, 1990) pp. 27–44 (on the advantages and limitations of court records).

4 On the 'new legal history' see, the following articles in this anthology: Baker, 'Two Decades of English Legal History'; Gordon, 'Tribute: E.P. Thompson's Legacies' and 'Introduction: J. Willard Hurst and the Common Law Tradition in American Legal Historiography'; Soifer, 'Beyond Mirrors'; Sugarman, 'Review Essays: By Horwitz', 'Simple Images and Complex Realities', and 'Writing "Law and Society" Histories'; Ernst, 'The Critical Tradition in the Writing of American Legal History'; Innes and Styles, 'The Crime Wave'; Schulze, 'European Legal History'; Friedman, 'Opening the Time Capsule'; and Tomlins, 'How Who Rides Whom'.

See, further, Friedman, Lawrence M., 'Some Problems and Possibilities of American Legal History', *The State of American History*, ed. Herbert J. Bass. (Chicago: Quadrangle Books, 1970); Friedman, Lawrence M., and Harry N. Scheiber, eds, *American Law and the Constitutional Order*, (Cambridge: Harvard University Press, 1978); Gordon, Robert W., 'Critical Legal Histories', *Stanford Law Review* **366** (1984): 57; Hoeflich, M.H., 'A Renaissance in Legal History?', *University of Illinois Law Review* (1984): 507; Holt, Wythe, 'Now and Then: The Uncertain State of Nineteenth-Century American Legal History', *Indiana Law Review* **7** (1974): 615; Hunt, Alan, 'The New Legal History: Prospects and Perspectives', *Contemporary Crises* **10** (1986): 201; Hurst, James Willard, 'Legal Elements in United States History', *Law in American History*, ed. Donald Fleming, and Bernard Bailyn. (Boston: Little, Brown and Co., 1971): 3; Knafla, Louis A., and Susan W.S. Binnie, 'Beyond the State: Law and Legal Pluralism in the Making of Modern Societies', *Law, Society and the State: Essays in Modern Legal History*, ed. Louis A. Knafla, and Susan W.S. Binnie. (Toronto: University of Toronto Press, 1995): 3; Momigliano, A.D., 'The Consequences of New Trends in the History of Ancient Law', *Rivista Storica Italiana* **LXXVI** (1964): 133; Sugarman, D., 'Theory and Practice in Law and History: A Prologue to the Study of the Relationship between Law and Economy from a Socio-Historical Perspective', *Law, State and Society*, ed. B. Fryer *et al.*, (London: Croom Helm, 1981): 70; Sugarman, D. and G.R. Rubin, 'Towards A New History of Law and Material Society in England, 1750–1914, *Law, Economy and Society: Essays in the History of English Law, 1750–1914*, ed. G.R. Rubin, and David Sugarman. (Abingdon: Professional Books, 1984): 1; Wright, Barry, 'An Introduction to Canadian Law in History', *Canadian Perspectives on Law and Society: Issues in Legal History*, ed. W. Wesley Pue, and Barry Wright. (Ottawa: Carleton University Press, 1988): 7; Steinmetz, Willibald, 'Law, Crime and Society in England 1750–1950', *German Historical Institute London Bulletin* **XVI** (1) (1994): 3;

5 I have, for example, tended to exclude those articles that have been published elsewhere in the *International Library of Essays in Law and Legal Theory*. Fisher III, William W., 'Making Sense of Madison: Nedelsky on Private Property', *Law and Social Inquiry* **18** (1993): 547.

6 See, Certeau, Michel de, *The Writing of History*, (New York: 1988); Garland, David, *Punishment and Welfare: A History of Penal Strategies*, (Aldershot: Gower, 1985); Poster, Mark, *Foucault, Marxism and History*, (Cambridge: Polity Press, 1984); McGowen, Randall, 'Power and Humanity, or Foucault Among the Historians', *Reassessing Foucault: Power, Medicine and the Body*, ed. Colin Jones, and Roy Porter. (London: Routledge, 1994) 91; Rose, Nikolas, *Governing the Soul: The Shaping of the Private Self*, (London: 1990); Goodrich, Peter, *Languages of Law*, (London: Weidenfeld, 1990); Goodrich, Peter, *Oedipus Lex: Psychoanalysis, History, Law*, (Berkeley: University of California Press, 1995); Norrie, Alan, *Crime, Reason and History: A Critical Introduction to Criminal Law*, (London: Weidenfeld & Nicholson, 1993).

See, also, the articles by Murphy, Farmer and Goodrich in this collection.

7 See Kelley, 'Hermes, Clio, Themis' and Murphy, 'The Oldest Social Science?' in this anthology.

See, further, Berman, Harold, *Law and Revolution: The Formation of the Western Legal Tradition*, (Cambridge, Mass: Harvard University Press, 1983); Kelley, Donald R., *Foundations of Modern Historical Scholarship: Language, Law and History in the French Renaissance*, (New York: Columbia University Press, 1970) and *The Human Measure*, (Cambridge: Harvard University Press, 1993); Shapiro, B.J., *Probability and Certainty in 17th Century England: A Study of the Relationships Between Natural Science, Religion, History, Law and Litigation*, (Princeton: Princeton University Press, 1983) and *Beyond Reasonable Doubt and Probable Cause: Historical Perspectives on the Anglo-American Law of Evidence*, (Berkeley: University of California Press, 1991); Iggers, Georg G., *The German Conception of History*, (Middletown, CT.: Wesleyan University Press, 1968); Cousins, Mark, 'The Practice of Historical Investigation', *Poststructuralism and the Question of History*, ed. D. Attridge, and *et al.* (Cambridge: Cambridge University Press, 1987); Nerhot, Patrick, *Law, Writing, Meaning: An Essay in Legal Hermeneutics*, (Edinburgh: Edinburgh University Press, 1992) chap. 15.

8 Anderson, B., *Imagined Communities*, (London, Verso, 1983).

9 Burrow, J.W., *Evolution and Society: A Study of Victorian Social Theory*, (Cambridge: Cambridge University Press, 1966) and *A Liberal Descent: Victorian Historians and the English Past*, (Cambridge: Cambridge University Press, 1981); Blaas, P.B.M., Continuity and Anachronism: Parliamentary and Constitutional Development in *Whig Historiography and in the Anti-Whig Reaction between 1890 and 1930*, (The Hague: Martinus Nijhoff, 1978); Collini, Stefan, Donald Winch, and John Burrow, *That Nobel Science of Politics: A Study in Nineteenth-Century Intellectual History*, (Cambridge: Cambridge University Press, 1983); Collini, Stefan, *Public Moralists: Political Thought and Intellectual Life in Britain, 1850–1930*, (Oxford: Clarendon Press, 1991); Novick, Peter, *That Nobel Dream: The 'Objectivity Question' and the American Historical Profession*, (Cambridge: Cambridge University Press, 1988); Ross, Dorothy, *The Origins of American Social Science*, (Cambridge: Cambridge University Press, 1991); Bann, Stephen, *The Inventions of History: Essays on the Representation of the Past*, (Manchester: Manchester University Press, 1990); Soffer, Reba, *Discipline and Power: The University and the Making of an English Elite, 1870–1930*, (Sanford: Sanford University Press, 1994); Vernon, James, 'Narrating the Constitution: The Discourses of "The Real" and the Fantasies of Constitutional History', *Re: Reading the Constitution*, ed. James Vernon (Cambridge: Cambridge University Press, in press).

10 Gordon, R.W., 'Historicism in Legal Scholarship', *Yale Law Journal* **90** (1981): 1017; Finkelman, Paul, 'The Constitution and the Intentions of the Framers: The Limits of Historical Analysis', *University of Pittsburgh Law Review* **50** (1989): 349; Siegel, Stephen, 'Historicism in Late Nineteenth-Century Constitutional Thought', *Wisconsin Law Review* (1990): 1431; Kammen, Michael, 'A Machine That Would Go Itself' in this anthology.

11 Hill, C., *Intellectual Origins of the English Revolution*, (Oxford: Clarendon Press, 1980).

12 Reynolds, Susan, *Fiefs and Vassals: The Medieval Evidence Reinterpreted*, (Oxford: Oxford University Press, 1994).

13 Wiecek, William M., 'Clio As Hostage: The United States Supreme Court and the Uses of History', *California Western Law Review* **24** (1988): 227, 227–278.

14 See, further, Goodrich, Peter, *Languages of Law*, (London: Weidenfeld, 1990) pp. 84–86.

15 Sugarman, David, 'The Legal Boundaries of Liberty: Dicey, Liberalism and Legal Science', *Modern Law Review* **46** (1983): 102 and 'Legal Theory, the Common Law Mind and the Making of the Textbook Tradition', *Legal Theory and Common Law*, ed. William Twining. (Oxford: Blackwell, 1986): 26; Collini, Stefan, *Public Moralists*. Cf. Whitman, James Q., *The Legacy of Roman Law in the German Romantic Era: Historical Vision and Legal Change*, (Princeton: Princeton University Press, 1990).

16 This paragraph draws upon Sugarman, David, 'Law', *The Blackwell Companion to the Enlightenment*, ed. John W. Yolton *et al.* (Oxford: Blackwell, 1991) 275.

See, further, Higham, J. *et al.*, (ed.), *History*, (Princeton: Princeton University Press, 1965); Stein, Peter, *Legal Evolution, the Story of an Idea*, (Cambridge: Cambridge University Press, 1980); Starobinski, Jean, *Montesquieu*, (Paris: Seuil, 1987); Burrow, J.W., *Whigs and Liberals: Continuity and Change in English Political Thought*, (Oxford: Clarendon Press, 1988); Hont and Ignatieff eds, *Wealth and Virtue*.

17 But Weber qualified his assertion of the causal importance of 'rational law' in several respects. In particular, his study of the history of English law and society convinced him that English law did not meet this criterion of formally rational law. Instead, he contrasted the logical formalism of Continental law with the relatively irrational (what he termed 'empirical') legal system in England.

See, generally, Rheinstein, M., ed., *Max Weber on Law in Economy and Society*, (Cambridge: Harvard University Press, 1954); Trubek, David, 'Max Weber on Law and the Rise of Capitalism', *Wisconsin Law Review* (1972): 720; Kronman, A.T., *Max Weber*, (London: Edward Arnold, 1983); Sugarman, David, *In the Spirit of Weber: Law, Modernity and 'the Peculiarities of the English'*, Institute for Legal Studies, Madison, Wisconsin, Working Papers Series 2:9 (Madison: Institute for Legal Studies, Wisconsin University, 1987); van Caenegem, R.C., *Legal History: A European Perspective*, (London: The Hambledon Press, 1991) pp. 201–222; Whimster, Sam, and Scott Lash, eds, *Max Weber, Rationality and Modernity*, (London: Allen & Unwin, 1987).

18 See, Gordon, 'Introduction: J. Willard Hurst and the Common Law Tradition in American Legal Historiography' in this anthology. See also, Boorstin, Daniel J., 'Tradition and Method in Legal History', *Harvard Law Review* **54** (1951): 421; Horwitz, Morton J., 'The Conservative Tradition in the Writing of American Legal History', *American Journal of Legal History* **17** (1973): 275.

19 Thompson, E.P. *Whigs and Hunters: The Origins of Black Act*, (London: Allen Lane, 1975 reprinted with a new postscript, Harmondsworth, Penguin, 1977), 'The Grid of Inheritance: A Comment, Family and Inheritance: Rural Society in Western Europe 1200–1800', ed. Jack Goody, Joan Thirsk, and E.P. Thompson. (Cambridge: Cambridge University Press, 1976): 328, *The Poverty of Theory and Other Essays*, (London: Merlin, 1978), and *Customs in Common*, (London: Merlin Press, 1991).

See, generally, Gordon, 'Tribute: E.P. Thompson's Legacies' and Sugarman, 'Writing "Law and Society" Histories' in this collection. See, also, Kaye, Harvey J., and Keith McClelland, eds, *E.P. Thompson: Critical Perspectives*, (Cambridge: Polity Press, 1990).

20 Burrow, *A Liberal Descent*, and *Whigs and Liberals*; Collini, Stefan, Donald Winch, and John Burrow, *That Nobel Science of Politics*; Collini, Stefan, *Public Moralists*; Davis, Natalie Zemon, *Fiction in the Archives: Pardon Tales and Their Tellers in Sixteenth-Century France*, (Stanford: Stanford University Press, 1987); Kelley, Donald R., *The Human Measure*; MacFarlane, A., *The Origins of English Individualism*, (Oxford: Blackwell, 1978) and *The Justice and the Mare's Ale: Law and Disorder in Seventeenth-Century England*, (Oxford: Basil Blackwell, 1981); Pocock, J.G., *The Ancient Constitution and the Feudal Law. Reissue with Retrospect*, (Cambridge: Cambridge University Press, 1987), *Virtue, Commerce and History: Essays on Political Thought and History, Chiefly in the Eighteenth Century*, (Cambridge: Cambridge University Press, 1985), and Pocock, J.G.A., ed., *The Varieties of British Political Thought, 1500–1800*, (Cambridge: Cambridge University Press, 1993); Shapiro, B.J., *Probability and Certainty in 17th Century England* and *Beyond Reasonable Doubt and Probable Cause*; Stone, Lawrence, *Uncertain Unions: Marriages in England 1660–1753*, (Oxford: Oxford University Press, 1992), *Road to Divorce in England 1530–1987 and Broken Lives*, (Oxford: Oxford University Press, 1993); Thompson, E.P., *Whigs and Hunters*, 'The Grid of Inheritance: A Comment', 'The Poverty of Theory' and *Customs in*

Common; Wiener, M.J., *Reconstructing the Criminal: Culture, Law and Policy in England, 1830–1914*, (Cambridge: Cambridge University Press, 1990).

Beyond Anglo-American history writing see, for example, Ladurie, Le Roy, Montaillou, and Ginzburg, Carlo, *The Cheese and the Worms*.

21 One manifestation of this trend is an increasing interest in the visual dimensions of law. See, for example, Brownlee, David B., *The Law Courts: The Architecture of George Edmund Street*, (New York: The Architectural Foundation, 1984); Curtis, D., and J. Resnick, 'Images of Justice', *Yale Law Journal* (1986): 1727; Dickinson, H.T., *Caricatures and the Constitution*, (Cambridge: Chadwick-Healey, 1986); Evans, R., *The Fabrication of Virtue: English Prison Architecture 1750–1840*, (Cambridge: Cambridge University Press, 1982); Manchester, A.H., 'An Introduction to the Iconographical Studies of Legal History: England and Wales', *Legal History in the Making*, ed. W.M. Gordon, and T.D. Fergus (London: The Hambledon Press, 1991): 85; Watkin, T.G., 'Tabula Picta: Images and Icons', *Studia et Documenta et Iuris* **50** (1984): 383; Sharpe, J.A., *Crime and the Law in English Satirical Prints 1600–1832*, (Cambridge: Chadwyck Healey, 1986); Goodrich, Peter, *Languages of Law*; Ribner, Jonathan P., *Broken Tablets: The Cult of the Law in French Art from David to Delacroix*, (Berkeley: University of California Press, 1993); Taylor, Katherine Fischer, *In the Theatre of Criminal Justice: the Palais de Justice in Second Empire France*, (Princeton: Princeton University Press, 1993); Bender, John, *Imagining the Penitentiary: Fiction and the Architecture of Mind in Eighteenth-Century England*, (Chicago: Chicago University Press, 1987); Jacob, Robert, *Images de la Justice: Essai sur l'iconographie du Moyen Age à l'age classique*, (Paris: Leopard d'Or, 1994).

22 See Skinner, Quentin, 'Introduction: the Return of Grand Theory', *The Return of Grand Theory in the Human Sciences*, ed. Quentin Skinner. (Cambridge: Cambridge University Press, 1985): 1; Marcus, George E., and Michael J. Fisher, *Anthropology as Cultural Critique: An Experimental Movement in the Human Sciences*, (Chicago: University of Chicago Press, 1986); Appleby, Joyce, Lynn Hunt and Margaret Jacob, *Telling the Truth About History*, (New York: Norton & Company, 1994); Chartier, Roger, 'Intellectual History or Sociocultural History? The French Trajectories', *Modern European Intellectual History: Reappraisals and New Perspectives*, ed. Dominick LaCapra, and Steven Kaplan, (Ithaca: Cornell University Press, 1983): 13; Hunt, Lynn, *Politics, Culture, and Class in the French Revolution*, (Berkeley: University of California Press, 1984); Clifford, James and George E. Marcus, eds, *Writing Culture: The Poetics and Politics of Ethnography*, (Berkeley: University of California Press, 1986); Chartier, Roger, *Cultural History*, (Cambridge: Polity Press, 1988); Hunt, Lynn, ed., *The New Cultural History*, (Berkeley: University of California Press, 1989); Veeser, H. Aram, ed., *The New Historicism*, (New York: Routledge, 1989); Chartier, Roger, *The Cultural Origins of the French Revolution*, (Durham: Duke University Press, 1991); Burke, Peter, ed., *New Perspectives on Historical Writing*, (Cambridge: Polity Press, 1991); Corfield, Penelope J., ed., *Language, History and Class*, (Oxford: Blackwell, 1991); Porter, Roy, 'Introduction', *Language, Self and Society: A Social History of Language*, ed. Peter Burke, and Roy Porter, (Cambridge: Polity Press, 1991): 1; Wilson, Adrian, ed., *Rethinking Social History: English Society 1570–1920 and its Interpretation*, (Manchester: Manchester University Press, 1993); Pocock, J.G.A., *Politics, Language and Time: Essays on Political Thought and History*, (London: Methuen, 1972); Higham, John and Paul K. Conkin, eds, *New Directions in American Intellectual History*, (Baltimore: Johns Hopkins University Press, 1979); Pocock, J.G.A., *Virtue, Commerce and History: Essays on Political Thought and History, Chiefly in the Eighteenth Century*, (Cambridge: Cambridge University Press, 1985) see 'Introduction: The State of the Art', pp. 1–36; LaCapra, Dominick, ed., *Rethinking Intellectual History: Texts, Contexts, Language*, (Ithaca: Cornell University Press, 1983); LaCapre, Dominick and Steven Kaplan, eds, *Modern European Intellectual History: Reappraisals and New Perspectives*, (Ithaca: Cornell University Press, 1983) (the essays by Martin Jay and Keith Michael Baker in this collection are especially recommended for their lucid treatment of the 'linguistic turn' as it applies and might be applied to intellectual history); Kelley, D., 'Horizons of Intellectual History', *Journal of the History of Ideas* **48** (1987): 143; Tulley, James, ed., *Meaning and Context: Quentin Skinner and His Critics*, (Cambridge: Polity Press, 1988); Kelley, D., 'What is Happening to the History of Ideas?', *Journal of the History of Ideas* **51** (1990): 3; Jenkins, Keith, *Re-thinking History*, (London: Routledge,

1991); Jenkins, Keith, *On What is History? From Carr and Elton to Rorty and White*, (London: Routledge, 1995); Attridge, Derek, Geoff Bennington and Robert Young, ed., *Post-Structuralism and the Question of History*, (Cambridge: Cambridge University Press, 1987); Derrida, Jacques, 'Force of Law: the Mystical Foundation of Authority', *Cardozo Law Review* **11** (1990): 921; Patterson, Thomas C., 'Post-structuralism, Post-modernism: Implications for Historians', *Social History* **14** (1) (1989): 83; Joyce, Patrick, 'The End of Social History?', *Social History* **20** (1995); Joyce Patrick, 'The End of Social History?: A Brief Reply to Eley and Nield', *Social History* **21** (1996): 96; Eley, Geoff, and Keith Nield, 'Starting Over: the Present, the Post-Modern and the Moment of Social History', *Social History* **20** (1995); White, Hayden, *The Content of the Form: Narrative, Discourse and Historical Representation*, (Baltimore: Johns Hopkins University Press, 1987); Ankersmit, Frank and Hans Kellner, eds, *A New Philosophy of History*, (Chicago: University of Chicago Press, 1995); Appleby, Joyce, *et al.*, eds, *Knowledge and Postmodernism in Historical Perspective*, (London: Routledge, 1996); Sewell, William H., *A Rhetoric of Bourgeois Revolution: The Abbe Sieyes and What is the Third Estate?*, (Durham: Duke University Press, 1994); Mertz, Elizabeth, 'A New Social Constructionism for Sociolegal Studies', *Law and Society Review* **28** (1994): 1243; Minder, Gary, *Postmodern Legal Movements*, (New York: New York University Press, 1995).

23 See, for example, Ernst, 'The Critical Tradition in the Writing of Legal History', Innis and Styles, 'The Crime Wave', Tomlins, 'How Who Rides Whom' and Sugarman, 'Writing "Law and Society" Histories' in this anthology. See, also, the material in note 22.

24 With respect to women and the law, the following is merely a small sample of this ever increasing and important literature: Berns, Sandra S., 'Women in English Legal History: Subject (Almost), Object (Irrevocably), Person (Not Quite)', *University of Tasmania Law Review* **12** (1) (1993): 26; Clark, Elizabeth B., 'Matrimonial Bonds: Slavery and Divorce in Nineteenth Century America', *Law and History Review* **8** (1) (1990): 25; Staves, S., *Married Women's Separate Property in England, 1660–1833*, (Cambridge: Harvard University Press, 1989); Backhouse, Connie, *Petticoats and Prejudice*, (Toronto: Women's Press, 1991); Spring, Eileen, *Law, Land and Family: Aristocratic Inheritance in England, 1300 to 1800*, (Chapel Hill: University of North Carolina Press, 1993); Erickson, Amy Louise, *Women and Property in Early Modern England*, (London: Routledge, 1993); Frost, Ginger S., '"I Shall Not Sit Down and Crie": Women, Class and Breach of Promise of Marriage Plaintiffs in England, 1850–1900', *Gender and History* **6** (2) (1994): 224; Gavigan, Shelley, 'Petit Treason in Eighteenth Century England: Women's Inequality Before the Law', *Canadian Journal of Women and the Law* **3** (1989): 335; Gowing, Laura, 'Gender and the Language of Insult in Early Modern London', *History Workshop* **35** (1993): 1 and 'Language, Power and the Law: Women's Slander Litigation in Early Modern London', *Women, Crime and the Courts in Early Modern England*, ed. J. Kermode, and G. Walker, (London: UCL Press, 1994) 26; Hartog, Hendrick, 'Mrs Packard on Dependency', *Yale Journal of Law and the Humanities* **1** (1988): 79 and 'Abigail Bailey's Coverture: Law in a Married Woman's Consciousness', *Law in Everyday Life*, ed. Austin Sarat, and Thomas R. Kearns. (Ann Arbor: University of Michigan Press, 1993) 63; Kuehn, Thomas, *Law, Family and Women: Toward A Legal Anthropology of Renaissance Italy*, (Chicago: University of Chicago Press, 1991); Shanley, Mary Lyndon, *Feminism, Marriage and the Law in Victorian England*, (Princeton: Princeton University Press, 1989); Sharpe, J.A., *Defamation and Sexual Slander in Early Modern England: The Church Courts at York*, (York: Borwick Papers, 1980): 58; Ingram, M., *Church Courts, Sex and Marriage in England, 1570–1640*, (Cambridge: Cambridge University Press, 1987); Stretton, Tim, 'Women and Litigation in the Elizabethan Court of Requests', Ph.D. Cambridge, 1993; Zedner, Lucia, *Women, Crime and Custody in Victorian England*, (Oxford: Oxford University Press, 1991); Siegel, Reva, 'Home as Work: the First Woman's Rights Claims Concerning Wives' Household Labor, 1850–1880', *Yale Law Journal* **103** (1994): 1073; Arnaud-Duc, Nicole, 'The Law's Contradictions', *A History of Women in the West*, ed. Genevieve Fraisse, and Michelle Perrot, (Cambridge: Harvard University Press, 1993) vol. IV: 'Emerging Feminism from Revolution to World War': 80; Walkowitz, Judith R., 'Dangerous Sexualities', *A History of Women in the West*, ed. Genevieve Fraisse, and Michelle Perrot. (Cambridge: Harvard University Press, 1993) IV: 'Emerging Feminism from Revolution to World War': 80; Rose, Carol M., *Property and Persuasion: Essays on the*

History, Theory and Rhetoric of Ownership, (Boulder: Westview Press, 1994); Goodrich, Peter, *Oedipus Lex*, ch. 6.

25 'Culture', like 'language' and 'discourse', is one of the banners of the new historical writing. It may be used in a rather loose fashion so as to mean almost anything. On the concept of 'culture' and its capacity to reintegrate diverse approaches to history writing see Kammen, Michael, 'Extending the Reach of American Cultural History', *American Studies* **29** (1984): 19. For a useful discussion of the virtues and limits of the concept of 'culture' and cultural approaches in history writing see, Burke, Peter, *History and Social Theory*, (Ithaca: Cornell University Press, 1992) pp. 118–126; and on the confines of the concept of 'culture' in the context of the comparative sociology of law see Cotterrell, Roger, 'The Concept of Legal Culture', *Comparing Legal Cultures*, ed. David Nelken. (Aldershot: Dartmouth Publishing, 1996).

26 Cf. Rowbottom, Sheila, *Hidden From History: 300 Years of Women's Oppression and the Fight Against It*, 3rd edn, (London: Pluto Press, 1977).

27 Wrightson, Keith, 'The Enclosure of English Social History', *Rethinking Social History: English Society 1570–1920 and its Interpretation*, ed. Adrian Wilson. (Manchester: Manchester University Press, 1993): 63 (making this criticism with respect to the development of social history).

28 Starr, June, and Jane F. Collier, 'Introduction: Dialogues in Legal Anthropology', *History and Power in the Study of Law*, ed. June Starr, and Jane F. Collier, (Ithaca: Cornell University Press, 1989) 1–28, 25.

29 Thompson, E.P., 'Time, Work-Discipline and Industrial Capitalism', *Past and Present* **38** (1967); Pocock, J.G.A., *Politics, Language and Time*; Ladurie, E. Le Roy, *The Territory of the Historian*, (Hassocks: Harvester, 1972) pp. 111–132; Goff, Jacques Le, *Time, Work and Culture in the Middle Ages*, (Chicago: University of Chicago Press, 1980); Geertz, Clifford, *The Interpretation of Cultures*, (New York: 1973) 360; Barthes, Roland, 'History as Discourse', *Structuralism; A Reader*, ed. Michael Lane (London: Cape, 1970): 145; Ricoeur, P., *Time and Narrative*, 3 vols. (Chicago: University of Chicago Press, 1984–88); Carr, David, *Time, Narrative and History*, Indiana University Press, 1986); Goff, Jacques Le, *History and Memory*, (New York: Columbia University Press); Greenhouse, Carol J., 'Just in Time: Temporality and the Cultural Legitimation of Law', *Yale Law Journal* **98** (1989): 1631.

30 For example, the new legal history has played an important role in the renaissance of historical work on early modern Britain, particularly the so-called 'long eighteenth century'. Cf. Wrightson, 'The Enclosure of English Social History' pp. 62–63 on the phenomenon of 'compartmentalisation by period' in the field of social history.

31 Some of the building blocks that might be utilized include: Moore, R.I., *The Formation of a Persecuting Society: Power and Deviance in Western Europe, 950–1250*, (Oxford: Clarendon Press, 1987); Davis, David Brion, *The Problem of Slavery in Western Culture*, (Ithaca: Cornell University Press, 1966); Hall, Catherine, *White, Male and Middle Class: Explorations in Feminism and History*, (Cambridge: Polity Press, 1992) and 'Imperial Man: Edward Eyre in Australasia and the West Indies, 1833–66', *The Expansion of England: Race, Ethnicity and Cultural History*, ed. Bill Schwarz, (London: Routledge, 1996): 130; Grant, Alexander and Keith J. Stringer, eds, *Uniting the Kingdom? The Making of British History*, (London: Routledge, 1995); Gilroy, Paul, *'There Ain't No Black in the Union Jack'. The Cultural Politics of Race and Nation*, (London: Hutchinson, 1987) and *The Black Atlantic: Modernity and Double Consciousness*, (Cambridge: Harvard University Press, 1993); Craven, Paul, and Douglas Hay, 'Master and Servant in England and Empire: A Comparative Study', *Labour/Le Travail*, Spring (1993): 175; Craven, Paul, and Douglas Hay, 'The Criminalization of "Free" Labour: Master and Servant in Comparative Perspective', *Slavery and Abolition* **15** (1994): 71; Colley, Linda, *Britons: Forging the Nation 1707–1837*, (New Haven: Yale University Press, 1992); Cocks, R.C.J., *Sir Henry Maine: A Study of Victorian Jurisprudence*, (Cambridge: Cambridge University Press, 1988); Cain, P.J., and A.G. Hopkins, *British Imperialism*; Brogden, Michael, 'The Emergence of the Police: the Colonial Dimension' (in this anthology); Hobsbawm, Eric and Terrence Ranger, eds, *The Invention of Tradition*, (Cambridge: Cambridge University Press, 1983); Stokes, Eric, *The English Utilitarians and India*, (Oxford: Clarendon Press, 1963); Samuel, Raphael, ed., *Patriotism: The Making and Unmaking of British National Identity*, 3 vols., (London: Routledge, 1989); Cairns, John W.,

'Blackstone, and English Institutist: Legal Literature and the Rise of the Nation State', *Oxford Journal of Legal Studies* **4** (1984): 318; Canny, N. and A. Pagden, eds, *Colonial Identity in the Atlantic World, 1500–1800*, (Princeton: Princeton University Press, 1987); Marquis, Greg, 'Doing Justice to "British Justice": Law, Ideology and Canadian Historiography', *Canadian Perspectives on Law and Society: Issues in Legal History*, ed. W. Wesley Pue, and Barry Wright, (Ottawa: Carleton University Press, 1988) 43; Newman, Gerald, *The Rise of English Nationalism*, (New York: St Martin's Press, 1987); Stone, Lawrence, ed., *An Imperial State at War: Britain from 1689 to 1815*, (London: Routledge, 1994); Wesseling, Henk, *'Overseas History', New Perspectives on Historical Writing*, ed. Peter Burke. (Cambridge: Polity Press, 1991): 67; Bhaba, Homi K., ed., *Nation and Narration*, (London: Routledge, 1990); Maurer, Bill, 'Writing Law, Making a "Nation": History, Modernity, and Paradoxes of Self-Rule in the British Virgin Islands', *Law and Society Review* **29** (1995): 255; Kearney, Hugh F., *The British Isles: A History of Four Nations*, (Cambridge: Cambridge University Press); Reynolds, S., *Kingdoms and Communities in Western Europe 900–1300*, (Oxford: 1984); Clark, J.C.D., *The Language of Liberty 1660–1832: Political Discourse and Social Dynamics in the Anglo-American World*, (Cambridge: Cambridge University Press, 1994); Davies, R.R., 'Domination and Conquest: The Experience of Ireland, Scotland and Wales, 1100–1300', (Cambridge: Cambridge University Press, 1990); Davies, R.R., 'The Peoples of Britain and Ireland, 1100– 1400, Identities', *Transactions of the Royal Historical Society*, Sixth Series, (London: Royal Historical Society, 1994): iv: 1; Pocock, J.G.A., ed., *Three British Revolutions: 1641, 1688, 1776*, (Princeton: Princeton University Press, 1980); Bailyn, B. and P.D. Morgan, eds, *Strangers Within the Realm: Cultural Margins of the First British Empire*, (Chapel Hill: University of North Carolina Press, 1991); Fisher, D.H., *Albion's Seed: Four British Folkways in America*, (New York: 1989); Bayly, C.A., *Indian Society and the Making of the British Empire*, (Cambridge: Cambridge University Press, 1988); Bayly, C.A., *Imperial Meridian: The British Empire and the World, 1780–1830*, (London: 1989); Levack, B.P., *The Formation of the British State: England, Scotland and the Union of 1603*, (Oxford: Clarendon Press, 1987); Brubaker, Rogers, *Citizenship and Nationhood in France and Germany*, (Cambridge: Harvard University Press, 1992); Greenfeld, Liah, *Nationalism: Five Roads to Modernity*, (Cambridge: Harvard University Press, 1992); Prakash, Gyan, ed., *After Colonialism: Imperial Histories and Postcolonial Displacements*, (Princeton: Princeton University Press, 1995); King, Anthony D., ed., *Culture, Globalisation and the World-System*, (London: Macmillan, 1991). See, also, the references in note 2.

32 Burns, J.H., and with the assistance of Mark Goldie, ed., *The Cambridge History of Political Thought 1450–1700*, p.5 (discussing the history of political thought).

Beyond this Collection

The following material is intended to provide information on some of the many other histories of law and society that I was unable to include or consider in this collection.

Law, Ideas, Politics, Economy and Society

Alexander, Gregory, 'The Dead Hand and the Law of Trusts in the Nineteenth Century', *Stanford Law Review* **37** (1982): 1189.

Abraham, David, 'Liberty and Property: Lord Bramwell and the Political Economy of Liberal Jurisprudence: Individualism, Freedom and Utility', *American Journal of Legal History* **38** (1994): 288.

Atiyah, P.S., *The Rise and Fall of Freedom of Contract*, (Oxford: Clarendon Press, 1979).

Baker, G. Blaine, 'The Reconstruction of Upper Canadian Legal Thought in the Late-Victorian Empire', *Law and History Review* **3** (2) (1985): 219.

Baker, J.H. ed., *The Reports of Sir John Spelman* (Volume II), (London: Seldon Society, 1978).

Bartrip, P.W.J. and Burman, S., *The Wounded Soldiers of Industry: Industrial Compensation Policy, 1833–1897*, (Oxford: Oxford University Press, 1983).
Berman, Nathaniel, '"But the Alternative is Despair": European Nationalism and the Modernist Renewal of International Law', *Harvard Law Review* **106** (1993): 1795.
Biagini, Eugenio F. and Alastair J. Reid, eds, *Currents of Radicalism: Popular Radicalism, Organised Labour and Party Politics in Britain, 1850–1914*, (Cambridge: Cambridge University Press, 1991).
Bonfield, L., ed., *Marriage, Property, and Succession*, (Berlin: Duncker & Humblot, 1992).
Brand, Paul, *The Making of the Common Law*, (London: The Hambledon Press, 1992).
Brundage, James A., *Medieval Canon Law*, (London: Longman, 1995).
Clanchy, M.T., *From Memory to Written Record*, (London: Methuen, 1979).
Coleman, P.J., *Debtors and Creditors in America: Insolvency, Imprisonment for Debt and Bankruptcy, 1607–1900*, (Madison: State Historical Society of Wisconsin, 1974).
Coombe, Rosemary J. '"The Most Disgusting, Disgraceful and Iniquitous Proceeding in Our Law": the Action for Breach of Promise of Marriage in the Nineteenth Century Ontario', *University of Toronto Law Journal* **38** (1988): 64.
Conrad, Stephen A., 'Metaphor and Imagination in James Wilson's Theory of Federal Union', *Law and Social Inquiry* **13** (1988): 1.
Davis, Paul, and Mark Freedland, *Labour Legislation and Public Policy*, (Oxford: Clarendon Press, 1993).
Doggett, Maeve, *Marriage, Wife-Beating and the Law in Victorian England*, (London: Wiedenfeld and Nicolson, 1992).
Ernst, Daniel R., *Lawyers Against Labor: From Individual Rights to Corporate Liberalism*, (Urbana: University of Illinois Press, 1995).
Fisher, William, 'Ideology, Religion and the Constitutional Protection of Private Property: 1760–1860', *Emory Law Journal* **39** (1990): 65.
Flaherty, David, ed., *Essays in Canadian Law*, vols I and II, ed. David Flaherty, (Toronto: Osgoode Society, 1981–83).
Forbath, William, 'Why is this Rights Talk Different from All other Rights Talk? Demoting the Court and Reimagining the Constitution', *Stanford Law Review* **46** (1994): 1771.
Francis, C.W., 'Structure of judicial administration and the development of contract law in 17th century England', *Columbia Law Review* **83** (1983): 36.
Francis, C.W., 'Practice, strategy and institution: debt collection in the English common law courts, 1740–1840, *North Western University Law Review* **80** (1986): 807.
Freyer, Tony, *Regulating Big Business: Antitrust in Great Britain and America 1880–1990*, (Cambridge, Cambridge University Press, 1992).
Gaines, Jane, *Contested Culture: The Image, the Voice and the Law*, (Chapel Hill: University of North Carolina Press, 1991).
Getzler, Joshua, 'Theories of Property and Economic Development', *Journal of Interdisciplinary History* **26** (1996): 639.
Gordon, Robert W., 'Legal Thought and Legal Practice in the Age of the American Enterprise, 1870–1920', *Professions and Professional Ideologies in America*, ed. G. Geison, (Chapel Hill: University of North Carolina Press, 1983).
Gordon, Robert W., ed., *The Legacy of Oliver Wendall Holmes, Jr.*, (Stanford: Stanford University Press, 1992).
Greenwood, F. Murray, *Legacies of Fear: Law and Politics in Quebec in the Era of the French Revolution*, (Toronto: University of Toronto Press for the Osgoode Society, 1993).
Grossi, Paolo, *An Alternative to Private Property: Collective Property in the Juridical Consciousness of the Nineteenth Century*, (Chicago: University of Chicago Press, 1981).
Hartog, Hendrik, *Public Property and Private Power: The Corporation of the City of New York in American Life*, (Chapel Hill: University of North Carolina Press, 1983).
Helmholz, R.H., ed., *Canon Law in Protestant Lands*, (Berlin: Duncker & Humblot, 1992).
Hill, Christopher, *Liberty Against the Law: Some Seventeenth-Century Controversies*, (London: Allen Lane: The Penguin Press, 1996).
Horwitz, Morton J., 'Forward: The Constitution of Change: Legal Fundamentality Without

Fundamentalism', *Harvard Law Review* **107** (1993): 30.
Hovencamp, Herbert, *Enterprise and American Law, 1836–1937*, (Cambridge, Mass: Harvard University Press, 1991).
Hull, N.E.H., 'Networks and Bricolage: A Prolegomenon to a History of Twentieth-Century American Academic Jurisprudence', *American Journal of Legal History* **35** (1991): 307.
Hyams, P.R., *Kings, Lords and Peasants in Medieval England: The Common Law of Villeinage in the 12th and 13th Centuries*, (Oxford: Clarendon Press, 1980).
Johnson, Paul, 'Class Law in Victorian England', *Past and Present* **141** (1993): 147.
Kantorowicz, Ernst H., *The King's Two Bodies: A Study in Medieval Political Theology*, (Princeton: Princeton University Press, 1957).
Kelley, Donald R., *Historians and the Law in Postrevolutionary France*, (Princeton: Princeton University Press, 1984).
Kennedy, D., 'The Structure of Blackstone's Commentaries', *Buffalo Law Review* **28** (1979): 205.
Kennedy, D., 'Toward an Historical Understanding of Legal Consciousness', *Research in Law and Sociology*, **3**, ed. S. Spitzer (Greenwood: JAI Press, 1980).
Kelman, Laura, *The Strange Career of Legal Liberalism*, (New Haven: Yale University Press, 1995).
King, Andrew J., 'Constructing Gender: Sexual Slander in Nineteenth-Century America', *Law and History Review* **13** (1995): 63.
Konefsky, Alfred S., 'Law and Culture in Antebellum Boston', *Stanford Law Review* **40** (1988): 1119.
Lieberman, David, *The Province of Legislation Determined*, (Cambridge: Cambridge University Press, 1989).
McEvoy, Arthur, *The Fisherman's Problem: Ecology and the Law in the California Fisheries 1850–1980*, (Cambridge: Cambridge University Press, 1986).
McIntosh, M.K., *Autonomy and Community. The Royal Manor of Havering 1200–1500*, (Cambridge: Cambridge University Press, 1986).
McIntosh, M.K., *A Community Transformed: The Manor and Liberty of Havering, 1500–1620*, (Cambridge: Cambridge University Press, 1991).
McLaren, John P.S., 'Nuisance Law and the Industrial Revolution – Some Lessons from Social History', *Oxford Journal of Legal Studies* **3** (1) (1983): 155.
MacLeod, Christine, *Inventing the Industrial Revolution: The English Patent System 1660–1800*, (Cambridge: Cambridge University Press, 1988).
Mensch, Elizabeth, 'The Colonial Origins of Liberal Property Rights', *Buffalo Law Review*, **31** (1983): 635.
Merritt, Adrian, 'The Historical Role of Law in the Regulation of Employment – Abstentionist or Interventionist?', *Australian Journal of Law and Society* **1** (1) (1982): 56.
Mertz, Elizabeth, 'The Uses of History: Language, Ideology and the Law in the United States and South Africa', *Law and Society Review*, **22** (4) (1988): 661.
Minow, Martha, '"Forming Underneath Everything that Grows": Toward a History of Family Law', *Wisconsin Law Review*, (1985): 819.
Muldrew, Craig, 'Interpreting the Market: the Ethics of Credit and Community Relations in Early Modern England', *Social History*, **18** (2) (1993): 163.
Nenner, H., *By Colour of Law: Legal Culture and Constitutional Politics in England, 1660–1689*, (Chicago: University of Chicago Press, 1977).
Novak, William J., 'Public Economy and the Well-ordered Market: Law and Economic Regulation in 19th-Century America', *Law and Social Inquiry*, **18** (1) (1993): 1.
Palmer, R.C., *English Law in the Age of the Black Death, 1348–1381: A Transformation of Governance and Law*, (Chapel Hill, N.C.: University of North Carolina Press, 1993).
Poni, Carlo, 'Norms and Disputes: the Shoemakers' Guild in Eighteenth-century Bologna', *Past and Present* **123**.
Reimann, Mathias, ed., *The Reception of Continental Ideas in the Common Law World 1820–1920*, (Berlin: Duncker & Humblot, 1993).
Risk, Richard, and Robert C. Vipond, 'Rights Talk in Canada in the Late Nineteenth Century: "The Good Sense and Right Feeling of the People"', *Law and History Review*, **14** (1996): 1.

Romney, Paul, 'From Constitutionalism to Legalism: Trial by Jury, Responsible Government, and the Rule of Law in the Canadian Political Culture', *Law and History Review*, **7** (1) (1989): 121.
Rose, Mark, *Authors and Owners: the Invention of Copyright*, (Cambridge: Harvard University Press, 1993).
Ross, Richard, 'The Legal Past of Early New England: Notes for the Study of Law, Legal Culture and Intellectual History', *William and Mary Quarterly*, 3d ser., **50** (1993): 40.
Rubin, G.R., *Private Property, Government Requisition and the Constitution, 1914–1927*, (London: The Hambledon Press, 1994).
Scheiber, H.A., 'Regulation, Property Rights and Definition of the Market', *Journal of Economic History*, (1981): 103.
Schlegel, John Henry, *American Legal Realism and Empirical Social Science*, (Chapel Hill: University of North Carolina Press, 1995).
Sharpe, J.A., 'The People and the Law', *Popular Culture in Seventeenth Century England*, ed. Barry Rea, (London: Croom Helm, 1985): 244.
Siegel, Stephen A., 'Joel Bishop's Orthodoxy', *Law and History Review*, **13** (1995): 215.
Simpson, A.W. Brian, *Cannibalism and the Common Law*, (Harmondsworth: Penguin Books, 1986).
Simpson, A.W.B., *Leading Cases in the Common Law*, (Oxford: Clarendon Press, 1995).
Singer, Joseph William, 'The Legal Rights Debate in Analytical Jurisprudence from Bentham to Hohfeld', *Wisconsin Law Review*, (1982): 975.
Sklar, Martin J., *The Corporate Reconstruction of American Capitalism, 1890–1916*, (Cambridge: Cambridge University Press, 1988).
Somers, Margaret R., 'Citizenship and the Place of the Public Sphere; Law, Community and Political Culture in the Transition to Democracy', *American Sociological Review* **58** (1993): 587.
Staves, Susan, 'Chattel Property Rules and the Construction of Englishness', *Law and History Review*, **12** (1) (1994): 123.
Sugarman, David, and Ronnie Warrington, 'Land Law, Citizenship and the Invention of "Englishness": The Strange World of the Equity of Redemption', *Early Modern Conceptions of Property*, ed. John Brewer and Susan Staves, (London: Routledge, 1995) 111.
Tierney, B., *Religion, Law and the Growth of Constitutional Thought 1150–1650*, (Cambridge: Cambridge University Press, 1982).
Walker, Sue Sheridan, ed., *Wife and Widow in Medieval England*, (Ann Arbor: University of Michigan Press, 1993).

Judges, Courts, Lawyers, Legal Institutions and Society

Abel-Smith, B., and R. Stevens, *Lawyers and the Courts: A Sociological Study of the English Legal System, 1750–1965*, (London: Hutchinson, 1967).
Arthurs, H.W., *Without the Law: Administrative Justice and Legal Pluralism in Nineteenth Century England*, (Toronto: University of Toronto Press, 1985).
Bartlett, R., *Trial by Fire and Water: the Medieval Judicial Ordeal*, (Oxford: Clarendon Press, 1986).
Beattie, J.M., 'Scales of Justice: Defence Counsel and the English Criminal Trial in the Eighteenth and Nineteenth Centuries', *Law and History Review*, **9** (2) (1991): 221.
Brand, Paul, *The Origins of the English Legal Profession*, (Oxford: Blackwells, 1992).
Brooks, C.W., *Pettyfoggers and Vipers of the Commonwealth: The 'Lower Branch' of the Legal Profession in Early Modern England*, (Cambridge: Cambridge University Press, 1986).
Brooks, C.W., 'Interpersonal Conflict and Social Tension: Civil Litigation in England, 1640–1830', *The First Modern Society*, ed. A.L. Beier, D. Cannadine, and J. Rosenheim. (Cambridge: Cambridge University Press, 1989): 357.
Constable, Marianne, *The Law of the Other: The Mixed Jury and Changing Conceptions of Citizenship, Law and Knowledge*, (Chicago: University of Chicago Press, 1994).
Cover, R., *Justice Accused*, (New Haven: Yale University Press, 1978).
Ferguson, R.B., 'The Adjudication of Commercial Disputes and the Legal System in Modern England', *British Journal of Law and Society*, **7**, Winter (1980): 141.

Fifoot, C.H.S., *Judge and Jurist in the Reign of Victoria*, (London: Stevens, 1959).
Goodrich, Peter, 'Eating Law: Commons, Common Land, Common Law', *Journal of Legal History*, **12** (1991): 246.
Grossberg, Michael, 'Institutionalizing Masculinity: the Law as a Masculine Profession', *Meanings of Manhood: Constructions of Masculinity in Victorian America*, ed. Marc C. Carnes, and Clyde Griffen (Chicago: University of Chicago Press, 1990).
Karpik, Lucien, *Les Advocats*, (Paris: Gallimard, 1995).
Konefsky, Alfred S., and Andrew J. King, ed., *The Papers of Daniel Webster*, 3 vols, (Hanover, New Hampshire: University Press of New England, 1982–84).
Kostal, Rande, *Law and English Railway Capitalism, 1825–1875*, (Oxford: Oxford University Press, 1994).
Levack, B.P., *The Civil Lawyers in England 1603–1641*, (Oxford: 1973).
Muldrew, Craig, 'Credit and the Courts: Debt Litigation in a Seventeenth-Century Urban Community', *Economic History Review*, **XLVI** (1) (1993): 23.
Muller, Ingo, *Hitler's Justice: The Courts of the Third Reich*, (Cambridge: Harvard University Press, 1991).
Newmyer, R. Kent, *Supreme Court Justice Joseph Story, Statesman of the Old Republic*, (Chapel Hill: University of North Carolina Press, 1985).
Offer, A., *Property and Politics 1870–1914: Landownership, Law, Ideology and Urban Development in England*, (Cambridge: Cambridge University Press, 1981: reprinted, with a new preface, Hampshire: Gregg Revivals, 1992).
Oldham, James, *The Mansfield Manuscripts and the Growth of English Law in the Eighteenth Century*, (Chapel Hill, N.C.: University of North Carolina Press, 1992).
Phillipson, N.T., 'Lawyers, landowners and the civil leadership of post-Union Scotland: an essay on the social role of the Faculty of Advocates 1661–1830 in 18th century Scottish Society', *Juridical Review*, **21** (1976): 97.
Prest, W.R., *The Rise of the Barristers: A Social History of the English Bar, 1590–1640*, (Oxford: Clarendon Press, 1986).
Pue, W. Wesley, 'Moral Panic at the English Bar: Paternal v Commercial Ideologies of Legal Practice in the 1860's', *Law and Society Inquiry*, **15** (1990): 49.
Pue, W. Wesley, 'In Pursuit of Better Myth: Lawyers' Histories and Histories of Lawyers', *Alberta Law Review*, **33** (1995): 730.
Siegrist, Hannes, *Advokat, Burger und Staat: Sozialgeschichte der Rechtsanwalte in Deutschland, Italien und der Schweiz (18.–20. Jh)*, (Frankfurt-am-Main: Vittorio Klostermann, 1996).
Simpson, A.W. Brian, *In the Highest Degree Odious: Detention Without Trial in Wartime Britain*, (Oxford: Clarendon Press, 1992).
Smith, J. Clayton, *Emancipation: The Making of the Black Lawyer, 1844–1944*, (Philadelphia: University of Pennsylvania Press, 1993).
Sonenscher, Michael, *Work and Wages: Natural Law, Politics and the Eighteenth-century French Trades*, (Cambridge: Cambridge University Press, 1989).
Sugarman, David, 'Bourgeois Collectivism, Professional Power and the Boundaries of the State: The Private and Public Life of the Law Society, 1825–1914', *International Journal of the Legal Profession* **3** (1996): 81.
White, G. Edward, *Justice Oliver Wendall Holmes: Law and the Inner Self*, (New York: Oxford University Press, 1993).

Crime, Punishment and Policing

Andrews, Richard Mowery, *Law, Magistracy, and Crime in Old Regime Paris, 1735–1789*, (Cambridge, Cambridge University Press, 1994).
Barrell, John, 'Imaginary Treason, Imaginary Law: the State Trials of 1794', in his *The Birth of Pandora and the Division of Knowledge*, (London: Macmillan, 1992) 119.
Dubinsky, Karen, *Improper Advances: Rape and Heterosexual Conflict in Ontario, 1880–1929*,

(Chicago: University of Chicago Press, 1993).
Friedman, Lawrence, *Crime and Punishment in American History*, (New York: Basic Books, 1993).
Gatrell, V.A.C., 'The Decline of Theft and Violence in Victorian and Edwardian England', *Crime and the Law: The Social History of Crime in Western Europe Since 1500*, ed. B. Lenman and G. Parker, V.A.C. Gatrell, (London: Europa, 1980).
Gatrell, V.A.C., 'Crime, Authority and the Policeman-State', *The Cambridge Social History of Britain 1750–1950*, Volume Three, ed. F.M.L. Thompson, (Cambridge: Cambridge University Press, 1990): 243.
Gatrell, V.A.C., *The Hanging Tree: Execution and the English People 1770–1868*, (Oxford: Oxford University Press, 1994).
Green, T.A., *Verdict According to Conscience*, (1985).
Harris, Ruth, *Murders and Madness: Medicine, Law and Society in the 'Fin de Siècle'*, (Oxford: Oxford University Press, 1989).
Hay, Douglas, 'War, Dearth and Theft in the Eighteenth Century: The Record of the English Courts', *Past and Present*, **95** (1982): 117.
Hay, Douglas, 'Time, Inequality, and Law's Violence', *Law's Violence*, ed. Austin Sarat, and Thomas R. Kearns. (Ann Arbor: University of Michigan Press, 1992): 141.
Hay, Douglas and Francis Snyder, eds, *Policing and Prosecution in Britain 1750–1850*, (Oxford: Clarendon Press, 1989).
Herrup, Cynthia, *The Common Peace: Participation and the Criminal Law in 17th Century England*, (Cambridge: Cambridge University Press, 1987).
Herrup, Cynthia, 'The Patriarch at Home: The Trial of the Second Earl of Castlehaven for Rape and Sodomy', *History Workshop*, **41** (1996): 1.
Jones, D., *Crime, Protest, Community and Police in 19th Century Britain*, (London: Routledge and Kegan Paul, 1982).
King, P., 'Gleaners, farmers and the failure of legal sanctions in England 1750–1850', *Past and Present*, (1989): 116.
Knafla, Louis A., *Kent at Law 1602: Volume 1, The County Jurisdiction: Assizes and Sessions of the Peace*, (London: HMSO, 1995).
Linebaugh, Peter, *The London Hanged: Crime and Civil Society in the Eighteenth Century*, (London, Penguin, 1991).
Morris, Norval and David J. Rothman, eds, *The Oxford History of the Prison*, (Oxford: Oxford University Press, 1995).
Petrow, Stefan, *Policing Morals: The Metropolitan Police and the Home Office 1870–1914*, (Oxford: Clarendon Press, 1994).
Phillips, Jim, Tina Loo and Susan Lewthwaite, eds, *Essays in the History of Canadian Law Vol. 5, Crime and Criminal Justice*, (Toronto: The Osgoode Society, 1994).
Portelli, Alessandro, 'Oral Testimony, the Law and the Making of History: The "April 7" Murder Trial', *History Workshop Journal*, **20** (1985): 5.
Smith, Roger, *Trial by Medicine: Insanity and Responsibility in Victorian Trials*, (Edinburgh: Edinburgh University Press, 1981).
Walkowitz, Judith R., *City of Dreadful Delight: Narratives of Sexual Danger in Late Victorian London*, (Chicago: University of Chicago Press, 1992).

Part I
Law and Society in Pre-Industrial England

[1]

Frederic William Maitland

† 21 December 1906.

A GREEK myth tells us of a king at whose touch all objects, however homely, were turned into gold. We do not see such transformations nowadays, but we know another king at whose touch every living being, however noble, is turned into dust. King Death has touched with his wand one of the most subtle and profound thinkers of our time, and stores of patiently accumulated knowledge, marvellous designs of a creative intellect have disappeared for ever from this world of ours. The best thing we have to do is to look for moral support to the example of the fallen champion, to his indomitable energy and absorbing devotion to his task through a life of pains and forebodings which might have crippled a less courageous nature. Of late years he was walking in the shadow of death in a more manifest sense than most of us, but he was too proud and strong to slacken in his efforts.

It is not my intention in the present notice to give anything like a complete account and estimate of Maitland's achievement; it is too early yet to condense its value in a short summary, and in one way or another all students of English law and history must realise constantly the importance of his bequests in the course of their own work. I should like merely to tell the readers of this Review of some impressions created by his personality and his writings in the mind of one who has had many opportunities to study both. It has been my privilege to stand very near Maitland in the early stage of his career, and since then our friendly intercourse has never been interrupted, in spite of the fact that I lived most of the time in another country and our personal interviews were not very frequent. I met him the first time at a friend's house in London in the beginning of 1884. It was at a dinner party, at which Sir Henry Maine was present. Maitland did not take much part in the talk, and listened modestly, but when we went home together we had some interesting conversation on the subject of our studies. He said, among other things—and he often repeated to me afterwards—that he would much rather devote his life to the historical study of English law than watch in his chambers in Lincoln's Inn for the footsteps of the client who never comes. Since that day we met often, and I always look with a peculiar feeling on the *Gloucester Pleas of the Crown*, the *Note Book of Bracton*, the *Rolls of King's Ripton*, and many pages of my own book on *Villainage*. They recall to my mind endless talks on remote problems of legal and social history; there are many personal traits about them which the duty of addressing a large audience of strangers has not entirely wiped out.

I am, perhaps, dwelling too long on these recollections, which concern chiefly myself. To his ever increasing public of readers and pupils the great scholar stood also in a kind of special, personal relation through his style, the literary presentment of his subject. The French saying, *Le style c'est l'homme*, seems true in more ways than one. A writer's style is not only a significant expression of his character and moods; it constitutes a sort of medium between him and his audience; it may attract and electrify, or, on the contrary, it may jar on them. It is not for me to speak of the idiomatic pith, the boldness and picturesqueness of Maitland's style; but I may be allowed to dwell on a feature which has been often noticed by more competent judges: one of the qualities which contributed most to attract his readers and to dispose them towards admiration and persuasion was the wealth of humour that pervaded all his writings, in spite of their severe aims and their highly technical details. It is certainly not of smoothly polished classical patterns that one is reminded when reading brilliant pages on Anglo-Saxon hides, medieval modes of pleading, or German juridical theories. The poignant sense of the irony of life makes one rather think of Shakespeare, the continual shifting of colour and light of Sterne, the coruscating epigram of Meredith. One may take illustrations almost at random, and I do not try to select an especially happy one by quoting a passage from the introduction to Gierke's *Political Theories of the Middle Age*.

The Realist's cause would be described by those who are forwarding it as an endeavour to give scientific precision and legal operation to thoughts which are in all modern minds and which are always displaying themselves especially in the political field. We might be told to read the leading article in to-day's paper and observe the ideas with which the writer 'operates': the will of the nation, the mind of the legislature, the settled policy of one State, the ambitious designs of another: the praise and blame that are awarded to group-units of all sorts and kinds. We might be asked to count the lines that our journalist can write without talking of organisation. We might be asked to look at our age's criticism of the political theories and political projects of its immediate predecessor and to weigh those charges of abstract individualism, atomism, and macadamisation that are currently made. We might be asked whether the British Empire has not yet revolted against a Sovereign that was merely Many (a Sovereign Number as Austin said) and in no sense really One; and whether 'the People' that sues and prosecutes in American courts is a collective name for some living men and a name whose meaning changes at every minute. We might be referred to modern philosophers: to the social tissue of one and the general will, which is the real will, of another. Then, perhaps, we might fairly be charged with entertaining a deep suspicion that all this is a metaphor: apt perhaps and useful, but essentially like the personification of the ocean and the ship, the storm and the stormy petrel.[1]

One of the most marked peculiarities of such a style is its vividness, the power of closing abstract reasoning into forms taken from the living world of shapes and sounds. The wealth of concrete illustration was not suggested in this case merely by artistic taste. It corresponded to a constant striving of the mind to obtain a full and close grasp of the subject studied. Powerful though he was in abstract speculation and dialectic analysis, what Maitland wanted most was to trace ideas to their embodiment in facts, to sketch their ramifications and complications in practice. Therefore he never fell a prey to those scholastic formulae in which analytical jurists often delight. It is interesting to watch him in close proximity to prominent German jurists.

He much admired the work of Gierke, for instance, and fully appreciated the part played by the 'Germanists' in the remodelling of their country's private law. Of late years he had begun studying very attentively the German civil code,[2] and even, I believe, to translate portions of it in his spare moments. But the reading of his preface to the *Political Theories of the Middle Age* suggests interesting comparisons with the main text of the German writer; the latter is, after all, a masterly exposition of formulae and principles, while the English introduction tries to reduce all theories to their practical consequences, and to sketch their evolution in all the complexity of their natural environment. Of Jellinek's dogmatic constructions and of his deductive 'Study of the State' Maitland never had occasion to speak; but in a recent production of one of Jellinek's pupils, Hatschek's Handbook of English Public Law, much is said about coincidences with Maitland's views in regard to English public bodies as representing 'passive unions' (*passive Verbände*) in contrast with 'active' ones.[3] There is good reason to believe that this pitting of abstract categories against one another did not meet with

[1] *Political Theories of the Middle Age*, pp. xl, xli.

[2] See, e.g., the address published in the *Independent Review*, August 1906.

[3] E.g. *Englisches Staatsrecht*, vol. i. For a thoroughly competent estimate of this book see *Law Quarterly Review*, xxi. 309–313, 1905.

Maitland's approval, and the latter's masterly analysis of the life of English townships and parishes, boroughs and counties, certainly does not lend itself to such scholastic distinctions. He laid stress on their responsibilities in regard to the State, but did not consider them as produced by outside pressure or void of active interests and life. In this case, as in the study on trusts,[4] Maitland was chiefly concerned to show by what legally imperfect and clumsy means the need for corporate organisations is sometimes met in practice, and how slowly a clear conception of the principles of an institution ripens in the course of its historical life. A London club or an Inn of Court serves the purposes of a social or collegiate group, although the technical principle of the corporation is absent in this and in many other similar cases. Even so the vill and the county were certainly groups with independent cohesion and real interests; but it was important to show to what extent their self-government was determined, among other things, by the requirements of central government. It may perhaps be urged that Maitland's statements are somewhat eccentric in form and influenced by his desire to avoid commonplaces, but they do not fit into the pigeon-hole of the *passiver Verband*.

Even so the attention bestowed on the concrete, the interest for first-hand evidence, the disinclination to deal in other people's words made it impossible for our scholar to sympathise either with the old-fashioned doctrines of Austinian jurisprudence which he found to be 'nature-rightly'[5]—that is, outside the frame of space and time—or with grandiloquent 'sociology,' piling up hollow terms and pretentious generalisations on very slight foundations of fact. He was emphatically *an historian*, a student of actual development in the past. Although his work never stuck in details for their own sake, it will always remain an example of what a thorough grasp of details and keen investigation of all the particulars of a case can mean in the research of scientific truth. For a teacher of this kind the drudgery of special disquisitions did not exist, because every minute observation connected itself with other observations on the lines of a profound insight into general processes. He shared the enthusiasm of the naturalist who is not repelled by the mean or the insignificant, for whom such terms have, in truth, no meaning; so he thoroughly realises that a microscopic study of tissues, a patient observation of the structure and doings of infinitesimal *protozoa* is as essential as the description of mighty and beautiful specimens. And Maitland was not scared when, in order to read and to publish Year Books, he, the jurist,

[4] 'Korporation und Trust,' in Grünhut's *Zeitschrift für das Privat- und Öffentliche Recht der Gegenwart*, 1903.

[5] *Political Theories*, p. xliv.

had to build up a grammar of corrupt law French and to fathom the inadvertences and blunders of fourteenth-century legal students taking hurried notes in court.

On the other hand he was not likely to rest content with supposed juridical notions of a permanent nature. Wielding the sharp scalpel of the lawyer with consummate ability within given surroundings, he was never oblivious of the relative and changeable character of the first principles from which legal analysts have to evolve their arguments. The most fascinating task of the legal historian was to watch the gradual modification of legal rules, the half-instinctive adaptation of legal theory to the promptings of business or to the interests represented by conflicting social forces. We should claim on behalf of the Year Books that

> . . . they show us a marvellous deal of the play of those moral and economic forces of which legal logic is the instrument, and, often, if we may say, the reluctant instrument. Our old lawyers were fond of declaring 'that the law will suffer a mischief rather than an inconvenience,' by which they meant that it will suffer a practical hardship rather than an inconsistency or logical flaw. But . . . we are forcibly told where the mischief lies, where the shoe pinches, even when we are also told that the unconformist foot that will not fit the shoe is a bad foot and ought to be pinched. And then, as we compare case with case, we see that more commodious shoes are made for growing feet: logic yields to life, protesting all the while that it is only becoming more logical.[6]

The touch of irony so characteristic of Maitland's style is certainly not the product of literary mannerism. Its effectiveness depends on habits of mind, which led him to approach most subjects in a sceptical mood. He seems to be wandering in a strange world, crowded with fancies and shams. He is constantly on the alert against traditions kept up out of sheer indolence of mind, against political and religious prejudice, against complex theories devoid of foundation in reality. And his criticism generally illustrates the maxim, *Suaviter in modo, fortiter in re*. With all reverence to acknowledged authorities he is often able to show that many of their constructions are hollow, and do not stand a searching examination. In the essays on *Canon Law*, for instance, Maitland, though dissenting from all churches, supports in substance the contentions of Roman catholic scholars against a kind of antedated Anglicanism favoured by Bishop Stubbs. The genuine respect felt by Maitland for this eminent man did not prevent the critic from exposing pitilessly the gaps and inconsistencies of the evidence appealed to.[7] One of the motives for drawing a remarkable parallel between Azo and Bracton was the desire to enter a protest

[6] Introduction to *Year Books*, vol. i. pp. xviii, xix.

[7] E.g. *Roman Canon Law in the Church of England*, pp. 52, 53.

against a view propounded by Maine with more assurance than discretion in regard to the influence of the civilian on the English lawyer.[8] Altogether the principles and methods of the school of comparative jurisprudence as expounded by Maine did not find much favour with our scholar. He was too exacting in his handling of evidence and too distrustful of general assumptions to let pass without a challenge wide statements more often supported by allusions than by definite proofs. Moreover it seemed to him that one of the leading ideas of the school—namely, the view that different nations pass approximately through the same stages of evolution—was fundamentally wrong. Races and nations do not travel by the same roads and at the same rate; each chooses its own direction and traverses the country at a different speed. The interest of history lies in taking note of these different records and not in grinding down characteristic varieties to colourless uniformity.[9]

On several very important points Maitland criticised the teaching of investigators hailing from the comparative school. He was, for instance, opposed to the idea of a primitive collectivism shaping the early land law of Indo-European nations, and of England in particular. He looked at the old English townships from a point of view acquired in the course of a study of medieval law in its express manifestations. They appeared to him chiefly as organisations for the collection of dues, the assumption of responsibilities, and the management of some economic concerns with but a slight legal admixture. Communalism evaporates at the touch of legal doctrine,[10] as he puts it. No evidence of a township moot as distinct from the manorial court is forthcoming; the doctrine of corporation appears altogether unfit to explain the ties between villagers. Economic and legal development starts from the notion of 'mine' and not from that of 'ours.'

What may be called Maitland's antiquarian individualism brought him into collision with the teaching about tribal as well as about agrarian communities. Evidence supplied by Celtic material never seemed quite satisfactory to him; it was too illogical, too incoherent, presented in too uncritical a manner.[11] And the fundamental conception of agnatic kinship was dissolved for him by the consideration that relationship through women, necessarily divergent, appears as the earliest form of relationship.[12] Thus Maitland was always inclined to follow individualistic lines when explaining ancient society, although he admitted that the influence

[8] *Bracton and Azo* (Selden Soc., vol. viii.) p. xiv.
[9] *Domesday Book and Beyond*, pp. 345, 346.
[10] *History of English Law*, i. 619; *Domesday and Beyond*, p. 150.
[11] Review of Seebohm's 'Tribal System in Wales,' *Economic Journal*, vol. v.
[12] *History of English Law*, ii. 238 ff.

of groups made itself felt, to a certain extent, in a loose and extra-legal way. Fustel de Coulanges's clear-cut individualism did not suit him. He often said, in conversation, that the great French *savant* had probably never vouchsafed to look at the map of an open-field country.

Although Maitland's teaching thus ran counter to some of the views held by Maurer and the Germanists on the one hand, Maine and the comparative jurists on the other, he was in no way at one with the exaggerated reaction produced by these views. Neither wholesale Romanism, with the derivation of the manor from the Roman villa, nor the device of treating Old English society as a ring of slaveholders gradually losing their grasp over their dependents was to his taste. He refused to consider the Saxon conquest as achieved by a handful of chieftains without followers,[13] and declared emphatically in favour of the prevalence of Germanic tradition in Old English development.[14] As for the free elements of the population and the rise of the manorial system, his treatment of the problem reckoned materially with the heterogeneous character of Old English society and the degradation of an originally free class.

It is not my object in the present instance to enter into any discussion of Maitland's views on subjects which have called forth protracted literary controversies. I have had occasion to state that I dissent from some of his doctrines on these points. Others may urge objections on their side. But no one can deny, I think, that the sharpness of Maitland's criticism, his high standard of evidence, the thoroughness of his methods of investigation have done more to clear up the difficult problems in question than most dutiful repetitions of time-honoured theories. Whatever may be the ultimate outcome of the controversy, neither the doctrine of early collectivism nor that of tribal development, nor that of gradual emancipation can afford to disregard the exact study of documents and the close reasoning brought to bear on the problems by the late Downing professor. And although the comparative method has certainly not been exploded by his distrust for its applications, those who have to make use of it may do worse than take a warning from his protest against the sliding analogies and sweeping generalisations which are least permissible to a school which claims to do its work on scientific principles.

A touch of good-humoured sarcasm was perhaps more appropriate to Maitland's countenance than other expressions. Some of his most striking appreciations of persons and institutions savour of a rather irreverent frame of mind. But he would go far wrong who supposed, on the strength of sceptical and sarcastic passages, that the sharp glance of the great scholar was apt to

[13] *Domesday Book and Beyond*, p. 232. [14] *Ibid.* 222 ff.

discover nothing but the seamy, the incongruous aspect of things. Maitland had gifts of devotion and enthusiasm which acted as a powerful set-off to his Mephistophelian faculties. No one of the dissonances of history escaped his ear, but he did not fail either to catch the strange harmony of the concert. The grand way in which he clung to study and mastered knowledge enabled him to realise fully the majesty of history as a whole. Two favourite passages close the general introduction to the *Study of the Year Books*. They were not composed but treasured by him, and they are indeed an honour both to those who wrote them and to the one who took them up as noble *dicta*. One is of Justice Holmes, the other of Albert Sorel. I may be allowed to quote at least one of them.

> When I think thus of the law I see a princess, mightier than she who once wrought at Bayeux, eternally weaving into her web dim figures of the ever lengthening past—figures too dim to be noticed by the idle, too symbolic to be interpreted except by her pupils, but to the discerning eye disclosing every painful step and every world-shaking contest by which mankind has worked and fought its way from savage isolation to organic social life.[15]

In every special case, in the treatment of any great doctrine, or institution, or epoch, Maitland has a manner of starting with disconcerting critical observations and of noticing at the outset contradictions and confusion, but then he feels his way, as it were, like a musician running his fingers over the keys in an improvised prelude, towards leading ideas and harmonious combinations. Read his chapters on such subjects as military tenure, or inheritance, or municipal institutions: the dry material becomes curiously attractive through the reflexion of a kind of organic process in the mind of the scholar creating order and sense in the midst of confusion.

Nor were the interests of this thinker solely directed to the study of impersonal evolution. The kindest and most generous of men in personal intercourse, he was keenly appreciative of any merit or achievement of those with whom he came in contact. He was always on the look-out for genuine research, and acknowledged his debts in regard to those from whom he had learnt with ungrudging warmth. The article in the *Quarterly Review*[16] on Liebermann's *Anglo-Saxon Laws* must have brought the proudest reward to the Berlin editor for his masterly work, and many other scholars can look with gratification on sentences in Maitland's books which weigh more than undiscerning praise. I was often struck by the fact that a man of so critical a mind was often almost too apt to admire books which he had just finished reading. He

[15] *Year Books*, vol. i. (Selden Soc. xvii.), p. xx.
[16] Vol. cc. pp. 139–157, July 1904.

recovered soon enough from some of his *engouements*, if I may be allowed to use the untranslatable French expression; but they showed, as it seems to me, that his artistic nature was apt to take for a time the strain of a fine performance, and that critical dissent came almost as an afterthought. Criticism was not less effective for that, but it was never spoiled by the niggardly obtuseness which seeks not to estimate but to harm.

Maitland's learning was anything but insular. He followed with keen interest and unfailing judgment the main currents of legal and historical literature on the continent. In regard to some of his best known theories there may be traced the influence of suggestions received from fellow-workers' writings. We have to note, for instance, how his views as to corporations were influenced by Gierke; in what a remarkable way he developed for England Keutgen's [17] garrison explanation of the rise of boroughs; how he adopted and strengthened Ficker's [18] and Heusler's [19] teaching on early kingship. Thus, although not addicted to comparative legal history in the general sense of the word, he fully realised the importance of analogies for suggesting explanations and filling up gaps in the evidence.

It would be out of the question to state in a short notice, written under the impression of a recent death, what the principal achievements of such a life's work have been. Scholars of the twenty-first century will be in a better position to pronounce a verdict in this respect, as we are nowadays better able to speak of Selden and Blackstone than their own contemporaries. But some lines of appreciation are so clearly indicated even now that it seems natural to allude to them. It is no exaggeration to say that we have known and lost the greatest historian of the law of England, one who not only surpassed all predecessors in this domain but is not likely to be surpassed soon in the course of succeeding generations. As the principal contributor to the monumental *History of English Law*, as the editor of Bracton's *Note Book* and *the Year Books of Edward II*, as the writer of innumerable and invaluable articles for learned periodicals, Maitland has practically remodelled our knowledge of English law at the most important period of its existence. To realise his achievement in this respect one need only think of the standard books of the pre-Maitlandian age—the uncritical, scanty compilation of Reeves and Finlason, the brilliant but all too brief sketch of O. W. Holmes, the fragmentary and ill-balanced attempts of Palgrave and Sir J. Stephen. What we have now is the production of a writer steeped in the original lore of mediæval common law. Bracton and Martin of Pateshull

[17] *Untersuchungen über den Ursprung der deutschen Stadtverfassung.*

[18] *Untersuchungen zur germanischen Rechtsgeschichte.*

[19] *Institutionen des deutschen Privatrechts.*

would certainly not have rejected him as a colleague, and, on the other hand, he stands hand in hand with the leading representatives of European learning at the eventful turn from the nineteenth century to the twentieth.

His intimate knowledge of the thirteenth-century world brought him much nearer to the life of the middle ages than any one else can pretend to be, and we cannot wonder that the great lawyer reveals himself as a great historian. In *Domesday Book and Beyond* he took up a task which led him to examine some of the most complicated and contested problems of social history, and here again his trained and piercing eye did not fail not only to discover new facts, but to co-ordinate them in an unexpected manner. I cannot help thinking that one of the limitations inherent in human work is noticeable in the natural bent of a mind exercised on common-law problems to explain earlier periods mainly in the light of a conflict between individualistic rights and forces. And the standards of criticism and evidence are perhaps too stringent for the case of primitive institutions and the confused fermentation of nationalities in the making. But I need not dwell on disputed points. Even what has been said in these few pages may be sufficient to recall to the memory of European scholars that we have to mourn a real leader of thought. Lawyers, historians, and sociologists are equally indebted to him—lawyers because of his subject, historians because of his methods, sociologists because of his results.

P. VINOGRADOFF.

[2]

L. R. Poos and Lloyd Bonfield

Law and individualism in medieval England

In *The Origins of English Individualism*, Alan Macfarlane has questioned the fundamental evolutionary vision of English society held by both medieval and early modern historians. To replace current theories that stress social change over time, he sketches one of continuity, arguing that a cluster of social and cultural attributes epitomized by the concept of 'individualism' can be discerned among English rural dwellers from as early as the thirteenth century.[1] The forcefulness with which he puts forward his thesis, its polemical tone, and the flawed handling of many particular issues have engendered sharp reactions, particularly among medieval social historians.[2] Equally strong challenges to Macfarlane's theory have been made in a far-reaching and thoughtful review essay by Stephen D. White and Richard T. Vann, two historians whose interests collectively broach the modern divide.[3] The tenor of White and Vann's reflections, however, is not totally negative; for example, they have agreed with Macfarlane that synthetic theories of social change have not yet assimilated the recent rapid progress of empirical research on both sides of this chronological divide.

Perhaps the feature of Macfarlane's thesis which has attracted most fire from his critics, including White and Vann, is his construction of a model 'peasant' society, incorporating a number of elements (particular configurations of family relationships and rights, absence of 'markets' in land and labour), against which to compare medieval English rural society. As White and Vann properly point out, no social historian conversant with the medieval sources or current historiography would recognize a medieval England exclusively comprising the 'peasant' characteristics which Macfarlane selects. And yet Macfarlane, albeit in a sometimes opaque fashion, has raised issues of definition regarding pre-industrial social structure that clearly require stricter specification. For example, both medievalists and early modernists conceive of rural households as basic units of production and consumption, with wage labour or servanthood and participation in product marketing as incremental adjuncts to this basic function; in this respect the

[1] Alan Macfarlane, *The Origins of English Individualism: the family, property, and social transition* (Oxford, 1978).

[2] E.g. R. H. Hilton, 'Individualism and the English peasantry', *New Left Review*, CXX (1980), 109–11.

[3] Stephen D. White and Richard T. Vann, 'The invention of English individualism: Alan Macfarlane and the modernization of pre-modern England', *Social History*, VIII (1983), 345–63.

medieval/early modern divide may now appear one less of kind than of degree.[4] Similarly, although Macfarlane's choice of eastern Europe as a paradigm for all 'peasant' societies may be misplaced, fundamental and long-enduring differences in household structure and associated demographic, economic and legal attributes have nevertheless been delineated among north-western, southern and eastern Europe, with profound implications for these regions' subsequent development.[5] Despite the shortcomings of Macfarlane's absolute, 'straw man' approach, and his flawed discussion of technical matters, he has provoked historians on all sides of these chronological and geographic divides to define and measure more rigorously their chosen indices of change and contrast.

In their review essay, White and Vann deal extensively with Macfarlane's methodology; we wish to turn to another aspect of the thesis which has been treated less satisfactorily: the role of law in pre-industrial English society. Although Macfarlane's arguments about the nature of 'individualism' touch upon a wide variety of issues, from demography to economics to culture, his substantive argument is supported by evidence derived from law and legal institutions. In particular, he stresses that individuals in medieval English rural society had an absolute right in law to control the disposition of their property in the face of what are often believed to have been the contraposed rights or interests of family, community, lord or state. Yet if one accepts the premise that a society's law can serve as a barometer for so wide a range of that society's other qualities, it is necessary to be quite specific about assumptions regarding the nature of law, and how they may be related to these social and cultural attributes.

Analysis of the relationship between law and society is inevitably rendered complex by the nature of evidence with which historians must labour. In the main, our evidence was generated by the legislative or adjudicative process, which over the course of time itself underwent structural change. Historians must therefore isolate institutional alterations because modifications in administrative practice need not necessarily foretell or demonstrate substantive changes in either law or the structure of society. Indeed, institutional developments may mask or distort reality, while significant substantive change can occur within the context of administrative continuity. Our purpose in this essay is therefore not to explore administrative frameworks, but to examine what we believe is a shared conception of substantive law accepted by both the polemicist and his critics. We wish to

[4] For a succinct statement of this principle for medieval England see R. H. Hilton, *The English Peasantry in the Later Middle Ages* (Oxford, 1975), 13. Recent discussions of this function of household economies in early modern Europe include Michael Anderson, *Approaches to the History of the Western Family* (1980), 69–84; F. F. Mendels, 'La composition du ménage paysan en France au xixe siècle: une analyse économique du mode de production domestique', *Annales: Economies, sociétés, civilisations* (1978), 780–802; H. Medick, 'The proto-industrial family economy: the structural function of household and family during the transition from peasant society to industrial capitalism', *Social History*, 1 (1976), 291–315.

[5] Among recent synthetic essays, see in particular J. Hajnal, 'Two kinds of pre-industrial household formation system', and Peter Laslett, 'Family and household as work group and kin group: areas of traditional Europe compared' in Richard Wall (ed.), *Family Forms in Historic Europe* (Cambridge, 1983), 65–104, 513–63.

explore the role of law, not only in reflecting collective cultural values but also in determining behaviour, and further to ponder its suitability as a vehicle for understanding medieval English society.

I

Despite differences in interpreting legal doctrines which form the evidentiary basis of Macfarlane's thesis, Macfarlane (as well as George Homans, whose earlier work forms the backdrop against which much of his attack is launched),[6] and even to a certain extent White and Vann, appear to envisage a deterministic influence by the forces of what may be termed *positive law* upon the practices, beliefs and assumptions which comprise social structure. Our understanding of positive law is that it consists of a set of strictures, prohibitions and coercions which can be sought in definitive statements and applied to particular circumstances. Macfarlane, White and Vann appear to ask: 'What does the law *direct* in this given situation?' Accordingly, they assume behaviour is governed by rules that can be ascertained by reference to a collective source akin to a modern statute book. Law is derived from conflict, and is found in appropriate sources; the historian then proceeds to deduce the attitudes, behaviour or practices which are assumed to reflect the collective personality of pre-industrial English society.

This approach, as White and Vann point out, carries a strong 'odour of structuralism'.[7] Moreover, such a perception of law tends to focus on conflict, and to render law arid and static, immune to economic or demographic influences upon the various strategies of production and reproduction which individuals and families might employ. Perhaps most seriously, if taken to its ultimate extreme, this conceptualization views English villagers as trapped in an orbit determined by rules made by others, and lacking the potential to effect strategies of production and reproduction of their own volition.

We shall argue below that White and Vann, as well as Macfarlane, have erred in their specific interpretations of the positive law of medieval English manorial courts. But here we would question whether their search for positive law is the appropriate manner for evaluating ordinary English people's experience in the past. For legal systems can allow room for manoeuvre, even for a 'peasantry' subject to medieval English customary law. Positive law (again even in the guise of manorial customary law) could, and did, evolve and change in response to influences both internal and external to the law.

Accordingly, we would suggest that the approach to understanding the relationship between law and society is to observe *actual practice*; the question ought to be: 'What *does* happen in a given situation?' Historians must ascertain what different alternatives were taken with what frequencies under what circumstances over time and by various people. White and Vann, while articulating this distinction, have none the less chosen to pursue the quest for fixed rules of positive

[6] George C. Homans, *English Villagers of the Thirteenth Century* (reissued, New York, 1960).

[7] White and Vann, 'English individualism', 356.

law by criticizing Macfarlane's use of medieval evidence, rather than by considering its appropriateness. While arguing that Macfarlane neglects current research on actual peasant practice, White and Vann themselves underemphasize practice in their search for broadly based principles of positive law to illuminate the social structure. We shall employ the same documentary sources scrutinized for principles of positive law by this debate's participants, and suggest that concern with distilling definitive principles has led them seriously astray by failing to appreciate the diversity of actual practice within the structure of customary law.

Delineating patterns of actual practice in property tenure and transmission has, in fact, been central to the approaches of current writers on the subject of rural English social structure, both before and after the medieval/early modern divide.[8] But even these patterns do not yet amount in themselves to what we understand to be an ultimate objective of Macfarlane's quest, the establishment of a set of cultural attitudes and associated practices that comprises 'individualism'. From positive law and actual practice, then, we would further distinguish what may be termed *normative rules*. By this we mean cultural principles regarded by a society's members as defining proper or desirable action to be taken in particular contexts – 'What do the cultural values of the society in question say *should* happen in a given situation?'[9]

As an illustration of the nuances among these concepts, one may take the problem of a father considering the transmission of his property to his offspring under common law rules of inheritance in early modern England.[10] Positive law allowed him under most circumstances to disinherit his children altogether if he wished by selling his land during his lifetime, but it provided that his eldest son would inherit all real property of which he died seised. Normative rules, though, appear to have dictated that daughters and younger sons ought to be given whatever endowment in real or personal property was feasible without seriously compromising the primary heir's position. Actual practice, when observed in operation among many fathers over many decades, inevitably comprised a variety of formal and informal strategies utilizing conveyancing techniques, and depending upon a myriad of factors in individual cases: number and sex of surviving

[8] These will be cited in more detail below; see fns 14 and 18.

[9] We would emphasize that our concept of normative rules includes (though it is not limited to) principles which may be *unconsciously* adhered to and indeed may never be articulated, but can still operate in practice as collectively held values. We have adapted this concept in part from Peter Laslett, 'Demographic and microstructural history in relation to human adaptation: reflections on newly established evidence' in Donald J. Ortner (ed.), *How Humans Adapt: A Biocultural Odyssey* (Washington, 1983), 343–70, although it is used here in a somewhat different context from Laslett's.

[10] For a general discussion of inheritance strategy, see Jack Goody, 'Strategies of heirship', *Comparative Studies in Society and History*, xv (1973), 3–20 and his *Production and Reproduction: a comparative study of the domestic domain* (Cambridge, 1976); and in the context of early modern England see Lloyd Bonfield, 'Marriage, property, and the "affective family"', *Law and History Review*, 1 (1983), 297–312, and also '"Contrasting sources": court rolls and settlements as evidence of hereditary transmission of land among small landowners in early modern England', *University of Illinois Law Review* (1984).

offspring, financial exigencies, nature of property, even emotional quality of family relationships.

The options selected may therefore follow positive law; but they may also circumvent law to accommodate normative rules. Indeed, positive law may ultimately fall into desuetude or be formally abrogated in response to cultural or social change. Because there is little direct evidence articulating normative rules among medieval villagers, these rules can therefore only be inferred by observing actual practice and attempting to isolate influences bearing upon it. It is in this perspective that we propose to consider a pivotal issue regarding rights in property on which much of this debate has crystallized: alienations by manorial tenants who held land upon terms subject to customary law. (Throughout this discussion we refer to 'manorial tenants' as those who held rights in property defined by customs enunciated in local manorial courts. As will become apparent in the course of our essay, the gist of the debate in which we are engaged centres upon the extent to which this customary tenure approximates to modern conceptions of ownership.) Thereafter, we shall consider how free alienation of these customary tenements enabled villagers, through the use of entail, a broader scope for fashioning personalized strategies of property transmission. Instead of asking the question 'could peasants alienate', we shall consider whether they did alienate and how, in order to consider some of the forces that drove them to dispose of land. In so doing, we shall sketch a very different picture of the nature of law and its role in the social structure of pre-industrial society.

II

The central plank of Macfarlane's argument for the primacy of individualist over collectivist initiative in medieval English rural society concerns the implications of what he argues were essentially absolute rights in property, tantamount to ownership in the modern sense of the term. Because this quasi-ownership was vested in individuals rather than families, and implied the right to sell, give, lease or otherwise make permanent dispositions of land without reference to the interests of immediate or wider kin or the 'community', Macfarlane argues that self-interest or 'rampant individualism' epitomized the interactions and emotions of English people from as early as the thirteenth century, predisposing them to their own, particularistic, subsequent role as first developers of capitalism.[11]

We shall return later to the logical leap which Macfarlane makes from the mere *existence* of individual rights to individualism. Although Macfarlane has also been rightly censured for confusing practices and strictures relating to customary tenure, governed by local custom and manorial jurisdiction relating to serfdom, with the freehold tenure of Bracton's treatise and common law courts, we wish to take particular issue with the comments which White and Vann make regarding Macfarlane's discussion of customary law, before shifting attention from positive law to actual practice.

[11] Macfarlane, *English Individualism*, 102–30.

Homans' *English Villagers of the Thirteenth Century* remains an influential discussion of medieval English rural society, and Macfarlane devotes considerable attention to the arguments and evidence which Homans used. Homans' pioneering sociological analysis was informed in many ways by parallels with other pre-industrial societies that in retrospect appear inappropriate. But White and Vann have questioned specific points of customary law raised by Macfarlane's treatment of Homans, and have proposed counter-interpretations which we believe are untenable.

Homans' original work cited a number of land-tenure disputes heard in medieval English manorial courts, which he regarded as explicit statements that under the customary law of the manors in question individual tenants were incapable of alienating or otherwise disposing of their land permanently. Homans regarded these statements as legal expressions of the cultural principle, common to 'traditional' societies, that the bond between family and family land must not be broken; as Homans put it, the land must be kept 'in the blood'. Macfarlane suggested that Homans took as definitive statements of positive law what were in reality verdicts arising from previous land grants to which restrictive conditions had been attached. Therefore, these statements cannot correctly be read as principles governing customary tenure in general. In their turn, White and Vann have not only objected to Macfarlane's extrapolation from the mere existence of monetarized, permanent land transfers to market-centred exchange networks, but have also taken issue with Macfarlane's narrow textual interpretation, which they find 'not successful' and 'unconvincing'. Rather they actually appear to imply that on many medieval English manors customary law did prohibit permanent alienation.[12]

The original manuscripts with which Homans dealt explicitly contradict this, as do similar contemporary sources from other manors. One instance cited by Homans, Macfarlane, White and Vann comes from a case in the manorial court of Burley (Rutland) in 1298.[13] One Richard ate Mere came into court to claim land which a by-then-deceased woman, Juliana Joye, had previously acquired from William ate Mere. William was almost certainly a relative of Richard, as the latter claimed to be heir to the land. The court said that Juliana could not 'sell, bequeath, or assign' the land after her death and granted Richard seisin. Three different interpretations of this case have been offered by the debate's participants: Homans, that the text proved medieval customary tenants were not allowed to alienate land permanently outside the family, and thus did not 'acquire the rights which go with purchase in our modern sense of the word'; Macfarlane, that the principle in this case was a prohibition against disposal *post mortem*, i.e. by will, but that this did not prevent permanent sales *inter vivos*; and White and Vann, that the Latin text may have read that *William* was unable to alienate beyond *his*

[12] Homans, *English Villagers*, 195–207; Macfarlane, *English Individualism*, 102–30; White and Vann, 'English individualism', 354–5.

[13] Public Record Office, London (hereafter PRO), SC2.197.81 (Burley court, 21-6-1298); text given in Homans, *English Villagers*, 196, 442; cf. Macfarlane, *English Individualism*, 114–15; White and Vann, 'English individualism', 355.

lifetime, and therefore that Homans was essentially correct after all. But the text also explicitly states that Juliana's tenure was only for her lifetime (*toto tempore vite sue*). It therefore seems clear that this case was the resolution of a previous grant to which restrictions had been attached at its inception (in this instance, Juliana had received a life interest or lease, which is why she could not dispose of the land beyond her lifetime), and can hardly be taken as a definitive statement of prohibition against permanent alienation *per se*. Such situations can be paralleled in any number of other manorial court rolls. To prove conclusively that this was the issue in this case would require the text of Juliana's original acquisition, which has not survived in the original documents. But the point appears moot, because the very same court roll from which this case comes records transfers from one individual to another, in the form of surrender and admission 'to X and his heirs' employed in permanent *inter vivos* alienations in medieval English manor court rolls.[14]

Another case cited in all three contributions to the debate, recorded in 1296 at the court of Halton (Buckinghamshire), a manor of Christ Church Priory, Canterbury, superficially appears to support Homans' position.[15] The jury stated that 'no tenant of the lord can demise (*dimittere*) his land except for his lifetime, and the heir is not bound to warrant'. Macfarlane noted, quite correctly, that *dimittere* is usually employed in medieval terminology to denote leases rather than permanent alienations. Indeed, Homans himself recognized that this was a lease, but inexplicably claimed that this rule 'would prevent any permanent alienation'. But White and Vann question whether 'lease' is to be understood in this case, and furthermore find it difficult to believe that restrictions of this sort would be found on leases. The first question is easily resolved by the terminology of this same case, which makes it clear that a lease for a limited term of years is at issue: the inquisition was called to determine 'if any tenant of the lord demises his land for a fixed term (*ad certos terminos*) and the tenant died within the term, who ought to fulfil the agreement after the grantor's death?' Another lease recorded on the Canterbury estate at about the same time suggests, moreover, that such conditions might conventionally be applied to leases made under this lordship: one man leased (*dimisit*) ten acres to another for six years, with the stipulation that if the lessor died before the lease was completed the lessor's pledges would acquit the

[14] E.g. PRO, SC2.197.81 (Burley court, 12-12-1297): *Simon Aunsel venit et reddit sursum in manus domini iij rodas terre vocatas Denacre ad opus Roberti Scoltone et heredum suorum. Et idem Robertus dat domino pro introitu xij d...* For discussions of the legal implications of alienation of customary lands by surrender and regrant see John Beckerman, 'Customary Law in English Manorial Courts in the Thirteenth and Fourteenth Centuries' (unpublished Ph.D. dissertation, University of London, 1972), 138–9; P. R. Hyams, 'The origins of a peasant land market in England', *Economic History Review*, 2nd ser., XXIII (1970), 18–31; P. R. Hyams, *King, Lords, and Peasants in Medieval England* (Oxford, 1980), 39–40; R. M. Smith, 'Some thoughts on "hereditary" and "proprietary" rights in customary land in thirteenth- and fourteenth-century England', *Law and History Review*, 1 (1983), 95–128.

[15] Cathedral Archives and Library, Canterbury (hereafter CALC), Eccl. 1.16.43 (Halton court, 24-5-1296); text given in Homans, *English Villagers*, 196, 442; cf. Macfarlane, *English Individualism*, 114; White and Vann, 'English individualism', 354–5.

lessee for loss of the remaining term.[16] A similar provision appears to have been operative in deciding yet another case cited by Homans and taken up by Macfarlane, when a lease was voided by the lessor's death (again, at a Christ Church manor).[17] Here also, as Macfarlane correctly pointed out, Homans interpreted limitations upon leases with restricted terms as paradigmatic of all *inter vivos* transfers.

Although further examples of permanent alienations of customary land could be drawn from any surviving series of medieval English manorial court rolls, we have no wish here to flog a technical issue of legal history. But because Macfarlane's handling of this issue is itself technically flawed, and White and Vann have apparently misrepresented a well-established point of customary law, we would reiterate that, on the narrow topic of individuals' rights under manorial law to make permanent, extrafamilial alienations of customary land, Macfarlane is clearly correct. As White and Vann point out, though, the mere existence of this right says very little about how frequently it was exercised and how its employment coincided with the social or cultural attitudes of English rural society.

To what extent can the existence or even the exercising of this right be equated with a 'market' in land? Macfarlane would define a land 'market' as an exchange network which 'treats land as just another commodity', and which would on his terms be antithetical to a 'peasant' society. But in the looser sense of an arena in which some people sold and some bought land, money was exchanged for property, and the configuration of transactions, participants and levels of prices or entry fines can be described in analytical terms, exchange networks in customary land were an integral feature of medieval English village society and are central to current historiography on the period.

The contexts within which such exchanges took place were diverse and complex, and the quest for explicit statements of positive law or custom, with its attendant quality of textual interpretation of the variety with which Homans, Macfarlane and, to a lesser extent, White and Vann have been concerned, obscures the multifaceted reality over which positive law presided.[18] *Inter vivos* transfers,

[16] CALC, Eccl. 1.26.30 (Newington, Oxon., court, 14-9-1293): *Coventum est inter Nicolaum Trote et Johannem de Samerugg ita quod dictus Nicolaus dimisit dicto Johanni decem acras terre...donec idem Johannes de predicta terra sex vesturas plene percepit...et si dictus Nicolaus infra terminum predictum obierit invenit eidem Johanni plegios...ad solvendum eidem Johanni quantitatem catalli sui quod iuste aretrum fuerit...*

[17] CALC, Eccl. 1.26.29 (Newington court, 30-4-1293); text given in Homans, *English Villagers*, 197–8, 442–3; cf. Macfarlane, *English Individualism*, 115–16. In this case the plaintiff, Thomas le Northerne, claimed that his father John had leased land for his (John's) lifetime to another couple, and now Thomas reclaimed the land after John's death, his claim being upheld by the jury.

[18] For discussions of the different contexts in which these transfers took place, see essays in R. M. Smith (ed.), *Land, Kinship, and Life-Cycle* (Cambridge, 1984); L. R. Poos, 'Population and Resources in Two Fourteenth-century Essex Communities: Great Waltham and High Easter 1327–1389' (unpublished Ph.D. dissertation, University of Cambridge, 1984), 190–255; Hyams, 'Peasant land market'; Smith, '"Hereditary" and "proprietary" rights'; L. R. Poos and R. M. Smith, '"Legal windows onto historical populations?" Recent research on demography and the manor court in medieval England', *Law and History Review*, II (1984),

whether to kin or non-kin, could form part of the devolution process from generation to generation, and therefore would proceed at least partly along life-cyclical patterns; pre-mortem intervention might also be used to modify or circumvent received inheritance custom, or to secure provision of maintenance for the elderly from relatives or non-relatives. Demographic variables play a central role in shaping strategies: rates of heirship failure resulting from mortality/fertility combinations helped to dictate the frequency with which property might be disposed of outside normal heirship channels. Homans apparently never conceived of this possibility, inevitable on a greater or lesser scale due to demographic reality.

Economic or even ecological circumstances might conspire to accelerate differentiation among village strata, and in certain well-documented situations such as the agrarian crisis of 1315–17 were responsible for sharp upsurges in quantities of property coming into the 'market' (as customary tenants holding land insufficient to cushion against harvest failure were forced to sell) and for a pattern of net acquisition by the richer at the expense of the poorer. The surviving records of most villages produce examples of kulak-like accumulators, often involved in creditor roles as well, whose activities did transcend simple household-scale production. Finally, it would be misconceived to envisage the weight or direction of seigneurial interest and intervention in exchanges of customary land as monolithic; while traditionally seen as largely directed against unrestrained alienation of servile property, seigneurial interest itself has been shown to have been more complex, and in some situations to have countenanced large volumes and frequencies of transfers as an elastic source of curial revenue. It is from analyses of temporal and interpersonal patterns of property transactions in these contexts that new syntheses of medieval English rural society, and resolutions of the problems raised by Macfarlane and others, will be (and are being) produced.

Preoccupation with refining principles of positive law also obscures the range of options which were open to individuals in this society and ignores the extent to which normative rules govern behaviour. No legal or social historian would ascribe to customary tenure, with its inbuilt limitations which seigneurial authority posed (at least as ultimate threat even if not regularly exercised), the full 'quasi-ownership' quality Macfarlane imports. And yet the accumulation of recorded decisions which came to carry in some degree the binding force of custom in manorial courts over the later thirteenth and fourteenth centuries also entailed a degree of *de facto* and enforceable security of tenure. One aspect of this security was the development of provisions under customary law which allowed transfers with restricted terms, and therefore permitted individuals to exercise greater latitude in property dealings. Ironically, then, 'absolute' 'individualistic' property rights also implied the right to impose conditions limiting the 'absolute' nature of tenurial security. Some examples have already been touched upon in the cases discussed above; a more complex example is that of entails.

128–52; J. Hatcher, 'English serfdom and villeinage: toward a reassessment', *Past and Present*, XC (1981), 3–39; A. De Windt, 'A peasant land market and its participants: King's Ripton 1280–1400', *Midland History*, IV (1978), 142–59; and the studies contained in P. D. A. Harvey (ed.), *The Peasant Land Market in Medieval England* (Oxford, 1984).

III

We have suggested that the issue of free alienability is multifaceted. While our reading of the cases which Macfarlane cites in manorial court rolls supports the proposition of alienability, we have argued that external pressures on customary tenants imposed by seigneurial authority and internal constraints posed by economic and demographic forces suggest caution in relying too heavily upon random examples from particular manors at given times before translating the potential to alienate into 'individualism'. In this section we shall demonstrate the limitations of basing theses upon assumptions regarding law rather than enquiries into actual practice in fashioning a conception of rights in property in medieval England by illustrating how the power of alienation in conjunction with another legal development, that of entail, enabled small landholders to effect strategies of heirship which might restrain their successors' powers to deal with their inheritance. In short, we shall see how one generation used its powers of alienation to limit alienation in the next.

In addition to the court rolls used by Homans, Macfarlane has recourse to another body of evidence to support his proposition that absolute ownership could be vested in an individual: the commentators upon royal law, and in particular Bracton.[19] White and Vann criticize reliance upon Bracton, arguing that few English villagers were conversant with the text.[20] This was undoubtedly true; however, it does not necessarily follow that the rules which Bracton described did not also reflect peasant practice under customary law. Similar social, economic or cultural forces that interacted to fashion the common law principles which commentators described may well have produced like practices among the peasantry. In short, Macfarlane's search for binding legal authority and White and Vann's theoretical rejection symbolize the shortcomings of the debate: it assumes that 'law' can be found and, once in hand, practice must follow in conformance. We believe that recourse to texts is not unwarranted, but that exclusive reliance is misplaced. Macfarlane's use of Bracton is flawed, not because English villagers were unfamiliar with the text, but because he believes that the notations contained therein directed practice.

Furthermore, Macfarlane misunderstands the context of Bracton. Unlike Macfarlane, Bracton sketches thirteenth-century law as dynamic rather than static.[21] This is crucial; because Macfarlane chooses to stress continuity in law he assumes that Bracton's statements reflect the law in the generations following its compilation. We shall highlight the way in which legal developments limited free alienability, the crucial component of Macfarlane's 'individualism'.

At first blush, Macfarlane's use of Bracton is persuasive. In England, land at common law could be held in fee simple, the equivalent of modern freehold. Where land is granted to 'A and his heirs', it is by the close of the thirteenth century

[19] Macfarlane, *English Individualism*, 105, 120–1.

[20] White and Vann, 'English individualism', 356.

[21] T. F. T. Plucknett, *Early English Legal Literature* (Cambridge, 1958), 60 77; J. H. Baker, *An Introduction to English Legal History*, 2nd edn (1979), 162.

alienable and hereditable. To this point, the legal historian can have no quibble. Yet Macfarlane exhibits a cavalier attitude towards fine distinctions in the law of property. Not only does he consider the customary tenure of the thirteenth century to be tantamount to sixteenth-century copyhold, he seems to equate it with freehold. The alienable and hereditable fee which Bracton at times discusses is a freehold estate. In order to find support in Bracton, Macfarlane must be suggesting that many, most or nearly all of his 'individualists' held freehold land, or else the rules governing the two types were similar.

Neither option, of course, was the case. Despite the legal complication which could arise from holding both free and customary land, the assarting of land in the twelfth and thirteenth centuries did produce customary tenants holding non-customary land. Moreover, many peasants held only parcels of freehold.[22] These men, though technically of different status, were in an economic sense indistinguishable from customary tenants. Yet the majority of 'rustics' which Macfarlane discusses could not have been primarily freeholders and were therefore untouched by the law regarding free tenants, upon which Bracton elaborates. While certain common law principles may have been absorbed into customary law, their reception must be verified by practice in the manor court and not merely assumed.

Moreover, Macfarlane's insistence upon alienability as the focus of property law ignores the diversity and flexibility of the common law described by Bracton. According to Bracton estates might also be conditional.[23] By agreement, a donee or heir might be limited in his powers to deal with the estate even though such provisions were contrary to law. A perusal of Bracton reveals examples of limitations on alienation by the use of reversions and remainders.[24]

Thus Macfarlane, in his search for a unified body of positive law to support his assertions regarding free alienability, both assumes that customary law was indistinguishable from common law and ignores the potential diversity of common law estates in land. His misunderstanding of common law, however, goes even further when he formulates the law with respect to real property as static, and suggests that: 'The only major change between the thirteenth and sixteenth century was that by the Statute of Wills...a parent could...disinherit his heirs.'[25]

Perhaps the most significant alteration in the land law during the period after Bracton was the development of entail. An entail was a fee interest in land, but with a limitation that the estate descend to a particular category of heir. For example, suppose a father wished to grant land to his daughter on her marriage, but on her death he wanted to direct the estate to descend only to male children produced by the daughter's union; if none survived he wanted the estate to revert to his son and the latter's heirs. He might grant land he held in fee as follows: to daughter and son-in-law and the heirs male of their body. What is ironic is that

[22] M. M. Postan, *The Medieval Economy and Society* (1972), 145–7; E. A. Kosminsky, *Studies in the Agrarian History of England in the Thirteenth Century* (Oxford, 1956), 203–23.

[23] G. E. Woodbine (ed.), *Bracton on the Laws and Customs of England*, trans. S. E. Thorne (Cambridge, Mass., 1968), II, 66–84.

[24] *Ibid.*, 70, 106.

[25] Macfarlane, *English Individualism*, 82.

the very freedom to dispose which Macfarlane abstractly discusses could be manipulated through the employment of entail to limit that power in subsequent holders; in our example, the daughter cannot alienate in fee.[26]

In arguing for continuity in the land law Macfarlane dismisses entails as artificial. Moreover, he argues that they could be 'broken'.[27] This was not the case in medieval England. Entails were protected by statute. The intent of Parliament was clearly expressed: alienation of estates limited in this fashion was not to be permitted, because to allow such action was contrary to the wishes of the grantor, which should be respected. Admittedly the entail could be barred, and therefore broken, and the land under entail alienated, by fine and recovery, but this did not occur until the close of the fifteenth century. Thus for about two centuries considerable quantities of land were held in this 'artificial' way, theoretically inalienable, and in practice these entails were allowed to run their course.[28]

It was suggested above that Macfarlane incorrectly assumed that common law doctrine applied to customary estates. Entails were likewise freehold interests, and it could therefore be argued that customary land held by peasants was not similarly limited. Yet a glance through manor-court rolls suggests that entails were fashioned in these tribunals also. For example, in the Wakefield court roll of 4 September 1332 John Tubbyng surrendered to the lord two acres and a rood of land, which were regranted to 'Thomas son of the same John to be held by him and the heirs of his body. And if he dies without heirs the land reverts to John and his right heirs.'[29] Entails were likewise created, including a limitation to the grantor's spouse or daughter-in-law to provide successive interests in possession should the wife survive her husband. It is striking to the legal historian how soon entails appeared in customary land transactions after the statute *De Donis* (1285)

[26] The Statute *De donis* (13 Edw I, c. 1 (1285)) was passed in order to protect the interest in the male heirs from being defeated by an alienation by their parents. Although the statute was silent as to the number of subsequent generations that were protected from parental alienation, the entail was finally interpreted as inalienable for ever. Protection of subsequent issue was provided for in the statute by a writ known as formedon in the descender; the heir could recover from his parent's grantee. Thus, by employing entail a father could circumscribe the power of alienation in subsequent generations. By the last quarter of the fifteenth century entails could be barred by fine and recovery. For a more detailed discussion, see S. F. C. Milsom, *Historical Foundations of the Common Law*, 2nd edn (1981), 72–89. Thereafter, lawyers contrived other mechanical devices to restrain alienation in perpetuity. For a discussion of these conveyancing techniques, see Lloyd Bonfield, *Marriage Settlements, 1601–1740: the Adoption of the Strict Settlement* (Cambridge, 1983), 11–45.

[27] Macfarlane, *English Individualism*, 105.

[28] This statement cannot be supported by reference to a broadly based study. However, historians undertaking research into various landed families have suggested that entails were generally respected. Cf. J. M. W. Bean, *The Estates of the Percy Family, 1416–1537* (Cambridge, 1958), 121; J. P. Cooper, 'Patterns of inheritance and settlement by great landowners from the fifteenth to the eighteenth centuries' in Jack Goody, Joan Thirsk and E. P. Thompson (eds), *Family and Inheritance: Rural Society in Western Europe 1200–1800* (Cambridge, 1976), 201.

[29] Sue Sheridan Walker (ed.), *The Court Rolls of the Manor of Wakefield from October 1331 to September 1333* (Leeds, 1983), 108.

protected them at common law; Maitland observed this point in reproducing an entail recorded in the court rolls of Weedon Beck (Northamptonshire) in 1291.[30]

The employment of entails was one method of fashioning flexible transmission strategies, which we believe was the thrust behind many land transfers. Other customary tenants employed cross-remainders where they wished to provide for more than one child but desired that the holding be reunited if one child died without issue.[31] Such limitations would restrain alienation in the second generation. While such strategies may have been limited to more prosperous landholders, the flexibility infused into customary law by the acceptance of entail and remainders/reversions provided the customary tenant with the opportunity to direct dispositions in succeeding generations, and therefore circumscribe their heirs' powers of alienation.

It may be argued that the mere existence of limitations in admittances in manorial court rolls similar to entails does not prove that tenants could limit their successors' powers of disposition. Rather, examples of the actual enforcement of the restraint on alienation directed by entail are required to establish a persuasive case. This would require a survey of land disputes in a number of manorial court rolls. Our preliminary research into customary practice suggests, however, that the restraint upon alienation which entail sought to promote was sanctioned. A detailed illustration of the employment and protection of an entail in the manor of Codicote in Hertfordshire may provide an example. In the court of 27 October 1292, customary land which had been held by his wife Eleanor's father was granted to Robert, son of William Pani of Watton and 'the heirs issuing from them'.[32] Robert had recently married Eleanor and the land must have been Eleanor's inheritance. The terms of the limitation are worth reciting in detail:

> And if it happens that the said Eleanor dies without an heir between the said Robert and the said Eleanor the said Robert will hold the said land for his lifetime...And after the death of the said Robert, if he die without heir as aforesaid, the land will revert to the true heirs of the said Richard if there be any.[33]

Thus, during their lifetimes, alienation was proscribed: at their death the land was to descend to their children; if they died without issue the land was to pass to the grantor's heirs.

Despite the limitation, some fourteen years later Robert and Eleanor surrendered one message with curtilage to Margery and Agnes, daughters of Eleanor

[30] F. W. Maitland (ed.), *Select Pleas in Manorial and other Seignorial Courts*, Selden Society, vol. 2 (1889), 40.

[31] For particular examples, see the cases discussed in Poos, 'Population and resources', 204–17.

[32] British Library, Stowe MS, 849 (Manor of Codicote, court book) fo. 21v: *sibi et heredibus ex se ipsis provenientibus*...

[33] *Ibid. Et si contingat quod dicta Helienora sine herede inter ipsum Robertum et dictam Helienoram decedat dictus Robertus quo ad vixerit dictam terram tenebit....Et post mortem dicti Roberti si sine herede decedant ut supradictum est terra revertatur ad veros heredes dicti Ricardi si sint.*

by a previous marriage, while retaining life interests in themselves.[34] Thereafter, in 1334, Robert and Eleanor surrendered all lands 'from the inheritance of the said Eleanor in Codicote' to one Simon at Watteredelle in return for 'sufficient sustenance'.[35] The transfer was in the nature of a retirement arrangement, whereby Simon was admitted in fee in return for the annual rendering of various quantities of grain to Richard and Eleanor for their lifetimes.

Upon the death of Eleanor, however, the arrangement was challenged.[36] Alice Sawyne and her husband Adam appeared in court claiming that she was the legitimate daughter of Robert and Eleanor and that the alienation to Simon was made in derogation of the grant. Alice prevailed and also recovered the messuage and curtilage alienated to Margery and Agnes made 'against the first form of the grant'.[37]

This complex case suggests that entails were created in the late thirteenth century in order to effect individual inheritance strategies, and that the restraint directed was respected. Further research may demonstrate how widely the freedom of alienation which Macfarlane rightly suggests existed among some customary tenants in medieval England was manipulated by entail to deprive successors of similar latitude. At this juncture it is clear that the abstract principles elaborated upon by Bracton which Macfarlane selected cannot be employed to fashion an argument for plenary powers of disposition. It is only through exploration of peasant practice that the extent of alienation can be ascertained, its purposes delineated, and the argument for individualistic conceptions of property sustained.

IV

Our purpose in this essay has been to explore the conception of law embraced by Alan Macfarlane in constructing a thesis of continuity in pre-industrial English social structure. Macfarlane, as well as White and Vann, strives to find principles of positive law articulated in cases and the legal commentators to support his view of the social, economic and cultural attributes of English society. By focusing on the pivotal issue of freedom of alienation, we have illustrated the shortcomings of such an approach. Accordingly, we have suggested that Macfarlane may be correct in proffering wide latitude in alienation, but before this can be translated into 'individualism' the variety of actual practice must be observed. Within the strictures of positive law, be it common law or customary law, and perhaps even outside it, the peasantry responded to economic and demographic variables producing a variety of inheritance strategies. At times it would appear that some peasants employed sophisticated legal devices such as entails to effect a desired distribution that circumscribed their successors' freedom of alienation.

Preferences in inheritance strategies were as likely to have been governed by self-generated normative rules as to have been directed from above by positive

[34] *Ibid.* (6 Oct. 1306), fo. 29v.

[35] *Ibid.* (21 Apr. 1334), fo. 58v: *sustentacionem sufficientem.*

[36] *Ibid.* (15 Oct. 1338), fos. 63v, 64r.

[37] *Ibid.*, fo. 64r: *et contra primam formam donationis etc.*

law. Seigneurial control may have played some role, but only to the extent necessary to protect their interests. Normative rules must be inferred from broadly based studies of actual inheritance practice. Until such research is undertaken, the argument that English society consisted of 'rampant individualists' who dealt with their property untouched by societal and familial expectations must be treated with healthy scepticism. In our view it is as unrealistic to assume that pronouncements of law control behaviour as it is to dismiss lordship and the greater or lesser degree of collectivist interaction which characterized medieval English village society.

Principles of positive law cannot be ignored, but attempts to establish them should not serve either to direct or to limit historical discussion. Our aim must be to broaden conceptions of law beyond the statutes, the cases and the commentators to include actual practice. By so doing we can observe the inherent contradictions in what appears to be a straightforward body of law. Ultimately, our focus will then return to the economic, structural and demographic variables that interacted with the process of rule-making in pre-industrial English society.

Tulane University Law School, New Orleans
Catholic University of America, Washington

[3]

MEMORANDA AND DOCUMENTS

A NEGLECTED ASPECT OF THE RELATIONS BETWEEN ECONOMIC AND LEGAL HISTORY

IN the course of my studies in legal history I have been struck by the fact that many of the rules of English law have an economic origin. This is true both of the enacted and the unenacted law. At all periods in the history of English law the group of statutes on economic subjects surpass in bulk the statutes on any other subject; and some of these statutes have given rise to technical developments in the law, which have had a longer life than the statute itself. Similarly, there are a number of rules of the common law, which owe their origin to some economic idea or necessity existing at the period when they first appeared; and these rules have often survived the idea or necessity to which they owed their origin, and have developed in unexpected directions. This phenomenon is, it seems to me, a neglected aspect of the relations of economic and legal history. It is this neglected aspect of their relations that is the subject of this paper.

To illustrate this aspect of the interrelation of rules of English law, statutory and otherwise, and economic conditions I propose to take three sets of instances: (1) the Statutes of Labourers and the labour legislation of Elizabeth's reign; (2) the agitation against monopolies in Elizabeth's reign, and James I.'s Statute of Monopolies; and (3) developments in the land law.

1. *The Statutes of Labourers and the labour legislation of Elizabeth's reign.*

I do not intend to undertake an exhaustive examination of the provisions of the Statutes of Labourers, nor of the Elizabethan Statute of 1562–63,[1] in which they were codified and adapted to the needs of the sixteenth century. I only want to call attention to two cases—one of very minor importance, and one of very great importance—in which this legislation has given rise to technical rules of law. I will take first the rule of minor importance.

It was laid down in 1824 by Lord Denman, C.J., in the case of *Fawcett v. Cash*,[2] that "if a master hire a servant, without mentioning the time, that is . . . in point of law, a hiring for a year." This I think is due to the fact that, under the Statutes of Labourers, the hiring must be for a year or six months; and under the Statute of Elizabeth there

[1] 5 Eliz., c. 4.

[2] 5 Barnewall and Adolphus, 907.

were a large number of employments in which the hiring must be for a year. Sir Edward Coke, whose legal history is not always erroneous, said: "If a man retains a servant generally without expressing any time, the law shall construe it to be of one year";[1] and then he cites the Statutes of Labourers—beginning with the ordinance of 23 Edward III.

I turn now to the more important rule. In the fourteenth century the courts held that, as the result of the Statutes of Labourers, civil proceedings, in the form either of an action of trespass, or an action of trespass on the case, could be taken, not only against a servant who left his master's service, but also against a person who enticed him away. In Elizabeth's reign the courts held that the right of action against a person, who enticed another person's servant away, was not affected by the repeal of the Statutes of Labourers by Elizabeth's Statute of 1562–63; and it was held in later cases that an action would lie, not only if A enticed B's servant away, but also if he retained B's servant knowing him to be B's servant. Now I think that the idea of the courts was this: they considered that though the relation between master and servant was contractual in its origin, yet that the contract of employment, like the contract of marriage, gave rise to a status of a peculiar kind; and that the rights and duties involved in this status must be protected by actions against persons who interfered with them. But, in the nineteenth century, the tendency was to regard the contract of employment simply as a contract and nothing more. Therefore, the cause of action against a person who procured a servant to leave his master's employment came to be regarded as simply an action for causing a breach of contract. This paved the way for the decision in 1853, in the case of *Lumley v. Gye*,[2] that the procuring of the breach of any contract gives a cause of action—that it is, in other words, an actionable wrong. I need not dwell on the practical importance of this decision at the present day. What I want to emphasize is the fact that this modern rule of law is derived directly from the industrial legislation of the Middle Ages and Elizabeth's reign. And in this connection it may be noted that, in the case of *Lumley v. Gye*, the only cases cited in support of the modern rule that persuasion to break a contract is an actionable wrong were, apart from cases of procuring a breach of the contract of marriage, contracts of service to which the Statutes of Labourers applied. I think that, historically, there is much to be said for Coleridge, J.'s, dissenting judgment, to the effect that, apart from the Statutes of Labourers, the common law gave no action for procuring a breach of contract. However that may be, it is clear that this industrial legislation is at the root of a principle of enormous importance in our modern law. I pass now to my second set of illustrations.

[1] Coke upon Littleton, 42*b*.

[2] 2 Ellis and Blackburn, 216.

2. *The agitation against monopolies in Elizabeth's reign, and James I.'s Statute of Monopolies.*

It is well known that the agitation against monopolies at the latter part of Elizabeth's reign was the first serious opposition, of a non-religious kind, that the Queen had been called upon to face. The agitation raised all sorts of questions as to the Crown's power to make grants of monopolies, and to grant privileges to trading companies. Elizabeth won a great diplomatic triumph when she persuaded parliament to abandon a projected bill on this topic, which would have raised serious constitutional questions, and to leave the validity of these monopolies to be tried by the common law courts. The views of the common lawyers are to be found in the case of *Darcy v. Allen* (1602), which is reported by three reporters—Coke, Moore, and Noy[1]—and also in other cases of the early years of the seventeenth century.

The question of the validity of these monopolies, and of grants of trading privileges to companies, municipal corporations, and others, was eminently an economic question, which depended a good deal upon current views as to economic expediency. Naturally the opinions expressed by the judges of the courts of common law to some extent reflected these views; but equally naturally the judges expressed their opinions in the technical language, and from the technical point of view, of the lawyers. I shall take five illustrations of the fact that their consideration of these economic questions from this technical angle both illustrates the economic origin of certain rules of English law, and has given rise to some important rules in different branches of English law.

(i.) It was admitted that a monopoly was valid if the grantee had introduced a new invention into the kingdom and had thereby created a new industry. Statutory effect was given to this rule in 1624 by James I.'s Statute,[2] which is the foundation of our modern patent law.

(ii.) It was admitted that the Crown might grant privileges restrictive of trade, in order that trade might be properly organized and governed. In *The City of London's Case* (1610)[3] Coke said that privileges were valid if granted to "a fraternity society or corporation of merchants to the end that good order and rule should be by them observed for the increase and advancement of trade and merchandise"; and the legislature agreed. James I.'s Statute of Monopolies[4] excepted from its operation charters granted to corporations and companies "for the maintenance enlargement or ordering of any trade of merchandise." In 1684 the extent of the powers which this exception

[1] 11 Coke's Reports, 84*b*; Moore, King's Bench, 671; Noy, 173.
[2] 21 James I., c. 3. [3] 8 Coke's Reports, 125*a*. [4] 21 James I., c. 3, § 9.

from James I.'s Statute gave to the Crown was exhaustively discussed in the case of *The East India Company v. Sandys*,[1] or, as it is sometimes called, the "Case of Monopolies." The case arose in this way. The East India Company had been granted by their charter an exclusive right to trade to the East Indies. The defendant infringed this right by trading in the East Indies without a license. The plaintiff company sued him for damages. The defendant contended that the grant by the Crown of this exclusive right to trade was void, because it was a monopoly. The principal judgment was given by Jeffreys, C.J.; and it constitutes one of the strongest pieces of evidence that Jeffreys, in spite of his very numerous failings, was a learned lawyer. He held that the charter of the East India Company was valid, because the common law gave the Crown large and indefinite powers to regulate and govern foreign trade. I think that we may fairly say that this decision is an illustration of the way in which economic ideas have influenced that branch of constitutional law which is concerned with the prerogative. And it should be noted that there was no complaint of the correctness of this decision at the Revolution. Therefore, the idea that the Crown had large and vague powers to regulate foreign trade did not disappear. In 1718 Mr. West, the counsel of the board of trade, summed up the views then generally held as to the extent of this prerogative. He said:[2] "That particular subjects should have an uncontrollable liberty of all manner of trading, is not only against the policy of our nation, but of all other governments whatsoever. I do, therefore, take it to be law, that the Crown may, upon special occasion, and for reasons of state, restrain the same; and that not only in cases of war, plague, or scarcity of any commodity, of more necessary use at home, for the provision of the subject, or the defence of the kingdom, etc. . . . but even for the preservation of the balance of trade; as suppose a foreign prince, though in other respects preserving a fair correspondence and in amity with us, yet will not punctually observe such treaties of commerce as may have been made between the two nations; or, in case there are no such treaties existing, refuses to enter into such a regulation of trade as may be for the mutual advantage and benefit of both dominions. On such occasion, I am of opinion that the king, by his prerogative, may prohibit and restrain all his subjects, in general, from exporting particular commodities, etc., or else, generally from trading to such a particular country or place. . . . Without such a power it is obvious that the government of England could not be upon equal terms with the rest of its neighbours, and since trade depends principally upon such treaties and alliances as are entered

[1] 10 State Trials 371.

[2] Forsyth, *Cases and Opinions on Constitutional Law*, 423-27.

into by the Crown with foreign princes; and, since the power of entering into such treaties is vested absolutely in the Crown, it necessarily follows that the management and direction of trade must, in a great measure, belong to the king. Things of this nature are not to be considered strictly according to those municipal laws, and those ordinary rules, by which the private property of subjects resident within the kingdom is determined; but a regard must also be had to the laws of nations, to the policy and safety of the kingdom; the particular interest and advantages of private men must, in such cases, give way to the general good; and acting against that, though in a way of commerce, is an offence punishable at the common law. Foreign trades carried on by particular subjects for their private advantage, which are really destructive unto, or else tending to the general disadvantage of the kingdom, are under the power of the Crown to be restrained or totally prohibited. . . . Carrying on such trades is, in truth (what some acts of parliament have declared some trades to be), being guilty of common nuisances; and if the Crown, which in its administration of government is to regard the advantage of the whole realm, should not be invested with sufficient power to repress and restrain such common mischiefs, it has not a power to do right to all its subjects." In fact, this idea that the king, by virtue of his prerogative, has large powers to regulate foreign trade came very naturally to an age which believed that foreign trade should be so regulated as to increase the strength of the nation. It is true that after the Revolution the tendency was to vest the power of making these regulations in parliament rather than in the king. In 1693 parliament resolved that "it is the right of all Englishmen to trade to the East Indies, or any part of the world, unless prohibited by act of parliament." But parliament often acted upon the principles set out in Mr. West's opinion. And so we get a body of rules as to regulation of trade, statutory and otherwise, which are based on this economic theory. They did not disappear till those ideas disappeared under the influence of very different economic theories—so that here again we see a striking instance of the influence of economic ideas on legal rules.

(iii.) It was admitted by the common lawyers that various privileges granted to boroughs and gilds in mediæval times, though they would have been invalid if newly granted by royal charter, could be justified by custom. Thus in *The City of London's Case* (1610)[1] it was held that a custom in the city of London that no foreigner—*i.e.*, no one not a freeman of the city—should keep any shop, or use any trade in London, was a valid custom; and that a bye-law which imposed a penalty for the infringement of the custom was a valid bye-law. Privileges such

[1] 8 Coke's Reports, 121*b*.

as these, which represent mediæval economic ideas, having been thus held to be valid in the seventeenth century, continued to be upheld until they were finally abolished by § 14 of the Municipal Corporations Act, 1835. Here, then, we see an instance of the survival of a rule, founded on mediæval economic ideas which had long passed away, because it had given rise to a rule of law. It survived till it was swept away in obedience to a totally different set of economic ideas.

(iv.) It was admitted that the Crown might impose restrictions on the freedom of trade in the interests of the State. Thus, in the first place, it might grant a monopoly of the sole printing of books;[1] and this view of the law was confirmed by the legislature in James I.'s Statute of Monopolies.[2] As I have elsewhere shown, this prerogative of the Crown is one of the roots of the law of copyright.[3] In the second place, in the interests of the defence of the realm, a monopoly of saltpetre was held to be valid.[4] That prerogative was dealt with at length by Coke in *The Case of the King's Prerogative in Saltpeter* (1607).[5] And the dicta in that case were relied on by the court in the *Shoreham Aerodrome Case*[6] to prove that, in a time of emergency, the Crown had extensive powers to requisition property without paying compensation. In view of *The De Keyser's Hotel Case*,[7] it is probable that the Shoreham Aerodrome Case was wrongly decided. But it is clear that here again we have an important instance in which economic ideas, as to the extent of the Crown's powers to regulate trade and industry, have contributed to the making of our constitutional law.

(v.) It was assumed by Coke and the common lawyers in the case of *Darcy v. Allen* that trade ought to be free. Now it is clear from what has been already said that, when the common lawyers talked of freedom of trade, they did not attach to that phrase the meaning which we attach to it to-day. What they meant was that trade ought to be free from arbitrary restrictions unknown to the common law of that day. We have seen that they were prepared to admit that the common law of that day sanctioned all kinds of restrictions which are not now recognized; and it is clear that those restrictions reflected the economic ideas of the middle ages and the sixteenth century, which admitted that the Crown had large powers to act in the commercial interests of the nation. But to-day, when freedom of trade has, under the influence of a different set of economic ideas, come to mean something very different, these old phrases about freedom of trade have been cited for propositions which Coke would probably have denounced as

[1] Moore, King's Bench, 673.
[2] 21 James I., c. 3, § 10.
[3] History of English Law, VI., 365-36, 376-74, 378-79.
[4] Moore, King's Bench, 831.
[5] 12 Coke's Reports, 12.
[6] Law Reports [1915], 3 K.B., 649.
[7] Law Reports [1920], A.C., 508.

far too wide. Take this statement, for instance, from the judgment of Lord Parker in the case of *The Attorney-General of the Commonwealth of Australia v. Adelaide Steamship Company*:[1]

"At common law every member of the community is entitled to carry on any trade or business he chooses and in such manner as he thinks most desirable in his own interests, and inasmuch as every right connotes an obligation, no one can lawfully interfere with another in the free exercise of his trade or business, unless there exists some just cause or excuse for such interference. Just cause or excuse for interference with another's trade or business may sometimes be found in the fact that the acts complained of as an interference have all been done in the bona fide exercise of the doer's own trade or business, and with a single view to his own interests.[2] But it may also be found in the existence of some additional or substantive right conferred by letters patent from the Crown or by contract between individuals. In the case of letters patent from the Crown this additional or substantive right is generally described as a monopoly. In the latter case the contract on which the additional or substantive right is founded is generally described as a contract in restraint of trade. Monopolies and contracts in restraint of trade have this in common, that they both, if enforced, invoke a derogation from the common law right, in virtue of which any member of the community may exercise any trade or business he pleases and in such manner as he thinks best in his own interests."

It is clear from Lord Parker's statement that to Coke and the lawyers of his day, the phrase "freedom of trade" meant something very different to that which the phrase means to the lawyers of to-day. The old cases are cited, but a new meaning is given to them; and this change of meaning has been caused by a change in economic ideas. As O. W. Holmes once said very truly:[3] "When ancient rules maintain themselves . . . new reasons more fitted to the time have been found for them, and they gradually receive a new context, and at last a new form, from the grounds to which they have been transplanted."

I now pass to the third of my series of illustrations—developments in the land law.

3. *Developments in the land law.*

I propose to take three illustrations of the manner in which economic ideas have influenced the development of the land law—one from the middle ages; another, closely connected with the first, from the sixteenth century; and a third from modern times.

[1] Law Reports [1913], A.C., 793-94.
[2] *The Mogul Steamship Case*, Law Reports [1892], A.C., 25.
[3] *The Common Law*, 36.

(i.) It is well known that two fundamental dividing lines in the land law, which lasted until 1926, were, first, the division of interests in land into freehold interests, which fell into the category of real property, and interests for terms of years, which fell into the category of personal property; and second, the division between land held by free, and land held by unfree or villein tenure. Now the first of these dividing lines—the distinction between freehold interests and interests for terms of years—was, in its origin, not due to economic causes. It was due to an unfortunate adaptation of the rules of Roman law. Maitland has said:[1] " The only explanation that the lawyers have to give is a romanesque explanation." They followed, or thought they followed, the Roman law of possession, when they treated the lessee as a mere *conductor* who had merely a personal right as against his landlord, but no possession. Hence the interest of the lessee for years, being protected by the personal and not by real actions, fell into the category of personal property; and so the English land law was split into two halves—" English law for six centuries and more will have to rue this youthful flirtation with Romanism."

But the law soon came to the conclusion that the lessee had something very much more than a merely personal right as against his lessor. It was recognized that he had a proprietary right. Why, then, was it never protected by the real actions and classed as real property ? Why did it continue to be protected by personal actions and to be classed as personal property ? The answer to this question, Maitland thinks, depends upon economic reasons. These leases very often represented investments of capital. If they had been regarded as real property they could not have been left by will. But as Maitland says: " It is very natural that a man who invests a round sum should wish for a power of bequest. The invested sum is an utterly different thing from the landed estate which he would desire to keep in his family."[2]

I pass to the second of these distinctions—the distinction between land held by free, and that held by unfree, tenure. The question at what point the courts drew the line between free tenure, which connoted protection by the royal courts and the common law, and unfree tenure, which connoted the absence of this protection, is by no means easy to state confidently. The best opinion is, I think, this: a tenure which compelled the tenant to do any large amount of labour services for his lord, which put him in effect in the position of one of the hands by which the lord's demesne was cultivated, was classed as unfree. The courts had gone great lengths in ousting the lords' jurisdiction by protecting all free tenants. Having regard to the labour service system, by which the lord cultivated his demesne, it may well have

[1] Pollock and Maitland, ii., 114 (2nd ed.). [2] *Ibid.*, ii., 117.

seemed to these royal courts that, if they still further extended their jurisdiction, and protected unfree as well as free tenants, they would have deprived landowners of proper control over the management of their estates. If this is so, the line which the royal courts drew in the twelfth and thirteenth centuries between free and unfree tenure is due to economic causes—so that it may be said that the economic conditions prevailing in those centuries are the cause for this salient distinction in the English land law between freehold and copyhold, which lasted until 1926.

I pass now to the sixteenth century.

(ii.) It is well known that, at the end of the fifteenth and the beginning of the sixteenth centuries, the evil effects of depopulation, caused by the conversion of arable land into sheep farms, were exercising the mind of the government. Now it is quite clear that the denial to the lessee for years of a remedy, which would enable him to recover his land if he were wrongly turned out of his farm, and the denial to the copyholder of any remedy in the king's court if he were ejected, facilitated the operations of landlords who wished to turn out their tenants, and use their property as pasture for sheep. It is, I think, for this reason that the lawyers, at the end of the fifteenth century, decided to allow the lessee for years, who had been ejected, to recover, not only damages, but also the land itself; and that they decided to give the copyholder a similar remedy, if the lord ejected him in defiance of the custom of the manor. Here, then, we have two changes in the law, which had large indirect effects on the development of the land law, due mainly to economic causes. I pass now to my last instance, which comes from modern times.

(iii.) The evils of the system of strictly settling property came to be more and more felt, as, in the course of the nineteenth century, England became industrialized. These evils have been admirably stated by Sir Arthur Underhill:[1]

" If the estate consisted of a large tract of poor country, fruitful in dignity but scanty in rent, and especially if the portions of younger children charged on it were heavy, he too often found it a *damnosa hereditas ;* the rents, after payment of interest on the portions, leaving a mere pittance for the unfortunate life tenant to live upon, and quite disabling him from making improvements, or even keeping the property in a decent state of repair. Nay, more, if he did spend money in improvements, the money was sunk in the estate to the detriment of his younger children. He could not pull down the mansion house, however old and inconvenient it might be, nor even, strictly, make any substantial alteration in it. Unless expressly made unimpeachable for

[1] *A Century of Law Reform*, 284-85.

waste, he could not open new mines. But, in addition to these disabilities, what pressed still more hardly upon him, and on the development of the estate generally, was his inability to make long leases. Consequently, when valuable minerals lay beneath a settled property, or the growth of a neighbouring town made it ripe for building sites (the rents for which would greatly exceed the agricultural rent), nothing could lawfully be done. The tenant for life could not open the mines himself even if he had the necessary capital for working them; nor, even if unimpeachable for waste, could he grant leases of them to others for a term, which would repay the lessees for the necessary expenditure in pits and plant; nor could he grant building leases or sell for building purposes at fee farm rents."

It was these economic evils which produced the settled land acts, 1882–90. As Lord Macnaghten said in *Bruce v. Marquis of Aylesbury*:[1] "The act of 1882 differs from all previous legislation in regard to settled land. . . . A period of agricultural depression, which showed no sign of abatement, had given rise to a popular outcry against settlements. The problem was how to relieve settled land from the mischief which strict settlements undoubtedly did in some cases produce, without doing away altogether with the power of bringing land into settlement. That was something very different from the task to which parliament addressed itself in framing the settled estates acts. In those acts the legislature did not look beyond the interests of the persons entitled under the settlement. In the settled land acts the paramount object of the legislature was the well-being of the settled land." In other words, economic reasons produced the scheme of the settled land acts, under which the tenant for life under a settlement was given very many of the powers of an absolute owner, in order that the best use might be made of the property, in the interests both of the general public and of the beneficiaries under the settlement.

This paper has been rather in the nature of an array of scattered instances. I hope that it has demonstrated the close connection which exists between legal and economic history. That connection is so very close that I do not think that either the legal or the economic historian can do justice to his subject without extensive borrowings from the other's learning—that, at any rate, is the experience of one legal historian.

W. S. Holdsworth.

[1] Law Reports [1892], A.C., 364-65.

[4]

Book Reviews

An Old Play in Modern Dress

The Death of Contract. By Grant Gilmore. *Columbus, Ohio: Ohio State University Press,* 1974. Pp. 151. $8.00.

Reviewed by S.F.C. Milsom†

The reviewer determined to complain about something had better pick on the title. The death in question, like Mark Twain's, may turn out to have been exaggerated. Mr. Gilmore's book is as much about the birth of contract as its death. And in a deeper sense it is not about the death of anything, but about the way in which the common law lives, perhaps the way in which any system of law lives.

To this improbable reviewer, a legal historian practicing mostly in the Middle Ages, it has given that rare and unnerving pleasure experienced by lecturers who suddenly, in full cry, understand what they are saying. From time to time, pretending that he belongs in a law school, the medievalist puts on a course with some such title as "mechanics of legal development." Part of it goes like this. The law is a reiterated failure to classify life. There have always been categories like tort and contract (the medieval words were trespass and covenant); each cycle begins with fact situations being pinned up under the one or the other without much need for thought. Under each heading, the preoccupations of the formative period dictate more or less clear rules; and the system as a whole acquires mathematical force. But as soon as the force is compelling, the system is out of date. Both the classification itself and the rules within each category formed around yesterday's situations; when today's are pinned up on the same principles, they are subjected to rules and yield results no longer appropriate. The individual lawyer cannot hope to get the rules changed for his client, but he can often try to have his case reclassified. No doubt a promise is a promise: but it may also be or imply a statement, and if the rules of contract do not effectively enforce the promise, the statement may still trigger essentially tortious rules about reliance. This is how *as-*

† F.B.A., Professor of Legal History, University of London; Visiting Professor of Law, Yale University.

The Yale Law Journal Vol. 84: 1585, 1975

sumpsit began, not, of course, as the conscious device of a profession suddenly aware that its rules of contract were out of date, but as a back door to justice in a few hard cases. For the front door, the law of contract governing at the time, you needed a document under seal; this once sensible requirement of proof for large transactions was being forced upon small ones by economic and jurisdictional changes, hitting first and worst those who themselves acted on their agreements but had no document with which to attack the other side. It was for such victims that lawyers first sought out a backdoor "tort theory." But the inappropriateness of sealing wax for daily business turned it into the main entrance: most agreements were made on the footing that any litigation would be in *assumpsit,* and the document under seal came to be used only for special transactions. And so our first law of contract died its death, and there was conceived that which was to flourish in the late 19th and early 20th centuries and to die so opportunely under the eyes of Mr. Gilmore.

The medievalist's offering is of course a little fraudulent: already uncomfortable as the 17th century looms up, he never reaches the 19th, let alone today; names like 'promissory estoppel' and 'products liability' have hitherto been dropped to suggest that it all belongs together and that the past can illuminate the present.[1] Now it turns out that it all does indeed belong together, and that the present can also illuminate the past. One might say that Mr. Gilmore has almost produced this play again in modern dress, but with the richness of ascertainable detail, the immediacy of Corbin's recollections, and the solidity of Mr. Fuller's reliance cases[2] instead of those shadowy early *assumpsits.* But one difference deserves discussion. The mechanism depends upon there being clearly separate categories within which rules are insulated, and the early *assumpsit* cases seem to have been truly seen or at least truly presented as trespass rather than covenant, in our language tort rather than contract. It was this that warded off the requirement of a seal, and development would have been crippled by a suggestion which left some traces in the year books: that even in the tort action a plaintiff relied upon the contract as a factual ingredient, must prove it appropriately.[3] The modern analogue, presumably, would be a holding that reliance entitled you to reliance damages, but did not absolve you from the need to prove consideration.

1. On all the foregoing, see the present reviewer's HISTORICAL FOUNDATIONS OF THE COMMON LAW (1969) and *Reason in the Development of the Common Law*, 81 LAW Q. REV. 496 (1965).
2. Fuller & Perdue, *The Reliance Interest in Contract Damages*, 46 YALE L.J. 52, 373 (1936).
3. Y.B. Mich. 2 Hen. 4, f. 3d, pl. 9; Y.B. Mich. 11 Hen. 4, f. 33, pl. 60.

A Pageant in Modern Dress

But the development described by Mr. Gilmore began entirely in contract, the separate categories being epitomized by two sections of the first *Restatement of Contracts,* § 75 (consideration) and § 90 (reliance). His account of their genesis is perhaps the most absorbing passage in this absorbing book. He also gives as good an explanation as we can hope for of the paradoxical fact of the two sections in the same document: the text and illustrations of § 90 suggest "that no one had any idea what the damn thing meant";[4] it was compelled by a line of cases won by plaintiffs who could plainly show no consideration within the meaning of § 75, in many of which the courts had resorted to talk of estoppel, "which is simply a way of saying that, for reasons which the court does not care to discuss, there must be judgment for plaintiff."[5] Section 90, in short, represents a sensible, practical view taken in hard cases. "A sensible, practical view it may be," wrote the greatest of legal historians about a very different development, "but legal principle avenges itself."[6] Mr. Gilmore mentions recent suggestions that a recovery based on the principle behind § 90 is not a contract recovery at all.[7] As a practical matter, of course, such recovery accommodates plaintiffs who lack some component in the contract package other than consideration; it would also lead to greater flexibility over damages (a need, incidentally, which seems to have helped the beginning of *assumpsit*). But the compulsion to intellectualize is surely playing its part. Of §§ 75 and 90 Mr. Gilmore says that "these two contradictory propositions cannot live comfortably together: in the end one must swallow the other up."[8] Or push it out into a different compartment of the law? The animals can live at the same time provided they are in separate cages.

And it remains astonishing that they have for quite a long period lived together as incompatible principles in the same compartment; and here a geographical rather than a historical comparison may be helpful. This vigorous coexistence has not happened in England, and could not have happened. The English promissory estoppel is an anemic creature able only to release obligations; it cannot replace consideration in creating liability. Mr. Gilmore charitably attributes this difference to a more relaxed English view of consideration,[9] but the

4. G. Gilmore, The Death of Contract 65 (1974) [hereinafter cited to page number only].
5. P. 64.
6. 1 F. Maitland, The Collected Papers of Frederic William Maitland 447 (1911).
7. Pp. 66, 72.
8. P. 61.
9. P. 100; *see also* p. 129 n.145.

The Yale Law Journal Vol. 84: 1585, 1975

offended reaction when the pale English estoppel was introduced, less than 30 years ago,[10] suggests that here he is overgenerous. The likely explanation, and one which gives the story a new juridical twist, is that the English have been hidebound enough never to do anything about sealing wax. It remained possible to embody an agreement in a document under seal, and so long as the forms of action mattered the chief result was that litigation would be in one of the old actions rather than in *assumpsit*. The chief result today is that one can make a promise binding without any consideration. The kind of case in which American courts first resorted to promissory estoppel, for example, the promised benefaction, would therefore look less hard in England: the benefactor could have made a binding promise under seal, and the beneficiary relied on anything less at his own risk.

But what actually happened or not is less important than what could have happened, and however pressing the need, things could not have happened in England quite as they did in the United States. There could not have been a *Restatement* enunciating contradictory principles because there could not have been a *Restatement* at all. It is a larger proposition than it sounds. There is no room for a *Restatement* in a single jurisdiction with a clear hierarchy of courts and the rigid adherence to a monolithic precedent that is its product. There is no room either for that vitalizing competition between ideas and approaches so strikingly exemplified by the American story. Multiplicity of jurisdictions does not alter the basic mechanism of change, but it enables it to respond much faster.

The English experience may be relevant to another aspect of Mr. Gilmore's story, namely the 19th-century appearance of contract as a system, a subject in itself. He attributes to Langdell's casebook, first published in 1871, and in particular to a summary appended to the second edition in 1880, "the idea that there was—or should be—such a thing as a general theory of contract,"[11] and to Holmes and then Williston the enunciation and elaboration of that theory; Holmes's formulation in particular is beautifully expounded. But these system-builders may have found more spadework done than is here suggested, and more by way of foundations already laid. Mr. Gilmore[12] remarks that many of Langdell's cases were English, and that the jurisdictional unity in England makes for doctrinal coherence. "English case law is manage-

10. Central London Property Trust Ltd. v. High Trees House Ltd. [1947] K.B. 130.
11. Pp. 13-14.
12. P. 13.

A Pageant in Modern Dress

able in a way that American case law has never been."[13] Another adjective would be "stifling." But it is certainly manageable for the writers of textbooks, and a cursory glance suggests that they may by the date of Langdell's book and summary have come closer than their American counterparts to formulating a theory of contract, or at any rate to assuming that there was such a thing. Where did the idea come from? It may not be irrelevant that among the earliest treatises on contract to be published in English were translations of Pothier.[14] But we would be as wrong to think of a civilian idea being casually taken up, as Mr. Gilmore may be wrong in seeing a like idea as coming out of the blue to Langdell. History had left a vacuum to be filled and lawyers' thinking necessarily requires the kind of classification with which this review began.

The Middle Ages had a concept like our contract, or rather had two concepts. Their "covenant" was about the enforcement of agreements as such. And their "contract," confusingly different from ours, was something like the Roman contract *re:* it was about the duties arising when certain transactions were executed on one side, most obviously loans. But these concepts were submerged by *assumpsit,* which expressed the matter in tort: even in the early 19th century, for example, the contractual defendant would be charged with deceit, though so formally that he did not even take offense. This made the old concepts unusable. Trespass and covenant became the names of actions and for a century or so legal thought proceeded in terms not of separate abstract categories but of separate "forms of action." The assumption that such thought is as old as the common law writs has done much to make our legal history seem unsatisfying; indeed the thought itself must have been unsatisfying too. The rise of our own ideas can be traced in the titles of books. 'Tort' was a newcomer in such a role, and at first needed a subtitle explaining torts as wrongs.[15] But 'contract' had only to be expanded from its old sense. Powell in 1790 on the *Law of Contracts and Agreements* was followed in 1807 by Comyn

13. P. 55.

14. The earliest translation of R.J. Pothier's *Treatise on Obligations* was American, but was presumably done not just to satisfy juridical curiosity: It was published in 1802 by F.X. Martin, who also wrote on the laws of North Carolina and of Louisiana. Another translation was published in London in 1806 by W.D. Evans, who admired the cosmopolitan learning of Lord Mansfield and saw the value of comparative study; this edition was reproduced 20 years later in Philadelphia.

15. The lateness of books on torts is interesting. The earliest was American. F. Hilliard, Law of Torts or Private Wrongs (1859). In England, instructive titles are C.G. Addison, Wrongs and their Remedies, being the Law of Torts (1860) (15 years after his contract book); A. Underhill, Law of Torts, or Wrongs independent of Contract (1873). Even F. Pollock, Law of Torts (1887) has a subtitle referring to 'Civil Wrongs.'

The Yale Law Journal Vol. 84: 1585, 1975

on *Law of Contracts and Agreements not under Seal,* and the additions were evidently needed to bring in the original idea of 'covenant.' But for Chitty in 1826, Addison in 1845, Smith in 1847 and Leake in 1867, *Law of Contracts* by itself was enough to mark out the field. Pollock in 1876 and Anson in 1879 both expressly endowed it with "principles." Pollock, in fact, took a further step relevant to Mr. Gilmore's theme: he went into the singular with *Principles of Contract.*[16]

Pollock must bring us back to his great friend Holmes, and to another dimension of a book which could take on a team of reviewers and entice each into a different sort of irrelevance. This notice has sought to place Mr. Gilmore's insights about contract in the context of centuries. To others, the main interest will not be in contract at all, but in his picture of the American legal scene in the last hundred years. It comes almost in throwaway sketches: Williston and Corbin; the making of the *Restatements;* Holmes's dramatic lectures on the common law. A line here and a line there, and that is what people were like and how things happened. The life of the law may be all sorts of solemn things, but in court and classroom it can also be seen as something which hardly ever comes through in print: sheer pleasure in predicaments and solutions, in the economy of ideas. It is this which makes Mr. Gilmore's so perceptive as well as so enjoyable a book.

16. A subtitle notes that references are made to American law, as well as to Roman and European law and to the Indian Contract Act of 1872.

[5]

JOHN H. BAKER, Cambridge

Two Decades of English Legal History*)

1. Chronological survey

The last twenty years have seen a resurgence of interest in English legal history, not only in law faculties but also among historians whose primary training has not been in law. The phenomenon as experienced in law faculties is at least partly due to the publication of an outstandingly original and important new textbook, by Professor *S. F. C. Milsom*[1]); while in history faculties it seems to have been caused primarily by a growing concern with the social history of crime, and also with patterns of land ownership. Both schools have been brought together in a successful series of *legal history conferences*, the first of which was held at Aberystwyth in 1972. Seven such conferences have now been held, at different British universities, and six volumes of proceedings are in print[2]). Two new *journals of legal history* have appeared[3]), and the number of legal history contributions to other journals seems to have increased[4]). There have also been two new student textbooks[5]). The subject is still rather a minority interest in universities – it is estimated that only one law student in seven studies it – but at least it is now found on the curriculum of most English law schools.

---

*) This paper does not deal with parliamentary and constitutional history, in which fields much progress has been made in recent years. The emphasis here is on law courts and legal doctrine, especially in the period 1500–1800.
Die Fußnoten folgen der englischen Zitierweise; Titel zwischen '...' bezeichnen Beiträge in Periodika. Folgende Abkürzungen wurden verwendet:

AJLH:	cf note 17	JSPTL:	cf note 10
CLJ:	cf note 8	LQR:	cf note 10
EHR:	cf note 17	OJLS:	cf note 18
JLH:	cf note 3	Spelman:	cf note 8

1) Historical Foundations of the Common Law (1969; 2nd ed, 1981).

2) *D. Jenkins* ed, Legal History Studies 1972 (1975); *J. H. Baker* ed, Legal Records and the Historian (Royal Historical Soc, Studies in History, no 7, 1977); *A. Harding* ed Law-making and Law-makers in British History (Studies in History, no 22, 1980); *E. W. Ives–A. H. Manchester* ed, Law, Litigants and the Legal Profession (Studies in History, no 36, 1983); *J. A. Guy–H. Beale* ed, Law and Social Change in British History (Studies in History, no 40, 1984); *A. Kiralfy–M. Slatter–R. Virgoe* ed, Custom, Courts and Counsel (5 Journal of Legal History, no 3, 1984). The seventh conference was held at Canterbury in 1985, and the eighth will be at Cardiff in 1987.

3) The J[ournal of] L[egal] H[istory] (London, since 1980); Law and History Review (Ithaca, N.Y., since 1983). Of more specialist interest, there is also Criminal Justice History (New York, since 1980).

4) Since 1975 useful annual bibliographies have appeared in the Cambrian Law Review. Articles in periodicals may also be traced through the appropriate headings in Harvard Law School Library, Annual Legal Bibliography (discontinued 1981); *G. R. Elton* ed, Annual Bibliography of British and Irish History (Royal Historical Soc, since 1975); Index to Legal Periodicals; The Humanities Index.

5) *A. Harding*, A Social History of English Law (1966); *J. H. Baker*, An Introduction to English Legal History (1971; 2nd ed, 1979).

Much of the broad theoretical writing has concentrated on the sixteenth century, and in particular on the themes raised in *Maitland's* famous lecture: English Law and the Renaissance (1901). There is still some controversy as to the precise nature of *Maitland's* thesis[6]), but the present writer has taken the view that *Maitland's* question may have been based on a false premise. *Maitland* began by asking why English law had not succumbed to the Reception of Roman Law, which had "driven German law out of Germany". But it now seems that Roman law did not simply replace national law in Germany, nor in France and Italy. The principal change in the fifteenth and sixteenth centuries was that legal questions were increasingly cast upon new royal courts composed of doctors of law, courts which would naturally use Civilian techniques and learning in answering those questions, but without any thought of displacing national law[7]). England underwent a closely similar process, save in the important respect that the royal courts in England were composed of judges trained in the inns of court and not in Roman law. More questions were thrown upon the central courts, and more new law was made: there was in a sense a *reception in England*, but it was a Reception of Inns of Court Law[8]). This conclusion is not contrary to *Maitland's*, because he also stressed the importance of the inns of court in preventing Roman influence: "law schools make tough law"[9]). The inns of court hold the key to the distinct character of English law, and its insularity; and they are coming to receive more scholarly attention than in the past[10]). Nevertheless, *Maitland's* question has lost much of its point. Legal historians are now less concerned with explaining the resistance of the common law to Romanism than with investigating the great reformation of the common law which occurred in the sixteenth century.

The *seventeenth century* has offered similar opportunities for broad theorising in connection with the work of individual writers, and also with the law-reform movement of the Civil War and Interregnum period (1640–60). Of interest in the former category are studies of Sir Henry Finch (d 1625) and his reliance on Ramist methods of dialectic learned at Cambridge[11]); and of Sir Matthew Hale (d 1676)[12]) and William Sheppard (d 1674)[13]),

---

6) *D. Jenkins*, 'English Law and the Renaissance. Eighty years on: in defence of Maitland' (1981) 2 JLH 107–142 (reviewing earlier literature); *G. R. Elton*, F. W. Maitland (1985), pp 79–88.

7) For summaries in English of recent revisionary writing, see *C. C. Turpin*, 'The Reception of Roman Law' (1963) 3 Irish Jurist N.S. 162–174; *W. Kunkel* and *G. Dahm* in *E. Strauss* ed, Pre-Reformation Germany (1972), pp 263–315.

8) *J. H. Baker*, 'English Law and the Renaissance' [1985] C[ambridge] L[aw] J[ournal] 46–61. See also 'English Law and the Renaissance' in *Baker* ed, The Reports of Sir John Spelman, vol II (Selden Soc vol 94, 1978), introduction, pp 23–51 (hereafter cited as 'Spelman').

9) English Law and the Renaissance (1901), p 25.

10) For the early Tudor inns, see Spelman, II, 125–137; *D. S. Bland*, 'Henry VIII's Royal Commission on the Inns of Court' (1969) 10 J[ournal of the] S[ociety of] P[ublic] T[eachers of] L[aw] 179–194; *A. W. B. Simpson*, 'Early Constitution of the Inns of Court' [1970] CLJ 241–256; 'Early Constitution of Gray's Inn' [1975] CLJ 131–150; *J. H. Baker*, 'The Old Constitution of Gray's Inn' (1978) 81 Graya 15–19; 'The Old Moot Book of Lincoln's Inn' (1979) 95 L[aw] Q[uarterly] R[eview] 507–512; *D. S. Bland*, 'Learning Exercises and Readers at the Inns of Chancery' (1979) 95 LQR 244–252; *E. W. Ives*, The Common Lawyers in pre-Reformation England (1983), pp 36–59. For the later inns, see note 52, below.

11) *W. R. Prest*, 'The Dialectical Origins of Finch's Law' [1977] CLJ 326–352. See also *R. J. Terrill*, 'Humanism and Rhetoric in Legal Education: the contribution of Sir John Dodderidge' (1981) 2 JLH 30–44.

12) *C. M. Gray*, Hale's History of the Common Law of England (1971); *D. E. C. Yale*, 'Hobbes and Hale on Law, Legislation and the Sovereign' [1972B] CLJ 121–156; Hale's Prerogatives of the King (Selden Soc vol 92, 1975); Hale as a Legal Historian (Selden Soc lecture, 1976). See also *M. Heward*, Mathew Hale (1972).

13) *N. J. Matthews*, William Sheppard, Cromwell's Law Reformer (1985).

both of whom were involved in law reform in the 1650s. Hale was the greatest of these. He wrote at length, with immense clarity and erudition, and after deep reflection; but he did not favour publication of his writings, and some are still unpublished[14]). Of similar stature was John Selden (d 1654). Most of his works were published, albeit in very old editions, but a full biography is still required[15]). Even more requisite is a full biography of Sir Edward Coke[16]), who was probably the most influential judge and legal writer during the seventeenth century. As for law reform, a good deal of illuminating research has now been done on the fugitive literature and on the minutes of Hale's law reform commission, and there has been speculation as to the reasons for the movement's ultimate failure[17]).

The *eighteenth century* remains the most neglected in English legal history. Blackstone continues to provide stimulation[18]); and work has begun on the judicial career and achievements of Lord Mansfield (Chief Justice of the King's Bench 1756–88), who transformed English commercial law during his thirty years in office[19]). Yet so far, remarkably, no major work has been published on the court records or unpublished manuscripts of the period. There are many questions calling out for investigation, not least of which is the establishment of the tort of negligence.

The *nineteenth century* is at last being opened up by legal historians, and in recent years we have been provided both with a student's textbook[20]) and with a valuable critical survey of what has so far been achieved and what ought to be done[21]). Modern legal history – that is, the period after Blackstone (1765) or after 1800 – is now taught as an undergraduate course in several English law schools, though it still suffers from a dearth of original research in significant areas. Interest in the legal philosophy of the period has been centred on Jeremy Bentham (d 1832), whose collected works are being published in a full new edition[22]). There has also been some controversy – rare in English legal history – about the economic, social and intellectual forces behind certain nineteenth-century legal

---

14) Mr *Yale* is editing some of these unpublished writings.

15) Professor *D. S. Berkowitz* collected much material for such a life, but died before its completion. See his 'Projects for a Biography and Edition of John Selden's Works 1654–1766' (1974) 4 Quaerendo 247–257.

16) There is a study of his parliamentary career: *S. D. White*, Sir Edward Coke and The Grievances of the Commonwealth (1979). For his notebooks, see note 30, below. *J. Beauté*, Un grand juriste anglais: Sir Edward Coke (1975) is a brief summary based on rather dated printed sources.

17) *S. E. Prall*, Agitation for Law Reform during the Puritan Revolution 1640–1660 (1966); *M. Cotterell*, 'Interregnum Law Reform: the Hale Commission of 1652' (1968) 83 E[nglish] H[istorical] R[eview] 689–704; *D. Veall*, The Popular Movement for Law Reform 1640–1660 (1970); *B. Shapiro*, 'Law Reform in 17th Century England' (1975) 19 A[merican] J[ournal of] L[egal] H[istory] 280–312; 'Codification of the Law in 17th Century England' (1974) Wisconsin Law Rev 428–465; 'Sir Francis Bacon and the mid-17th Century Movement for Law Reform' (1980) 24 AJLH 331–362.

18) See especially *D. Kennedy*, ,The Structure of Blackstone's Commentaries' (1979) 28 Buffalo Law Review 205–382; *S. F. C. Milsom*, 'The Nature of Blackstone's Achievement' (1981) 1 O[xford] J[ournal of] L[egal] S[tudies] 1–12. A reprint of the 'Commentaries' by the University of Chicago (1979) contains short new introductions in each volume. See also *G. H. Jones*, The Sovereignty of the Law (1973).

19) See *E. Heward*, 'Lord Mansfield's Notebooks' (1976) 92 LQR 438–455; Lord Mansfield (1979). An edition of cases from the notebooks is being prepared by Professor *J. C. Oldham*.

20) *A. H. Manchester*, A Modern Legal History of England and Wales 1750–1950 (1980).

21) *G. R. Rubin & D. Sugarman*, Law, Economy and Society: essays in the history of the common law (1984), pp 1–123.

22) *J. H. Burns* and *J. R. Dinwiddy* ed, The Collected Works of Jeremy Bentham (1968). It has been questioned whether Bentham had as much influence on legal change as was once imagined: *H. Beynon*, 'Mighty Bentham' (1981) 2 JLH 62–76.

developments[23]). Research in the raw sources, however, is daunting and has until very recently been largely avoided. In addition to the voluminous court records, there are far more opportunities in this period for uncovering government memoranda, private papers, correspondence, periodical literature, newspaper reports, and the like, all of which can throw new light on legal changes. Just what can be achieved with such material has been shown by Professor *A. W. B. Simpson* in a number of exciting pioneering studies[24]).

2. Sources of the Law

During the last twenty years the publication of facsimile reprints has made many older legal texts freely available[25]), and the patient industry of bibliographers has also facilitated research in printed materials[26]). But the principal development has been in the attention now paid to unpublished sources. Some records and manuscript materials have been made available on microfiche[27]) and microfilm[28]), and attempts are being made to locate and list English legal manuscripts so that they may more easily be found and used[29]). Scholars have given attention not only to the traditional sources – the reports of cases in the king's courts[30]) – but also to the influence of lecturers in the inns of court and treatise writers[31]), and the importance of practitioners' reference works[32]). There have, nevertheless, been surprisingly few edited texts published in the last two decades; editing still seems to be regarded as the peculiar province of the medievalist. The Selden Society has published

---

[23]) Eg, *A. W. B. Simpson*, 'The Horwitz Thesis and the History of Contract' (1979) 46 Chicago Univ Law Review 533–601; 'Contract: the twitching corpse' (1981) 1 OJLS 265–277; *J. H. Baker*, Review of P. S. Atiyah, Rise and Fall of Freedom of Contract (1979), in (1980) 43 Modern Law Review 467–469.

[24]) Cannibalism and the Common Law (1984); 'Legal Liability for Bursting Reservoirs: the historical context of Rylands v Fletcher' (1984) 13 Journal of Legal Studies 209–264; The Case of *The Franconia* and the Rule of Law (Selden Soc lecture, 1985, in the press). See also note 76, below.

[25]) The principal series are 'Classical English Law Texts' (by Professional Books Ltd), which includes the main treatises on criminal law and the vulgate year books; and 'Classics of English Legal History in the Modern Era' (by Garland Publications Inc).

[26]) For the 18th century we now have *J. N. Adams & G. Averley*, A Bibliography of 18th Century Legal Literature (1982). The period before 1700 is covered by the Short Title Catalogues of *Pollard & Redgrave* (to 1640) and *Wing*. Both catalogues are being revised, and important new editions have been brought to light.

[27]) The 'English Legal Manuscripts' series (by Inter Documentation Co, Leyden) has published the manuscript law reports, readings and moots in the Harvard Law School, Yale Law School, Bodleian Library, Lincoln's Inn and Gray's Inn. Over 100 printed books are also available in the 'English Legal Sources' series.

[28]) Eg, the manuscripts in the Inner Temple (World Microfilms); the papers of Sir Julius Caesar, the Old Bailey proceedings 1714–1834, and various ecclesiastical court records (Harvester Microform), and the records of the Court of Arches (Chadwyck-Healey). For an experiment in computerising records, see note 43, below.

[29]) *J. H. Baker*, English Legal Manuscripts, vol I (1975) and II (1978); English Legal Manuscripts in the U.S.A., vol I (1985). Only one legal library has been fully catalogued: *J. Conway Davies*, Catalogue of Manuscripts in the Inner Temple Library (1972).

[30]) *J. P. Dawson*, Oracles of the Law (1968); *L. W. Abbott*, Law Reporting in England 1485–1585 (1973); *J. H. Baker*, 'Coke's Notebooks and the Sources of his Reports' [1972 A] CLJ 59–86; 'Sir Thomas Robinson, Chief Prothonotary of the Common Pleas' (1978) 10 Bodleian Library Record 27–40; *Spelman*, II, 159–178.

[31]) *A. W. B. Simpson*, 'The Rise of the Legal Treatise' (1982) 48 Univ Chicago Law Rev 632–679; *J. H. Baker*, 'The Newe Littleton' [1974] CLJ 145–155; 'English Law and the Renaissance' [1985] CLJ at pp 51–53; notes 11–15, 18, above.

[32]) Eg, *F. L. Boersma*, An Introduction to Fitzherbert's Abridgment (1981); *E. Poole*, 'West's Symboleography, an Elizabethan Formulary' in Law and Social Change (note 2, above), pp 96–106.

only two post-medieval treatises[33]), and two judicial notebooks[34]). It is very much to be hoped that new editors will volunteer to tackle more later texts. There is a tremendous mass of unpublished material[35]), some of which remains almost unusable without the apparatus which an editor provides.

3. The Courts

Legal and social historians share an interest in what courts of law did, the former being most interested in the variety of cases, in procedure, and in the precedents to be found in the records, while the latter are more interested in the volume and dispatch of business, the social distribution of litigants and the economics of litigation. This shared interest has stimulated some valuable monographs on the work of particular courts, especially those outside the regular common-law system.

Professor *W.J. Jones's* study of the *Elizabethan Court of Chancery*[36]) set a high standard, by showing how the procedure and workings of a court can only be unterstood through a minute study of its records and personnel. It has been followed by even more detailed work on the Chancery in the early sixteenth century[37]), when business increased dramatically and the jurisdiction in „equity" was settled. Other work on the early-modern Chancery has focused on the careers and personalities of individual chancellors[38]), and also on the debates over the relationship between law and equity in the chancellorships of Sir Thomas More (d 1535) and Lord Ellesmere (d 1617). The earlier debate seems to have been more philosophical and to have defined the function and character of equity in the English legal system[39]), whereas the crisis of 1616 seems to have resulted rather from a clash of powerful personalities (including Coke, Ellesmere and Sir Francis Bacon) and to have had less lasting significance[40]). The *Chancery of the Restoration period* (1660s and 1670s) has been the subject of a masterly survey by *D.E.C. Yale*[41]), since

[33]) *T.F.T. Plucknett* and *J.L. Barton* ed, St German's Doctor and Student (vol 91, 1974); *D.E.C. Yale* ed, Hale's Prerogatives of the King (vol 92, 1975). Currently in the press is *J.A. Guy* ed, Christopher St German on Chancery and Statute (Supplementary Series vol 6, 1985).

[34]) *J.H. Baker* ed, The Reports of Sir John Spelman (vols 93-4, 1977–78); The Notebook of Sir John Port (vol 102, in the press).

[35]) For a brief indication of the range of sources for the early-modern period alone, see 'The Dark Age of English Legal History' in Legal History Studies 1972 (note 2, above), pp 1–27.

[36]) *W.J. Jones*, The Elizabethan Court of Chancery (1969).

[37]) *F. Metzger*, Das Englische Kanzleigericht unter Kardinal Wolsey 1515–29 (Erlangen Ph D 1976); 'The Last Phase of the Medieval Chancery' in Law-making and Law-makers (note 2, above), pp 79–89; *J.A. Guy*, 'Thomas More as Successor to Wolsey' (1977) 52 Thought 275–292; The Public Career of Sir Thomas More (1980), pp 35–93; 'The Development of Equitable Jurisdiction 1450–1550' in Law, Litigants and the Legal Profession (note 2, above), pp 80–86.

[38]) Eg, *R. Tittler*, 'Sir Nicholas Bacon and the Reform of the Tudor Chancery' (1973) Univ Toronto Law Journal 383–395; *L.A. Knafla*, Law and Politics in Jacobean England: the tracts of Lord Chancellor Ellesmere (1977).

[39]) *D.E.C. Yale*, 'St German's Little Treatise concerning Writs of Subpoena' (1975) 10 Irish Jurist 324–333; Spelman, II, 37–43, 74–83; *Z. Rueger*, 'Gerson's Concept of Equity and Christopher St German' (1982) 3 History of Political Thought 1–30; *J.A. Guy*, St German on Chancery and Statute (note 33, above).

[40]) *J.H. Baker*, 'The Common Lawyers and the Chancery: 1616' (1969) 4 Irish Jurist 368–392; *G.W. Thomas*, 'James I, Equity and Lord Keeper Williams' (1976) 91 EHR 506–528; *Knafla*, op cit in note 38, above, pp 123–181. See also (on the conciliar courts) *C.M. Gray*, 'The Boundaries of the Equitable Function' (1976) 20 AJLH 192–226.

[41]) Lord Nottingham's Chancery Cases (Selden Soc vols 73, 79, 1954–62); Lord Nottingham's 'Manual of Chancery Practice' and 'Prolegomena of Chancery and Equity' (1965). For the interregnum period, see *A.J. Busch*, 'Bulstrode Whitelocke and early Interregnum Chancery Reform' (1979) 11 Albion 317–330; 'The Chancery Petty Bag Office during the Interregnum' (1982) 3 JLH 263–273.

when very little new work has been done on the later Chancery. The reason for this neglect is almost certainly the frightening bulk of Chancery records: but it is a serious gap, which someone should attempt to fill. A possible approach may be through the unpublished Chancery reports, and a project to find and transcribe these is under way.

The *Star Chamber* has always interested historians because of the rich variety of cases which passed through it, and its records have been subjected to similar close study for certain periods. As yet there is no full-length history of the court, but *J. A. Guy* has produced a useful guide to its earlier archives and a thorough account of Cardinal Wolsey's part in establishing the court as a jurisdiction of constant resort in the 1520s[42]). The seventeenth-century Star Chamber has been fully investigated by Professor *T. G. Barnes*, and some of his conclusions have begun to appear[43]). Although the Star Chamber was supposed to be an extraordinary court for cases of particular difficulty or delicacy, it has now been shown how far it was used by ordinary litigants in ordinary disputes – frequently in order to bolster up suits depending in other courts. Full-blown litigation in the period 1550–1650 was a matter of using, simultaneously, every procedure and jurisdiction which seemed to offer an advantage. To study any one court in isolation is now dangerously myopic.

By way of contrast with these courts, relatively little comparable work has been done on the central courts of common law, even though most writing on the substantive law has been concerned with the decisions of these courts. The King's Bench plea rolls have been searched for the purpose of identifying major innovations in the common law between 1490 and 1540; there has been a constructive debate about the causes and extent of the expansion of King's Bench business in the sixteenth century; and the complex series of King's Bench files has been carefully sorted and arranged for future use[44]): but there is still no major institutional history such as we have for the Chancery, and the work of the court after 1550 – when it was even more important – has been seriously neglected. The *Common Pleas*, because of the bulk of its rolls, has been still more neglected. The records of these courts occupy several miles of parchment, in abbreviated Latin, for every year. It seems impracticable to think of filming them, let alone indexing them or putting their contents into a computer. They remain a largely unexplored treasure-house, and yet it is difficult to see how the situation can be remedied.

The fullest institutional study on the common-law side is Professor *J. S. Cockburn's* account of *the assizes* between 1558 and 1714, coupled with his painstaking edition of the gaol-delivery records of the *Home Circuit* during the same period[45]). There have been

42) *J. A. Guy*, The Cardinal's Court (1977); The Court of Star Chamber and its Records to the Accession of Elizabeth I (1985).

43) Eg, 'Star Chamber and the Sophistication of the Criminal Law' [1977] Criminal Law Rev 316–326; 'Star Chamber Litigants and their Counsel' in Legal Records and the Historian (note 2, above), pp 7–28. Professor *Barnes's* experiment in computerising the records for James I's time has been published by the American Bar Foundation: List and Index to the Proceedings in the Star Chamber for the Reign of James I (1975).

44) Spelman, II, introduction; *M. Blatcher*, The Court of King's Bench 1450–1550: a study in self-help (1978); *C. A. F. Meekings*, 'King's Bench Files' in Legal Records and the Historian (note 2, above), pp 97–139; *E. W. Ives*, The Common Lawyers of pre-Reformation England (1983), pp 189–221.

45) *J. S. Cockburn*, A History of English Assizes 1558–1714 (1972); 'Early-modern Assize Records as Historical Evidence' (1975) 5 Journal of the Society of Archivists 215–231; Calendar of Assize Records: Home circuit Indictments (1975–85), 10 vols and introduction.

smaller, but valuable, studies of the Exchequer[46]), the ecclesiastical courts[47]) and local courts[48]); and of the nineteenth-century *Admiralty*[49]), *Privy Council*[50]) and *House of Lords*[51]).

4. The Legal Profession

It would require a separate paper to review adequately all the work that has been done on the English legal profession over the last twenty years. We now have two reliable books on the early-modern inns of court[52]), an account of the development of the distinction between *barristers and solicitors*[53]), a history of the serjeants at law[54]), outline social histories of the legal profession in the sixteenth and seventeenth centuries[55]), discussions of the independence of the judiciary in the same period[56]), and illuminating studies of bench and bar in the eighteenth and nineteenth centuries[57]). Besides the common-law profession, we also have two full-length monographs on the Civilian advocates and their college, Doctors' Commons[58]). The tendency of recent research has been towards proso-

---

[46]) *W.H. Bryson*, The Equity Side of the Exchequer (1975); *D.J. Guth*, 'Notes on the early Tudor Exchequer of Pleas' in *A.J. Slavin* ed, Tudor Men and Institutions (1972), pp 101–122; *D. Lidington*, 'Mesne Process in Penal Actions at the Elizabethan Exchequer' (1984) 5 JLH 33–38.

[47]) Eg, *R.A. Marchant*, The Church under the Law 1560–1640 (1969); *G.I. Duncan*, The High Court of Delegates (1971); *R. Houlbrooke*, Church Courts and People ... 1520–1570 (1979); *R. Wunderli*, London Church Courts and Society on the Eve of the Reformation (1981).

[48]) Eg, *R.R. Pennington*, Stannary Law (1973); *C. Carlton*, The Court of Orphans (1974); *D.G. Greene*, 'The Court of Marshalsea in late Tudor and Stuart England' (1976) 20 AJLH 267–281; *M.K. McIntosh*, 'Social Change and Tudor Manorial Leets' in Law and Social Change (note 2, above), pp 73–81; *K. Emsley* and *C. Fraser*, The Courts of the County Palatine of Durham (1984); *M. Slatter*, 'The Norwich Court of Requests' (1984) 5 JLH 97–107; *H.W. Arthurs*, 'Courts of Local and Special Jurisdiction in 19th Century England', ibid, 130–149; various essays in Law, Economy and Society (note 21, above), pp 321–411.

[49]) *F. Wiswall*, The Development of Admiralty Jurisdiction and Practice since 1800 (1971).

[50]) *P.A. Howell*, The Judicial Committee of the Privy Council 1833–76 (1979).

[51]) *R. Stevens*, Law and Politics: the House of Lords as a judicial body 1800–1976 (1979). For a much earlier period, see also *J.S. Hart*, 'Judicial Review in the House of Lords 1640–43' (1984) 5 JLH 65–78.

[52]) *W.R. Prest*, The Inns of Court 1590–1640 (1972); *W.C. Richardson*, A History of the Inns of Court (1978). Prest's book contains more new material, but there are many useful references in the other (especially in connection with drama).

[53]) *J.H. Baker*, 'Counsellors and Barristers' [1969] CLJ 205–229; 'Solicitors and the Law of Maintenance' [1973] CLJ 56–80.

[54]) *J.H. Baker*, The Order of Serjeants at Law (Selden Soc Supplementary Series vol 5, 1984).

[55]) *W.R. Prest* ed, Lawyers in early modern Europe and America (1981); *E.W. Ives*, The Common Lawyers of pre-Reformation England (1983).

[56]) Spelman, II, 137–142; *D.A. Rubini*, 'The Precarious Independence of the Judiciary 1688–1701' (1967) 83 LQR 343–345; *W.J. Jones*, Politics and the Bench (1971); *S.F. Black*, 'Coram Protectore: the judges of Westminster Hall under the Protectorate of Oliver Cromwell' (1976) 20 AJLH 32–64.

[57]) *B. Abel-Smith & R. Stevens*, Lawyers and the Courts (1967); *D. Duman*, 'The English Bar in the Georgian Era' in Lawyers in early modern Europe (note 55, above), pp 86–107; 'The late Victorian Bar' in Law, Litigants and the Legal Profession (note 2, above), pp 140–154; The Judicial Bench in England 1727–1875 (Royal Historical Soc, Studies in History, no 29, 1982); The English and Colonial Bars in the 19th Century (1983); *R. Cocks*, Foundations of the Modern Bar (1983).

[58]) *B.P. Levack*, The Civil Lawyers in England (1973); *G.D. Squibb*, Doctors' Commons (1977). See also *D.E.C. Yale*, 'A View of the Admiral Jurisdiction: Sir Matthew Hale and the Civilians' in Legal History Studies 1972 (note 2, above), pp 87–109; *B.P. Levack*, 'The English Civilians 1500–1750' in Lawyers in early modern Europe (note 55, above), pp 108–128; *D.R. Coquillette*, 'Legal Ideology and Incorporation I: the English Civilian Writers 1523–1607' (1981) 61 Boston Univ Law Rev 1–89.

pography, and there is reason to think that within a decade or so the pursuit of this method will reveal much that is new about the composition, social and geographical distribution, and career patterns of English lawyers. A more difficult task will be to relate this new information to changes in patterns of litigation[59] and in the law itself.

5. Land Law

The land law must have occupied more than nine-tenths of the whole law before the last century, and yet it has never occupied quite the same prominence in the work of post-medieval legal historians. This must be partly because of the recondite and complex nature of the subject. Not only the minutiae, but even some of the leading principles, have seemed remote from the interests of history departments. Historians are, nevertheless, coming to realise that English society cannot be understood without a knowledge of its property arrangements. Social and economic historians, to their dismay, have found that they must read law; while historians, to their almost equal dismay, are being confronted with labyrinthine problems thrown up by the study of actual estates and property transactions.

The principal subject of interest in the sixteenth century has been the *Statute of Uses* (1536), which turned uses into legal estates and had profound effects – some unintended. The story of its passage through Parliament was suddenly illuminated in 1957 by the discovery of a report of *Lord Dacre's Case* (1535), written by *Sir John Spelman*[60], which has been discussed by several recent writers. From this report it appeared that the judges were persuaded to decide that wills of land held in use were invalid. Since lands had been placed in use primarily in order to enable wills to be made, this devastating decision undermined the opposition to the king's proposal to abolish uses and wills and thereby restore feudal revenues. The passing of the statute the following year is now seen less as a favour to the king than as a desperate measure to preserve the status quo, so that titles depending on earlier wills would not be overthrown[61].

There have been some conjectures about the re-emergence of equitable interests (as „trusts") after the Statute of Uses[62]; but the origins of the modern trust remain obscure, and will linger in obscurity until someone tackles the Chancery records in conjunction with surviving Elizabethan conveyances[63].

The chief interest in the seventeenth and eighteenth centuries has been *the family settlement*[64]. An examination of a wide sample of deeds of settlement, found in record offices

59) For a preliminary attempt, see *C. W. Brooks*, 'Litigants and Attorneys in the King's Bench and Common Pleas 1560–1640' in Legal Records and the Historian (note 2, above), pp 41–59.

60) *A. W. B. Simpson*, 'The Reports of John Spelman' (1957) 72 LQR 334–338; now printed in Spelman, I, 228. Spelman was one of the judges in the case.

61) *E. W. Ives*, 'The Genesis of the Statute of Uses' (1967) 82 EHR 673–697; *J. M. W. Bean*, The Decline of English Feudalism 1215–1540 (1968), pp 257–305; *J. H. Baker*, 'Uses and Wills' in Spelman, II, 192–203; Introduction to English Legal History (2nd ed), pp 213–219.

62) *J. L. Barton*, 'The Statute of Uses and the Trust of Freeholds' (1966) 82 LQR 215–225; *J. H. Baker*, 'The Use upon a Use in Equity 1558–1625' (1977) 93 LQR 33–38; Introduction to English Legal History (2nd ed), pp 242–245; *Milsom*, Historical Foundations (2nd ed), pp 233–239. For charitable trusts, see *G. H. Jones*, History of the Law of Charity 1532–1827 (1969). The married woman's separate use is considered in *M. Cioni*, Women and Law in Elizabethan England (Cambridge Ph D, 1974).

63) *C. M. Gray*, Equity, Copyhold and the Common Law (1963); *J. H. Baker*, 'Agrarian Changes and Security of Tenure' in Spelman, II, 180–192.

64) For the period before 1550, see *J. H. Baker*, 'Family Settlements' in Spelman, II, 204–209. For the later law, see *M. R. Chesterman*, 'Family Settlements on Trust: landowners and the rising bourgeoisie' in Law, Economy and Society (note 21, above), pp 124–167. An introduction (with useful bibliography) has also been written for the general reader: *B. English* and *J. Saville*, Strict Settlement: a guide for historians (1983).

across the country, has enabled some traditional assumptions to be questioned. It has often been supposed that settlements were forced by fathers on eldest sons when the latter came of age, in order to ensure the devolution of the patrimony in the main line of descent. It now seems in fact to have been relatively unusual for sons to come of age in their father's lifetimes, and that most settlements were made on marriage, with the principal object of securing and defining the bride's jointure. Provision of portions for younger children became increasingly common, especially in the eighteenth century, and yet it worked against the dynastic scheme by imposing heavy burdens on the inheritance. It is therefore no longer certain that the main object of the strict settlement was to shackle property to a succession of eldest sons. It may rather represent a compromise between all the interests of the wider family[65]). This thesis has provoked a debate which will certainly continue.

6. The Law of Contract

More space has been devoted to *the action of assumpsit* in the last twenty years than to any other particular branch of legal doctrine[66]). Most of the new work has exploited manuscript law reports and plea rolls, and this technique has shown in this field perhaps more than others how unsafe it is to rely on printed books alone. An illustration is provided by the story of *Slade's Case* (1602), which ended a prolonged debate between the King's Bench and Common Pleas over the use of assumpsit to recover debts. Twenty years ago there appeared in print a very scholarly account of this case, together with speculations as to its effect on seventeenth-century developments in pleading in contract cases[67]). The arguments were perfectly convincing in themselves, and were meticulously reconciled with all the traditional sources. Since then, however, work on manuscript sources has suggested that the writer was misled by his (printed) sources both as to what was in issue in Slade's Case and as to its effect[68]). Much of the blame rests with Sir Edward Coke, whose report of the case (printed in 1604) treated his own arguments for the plaintiff as if they were „resolutions" of the court, and omitted some of the arguments on the other side. It was Coke's report, of course, which governed later history; and historians of later law will still look to Coke rather than the manuscripts. In assessing the case itself, however, all the available evidence is needed. The historian of the common law can no longer, like *Sir William Holdsworth* (d 1944), stop at the printed word.

Similar investigation of unpublished sources has brought to light a few more facts in the history of *the doctrine of consideration*, and has given this topic a chronological frame-

65) *L. Bonfield*, 'Marriage Settlements and "The Rise of the Great Estates": the demographic aspect' (1979) 32 Economic History Rev (2nd series) 483–493 (with reply in vol 33, pp 556–558); Marriage Settlements 1601–1740 (1983); 'Marriage, Property and the Affective Family' (1983) 1 LHR 297-312; *C. Clay*, 'Property Settlements ... 1660–1790' (1981) 21 Journal of British Studies 18–38; *E. Spring*, 'The Family, Strict Settlements and Historians' in Law, Economy and Society (note 21, above), pp 168–191. For a specific aspect, see also *S. Staves*, 'Pin Money' (1985) 14 Studies in 18th Century Culture 47–77.

66) General accounts may be found in *A. W. B. Simpson*, History of the Common Law of Contract: the rise of assumpsit (1975); *S.J. Stoljar*, History of Contract at Common Law (1975); *Milsom*, Historical Foundations (2nd ed), pp 314–360; *Baker*, Introduction to English Legal History (2nd ed), pp 273–290; 'The Establishment of Assumpsit for Nonfeasance' in Spelman, II, 255–298; *D.J. Ibbetson*, The Development of the Action of Assumpsit 1540–1620 (Cambridge Ph D 1980).

67) *H.K. Lücke*, 'Slade's Case and the Origin of the Common Counts' (1965–66) 81 LQR 422–445, 539–561; 82 LQR 81–96.

68) *J.H. Baker*, 'New Light on Slade's Case' [1971] CLJ 51–67, 213–236; *D.J. Ibbetson*, 'Assumpsit and Debt in the early 16th Century: the origins of the indebitatus count' [1982] CLJ 142–161; '16th Century Contract Law: Slade's Case in perspective' (1984) 4 OJLS 295–317.

work. Probably there will never be complete agreement on the origins of consideration, which seems to have sprung from more than one source[69]). A preliminary attempt has also been made to investigate – necessarily from manuscript sources, since there is scarcely anything in print – the first stages in the adaptation of common-law remedies to enforce obligations arising from negotiable instruments. Traditional learning supposed a pre-existing body of "law merchant", which the common law simply "incorporated" when the time came, somewhere in the seventeenth or eighteenth century. The new material suggests rather that the common lawyers edged their way forward slowly and in their own way, using pleading devices of considerable subtlety, and seeking to give effect to the commercial opinion of the day, rather than receiving a system of ready-made law[70]). The development changed course in the time of Lord Mansfield, who used new techniques to put commercial law on a sounder footing. Lord Mansfield tried to assimilate English commercial law to that of continental countries, and the new awareness of foreign law which resulted was marked in 1806 – at the height of the Napoleonic War – by the publication of an English edition of Pothier. It is now clear that many of the general principles of the English law of contract, which were first settled in the nineteenth century, owe more to Pothier than to previous English legal scholarship[71]).

7. The Law of Tort

The law of tort has not, as a whole, received so much recent attention as contract. The most obvious need is for a history of the law of negligence: both the origins of the tort, as an entity distinct from assumpsit[72]), and its steady expansion in the nineteenth and twentieth centuries. The tort which has received the most attention is defamation, which the central courts first remedied at the beginning of the sixteenth century. The establishment of the action on the case for words, the principles behind it, and the campaign to narrow its scope, have all been explored in some detail by using manuscript sources[73]); and we have been provided with the first convincing explanation of the distinction between libel and slander[74]). A few other torts have been traced to their origins in the early sixteenth century[75]). But some of the best recent work on tort has been on the nineteenth century, and the reaction of the courts to problems created by the industrial revolution[76]).

[69]) *J.H. Baker*, 'Consideration' in Spelman, II, 286–297; 'Origins of the „Doctrine" of Consideration' in *M.S. Arnold* and others ed, On the Laws and Customs of England: essays in honor of S.E. Thorne (1981), pp 336–358. For a different view, and a full analysis of the printed cases, see also *Simpson*, History of Contract, pp 406–488.

[70]) *J.H. Baker*, 'The Law Merchant and the Common Law before 1700' [1979] CLJ 295–322. For an excellent account of the traditional view, see *D. Coquillette*, 'Legal Ideology and Incorporation II: Sir Thomas Ridley, Charles Molloy and the literary battle for the law merchant' (1981) 61 Boston Univ Law Rev 315–371. For the techniques used by Lord Mansfield, see *J.C. Oldham*, 'Origins of the Special Jury' (1983) 50 Univ Chicago Law Rev 137, especially at pp 140 n 13, 210.

[71]) *A.W.B. Simpson*, 'Innovation in 19th Century Contract Law' (1975) 91 LQR 247–278.

[72]) For summaries of what is known, see *Milsom*, Historical Foundations (2nd ed), pp 392–400; *Baker*, Introduction to English Legal History (2nd ed), pp 336–350; Spelman, II, 220–230.

[73]) *Milsom*, Historical Foundations (2nd ed), pp 379–392; *J.H. Baker*, 'Defamation' in Spelman, II, 236–248; Introduction to English Legal History (2nd ed), pp 364–374; *R.H. Helmholz* and *T.A. Green*, Juries, Libel and Justice (1984); *R.H. Helmholz*, Select Cases of Defamation to 1600 (Selden Soc vol 101, for 1985, in the press).

[74]) *J.M. Kaye*, 'Libel and Slander – Two Torts or One?' (1975) 91 LQR 524–539.

[75]) Eg, Spelman, II, 60 (malicious prosecution, extortion), 61 (enticement), 244 (slander of title), 248–253 (trover and conversion), 254 (procuring a breach of contract).

[76]) *J.F. Brenner*, 'Nuisance Law and the Industrial Revolution' (1974) 3 Journal of Legal Studies 403–433; *J.P.S. McLaren*, 'Nuisance Law and the Industrial Revolution' (1983) 7 OJLS 155–221; *A.W.B. Simpson*, 'Legal Liability for Bursting Reservoirs' (1984), note 24, above; *J.L. Bar-*

8. Criminal Law

One of the biggest growth areas in history – not only in England – has been the history of crime. It has been an area of fruitful contact between social and legal historians, though much of the work on crime as a social phenomenon is beyond the scope of the present survey[77]. In recent years we have come to learn a great deal – from a wide range of previously untapped sources – about criminal trials and the development of rules of procedure, especially in the eighteenth century[78]. We have also learned more about the development of the substantive criminal law, especially in connection with *treason*[79], *homicide*[80], *theft*[81], and *the defence of insanity*[82]. But a third, and more novel, area of concern to lawyers has been the means by which *criminal legal doctrine* was developed[83]. The story is quite different from that of private law, because of the differences of jurisdiction and procedure, and especially the absence from criminal courts of counsel and special pleading. The present writer has argued that before the mid-sixteenth century the basic principles of criminal law were discussed and refined in the inns of court as much as in the courts, and has shown that the unpublished lectures given in the inns during the period 1450–1550 contain many detailed and surprisingly sophisticated expositions of this branch of the law[84]. From the early sixteenth century, informal meetings of judges began to take over this function; and, although most of the reports of these meetings remain unpublished, some of the writers mentioned in the preceding footnotes have made use of them in manuscript. Finally, in an important new work on the jury in criminal trials, Professor *T.A. Green* has shown how permanent changes in criminal law and administration were sometimes rooted in the general practices of jurymen in exercising their discretion to mitigate or obstruct strict law[85].

---

ton, 'Liability for Things in the 19th Century' in Law and Social Change (note 2, above), pp 145–155. For good recent examples of even more modern history, see *M. Davies*, 'The Road from Morocco: Polemis through Donoghue to No-fault' (1982) 45 MLR 534–555; *J. R. Spencer*, 'Motor Cars and the Rule in Rylands v Fletcher: a chapter of accidents in the history of law and motoring' [1983] CLJ 65–84.

77) For a bibliography down to 1977, see *L.A. Knafla*, 'Crime and Criminal Justice: a critical bibliography' in *J.S. Cockburn* ed, Crime in England 1550–1800 (1977), pp 270–298. It has been brought up to date by Professor *Knafla* in Crime and Criminal Justice in Europe and Canada (2nd ed, 1985), pp vii–xxix.

78) See, eg, *J.H. Langbein*, Prosecuting Crime in the Renaissance (1974); 'The Criminal Trial before the Lawyers' (1978) 45 Univ Chicago Law Rev 263–316; 'Shaping the 18th Century Criminal Law: a view from the Ryder sources' (1983) 50 Univ Chicago Law Rev 1–136; *J.H. Baker*, 'Criminal Justice at Newgate 1616–27' (1973) 8 Irish Jurist 307–322; 'Criminal Courts and Procedure at Common Law' in Crime in England (last note), pp 15–48; *J.S. Cockburn*, 'Trial by the Book? Fact and theory in the criminal process 1558–1625' in Legal Records and the Historian (note 2, above), pp 60–79, and op cit in note 45, above; *J.M. Beattie*, 'Crime and the Courts in Surrey' in Crime in England (last note), pp 155–186; Crime and the Courts in England 1660–1800 (1985); *D.R. Ernst*, 'The Moribund Appeal of Death' (1984) 28 AJLH 164–188.

79) *G.R. Elton*, Policy and Police (1972); *J.M. Derrett*, 'The Trial of Sir Thomas More' in *R.S. Sylvester* and *G.P. Marc'hadour*, Essential Articles for the Study of Thomas More (1977), pp 49–78; *J.G. Bellamy*, The Tudor Law of Treason (1979).

80) *J.M. Kaye*, 'Early History of Murder and Manslaughter – Part II' (1967) 83 LQR 569–601; *J.H. Baker*, 'Homicide' in Spelman, II, 303–316.

81) *G.P. Fletcher*, 'The Metamorphosis of Larceny' (1976) 89 Harvard Law Rev 469–530; *J.H. Baker*, 'Theft' in Spelman, II, 316–323.

82) *N. Walker*, Crime and Insanity in England. Volume One: the historical perspective (1968).

83) For a survey of the methods used, see *J.H. Baker*, 'The Refinement of English Criminal Jurisprudence 1500–1848' in Crime and Criminal Justice (note 77, above), pp 17–42; and Spelman, II, 300–303.

84) Spelman, II, 299–350.

85) *T.A. Green*, Verdict according to Conscience: perspectives on the English criminal trial jury 1200–1800 (1985).

[6]

E.P. Thompson's Legacies

ROBERT W. GORDON*

Edward Thompson was by common agreement the greatest English-speaking social historian of his age, the presiding genius of an entire generation of historians of the 1960s and after who determined to write history "from the bottom up," through the eyes of people who had been crushed under the wheels of history, especially the wheels of economic "progress." It was Thompson more than anyone else who rescued the lower orders from "the enormous condescension of posterity,"[1] from their reputation as a dumb, illiterate, and violence-prone mob—Burke's "swinish multitude," or less pejoratively but almost as anonymously, Marx and Engels' faceless, mutely suffering "proletariat"—and who showed the New Social Historians how to perform patient, exhaustive archival excavations; whose work gradually revealed a whole underground world of articulate, thoughtful laboring men and women, architects of their own consciousness, active agents who well understood and fiercely resisted the catastrophic changes that were carelessly sweeping them onto history's scrap-heap. It was Thompson whose slashing and passionate, while surprisingly precise and delicate, narrative style could make any reader feel—and resolved many to act on the feeling—that writing social history to recruit the understanding of past struggles to present-day social understanding and political action was one of the most important things one could do with one's life.

Thompson's masterpiece, *The Making of the English Working Class*, first appeared over thirty years ago. Reading it through again is like resuming a very old friendship, which intervening time and experience have only improved. The prose is as fresh as ever; the English artisans, laborers, and peasants of 1790-1830 are made as real and immediate as any present-day social movements. All over again one experiences, through Thompson's power of sympathetic recreation, his admiration for their irreverent wit and courage, and his scorn and indignation for the landowners, employers, and magistrates who harassed them endlessly and ultimately wore them out.

Yet at this later re-reading still other qualities, which I was not really equipped to appreciate the first time around, emerge from Thompson's work. One such quality is Thompson's sheer amazing craftsmanship as historian, shown in the hundreds of thousands of scraps of notes from local archives and obscure sources that he gathered and wove into narratives both coherent and grippingly dramatic; in his refusal to be confined by

---

* Adelbert H. Sweet Professor of Law, Stanford University.

1. E.P. THOMPSON, THE MAKING OF THE ENGLISH WORKING CLASS 12 (1963).

discipline or specialty and his ability to draw freely upon economic, legal, intellectual, political, and social perspectives; in his complete mastery of high and popular cultures reflected in the scraps of poetry, belles-lettres, ballads, and political songs scattered like jewels over every page; and in the intense but restrained (and, for so engaged a writer, remarkably judicious) critical scrutiny that he repeatedly brought to bear on technical and historiographical quarrels. Thompson wore his learning lightly; he almost never (save when exposing an opponent as an ignorant twit) showed off how hard he had been working, what deep quarries of research and theoretical synthesis lay just out of sight, behind his monumental art.

On this re-reading yet another facet of Thompson's work—one of special interest to this readership of lawyers and legal scholars—also becomes more visible: his extremely sophisticated understanding of the many social roles of law. Like other social critics schooled in Marxist traditions of history and theory, Thompson was well aware of the instrumental functions of law as a bag of weapons and tricks for the rich and powerful to use against the poor. In the period of his special interest, such instrumental uses of law could hardly have been ignored, since they were everywhere: the criminalization of customs, whereby exercises of ancient right such as grazing or deer-taking in common fields and forests were curbed by enclosure; the death penalty; the Combination Acts passed to break up workingmen's associations; and the great wave of repressive statutes and prosecutions of "Jacobin" societies and organizations for sedition and riot in England during its early nineteenth-century Red Scare.[2] Thompson's period of interest provided numberless examples of the cynical manipulation and deployment of law by a ruling elite to maintain its privileges and to shatter the leadership, morale, and cohesion of working-class organizations.

Thompson, however, never succumbed to a crudely instrumentalist view of law, or to the dismissal of law altogether as expressing merely "bourgeois rights." As always, he drew insight from the radical traditions he admired, and in those traditions law appears in many forms besides class trickery and repression. Law appears, most importantly, as customary right. The claims of easement, or of use-rights such as gleaning, grazing, and taking of fish and deer, made by cottagers, villagers, and tenants upon farmer and gentry landowners were, of course, legal claims—claims *to* rights of property, not in defiance of property.[3] The claims made by defendants at trials for sedition and riot, for free speech and assembly, free press, fair procedure, and trial by jury were legal claims as well, claims to the rights of "free-born Englishmen" that every radical asserted as his

2. *See generally id.* at chs. 4, 5, 14, 15; E.P. THOMPSON, WHIGS AND HUNTERS: THE ORIGIN OF THE BLACK ACT (1975).

3. *See* E.P. Thompson, *Custom, Law, and Common Right, in* CUSTOMS IN COMMON 97 (1991).

heritage. The eighteenth-century crowd resorted to riot, more often than not, as a carefully regulated remedy aimed at restoring a status-quo-ante after some violation of legal right that regular legal institutions would not or could not redress. Undoubtedly Thompson's famous, spirited defense in *Whigs and Hunters*[4] of the "Rule of Law" as an "unqualified human good" and permanently valuable legacy of Western culture, despite all the long history of law's abuse by rulers and the wealthy for their own ends, draws upon this rich tradition of legalism in English radical dissent.

Seeing law in every corner of social life, Thompson never made the mistake of supposing law was only epiphenomenal, a mere rationalizing ideology or "superstructure" erected on the "real," "material" bases of social life such as technology, relations of production, market structures, or power relations. Law was a crucial element in the constitution of markets and relations of power and of production:

> I found that law did not keep politely to a "level" but was at every bloody level; it was imbricated within the mode of production and productive relations themselves (as property-rights, definitions of agrarian practice) and it was simultaneously present in the philosophy of Locke; it intruded brusquely within alien categories, reappearing bewigged and gowned in the guise of ideology; it danced a cotillion with religion, moralising over the theater of Tyburn; it was an arena of politics and politics was one of its arms; it was an academic discipline, subjected to the rigour of its own autonomous logic; it contributed to the definition of self-identity both of rulers and of ruled; above all, it afforded an arena for class struggle, within which alternative notions of law were fought out.[5]

Still another aspect of Thompson's work that I better understand now is also one of Thompson's most valuable qualities for present day use—a quality that might be called humanistic concreteness, or particularism. Thompson never wrote a page of history that was not exceptionally dense in detail, in the proper names of persons and places, customs and trades, numbers and events, and quotations from participants. Sometimes he mocked his own habit: "[D]oes it matter a damn who gave Parson Power his instructions; which forms brought 'Vulcan' Gates to the gallows; or how an obscure Richmond publican managed to evade a death sentence . . .?"[6] The answer, as he well knew, is that it does matter, for (as usual) a complex variety of reasons. One reason was simply fidelity to his project and materials: he was writing about and taking the side of people who were defending against erosion their intensely particular trades, intensely local customs. Not just their livings, but also their dignity and identity,

---

4. WHIGS AND HUNTERS, *supra* note 2, at 258-69.
5. E. P. THOMPSON, THE POVERTY OF THEORY AND OTHER ESSAYS 96 (1978).
6. WHIGS AND HUNTERS, *supra* note 2, at 260.

their sense of the right and moral, were all bundled up in these particularities. To understand their situation the historian has to recreate their world in the details that mattered *to them*—especially because as progress swept them away they mattered not at all to anyone else. One cannot represent men and women as agents unless one can make the reader understand them as real, and reality resides in the details. Thompson learned this lesson from the great Radical polemicists of the period he made his own, especially William Cobbett.[7] Thompson's radicalism, like that of the other great lettered English radicals such as Cobbett, William Morris, R.H. Tawney, or George Orwell, was entirely and doggedly English. Without being chauvinistic or intellectually provincial, Thompson sought to elaborate the distinctness, the local and decentralized nature, the "peculiarities" of English dissent both as factors explaining England's special history and as sources of values worth preserving.

In this celebration of the particular there is concealed, it seems to me, an important and quite general message. Virtually everything Thompson wrote consists as part of a running argument against a kind of reductionist abstraction-mongering, which Thompson truly loathed and believed to be dangerously anti-human wherever it was adopted and applied.[8] In the early-industrial period of his main historical interest, this noxious form of intellectual practice was mainly represented by classical political economy and utilitarian theory and policy; in his own time, by the modern version of the same things—neo-liberal political economy—but also by functionalist sociology and structuralist Marxism.

The Making of the English Working Class is, among other things, a sustained polemic against impersonal models of "industrialization," "modernization," or "capitalist development," especially the complacent ones like those of F.A. Hayek, T.S. Ashton, R.M. Hartwell, and their school.[9] These writers argued that although the natural workings of markets in the Industrial Revolution may have temporarily displaced a few marginal occupations like cottagers and technologically-obsolete craftsmen, "free markets" had also produced a generally higher standard of living for everyone. Thompson set out to refute this smug cost-benefit analysis. The main technique he used was the method of detail—disaggregation of gross statistical claims, of large and lazy economic generalities. He asked, who

7. For Thompson's tribute to Cobbett, see THE MAKING OF THE ENGLISH WORKING CLASS, *supra* note 1, at 746-52. Though Thompson's style resembles Cobbett's in its attachment to particularity and proper names, it is actually quite different from Cobbett's, much more ironic, cosmopolitan, and allusive, and in fact more like that of the essayist William Hazlitt, whom Thompson admired as well.

8. *See, e.g.*, THE MAKING OF THE ENGLISH WORKING CLASS, *supra* note 1, at 267-68, 776-79 (nineteenth-century utilitarians and political economists); THE POVERTY OF THEORY AND OTHER ESSAYS, *supra* note 5, at 140, 153, 168 (Stalinism and scientism); *The Moral Economy Reviewed*, *in* CUSTOMS IN COMMON, *supra* note 3, at 259, 303-05 (modern economists).

9. *See* CAPITALISM AND THE HISTORIANS (F.A. Hayek ed., 1954).

exactly were the people displaced, how many of them actually were there, and—above all—how did *they* experience their displacement? He insisted on describing human welfare in non-reductive terms—not just as money incomes, but as independence, dignity, autonomy, and pride in craft. He peered closely at the "natural workings of market forces" and exposed the pervasive coercion behind them—the manipulation of law to reassign property from ancient rights to entrepreneurial uses; the recruitment of tort, trespass, and criminal law to defeat customary practices; the massive repression of political dissent and labor combinations. And indeed Thompson's case is overwhelming that, seen through the eyes of the men and women who lived through them, the Industrial Revolution and the political counter-revolution that accompanied it were nothing short of catastrophic.

Thompson was often accused of being a "romantic," of sentimentalizing obsolete and pre-industrial forms of community. It is certainly true that he saw value in the lives his subjects had assembled around their customs and trades, and irrecoverable losses—losses not easily valued in a cost-benefit accounting and usually not attempted to be valued at all—in the disappearance of those customs and trades. Though formally a socialist, he was at bottom a Romantic radical in sensibility; he despised both Stalinism and bureaucratic capitalism for their crushing of human personality, especially the eccentric, cantankerous, combative, and lyrical fighting spirit of the sort of radicalism he himself personified.

But to think of Thompson exclusively in this way—for example, as someone who preferred to depict reality with the personal stories of underdogs rather than with abstract models of impersonal processes—is to marginalize him unduly and greatly to underrate his importance as a social thinker. Thompson was a better social analyst, most of the time, than his reductionist opponents because he was a more accurate observer and more hard-headed theorist. He did not disdain economic theory and statistical indices; he used them in his own work, but broke them down, critiqued them, and refined them. He did not suppose that the emphasis he gave to agency in his histories denied the existence or importance of processes or structures. Indeed, one of his persistent criticisms of the New Leftists of 1968 was of their utopian voluntarism, their notion that the world can always spontaneously be remade if you only will it hard enough. But he thought that both economists and structuralist Marxists persistently *misdescribed* those processes because they were too lazy, or blinded by ideology, to look at them *in detail*.

Economists, for example, repeatedly asserted that successful forms of capitalist development require markets constituted by fixed and stable legally-defined rights of property, and illustrated this proposition with historical examples of societies in which, they contended, such rights had emerged (such as early-modern England). Thompson, sometimes patiently and sometimes not, would respond that there was never anything very fixed about the rights pointed to; that they were a version of rights favored by some courts and social groupings but not others; that they existed in conflict with well-established claims of competing rights; that in any case they were constantly being fought over and renegotiated with every shift in the balance of economic and social power; and that we could not begin to understand property rights until we also understood the webs of local custom, religion, magic, and politics in which they were embedded. Moreover, the webs of customary practice were not just reactionary drags on free markets; but were often highly functional in their own way. For instance, the moral economy of the English crowd in Thompson's classic essay of that title,[10] using law, custom, and calibrated rioting to regulate the price and supply of staple commodities, represented a functional system for preventing famine in times of dearth.[11]

It is heartening to see, in recent economic theorizing and historiography among other places, some tendencies even in the reductionist disciplines to begin to recognize the importance of custom, culture, moral norms, path-dependent institutional forms, religious and family ties, and other solidarities in the formation and enforcement of legal claims and the constitution of markets—in short, to see social science working its long, slow, painful way back to the insights E.P. Thompson had already achieved in 1963. Social-legal historians, who like everyone else familiar with Thompson's work, could hardly avoid being inspired by it, have profitably lived off those insights for some time.[12] But now more than ever the terrible simplifiers are roaming the globe, prescribing "shock therapies" for economic stagnation in post-Communist societies and the Third World in the form of "fixed and stable property rights," "privatization," and "free markets." Evidently, they are without the faintest knowledge of the political, legal, and cultural contingencies in which such institutions developed even in the Western capitalist economies—not to mention the human wreckage such development often entailed—and certainly without the slightest reflection on the indigenous political and cultural contexts of their new experiments. More than ever, therefore, social thinkers and social activists, perhaps especially legal thinkers and activists, will have need of Thompson's patient attention to detail, his polemical talent for attacking ideological abstractions and his analytic talent for picking them apart, his engaged

10. *See The Moral Economy of the English Crowd in the Eighteenth Century, in* CUSTOMS IN COMMON, *supra* note 3, at 185-258.

11. In a fascinating reply to critics of his thesis on *The Moral Economy of the English Crowd,* Thompson enriched the thesis by comparisons to similar moral-economies at work elsewhere in the world, especially in India. *See The Moral Economy Reviewed, supra* note 8, at 259-351.

12. Among the legal historians who have seemingly been strongly influenced by Thompson, one thinks of William Forbath, Douglas Hay, Hendrik Hartog, Morton Horwitz, Alfred Konefsky, Elizabeth Mensch, William Novak, Carol Rose, Richard Ross, David Sugarman, and Christopher Tomlins.

sympathy with the men and women whom structural changes leave flattened in their path, and his sharp, disciplined moral indignation. These are his legacies: to strive to imitate his methods, in the service of his ideals of social decency and the most exacting standards of craft, is the best tribute we could pay him.

Part II
Theory and Politics in American Legal History

[7]

INTRODUCTION: J. WILLARD HURST AND THE COMMON LAW TRADITION IN AMERICAN LEGAL HISTORIOGRAPHY*

ROBERT W. GORDON

State University of New York at Buffalo

In 1963 the Italian historiographer Arnaldo Momigliano told an assembly of legal historians that they were gathered to celebrate "a historical event of some importance, the end of history of law as an autonomous branch of historical research." At least in the historiography of ancient law, he said, "the elimination of history of law as independent history now seems to me to be settled."

> Nor is it important to debate whether it was Max Weber or the French school of sociology or the teaching of Marx and Engels or, finally, the influence of Marc Bloch that precipitated this solution. It is inherent in the general recognition that law, as a systematization of social relations at a given level, cannot be understood without an analysis of the sexual orientations, the moral and religious beliefs, the economic production and the military forces that characterize a given society at a given moment, and are expressed in associations of individuals and in conflicts. It is conceivable today that history of literature, history of art, history of science, and history of religion can each retain some sort of autonomy, inasmuch as each is concerned with a specific activity of man. But what is no longer conceivable is that history of law should be autonomous; for by its very nature it is a formulation of human relations rooted in manifold human activities. And if, in some civilizations, there is a class of jurisconsults with special rules of conduct and of reasoning, this too is a social phenomenon to be interpreted.[1]

In the historiography of American law, the process Momigliano thus described as completed is only just beginning, for American legal historians have usually worked on the assumption that, at least for the purpose of dividing academic labor, it makes sense to identify a sphere of "legal" phenomena in society, and to write about how these have changed over time. It has never, of course, been possible to mark off the precise boundaries of such a field, but as a practical matter it almost inevitably turns out that they are drawn around the institutions,

---

* This essay owes much to conversations with Paul R. Duggan, Marc Galanter, David Hollinger, Stewart Macaulay, John Henry Schlegel, David Trubek and Mark Tushnet, and to the members of the Faculty Seminar on Law and Development of the SUNY at Buffalo Law School, who heard and criticized an earlier version. They do not by any means all share the views reported here; and are not responsible for errors and distortions.

1. A.D. Momigliano, "The Consequences of New Trends in the History of Ancient Law," in Momigliano, *Studies in Historiography* 239, 240-241 (1966).

the occupations, the ideas and the procedures that have the appearance at any one time of being *distinctively legal.*[2] One might crudely represent this way of looking at law in society as follows:

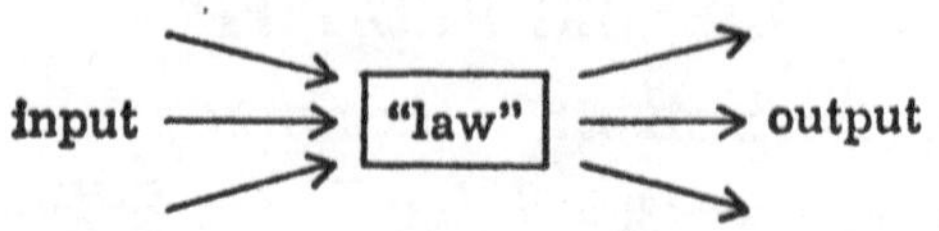

Inside the box is "the law," whatever appears autonomous about the legal order—courts, equitable maxims, motions for summary judgment; outside lies "society," the wide realm of the nonlegal, the political, economic, religious, social; the "inputs" are social influences upon the shape of the mass of things inside the law-box, the "outputs" the effects, or impact, of the mass upon society. Within the structure of this crude model there is, of course, a great range of possible theories of law, from a theory asserting that law derives its shape almost wholly from sources within the box (i.e. that it is really autonomous as well as seeming so), to one claiming that the box is really empty, the apparent distinctiveness of its contents illusory, since they are all the product of external social forces. Yet even those who incline to the latter view[3] take the contents of the box, epiphenomenal

---

2. This would seem to imply that no one could write the legal history of a society that had no notion of "law" as a bundle of specialized activities distinct from, and to some extent autonomous of, other social phenomena—e.g., a society that did not distinguish between legal and religious norms. Legal historians usually solve this problem by treating of the aspects of such societies that appear to serve counterpart social functions to those of the relatively autonomous legal systems. For example, courts perform certain dispute settlement functions in modern Western societies which might, in other societies of the past, have been performed by councils of warriors or village elders. The warriors or elders will therefore be treated in the legal history of the other society. Yet though dispute settlement may be done by warriors or elders in modern Western societies also, that is not "law" and is therefore usually of no interest to legal historians This somewhat curious manner of defining the field of specialization is partly responsible for the fact that focus abruptly shifts (and narrows) whenever a society exhibits traces of an autonomous legal order. On this point, see text at notes 29-31, 40-44, *infra*. On the emergence of "autonomous" legal orders in modern societies, see *Max Weber on Law and Economy in Society* (Rheinstein ed. 1954), especially chs. 7-9, 11; for a brilliant recent reinterpretation, Roberto Mangabeira Unger, *Law in Modern Society* (forthcoming, 1976), especially at 52ff.

3. Lawrence M. Friedman probably inclines as far as anyone. See e.g., his *History of American Law* (1973):

> This book treats American law . . . not as a kingdom unto itself, not as a set of rules and concepts, not as the province of lawyers alone, but as a mirror of society. It takes nothing as historical accident, nothing as autonomous, everything as relative and molded by economy and society. . . . The [legal] system works like a blind, insensate machine. It does the bidding of those whose hands are on the controls. . . . [T]he strongest ingredient in American law, at any given time, is the present: current emotions, real economic interests, concrete political groups.

though they may be, as the main subject-matter of concern to the legal historian. Not that this is the only way of treating law historically, as Momigliano's words make clear;[4] but it probably *is* the only way for someone who defines himself as a "legal" historian; he has no choice.

Where he does have a choice, and an important one, is between writing internal and external legal history.[5] The internal legal historian stays as much as possible within the box of distinctive-appearing legal things; his sources are legal, and so are the basic matters he wants to describe or explain, such as changes in pleading rules, in the jurisdiction of a court, the texts assigned to beginning law students, or the doctrine of contributory negligence. The external historian writes about the interaction between the boxful of legal things and the wider society of which they are a part, in particular to explore the social context of law and its social effects, and he is usually looking for conclusions about those effects.

Up until very recently, and with few exceptions, American legal history has been of the internal kind. From time to time the few proponents of external history would direct an exasperated complaint against this situation, without much altering it.[6]

Id. at 10, 14. Professor Friedman acknowledges the existence of legal phenomena that are purely "internal" or "formal"—technical aspects of the system that can be altered or adjusted without affecting much (if at all) the outside society. See his "Law Reform in Historical Perspective," 13 *St. Louis U.L.J.* 351 (1969). He also recognizes that people living in some societies may perceive their legal order to be autonomous and to associate autonomy with legitimacy; he would classify such beliefs as part of a society's "legal culture"—"values and attitudes which . . . determine the place of the legal system in the culture of the society as a whole." See his "Legal Culture and Social Development," 4 *L. & Soc'y. Rev.* 29, 34 (1969).

4. Some scholars would go further than Momigliano; see, e.g., Richard L. Abel, "A Comparative Theory of Dispute Institutions in Society," 8 *L. & Soc'y Rev.* 217, 221-224 (1973), for the views of a legal anthropologist who has given up on "law" altogether as a useful organizing concept in social research.

5. These terms are borrowed from T.S. Kuhn's treatments of (remarkably similar!) problems in the historiography of science. See especially his "Relations between History and History of Science," 100 *Daedalus* 271, 279 (1971). "External history" seems to me a better label than "social" history because it is more inclusive; specifically, it includes intellectual and cultural history.

6. The best of these are, I think, Daniel J. Boorstin, "Tradition and Method in Legal History," 54 *Harv. L. Rev.* 424 (1951); George L. Haskins, "Law and Colonial Society," 9 *Am. Q.* 354 (1957); Stanley N. Katz, "Looking Backward: The Early History of American Law," 33 *U. Chi. L. Rev.* 867 (1966); Lawrence M. Friedman, "Some Problems and Possibilities of American Legal History," in *The State of American History* 3 (Bass ed. 1970); Morton J. Horwitz, "The Conservative Tradition in the Writing of American Legal History," 17 *Am. J. Leg. Hist.* 275 (1973); Herbert Alan Johnson, "American Colonial Legal History: A Historiographical Interpretation," in *Perspectives on Early American History* 250 (Vaughan & Billias eds. 1973), hereinafter Johnson, "Colonial Legal History"; and the many

As it happens, I tend to sympathize with most of these complaints, but writing another one is not my present purpose, since others have already said trenchantly what needed to be said; and in any case the situation is rapidly improving and there is no need for one. At this point it is more interesting to ask how the tradition of internal historiography got itself established, how it managed to last so long, and what the consequences of its ascendancy were for historical writing about American law. With that kind of perspective it might be possible adequately to assess the achievement of James Willard Hurst, the legal historian who broke decisively with the main tradition over thirty years ago, and who has since become the leading exponent and practitioner of an external historiography.

With the purpose of attempting that assessment in mind, the brief essay that follows tries to sketch the broad outlines of the paths taken by American legal historians since the beginnings of their discipline in the 1880's.[7] As I see it, there was a Classical Period from about 1880 to 1900, followed by a long slump lasting until about 1930; a First Revival of interest and activity in legal-historical studies from the 1930's through the early 1960's; then a Second Revival starting around 1970 and still going strong.[8]

---

historiographical contributions of Willard Hurst, of which the most comprehensive, as well as the most recent, is "Legal Elements in United States History," in *Law in American History* 3 (Fleming & Bailyn eds. 1971), hereinafter Hurst, "Legal Elements." Much acerbic and astute criticism of the state of the art has appeared over the years in the *Annual Survey of American Law's* "Legal History" sections written by John Phillip Reid (1962-66); Reid and William E. Nelson (1969-70); and Nelson (1967-69; 1973-present). I am very indebted to all the articles cited here. One of the many ironies connected with American legal history is that its shortcomings have called forth so useful a historiographical literature.

7. See Calvin Woodard, "History, Legal History, and Legal Education," 53 *Va. L. Rev.* 89 (1967) for a similar sketch arriving at somewhat different conclusions.

8. Some readers may find my idea of what constitutes "American legal history" idiosyncratic—both too inclusive and too exclusive. It includes studies in *English* legal history in the 1880s and 90s, but then drops these; and excludes constitutional, administrative, and other plausible candidates for the category of American legal history throughout. Let me try to justify this. Hardly anything one could call American legal history was written in the 1880s and 90s, but one has to say something about the legal history that was written (English, mostly), because it exerted such a strong influence on what came later. After that I try to stick to the American side, including in the "legal history" field whatever contemporaries were likely to include, which until recently meant the history of "private law" subjects and not much else except perhaps constitutional history, which I do not feel competent to discuss, but which I gather has suffered from comparable if considerably less severe limitations. See the bibliographical note, and sources there cited, in Harold M. Hyman, *A More Perfect Union* 557-560 (1973). Notions of what legal history is about are, of course, rapidly changing (as witness the essays in this issue) thanks in large part to the work of Willard Hurst and his school. See text at notes 132-135, *infra*.

Some hedges and qualifications are in order. I do not try here to provide a comprehensive bibliographical survey; there are several excellent ones available.[9] I shall have very little to say about the literature of the Second Revival, contemporary historiography, since I plan to write about that on another occasion. And I can't do here what really ought some day to be done: a full-blooded social history of legal historiography in this country, showing the relationship of attempts to reconstruct the legal past to changes in the situation of lawyers generally, not only in the schools but in practice and in politics; and to intellectual developments outside the law, especially in philosophy and the social sciences.[10] In other words, this story is properly a minor subtheme of a much larger one—which remains untold because its telling has had to wait upon the development of an external legal historiography.[11] In this piece there are

---

9. See, e.g., Reid & Nelson, *Ann. Survey Am. L., supra*, note 6; Friedman, *History of American Law, supra*, note 3, at 596-621; Friedman *supra*, note 6; Johnson, "Colonial Legal History"; David H. Flaherty, "An Introduction to Early American Legal History," in *Essays in the History of Early American Law* (Flaherty ed. 1969); Wythe Holt, "Now and Then: The Uncertain State of Nineteenth Century American Legal History," 7 *Ind. L. Rev.* 615 (1974); and Harry N. Scheiber, "Federalism and the American Economic Order," 10 *L. & Soc'y Rev.* 57 (1975) (in this issue, *infra*).

10. For an example of the exciting possibilities of a historiography relating law and lawyers to a wider culture, see William J. Bouwsma, "Lawyers and Early Modern Culture," 73 *Am. Hist. Rev.* 303 (1973) and the contributions already made to such a history cited in *id.* at 304 n.4.

11. Friedman, *History, supra*, note 13, at 567-595 sketches a provocative brief outline of 20th century American legal history. The best general secondary treatment of the history of the American bar remains, 25 years later, Willard Hurst, *The Growth of American Law: The Lawmakers* [hereinafter Hurst, *Lawmakers*] 249-375 (1950), a circumstance that probably gives the author little satisfaction. The history of legal education has been well treated recently in Robert Stevens, "Two Cheers for 1870: the American Law School," in *Law in American History* 405, *supra*, note 6; Jerold S. Auerbach, "Equity and Amity: Law Teachers and Practitioners, 1900-1922," *Id.* at 551; and William Twining, *Karl Llewellyn and the Realist Movement* (1973). Two books are especially successful at relating legal to philosophical thought in the 20th century: Morton White, *Social Thought in America: The Revolt Against Formalism* (2d ed. 1957) and David A. Hollinger, *Morris R. Cohen and the Scientific Ideal* (1975). There are several studies of Realism: among them Wilfrid E. Rumble, Jr., *American Legal Realism: Skepticism, Reform, and the Judicial Process* (1968); Calvin Woodard, "The Limits of Legal Realism; an Historical Perspective," 54 *Va. L. Rev.* 689 (1968); Twining, *supra*, this note; Edward A. Purcell, Jr., *The Crisis of Democratic Theory* (1971); and G. Edward White, "From Sociological Jurisprudence to Realism: Jurisprudence and Social Change in Early Twentieth Century America," 58 *Va. L. Rev.* 999 (1972). This literature on Realism, though interesting and useful, still leaves one with the feeling that something important has been left out. Except for Twining, the authors tend to treat the Realists as (rather inept) legal philosophers, quoting from their more speculative work and from their debates on the nature of law with critics like Roscoe Pound and Morris Cohen. What gets slighted in the process is most of the stuff that the Realists themselves considered their most important work: their studies of subjects like procedure and commercial law. Research

hints and whispers about the important relationships, but nothing more.

I

At the beginning of professional legal historiography in the United States which, for convenience, may be taken to be the publication by Henry Adams and his students of their *Essays in Anglo-Saxon Law* in 1876, nobody would have drawn a distinction between legal history and any other kind. For the first generation of professional historians in this country borrowed from Germany not only the name and method of "scientific" historiography, but also the idea of the proper subject-matter of that science: the development of political institutions from their remotest origins to the present. In the hands of the leading professionals in England like Freeman and Stubbs, and in America like Herbert Baxter Adams and John W. Burgess, this turned out to mean that virtually all history was to be legal and constitutional history: they were going to do for Anglo-American political forms what their German models had done for the Roman. Thus there was nothing eccentric about the young Henry Adams's choice of Anglo-Saxon law as his Harvard seminar project in medieval history, or about the young O.W. Holmes's decision to study first Roman law and then the early forms of common law: the most exciting intellectual problems of the day were problems concerning origins of present political and legal forms, and the hottest debates over whether these origins were Roman or Teutonic.[12]

This preoccupation with origins resulted, of course, from the subscription of 19th century historians to various kinds of evolutionary assumptions about the development of political institutions. These assumptions varied greatly in their particulars and patrimony from historian to historian: some learned an idealist historical jurisprudence from Savigny; others picked up Freeman's idea of history as the gradual unfolding of political liberty; still others borrowed metaphors from anthropology or comparative philology. At the common core of these theories were the assumptions that all societies undergo comparable processes of development from the simple to the complex, the

now being done by John Henry Schlegel should help to correct this. Jerold S. Auerbach, *Unequal Justice: Lawyers and Social Change in Modern America* (1976) appeared too late to be consulted for this essay.

12. On the significance of Henry Adams' seminar, see Helen M. Cam, *Law Finders and Law-Makers* 176-182 (1962); on the influence of German writers on Holmes, Mark DeWolfe Howe, *Justice Oliver Wendell Holmes: The Proving Years, 1870-1882*, ch. 5 (1963).

primitive to the civilized; that these processes are continuous and progressive; and that the business of scientists was to discover, through the comparative study of developed and undeveloped peoples, the laws governing the growth of civilizations.[13] The particular business of historians was to trace the development of customs and ideals of already developed civilizations back to their ancient beginnings. For the extremely influential historians H.B. Adams and Burgess, who were especially impressed by German conceptions of history as the science of the state, this program dictated studying the development of political institutions, in their legal and constitutional forms.[14] National and racial ethnocentrism then combined to make Anglo-American civilization the focus of study; and this in turn made of the historiography of North America simply the study of the most recent stages of a long, continuous process beginning in the ancient Teutonic forests.[15]

Institutional-evolutionary studies in legal history flourished in the law schools too in the 1880s and 90s, especially at Harvard; it was under the influence of this school (to varying degrees) that Holmes, Bigelow, Thayer and Ames made their contributions to the study of early English law.[16] The point of dwelling on the assumptions of the historical school is not to depreciate the achievement of these men, who were among the few people Maitland found it worthwhile to correspond with on professional subjects;[17] it is that these assumptions have continued to linger around the law schools to the present day, like radio-active matter with an abnormally long half-life. Professional histor-

13. J.W. Burrow, *Evolution and Society, A Study in Victorian Social Theory* (1966) emphasizes the variety of 19th century evolutionary theories; Robert A. Nisbet, *Social Change and History* 166-188 (1968), their similarity.

14. See especially Jurgen Herbst, *The German Historical School in American Scholarship* 112-116 (1965); and John Higham, *History: Professional Scholarship in America* 158-161 (1965). Out of 15 history courses given at Harvard in 1890-91, "twelve were wholly or partly concerned with constitutional development." Cam, *supra*, note 12, at 182.

15. The titles of some of H.B. Adams' articles will convey the flavor of some of his scholarship: "The Germanic Origin of New England Towns," *Johns Hopkins Studies in History and Political Science* (ser. 1, no. 2, 1882); "Saxon Tithing-Men in America," *id.* (ser. 1, no. 4, 1882); "Norman Constables in America," *id.* (ser. 1, no. 8, 1883).

16. James Barr Ames, *Lectures on Legal History and Miscellaneous Legal Essays* (1913); Melville M. Bigelow, *Placita Anglo-Normannica* (1879) and *History of Procedure in England from the Norman Conquest* (1880); O.W. Holmes, Jr., *The Common Law* (1881); James Bradley Thayer, *A Preliminary Treatise on Evidence at the Common Law* (1898).

17. See C.H.S. Fifoot, *Frederick William Maitland: A Life*, at viii, 69-70, 75-76, 80 (1971).

ians—helped and sometimes led by the legal historians—soon repudiated the simpler tenets of this school, such as the theories of a unilinear evolutionary development and of the Teutonic origins of Anglo-Saxon civilization; and most of them went on to shake off its influence almost entirely. What we have to account for is the survival of 19th century evolutionary theory not only in amateur legal writing—the brief "historical introductions" to textbook or article—but in various indirect ways in monographic legal history as well.[18]

The solution to the puzzle lies, I think, in the reasons that the new law schools were so hospitable to legal-historical studies in the first place: their faculties (at least initially) perceived no conflict between historical research and the strictly professional ambitions of the schools. To be sure, the founding generation of law teachers defined a role for themselves in the profession differing from the practitioner's. The legal scholar was not simply to train his students in the law as it was, but to ascertain the principles truly underlying the law through scientific research, to the end of reforming existing law by bringing it into conformity with those principles.[19] History was supposed to be the primary field of research. But ultimately the results of research were to be grist for the judicial mill. Ames, for example, thought of historiography simply as one of the useful lawyer's tasks that the professor, because of his freedom from the press of business, could attend to with the greater efficiency that comes from specialization of function. What was wanted was:

> a high order of treatises on all the important branches of the law, exhibiting the historical development of the subject and containing sound conclusions based on scientific analysis. . . . Too often the just expectations of men are thwarted by the action of the courts, a result largely due to taking a partial view of the subject, or to a failure to grasp the original development and true significance of the rule which is made the basis of the decision.

As an instance he cites the rule denying enforceability to creditor's agreement to release debtors on part payment of the debt: this "unfortunate rule", says Ames, "is the result of misunderstanding a *dictum* of Coke. In truth Coke, in an overlooked case, declared in unmistakable terms the legal validity of the creditor's agreement."[20]

---

18. See text at notes 23-27, 32-44, *infra*.
19. See Auerbach, "Equity and Amity," *supra*, note 11 at 553-72.
20. James Barr Ames, "The Vocation of the Law Professor," in Ames, *supra*, note 16 at 366. [The reference is clearly to Foakes v. Beer, 9 App. Cas. 605 (1884), *citing* Pinnel's Case, 5 Co. Rep. 117a (1602).]

If only historians had earlier brought to light Coke's other case! Ames, plainly, felt none of Maitland's skepticism about the results of mixing legal dogma and legal history. Maitland said: "The lawyer must be orthodox otherwise he is no lawyer; an orthodox history seems to me a contradiction in terms."[21] Like most of his colleagues, Ames did not see the contradiction. He hoped to subordinate the development of dogma to historical science. In fact, things turned out exactly the opposite: legal history was subordinated to legal technique, the immediate needs of the profession to keep current dogma rationalized in line with past authority. The historical school's view of law as the continuous development of institutional forms lent itself beautifully to these needs, since that view made it easy to confuse the history of law with the "common law tradition"—the fictional continuity that each generation of common lawyers imposes, in its own fashion and for its own ends, on the development of judicial doctrine.[22]

Institutional-evolutionary studies prospered in the law schools because they had something to offer the profession: documentation of the unbroken chain of connection between living lawyers and an ancient tradition. The successors in historiographical fashion to the historical school, however, could offer nothing of the kind. The second generation of American institutional historians, C.M. Andrews and H.L. Osgood in particular, rejected the idea of universal and necessary legal development; and picked up from the research of Maine, Brunner, Maitland,

---

Ames also saw a role for the law professor as an "expart counselor in legislation," by which he meant advisor on technical law reform. *Id.* at 367-68.

21. "Why the History of Law Is Not Written," *Collected Papers*, I, 480, 493 (1911).

22. Horwitz, *supra*, note 6 at 282-83, calls attention to the "incredibly striking" parallels between lawyer's legal history and scientists' history of science, quoting T.S. Kuhn, *The Structure of Scientific Revolutions* 137-38 (2d ed. 1970):

> Textbooks . . . begin by truncating the scientist's sense of his discipline's history and then proceed to supply a substitute for what they have eliminated. Characteristically, textbooks of science contain just a bit of history, either in an introductory chapter or, more often, in scattered references to the great heroes of an earlier age. From such references both students and professionals come to feel like participants in a long-standing historical tradition. Yet the textbook tradition in which scientists come to sense their participation is one that, in fact, never existed . . . [S]cience textbooks . . . refer only to that part of the work of past scientists that can easily be viewed as contributions to the statement and solution of the text's paradigm problems. . . . No wonder that textbooks and the historical tradition they imply have to be rewritten after each scientific revolution. And no wonder that, as they are rewritten, science once again comes to seem largely cumulative.

and Vinogradoff (among others) the program of studying the effects upon legal forms of specific and local variations in social environment.[23] Meanwhile the New, or Progressive historians led by Turner and Beard were carrying off much of the historical profession in their challenge to the primacy of the study of the development of political institutions, insisting that legal and constitutional forms were only secondary derivatives of economic and social forces. Beard was of course the most influential proponent of a revised notion of law as the expression, not of the evolving ethical ideals of the Anglo-Saxon race, but of economic interests pursued through factional politics.[24]

The law schools had small use for either of these modes of practising history, even though Holmes and Pound, both law teachers, had been instrumental in promoting them. Very little American history of any distinction in the institutional vein of Andrews and Osgood was written in the law schools between 1900 and the revival of legal-historical studies in the 1930's; this is probably because history, like liberal learning generally in that period, fell victim to the case method's exclusive claim on the undergraduate law curriculum. Moreover the institutional approach demanded long and patient study in primary materials, time taken away from, and not yielding any particularly valuable results in aid of, treatise and case-book writing.[25] As for Pro-

23. On the new institutional (or "imperial") historians, see Higham, *supra*, note 14 at 162-166; Johnson, "Colonial Legal History." Maine is usually thought of as an evolutionist; but Kenneth E. Bock has persuasively argued that he was an opponent of the theory of a unilinear evolutionary development, and not interested in hunting for origins among primitive peoples, but instead was concerned to study law in relation to the entire surrounding culture, including its "relatively recent history." (I.e., Maine was disposed to explain ancient law by ancient history, but not modern law.) "Comparison of Histories: The Contribution of Henry Maine," 16 *Comp. Stud. in Soc'y & Hist.* 232, 247 (1974).

24. On the Progressives, see Richard Hofstadter, *The Progressive Historians* (1968), especially 181-218; and Higham, *supra*, note 14 at 171-182.

25. The case method, in Langdell's original conception a way of getting across the basic principles of legal science, rapidly acquired its present-day justification as a pedagogic vehicle for the teaching of legal method. Thus justified, it became the device for teaching every undergraduate law course, tending to drive out subjects (such as legal philosophy and history) not suited to being so taught. See Stevens, *supra*, note 11 at 435-449. In 1960, commenting bitterly on the anti-intellectualism accompanying the spread of the Harvard method in the late 19th and early 20th centuries, Karl Llewellyn recounted that when

> [William A.] Keener was called to Columbia in 1890 to put that law school on a footing worthy of a great University, he brought with him two policies: (1) "The" case-system . . . (2) All that noise which is not "law" must go out; a "law" curriculum must cast out Ishmael. Columbia . . . had therefore to amputate from any official "law"-connection what became the Department of Political Science. Thus the Roman Law Perspective of a Munroe Smith, the scholarship

gressive history, it was simply anathema. When the Progressives took over American constitutional history they pretty well wiped out internal—doctrinal and intellectual—approaches among the historians, leaving these to be cultivated (with great distinction, as it turned out) by political scientists like Corwin and McIlwain.[26] They could obviously not have converted many lawyers to their method in the early part of this century, since in its extreme forms it denied the existence of any autonomous content to law, and hence any meaning to legal historiography as traditionally practiced. The Progessives did not themselves produce (at least, until Willard Hurst began to write) any significant body of work on private law; but their hostility helped effectively to split off legal history from the main action in American scholarship and to isolate it in the law schools.[27]

Confined to the law faculties, reduced to the status of auxiliary service for strictly professional tasks, and written for the most part by amateurs, legal historiography suffered a rapid narrowing of scope. The old historical school had held out the promise of connecting the history of law and of society. In the study of medieval English law, that promise was being fulfilled. In America it was cut short, and legal history was reduced to internal history.

In part this happened because the historical school's organic theory of culture paradoxically encouraged scholars to disregard the social context of law, just as the "comparative method," by generalizing patterns of development in a single civilization to

> and vision of a [Frank J.] Goodnow, the power and range of our greatest international lawyer, John Bassett Moore [who trained, among others, Julius Goebel, Jr.], flourished not within the law curriculum, nor for it, but across the barbarian border . . . . In 1915, when, already our foremost jurisprude, [Roscoe Pound] became Dean at Harvard Law School, he deliberately took his own Jurisprudence course *out of the undergraduate curriculum.* He kept it out, lest his bulk of graduates be distracted—or contaminated.

Llewellyn, "The Study of Law as a Liberal Art," in *Jurisprudence* 375, 377-78 (1962). [Italics Llewellyn's; interpolations mine.]

26. See generally, Herman Belz, "The Realist Critique of Constitutionalism in the Era of Reform," 15 *Am. J. Leg. Hist.* 288 (1971); Paul L. Murphy, "Time to Reclaim: The Current Challenge of American Constitutional History," 69 *Am. Hist. Rev.* 64 (1963).

27. It is not always appreciated how wide the split was. One can get some sense of it from casual remarks made recently by non-lawyer historians who have become interested in law. For example: (a) Eugene Genovese: "[T]he fashionable relegation of law to the rank of a superstructural and derivative phenomenon obscures the degree of autonomy it creates for itself." *Roll, Jordan, Roll* 25 (1974). (b) Harry N. Scheiber, speaking of recent developments in economic history, refers to "*new* lines of inquiry that stress institutional and doctrinal development in American law . . ." "Government and the Economy: Studies of the 'Commonwealth' Policy in Nineteenth Century America," 3 *J. Interdisc. Hist.* 135, 151 n. 44 (1972) [Italics added]. Historians are discovering law, lawyers society.

all others, in fact justified ethnocentricity. James Coolidge Carter, Savigny's chief popularizer in this country, give the game away when he said that the field of research for judges trying to locate the true or just rule of law for a case by the historical method was "the habits, customs, business and manners of the people, *and those previously declared rules which have sprung out of previous similar inquiries into habits, customs, business, and manners.*"[28] This was certainly a convenient method for legal scholars: it meant that in practice they carried no greater research burden than would any legal positivist, for whom legal history was only the history of past state commands, rather than the history of an entire culture.

But of course the main reason lawyer's history became, and remained, internal—confined to the boxful of distinctively legal things—is that it was written from inside the box, was itself a "form of professional activity within the legal system—like adjudication, or advocacy, or counseling."[29] As long as the common law tradition was a source of normative authority, the doing of legal history was conceived to be a professional task; as long as it was a professional task it was bound to be internal. Legal scholars not only took the boxful of legal things as their exclusive subject-matter, but whenever possible adduced as factors explaining the development of legal things only *other* legal things. The rule seemed to be: stay inside the box; the most common application of the rule was explanation of current case-law doctrine by means of prior case-law doctrine.

This is why, long after the discrediting of evolutionary theories of history, legal history was still so frequently written as if these theories still held sway. For the historian who restricts his sources to the strictly legal, there often is no explanation available other than the genetic. Suppose one wanted to explain the use of the "fellow-servant" rule to limit liability of employers for the costs of industrial accidents in the 19th century, and one's search were confined to the rule's predecessors in form. One would learn a good deal about the common law of master and servant and the writ of trespass on the case, but

28. *The Ideal and the Actual in Law* 10-11 (1890).

29. This is how Richard L. Abel describes a "law book," a "study [that] identifies, defines, organizes the rules [that legal institutions apply] by means of criteria proper to the legal system—it *rationalizes* them in Weber's sense." He contrasts such a "law book" to a "book about law," which is a "mode of *reflection* upon the legal system". "Law Books and Books About Law," 26 *Stan. L. Rev.* 175, 176 (1973) [Italics Abel's]. This is another (and very effective) way of stating Maitland's distinction between legal history and legal dogma, text at note 21, *supra*.

nothing about the 19th century industry, however useful such knowledge might be.[30]

Limitations of method thus kept driving American lawyers backwards in search of the ancestors of current legal categories in early English forms. When they got there they found a historiography that was often extremely technical, but not internal; the further back one went, the more one found law connected to social structure, economic organization, agricultural method, administrative practice, currents of religious and philosophical speculation. The great researchers of the classical period and their successors had given medieval law a context. But as one approached more recent times, legal history started to thin out to the distinctively "legal" again, and explanations for the shape of legal things to revert to the genetic.

Around 1900 then, at the point serious work in legal history slumped in American law schools, scholarly convention in the field suggested it was all right to try to account for old law by external circumstance, but not new law. This way of looking at things matched nicely with the contemporary jurisprudential theory that the common law, though it had started out derived from Custom, had come, as its administration was brought under a professional judiciary, to be based upon Reason.[31] It is tempting to suggest that the law schools were not interested in developments in historiography that would tend to controvert this theory. At any rate, the configurations that legal-historical

---

30. The late Professor Goebel employed his gift for Latinate astringency to characterize this method as treating

> the growth of doctrine as something projected on a horizontal plane of rational manipulation unmindful of its perpendicular support in time or circumstance. In expositions of the doctrine of consideration, the judgments of his majesty's judges in the seventeenth century rub shoulders with those from the American backwoods two hundred years later. To legitimate the control of business, Tudor sumptuary statutes are forcibly wedded to the legislative indiscretions of the seventy-third Congress . . .
>
> That so fantastic a conception of history should prevail as a convention in the bulk of our legal literature is attributable in some degree to the intellectual tyranny which the judicial opinion exerts. It is a truism that to know the common law its history must be known. Our courts, however, seek enlightenment on the past chiefly in the judgments of their predecessors. These judgments are rarely treated as single but complex assessable facts, for the mass of relevant data of which they are merely parts is usually ignored. In consequence, the antecedent judicial opinion is elevated to a status of preposterous importance as a source. . .

Julius Goebel, Jr., *Felony and Misdemeanor* xvii-xviii (1937).

31. Beale was expounding this theory to Harvard law students in 1909, according to notes taken by Robert Lee Hale of his lectures on jurisprudence in that year. These notes are published, with an introduction, in Warren J. Samuels, "Joseph Henry Beale's Lectures on Jurisprudence, 1909," 29 *U. Miami L. Rev.* 260 (1975). See *id.* at 288-293.

scholarship achieved by 1900 were decisive for the future shape of the field—especially in American legal history.

Look for example at the Association of American Law Schools' *Select Essays in Anglo-American Legal History* (1907), which purported to collect in three volumes the cream of current scholarship in the field.[32] This includes some wonderful stuff—e.g. Maitland's famous essay on "English Law and the Renaissance"—but is mostly interesting now for the subjects it includes. Most of the essays (after the traditional start with Teutonic Law) have to do with English law; after some broad surveys, the essays tend to be organized by type of court (Chancery, Admiralty, etc.) and doctrinal field (assumpsit, agency, trover, defamation, etc.). The stress is on the common law, though equity receives seven essays in all, and there are brief treatments of canon law, admiralty, and the law merchant. With very few exceptions, the essays are concerned with tracing the early forms of modern practice categories—"The Historical Development of Code Pleading"—"Early Forms of Partnership"—"The Early History of Negotiable Instruments"—and the exceptions are the essays set in early English history and unabashedly making no pretence at current relevance.

The American entries are of most interest. They cluster around colonial legal history and are primarily devoted to exploring the extent to which colonial law was influenced or determined by English models. Then there are treatments of 19th century attempts at procedural reform in the common law, dealing with proposals to simplify pleading and the organization of courts and with the fate of schemes to codify the common law in whole or in part, from Bentham to David Dudley Field. Lacking (as yet) only the addition of something on the reception of English law after the Revolution, the basic canon of American legal history was fixed—and fixed almost before any work had been done!—upon transplantation to America of the common law and the subsequent challenge and defeat, save for partial accommodation in the form of Code Pleading, of the common law's arch rival, codification. Even to the present, general surveys and collections of materials on American legal history are faithful to the broad outlines of this canon. This is a wonderful example of the survival of form beyond its inspiring context, for these

32. And did so in fact. Its nearest rival was a compilation of essays in American legal history put out by members of the Yale Law School faculty, *Two Centuries' Growth of American law, 1701-1901* (1901), sketching the antecedents of some 18 fields of contemporary practice, and now interesting mostly as revealing how little access even learned lawyers had to their own past.

subjects are the vital ones of American experience only within a theory such as the old historical school's—by which American history simply records the later stages of the common law's triumphant struggle for continuous development through Anglo-Saxon civilization.

There were two jarring notes in this collection. One was the famous attempt by Reinsch, a disciple of Turner's at Wisconsin, to demonstrate the domination of colonial law not by English models but the primitive law of the frontier.[33] Oddly enough this environmental (and later proved erroneous[34]) explanation was absorbed along with the rest of the 1907 collection into the orthodox view of the American past. The assumption of the continuity of Anglo-American legal development was neatly rescued despite the Reinsch theory by Roscoe Pound, who simply moved up the period of "reception" of English law in America to a "formative era" after the Revolution.[35] The other oddity in the collection was the presence of contributions by Simeon Baldwin and the young Samuel Williston on early corporation law.[36] Corporation law too was to find a niche in the permanent canon of appropriate subjects, either as a subspecies of commercial law or on its own. These particular articles, like the others, tended to emphasize the most formal aspects of corporations and the earliest forms at that; there was nothing here like Maitland's speculations on the social functions of different forms of group legal personality.[37] Nonetheless, corporation law had so obviously responded to political and economic pressure in recent history that the inclusion of it in the standard canon was prophetic. Sooner or later, it would be the most promising candidate for external historiographical treatment; and so it eventually proved to be.[38]

33. Paul Samuel Reinsch, "English Common Law in the Early American Colonies," *Select Essays in Anglo-American Legal History*, I, 367 (1907).

34. By the work of Goebel, Morris, and Haskins in particular. See Johnson, "Colonial Legal History," and the essays collected in Flaherty, *supra*, note 9.

35. Pound, *The Spirit of the Common Law* 113-118 (1921); *The Formative Era of American Law* 6-12, *et passim* (1938). For an account of Pound's "enormous influence on the study of American law" with these two books, see Michael G. Kammen, "Colonial Court Records and the Study of Early American History: A Bibliographical Review," 70 *Am. Hist. Rev.* 732, 738 (1965); and Katz, *supra*, note 6.

36. Baldwin, "History of the Law of Private Corporations in the Colonies and States," in *Select Essays*, *supra*, note 33, at III, 236; Williston, "The History of the Law of Business Corporations before 1800," *id.* at III, 195.

37. Maitland's essays on trusts, corporations, and unincorporated bodies are all collected in *Maitland: Selected Essays* (Hazeltine, Lapsley & Winfield eds. 1936), as well as in Maitland, *supra*, note 21.

38. There is a fuller literature on the history of the American corporation

Anyone who is skeptical about the extraordinary persistence through our time of this late 19th century view of the proper scope of legal history should pick up any of the standard history texts published for law students.[39] Or he might look at the historical section of any recent law review article. I am looking at one now, chosen because it is near at hand and because it is one of the best things of its kind, not one of the worst: an excellent synthesis of anthropological and historical literature about contract law.[40] The article is explicitly evolutionary; it begins with economic transactions in "primitive" societies and ends with 20th century American contracts; in between lie ancient Rome, England from medieval to modern times, and 19th century America. The sections on primitive society are rich in detail about the relation of forms of transactions to social life—to kinship systems, religion, land tenure, warfare.[41] Even by the time he reaches medieval England, the author is still interested in externals: we learn for example something about theological views of contract.[42] But from the moment the common law courts get into the picture, the focus of the narrative shifts almost exclusively to institutional and doctrinal forms: case, assumpsit, indebitatus assumpsit, consideration, up to Slade's Case in 1602, whereupon, saving a brief "Epilogue", the article ends![43] It ends presumably because the story of doctrinal developments is now complete; the Epilogue treats summarily of the high point of "freedom of contract" in the 19th century and of the tendency in the 20th to limit this freedom by legislation.[44] Except for passing references to the work of Weber, Hurst, and Lawrence Friedman, there is scarcely a word on the tremendous changes that have taken place in the nature of economic exchange relationships between the 17th century and the present, no allusion even to the standard economic histories of Europe and America for that time. It would be absurd to

---

than on any other subject that plausibly belongs in the field of American legal history. See the bibliography in Willard Hurst, *The Legitimacy of the Business Corporation in the Law of the United States, 1780-1970* at 165 (1970).

39. See, e.g., William F. Walsh, *A History of Anglo-American Law* [Bobbs-Merrill] (2d ed. 1932); Max Radin, *Handbook of Anglo-American Legal History* [West Hornbook Series] (1936); Frederick G. Kempin, Jr., *Historical Introduction to Anglo-American Law in a Nutshell* [West Nutshell Series] (1973). Of course these vary greatly in quality: Radin's is the outstanding one.

40. E. Allan Farnsworth, "The Past of Promise: An Historical Introduction to Contract," 69 *Colum. L. Rev.* 576 (1969).

41. *Id.* at 578-88.

42. *Id.* at 591.

43. *Id.* at 592-99.

44. *Id.* at 599-607.

blame this situation on the author, who is a scholar of distinction; he was working with materials that are at hand to tell the story that has commonly been thought the one worth telling. The point is to show how deeply ingrained in the consciousness of the modern lawyer is the late 19th century's subordination of legal history to the common law tradition.

II

American legal historiography began to revive in the late 1920's. It is not clear why this happened. Perhaps in part it was simply because the students whom Andrews and Osgood had interested in the study of primary source material on British imperial administration were starting to turn out their own work; in part because some of the younger law teachers, especially at Columbia, were trying to break down the hedges that had grown up between other university departments and the law schools. In 1930 the American Historical Association organized a conference of lawyers and historians to draw up a program to publish American legal source materials: this resulted in the American Legal Records series.[45] In the same year, private and foundation gifts established the Foundation for Research in Legal History at Columbia Law School, under the direction of Julius Goebel, Jr., which underwrote research and publication expenses of new secondary work.[46]

For the purposes of this essay, the most interesting aspect of this period of revival, which lasted through the mid-1960's (and is perhaps still going on—these periodizations never work out very neatly), is that its scholarship did not bring about any very substantial redefinition of the field of legal history. (There were exceptions, which will be noted). On the face of it, this is rather surprising. The period was dominated by work in colonial law done by historians of formidable talent—Goebel, George L. Haskins, Mark DeWolfe Howe, Richard B. Morris, Joseph H. Smith. None of these historians believed that law develops primarily according to the logic of an internal dynamic, independently of surrounding political, social, and economic con-

45. The committee consisted of Charles McLean Andrews, Carroll T. Bond (Chief Judge of the Maryland Court of Appeals and editor of the first volume in the series), John Dickinson, the ubiquitous Felix Frankfurter, Evarts B. Greene, and Richard B. Morris. See Evarts B. Greene, "Foreword" to *Proceedings of the Maryland Court of Appeals, 1695-1729* (American Legal Records, I; Bond ed. 1933). Greene acknowledged "the encouragement, given at an early stage of the development of this project, by Mr. Justice Brandeis . . ." *Id.* For a list of publications in the series, see Kammen, *supra*, note 35 at 733.

46. See Goebel, *supra*, note 30 at ix.

ditions; indeed each thought that belief one of the failings of the amateur historiography of the early 20th century, for among other errors it propagated the theory of the process of reception and development of English law taking place in a uniform manner and rate across all of early America. Though some members of this fresh group of colonial historians, notably Morris,[47] were eventually again to emphasize similarities among colonial legal patterns, all of them recognized that any generalizations would have to be based upon archival study of local materials in individual colonies.

Yet though a conviction of the importance of the influence of social surroundings on law was what drove historians of this period to research in local sources in the first place, it did not carry most of them so far as to write external legal history. They stayed chiefly within the orthodox canon of subjects—the reception of English common law in America and its 19th century rivalry with "codification"—and continued to take their materials from the box of distinctively legal things. Their teaching materials, enriched by the results of their research in primary sources, were enormously more sophisticated than similar products of the old institutional-evolutionary school; but they were organized by the same categories as the old school's (reception, codification, corporations, etc.), and the detail filling the old categories, though new, was all *legal* detail.[48] Symbolically, the most important collective effort of professional American legal historians at the end of the period was of the same kind as at the beginning—publication of colonial legal records.[49]

One must point out immediately that there were significant exceptions to this pattern; and that historians of this period did make major contributions to an external legal historiography. Daniel Boorstin's study of Blackstone's *Commentaries* and Mark

47. See his *Studies in the History of American Law* (1958); and Johnson, "Colonial Legal History" at 258-261.

48. See, e.g., Julius Goebel, Jr., *Cases and Materials on the Development of Legal Institutions* (2d ed. 1937) [*but see* Ch. 3 of this book, on "Social, Economic and Intellectual Factors Conditioning Legal Development," which mostly accords with tradition in confining discussion of such factors to the earlier English law, but not entirely: cf. *id.* at 620-626 on American corporations]; Mark DeWolfe Howe, *Readings in American Legal History* (1949); and Joseph H. Smith, *Cases and Materials on the Development of Legal Institutions* (1965).

49. The William Nelson Cromwell Foundation underwrote in whole or in part: *Colonial Justice in Western Massachusetts (1639-1702): The Pyncheon Court Record* (Smith ed. 1961); *Legal Papers of John Adams* (Wroth & Zobel eds. 1965); and *The Law Practice of Alexander Hamilton* (Goebel *et al.*, eds. 1964-). I am not complaining about this; these volumes are superbly edited, and if there is one place where lavish spreading of technical detail is surely justified, it is in the edition of a primary text.

DeWolfe Howe's of Holmes's *Common Law* both succeeded in connecting law books to wider regions of the thought of their time.[50] After a series of monographs written in a more cautious mode, George L. Haskins built a new framework for colonial legal studies by taking as his subject not the specialized concerns of lawyers, but the whole governmental and clerical apparatus of social control in 17th century Massachusetts.[51]

But these, like the work of Hurst and his followers to be discussed later, were exceptions. The main business of the period was to make a start at giving American law historicity, localizing it to specific times and places. Under the spell of evolutionism and professional habit, the earlier school of lawyer-historians had ransacked the past for ancestors of their own day's categories, though these categories might have possessed no significance, or a very different one, for the previous generations back through whom they were traced. The researchers of the 1930's and onward corrected this by showing us colonial law through the eyes of contemporaries—but usually through the eyes of contemporary lawyers, and abnormally bookish lawyers at that. Research that adopted a different perspective was not likely to be considered "legal" history at all, even if it relied primarily on legal sources as evidence—e.g. Richard Morris's great study of colonial labor conditions and regulation[52] or the studies of 19th century "public policy" in the states.[53]

What can account for the almost unrelenting preoccupation with internals? Daniel Boorstin and Calvin Woodard, who at different times both called for a more catholic vision of the scope of legal history, both attributed its unsatisfactory state in part to the pragmatic temper of legal studies since the 1930's. Boortin said: "[N]early every American contribution to legal history which ought to be considered a classic was made *before* the movement [to integrate law and the social sciences]"; he blamed the law schools' fads for policy science, social science, and clinical education.[54] Woodard reproached legal scholars "somewhat intoxicated with the delusion of complete freedom from the past" for promoting among students the view that law

---

50. Boorstin, *The Mysterious Science of the Law* (1941); Howe, *supra*, note 12.
51. Haskins, *Law and Authority in Early Massachusetts* (1960). The influence of this approach may be detected in the range (as well as the title) of a recent collection of essays, *Law and Authority in Colonial America* (Billias ed. 1965).
52. *Government and Labor in Early America* (1946).
53. See Scheiber, *supra*, note 27.
54. "The Humane Study of Law," 57 *Yale L.J.* 960, 963-64 (1948).

is merely "engineering," or "the vector of so many mid-20th century social forces rationalized in accordance with the personal preference of so many contemporary judges and legislators."[55]

The trouble with this explanation is that it was precisely those people who took the most pragmatic view of present law that tended to urge the study of the past—urged it, indeed, partly for the sake of ridding the present of the deadwood of irrelevant survivals. Maitland took this view, for example;[56] so did Holmes, the founder of American pragmatic legal thought.[57] In fact a very large number of lawyers associated with the pragmatic movement[58] took more than a passing interest in legal history. Pound's lectures on the "formative era of American law" influenced several generations of historians;[59] Frankfurter was not only instrumental in obtaining research funding for legal history, but also wrote histories of the Commerce Clause, and (with others) of federal jurisdiction and labor injunctions;[60] Karl Llewellyn, Jerome Hall, Walton Hamilton, Walter Nelles, and Hessel Yntema, all Realists, all did some of their own work in history[61] and followed closely what was done by others.

55. Woodard, *supra,* note 7 at 110-114.

56. See, e.g., Maitland writing to Dicey in 1896 (cited in Fifoot, *supra,* note 17 at 143):

> The only direct utility of legal history (I say nothing of its thrilling interest) lies in the lesson that each generation has an enormous power of shaping its own law. I don't think that the study of legal history would make men fatalists; I doubt it would make them conservatives. I am sure it would free them from superstitions and teach them that they have free hands.

57. See, e.g., "Law in Science and Science in Law [1899]", in Holmes, *Collected Legal Papers* 210, 225 (1920):

> From a practical point of view, [the use of history] is mainly negative and skeptical . . . [I]ts chief good is to burst inflated explanations. Everyone instinctively recognizes that in these days the justification of a law cannot be found in the fact that our fathers have always followed it. It must be found in some help which the law brings toward reaching a social end which the governing power of the community has made up its mind that it wants . . . [H]istory is the means by which we measure the power which the past has had to govern the present in spite of ourselves, so to speak, by imposing traditions which no longer meet their original end.

58. This phrase seems broad enough to encompass Holmes's pragmatism, Pound's sociological jurisprudence, and the many varieties of legal Realism.

59. See note 35, *supra.*

60. Frankfurter, *The Commerce Clause under Marshall, Taney, and Waite* (1937); Frankfurter and James M. Landis, *The Business of the Supreme Court, A Study in the Federal Judicial System* (1928); Frankfurter and Nathan Greene, *The Labor Injunction* (1930).

61. Llewellyn: "On Warranty of Quality and Society," (Pts. 1 & 2) 36 *Colum. L. Rev.* 699 (1936), 37 *Colum. L. Rev.* 341 (1937); "Across Sales on Horseback," 52 *Harv. L. Rev.* 725 (1939); "The First Struggle to Unhorse Sales," 52 *Harv. L. Rev.* 874 (1939). (This superb quartet on the history of sales law may be Llewellyn's most

Pragmatic legal studies were at their height during the revival of professional legal historiography in the 1930's; Goebel was one of the young Turks at the Columbia Law School; Howe was a clerk to Holmes and protégé of Frankfurter's; Haskins was inspired by Pound's theory of interests; and —as will be seen— Hurst's work is written out of an explicitly pragmatic theory of law. The failure of the period of revival to develop an extensive external historiography of law does not stem from pragmatic thinking, but—I am persuaded—from loss of nerve in the face of the implications of that thinking; not from reckless disregard of the common law tradition, but from an anxious solicitude to preserve it.

The program set forth by pragmatists like Holmes and Pound for development of a science of law called for reconnecting legal

---

durable work. Yet he said [of "Warranty of Quality," Pt. 1, *supra* this note at 699 n.*] he was not writing "history, . . . [but] an appeal for history. It is a sad commentary on our dogmatics that sales cases over a hundred and fifty years and more than fifty jurisdictions have been treated as if they floated free of time, place and person. Whereas it is time, place, person and circumstance which give them meaning. A few major trends are here presented. But not as history. History calls for detailed knowledge, for detailed background, and for discrimination even more detailed.")

Hall: *Theft, Law and Society* (1935).

Hamilton: "The Ancient Maxim *Caveat Emptor*", 40 *Yale L.J.* 1133 (1931).

Nelles: *"Commonwealth v. Hunt,"* 32 *Colum. L. Rev.* 1128 (1932); "Towards Legal Understanding," (Pts. 1 & 2), 34 *Colum. L. Rev.* 862, 1041 (1934).

Yntema: *Sourcebook on Roman Law* (1929) (with A. Arthur Schiller).

But see Grant Gilmore, Book Review, 21 *The Law School Record* (Chicago) 38 (Summer, 1975):

> When I studied law at Yale in the early 1940's there was no suggestion, in any of the instruction which I received, that there was any point in thinking about law as a historical process. The implicit philosophical or jurisprudential bias which the entire law faculty seemed to share was that law was a sort of mystical absolute waiting to be discovered, described, catalogued, mapped out, so to say, reduced to possession. [Gilmore adds that his instructors included some noted Realists.] It was not until considerably later—if we must have a date, 1960 will do as well as any—that a historical approach to law seemed, almost overnight, to become fashionable, at least among academic theorists.

The absence of a historical approach at Yale in the 1940's does not surprise me; the intellectually curious and innovative phase of legal pragmatism was by then over. I am somewhat perplexed by the reference to a new fashion for history starting about 1960. In 1963 Edward Re surveyed law school curricula to find legal history courses other than "development of Anglo-American legal institutions" (often shortened to DLI) virtually non-existent; and even DLI was rare. (DLI was sometimes real history camouflaged as evolutionism, as in John P. Dawson's splendid Harvard Law School version; more often [to judge from course descriptions cited in Re] simply orthodox evolutionism.) Of course this is not necessarily inconsistent with Gilmore's recollection; "a historical approach to law" does not have to mean legal history courses. But legal history courses provide some evidence of the seriousness of commitment to the approach. See Re, "Legal History Courses in American Law Schools," 13 *Am. Univ. L. Rev.* 45 (1963).

to social history, since the contribution of historical study to the program was to liberate the present from law that had arisen out of entirely different social contexts and modes of thought and was not, as a consequence, necessarily suited to modern needs. This was potentially quite a radical view, since it repudiated the whole concept of tradition. Scholars like Langdell (and to a lesser extent Ames) tended to equate historical method and legal science: accurate tracing of the historical development of rules would reveal their immanent principles. Holmes and Pound said that since the end of law was the efficient adjustment of conflicting social interests, *real* legal science consisted in accurate measurement of those interests. The role of history was the important but auxiliary one of clearing away the rubbish of pointless old law.[62]

Outside the law schools these ideas had considerable influence on historians, especially constitutional historians, among whom the impact of economic, social and political factors upon judicial decision-making was a commonplace idea well before the ascendancy of legal Realism.[63] Yet among the lawyers the pragmatic prescription for legal science, assisted by a historiography devoted to destroying instead of beatifying the common law tradition, perhaps not surprisingly failed to make complete converts even of its chief proselytizers. Without knowing for sure what cut short the pragmatic movement as a whole, it is hard to tell what happened to the minor appendage of a program for an external historiography. But here are some ideas.

Training in the common law tradition was what gave a significant elite of the American bar its sense of identity as a mandarinate of masters of an ancient technique; the tradition associated law with both science and high culture, and justified

62. See Pound, *Interpretations of Legal History* 152 and Ch. 7 *passim* (1923); Holmes, "The Path of the Law [1897]," in *supra*, note 57 at 167, 191-195. The difference between Holmes's and Ames's views on tradition and function in law is really only one of emphasis: in practice they often arrived at the same conclusion. Ames believed that traditional authority, accurately interpreted by means of scientific historiography, would also produce the socially functional results he thought desirable. Holmes rejected, of course, the idea that the past could supply "correct" legal doctrine, but argued nonetheless for judicial conservatism towards reforming traditional doctrine—". . . because I believe the claim of our especial code to respect is simply that it exists, that it is the one to which we have become accustomed . . ." "Law in Science," *supra*, note 57 at 239.

63. See Herman Belz, *supra*, note 26 and "The Constitution in the Gilded Age: The Beginnings of Constitutional Realism in American Scholarship," 13 *Am. J. Leg. Hist.* 110 (1969); Richard Hofstadter, *The Progressive Historians* 200-202 (1968). Charles Beard acknowledged Holmes, Pound and Goodnow as forerunners in *An Economic Interpretation of the Constitution of the United States* 9 (1913).

the prestige and power of its practitioners.[64] Law was authoritative because autonomous; and its autonomy derived from two sources, its formality (or technicality) and its antiquity. An evolutionary and internal legal historiography contributed, like legal scholarship generally, to reinforcing the tradition.[65] To deprive lawyers of the tradition entirely, as the pragmatists apparently (but, as will be seen, only apparently) proposed to do, was to make orphans of them. It was a threatened professionalism, among other things, that squashed legal pragmatism in the end.

This professionalism more likely arose from within than without the law schools. I doubt that the common law tradition had much mythic significance for the great majority of American lawyers, who probably were content to think of themselves as technicians rather than mandarins.[66] Even among the elite practitioners there can have been few who knew or cared much about the kind of legal history that was being done at the law schools; though if they had known it is entirely possible that they would have favored inculcation of the text-

64. Beale: "[L]aw is a traditional manner of thought about right behavior; the lawyers and judges are experts in it." *A Treatise on the Conflict of Laws* xiii (2d ed. 1935). He developed the idea in his 1909 lectures (Samuels, *supra*, note 31 at 292-93):

> [The principal characteristic of the common law] is that it requires a scientific knowledge on the part of a legal caste, thus coming back to a characteristic of the most ancient times, where it was in the knowledge of a priestly caste. . . . How can you tell what is the law of Massachusetts today? You can of course ask the judges, as special experts; but they will not say unless a case is brought before them. The law of Massachusetts is what the body of the Massachusetts bar thinks it is.

I use Beale to stand for orthodoxy because the Realists, especially Frank, did so; and Beale did not seem to mind. How seriously members of the bar took the image of a priesthood is another question, which would require much more research to answer.

65. The point is forcefully made by Horwitz, *supra*, note 6, "The Conservative Tradition in the Writing of American Legal History," that preoccupation with formality and technique in legal history is ideological, in that it serves the interests of the profession to write about law as if it were autonomous from politics and inaccessible to the uninitiated. I think this is right but in some need of qualification and elaboration, which the text following this note tries to supply.

66. See Maxwell Bloomfield, "Law v. Politics: The Self-Image of the American Bar (1830-1860)," 12 *Am. J. Leg. Hist.* 306 (1968), a study of 19th century lawyers suggesting that most of them disavowed intellectual pretensions and presented themselves as practical businessmen and skilled craftsmen. Jerome Carlin's study of individual practitioners found that "[t]hese lawyers although generally handling matters that require little in the way of technical legal skill, still have fairly frequent contact with the courts and are thereby able to find a link with the most commonly accepted image of a lawyer . . . [T]he big firm lawyer, in their view, has not only lost his identity as a real lawyer by virtue of his more infrequent contact with the courts . . . but his independence as well." *Lawyers on Their Own* 187 (1962). In short, their identification is with the image of the trial lawyer, not with the more mandarin image of the appellate judge.

book view of Anglo-American legal "development" which still permeates legal rhetoric.[67] But law teachers too think of themselves as lawyers as much as professors, and usually more so;[68] it was the professional identities of the legal pragmatists themselves that the tendencies of their movement most threatened. As Leslie Stephen said of Gibbon: "Insects who are eating the heart out of an old tree are not generally gratified, it may be supposed, by the crash and thunder of the fall."[69]

The intellectual currents that eventually converged in Realism, one of which was the proposal for a legal historiography relativized to social and economic surroundings, challenged the professional viewpoint in several ways. (1) Pragmatism promoted research into non-legal materials. The amateur legal historians had stuck to the case reports; their professional successors had added legal manuscript sources of all kinds; but pragmatic legal history would apparently require the historian to step outside the box of distinctively legal things entirely. How far outside one could venture and remain a *legal* scholar? (2) Ames's conception of the legal-scholar-scientist gave him an inside role in the legal system, expert confidant to the judge (and in the extreme case where some statutory adjustment might be required) to the legislature. Pragmatic legal science offered at best a "negative and skeptical" role to the legal historian in present-day practice, whose relation to the judge would be the relatively indirect one of pointing out the irrelevance of the past to the solution of current problems—the role of an outsider, and a critical outsider at that. (3) The proposed field of research not only promised to transform legal scholars into some kind of subspecies of social scientist, but also to displace the judge from the center of the intellectual universe. The judge is of course the key figure in studies of the common law tradition, since he

---

67. See, e.g., William D. Guthrie, *Magna Carta and Other Addresses* (1916) and Elihu Root, *Addresses on Government and Citizenship* (1916), for a view of Anglo-American history as the progressive realization of the principle of individual liberty against the state. Guthrie and Root were the two leading Wall St. practitioners of their time. But it is dangerous to generalize too far. Some Wall St. men belong, now as then, to the quasi-acadmic bar, which restates the law in the American Law Institute, serves on law reform commissions and the Cromwell Foundation, takes an active and informed interest in the curricula of the schools, and is familiar with scholars' legal history. It is worth remembering that there are several elites of lawyers—a municipal bond elite, a trial elite, etc.—and that they are not much like one another.

68. I have no authority for this beyond my own observation of teachers and colleagues.

69. *History of English Thought in the Eighteenth Century*, I, 379 (1876). Stephen thought Gibbon's skeptical views had helped to bring about the French Revolution which horrified him.

is the carrier of the tradition. The pragmatic view of law—that it arises out of social needs and is to be evaluated by the efficiency with which it serves social functions—merges law into administration; the judge becomes simply one kind of official among many, and often not the most important. (4) Finally, and inevitably, the program of studying law in its social context opened up for discussion the whole explosive issue of the relationship between the inside and the outside of the law-box; of how far legal decisions are determined, or influenced by external pressures and how far by internal criteria; in short, of the reality of the idea of an autonomous legal order in modern society.

Social research in law along pragmatic lines was a quagmire for legal method and legal ideology. The program of investigating the social contexts and effects of law, to the end of discovering how efficiently it performed its social functions, made potentially relevant to legal study the entire universe of experience outside the law box. Some of those who ventured into that universe to gain broader perspectives on law never came back—Daniel Boorstin and David Riesman, for example. For others immersion in social research brought about something close to religious conversion: the story is told of Underhill Moore that he was found one day in his office,

> pulling drawers from his filing cabinets and dumping the contents into wastebaskets, cursing meanwhile most frightfully. The student inquired what was going on. "It's my life work," said Moore, "all the notes I have taken in a lifetime of research and it's all wrong." Moore had decided to discard everything he had ever done [he was an authority on Bills and Notes] and start over again, devoting the rest of his life to the experiments needed to work out a scientific theory of legal control in terms of behavioristic psychology.[70]

This episode took place at Columbia Law School in the 1920's, where Moore and others who were to form the core of the Realist movement made the first real attempt to institutionalize the "functional" study of law-in-society in a law school. This famous attempt failed; what is especially instructive about it for our purposes is that it began with the strictly professional purpose of reforming the curriculum to prepare students better for "the actual work in modern law practice";[71] and ended with many of its backers convinced that social research in law could not be performed in a professional setting at all.[72] (Some of

70. Julius Goebel, Jr. *et al.*, *A History of the School of Law, Columbia University* 251 (1955).

71. Stevens, *supra*, note 11 at 472 n. 28.

72. For the Columbia experiment, see especially Twining, *supra*, note 11, ch. 4 (and the annotations to that chapter at 399-402, which con-

them went off to found the short-lived Johns Hopkins Institute.) But most of the Columbia reformers—those who went off to Yale as well as those who stayed on—avoided falling into the quagmire by fashioning lifelines of limiting principles on the scope of their legal research, which kept them connected to traditional professional identities.

One such lifeline, for example, was the notion that the purpose of social research in law was to explore the gap between "law on the books and law in action," or the "limits of effective legal action." (Both these famous slogans were, of course, coined by Pound, who pioneered not only the pragmatic movement in law but the later retreat from it.[73]) This program solved two problems at one stroke. It gave the study of extralegal "action" a restricted scope symmetrically co-extensive with that of the law-box itself: one looked for the counterpart in "reality" of a law in the "book." It also annexed social research to a respectable professional and ideological purpose, i.e. closing the gap, making legal action more effective.[74] After the burst of empirical studies done at Yale in the 1930's, research in this mode largely vanished from the law schools. It never did much influence legal history, though it produced a large body of "impact research" in sociology and political science.[75]

The pragmatic lawyers soon found a lifeline that was stronger and more enduring. This was simply to revive Ames's conception of the law professor as a scholar who helps the judge ensure the sound development of case law, and thus to limit research to such social facts as were potentially relevant to judicial decision-making. To be sure, they expected such research to range farther afield than traditional research, because the judge, to be properly advised, would need to know much more than traditional research could tell him.[76] Julius Goebel,

---

tain some useful warnings against generalizing about the Realists too broadly).

73. See text at notes 88-96, *infra*.

74. For the preoccupation of social-legal research with the gap between law on the books and law in action, see Abel, *supra*, note 29 at 185-89 and Marc Galanter, "Notes on the Future of Social Research On Law" (unpublished ms. on file with the *Law & Society Review*).

75. For discussions of these impact studies, see Stephen L. Wasby, *The Impact of the United States Supreme Court: Some Perspectives* (1970); Richard Lempert, "Strategies of Research Design in the Legal Impact Study: The Control of Plausible Rival Hypotheses," 1 *L. & Soc'y Rev.* 111 (1966); Martin Shapiro, "The Impact of the Supreme Court," 23 *J. Leg. Ed.* 77 (1971).

76. This position probably came easiest to the teachers of commercial law, a field in which facts of business practice had been supposed to have some relevance to adjudication since Mansfield's time.

for example, thought the judge ought to have an immensely detailed acquaintance with 18th century criminal prócedure.

> Our law is one of the few occupations where history is of direct and specific utility. Traditionally it is by an inquiry into what the law was or has been that the solution of present perplexities is sought. The further back in time this quest is pressed, the more difficult is the finding, and it is then that the aid of the legal historian is sought. Where such a historian, therefore, undertakes to speak of the past, since it is something a future court may need and use, he assumes a responsibility not lightly to be dismissed. This is a moral obligation the implications of which are far-reaching, for not only must the judge put trust in his word, but the parties-litigant whose rights and whose fortunes will be affected by it . . .[77]

This was all the more astonishing as it came from someone who certainly could not have been accused of writing practitioner's history, and who was one of the fiercest critics of textbook legal history. Yet he was even more hostile to laymen's trespasses on law; for he felt himself to be first and foremost a lawyer. His work locates colonial law in its full political context of imperial administration and shows how much its forms owed to that context; yet the relation of lawyer's detail is so thorough and minute that it tends to occupy almost the whole foreground—presumably because it is the lawyer's detail that will most interest the 20th century judge.[78]

The instance of Goebel may seem unique, and in a way it is—no one had a greater command of the legal sources or delighted more in flourishing them in the faces of the ignorant[79] —but the strategy for saving professional identity was entirely typical. The persisting case-law centeredness of legal scholarship hardly needs documentation, but it is worth noting that all those commonly named as principals in the revolt against formalism—Holmes, Gray, Pound, Frank and Llewellyn—contributed to it;[80]

77. Goebel & T.R. Naughton, *Law Enforcement in Colonial New York* xxxiii-xxxiv (1944).

78. Goebel's legal history materials are the first to stress extralegal influences on law (*supra*, note 48); as director of the Foundation for Research in Legal History he sponsored the publication of studies of the history of corporations that were the most ambitious attempts yet to relate modern law to social and economic context [Armand DuBois, *English Business Companies after the Bubble Act* (1933); Shaw Livermore, *Early American Land Companies* (1939)]; and his background essays in *The Law Practice of Alexander Hamilton*, *supra*, note 49, especially those on "The Law and the Judicial Scene," *id.* at I, 1 and "The Economy in Hamilton's New York," *id.* at II, 29, reveal a grasp on extra-legal detail as sure as on the law. It is especially striking that someone with so much range should have deliberately unbalanced so much of his work towards the internal.

79. See, e.g. "*Ex parte Clio*," 54 *Colum. L. Rev.* 450 (1954), reviewing W.W. Crosskey, *Politics and the Constitution* (1953).

80. Frank did try to direct attention away from appellate and toward trial courts in *Courts on Trial* (1949). Llewellyn, in his general work in legal sociology, notably "What Price Contract —An Essay

and before long I hope a history of American legal pragmatism will properly stress its conservatism in this respect as much as its iconoclasm in others. Pound's life (1870-1964) spanned the entire period. His biographer has related how his professionalism, his dislike (heightened by the New Deal) of administrative regulation, and his increasingly uncritical admiration of the judiciary steadily narrowed his interests to the point where, in the late 1940's, the prophet of "sociological jurisprudence" stopped reading social science altogether in order to give his full time to Anglo-American case reports.[81] Pound had been one of the first to venture outside the law-box. After a while he did not like what he saw, so he went back in and slammed the door.

This was an extreme version of a common process of withdrawal. It is once again necessary to emphasize that this limitation of scope to gathering fodder for the judge, even the fantastically erudite and open-minded judge of the legal pragmatists' imagination, was, in view of their general intellectual program, almost completely arbitrary. They undertook to look at law from the point of view of the functions it performed in society: this led them to the position that for the purpose of organizing research, it was useful to think of law as a system of social control, or as what officials do about disputes, or lawyers do for a living. By any of these standards litigation in courts (especially litigation to appeal) was only a fragment of diverse complex processes, and through the 20th century a rapidly shrinking one; few of the graduates of the schools where the legal pragmatists taught were ever likely to have much contact with it.[82] Yet the continuing preoccupation of legal research, including legal history, with the work of judges is so taken for granted that its extraordinary perversity is rarely even noticed.

Why this should have happened remains something of a mystery. Undoubtedly the great success of the case method as a teaching device had something to do with it: practically the whole curriculum has been organized around criticizing the work of the appellate bench and this has carried over to research

in Perspective," 40 *Yale L.J.* 704 (1931), showed he was perfectly aware of the limits of the case-lawyers' view—which makes it all the more interesting that he settled down into that view in *The Common Law Tradition: Deciding Appeals* (1960). See text at notes 97-99, *infra*.

81. David Wigdor, *Roscoe Pound, Philosopher of Law* 207-81 (1974).

82. On changes in the role of courts and types of law practice, see Hurst, *Lawmakers* 85-87, 301-305; Robert T. Swaine, *The Cravath Firm and its Predecessors*, II, 461-66 *et passim* (1948).

because law professors tend to direct their research towards ultimate incorporation in teaching materials. But by itself this explanation will not serve. Judicial opinions cannot, for instance, be *that* much better teaching tools than administrative opinions, yet courses in Administrative Law tend to be about judicial review of administrative action. That is probably because judges have something administrators do not have: the capacity to represent the learned and cultivated side of law practice,[83] immunity from at least the more obvious kinds of client or constituent pressure, and the ideal of the law-giver who derives his authority from sources independent of the dominant forces in society. Yet the learning, immunity, and authority that judges were supposed to symbolize all followed from their expertise in the common law tradition, which the legal pragmatists had spent two decades deriding.[84] That was all right when their basic pro-

83. See the extraordinary elegy of Julius Goebel, Jr., "Learning and Style in the Law—An Historian's Lament," 61 *Colum. L. Rev.* 1393 (1961), in which the author calls up the classical learning of great past judges ("Diversion . . . was on a level almost incomprehensible to us. I cannot picture Holt, or Hardwicke, or Mansfield viewing a so-called 'better' program on television, or, if trapped into so doing, esteeming what they had looked upon to be a fit subject of conversation." *Id.* at 1395-96.); and contrasts it invidiously with the present situation:

> A reasoned opinion that rests upon impeccable authority and that carries conviction by reason of this and of its inner logic, unquestionably is difficult to compose. Fortunate it is that there are so many written. Such are, alas, much outnumbered by those patchworks of cases stated, passages from cyclopedias and snippets from a *Restatement*. This is a style highly esteemed in some trans-Appalachian jurisdictions . . . [This has been accompanied by] the descresence of allusive and epigrammatic writing, which so conduces to elegance . . .
>
> Surely the law must lose something of majesty if its oracles think of their pronouncements in terms of threading a pipe or of contriving a passable mitre joint. Let us leave such ideas to the legislators. To judges and lawyers the past calls out that we should cherish writing as the exercise of art. This let us not forget.

Id. at 1398-1400.

84. David Riesman pointed this out in 1951:

> To be sure, most lawyers today recognize that their most important work is done in the office, not in the courtroom; the elaborate masked ritual of the courtroom holds attraction only for the neophyte and the layman. Yet it is astonishing how strongly the image of the judge stands as the image of the lawyer-hero. While at the better law schools at least one and often nearly three years are spent in debunking upper-court opinions, in showing their largely derivative quality, their endless fallacies, their interminable self-confusion as to what they are "actually" deciding (as against what they say they are deciding), the better products of the better law schools want nothing more exciting when they get out than a chance to serve as clerk [as I did] to an appellate judge—the "upperer" the better. And as members of the bar they will move heaven and earth to get on the bench themselves (which is the source of much dirt in our political system, since many congressmen have partners who itch to be judges), although they know from prac-

gram was critical, e.g., revealing the personal and class bases of Supreme Court decisions invalidating social legislation, or the confusions and contradictions of Langdellian method. When the Court switched directions in 1937, the growth of executive power in the New Deal seemed to some lawyers to portend administrative tyranny unless checked by the courts; and when the Germans reduced their courts to tools of the Nazi Party, even the most skeptical lawyers felt compelled to reassert the idea of legal autonomy.[85] Under this compulsion, perhaps because no better substitute had been found in the meantime, perhaps no better could be found, the notion of the common law tradition revived.[86]

The revival took several forms, all the way from Catholic natural law theory and Hutchins' and Adler's neo-Artistotelianism to Thurman Arnold's view that the idea of neutral and wisely applied law above men is a myth, but one whose general acceptance (by powerholders as well as others) is necessary to civilized society.[87] Two forms that were especially significant for legal historiography found their archetypes in the work of Pound and Llewellyn.

> tical experience how little power the judge has under the American system and how skilled lawyers are in emasculating that little.

"Towards an Anthropological Science of Law and the Legal Profession," in Riesman, *Individualism Reconsidered* 440-41 (1954). See also *id.* at 462-63.

85. I am uttering here what is rapidly becoming the standard social-political explanation for the decline of Realism. See Edward A. Purcell, Jr., "American Legal Realism Between the Wars: Legal Realism and the Crisis of Democratic Theory," 75 *Am. Hist. Rev.* 424 (1969); G. Edward White, "The Evolution of Reasoned Elaboration: Jurisprudential Criticism and Social Change," 59 *Va. L. Rev.* 279, 281-285 (1973); both of which stress the attacks associating the positivism and skepticism of the Realist movement with fascism, and later with communism.

And yet I wonder. One might have thought that the rise of Nazism and Stalinism would as likely have promoted social research in law as put an end to it, would have encouraged Americans to investigate the sociological bases of the rule of law rather than simply to assert its autonomy from social conditions. This is the sort of work that C.J. Friedrich, Franz Neumann, and Friedrich Hayek all did (from rather different perspectives); was there similar work going on in the law schools? I am not sure, but I think the answer is not much even among the émigré lawyers. *The Journal of Legal & Political Sociology*, started in 1942, began to address these issues (Karl Llewellyn and David Riesman were among the first contributors), but it petered out after a few numbers. The retreat from external social perspectives on law in the late 1930s and 40s is only just beginning to be explained. We need to know a lot more about the politics of law teachers, their attitudes towards the New Deal, towards communism and civil liberties in the 1950s; more also about the contribution of the émigré scholars, about how they altered (and failed to alter) our perspectives on study of the legal system.

86. Or perhaps simply survived; it may never have been abandoned.

87. On the Catholic natural lawyers and Hutchins and Adler, see Purcell, *supra*, note 11; on Arnold, see his *Symbols of Government* (1962); Rumble, *supra*, note 11 at 217-220.

Pound's contribution was his famous idea of a "taught legal tradition." He began to develop this idea well before the general crisis of pragmatic thought in the 1930's (as has been mentioned already, his was one of the earliest retreats from pragmatism), as a method of attacking the "economic interpretation" of legal history, the domesticated and vulgarized Marxism of the historians who assumed law to be nothing more than an instrument for realizing the self-interest of a dominant class, wielded by judicial members of that class.[88] Proponents of this interpretation were most vulnerable when they were most specific, as when they tried to explain results in individual cases by reference to the class position of the winning party or the judge.[89] Pound was able to run rings aound them, showing that contemporary judges with the same backgrounds had reached opposite conclusions on the same issues; and that big economic interests had sometimes won in the courts and sometimes lost.[90] It was a completely sterile debate, since both sides assumed that decisions in the appellate courts accurately represent the extent to which the legal system responds to the claims of economic interests[91] (even if this were valid the case samples were too thin to prove anything either way). The interesting aspect of the debate was that when it provoked Pound into insistence upon a degree of autonomy for law, this is what he came up with:

> Tenacity of a taught tradition is much more significant in our legal history than the economic conditions of time and place. These conditions have by no means been uniform, while the course of decision has been characteristically steady and uniform, hewing to common-law lines through five generations of rapid political, economic, and social change, and bringing about a *communis opinio* over the country as a whole on the over-

88. For an early American version, see Brooks Adams, *Centralization and the Law* (1906). The "economic interpretation" was most effective in the robust muckraking and debunking histories of the Supreme Court: notably Gustavus Myers, *History of the Supreme Court of the United States* (1918) and Louis B. Boudin, *Government by Judiciary* (1932). Other reductionist theories of law prevalent in the 1930's, such as Watsonian behavioristic psychology, apparently failed to influence historical writing.

89. Francis H. Bohlen, "The Rule in *Rylands v. Fletcher*," 59 *U. Pa. L. Rev.* 298 (1911); Walter Nelles, "*Commonwealth v. Hunt*," *supra*, note 61.

90. Pound's attacks on the "economic interpretation" may be found in "Political and Economic Interpretations of Legal History," *Proc. Am. Polit. Sci. Ass'n* 95 (1912); *Interpretations of Legal History*, ch. 5 (1923); *The Formative Era of American Law*, *supra*, note 35; "The Economic Interpretation and the Law of Torts," 53 *Harv. L. Rev.* 365 (1940).

91. For example, Pound concluded from the fact that interpretations of corporate and partnership law restricted businessmen's choice of forms of doing business and of ways of operating across state lines that "capitalists" (whom he conceded were the dominant class at the end of the 19th century) had suffered as much from courts' hanging on to traditional forms as had "laborers." See his *Interpretations of Legal History*, *supra*, note 90, at 111-112.

> whelming majority of legal questions, despite the most divergent geographical, political, economic, social and even racial conditions . . . Economic and political conditions of time and place have led to legislative abrogations and alterations of rules and even at times to attempts to alter the course of the taught tradition. But such changes are fitted into the traditional system in their interpretation and application, and affect slowly or very little the principles, conceptions and doctrines which are the enduring law. The outstanding phenomenon is the extent to which a taught tradition, in the hands of judges drawn from any class one will, and chosen as one will, so they have been trained in the tradition, has stoood out against all manner of economically or politically powerful interests.[92]

Have we seen this before? Of course: it is our old friend, the common law tradition, the continuous, uniform development of law over time by masters of a method. The obviously political part of law, legislation, is "fitted into the traditional system" by interpretation, without much affecting it.[93] Otherwise, the only role for economic and social factors is that of supplying problems for the aloof inhabitants of the law-box to resolve by resort to their learned technique.[94]

The "economic interpretation" refused to concede any autonomy to law: your law-box, its authors said, is really empty. Pound rightly denied this, but when pressed to say what was in it, fell back on the old identification of legal autonomy with formal doctrinal development. This had two bad effects: it prevented the leading advocate of a sociological legal history (and most of the legal historians who followed him) from seeing how much American law *could* quite satisfactorily be explained as the outcome of organized economic interest-group pressure.[95] It

92. Pound, *Formative Era, supra*, note 35, at 83-84.

93. Pound explained the vulnerability of legislators to economic pressures by their lack of training in the tradition: "The legislator . . . has no settled habits of applying an authoritative technique to authoritatively given materials." "Economic Interpretation," *supra*, note 90, at 366. A colleague to whom I showed this passage suggested that since many judges are legislators who have failed of re-election, the critical training experience might be the crucible of failure.

94. The "taught tradition" idea seems particularly hard to square with Pound's historical account of various theories he supposed had influenced American judicial decision-making in the 19th century (law-of-nature theory, analytic and historical theories, etc.) or with his frequent criticisms (especially in his earlier years) of late 19th century courts on the grounds that they had prevented necessary adaptations to social and economic needs, including adaptations sought to be accomplished by legislation. He worked himself into the position of saying that the taught tradition, apparently proof against "all manner of economically or politically powerful interests," fell victim to the influence of any jurisprudential scribbler who happened to be in the neighborhood; and also that the autonomy of courts consisted in their being perpetually out of tune with modern needs—the very quality for which he had once attacked them.

95. For fine recent examples of what might be called a "neo-Progressive" approach, see Lawrence M. Friedman, "The Usury Laws of

also prevented them from inquiring further into what could not—into the ways in which the specialized activities inside the law-box might be variables independent of and directing, channelling, diverting or obstructing those pressures. If there was one thing that the realists had made clear, and left as their enduring legacy, it was that the autonomous element in law was *not*—at least not necessarily, not always—its surface formality; that indeed such formality was most likely to mask the unexamined (or at any rate unacknowledged) presence of outside political or economic influences. But if it wasn't that, what was it? Pound's regression to the "taught tradition" discouraged any attempt to find out.[96]

The other contribution that the pragmatic movement made to the eleventh-hour revival of the idea of tradition in law was given its best and fullest expression in the work of Llewellyn. He saw the "common law tradition" not as a continuously developing body of doctrine but as historically diverse methods ("craft-styles") of judicial decision-making:

> the general and pervasive manner over the country at large, at any given time, of going about the job, the general outlook, the ways of professional knowledge, the kinds of thing the men of the law are sensitive to and strive for, the tone and flavor of the working and of the results. [Craft-style] is well described as a "period-style"; it corrresponds to what we have long known as period-style in architecture or the graphic arts or furniture or music or drama.[97]

There were thus several traditions, each specific to a period; the period 1820-1860 having been dominated by a "grand style," 1880-1910 by a "formal style;" the period from 1930 onwards, Lewellyn believed, by a renaissance of the "grand style." (It is hopeless to explain Llewellyn's typology properly in a short space, but for those unfamiliar with it, here are the basics: a grand-style judge is concerned not only to harmonize his decisions, wherever feasible, with past case-law, but to justify them as functional; he tries to work out over time general approaches to handling recurrent types of dispute situations, approaches that will "make sense" to people in the disputants' positions. The formal-style judge, by contrast, cares only about making sure that each decision logically fits into a pre-existing doctrinal

Wisconsin: A Study in Legal and Social History," 1963 *Wisc. L. Rev.* 515; Robert S. Hunt, *Law and Locomotives* (1958).

96. I don't wish to imply that the *net* effect of Pound's influence on legal historiography was baneful. In this field as in so many others, he called attention to the right problems and pointed to suggestive lines of inquiry; and the fact that the Dean of the Harvard Law School uttered phrases like "sociological jurisprudence" gave social research in law respectability it could have acquired in no other way.

97. Llewellyn, *Common Law Tradition, supra*, note 80 at 36.

scheme: "the rules of law are to decide the cases; policy is for the legislature, not the courts."[98]) This was the most ingenious reconciliation yet of tradition and function in law. It did not turn its back on the idea of law as pragmatic method, social engineering; neither did it reject the work of past judges: it married the two in the tradition of the grand style. Tradition was preserved, but as exemplary rather than authoritative. Whatever its merits as jurisprudence,[99] this way of looking at law had incidental benefits for legal history. It encouraged the study of grand-style judges from the point of view of what made them exemplary, since the historian working in an age of unabashedly "policy-oriented" jurisprudence will try to bring out, rather than suppress as unfortunate or irrelevant, past judges' view of their society and of what law is needed for it. It is possible to see the two best judicial biographies of recent times, Levy's of Shaw and Reid's of Doe,[100] both grand-style judges, as reflecting the influence of pragmatic legal thought in treating their subjects as architects of bodies of socially serviceable case-law. Llewellyn also taught legal scholars to read judicial opinions more carefully, for rhetoric as well as result, for sources of analogy and authority, for facts used and facts ignored, and above all for the characterization of implications for future cases. (His own excursions into history are probably the best examples of the deployment of the method.)[101] Finally, the concept of period-style (though ahistorical in one of its premises, i.e., that present-day judges were recapturing the reasoning modes of 19th century ancestors fundamentally different in mental outlook)[102] suggested possibilities for historical-sociological theories of legal reasoning styles along the lines of Max Weber's, possibilities that are beginning to be realized in the work of Friedman, Horwitz, Nelson and Tushnet.[103]

---

98. *Id.* at 39. The most effective statement of the concept of craft-style is in Llewellyn, "On the Good, the True, the Beautiful in Law [1942]", in Llewellyn, *supra*, note 25 at 167.

99. For effective criticisms from differing perspectives, see Charles E. Clark & David Trubek, "The Creative Role of the Judge: Restraint and Freedom in the Common Law Tradition," 71 *Yale L.J.* 255 (1961); Duncan Kennedy, "Legal Formality", 2 *J. Legal Studies* 351 (1973).

100. Leonard W. Levy, *The Law of the Commonwealth and Chief Justice Shaw* (1957); John Phillip Reid, *Chief Justice: The Judicial World Of Charles Doe* (1967). Howe's biography of Holmes, *supra*, note 12, doesn't count as "judicial" biography because it ends before Holmes goes on the bench.

101. See Llewellyn articles cited *supra*, note 61.

102. Though perhaps not so different in their aspects with which Llewellyn was particularly concerned, as judges in commercial cases.

103. Lawrence M. Friedman, "On Legalistic Reasoning—A Footnote to Weber," 1966 *Wisc. L. Rev.* 148; Morton J. Horwitz, "The Emergence

Yet though Llewellyn's concept of tradition, unlike Pound's, pointed towards a more expansive historiography, it maintained the insider's perspective on law, specifically that of insider-as-advisor-to-the-judge. And there are disadvantages to the perspective even of the most social-context-conscious, cosmopolitan insider: everything gets filtered through the lens of professional working concerns and categories. This may have any or all of the following consequences.

(1) The insider's categories to which even extra-legal detail tends to be assimilated may, while rendering it familiar and manageable to lawyers, seriously distort it in other ways. A good illustration from our legal history is the category of "codification," under which has been subsumed a vast diversity of behavior: evangelical antilegalism; backwoods resistance to debt-collection; merchant creditors' pressure for more efficient debt-collection; anglophobe propaganda; small legal practitioners' complaints about pleading complexities; aesthetic distaste for the disordliness, and democratic distaste for the feudal origins, of the common law; Jefferson's, Bentham's, and Field's plans for codes; the Massachusetts Laws and Liberties of 1648, Field's procedural code, the Federal Rules of Civil Procedure, and the Uniform Commercial Code, not to mention the Law of the Twelve Tables and the BGB. There are few purposes indeed for which it makes any sense at all to lump all this stuff together; yet our historiography to a greater or lesser degree repeatedly did so, combining most of it into a single prolonged "codification movement" that supposedly lasted throughout the 19th century and achieved its greatest successes in the 20th.[104] Scholarship

of an Instrumental Conception of Law," 5 *Perspectives in Am. History* 287 (1971); William E. Nelson, "The Impact of the Antislavery Movement upon Styles of Judicial Reasoning in Nineteenth Century America," 87 *Harv. L. Rev.* 513 (1974); Mark Tushnet, "The American Law of Slavery 1810-1860: A Study in the Persistence of Legal Autonomy," 10 *L. & Soc'y Rev.* 119, *infra*. So far as I know, nobody has taken up Llewellyn's hint that it might be valuable to apply methods of art or architectural history to law.

104. The codification theme can be tracked from Charles M. Hepburn, "The Historical Development of Code Pleading in America and England," in *Select Essays*, *supra*, note 33 at II, 643; through Charles Warren, *A History of the American Bar*, Ch. 19 (1911), Alison Reppy, "The Field Codification Concept," in *David Dudley Field Centenary Essays* (Reppy ed. 1949); Pound, *Formative Era*, *supra*, note 35; and Howe, *supra*, note 48. The theme was picked up by Perry Miller in *The Life of the Mind in America* (1965) (Book 2, "The Legal Mentality"); and has recently been sounded again in Carl B. Swisher, *The Taney Period, 1836-64* at 339-56 (Oliver Wendell Holmes Devise History of the U.S. Supreme Court, V, 1974). One reason for what must be described as the obsession of our legal historians with this theme is that 19th century American lawyers were obsessed with it also; "codification" was the staple topic of their occasional essays, articles in law periodicals, and orations at bar dinners and memorials. They had as great a capacity to as-

is only recently beginning to break this "movement" up into its component parts.[105]

(2) Appellate case-law comes to stand for the whole "legal system." This would be troublesome if only for the obvious reasons that it limits research to the legal business that happens to flow into the appellate courts; prevents institutional comparisons showing how alike courts are to other parts of the system, and how different, and how power and business are allocated among the various parts. (Prevailing jurisprudential theories of appropriate institutional jurisdiction or competence are likely seriously to misrepresent historical actualities in these matters.) It can also lead to a tendency to overintellectualize, to see the law as a complex body of attempted judicial and academic solutions to a set of philosophic puzzles. Obviously an extremely elaborate jurisprudential literature is an important cultural product, worth studying on its own terms; but as an *exclusive* approach to legal history, this can result in a perception of law as an elevated activity engaged in for its own sake by the lawyers and their clients, and thus fundamentally betray the nature of the subject.

(3) Perhaps most important, history from the lawyer's perspective, if it pays any attention to the world outside the law-box, is bound to focus more closely on inputs than on outputs, and mostly on those inputs that the insiders consciously employ as materials of their craft. This is bound to leave out of consideration major (it is not necessary to argue primary) determinants of the shape and content of the law-box—the reasons for there being any law-box in the first place—i.e., what it is that people in society demand, or expect, of their legal order.

III

The readers of Willard Hurst's first major work, *The Growth*

similate everything to their own categories as we do. Even the great Haskins may have been somewhat taken in by the appeal of the "codification" category: compare his "Codification of Law in Colonial Massachussetts: A Study in Comparative Law," 30 *Indiana L.J.* 1 (1954) (Massachusetts Law and Liberties of 1648 is the first modern law code in the West) with Ronald G. Walters, 'New England Society and the Laws and Liberties of Massachusetts", 106 *Essex Inst. Hist. Coils.* 145 (1970) (the "Laws" is not "basically a code of law but rather something more mundane: a handbook for justices, an instrument for the use of a public and a body of magistrates likely to be of uncertain and conflicting knowledge." *Id.* at 167).

105. See especially Richard E. Ellis, *The Jeffersonian Crisis* (1971); William E. Nelson, *Americanization of the Common Law*, ch. 5 (1975); Friedman, "Law Reform," *supra*, note 3; Maxwell Bloomfield," William Sampson and the Codifiers: The Roots of American Legal Reform, 1820-1830," 11 *Am. J. Leg. Hist.* 234 (1967); Gerald W. Gawalt, "Sources of Anti-Lawyer Sentiment in Massachusetts, 1740-1840," 14 *Am. J. Leg. Hist.* 283 (1970).

of American Law (1950), could tell from the first few pages that although the book purported only to synthesize existing secondary materials, the synthesis represented something new in American legal history. This was a history of law-making agencies—not only courts, but constitutional conventions, chief executives, administrative agencies, and the bar—inquiring into the social functions these agencies had served since the founding of the Republic. Though described with an insider's understanding and grasp of detail, its perspective on the operations of the legal system was that of an outsider: it was a critical Inspector General's report on how legal institutions had served the society that supported them. Hurst had formulated and announced his program of defection from the main line of legal historiography as early as 1942.[106] *The Growth of American Law* was the cornerstone for the imposing body of external legal history that he, and the Wisconsin school of legal studies he founded,[107] have been writing since, and are still adding to.

This essay has advanced the argument that the actualization of pragmatic legal theory in historical writing was stunted and sometimes choked off entirely by the reluctance of legal scholars to shake off their old roles of interpreters of the common law tradition. But in Hurst's work pragmatic legal theory reached full flowering, probably unexcelled anywhere else in American legal scholarship. Others have appraised,[108] some of them brilliantly,[109] his work in general: my concern here is only to try to show how his ways of thinking about law dissolved the constraints most legal historians had felt upon taking an external approach.

For this purpose, it is useful to consider Hurst's work as an effort to apply the general insights of pragmatic theory, especially as formulated by John Dewey,[110] to the study of the

106. "Legal History: A Research Program," 1942 *Wisc. L. Rev.* 319.

107. The works of this school on Wisconsin legal history are: Lawrence M. Friedman, *Contract Law in America* (1965); Hunt, *supra*, note 95; Spencer Kimball, *Insurance and Public Policy* (1960); George J. Kuehnl, *The Wisconsin Business Corporation* (1959); James A. Lake, *Law and Mineral Wealth: The Legal Profile of the Wisconsin Mining Industry* (1962); Francis W. Laurent, *The Business of a Trial Court, 100 Yeors of Cases* (1959); Samuel Mermin, *Jurisprudence and Statecraft: The Wisconsin Development Authority and its Implications* (1963); Earl F. Murphy, *Water Purity* (1961).

108. See the "Bibliography", *infra*, this issue, § V.

109. The outstanding ones are both, as it happens, by contributors to this volume: Harry N. Scheiber, "At the Borderland of Law and Economic History: The Contributions of Willard Hurst," 75 *Am. Hist. Rev.* 744 (1969), and Mark Tushnet, "Lumber and the Legal Process," 1972 *Wisc. L. Rev.* 114.

110. There are other significant influences detectable in Hurst's work, notably Max Weber's; but as a factor shaping Hurst's external per-

specific historical phenomenon of American law in the 19th and 20th centuries. "Law" is here a general label for several species of applied social intelligence, which may be understood only by reference to the conditions out of which they are generated and by the consequences to which they give rise. The basic function of law, as of any other form of social intelligence, is to increase men's ability to achieve rational control over social change in order to liberate their natural capacity for growth. Men achieve rational control through experimental method, which expands their empirical appreciation of the consequences of their conduct; expanded awareness of consequences enlarges their ideas of what is desirable as well as of the most efficient means of attaining it; and this leads to growth in the range and quality of life experience, especially emotional experience, for "reason probably finds justification ultimately as an instrument by which men achieve more subtle, more varied and more shared emotion."[111]

The special focus of Hurst's attention is governmental activity, the work of agencies and of those who interpret and apply it; Hurst calls this "law." (It is not a definition of law, since Hurst does not try to define law; it is a term of convenience without any precise boundaries.) His reason for concentrating on official action is that the state possesses special characteristics that impart to the exercise of directive intelligence through its agencies an exceptional social significance. Of all associations in society, it is the public organized in the state, acting through the legal order, that stands the best chance of increasing rational control over social change. This is not to say that American law has lived up to its potential in this respect. Far from it: one of Hurst's main themes is that social change has usually been permitted to take place by "drift," "default," or "inertia," by which is meant experience transmuted into social action without the intervention of reflective intelligence. The consciousness from which people draw their desires and preferred means of satisfying them tends to be imprisoned in habitual modes and forms,[112] but old forms are continually coming up against and mixing with one another, in different combinations, thus con-

spective, American pragmatic thought seems to me to have been more significant.

111. Hurst, "The Law in United States History," 105 *Proc. Am. Phil. Soc.* 518, 519 (1960). For Dewey on the same themes, see, e.g., *Experience and Nature*, ch. 10 (2d ed. 1929).

112. For Hurst on drift, see *Law and Social Process in United States History* (1960), especially at 66-75; cf. Dewey on habit, *Human Nature and Conduct*, Pt. 1 (1922).

tinually producing a new social environment.[113] Acted upon by new conditions, the old forms will of course yield new consequences. Men's failure to subject new conditions to experimental evaluations means that they are constantly being surprised and baffled by experience, instead of being able to achieve some mastery over it in the interests of human growth.

For Hurst, as for American Progressives generally, the most conspicuous example of "drift" is the persistence through the late 19th and early 20th centuries of the habitual consciousness of private-market-and-business-oriented individualism.[114] In the early 19th century this had been a mode of thinking more functional for growth: it had released human talents and energies for the purpose of settling a continent and fulfilling the basic economic conditions for community existence. But at the same time it had defined business as the main arena for the exercise of talent, so that instrumental intelligence was rarely directed toward the elaboration of any but the most short-term economic consequences of social action. Private economic interests had thus in time come to overwhelm social life, with the results that: (1) men's consciousness of the desirable and how to reach it came to take account only of immediate economic costs and benefits (a method of thought Hurst calls "bastard pragmatism") and not of longer-run consequences for more various modes of growth; and (2) men had lost the talent for politics, that is, for organizing to promote, through the legal agencies of the state, ideas of the general good of their communities less parochial than purely economic interest.[115]

Hurst thus follows the main tradition of Progressive thought in relating the exercise of social intelligence to conditions of social organization: its effectiveness depends upon the wide dispersal of power among diverse solidary communities of shared values. Thus rational policy-making, dispersal of power, and community solidarity are all conditions of one another's existence; and all three are conditions of social growth.[116] The

113. This phrase tries very clumsily to give a brief impression of Hurst's intricate theoretical account of how imprisonment in habit produces social drift. For this account in its most developed form in Hurst's work, see his *Justice Holmes on Legal History* 11-13 *et passim* (1964).

114. For typical descriptions of this consciousness, see Hurst, *id.* at 39-50; *Law and Social Process, supra*, note 112 at 54-55.

115. Hurst's most powerful expression of these ideas remains that in the final chapter of his *Lawmakers, supra*, note 11, at 439-446 *et passim*; see also *Law and the Conditions of Freedom in the Nineteenth Century United States* (1967). Here the allegiance to Dewey is especially strong: see *The Public and its Problems* (1927).

116. Hurst, "Legal Elements," *supra*, note 6 at 88-89; see Dewey, *id.*, especially at chs. 5-6. There is an excellent discussion of this aspect

importance of law in society (though Hurst keeps insisting that like other forms of rational planning law can never have more than a marginal directive impact on social change) is that it has special equipment to help nudge these conditions into being. In particular, as the monopolist of legitimate force, the state has authority to hold private power accountable to the general welfare and in extreme cases to adjust its distribution in society, either by breaking up power centers or balancing them with countervailing powers. But perhaps the most important feature of state action is that it is normatively rational, is supposed to operate through forms and procedures designed to encourage deliberate, informed, and accountable decision-making. More than any other association the government is subject to expectations that its decisions will not be habitual reflexes, but will be mediated through careful reflection upon long-run consequences; and it has extraordinary resources (e.g. the ability to call upon a wide range of expert opinion representing diverse interests in legislative investigation, administrative rule-making, etc.) to generate the appropriate laboratory conditions for the operations of experimental intelligence. In other words, the norms of American constitutionalism ought to provide an especially favorable environment for pragmatic method.[117]

The legal historian's task, as Hurst sees it, is to measure the actual past performance of government against this potential. It takes a historian to do this, because only a perspective on several generations can reveal the habitual modes that have conditioned decision-making as well as the long-run consequences of the actual decisions. The present generation of lawyers needs to know, and needs history to inform it, which circumstances promote, and which prevent, intelligent direction of society in favor of growth. Hurst's rebellion against the dominant tradition in legal scholarship was not made in the name of disinterested reconstruction of the past; he is an intensely committed moralist, for whom the past is full of dreadful warnings.

But for the purpose of this essay, I want to look at these issues exactly backwards from the way Hurst does. He is always

---

of Progressive thought in David E. Price, "Community and Control: Critical Democratic Theory in the Progressive Period," 68 *Am. Polit. Sci. Rev.* 1663, 1672 (1974).

117. For a representative passage on the constitutional ideal, see Hurst, "Legal Elements", at 3-7. Hurst never goes quite so far as to equate constitutionalism and his own normative pragmatic method (though he is not entirely innocent of sometimes confusing them in his discourse), since the constitutional ideal has held officials and private holders accountable to serve *individual* life, but not (at least not consistently) to serve social or community life. See *Law and Social Process, supra*, note 112 at 3.

concerned to see how history can contribute to the living lawyer's exercise of pragmatic method in the public interest; but it is also worthwhile to ask how his vision of pragmatic method contributes to his work as a historian. I think the answer is that, while the general theoretical apparatus outlined above creates some troublesome problems of its own in Hurst's work, it is effective in freeing that work from the limitations of the insider's perspective.

For one thing, Hurst does not feel out of place or pulled apart by being an historian in a law school; he sees no opposition between social research in law and lawyer's business. His view is in keeping not only with Dewey's insistence on the unity of thought and action but with the "Wisconsin idea"—that social science research in the university should lead to social reform through legislation. Historical research and legislative drafting are just specialized aspects of the operations of instrumental intelligence. His paradigm example of law's working the way it should work is the development of workmen's compensation in Wisconsin in the early 20th century: John Commons's university research seminars helped Charles McCarthy's legislative research department develop the legislation; and advisory committees of employers, unions, insurance companies, and the public helped administer it.[118] In fact, if one had to sum up in a phrase Hurst's deviation from the mainstream of legal historiography, it would be that his allegiances are to the Wisconsin Progressive tradition of lawmaking instead of the common law tradition.[119]

This has important consequences for his work. His first book made clear that he had no interest in linking law practice to the authority and complexity of common law tradition, since he

118. Hurst, *Law and Social Process, supra*, note 112 at 37-41.

119. But it would be misleading to conclude that Hurst simply carried on a going tradition at the Wisconsin Law School, since the Law School was only really brought into the Wisconsin tradition after World War II. In the heyday of the Wisconsin idea before World War I, the faculty consisted mostly of part-time practitioners; after World War I, "the faculty's major service contribution related not to legislation, but to law in the courts," i.e., work on the Restatements. John E. Conway, "The Law School: Service to the State and Nation," 1968 *Wisc. L. Rev.* 345, 346. The "law-and-society" approach that now distinguishes the Wisconsin Law School was pioneered after World War II by men recruited to the faculty by Dean Lloyd K. Garrison just before it: notably Jacob H. Beuscher and Willard Hurst. See W. Scottt Van Alstyne, Jr., "The University of Wisconsin Law School 1868-1968: An Outline History," *id.* at 321, 330-31; and Fran Thomas, *Law in Action: Legal Frontiers for Natural Resources Planning—The Work of Professsor Jacob H. Beuscher* (Land Economics Monographs No. 4, 1972).

Hurst therefore had to cut all his own trails. But of course it is not likely that his enterprise could have prospered anywhere else as well as in Madison.

thought that a stubborn clinging to traditional images of the profession was in part responsible for the bar's failure since 1870 to realize its possibilities for exercising social leadership: there were too many lawyers who were just technicians with no sense of the larger social effects of their jobs.[120] (The bar's contributions to "law reform" with Restatements, uniform laws, and the like don't count; the Wisconsin Progressive wants social reform through law, not technical law reform.[121]) Nor does he need to preserve the centrality of courts in legal study for their symbolic capacity to legitimate the legal order as a whole through their claims to autonomy derived from the distinctiveness of their doctrines and procedures: since far from thinking law achieves its capacity for control over social change from its distinctive forms, he believes one of the common causes of "drift" is mindless adherence to such forms.[122] Like Llewellyn, he replaces tradition-as-doctrine with pragmatic method as the source of what little directive influence law is ever likely to achieve—you don't achieve control by denying you're part of society but by recognizing how much you are a part of it—but does not go on to equate pragmatic method with case-law craftsmanship; because although courts continue to have an important public role as protectors of liberties against arbitrary state action, their pre-Civil War careers as major planners and coordinators of state policy have long since ended.[123]

The great strength that his historical work derives from his pragmatist's vision is the outsider's perspective: everything is to be examined for what it tells us about law's capacity to overcome the heavy odds in favor of social drift. Hurst's masterwork, the huge study of the legal history of the Wisconsin lumber industry,[124] responds to a single accusing question: how did it come about that the legal system so failed in its job of providing rational processes to increase awareness of long-run consequences that it permitted Wisconsin lumbermen to cut 30 million acres of forest to exhaustion?[125] Answering this leads him

120. See Hurst, *Lawmakers* at 370.

121. For an illuminating discussion of the distinction, see Friedman, "Law Reform," *supra*, note 3.

122. See, e.g., *Law and Economic Growth: The Legal History of the Lumber Industry in Wisconsin, 1836-1915* (1964) [hereinafter, Hurst, *Law & Lumber*] at 99, 298.

123. See Hurst, *supra* note 82; and *Law & Lumber* 249-50 (on built-in institutional limitations of common law litigation as decisionmaking method).

124. *Law & Lumber*.

125. I do not mean that this book is accusing in tone; on the contrary it is a model of scholarly neutrality, full of warnings against applying the criteria of the present age to the 19th century. (The earlier

into (a) an account of the basic social and cultural conditions (scarcity of working capital, abundance of land, an aggressive manipulativeness towards nature, etc.) that engendered the consciousness of 19th century Wisconsin policy-makers; (b) a decription of the consciousness itself ("bastard pragmatism," measurement of benefits by short-term money yields); and (c) an analysis of the results of the applications of this consciousness to legal policy towards the lumber industry (fragmentation of decision-making into one-at-a-time resolution of strictly local problems; great ingenuity in promoting—finding non-monetary subsidies for, allocating power and resources in favor of, inventing financing devices to benefit—those interests believed most capable of getting timber cut, transported, and marketed; also complete failure to bring to awareness, and hence to deal with, problems like depletion of the forest or the conditions of lumber labor).

By his choice to organize his work around the concept of "law", Hurst has committed himself to a version of the box model of the legal order in society, but it is a wonderfully different box from those of the standard legal histories. It is much larger, of course, since it includes all official activity: its contents are the habitual modes and forms of official thought—dialect variations, as it were, of the dominant consciousness of the surrounding culture—such as a legislative disposition to protect working men through labor liens but not through state accident insurance. The dialects are significant data for Hurst if and only if they are likely to be consequential for a society's growth; this means that although his work is rich in detail, it is all detail accumulated towards generalization about its social function. As a result—

(1) It tends to be what we might call democratic detail. Legal historians have favored aristocratic detail, worked into intricate tapestries by jurisconsults out of the appellate case law; Hurst's concern is with the system's routine business. This is partly because the effectiveness of law as an instrument of growth has to be assessed by its impact on the ordinary people in society[126] but also because habitual consciousness is formed

---

Lawmakers is much more overtly didactic.) But it is a grim and passionate book all the same, the more impressively so for its outward reserve.

126. Cf. Hurst's very Brandeisian early statement of this position:

> Emphasizing the economic setting, [a legal history course] would deal [in part] with the security and values of individual personality in a world increasingly marked by centralized, large-scale power arrangements. The emphasis

out of the cumulation of tiny decisions. The study of big decisions fundamentally misleads, since it is only by tracking long sequences that it is possible to sketch the dynamics of drift.

(2) A remarkably small proportion of Hurst's detail consists of the technical stuff of doctrine and procedure beloved of internal legal historians. At least in 19th century Wisconsin law related to lumber, on which Hurst has read *everything*, and reported everything he thinks significant, the particular forms of lawyer's law simply do not seem to have possessed much social significance.[127] The legal variables that *do* matter by his criteria tend to be broader institutional or conceptual traits of the system—e.g. adversary process in litigation as a means of organizing facts and bringing them to the awareness of decision-makers; or the survival into new contexts of thought-patterns formed in old ones, such as the fee simple as the desirable mode of conveying timberland, or the English practice of treating standing timber as an ordinary commodity of trade.[128] And Hurst always makes it clear that peculiar dialect-forms of the legal order survive and flourish in part *because* of outside social conditions, not (as Pound's "taught tradition" theory holds) despite them; thus, for example, the 700 lumber-industry contract cases Hurst studies have autonomous characteristics (are "contract-law cases first, and lumber industry cases second" and doctrinally stable over the industry's lifetime) because the abstraction of contract doctrine met the industry's immediate needs for security of market dealings; and the lumbermen's modes of thought did not encourage them to seek anything beyond those needs.[129]

(3) Hurst's organization around the concept of social function encourages comparison among official institutions, and between official and unofficial institutions.

It must be added that Hurst's theory also has some disadvantages for his history.[130] Two of a general nature might be mentioned here:

(1) The theory associates normatively adequate exercise of pragmatic method, or instrumental intelligence, with growth, and

would be on the small man—laborer, white-collar worker, farmer, small business man.

Hurst, *supra*, note 106, at 331.

127. See, for one of the rare instances in which Hurst cites a pleading form as significant, *Law & Lumber* 354-55 (where he also points out that it wasn't *very* significant).

128. See citations to *Law & Lumber*, *supra*, notes 122, 123.

129. *Law & Lumber* 289-90.

130. For other criticisms (in the course of generally appreciative treatments) of Hurst's work as theory and history, see the articles by Scheiber and Tushnet, *supra*, note 109; Julius Stone, Book Review, 78 *Harv. L. Rev.* 1687 (1965); and Richard B. Abrams, Book Review, 24 *Stan. L. Rev.* 765 (1972).

failure adequately to exercise it with inertia and drift. This makes it hard to deal with historical situations in which, in retrospect, it appears that heightened awareness of consequences would have been dysfunctional for growth (as Hurst conceives it) and a relative lack of awareness functional. This is most likely to happen when people's interests are in fundamental opposition, but at least one side doesn't know that: and Hurst himself suggests this situation has been a common one:

> [O]n the whole contemporary community values supported, acquiesced in, or were indifferent or unseeing toward most of what private interest sought and obtained from law concerning exploitation of the Wisconsin forest. Undoubtedly there would have been more conflict, and more skulduggery, had contemporary attitudes and energies existed to bring more of these matters to explicit issue. . . . [But in this history] the limitations of men's perception, imagination, and will were more significant than their purposes.[131]

To the extent that a condition of growth is the accommodation of conflicting interests, it may be more functional for the legal system to obscure consequences rather than to reveal them,[131] to legitimate social change by pretending that it all accords with comfortable old forms. I am perhaps suggesting here that Hurst's normative view of the decision-making process may somewhat blunt a sense of historical irony.

(2) Hurst's history relies upon a model of the interaction of law and society drawn chiefly from the peculiar context of 19th century American state promotion and regulation of economic enterprise, which may be difficult to apply outside that context. In a way, Hurst has got hold of the easiest case: (a) the social actors to whom legal regulation is addressed may be counted on to look to extract short-term economic advantage from every decision; (b) they have relatively clear access to legal decision-makers (legislature and courts); (c) the decision-makers pretty much share their views of what is generally desirable for the society; they are really part of the same subculture of entrepreneurs; (d) the rest of society shares or passively accepts the same norms as they do; (e) regulation is almost all promotional and facilitative, rather than adversary; so that there are few significant problems of enforcement.

One could go on, but the point is that these particular conditions all combine to minimize the terrible problems of method faced by those who would practice an external historiography. They make it possible to infer social conditions and consequences

131. Tushnet, *supra*, note 109 at 125-26 points out in this connection (citing Albert Hirschman on unbalanced growth) that economic development may sometimes *depend* upon concealment of externalities.

to a large extent from the legal materials themselves:[132] which in other contexts, involving groups whose norms are alien to those of the decision-makers, or whose access is limited, or who seek symbolic legitimacy for themselves and condemnation of others rather than economic gain from the legal system, or seek nothing from it because they can get what they need outside it, or who resist compliance with its decisions, one cannot safely do.

But even for the study of contexts differing from those out of which he developed his theory, Hurst's milking of legal detail for every ounce of social significance has contributed not only a theoretical account of the social function of law, but some extremely refined techniques for what might be called the intellectual history of government action: how the state, through legal process, expresses social values; the devices by which it ratifies and legitimates certain values and ranks them in relation to others. These techniques—which enable the reader to discover basic notions about prevailing views of favored economic interests, the nature of property rights, or the appropriate role of government from such clues as how a statute allocates burdens of proof—are useful in their own right, whether or not the context also permits inferences as to the actual effects of law on social behavior.

Hurst's main contribution has been to expose the hitherto invisible ways in which the apparently most commonplace incidents of a legal order illuminate social values. By so doing he managed, almost single-handed, to lower from inside the drawbridge over the moat isolating American legal from general historiography.

Others had been bridging the moat from the outside—with studies of 19th century public policy and corporations, of public lands, and of administrative history[133]—but it required an in-

132. Tushnet, *id.* at 122, says that purely legal materials cannot adequately test even Hurst's theory, and that his "law centeredness seeems totally ingenuous." This is unfair. Hurst is acutely aware of the problems of law-centered research, and repeatedly qualifies the inferences he thinks permissible to draw from it. See, e.g., "Legal Elements" at 21-22; *Law & Lumber* at 225-227 (where Hurst also makes it clear he did not use business records because none existed). But *some* inferences about the effects of law on extra-legal behavior can be drawn from the legal sources: e.g., the output of the legal system may be supposed to be important, or at least to be thought important, to people who resort frequently to it (seek amending acts in the legislature, litigate in the courts); and less important to those who could use it but do not (like the big lumber companies that tended to refrain from litigation). *Law & Lumber* 200, 226, 321 *et passim.*

133. See Scheiber, "Federalism and the American Economic Order," *infra* at 57.

sider with unassailable lawyer's as well as historian's credentials to throw open the gates. For a time, Hurst's work was about the only view law students obtained on the social context of the history of their law.[134] But since what I have called the Second Revival of American legal history started a few years ago, his perspective is becoming the dominant one.[135] One of the events signifying the revival was the devotion of an issue of *Perspectives in American History* to legal history. That was a joint effort by lawyers and historians; and of course the leading article was written by Willard Hurst.[136]

I believe the present collection will also show how busily the traffic has been humming across the drawbridge between law and history. I think it best to let these essays, written by people trained in law, in history, and in both fields, speak to the reader for themselves, unmediated by any attempt on my part to generalize factitiously upon the relationships and resemblances among them. I am only sorry that in the nature of the case this collection could not include another contribution to the external historiography of American law by the field's most distinguished, most prolific and most active practitioner.

134. See Re, *supra*, note 61.

135. See, e.g., the large number of respondents stressing the necessity of an external approach to legal history (and taking such an approach in their courses and publications) in Joseph H. Smith, *Report on the Teaching of Legal History in American Law Schools* (AALS Legal History Section; Nov. 1973).

136. This is his "Legal Elements," *supra*, note 6.

[8]

BEYOND MIRRORS: LAWRENCE FRIEDMAN'S MOVING PICTURES

AVIAM SOIFER

> "L'exactitude ce n'est pas la vérité."
>
> Henri Matisse, quoted in Robertson Davies, *What's Bred in the Bone* 334 (New York, 1985)

> "[A] legal system . . . accommodates the equally exigent demands of being and meaning . . . in a universe in which what a thing does is only one of the things that it means, but everything that it means is something else that it does."
>
> Arthur Leff, "Law and . . . ," 87 *Yale Law Journal* 989 (1978)

Lawrence Friedman is a rare and remarkable phenomenon. He is a counter who thinks and a thinker who counts. He is aware of paradoxes such as the fact that "Everybody is an individual; everybody is also a conformist" (1985b: 102). More specifically, Friedman is particularly knowledgeable about the limitations and unpredictable consequences of efforts at legal reform. Yet, surprisingly, he seems somehow to be able to escape transforming his healthy skepticism into cynicism.

A list of Lawrence Friedman's publications would exhaust a large chunk of my word limit. But such a list would serve an important function. It would suggest the range of Friedman's scholarly interests as well as his astonishing productivity. Even the titles of Friedman's articles and books belie a curious but prevalent notion that Friedman leads an apocryphal band of reductionist-functionalist-instrumentalists. There is a good deal of talk, and a fair amount of scholarly critique published, attacking a group of legal historians who ignore or deny the idea that legal categories of thought have impact on society or that there are particularistic,

---

This essay was completed in the Fall of 1987. It is Lawrence Friedman's way to have published a half dozen or so articles since then, too late to be included in this discussion. The author thanks Daniel Offner for his research assistance and Kathy Abrams, Mary Dudziak, Chip Lupu, Martha Minow, David Seipp, Josephine Woll, Larry Yackle and, most particularly, Lance Cassak and Carol Weisbrod for reading drafts and discussing Lawrence Friedman's work with me.

LAW & SOCIETY REVIEW, Volume 22, Number 5 (1988)

changeable qualities in legal culture (Gordon, 1987; Vandevelde, 1980).

Yet in nearly-forgotten 1960s classics, for example, Friedman introduced theoretical categories and perceptive analysis concerning law reform and legal culture to legal history scholarship. He led discussion of how legal institutions "have a definite role, rather poorly understood, as instruments that set off, monitor, or otherwise regulate the fact or pace of social change (1969a: 29).[1] With his characteristic concern for the kinetic quality of law, Friedman provided important insights about desuetude, legalistic reasoning, and the many constraints on judicial discretion.

Critics tend to ignore Friedman's leadership on issues of methodology, theories of change, and questions of whether law follows, leads, or mirrors society. Friedman is hardly the simple and pure instrumentalist some describe.

To attempt to catch up only with what Friedman has done for us lately—e.g., a book on the legal issues of age discrimination and mandatory retirement; another on the tendency toward total justice and plural equality in the twentieth century; a chapter on changing legal consciousness concerning the rights of schoolchildren; a massive revision and expansion of his single-volume history of American law; articles on diverse additional subjects including, uncharacteristically, one that invades the turf of constitutional law (1984a, 1984c, 1985b, 1986; Friedman *et al.*, 1987)—suggests the enormous breadth of Friedman's careful, lucid, and adventurous scholarly achievements.

There can be little doubt that Friedman's work on the penetration of social, economic, and political factors into legal thought—and his less well known and, to be sure, his lesser emphasis on the reverse phenomenon—constitutes a remarkable, pioneering scholarly accomplishment. Today, however, there is significant controversy about Friedman's oeuvre overall. That controversy raises several questions worth pondering. Is Friedman's work appreciated as it should be? Why does he feel targeted in generational combat as one of "the dragons that need killing?"

---

[1] See, for example, Friedman's many articles in the 1960s discussing the relative power of legal ideas such as "Law Reform in Historical Perspective," 13 *St. Louis Law Review* 351 (1969); "Legal Culture and Social Development", 4 *Law & Society Review* 29 (1969); "Legal Rules and the Process of Social Change," 19 *Stanford Law Review* 786 (1967); with Ladinsky, "Social Change and the Law of Industrial Accidents", 67 *Columbia Law Review* 50 (1967); "On Legalistic Reasoning—A Footnote to Weber," 1966 *Wisconsin Law Review* 148. See also Friedman's discussion of the impact of legal ideas and the issue of legal change in his books of that period such as *Contract Law in America: A Social and Economic Case Study* (Madison, 1965) and *Government and Slum Housing: A Century of Frustration* (Chicago, 1968) and his chapters "Social Change Through Law" in *Law and Society: An Introduction* (Englewood Cliffs, N.J., 1977), and "Social Change and Legal Change" in *The Legal System* (New York, 1975).

(1984c: 573) And where does Friedman stand on the continuum of debate about the relative autonomy of law?

Throughout his work, on both micro- and macro-levels, Friedman has raised unanswered questions in regard to popular assumptions concerning historical causation. He has produced devastating critiques of formalistic approaches to legal history. Moreover, Friedman's descriptions of legal matters are peppered with vivid contextual details and with recognizable, unexceptional folks. Yet Friedman is the legal historian who deserves credit for introducing important Weberian notions long ago as well as for offering a sensitive critique of them. His work has demonstrated, early and often, that scholars have much to learn from a bottom-up approach to changes in legal ideas, as compared to more traditional tracking of doctrinal change in appellate opinions and treatises.

In a sense, Friedman can be considered the last of the real legal realists. But he also follows Willard Hurst as one of the first and few legal realist historians.[2] In emphasizing the dynamic quality of legal ideas, Friedman adapted and moved beyond Hurst's work. As does Hurst, whom Friedman described as "this greatest of legal historians [who] was not interested in law as such, but rather in what it did to, for, or against the rest of us" (1984c: 566), Friedman emphasizes factors outside the doctrinal law box.[3] Indeed, he directs witticisms at those who create fancy theories from appellate decisions. Friedman describes law libraries as less hard on the allergies than the down-and-dirty stuff of county court records and the like. Although he has been careful not to deny the symbolic aspect of law, Friedman concentrates on clashing interests; he finds law in corporate personnel policies, trial courts, and the hallways outside the courtrooms.

So why, one might ask, is Lawrence Friedman so alienated from the legal historians who work under the umbrella of critical legal studies? And why does his emphasis on competing interests as the moving force behind legal change not seem to appeal to the law-and-economics crowd? In this essay I suggest that Friedman is able to convey the problematic role of law-as-mirror with remark-

---

[2] The legal realists themselves were generally not seriously interested in history, with the possible exception of Walter Nelles and the great efforts at sweeping categorization by Karl Llewellyn and, later, Grant Gilmore. *See generally* John Henry Schlegel "American Legal Realism and Empirical Social Science: From the Yale Experience" 28 *Buffalo Law Review* 3 (1981) and "American Legal Realism and Empirical Social Science: The Singular Case of Underhill Moore" 29 *Buffalo Law Review* 2 (1980); Laura Kalman, *Legal Realism at Yale, 1927–1960* (1986).

[3] For a most useful historiographic map delineating variations on the internal/external theme concerning how legal history has been done, *see* Robert Gordon, "J. Willard Hurst and the Common Law Tradition in American Legal Historiography," 10 *Law & Society Review* 9 (1975). *See also* Steve Diamond, "Legal Realism and Historial Method: J. Willard Hurst and American Legal History," 77 *Michigan Law Review* 784 (1979); Calvin Woodard, "History, Legal History, and Legal Education," 53 *Virginia Law Review* 89 (1967).

able clarity, even as he anticipates the distorting quality of reflection and its possible influence on conduct. Friedman's word-pictures constantly remind us that neither life nor law is static, try as we might to freeze the frames of our existence.

I. THE IMPACT OF THE IDEAS OF A LAW PROFESSOR?

It is paradoxical to write about the impact of any academic's ideas, but the tensions are exaggerated when the subject is Friedman. One dare not speak of progress, but writers of legal history generally have moved past the purportedly clearcut categories of the lawyers who replaced parsons as described in Perry Miller's work. We no longer seem eager for the neat symmetry that turned Talcott Parson's tables. Today there is a serious, sometimes bitter split. Some scholars are concerned with the complexity and importance of inquiry about how an average person feels law and deals with it. Others wish to explore the inherent contradictions in, and presumed legitimating functions of, mandarin legal texts and techniques (Trubek, 1984: 575; Whitford, 1986: 75).

Some of Friedman's critics suggest that Friedman and others of the Wisconsin school are unconcerned with the impact of ideas generally and with the valuable cover story provided by legal mythology specifically. In response, Friedman and his law-and-society cohorts tend to denigrate the attention lavished by abstract thinkers on legal epiphenomena. Moreover, they doubt that exposing contradictions in learned journals does much to advance any radical cause or significantly aids any recognizable left or liberal agenda. But the argument is about more than tactics; it may even be over more than the traditional shadowboxing in internecine warfare on the left.

Throughout his work, Friedman has emphasized that elements other than the rare flowers cultivated in the hothouses of academe are crucial to how we, and, far more important, how others not members of our small professional cliques, perceive law and legal change. Repeatedly, in forceful metaphors, Friedman argues that society—the puppeter—pulls the strings and law responds. Law may be a peculiar dialect, but social and economic forces create and develop the language for law's development. It is, therefore, somewhat Dadaist to pursue Friedman's *influence* through selections culled from his extraordinary scholarly output. And it seems more than a trifle absurdist to violate Friedman's own careful, skeptical canons concerning what is actually safe to say about causation or intellectual influence.

What follows is a paradoxical, Pirandellian search for an author and his character. I begin by suggesting why any portrait of Friedman as foremost practitioner of some dominant functionalist or instrumentalist school of legal history committed to determinism or swaddled in teleological faith is largely a caricature. In doing so, I will pursue how legal ideas reflect and help create social change, with particular attention to Friedman's famous proclamation in *A History of American Law* that his book "treats American law . . . not as a kingdom unto itself, not as a set of rules and concepts, not as a province of lawyers alone, but as a mirror of society" (1985a: 12).

In surveying Friedman's contribution, I concentrate almost exclusively on the books Friedman has published in the past few years (1985b: 102; 1985a). (Even if Friedman did not write with extraordinary verve, and even if he did not combine his unusual clarity with a knack for uncovering memorable nuggets within the vast material he mines, news of Friedman's rate of scholarly output should obviously be kept from those who set salaries and grant tenure.) In the context of this "limited" sample of Friedman's work, I will consider competing notions of how mirrors function.[4]

Friedman is fascinated with change and with the problem of how the historian can detect it. He is also quite cautious about what we know and whether we have data to support how we know it. At the same time, he recently has explored ways in which deeply held, inconsistent, and frequently half-baked ideas about law reflect and also influence American culture and character.

Because of his abiding concern for the public, i.e., for what Everyperson believes about legal categories, whether she or he actually thinks about law or not, Friedman pays close attention to the audience for law. He rejects *auteur* theories of legal creation. Instead, he is fascinated with how feedback loops might work between society and the legal product. Friedman also manages to blend his wit and hard-bitten skepticism with social consciousness across a vast array of subjects. A central theme throughout Friedman's work is that law is shaped by the American public, but that law also has a lesser, but still significant, shaping effect on American life.

I will suggest in conclusion why it is appropriate to move beyond mirrors and metaphors to consider the Friedman phenomenon as some amazingly prolific, one-man major motion-picture studio. Friedman is most closely akin to Warner Brothers in the 1930s.

Warner Brothers' films generally managed to reflect changing popular ideology throughout the New Deal. In the process,

[4] I do so with the deference due both the great Groucho-in-a-nightcap sequence in "Night at the Opera" and Lewis Carroll's *Through the Looking Glass*. But, as Alice says about the house on the other side of the looking glass (Martin Gardner, ed., *The Annotated Alice* (New York, 1960: 180–182)):

> I can see all of it when I get upon a chair—all but the bit just behind the fireplace. Oh! I do wish I could see *that* bit! I want so much to know whether they've a fire in the winter; you never can tell, you know, unless our fire smokes, and then smoke comes up in that room too—but that may be only pretence, just to make it look as if they had a fire.

Warner Brothers neither created a false need nor falsely filled a real need (Roddick, 1983: 8). As in the best social conscience films of the 1930s for which Warner Brothers is famous, Friedman's work subtly but unmistakably reflects an important critical stance. It also shows several different facets of an abiding social concern.

II. MIRRORS AND MIRAGES

Friedman's commitment to writing a book about law rather than a law book (Abel, 1973: 175; Trubek, 1984: 575) is even clearer than his own image of the mirror might suggest. He continues, "[This book] takes nothing as historical accident, nothing as autonomous, everything as relative and molded by economy and society. This is the theme of every chapter and verse" (1985a: 12). It is this attitude that seems to infuriate many scholars or, in an ironic argument in the alternative, to be dismissed as a commonplace everybody already knows. Friedman's pathbreaking is often ignored because the trails he blazed are now so heavily traveled. Though Friedman's mirror analogy and his denial of legal autonomy stirred considerable controversy when they were first postulated, today hardly anyone argues that law is entirely autonomous or, for that matter, that law never channels thought and action.

If we are candid, we must concede all legal history is done with mirrors. Today's historiographic debates concern how dark the glass is, whether there is in fact any "there" out there to be reflected, and what to make of the inevitable distortion caused by use of a mirror. In several senses, reflection is an inevitable part of the legal historian's craft. But there are mirrors and then there are mirrors.[5] Moreover, what we seek tends to be what we get and may be all we can hope to see. So there is vigorous debate today among legal historians over the relative merits of contemplating a few navels or attending exclusively to mandarins. It is on issues such as these that Friedman often is caricatured (and sometimes sees himself) as an embattled, autumnal law-and-society archetype.

Friedman's work does not get the appreciation it deserves for several reasons. First, there is jealousy. Friedman is an exceptionally clear, compelling and prolific writer who seems to produce endless pages of luminous prose without the effort the rest of us require. The very fact that he writes so much about so many different topics also makes it difficult to pigeonhole Friedman. This,

[5] It may be that "Hell is—other people" particularly when one relies on someone else as a looking glass. Jean-Paul Sartre, "No Exit" in *No Exit and Three Other Plays* (New York, 1955: 20–21, 47). Moreover, as the adolescent who spends a great deal of time gazing at himself in mirrors tells his father in Peter Taylor's wonderful short story, "Promise of Rain": "[E]ven among mirrors there's a difference! Especially the big ones. They all give you different ideas of how you look." (Peter Taylor, *The Old Forest and Other Tales* (New York, 1985: 95). Cf. Richard Rorty, *Philosophy and the Mirror of Nature* (Princeton, 1979)).

in turn, frustrates our need for order as well as our desire to have time for things other than keeping up with the literature current in our professional fields. Next, because he often seeks and sometimes even finds an audience of nonspecialists, Friedman is derided as a popularizer and a mere synthesizer. Moreover, in a paradoxical bit of generational combat, Friedman is attacked by younger scholars both for lack of methodological sophistication and for insistence on methodological care. Friedman is said by some to be overly optimistic about incremental change while others find him overly dubious if not cynical concerning the possibilities of radical change.

To me what is most striking about Friedman's work, however, is the extent to which he has successfully moved beyond the traditional debates between idealists and materialists, intellectual historians and social historians. To a remarkable extent, Friedman's work already achieves what Wood (1979: 27) has argued is needed to meet the challenge of "nothing less than a revolution in our history-writing" (1979). Wood calls for "[A] kind of zoom lens that will enable us to move easily back and forth from the small, close-up world of unique events and individual volition where men try to use ideas for their own particular purposes to the larger aggregate and deterministic world of cultural conventions and collective mentalities where ideas control men" (1979: 37).

Friedman moves with confidence and clarity between memorable descriptions of actual people entangled in litigation and massive studies of what can be gleaned from litigation statistics over many decades. He interweaves humanistic and social science strands into vivid prose, often employing earthy imagery or flashes of wit premised on ironic insights. Jars of applesauce, for example, illustrate Friedman's points about safety regulation; our appetite for chickens illustrates the problematic issue of the demand and supply for legal resolutions.

What particularly distinguishes his work, however, is the extent to which it successfully anticipates the important historiographic point recently made by David Hall. In considering the overlapping worlds of print culture and collective mentality in seventeenth century New England, for example, and in an essay reviewing recent historical work on the New England Puritans, Hall points out that words and ideas mattered even to the unlettered laity. There were "affective, aesthetic, and ritual dimensions" to the multi-layered discourse of Puritanism as understood by both ministers and laity (Hall, 1987: 222). Hall notes that the newer historical work has "a new confidence in language, together with an understanding of language itself as essentially symbolic" (1979: 166).

This powerful point about Puritanism is, if anything, even more powerful in the context of American legal history. The common sense of Americans not trained in law includes important assumptions about what law will or will not, should or should not be.

Obviously, lawyers and judges constantly address and appeal to the perceptions of their lay audiences, albeit in varying degrees and in differing contexts. Those with legal training occasionally attempt to change common understandings of law, to be sure, but important legal disputes still echo the nursery cry, "Not fair" (Milsom, 1982: 272).

In fact, it is Friedman's concern for what the general population considers fair or not fair that sets his work apart from those who focus on legal doctrine. He emphasizes society and de-emphasizes the clout of the legal elite, bridging what has seemed an almost unbridgeable gulf between the two competing ideas as to which ideas count. Indeed, as Wood and Hall suggest, and as recent attempts to incorporate perceptions from anthropology and popular culture indicate, the gulf may be narrowing. Friedman's insistence on the many contributions to our understanding of community-structured legal life is part of that process.

It is difficult to pin down and criticize Friedman, as it is to criticize Maitland, in part "because of the caution with which he formulated his answers, a caution not at first apparent in the transparent lucidity of his style." It is also fair to say of Friedman that, as with Maitland, "[i]t is virtually impossible to be bored . . . even at his most technical, and seeing how very boring even good historians can be this gives him a remarkable advantage" (Elton, 1985: 35). Friedman is similarly able to convey "what lies concealed within the hard rind of legal history . . . the best, often the only evidence we have for social and economic history, for the history of morality, for the history of practical religion"[6] (Maitland, 1911: 485). Unlike Holmes and others who make a fetish either of constructing or demolishing doctrinal categories, Friedman has a social theory of law in which society plays a leading role. People peer out from behind the law he discusses.

Friedman echoes Maitland in other respects as well. (It may be more than mere coincidence that Friedman's first historical work in the 1950s was on English legal history, a realm in which "the further back one went, the more one found law connected to social structure, economic organization, agricultural method, administrative practice, currents of religious and philosophical specu-

---

[6] F.W. Maitland, 3 *Collected Papers* 485 (H.A.L. Fisher, ed. 1911). It may be more than coincidence that Friedman was attracted to English Legal History and got an L.L.M. in that subject from the University of Chicago in 1953. Before the contributions of William Hurst, and of his successors such as Lawrence Friedman and Harry Scheiber, "the further back one went, the more one found law connected to social structure, economic organization, agricultural method, administrative practice, currents of religious and philosophical speculation. The great researchers of the classical period and their successors had given medieval law a context. But as one approached more recent times, legal history started to thin out to the distinctly 'legal' again, and explanations for the shape of legal things to revert to the genetic." Gordon, *supra* note 3, at 21.

lation"[7] (Gordon, 1975: 21)). As with Maitland, there is "the directness with which he speaks to you through the printed page" (Milsom, 1982: 270) and the important sense in which he is able to "feel some sympathy for both sides" (Ibid.: 271) in the real or imaginary conflicts that lead people to legal entanglement. Most crucially, however, and perhaps more than even the great Maitland, Friedman has a remarkable "sense for common feelings" (Ibid.: 281). He maintains an outsider's perspective but is not condescending about the people whose worlds are reflected in the legal detritus he probes. Indeed, "the visions he communicates with such power are of people whose situation he sees so clearly that he feels their feeling." (Ibid.: 270). And Friedman discusses their messy interlocking worlds with considerable humor and flair.

A. Total Justice: *"An Epic Tale of Loss and Gain"*

Overall, *Total Justice* serves as a fine example of Friedman's clear, insightful, and provocative work (1985b). It is an exploration of a theory of change in American legal culture, moving from acceptance of the harsh uncertainty of life in the nineteenth century toward demands for legal remedies for greatly expanded categories of injuries or rights in the twentieth century. As always, Friedman emphasizes the impact of social change on legal change rather than the reverse. But his argument is anything but simple-minded determinism.[8] He insists, for example, that the choice of which particular tort doctrines prevailed out of the vast array available was neither primarily a product of the "taught tradition" Roscoe Pound emphasized, nor was the evolution of tort doctrine " 'inevitable' in a strict sense or 'determined' in every detail by economic needs; least of all does it mean that the class solidarity of judges shaped [tort doctrine] in a conscious way" (Ibid.: 56). Friedman suggests instead that the mentality of boosterism prevalent in nineteenth-century America was primarily responsible. An expanding, industrializing nation, in which sudden death and serious injury remained commonplace, got the tort law it seemed to want.

[7] It happens that Charles Beard also did his first work, and his doctoral thesis based on county histories and records, on "The Office of the Justice of the Peace in England: In Its Origin and Development," Ellen Nore, *Charles A. Beard: An Intellectual Biography* 18 (Southern Illinois University Press, 1983).

[8] Starting with his earliest work, Friedman has accepted the idea that legal ideas sometimes influence conduct, although his emphasis has always been on the much greater influence of conduct on legal ideas. His disagreement with those who today pursue the "relative autonomy of law" is not with use of the concept itself but rather with where on the autonomy scale law should be placed. (It is a given, after all, that relatives are not autonomous.) *See, e.g.*, Friedman, 1984a: 572–74 ("It is one thing to say that law is not *merely* instrumental; it is quite another to behave or write as if it is not instrumental at all, or as if its instrumental features do not matter as much as the rest of its work"); Friedman, 1985b: 28 ("Every scholar worth his salt would agree that the legal system has *some* autonomy; the question is, how much?").

Total Justice is full of insights ("lawyers both prevent redress and promote excessive redress" (Ibid.: 23); "[a] safety net encourages some people to swing on the trapeze, or walk the tight-rope, who would otherwise not dare" (Ibid.: 105) and strange-but-true concrete examples: liberality in workmen's compensation is illustrated with the case of an employee who prevails after being hurt while urinating from a moving truck; the persistence of moral and religious notions enforced by law is illustrated by a 1921 Maine Supreme Court decision upholding a conviction for blasphemy. Moreover, to oversimplify a richly textured argument, Friedman makes a powerful case that our current legal culture is composed of fewer "zones of immunity" (Ibid.: 82) protecting the discretion of government officials and civil defendants than it was in the nineteenth century. Instead, we have increased expectations for redress for a vast range of harms. But Friedman is careful to consider a counterexample—an increase in the delegalization of attitudes toward sexual conduct—and weaves that story into his rather sweeping general assessment of how "attitudes become processes and processes become institutions" (Ibid.: 148). Altered legal consciousness and changes in legal culture, Friedman suggests, do create tendencies to "bend toward the norm, like plants bending and growing toward the light" (Ibid.: 67).

It might appear that in *Total Justice* Friedman is responding to those who have criticized his emphasis on how social norms control law. This book emphasizes more than any of his earlier work what Friedman rather abstractly refers to as the effect of an "upward spiral" of alterations in social norms. But Friedman actually has long acknowledged the symbolic function of law and has taken into consideration what we have come to call the relative autonomy of legal ideas a focus of his work in the 1960s.

More significantly, Friedman continues to look for explanations. He tests his emphasis on the control of social forces over law by wrestling with legal categories in which, at least at first glance, it seems extremely difficult if not impossible to explain why some rules rather than others prevail. Friedman makes the point that it is difficult to tell who benefits from certain commercial law arrangements rather than others, for example.[9] He also

[9] "It is doubtful that majestic capitalism would have smothered in its crib without the rule of *caveat emptor*. It is doubtful whether specific doctrines of commercial law were cause, effect, or condition of American capitalism; or all or none of these." *History of American Law*, p. 264. As Gordon notes, in this respect—as in many others—Friedman does not fit the paradigm of the dominant vision of legal history, which Gordon terms evolutionary functionalism (36 *Stanford Law Review* 57, 76, n. 47). *See also*, e.g., Friedman and Macaulay agree with disengagement theory of autonomous law, positing that there is "law of leftovers," *id.*, p. 89, n. 79; Friedman shows in family law context that legal enactment may not have effect, since it merely ratifies social relationship already crystallized, *id.*, p. 91, n. 83; Friedman as an example of the "marvelous work" using a cultural anthropology approach, *id.*, p. 95, n. 89. All these footnotes make Friedman sound like a creative CLS type. But if it is not

recognizes that for every social trend there seems to be a countertrend (Friedman, 1985a as criticized by Tushnet 1977: 81; Friedman 1985b: 151). But generally Friedman sustains a rather sobering, and certainly humbling, argument that neither social engineering nor impressive theorizing is likely to cause major changes, unless external social factors are ripe for change.

Indeed, Friedman seems preoccupied by issues of legal change. He is unquestionably a worthy successor to Hurst, but Friedman seems less inclined than Hurst to accept consensus, inertia, and drift as dominant social forces. Perhaps as part of his own generational revolt, Friedman constantly stresses the dynamic quality of both social life and law. He perceives the world as somewhat akin to a beehive of activity, its action primarily competitive and chaotic, rather than harmonious and steady. Friedman does not sacrifice realism for resolution.

B. Your Time Will Come: The Law of Age Discrimination and Mandatory Retirement—*"And You Won't Have Everything!"*

To his credit, Friedman does not shy away from difficult tests for his hypotheses on the dominant role played by competing interests in changing the legal world. For example, in his book on the federal Age Discrimination Act of 1975—an act passed by Congress "in a fit of absentmindedness (perhaps)" (1984a: 16)—Friedman contends with a legal infant copied from a civil rights prototype. The Age Discrimination Act passed without significant support from identifiable pressure groups. In discussing this, as well as a 1967 Act that banned some additional forms of age discrimination in employment, Friedman points out that statutes often serve as surrogates for other, more deeply contested interests. Friedman speculates that concern over age discrimination is "a double stand-in." It approximates what he considers two important, albeit also largely unrecognized principles: the first is the *civil rights* principle, which attacks the use of any criterion considered to be unfair; the second is the *tenure* principle, which seeks to protect expectations developed over time.

Friedman is quick to point out that these two principles are largely unexamined and at least sometimes inconsistent. They are only half-conscious norms. Yet, as usual, the categories Friedman introduces provide useful scaffolding for organizing our thoughts. He distinguishes between unfairness, which is "not against the law, at least in so many words" and discrimination, "which is" (Ibid.: 48). Moreover, Friedman notes the symbolic function of antidiscrimination laws, but he suggests that it is patterns of conduct that

---

Friedman, then who is the target—the evolutionary functionalist—against which critical legal histories are to be arrayed?

provide both crucial evidence and crucial targets for Draconian legal change.

Friedman is again trailblazing in his attention to issues of age discrimination, his collection and vivid description of concrete examples, and his attempt to reach an audience beyond the law school professorate. Ultimately, however, in this book the somewhat abstract nature of the two categories he employs, coupled with the open-ended quality of the stand-in notion, seem less well grounded than does most of Friedman's work. Nonetheless, Friedman clearly advocates the use of law to help change consciousness, since "[i]n justice, as society defines it, is also a cost" and since "the sense of right has been a powerful motor force" (Ibid.: 52–54). "The source of all law is the normative climate," according to Friedman, but it is vital to recognize that "law crystallizes and formalizes lumpy or ghostly feelings, adrift in society; it hardens them into definite shapes; and it sets up machinery that people can use, to translate feelings into action" (Ibid.: 54, 66).

C. The Roots of Justice: Crime and Punishment in Alameda County, California, 1870–1910—*"Just the Facts, Ma'am"*

To be sure, some parts of Friedman's scholarly output—particularly the study of criminal records in Alameda County, California, he co-authored with Robert Percival—are so studiously grounded in minute factual detail about the machinery of law that at first glance they seem to cry out for more theory. Theory lurks in all historic writing, of course, but *The Roots of Justice* may contain too much data and too little explicit interpretation for readers who crave clear narrative development, if not fancy overarching theory. But the book is unquestionably a significant historical contribution, and it shows Friedman is not blinded by teleological faith.

Despite important variations in plea bargaining rates and approaches to guilty pleas in the period covered by the study, and despite other, more minor changes, the class structure behind the three-tiered criminal system a century ago in Alameda County seems distressingly similar to the modern criminal law system Friedman and Percival describe there today. We still use the formal criminal law process in diverse ways, depending on whether we employ it to process misfits; to administer punishments, for the most part without jury trials, for more serious offenses; or to perform an educative function in the most sensational cases in which lawyers dominate the process and we compose and broadcast the official rules about what process is due. We still rely on the police to help distinguish among these three categories, as well as to operate a fourth level of discretionary justice (Friedman and Percival, 1981: 315).[10] If anything, the storyline in *Roots of Justice* lacks reassuring movement. Neither clear progress nor clear regress leaps out at the reader. The central point the authors make, however, is that even low-visibility categories of legal culture are brimming over with so many variables as to make nice, neat generalizations impossible.

The Roots of Justice is rich in suggestive details. Its numerous tables include data ranging from arrests broken down by nationality and age group to less obvious categories such as the number of days between conviction and sentencing, broken down in terms of types of offenses and status of attorneys involved, and the percentages of total arrests for each offense class by time of day. We learn the ethnicity, gender, age, and occupation of those arrested for a number of different crime categories, that the successful prosecution of a typical license case actually cost Oakland more than seventy dollars in 1879, and even the number of arrests per police officer and per population.

Further, the monumental task involved simply in gathering the data for this study, with its relatively small yield of drama or glittering generalities, helps to underscore why few have heeded Friedman's perennial call to do the gritty work of digging out the "kilo-Ph.Ds" buried in every county courthouse. Yet despite his failure to win converts, Friedman remains not only remarkably versatile in his own legal history research, but unusually generous in his collaborations and in providing honorable mention to those who build theories, produce biographies, or otherwise toil throughout legal history's many rooms.

The glaring exception to Friedman's general generosity of spirit, beyond the occasional barbs he aims at what he considers the overly abstract meanderings of critical legal studies and the overly simple conceptualism of law and economics, is Friedman's general disdain for constitutional law. In this, he is undoubtedly

---

10 After Friedman and Percival published some of their preliminary data in "A Tale of Two Courts: Litigation in Alameda and San Benito Counties," 10 *Law & Society Review* 267 (1976), Richard Lempert wrote a lengthy article reanalyzing their data, controlling for adult population. Richard Lempert, "More Tales of Two Courts: Exploring Changes in the 'Dispute Settlement Function' of Trial Courts," 13 *Law & Society Review* 91 (1978). Lempert made the important point that paying attention to cases filed may miss an entire range of disputes that never made it to court in the first place. This point is not entirely lost on Friedman and Percival. And, as Lempert acknowledges, it is easy to criticize any collection of data for not collecting more or something else. Even the massive detail supplied by Friedman and Percival may be merely the tip of a peculiar iceberg, though they do an impressive job of supplementing their statistics with information culled from newspaper reports and other less obvious sources of social history as well. As Friedman once put it, "Reported cases, then, are always (or almost always) the tip of some sort of iceberg. That may be fine; after all . . . the bottom of an iceberg may be much like the top, that is, essentially ice. Reported cases, on the other hand, may or may not tell us much about unreported cases or ordinary complaints. . ." (Friedman, 1984a: 47).

true to the legal realist tradition (White, 1986: 452; Schlegel, 1984: 407–408; Llewellyn, 1934). In my view as a constitutional law teacher, Friedman here is too narrow-minded. Moreover, he contradicts his basic view that constitutional debate consists of poking away at "a kind of living fossil, the last and most vigorous survivor of conceptual jurisprudence" (Friedman, 1984c: 569), with his own constitutional insights in his magisterial *A History of American Law*. In his recent work, Friedman shows definite signs of dawning enlightenment concerning the worthiness of constitutional issues for serious consideration (1986: 1; 1985b).

D. A History of American Law: *"They Said It Couldn't Be Done!"*

A History of American Law is that part of Friedman's work (so far) for which he is most likely to be recognized. If there are legal historians in one hundred years—and if they are not all simply ferreting about in the dust of thousands of county courthouses—they will have to come to grips with both the details provided and the sweeping story told in this remarkable book. Friedman was probably a bit disingenuous when he offered his book as a "whipping boy" and "a primer" (1985a: 10), but he was surely accurate when he suggested that the book would provide "a shape for the field, even if others find it misshapen" (Ibid.). When first published in 1973, this snappy single-volume account provided marvelous, memorable, and detailed examples of the numerous ways in which American law was never immanent and hardly static.[11]

The enormous size, and considerable clout, of the landed middle class is the central thread in Friedman's impressively nuanced book. Friedman calls this "the master fact of American law and life" (1985a: 212). Perhaps it takes a mid-westerner fully to appreciate the phenomenon. This may help explain why a place such as Wisconsin nurtured the Hurst-Friedman school of legal history, with roots stretching directly back to populist historians such as

[11] The first edition received generally euphoric reviews, *see, e.g.*, W. E. Nelson, 18 *American Journal of Legal History* 182; H. A. Johnson, 23 *De Paul Law Review* 1086; E. D. Tucker, 86 *Harvard Law Review* 1625; W. A. Hill, 50 *N. D. L. Review* 147; S. J. Spitz, 36 *Ohio S. L. J.* 376; J. Lurie, 27 *Rutgers Law Review* 354; E. F. Murphy, 26 *Stanford Law Review* 701; C. A. Pierce, 42 *Tenn. Law Review* 615; J. H. Smith, 24 *University of Toronto Law Journal* 108; G. E. White, 59 *Virginia Law Review* 1130; J. W. Ely, Jr., 26 *Vand. Law Review*, a 'few balanced critiques'; S. B. Presser, 122 *University of Pennsylvania Law Review* 217; and L. J. Mazor, 60 *Minnesota Law Review* 147 and Mark Tushnet's "wonderfully, or awfully (take your pick), foul-tempered review," John Henry Schlegel, "Notes Toward an Intimate, Opinionated, and Affectionate History of the Conference on Critical Legal Studies," 36 *Stanford Law Review* 391, 408, discussing Mark Tushnet, "Perspectives on the Development of American Law: A Critical Review of Friedman's *A History of American Law*," 1977 *Wisconsin Law Review* 81. Thus far, the second edition has had less attention and more praise, *see, e.g.*, Calvin Woodard in *N.Y. Times*, Feb. 16, 1986, sec. VIII, p. 31.

Thorstein Veblen, Vernon Parrington, and, most significantly, Charles Beard. Life in the land of the Northwest Ordinance may go a long way toward immunizing historians against coastal neuroses. They are alerted to the power and the persistence of the great American Middle Class.

A Chicagoan only belatedly transplanted to America's dreamland, California, Friedman demonstrates across a range of legal subjects that middle-class dominance never was secure. In fact, if his book has a single central subtext, it is movement. Legal arrangements are seldom settled. The winners in legal contests are anything but permanently ascendant. This is a crucial aspect of Friedman's approach, an aspect that illuminates a great deal about his general approach to legal history.

Friedman does not merely show snapshots. The metaphor of moving pictures is more appropriate. Friedman explains why he thinks, or perhaps hopes, that intrumentalism in the long run is the enemy of what he calls "vertical pluralism," which is a concept close to what some of his critics would discuss in terms of hegemonic hierarchy,[12] provides a good illustration (1984a: 664). Reviewing what he has said about the nineteenth century, the period in which he has done most of his work, Friedman discusses "mobility for the few and dreams for the many" (Ibid.: 665). He writes in curmudgeonly language of a combination of factors that "acted as a brake on demands for redistribution of the social product" (Ibid.). But he also points out that the frontier was not the only safety valve: "there was also the hope of success, the culture and cult of opportunity," a metaphoric lottery for which tickets were hawked "on every corner, in every town" (Ibid.).

Friedman devotes attention throughout this book to those people he labels "The Underdogs" and to other victims of ascendant interests. Consistent with much of the rest of his scholarship, he reminds his readers of who got put down or kept down, even as he goes about the business of mapping how the law generally reflected hard-edged competition. It is also characteristic of Friedman to have raised doubts about the purportedly progressive motivation behind the Married Women's Property Acts, for example, before the recent outpouring of attention to the subject, but subsequently to have cited the new work and not his own original contribution.[13]

---

[12] See *A History of American Law*, 2d ed., p. 574 for a limited discussion of the issue.

[13] In "Law Reform in Historical Perspective," 13 *St. Louis Law Review* 351, 362–363 (1969), Friedman used Married Women's Property Acts as an example of a "hidden ratification," explainable neither in terms of a quiet yet significant revolution suggested by the bare legal record nor in terms of a response to pent-up social and economic pressure. He credited the unpublished thesis of Ellen Thurman, as well as the compilation of family law statutes in 3 Vernier, American Family Law 166 ff. (1935). Though Friedman makes no mention of the issue in the first edition of *A History of American Law*, he

In his recent work, Friedman often points out explicitly that cost-benefit analysis celebrating efficiency tends to omit unquantifiable, yet crucial, social costs. Ironically, this legal historian, seemingly so committed to hard data and empiricism, often appears to distrust profoundly the results of the marketplace. He refuses to accept the normative power of either the actual or the actuarial.

The irony may be resolved if we consider Friedman's empathy with those denied a fair place in the race of life and his sensitivity to the problematic nature of feedback loops.[14] For Friedman, law is a part of the cult of opportunity. But belief in the revolutionary power of law, or in the power of de-mystifying law, is belief in a flickering, chimerical image. What Roddick said of the Hollywood studios in the 1930s might be said about the legal system as well (1983: 11):

> The trends and events of public life provided the story material for and therefore strongly influenced the output of Hollywood; in turn, the image of themselves which the movies reflected back to the movie-going public exercised an influence on the same trends and events which had given birth to the image.

Friedman's work suggests that legal culture is similarly part of a circular relationship. There are obvious ideological overtones, but the perpetual loop depends on gauging and responding to audience needs in a sense that is largely manipulative, but also occasionally productive of an important focus for social consciences or even achievements. Like a great film such as *The Maltese Falcon*, *A History of American Law* has something for everyone: twists and turns in the plot, memorable characters, illuminating humorous moments, and vivid details that keep the viewer entranced. Both also respond to some of our deepest myths about individualism and society. And like Sam Spade, Friedman is hard-nosed and apparently beyond the fray. But his world-weary pose turns out to be just a pose when the crunch comes. He does the down and dirty work, but he also knows how to lead, perhaps even to inspire.

III. HOW DOES IT ALL COME OUT?

A major element in the criticism of Friedman's work involves dismay at his optimism. Friedman admits that he is in favor of gains, even symbolic gains, against discrimination. Indeed, he suggests, success may lie "precisely in the fact that the rules startle

cites generously to numerous recent studies in the 2d edition, pp. 208–211, but not to his own 1969 article.

[14] Even if "an exceedingly weak positive feedback loop" may be all that is necessary to explain the origin of life, T.F.H. Allen and Thomas B. Starr, *Hierarchy: Perspectives for Ecological Complexity* 49 (Chicago, 1982). Allen and Starr indicate the complexity of positive and negative feedback loops in the course of suggesting the importance of anticipation and purpose in "the evolved physical world [that] trades in futures." *Id.*, p. 60.

people" (1984a: 63). Friedman is a committed academic activist. His target, however, is more modest and almost certainly more realistic than the assault on paradigms favored by critical legal studies and by law and economics. Even Friedman's awareness of the folks who buy the tickets, his commitment to writing material that can be read by nonspecialists, appears to flow from a quiet zeal for reform.

Ironically, given the heat generated by the debate over what degree of relative autonomy one favors, Friedman quite clearly believes, as he has for a long time, that "[existing] structures of law and government, at least in the short run, exert a powerful influence on the way demands and attitudes become concrete" (1985b: 148). Additionally, he often expresses his willingness to accept inefficiency in exchange for gains in social justice (Ibid.: 151). He summarizes our legal culture's trend toward a total justice consciousness, a goal he notes can never be achieved, as follows: "I have to confess my personal sense of pleasure over many developments described. I like the spread of due process; I like the welfare state; I like justice for minorities; I like the broader meaning of equality, the great reach and depth of individual rights" (Ibid.).

Friedman does not believe that the social order is easily smashed. He has an explicitly organic view, even though he recognizes "the fallacy of extrapolation, expecting the future to be like the past, only more so" (Ibid.: 34). This makes him a reformer, not a revolutionary. It also helps explain why this tolerant scholar becomes somewhat intolerant of those who seem committed only to raising contradictions. To him, it is not difficult to do that. Nor is it at all clear that carefully-constructed deconstructions will somehow trickle into a torrent of radical change.

The history of legal change is very much Friedman's bailiwick. He has a sophisticated sense of the changes in the conditions of confinement in America's "iron grip of tradition in a rigid but comfortable prison of habits and norms." This helps Friedman elude common pitfalls. He does not cluck over a pattern of decline while romanticizing an earlier, more communal golden age, nor does he give way to despair. Friedman remains hopeful, despite the substantial congruence between his perspective and the bleaker point made by Grant Gilmore that "Law never creates society; society creates law. Law never makes society better; a better society will improve the law"[15] (1966: 7).

Like Charles Beard, Friedman seems painfully aware that historians necessarily "see what is behind our eyes" (Nore, 1983: 156).

---

[15] Grant Gilmore, "Law, Anarchy and History," 14 *University of Chicago Law School Record* 1, 7 (Autumn, 1966). The gap between the Friedman's still-hopeful skepticism and Gilmore's darker vision is illustrated by Friedman's puzzled response to Gilmore's work on the demise of contracts where Friedman says, "Gilmore's chief reason for regretting the death of contract theory seemed nothing more than nostalgic sentimentality—a sense of longing for the good old days, when scholars thought there was value in what they were do-

Not even historians, who of all people should be aware of what Graham Wallas termed the "paradox of unintended consequences," are able to "force the iron gates of the future" (Ibid.: 156). Nevertheless, Beard and Friedman share a commitment to the historian's professional search for "history-as-actuality" (Nore, 1983: 167), to taking an active role in public affairs, and to trying to reach a broader public than do most historians by writing and teaching with verve and clarity. Beard and Friedman are both famous for stressing the impact of economic interests on legal materials, but both are also frequently mischaracterized as believers in determinism. As does Beard, Friedman acknowledges subjectivity but celebrates the "inquiring spirit of science" (Ibid.: 166) as "the chief safeguard against tyranny of authority, bureaucracy, and brute power (Ibid.).

I have placed Lawrence Friedman in the august company of Maitland and Beard. This association of a very funny, impish Jewish fellow from Chicago with two austere WASP giants is obviously problematic in numerous details. Yet Friedman belongs in their company. He, too, deserves recognition for the clarity of his thought, the richness of his scholarly understanding of ideas in social context, and the lucidity of his astonishingly prolific writing.

IV. CONCLUSION

It may be whimsical to compare Friedman's work with the unmemorable films put out by Warner Brothers in the 1930s, but it is not entirely frivolous or inapt. Warner Brothers achieved fame and fortune for its gangster movies and newspaper films; social conscience films that attacked racism, fascism, inhumane prison systems and the like; "biopics" and more "classic" films. As Roddick put it: "[T]hose films marked both contemporary audiences in their attitude to the world and, in a different way, subsequent ideas of what is or is not a 'good' film"[16] (1983: 254). The same might be said of Friedman's legal history work.

Moreover, as did Warner Brother's social conscience pictures

ing." (Lawrence Friedman, "American Legal History: Past and Present" 34 *Journal of Legal Education* 563 (1984)).

The tension between the bleakness of what we think we know about law and the idea that we hope to do better than we think we can through law was explored with particular insight by Arthur Leff. As Leff put it, in a memorial issue for Gilmore, Gilmore's bleak vision is probably right, but we are "lutists of the unknowable" who, on our way to those final defeats, may sometimes have "some beautiful innings." (Leff, "Law and . . . ," 87 *Yale Law Journal* 1011 (1978)).

[16] For important recent work on the linkage and tension between popular culture and formal legal images of law, *see* David Papke, *Framing the Criminal: Crime, Cultural Work and the Loss of Critical Perspective* (Hamden, 1987); Stewart Macaulay, "Images of Law in Everyday Life: The Lessons of School, Entertainment, and Spectator Sports," 21 *Law & Society Review* 181 (1987); Anthony Chase, "Toward a Legal Theory of Popular Culture," 1986 *Wisconsin Law Review* 527.

such as *I am a Fugitive from a Chain Gang*, *Wild Boys of the Road*, *Angels with Dirty Faces*, and *Black Legion*, Friedman also assumes "the strengths of a basically sound if temporarily problem-ridden society" (Ibid.: 128). He also keeps an eye on the bottom and middle of the social order. What today may seem idiosyncratic about Friedman's work is his quiet confidence in being able to communicate to a broad audience about social problems, combined with a skeptical optimist's leap of faith in America's social conscience. In a sense, Friedman's understanding of the powerful strains of resistance and self-interest in American history liberate him to battle for improvement. He knows of the "generous concealment of mirrors" (Schwartz, 1987: 95). He also knows we need mirrors to perceive what we must take as real, so we can do something to change it.

The considerable achievement of these social conscience films was their blend of story-telling craft and powerful condemnation of social outrages such as the chain gang system. Friedman's scholarship also operates with power and persuasiveness on many levels of craft and social consciousness. His massive outpouring of scholarship surely enlightens all kinds of readers. Friedman's work may even move people past personal reflections of what has passed.

AVIAM SOIFER is Professor of Law at Boston University. He holds B.A., M. Urban Studies, and J.D. degrees from Yale University. His recent publications include: " 'Toward a Generalized Notion of the Right to Form or Join an Association': An Essay for Tom Emerson," 38 *Case Western Reserve Law Review* 641 (1988) and "Status, Contract, and Promises Unkept," 96 *Yale Law Journal* 1916 (1987).

REFERENCES

ABEL, Richard L. (1973) "Law Books and Books about Law," 26 *Stanford Law Review* 175.

ALLEN, T.F.H., and Thomas B. STARR (1982) *Hierarchy: Perspectives for Ecological Complexity*. Chicago: Chicago University Press.

AUERBACH, Jerold (1976) *Unequal Justice: Lawyers and Social Change in Modern America*. New York: Oxford University Press.

BERGMAN, Andrew (1971) *We're in the Money: Depression America and its Films*. New York: New York University Press.

CHASE, Anthony (1986) "Toward a Legal Theory of Popular Culture," *Wisconsin Law Review* 527.

DIAMOND, Steve (1979) "Legal Realism and Historical Method: J. Willard Hurst and American Legal History," 77 *Michigan Law Review* 784.

DIGGINS, John (1982) "Power and Authority in American History: The Case of Charles A. Beard and His Critics," 87 *American History Review* 701.

ELTON, G.R. (1985) *F.W. Maitland*. New Haven, Conn.: Yale University Press.

ELY, J.W., Jr. (1973) "Book Review," 26 *Vanderbilt Law Review*, 1353.

FRIEDMAN, Lawrence (1986) "A Search for Seizure: *Pennsylvania v. Mahon* in Context," 4 *Law and History* 1.

——— (1985a) *A History of American Law*, 2nd ed. New York: Simon & Schuster.

——— (1985b) *Total Justice*. New York: Russell Sage Foundation.

——— (1984a) *Your Time Will Come: The Law of Age Discrimination and Mandatory Retirement*. New York: Russell Sage Foundation (distributed by Basic Books).

——— (1984b) "Limited Monarchy: The Rise and Fall of Student Rights" in David L. Kirp and Donald N. Jensen, eds., *School Days, Rule Days, The Legalization and Regulation of Education*. London: Falmer Press.

——— (1984c) "American Legal History: Past and Present" 34 *Journal of Legal Education* 563.

——— (1977) *Law and Society: An Introduction*. Englewood Cliffs, N.J.: Prentice Hall.

——— (1975) *The Legal System*. New York: Russell Sage Foundation.

——— (1969a) "Legal Culture and Social Development," 4 *Law & Society Review* 29.

——— (1969b) "Law Reform in Historical Perspective," 13 *St. Louis Law Review* 351.

——— (1969c) "Legal Culture and Social Development," 4 *Law & Society Review* 29.

——— (1968) *Government and Slum Housing. A Century of Frustration*. Chicago: Rand McNally and Company.

——— (1967) "Legal Rules and the Process of Social Change," 19 *Stanford Law Review* 786.

——— (1966) "On Legalistic Reasoning—A Footnote to Weber," *Wisconsin Law Review* 148.

——— (1965) *Contract Law in America: A Social and Economic Case Study*. Madison: University of Wisconsin Press.

——— (1964) "Law and its Language," 33 *George Washington Law Review* 563.

FRIEDMAN, Lawrence, and Jack LADINSKY (1967) "Social Change and the Law of Industrial Accidents", 67 *Columbia Law Review* 50.

FRIEDMAN, Lawrence, and Robert V. PERCIVAL (1981) *The Roots of Justice: Crime and Punishment in Alameda County, California, 1870–1910*. Chapel Hill: University of North Carolina Press.

FRIEDMAN, Lawrence M., and S. WHEELER, B. CARTWRIGHT, R.A. KAGAN (1987) "Do the 'Haves' Come out Ahead? Winning and Losing in State Supreme Courts, 1870–1970," 21 *Law & Society Review* 403.

GILMORE, Grant (1966) "Anarchy and History," 14 *University of Chicago Law School Record* 1.

GORDON, Robert (1987) "Unfreezing Legal Reality: Critical Approaches to Law," 15 *Florida State University Law Review* 195.

——— (1984) "Critical Legal Histories," 36 *Stanford Law Review* 57.

——— (1982) "Holmes' *Common Law* As Legal and Social Science," 10 *Hofstra Law Review* 719.

——— (1975) "J. Willard Hurst and the Common Law Tradition in American Legal Historiography," 10 *Law & Society Review* 9.

HALL, David (1987) "On Common Ground: The Coherence of American Puritan Studies," 44 *William and Mary Quarterly 3rd Series* 193.

——— (1979) "The World of Print and Collective Mentality in Seventh-Century New England," in John Higham and Paul K. Conkin, eds., *New Directions in American Intellectual History*. Baltimore: Johns Hopkins University Press.

HILL, William A. (1973) "Book Review," 50 *North Dakota Law Review* 147.

HOFSTADTER, Richard (1968) *The Progressive Historians: Turner, Beard, Parrington*. New York: Knopf.

HOLMES, Oliver Wendell (1953) *Holmes–Laski Letters; The Correspondence of Mr. Justice Holmes and Harold J. Laski, 1916–1935*, Mark De Wolfe Howe, ed. Cambridge, Mass: Harvard University Press.

HORWITZ, M.J. (1977) *The Transformation of American Law*. Cambridge, Mass: Harvard University Press.

——— (1973) "The Conservative Tradition in the Writing of American Legal History," 17 *American Journal of Legal History* 275.

JOHNSON, Herbert (1974) "Survey of Legal Literature," 23 *DePaul Law Review* 1086.

KALMAN, Laura (1986) *Legal Realism at Yale, 1927–1960.* Chapel Hill: University of North Carolina Press.

LEFF, Arthur (1978) "Law and . . .," 87 *Yale Law Journal* 1011.

LLEWELLYN, Karl (1934) "The Constitution as an Institution," 34 *Columbia Law Review* 1.

LURIE, J. (1973) "Book Review," 27 *Rutgers Law Review* 354.

MACAULAY, Stewart (1987) "Images of Law in Everyday Life: The Lessons of School, Entertainment, and Spectator Sports," 21 *Law & Society Review* 181.

——— (1984), "Law and the Behavioral Sciences: Is There Any There There?, 6 *Law & Policy Quarterly* 149.

MAITLAND, F.W., (1911) *The Collected Papers of Frederic William Maitland*, H.A.L. Fisher, ed. Buffalo: W.S. Hein.

MANN, Bruce (1987) *Neighbors and Strangers: Law and Community in Early Connecticut.* Chapel Hill: University of North Carolina.

MAZOR, Lester (1975) "Book Review," 60 *Minnesota Law Review* 147.

MILLER, Perry (1969) "The Life of the Mind in America: From the Revolution to the Civil War," 77 *Yale Law Journal* 1244.

MILSOM, S.F.C. (1982 for 1980), "F.W. Milsom," Master-Mind Lecture, in *Proceedings of the British Academy.* London: Oxford University Press.

MURPHY, Earl (1974) "Book Review," 26 *Stanford Law Review* 701.

NELSON, William (1974) "Book Review," 18 *American Journal of Legal History* 182.

NORE, Ellen (1983), *Charles A. Beard: An Intellectual Biography.* Carbondale: Southern Illinois University Press.

PAPKE, David (1987) *Framing the Criminal: Crime, Cultural Work and the Loss of Critical Perspective, 1830–1900.* Hamden: Archon Books.

PIERCE, C.A. (1975) "Book Review," 42 *Tennessee Law Review* 615.

PRESSER, Stephen (1973) "Book Review," 122 *University of Pennsylvania Law Review*, 217.

RODDICK, Nick (1983) *A New Deal in Entertainment: Warner Brothers in the 1930's.* London: British Film Institute.

RORTY, Richard (1979) *Philosophy and the Mirror of Nature.* Princeton: Princeton University Press.

SARTRE, Jean-Paul (1955) "No Exit," in *No Exit and Three Other Plays.* New York: Vintage Press.

SMITH, J.H. (1974) "Book Review," 24 *University of Toronto Law Journal* 108.

SCHLEGEL, John Henry (1984) "Notes toward an Intimate, Opinionated, and Affectionate History of the Conference on Critical Legal Studies," 36 *Stanford Law Review* 391.

——— (1981) "American Legal Realism and Empirical Social Science: From the Yale Experience," 28 *Buffalo Law Review* 3.

——— (1980) "American Legal Realism and Empirical Social Science: The Singular Case of Underhill Moore," 29 *Buffalo Law Review* 2.

SCHWARTZ, Lynn Sharon (1987) "Killing the Bees," 2 *Tikkun* 92.

SPITZ, Stephen (1975) "Book Review," 36 *Ohio State Law Journal* 376.

TAYLOR, Peter (1985) *The Old Forest and Other Tales.* Garden City, N.Y.: The Dial Press.

TUCKER, Edwin (1973) "Book Review," 86 *Harvard Law Review* 1625.

TRUBEK, David (1984) "Where the Action Is: Critical Legal Studies and Empiricism," 36 *Stanford Law Review* 575.

TUSHNET, Mark (1977) "Perspectives on Development of American Law: A Critical Review of Friedman's *A History of American Law*," *Wisconsin Law Review* 81.

VANDEVELDE, Kenneth J. (1980) "The New Property of the Nineteenth Century: The Development of the Modern Concept of Property," 29 *Buffalo Law Review* 325.

WHITE, G. Edward (1986) "Looking at Holmes in the Mirror," 4 *Law and History Review* 439.

——— (1973) "Book Review," 59 *Virginia Law Review* 1130.

WHITFORD, William (1986) "Lowered Horizons: Implementation Research in a Post-CLS World," *Wisconsin Law Review* 75.
WOOD, Gordon (1979) "Intellectual History and Social Sciences," in John Higham and Paul K. Conkin, eds., *New Directions in American Intellectual History*. Baltimore: Johns Hopkins University Press.
WOODARD, Calvin in *N.Y. Times*, Feb. 16, 1986, sec. VIII, p. 31.
——— (1967) "History, Legal History, and Legal Education," 53 *Virginia Law Review* 89.

[9]

Book Reviews

The Transformation of American Law, 1780–1860. By M.J. HORWITZ.
(London: Harvard University Press 1977 xvii + 356 pp., £11.55 hard, £4.20 soft).

Do not let the title of this book mislead you. This work has a general appeal that far transcends the currently thriving world of American legal history. It is undoubtedly a seminal work — of profound importance to all those interested in the relationship between law and economy — and, in particular, the role played by law in the facilitation of industrial capitalism.

The Horwitz Thesis

Central to Horwitz's thesis is the notion that a radical break with pre-capitalist (pre-Revolutionary) society and its law occurred after 1790; and that in the period 1790–1860 the American common law courts engineered the facilitation and legitimation of industrial capitalism. The crux of his thesis is that the judges moulded the law so as to promote emergent mercantile interests at the expense of other weaker groups within the community, thereby resulting in a major redistribution of power and wealth. In order to support this thesis Horwitz draws upon an astonishing range of legal subject matter. He argues that in the period 1790–1850 the very conception and function of law changed. Eighteenth century law was conceived of as a static set of principles reflecting customary ideas of justice and practice derived from natural law. After 1790 this was supplanted by a more functional, "instrumental" conception of the common law. Judges "... came to think of the common law as equally responsible with legislation for governing society and promoting socially desirable conduct." (p.30) The instrumental approach adopted by the judiciary soon led to the transformation of private law. In one of his most impressive essays Horwitz describes the transformation of the idea of property "... from the eighteenth century view that dominion over land above all conferred the power to prevent others from interfering with one's enjoyment of property to the nineteenth century assumption that the essential attribute of property ownership was the power to develop one's property regardless of the injurious consequences to others."[1]

Common law rules which obstructed the demands of economic growth were repudiated or suitably amended. Eighteenth century law which imposed liability for interfering with the enjoyment of property or with another's livelihood irrespective of fault, was replaced by a lower level of duty in negligence. The desire to promote industrialisation caused the courts to alternate between protecting monopolies and encouraging competition. Whereas under eighteenth century law juries traditionally had a wide power to award damages on the basis of their own sense of fairness and equity, in the nineteenth century the courts shaped the new legal rules to restrict or eliminate that discretion. The judiciary were seeking to accommodate "...

[1] p. 99. Here Horwitz's thesis echoes the work of James Willard Hurst. Hurst distinguished between "static" and "dynamic" property. Static property was akin to absolute property rights. Hurst argued that in the early 19th century, American courts and legislatures tended to forego this conception of property rights in favour of a dynamic conception of property which abridged absolute conceptions of property where these impeded industrialisation. See *Law and the Conditions of Freedom in the Nineteenth Century United States* (1956) p.28. See also Scheiber, "The Road to Munn: Eminent Domain and the Concept of Public Purpose in the State Courts", in *Law in American History* (ed. D. Fleming and B. Bailyn, 1971).

the new insistence of entrepreneurial groups that certainty and predictability of legal consequences were essential for economic planning ...." (p.81)

A major facet of the transformation of private law after 1790 was "... the extent to which common law doctrines were transformed to create immunities from legal liability and thereby to provide substantial subsidies for those who undertook schemes of economic development." (pp.99–100) Examining the consequences of legal subsidisation, Horwitz argues that the courts imposed a disproportionate share of the cost of economic development "... on the weakest and least organized groups in American society."[2] Furthermore, subsidisation through technical legal doctrine mystified the underlying political choices. It avoided spreading the cost over a wider segment of society; and the more open public discussion and scrutiny that would have resulted if development had been encouraged by direct taxation.

Nowhere is Horwitz's analysis of the relationship between law and economy in nineteenth century America more striking than his essay on the transformation of contract law.[3] Eighteenth century law required that contracts be "fair" and generally permitted courts to set aside transactions that were unfair to one of the parties. In part, these principles mirrored a pre-capitalist economy characterised by local markets, relatively stable prices, a community sense of the "just price" and the virtual absence of complex executory bargains. The development of national markets after 1815, the increasing use of "futures" contracts (either to insure against fluctuations in the market or simply to speculate) and the needs of business for certainty and uniformity induced the courts to discard its judicial review of contracts where equity so demanded it and substitute in its place a body of doctrine embodying the philosophy of "buyer beware". The shift from basing contract upon communitarian notions of fairness and value to that more suited to the needs of market capitalism was brought about in two stages. In the early part of the nineteenth century, contract law doctrine increasingly adopted the position that all value was subjective and that the only basis of legal obligation was that the parties' minds "meet". By mid-century, legal doctrine was further transformed to accommodate the needs of trade and industry by grounding contractual obligations "objectively" in the light of

[2] p.101. A number of commentators have criticised this aspect of Horwitz's thesis and/or stressed that he provides no quantitive estimates of the changes in the distribution of wealth and power he posits: see, for example, Goldberg, (1979) 8 *J. Economic Issues* 200–205, 204–5; Williams, "Transforming American Law: Doubtful Economics Makes Doubtful History", (1978) 25 *U.C.L.A. Law Rev.* 1187–1218, 1206–1214. However, Horwitz can find some comfort in a recent study on American wealth holding by Edward Pessen. Pessen argues that that the rich in pre-Revolutionary America were already very rich; and that the Revolution actually consolidated their wealth. Pessen shows that in the period investigated by Horwitz, the rich in America were definitely getting richer; by 1850 wealth in the United States was more unequally distributed than ever before. See Pessen in *Wealth and the Wealthy in the Modern World* (ed. W.D. Rubinstein, 1980). How much, if any, of this American inequality was due to changes in the law remains to be established.

[3] The evidence for the analysis of contract has been questioned: see Baker, "From Sanctity of Contract to Reasonable Expectation?" (1979) *Current Legal Problems* 17–39, 19 and (1980) 43 *Modern Law Rev.* 467–9; and Simpson, "The Horwitz Thesis and the History of Contracts" (1979) 46 *Univ. Chicago Law Rev.* 533–601. In contrast, P.S. Atiyah's *The Rise and Fall of Freedom of Contract* (1979) affirms and develops a number of the theses espoused by Horwitz. Considerations of space forbids discussion of this controversy here: see further, Sugarman, "Horwitz, Simpson, Atiyah and the Transformation of Anglo-American Law", forthcoming.

commercial practice.[4] This embodied the fiction of freedom of contract: that equal bargaining power must normally be assumed to exist in all commercial transactions. In effect "... class legislation ..." (p.192) had been disguised. The new law favoured the "... commercially sophisticated insiders ..." (p.220) at the expense of labour and consumers. The doctrine of freedom of contract facilitated the incorporation of wide exemption clauses and in the context of employment contracts led to drastically reduced limits being imposed on the employees' right to sue their employer. The traditional aversion of the law to the principle of negotiability (as applied to bills of exchange and promissory notes) and usary almost dissolved under the impact of the newly ascendent contractual ideology. By 1850 this process of transformation was more or less complete.

However, it had generated both opposition and doubt within society. Pressure from a legal profession concerned to appear non-political, professionals and legal academics desirous to claim that their thought was "scientific" united with the obsession of both the legal profession and mercantile interests to depict law as neutral and thereby prevent other groups in society using the law-making power of the judges for more egalitarian purposes. After 1850, therefore, instrumentalism was supplanted by a more formalistic conception of law, one which de-emphasised judicial creativity and depicted law as impartial and apolitical.[5] Thus, legal doctrine was frozen at that very point in time at which it was most favourable to the newly emergent mercantile interests.

Horwitz argues that at the very heart of the metamorphosis of American law in the period 1780–1860 was an alliance between the legal profession and mercantile and entrepreneurial interests. Prior to 1790 lawyers and judges chiefly served the interests of the landed and were unsympathetic to the needs of commerce. After 1790, as it became clear where the future lucrative legal practice lay, the courts began to promote the emerging interests of trade and industry. As a result of this and other factors these interests increasingly looked to the courts for the facilitation and legitimation of their interests.

Comments

Although a number of strands of Horwitz's argument are not unfamiliar,[6] the breadth and scholarship of his work is prodigious. In attaching particular importance to the period *circa* 1780–1860, Horwitz follows in the trail of many American legal historians. However, he sets out to depict a very different landscape. At its simplest, most (but by no means all) histories of nineteenth century American law tend to fall within one of three interpretative frameworks. The first became known as the "economic interpretation" of legal history. Emerging in the early years of this century, this Americanised vulgar Marxism assumed that since devotion to economic self-interest was axiomatic, the class background of judges, legislators or winning

[4] The shift from standards of conduct conceptualised as private and ethics-based to standards of conduct conceptualised in a utilitarian and scientistic manner has also been discerned in American Administrative history: see Nelson, "Officeholding and Power-wielding: An Analysis of the Relationship Between Structure and Style in American Administrative History" (1976) 10 *Law and Society Rev.* 187–233. "Objective" or "external" standards of conduct came of age, jurisprudentially speaking, in Holmes's, *The Common Law* (1881). Here, Holmes sought to demonstrate historically that subjective or moralistic based standards of conduct had been replaced by objective standards of conduct so as to establish their legal pedigree and legitimacy.

[5] See further, Horwitz, "The Legacy of 1776 in Legal and Economic Thought", (1976) *J. of Law and Economics*, 621–632, 624 *et seq.*

[6] More recent examples would include, J.W. Hurst, *Law and the Conditions of Freedom in the Nineteenth-Century United States* (1956); K. Llewellyn, *The Common Law Tradition: Deciding Appeals* (1960); L.M. Friedman, *Contract Law in America, a Social and Economic Case Study* (1965) and G. Gilmore, *The Death of Contract* (1974).

litigants could explain the outcome of particular cases, or the enactment of specific legislation.[7]

Assailing this approach required little ingenuity. In the realm of legal history its most influential and ardent critic was Roscoe Pound.[8] In its place Pound posited a view of the development of an early nineteenth century law that was inherently schizophrenic. Pound celebrated the way in which, in the period after the Revolution, the courts recast English legal institutions and doctrines in a manner applicable to the conditions and needs of American society. This was the "formative" period or "Golden Age", as it was subsequently to be called, of American legal history.[9] But at the same time, Pound denied that much had substantially changed. As to the influence of economy and society, "tenacity of a taught legal tradition, is much more significant", he contended, "than the economic conditions of time and place."[10] In other words, historically speaking legal doctrine had evolved almost autonomously of economy and society. As Robert Gordon has observed:

> This had two bad effects: it prevented the leading advocate of a sociological legal history (and most of the legal historians who followed him) from seeing how much American law *could* quite satisfactorily be explained as the outcome of organised economic interest-group pressure. It also prevented them from inquiring further into what could not ....[11]

Pound's message was clear: the courts (and, by implication, the legal profession) had played a crucial and commendable role in the establishment of early modern American society.[12] Exercising that role, the courts (and, by implication, the legal profession) had been above "politics" and "economics". This exaltation of court-made law and legal professionalism, and the problematic of legal history it sought to advance and propagate resulted in "... a profoundly conservative interpretation of the role of law in ... society. Its basic categories contain fundamentally conservative political preferences dressed up in the neutral garb of expert and objective legal history ..."[13]

[7] The leading example is probably C.A. Beard's, *An Economic Interpretation of the Constitution of the United States* (1913). See also Bohlen, "The Rule in *Rylands v Fletcher*" (1911) 59 *Univ. Pennsylvania Law Rev.* 298–393 and 423–453; W. Nelles, "*Commonwealth v Hunt*", (1932) 32 *Columbia Law Rev.* 1128–1161.

[8] See, for example, *Interpretations of Legal History*, (1923) ch. 5; *The Formative Era of American Law* (1938) 83–91; "The Economic Interpretation and the Law of Torts" (1940) 53 *Harvard Law Rev.* 365–382.

[9] See R. Pound, *The Formative Era of American Law* (1938) and C.M. Haar (ed.), *The Golden Age of American Law* (1965).

[10] Pound, *ibid.*, p.82. Pound had greater difficulty explaining American legislation. For example, he conceded that, "Undoubtedly American legislation of the formative era may be understood to a large extent through a conventional economic interpretation": *Ibid.*, p.91.

[11] Gordon, "J. Willard Hurst and the Common Law Tradition in American Legal Historiography", (1975) 10 *Law and Society Rev.* 9–55, 40–1.

[12] See further Gordon, "Comment: John W. Johnson, 'Creativity and Adaptation: A Reassessment of American Jurisprudence, 1801–1857 and 1908–1940'," (1976) 7 *Rutgers-Camden Law J.* 648–654, 651 *et seq.*

[13] Horwitz, "The Conservative Tradition in the Writing of American Legal History" (1973) 7 *American J. Legal History* 275–294, 276. See generally Z. Bankowski and G. Mungham, *Images of Law* (1976) ch. 2; Duncanson, (1980) 15 *J. Society of Public Teachers of Law* 94–5; Gordon *op.cit. supra* n.11, 31 *et seq.*; Midgley, "The Role of Legal History" (1975) *Brit. J. Law and Society* 153–165.

A third interpretative framework has emerged since the 1950's, very largely as a result of the work of James Willard Hurst and his students.[14] Hurst's prolific output reflects both the strengths and weaknesses of American legal realism as applied to legal history. Amongst its virtues are its concern to grapple with the interaction between law and society, its emphasis on the need for historical work to transcend appeal court decision making and other litigation-centred activities; and its concern with how ordinary people perceived and utilised legal institutions. An important part of Hurst's writings constitutes a heady manifesto, a call for legal historians to re-direct their professional skills. His work has, undoubtedly, played a major role in the renaissance of modern American legal history. However, albeit unwittingly, the assumptions grounding Hurst's empirical work imbibes and reinforce a similar "world-view" to that of Pound's.

Sometimes in criticism, otherwise by way of approbation, Hurst details the ways in which legal change played a significant role in "the release of [productive] energy" in nineteenth century America.[15] What were the principal factors which induced that change? In essence, Hurst's methodology holds three factors were especially important in bringing law in line with the needs of industrial capitalism. First, he contends that Americans shared a desire to increase production, and that this was the pre-eminent value-consensus among Americans. As one commentator put it, he portrays "... the larger American society as communities of expectant capitalists."[16] Second, a further value-consensus was important. This he calls the "ideal of constitutionalism", that is, "... the desirability of broadly dispersed power, on the primacy of a popularly elected legislature, and on the availability of the courts to redress individual grievances ...."[17] Hurst recognises that this ideal "... often failed of realisation",[18] and that the demands of production and utility in practice often served to justify "... committing to private hands legally protected control over the bulk of economic resources."[19] Thirdly, Hurst contends that "drift" was significant in shaping the law. This term embraces a number of meanings. For example, it denotes the subordination of long-term gains to short-term limited ends, inflexibility as a result of habit and tradition, and the "... sloth, bafflement and weariness ..." which impedes individuals from undertaking rational planning.[20]

Like Pound, Hurst's analytic framework marginalises both the role played by economic interest groups in shaping American law; and the existence of divisions within American society concerning the economic, social and legal transition that characterised nineteenth century American society. As a result, legal development often appears de-politicised and antiseptic. Hurst probably takes us as far as one can go in milking a consensus-value framework of legal development from a historical perspective. Although a considerable advance on Pound's work,

[14] On Hurst's work see Gordon *op.cit. supra* n. 11, 44 *et seq.*; Scheiber, "At the Borderland of Law and Economic History" (1970) 75 *American History Rev.* 744–756; and Tushnet, "Lumber and the Legal Process", (1972) *Wisconsin Law Rev.* 114–132.

Lawrence Friedman is probably Hurst's most distinguished student: for a critical assessment of Friedman's pluralistic problematic see Tushnet, "Perspectives on the Development of American Law: A Critical Review of Friedman's 'A History of American Law' ", (1977) *Wisconsin Law Rev.* 81–110.

[15] See, for example, Hurst *op.cit. supra* n. 6 and *Law and Economic Growth: the Legal History of the Lumber Industry in Wisconsin, 1836–1915* (1964).

[16] Scheiber, *supra* n. 14, 747.

[17] Hurst, "Legal Elements in United States History" in *Law in American History* (ed. D. Fleming and B. Bailyn, 1971) 3–92, 3.

[18] *Id.*

[19] Hurst, *op.cit. supra* n. 6, 6.

[20] Hurst, *Law and Economic Growth: the Legal History of the Lumber Industry in Wisconsin, 1836–1915* (1964), 140.

ultimately Hurst also tends to convey a victor's view of legal history in which consensus is exaggerated and contemporary opposition to legal, economic and social development is given short-shrift.[21]

How does all this relate to Horwitz? Horwitz's work can be best understood in the context of the present conjuncture of orthodox Anglo-American legal history and its particular theoretical and ideological underpinnings. This is because *The Transformation of American Law* is not only a history. As I read Horwitz's work, it *also* represents an attempt to tease out and question the assumptions underlying orthodox legal history and expose the conservative ideology that lurks therein. His work is pedagogical and revisionist; it substitutes an alternative view of a period already much idealised in American legal historiography. His emphasis on the transformation of American law primarily as a result of the pressures of economic interests is, therefore, a conscious challenge to consensus legal historiography which regarded law as almost wholly autonomous from society and economy. By emphasising that this metamorphosis occurred in the face of resistance and disquiet his study constitutes an important counter to earlier Whiggish studies which have treated economic growth and industrialisation as unproblematical, simply reflecting a solid consensus of almost *volksgeist* proportions. As a result he rejects conventional historical wisdom which would take modernisation, uniformity and certainty to be inevitable and unqualified goods involving no underlying political or economic assumptions. Repeatedly he asks the question which often other legal historians have eschewed: in whose interest were laws forged? This is closely related to one of Horwitz's prime objectives: to challenge the tendency in orthodox historiography (and indeed legal scholarship generally) of treating law as morally and politically value-free.[22] Law, for Horwitz, was inevitably an active participant in the process of economic growth, the distribution of wealth and political power.

Horwitz's assessment of the consequences of the transformation of American law is "Dark and Doestoyevskyan".[23] In the light of Horwitz's researches, previous work which portrayed the period *circa* 1780–1860 as the "Golden Age" of American law appears complacent.[24] The achievement of the law economically, socially and politically is partially discredited. The sullied age that Horwitz portrays echoes (as does his title) Karl Polanyi's history of the desolation inflicted upon society by the growth of the "market economy".[25] Horwitz's work provides ammunition with which to challenge those who have represented the early nineteenth century

[21] Hurst's recent work has attempted to give greater attention to the relationship between economic conflict and legal change: see *Law and Social Order in the United States*, (1977) ch. "Consensus and Conflict" and "Old and New Dimensions of Research in United States Legal History" (1979) 23 *American J. Legal History* 1–20, esp. 9 *et seq.* However, this work does not represent a fundamental shift in his position, as his 1979 paper *Id.* testifies.

[22] See xii–xiii; also Horwitz *op.cit. supra* n. 5 and n. 13.

[23] Presser, "Revising the Conservative Tradition: Towards A New American Legal History", (1977) 52 *New York Univ. Law Rev.* 700–725, 700.

[24] An example of this previous work is A.H. Chroust, *The Rise of the Legal Profession in America* (1965).

[25] *The Great Transformation: The Political and Economic Origins of Our Time* (1944).

Ironically, Polanyi's work is being appropriated by those "new" economic historians who seek to replace the market model of resource allocation with that of a transaction cost model: see North, "Markets and Other Allocation Systems in History" (1977) 6 *J. European Economic History* 703–716.

as a period of *laissez-faire* in which law constituted a "spontaneous order."[26] In this sense, his study is a monumental effort of de-mystification.

The role of law in the process of capital accumulation has in the past been barely considered.[27] Horwitz's analysis directs attention as to how the legal system encouraged the transition from community rights to a reified conception of property ownership which defined labour as a "marketable commodity" and placed large property owners in a more advantageous position relative to small property owners. His study confirms the view that the modern law of contract and its ideology is historically closely related to classical economic theory; and that it dominated private law and practice during much of the nineteenth century.[28] As in the pioneering work of Willard Hurst and Lawrence Friedman, Horwitz's study represents a significant re-orientation in the sense that American historians, sociologists and criminologists have tended to concentrate on public law, i.e., constitutional and criminal law.[29] As he contends, private law (tort, contract, property and commercial law) constitutes "... an infinitely more typical pattern of the use of law .... By thus focusing on private law we can study the more regular instances in which law, economy and society interacted." (p.xii)

Whilst Horwitz's work is powerfully suggestive it is also open to question on a number of fronts. Horwitz's targets are clearly articulated: the conservative ideology of consensus historiography; and (implicitly) the blandness of pluralistic and other problematics which submerge causation. In his laudable desire to differentiate the materialistic wood from the trees, his more general conclusions tend to be premised upon an instrumentalist interpretative framework. This framework by definition imbibes a simplistic and ultimately reductionist view of the relationship between law and economy.[30] In all fairness, it must be stressed that there is in his study an important dichotomy between, on the one hand, the general conclusions he draws from his material and, on the other hand, his detailed analysis of the re-classification of specific legal doctrine. The former tends to portray legal development as simply generated by a

[26] See F.A. Hayek, *The Constitution of Liberty* (1960) and *Law, Legislation and Liberty* (1973).

For a thorough-going attempt to apply Hayek's notion of a spontaneous order to the realm of modern American legal history, in part, in order to criticise Horwitz's work, see R.V. Bridwell and R.V. Whitten, *The Constitution and the Common Law* (1977).

For an extremely crude application of Hayek's concept to English legal history see Hartwell, "Legal Change, Legal Reform and Economic Growth in England Before and During the Industrial Revolution", (1978) *International Economic History Congress* 216–222. For a detailed critique of the views there espoused see Sugarman, "Max Hartwell on Law and Economy During England's Industrial Revolution", (forthcoming).

[27] For a rare example, see Anderson, "The Attorney and the Early Capital Market in Lancashire" in *Capital Formation in the Industrial Revolution* (ed. F. Crouzet, 1972) 223–255.

[28] See *loc.cit. supra* n. 6. Also Kessler, "Contracts of Adhesion — Some Thoughts About Freedom of Contract" (1943) 43 *Columbia Law Rev.* 629–652; K. Llewellyn, "What Price Contract — An Essay in Perspective" (1931) 30 *Yale Law J.* 701–729 and J.P. Dawson, "Economic Duress — An Essay in Perspective" (1947) 45 *Michigan Law Rev.* 253–284.

[29] Re. Hurst see *loc.cit. supra* n. 15; re. Friedman, *loc.cit. supra* n. 6.

[30] Cf. Griffiths, "Is Law Important?" (1979) 54 *New York University Law Rev.* 339–374 and Summers, "Naive Instrumentalism and the Law" in *Law, Morality and Society* (ed. P.M.S. Hacker and J. Raz, 1977) 119–131.

wilful conspiracy between mercantile and legal interests.[31] However, these broad assertions are undercut by other statements that stress the influence of a multitude of complex economic changes on law, such as changes in technology and transportation. Thus, the more general Horwitz's assertions, the greater his tendency to deny the complex, contradictory and at times fortuitous way that history is made. In effect, one form of Whigg history has been supplanted by another. Of course, courts are not unfettered in their ability to shape the law to suit particular interests. The accident of litigation, the individual judge and counsel concerned, the shared expectations which circumscribe the judge's role, are but some of the restraints Horwitz tends to ignore.[32] As a consequence of casting his general thesis in an instrumentalist mould, Horwitz is forced to treat the relationship between the policy goals of courts and legislatures and the actual operation of law in practice as less problematical than it really is. Even when the specific end-results for which rules are created are not ambiguous or contradictory, in practice they may be put to use so as to negate the very purposes originally envisaged. For example, a legal rule may be developed in response to the needs of one section of the community only to be borrowed, or even turned against its originators, by another.[33] It is this "double-edged" sense of "the dialectics of history" which Eugene Genovese and E.P. Thompson have recently been at pains to stress; and which an instrumentalist analytical framework inevitably obscures and mystifies.[34]

Another unfortunate consequence of Horwitz's instrumentalism is his cursory treatment of law's ideological dimensions and the relative autonomy of law. Mostly, he conflates the whole sphere of the ideological and the relative autonomy of the law with ideology in one of its meanings, namely, as a "trick" which mystifies class self-interest. (p.viii) However, recent historical research in both America and England has, albeit in different ways, highlighted that law may develop relatively autonomously of economy.[35] As regards the law's ideological dimensions, there are a number of overlapping issues upon which it is unfortunate that Horwitz does not provide much needed historical data. These issues include: the extent to which different interest groups attached different symbolic significance to the instrumental concerns of laws; the role of law in institutionalising popular consent; the role of the state as "moral educator"; the extent to which legal ideology successfully penetrated the consciousness of the different interest groups and was modified and adapted to diverse conditions of existence; the relationship between dominant and legal ideology; and the extent to which legal ideology *limited* as well as legitimised the process of domination Horwitz describes. To take an example, "the triumph of contractarian ideology" (p.211) appears as a static, full-blown, end-product which simply mirrors instrumental concerns, rather than as a dynamic property whose form,

[31] Hay's attempt to define a ruling class conspiracy in such a way as to constitute an accurate historical description and not a deterministic epithet, might equally be used to justify Horwitz's thesis that something close to a conspiracy grounded the transformation of American law. See Hay, "Property, Authority and the Criminal Law" in *Albion's Fatal Tree* (ed. D. Hay *et al*, 1975) 17–63, 52–56. On Hay's methodology see Sugarman, "Theory and Practice in Law and History: A Prologue to the Study of the Relationship Between Law and Economy from a Socio-Historical Perspective" in *Law, State and Society* (ed. R. Fryer *et al*, 1981).

[32] See Tushnet, *loc.cit. supra* n. 14 (1977), 89, 90 and 93.

[33] See, for example, Neale in *Feudalism, Capitalism and Beyond* (ed. E. Kamenka and R.S. Neale) 84–103.

[34] E. Genovese, *Roll, Jordan, Roll* (1974) 25–49 and E.P. Thompson, "The Poverty of Theory" in *The Poverty of Theory and Other Essays* (1978), 288.

[35] For example, Klare, "Judicial Deradicalisation of the Wagner Act and the Origin of Modern Legal Consciousness, 1937–1941", (1978) 62 *Minnesota Law Rev.* 265–310; Tushnet, "The American Law of Slavery, 1810–1860" (1975) *Law and Society Rev.* 119–184; and White "The Intellectual Origins of Torts in America" (1977) 86 *Yale Law J.* 671–693.

substance and significance is constructed and built upon over the course of time by competing groups within and between classes in particular conflicts and struggles. What is omitted is a sense of limits of the powers of the power holders and those with whom they negotiated, and their respective use of negotiation, persuasion, threats and direct coercion.

Horwitz rightly argues that changes in legal doctrine "... reflected a variety of aspects of social struggle. That the conflict was turned into legal channels (and thus rendered somewhat mysterious) should not obscure the fact that it took place ..." (p.xvi) But his instrumentalism requires him to concentrate upon unmasking the struggle for power that underlay the ostensible "consensus" rather than also enquire into *how* private law mediated and navigated among the conflicting interests, simultaneously disguising the causes of conflict itself, whilst reinforcing and legitimising pre-existing inequalities. Perhaps his commendable desire to counter the prevailing view of the legal past, caused him to excessively de-emphasise the existence of "consensus" and, thereby, leave unexamined the role of the law in achieving that "consensus". In other words, he has much to tell us about the role of law in inducing social and economic change, but little about the role of law in the *production* of the *new* consensus or "social reality" that of necessity will accompany that transformation.

Another product of Horwitz's instrumentalism is his simplistic treatment of the divisions within American society: the men of commerce and industry and their legal allies versus "farmers, workers, consumers, and other less powerful groups". (pp.253–4) Unfortunately, these divisions are nowhere elaborated and refined; nor are they rooted in concrete social and economic historical data. Indeed, it is debatable how meaningful categorisation of such generality and historical abstraction really is. As at *circa* 1800 it is arguable, for instance, that those who regarded themselves as "weak" and oppressed included those same professional and mercantile groups whom Horwitz treats unproblematically as the "powerful". Until recently, historians of "the left", like their counterparts in criminology and sociology tended to concentrate upon the role played by law in the resolution and legitimation of *inter-class* conflict and correspondingly ignored the role of law *viz à viz intra-class* conflict. Whilst Horwitz's more general pronouncements also succumb to this error, his detailed researches do provide valuable data on the role of law in the resolution and legitimation of *intra-class* disputes too.

Horwitz's monolithic treatment of class also mars his discussion of the legal profession. As Maxwell Bloomfield's recent essays testify, the American legal profession of *circa* 1776–1876 was not a cohesive, homogeneous group.[36] Bloomfield's portraits reflect a diverse profession made up of philistine "plumbers" through to those who regarded themselves as cultured intellectuals. These contradictions and our lack of historical data make general characterisation of the American legal profession extremely difficult.

What is missing from Horwitz's picture of legal and economic transformation is the actual social, political, economic and religious clashes of the day. For example, would his portrayal of the rise of instrumentalism have appeared as irresistible if it had been related to contemporary controversies concerning the role of the judiciary in American society?[37] What kinds of opposition did the transformation of American law arouse?[38] Unfortunately, Horwitz's view of the relationship between law and economy appears to be wholly derived from legal sources, mostly law reports. Arguably, therefore, Horwitz draws conclusions that go far beyond his data. His more general conclusions must be treated as hypotheses whose proof is still, for the

[36] *American Lawyers in a Changing Society, 1776–1876* (1976).

[37] See, for example, R.E. Ellis, *The Jeffersonian Crisis: Courts and Politics in the Young Republic* (1971).

[38] Cf. recent historical work on American working-class culture and industrialisation, for example, H.G. Gutman, *Work, Culture and Society in Industrialising America* (1977); A. Dawley, *Class and Community: the Industrial Revolution in Lynn* (1976) and D. Montgomery, *Worker's Control in America: Studies in the History of Work, Technology and Labor Struggles* (1979).

most part, a matter of conjecture. Furthermore, because the bulk of his data derives from law reports the definition of "law" implicitly underlying his work is artificially circumscribed. As Hurst's work has stressed, any real understanding of the operation of law in practice requires that the focus of study shift from court decisions to, for instance, the actual practices and norms of regulatory bodies, companies and individuals.[39] Horwitz's exclusive use of "legal" material perhaps explains the arguably exaggerated view he has of the importance of law to trade and industry in the planning of their relationships. All the recent historical and empirical evidence suggests that businessmen pay little attention to the rules of commercial law, in a wide-range of situations; and that they have often shared a strong aversion to things "legal".[40] If this was the case, Horwitz's assumption that business and the legal profession tended to see their immediate interests as convergent requires some qualification.

Inevitably, for a book dealing with American legal history 1780–1860, the bulk of Horwitz's data derives from those eastern states that possessed vigorous commercial centres, especially Massachussets. Might we discover that those American states whose economies significantly differed from their industrialising counterparts in the east did not reproduce congruent legal systems? Indeed, is the legal change which Horwitz identifies an immanent dimension of the process of industrialisation in capitalist societies? If so, we might expect to discover analagous doctrinal re-classification occurring in other countries experiencing the rise of industrial capitalism. Despite the relative dearth of English data, the recent work of Richard Danzig and Patrick Atiyah provides strong comparative evidence in support of Horwitz's detailed analysis of the conceptual restructuring of the foundations of modern contract law and its close (but not symbiotic) relationship with the needs of the judiciary and entrepreneurs.[41]

By emphasising the *transformation* of American law, economy and society in the period 1790–1850, Horwitz exaggerates the nature and extent of the break between colonial and post-Revolutionary America and their law. Thus, a number of historians of colonial law have characterised much of this period as one of *transition* during which emergent and residual definitions of property and interest groups co-existed.[42] Indeed, Horwitz's detailed researches themselves (as distinct from his more general statements) testify that legal change in the early nineteenth century was slow; and that by the mid-century the metamorphosis of a number of legal doctrines still remained significantly incomplete. However, a methodology which stresses the centrality of "change" rather than "continuity" not only has the virtue of breaking with the dominant tradition in legal historiography. An historical account which thrusts "transformation" to the fore can also be justified in that "... the important thing is not to demonstrate (what we all know) that the garment of Clio is a seamless one, but to distinguish the different patterns into which it is woven."[43]

Horwitz also exaggerates both the communitarian nature of colonial America and the materialistic nature of the early post-revolutionary period. Here, perhaps, Horwitz was too influenced by the now partially discredited work of those who in a nostalgic and static fashion have portrayed colonial Massachussets as characterised by a political, economic and ethical

[39] See, for example, Hurst, "The Law in United States History", (1960) *Proceedings of the American Philosophical Society*, 518–26.

[40] See Friedman, *loc.cit. supra* n. 6; Beale and Dugdale, "Contracts Between Businessmen", (1975) *Brit. J. Law and Society* 45–60; Macaulay, "Non-Contractual Relations in Business" (1963) 28 *American Sociological Rev.* 55–66; Ferguson, "Legal Ideology and Commercial Interest", (1977) *Brit.J. Law and Society* 18–38.

[41] Danzig, "*Hadley v Baxendale*: A Study in the Industrialisation of the Law", (1975) 4 *J. Legal Studies* 249–284 and Atiyah *loc.cit. supra* n. 3. But cf. Baker, Simpson and Sugarman *loc.cit.supra* n.3.

[42] See, for example, Katz, "Looking Backward: The Early History of American Law" (1966) 33 *Univ. Chicago Law Rev.* 867–884.

[43] G. Barraclough, *An Introduction to Contemporary History* (1967), 19.

consensus.[44] Again, a number of historians have stressed the capitalist practices and attitudes of some areas of colonial New England.[45] Indeed, any attempt to generalise about the nature and application of law by the Colonial courts of, for instance, Massachussets is fraught with difficulty in that their judges did not regularly deliver written opinions.

Another frustrating consequence of Horwitz's instrumentalism is that the nature of state intervention in early industrial capitalism often has to be gleaned by way of implication. Horwitz is rightly sceptical of the value of contrasting *laissez-faire* with state intervention.(p.xv) As his study testifies, this dichotomy is misconceived "... since even *laissez-faire* capitalism depends, for the conditions of its existence, upon the state".[46] Thus, we must not assume that the role played by the state in the rise of the market economy in the eighteenth and nineteenth centuries was less vital than in contemporary state monopoly capitalism.[47] Unfortunately, the implication of Horwitz's wider statements is that the state was no more than a tool of capital — a characterisation which simply will not do. In history, as in theory, the problematical character of the state is increasingly being recognised. This has important ramifications for modern legal history. The formation of the modern state, the nature of state power and the role of law therein have been neglected by legal historians; and yet, these questions are especially important in understanding the origins and nature of the world in which we live today. Fortunately, E.P. Thompson's work on the English state in the eighteenth and early nineteenth centuries, Poulantzas's neo-Gramscian work on the state, hegemony and relative autonomy and recent studies on the capitalist state from a theoretical and historical perspective provide important building blocks for the future development of historical work on state formation, capitalism and law.[48]

It is important to see Horwitz's contrast between periods of instrumentalist and formalistic styles of judicial reasoning as both drawing upon and contributing to an on-going debate in which "... conflicting assertions abound."[49] Karl Llewellyn's work on appeal court decision-making stressed the "period style" of judgements. "I am referring", he said, "to a way of thought and work, not to a way of writing."[50] Like Pound, Llewellyn regarded the period

[44] See M. Zuckerman, *Peacable Kingdoms* (1970) and W.E. Nelson, *The Americanization of the Common Law* (1975).

For devastating criticisms of these works, see Zainaldin, "The New Legal History" (1978) 73 *Northwestern University Law Rev.* 205–225 and Zoebel (1977) 50 *New England Q.* 138–149 re. Nelson; and Murrin (1972) *History and Theory* 245–254 and Allen, "The Zuckerman Thesis and the Process of Legal Rationalization in Provincial Massachusetts", (1972) 29 *William and Mary Q.* 443–460 re Zuckerman.

[45] See, for example, B. Bailyn, *The New England Merchants in the 17th Century* (1955) and Lockridge, "Social Change in the Meaning of the American Revolution" (1973) 6 *J. Social History* 402–413.

[46] McIntosh, "The State and the Oppression of Women" in *Feminism and Materialism* (1978) 260, cited by P. Corrigan, in *Capitalism, State Formation and Marxist Theory: Historical Investigations* (ed. P. Corrigan, 1980) xxi–xxii.

[47] See further, *Id.*

[48] Thompson, "The Peculiarities of the English", in *The Poverty of Theory and Other Essays* (1978) 35–91; N. Poulantzas, *State, Power, Socialism* (1978) and "The Capitalist State" (1976) 95 *New Left Rev.*; the work discussed in B. Jessop and S. Stewart, *The Capitalist State* (1980); Corrigan, *op.cit. supra* n.46; T. Skocpol, *States and Social Revolutions* (1979); and P. Fitzpatrick, *Law and State in Papua New Guinea* (1980).

[49] R. Stevens, *Law and Politics: The House of Lords as a Judicial Body, 1800–1976* (1979) 77 n. 1.

[50] *Op.cit. supra* n. 6, 36.

1820–1860 as the highpoint of the "Grand Style" of the Common Law, when the courts overtly modified or invented doctrine where this was "needed". This style of reasoning was subsequently eclipsed by the "Formal Style" of judicial reasoning, akin to what Horwitz calls, "the rise of legal formalism". Since Llewellyn advanced his thesis, a number of American historians have resorted to analogous categories in order to distinguish discrete period styles of judicial law making.[51]

The problem with using terminology such as instrumentalism and formalism is that they are no more than a very general shorthand. In this respect, they resemble the term *laissez-faire*. Their meaning can often only be gleaned by way of inference. And there is no uniform usage of these terms. For instance, sometimes Horwitz seems to refer to the *style* or *form* of judicial reasoning (for example, whether judgements were overtly teleological, disencumbered by judicial precedent). On other occasions, his usage denotes the conscious use of doctrinal reclassification by judges to further certain *substantive* economic and political goals (for example, whether the courts were actively seeking to change the economic balance of power, or freeze it). Unfortunately, these two discrete meanings are not carefully distinguished. The result is sometimes confusing. Moreover, as yet, no agreement has emerged as to the precise chronology of these period styles, nor, indeed, as to whether such categorisation is an historically accurate description of judicial activity during the relevant periods. For example, some commentators have argued that instrumentalism continued after 1860; others have questioned the grounds offered to explain the rise of so-called formalism after 1850; whilst others have challenged the view that the late nineteenth century American legal system was "... the vessel of a legal formalism that did little to affect (certainly nothing to impede), economic development."[52] Horwitz's characterisations must be seen in the context of this debate. Certainly, like Llewellyn, his impressions seem to have some basis in fact. I suspect that whilst the style of judicial reasoning did become more relatively formalistic as the second half of the nineteenth century wore on, Horwitz exaggerates the divergencies between the styles of judicial reasoning during the former and latter halves of the nineteenth century. "Of course, there were many variations between court and court. Styles of decision were not uniform; neither was there a single conception of the judicial role."[53]

Horwitz frequently relies upon Blackstone's *Commentaries* as an accurate account of the "posessive individualism" of English law in the second half of the eighteenth century.[54] This is then measured against an American law that is increasingly less concerned with absolute property rights and more concerned with facilitating economic growth. Difficulties derive from this method, however, in that Blackstone's portrayal of English law has been criticised an an inaccurate or, at the very least, distorted synthesis deficient in detail, ignoring the realities of practice and idealising the *status quo* in the face of increasing change -legal, social and economic. As a result, Horwitz's portrayal of English pre-industrial law is too static; for English law too, it is more accurate to view the period *circa* 1750–1850 as one of "transition". During this period alternative forms of property and legal doctrine co-existed simultaneously at the same time that conceptions of property and the role of the jury were changing.[55]

[51] See, for example, Nelson, "The Impact of the Antislavery Movement Upon Styles of Judicial Reasoning in 19th Century America", (1974) 87 *Harvard Law Rev.* 513–549. Cf. Scheiber, "Instrumentalism and Property Rights" (1975) *Wisconsin Law Rev.* 1–17; R. Cover, *Justice Accused* (1975) 197–259; and Stevens, "Unexplored Avenues in Comparative Anglo-American Legal History", (1974) *Tulane Law Rev.* 1086–1098, 1093–97.

[52] Keeler, "Business History and Legal History", (1979) *Business History Rev.* 296–303, 297; and see the material *Id.*

[53] L. Friedman, *A History of American Law* (1973) 333.

[54] Sir W. Blackstone, *Commentaries on the Laws of England* (1765–1769).

[55] P.S. Atiyah *loc.cit. supra* n. 3 is more satisfactory on this account, than Horwitz.

Conclusion

None of my reservations, however, must be taken as detracting from the undoubted importance of Horwitz's monograph both as a stimulating and provocative portrait of law and economy; and a remarkable research resource for students of law, economics, history and the sociology of law.

Horwitz's work undoubtedly constitutes a significant event in the historiography of modern Anglo-American law. It represents an important attempt to depart from the analytic frameworks premising the work of Pound, Hurst and the bulk of conventional legal history. In particular, the relationship between legal development and economic interest group conflict has been vigorously re-asserted as a central feature and, therefore, concern of modern legal history. In this respect, Horwitz's work harks back to earlier "economic interpretations" of law. However, his work is much more insightful; and it involves a much larger sample of cases and legislation than has previously been investigated. Whether he has been wholly successful in breaking with earlier interpretations of the period 1780–1860 is a moot point. His instrumentalism and the case-centred nature of the bulk of his work has produced a study which may not be quite as novel in substance and in method as he may have originally envisaged. This would require an analytic framework more sensitive to the manifold functions and meanings of law, both instrumental and ideological, and which transcended the base-superstructure metaphor. E.P. Thompson's recent emphasis on the imbrication of law throughout society and economy is salutory in this respect.[56] At the level of method, there is a hint in Horwitz's more recent work that he has outgrown instrumentalism and now imbibes a more subtle problematic.[57] If this is the case, then given his formidable talent his future contributions to modern legal history could be very great.

For too long English legal scholarship has tended to be ahistorical. The real value of Horwitz's work on this side of the Atlantic may be to convince those who previously wrote-off legal history as irrelevant, of the importance of the socio-historical perspective in furthering our understanding of the processes of doctrinal innovation, growth and decay; and stimulate long overdue research on the relationship between law and industrialisation in eighteenth and nineteenth century Britain. The kind of questions his work suggests for British historians include: was the law and legal institutions of central importance to business and trade in 19th century Britain; what were the attitudes of business to law; to what extent did they utilise and manipulate legal forms and institutions; what was the relationship between the world of business and the legal profession; did the style of judicial reasoning in Britain reflect a shift from instrumentalism to formalism; it has been argued that economic inequality in Britain increased in the 19th century up to the 1850's levelling out thereafter: if this is correct, how much of British inequality was due to inherent aspects of industrialisation, how much to changes in law, how much to demographic forces, and how much to chance;[58] how did the legal profession and legal education change in response to industrialisation; to what extent did the demands of legal professionalism and technique cause the law and legal institutions to operate in a fashion where, at least in the short term, law appeared relatively autonomous of economy; what was the relationship between legal change and the formation of the modern state; what was the attitude of the working-classes to the law, how did the law affect them and how did their conceptions of legality change as the 19th century wore on? These are just a few of the more general (not to say, cosmic) questions prompted by Horwitz's work, as applied to the British context. These are also questions touching upon issues that British historians in the past have been notably deficient in addressing.

[56] See Thompson *loc.cit. supra* n. 34.

[57] See, Horwitz, "The Rule of Law: An Unqualified Human Good?" (1977) *Yale Law J.* 561–66.

[58] See, for example, Williamson, "Earnings Inequality in 19th Century Britain", (1980) *J. Economic History* 457–475.

Furthermore, by overtly challenging consensus-value and pluralistic accounts of the legal past, Horwitz's work requires legal historians to address a host of historiographical and theoretical issues which conventional legal history, at least in Britain, has almost wholly neglected:[59] For example, to what extent can, and should, legal historians borrow the concepts and methods of other social sciences; what are the methodological and theoretical problems that arise once one seeks to explain legal phenomena other than by distinctively "legal" phenomena; how is it possible to reconcile the need for generalisation and abstraction with the necessity for the extensive and detailed research of primary materials (legal and extra-legal)? In sum, the ultimate virtue of Horwitz's work — and the work of some of his other North American colleagues[60] — may be to spur us to consider anew what legal historians are doing; and what it is they should be doing.

DAVID SUGARMAN*

*Principal Lecturer in Law, Middlesex Polytechnic.

[59] Cf. the material in *loc.cit. supra* n. 3; Duncanson, (1976) 39 *Modern Law Rev*. 741–742; and Sugarman, *loc.cit. supra* n. 3 and n. 31.

[60] The work of Robert Gordon, Karl Klare, Duncan Kennedy, J.T. Noonan and Mark Tushnet, for example, is particularly suggestive because it treats "history" and "theory" as inseparable. See Gordon *loc.cit. supra* n. 11 and n. 12; Klare *loc.cit. supra* n. 35 and "Law-Making As Praxis" (1979) *Telos* 123–135; Kennedy, "Form and Substance in Private Law Adjudication" (1976) *Harvard Law Rev*. 1685–1778 and "The Structure of Blackstone's Commentaries" (1979) *Buffalo Law Rev*. 205–382; Noonan, *Persons and Masks of the Law* (1976); and Tushnet, *loc.cit. supra* n. 14 and n. 35.

All page references are to *The Transformation of American Law, 1780–1860* unless otherwise indicated.

[10]

Review Essays

An Exchange on Critical Legal Studies between Robert W. Gordon and William Nelson

Letter to William Nelson from Robert W. Gordon

I have been reading the book collecting the bibliographic essays on legal historiography that you and John Reid have been contributing since 1962 to the *Annual Survey of American Law.*[1] Although I'm writing to you because of an outraged response to one of the chapters in your book,[2] I must allow that it is nice to see all these pieces in one place, because for years they have provided one of the most useful (if inevitably idiosyncratic) reference guides to current work in our field ("I'm glad," I've often said to myself, "that *somebody* is reading all this stuff").

In its early years the series could also be relied on for an acidic stream of comments on the abuses of legal history by lawyers and the courts; although more recently, as the authorship shifted from Reid to you, I thought I saw a definite alteration in this line. Reid's early essays (for 1962-66) are savagely critical of the two common lawyers' modes of historiography: 1) "originalism," in which the lawyer seeks to establish the "original intent" of the framers of a text as defining its appropriate current meaning, and in so doing researches only the formal sources surrounding the text and usually ends up reading it anachronistically, as if it had been uttered in his own time; and 2) "Whig history," in which the lawyer draws a trend line between old law and modern law and sees the past as an embryonic form of the present, or the present as a fulfillment of the past. Reid is especially irritated by the attempts of the Warren Court and its supporters to adduce historical authority for the liberal civil rights decisions of the 1960s (51, 53, 70, 80-81, 85). It is not completely clear to me whether Reid believes that lawyers have invented bad history, where they could have used good history instead, to justify current decisions, or more sweepingly that good history can

Law and History Review Spring 1988, Vol. 6, No. 1

never serve as current authority because faithful reconstruction will invariably yield an unusable product—will yield a view of the original text's meanings as multiple, complex, ambiguous, and dependent upon an alien and vanished context. According to this latter view the only fair instrumental use of history would be negative and critical: to explode any pretended historical justifications for current practices by showing how much times had changed and historical meanings had varied, to demonstrate in short the *irrelevance* of the past.

Your own early essays (1966, 1967) continue this vein of historicist critique, pointing out that modern lawyers often behave as if past legal texts were intended to address the same problems as their current forms, whereas in fact their framers were often asking different questions entirely (e.g., 121-24: if the First Amendment were only intended to restrict federal power to regulate speech, historical exegesis cannot inform us how far its framers favored libertarian or restrictionist views of free speech). By 1973–74, however, your own historicism has started to trouble you. Your worry seems to be that a "realist" commitment to studying law in social context entails the view that law is determined by that context, that its rules "merely reflect current policy preferences of politically dominant groups" (185), as opposed to the "formalist" or "idealist" view that law is the product of a profession rationally working out its principles through cases. If historians promote this sort of "realism," they will encourage judges to believe that "the law takes its content solely from the political and economic goals of society" (leading them slavishly to follow the dominant will as they did in the Japanese internment cases), whereas what judges really should do is to "incorporat[e] into our jurisprudence autonomous moral values that can serve as restraints upon legal decision-making" (194). How can historians help locate these values? Not by discovering them in the "original understandings" of legal texts—you continue to think that is a naive and fruitless venture. But: "Historians may . . . be able to help by identifying those legal traditions which are an essential part of our legal culture. For if those traditions can be identified, judges and other decisionmakers . . . will feel constrained to follow them in order to avoid initiating revolutionary changes in that culture" (197). One such tradition that you suggest is likely to be revealed by historical study is that of the "hegemony of the individual" (200) over nature, government, and the community.

Despite many problems[3] I might want to raise with your way of formulating it, I sympathize in principle with your program. What you seem to be proposing is a sort of method not so much for history as for historical jurisprudence: What uses should lawyers and judges (and legislators and administrators too—for some reason we keep forgetting them) make of history? Just appreciating its historicity, its inability to speak directly and unambiguously to present problems, while very important, isn't enough. Policymakers live in history whether they want to or not; and they can't help appealing to history for inspiration or justification in a society such as ours in which certain mythic moments (The Migrations, The Founding) and teleologies (The Democratic Mission) have been endowed with significant cultural authority. Decisionmakers are constantly remaking the past, synthesizing traditions that provide normative standpoints, sources of public values, for justifying or criticizing current policies. As the Progressive paradigm that so long dominated official-legal discourse has begun to fade out, scholars of various views have begun to propose alternative interpretations of our historical "traditions." Among the most interesting of these are: 1) The Chicago School's resurrection of a (considerably mythified) pre-Progressive common-law laissez-faire Era as a Golden Age of Liberty and Efficiency, from whence all regulatory activity since represents an unfortunate Fall;[4] 2) Bruce Ackerman's attempt to mediate between the poles of a pure universalism (our constitutional values have always remained the same) on the one hand and pure contingency (they are always in flux, so history teaches nothing) on the other, through the notion that the U.S. has had three different Constitutions, each produced by a separate crisis of revolutionary upheaval (the Founding; Civil War and Reconstruction; the New Deal);[5] 3) and the efforts of Frank Michelman, Richard Parker, Cass Sunstein, and Mark Tushnet to build an alternative jurisprudence upon America's "republican" traditions, which stress the values of civic commitment, a rough equality of property, and participatory politics in counterpoint to some "liberal" conceptions of law as primarily an instrument for the promotion of individual self-interest.

A fourth novel source of perspectives upon the American legal past, developed in the service of current political and jurisprudential aims, is the historical work of scholars affiliated with the critical legal studies movement. And it's this work that I'm primarily concerned to write you about, because it's this work (nominally, anyway) that suddenly becomes central to your book (chapter 16: Report for 1981-84) as the object of a fierce, forty-two page polemic of denunciation, comparing "traditional" and "critical" legal historiography to the severe discredit of the latter brand. When I saw myself appointed as an "eloquent spokesman" of critical legal studies (CLS) on your very first page, I was naturally eager to see what you, by common consent one of our preeminent legal historians, had to say about all of "us" (if I may continue to speak for such a ragtag army of misfits as CLSers are). Since I finished the chapter, amusement and irritation, both intense, have been competing for dominance of my reaction to it. My first (and possibly wisest) instinct was not to respond at all, but then I thought, "My God, suppose people read this and accept it as a serious account of what CLS is all about? What if they start quoting it as authority on the subject"? So I thought I'd better write something.

The core thesis of your piece is that "critical" legal historians work from values, premises, and methods that are to some extent fundamentally incompatible with those of "traditional" legal historians; so that a historian must make a choice between the two modes of traditional and critical historiography, and he or she should choose the traditional mode, because it's better. In the context of the rest of your book, especially the 1973-74 Report where you announce your program for recovering the essential traditions, notably those of "individualism," embedded in our law, it's clear that you identify traditional history with your own program, and critical history with an exaggerated form of the "realism" that denies any autonomous content to law.

Your conclusion is certainly disturbing, but less disturbing than the methods used to arrive at it.

To begin with a rather basic complaint, there's an elementary and entirely "traditional" convention governing critical reviews such as yours that when you attack a body of work, you are supposed to pick on examples that are fairly representative of it. In the piece of mine you cite on "Critical Legal Histories"[6] I pointed out that there were *many* modes of "critical" historiography, but identified as what I thought the most distinctive and novel of such modes the history-of-doctrinal-contradictions-and-their-mediation school founded by Duncan Kennedy's seminal "Structure of Blackstone's Commentaries."[7] You seemed to concur when you listed some of the products of this school in your footnote 6 (262). One might therefore have expected your article to take on Kennedy's article or others in his school, some of the other "critical" work I cited, or perhaps some of the entries in the *Yale Law Journal* bibliography of CLS.[8] Yet in fact, in your entire article you discuss neither these works *nor any others by a CLS affiliated person,* except Mark Tushnet's book on slavery (266),[9] which you imply is distorted history without even briefly indicating how, and Jim Kainen's piece on vested rights,[10] which you mention in passing (290 n. 154) as an example of "traditional" legal history. Instead your leading examples of CLS work turn out to be books by Jerry Auerbach,[11] William Chase,[12] and Judith Baer,[13] none of whom has ever identified himself or herself with CLS and whose intellectual and political commitments are related only vaguely to those of most CLS people in that they are left-of-center (Auerbach and Baer) or adopt negative views (such as Chase's hostility to modern administrative law theory and the Harvard Law School) toward some twentieth-century legal institutions[14] (a criterion that would make Posner and Epstein into CLSers!). I think you picked these books, even though they don't have any connection to CLS, because some things about them summoned up in your mind images of what you *think* CLS is all about, and that you don't like.

So let's go on to those images, and the contrasting good images of "traditional" (Trad.) historiography. Your descriptions of *both* modes strike me as highly confusing, especially that of the traditional mode, which seems contradictory as well. Anyway, here are some of the contrasts, as you present them:

1. *Trad. history is neutral, objective, and factual; CLS history is partisan, political, and distorted because of its commitment to Marxism.* "I wonder whether the [high school] students who read [Mark Tushnet's book on slavery] appreciate that they are assimilating not the objective facts . . . but a Marxist interpretation of those facts" (266). I would expect better of you, especially since elsewhere in the book you fervently proclaim a set of your own political commitments out of which you think history *should* be written (commitments to American constitutionalism, individualism, etc.). In your concluding chapter on "Standards of Criticism," in fact, you argue that hostile reviewers of other historians' work ought to be sensitive to the fact that they may hate the work because of fundamental disagreements with its political or jurisprudential presuppositions; and you imply, very sensibly, that critics ought to understand and evaluate such work on its own terms, or try to find criteria of historical worth that bridge the political gulf. So what is the point of this dig of yours at Tushnet? You can't mean, "History should be a recitation of uninterpreted brute data," since that would be idiotic; you must simply mean, "Marxists (or at least "self-proclaimed" ones—266, n.30) can't write reliable history; only liberals can." This is positively libellous. You must be aware that you're taking on here not just (or even primarily) CLS historians (most of whom are extremely critical of orthodox Marxist historiography—more on this in a moment) but a long and extremely distinguished tradition of historical work: that of Marx himself (on "The Civil War in France"), R. H. Tawney, Christopher Hill, Albert Soboul, M. I. Finley, Eric Hobsbawm, E. P. Thompson, David Montgomery, and Gareth Stedman Jones, not to mention Tushnet's own teacher, Eugene Genovese, a Gramscian Marxist commonly acknowledged by bourgeois as well as radical scholars to be among the great historians of American slavery. If you really

want to take on Marxist historiography, I think you have at least to specify what you think it is, there being so many varieties of Marxism around in the modern world. One might have hoped that the time had long since passed in American letters when a scholar could use the word *Marxist* in the confident expectation that the mere adjective was enough to dismiss a piece of work as an absurd distortion.

2. *Trad. historians are cautious and restrained in tone; CLS historians are "strident."* The authority cited on stridency is Schlegel, but no examples are quoted in the text,[15] and I rather doubt that you could find many. The Kennedy school of doctrinal history is on the whole rather abstract and dry in tone. There is a tradition of radical—especially labor—historiography represented by some members of CLS (Konefsky and Klare come especially to mind) deriving from Engels, Tawney, and Thompson, which is suffused with sympathy for the poor and laboring classes and admiration of their heroic qualities, and with indignation at propertied or governing classes who exploit their misery or are indifferent to it. I would call this "moral passion" rather than stridency, and find it hard to think of as a *defining* characteristic of the genre.

3. The following seems to be your more substantial complaint: *CLS historians have an "instrumental" view of law, meaning that they think that law and legal change are best explained as deliberately manufactured for their own ends by social, economic, or political interests: doctrine is only "rationalization" or "ideological superstructure." Trad. historians believe that law has an autonomous content, that is, one not reducible to the pressure of interests, but at least to some extent to be appreciated as an integral system standing above or apart from the immediate pressures of politics and social struggle.*

If this is what you mean, it seems to me to rest on a most peculiar and partial view of what traditional legal history is all about, and a staggering misconception of the aims of CLS historians. Let me try to sort this out:

(a) There is of course one tradition in legal historiography—we could call it classical legal history—that treats solely of the evolution of legal doctrine as an almost wholly self-contained process, unconnected to social context. This still attracts some very able historians, especially in England; but I assume this is *not* the tradition you are concerned to defend, because you cite with approval so many studies connecting legal to political, social, and economic change and have written such studies yourself.

(b) Among historians of law who *are* interested in its social context, surely the dominant approach has for some decades now been a thoroughly instrumentalist one. Willard Hurst explains nineteenth-century law primarily as responsive to the demands of entrepreneurs pressuring for a legal framework facilitating rapid growth. Lawrence Friedman's work takes as its premise that the legal system is not autonomous but serves the dominant interest groups of society. Instrumentalism cuts across political affiliations. Orthodox Marxists see law as the repressive weapon of the ruling class. Populists and Progressives see it alternatively as the product of political initiatives by plutocratic elites or of reform movements of the masses; liberal pluralists as the vector sum of interest group pressures. Right-wing legal economists see common law as responsive to (wealth or utility-maximizing) interests in efficient cost-reduction, legislation to politically dominant interest groups.

(c) By contrast, most of the recent CLS history has been concerned to *reject* the instrumentalist and functionalist premises of this dominant tradition. Kennedy has said in as many ways as he can think of saying it that law has to be understood as embedded in relatively autonomous structures; and that is why he and his school have for the most part felt able to confine themselves to writing doctrinal history (and been severely criticized by instrumentalist-Marxist historians for their "idealism" in doing so). Your paraphrase of the quotation from my article (you write [262]: "Since law is indeterminate and thus incapable of autonomous development, critical legal studies historians striving to understand the law focus on its political roots") has things exactly backward: in fact it's *because* many CLS historians think legal principles are "indeterminate" that they think law *can't* adequately be explained as the product of interest-group or ruling-class pressures, or the "functional needs" of capitalism, economic growth, etc. For example, a fault-based standard of liability is so mushy and manipulable that in principle it could serve anyone's interest or any set of social needs. And that is why many CLS historians have instead tried to understand the fault principle as an expression of a complex legal consciousness rather than as an instrument of economic growth or of the railroad bosses.

I must say I feel a real sense of grievance here, having devoted by far the largest part of the article you cite to trying to show how critics had undermined instrumentalist accounts of law and had insisted upon respecting its autonomy as an object of study. Kennedy's work on "classical legal thought,"[16] or for that matter my own on late-nineteenth-century lawyers,[17] have made it as clear as we possibly can that we reject the standard, *traditional* Progressive interpretation of elite jurists of that time as nothing more than tools of large corporate interests. At 287 you attribute to CLS writers the comic-book legal-realist view that judicial decisions are grounded "only in the self-interest or political values of judges." This again is absurd (save in the sense in which it's self-evidently true that the "political values" of judges will inform their practices) to anyone who knows CLS work. Kennedy's writing in particular has been devoted to elaborating the structures of the legal consciousness underlying decisional law; he shows, for example, how *Lochner v. New York* is not just an outbreak of piggishness among a few reactionary judges, but fits into the logic of the "classical" categorical schemes and modes of reasoning.[18] CLS work emphasizes—most of its knowledgeable critics claim overemphasizes—the imbrication of everyday social practices in such belief-systems. This is precisely the *opposite* of the view that doctrinal systems are merely rationalizations or masks of naked interests;[19] it is the view that the formation of "interests" themselves is saturated in some of the basic categories and assumptions of law.

What is fascinating to me about this basic misapprehension of yours with respect to CLS work is that you are hardly alone in it, but share it with many other critics of CLS.[20] The reasoning process seems to be something like this: CLS people identify themselves as on the Left; Left means Marxism; Marxism means a vulgar-instrumentalist view of law. Quite aside from the fact that Western Marxists have for decades been moving away from instrumentalism—so far away, in fact, that in current academic debate you can often identify the Marxist in the room as the person insisting upon the importance of ideology, culture, political language, or autonomous concerns of bureaucracies as independent variables—most CLS writing routinely rejects vulgar-instrumentalist explanations, whether they take orthodox Marxist, liberal pluralist, or Chicago-economistic forms. Why is it so hard for outside readers to see that? The usual answer is, "The Jargon. That awful Jargon." (See your p. 269, where to your credit you call this a "trivial objection.") This I think simply a *canard*: I challenge anyone to find more than the normal academic quota of jargon in my work or that of Kennedy, Horwitz, Klare, Konefsky, Feinman, Mensch, Tony Chase, Stone, Singer, or Tushnet, for example. Every year I see many quite ordinary second- and third-year law students, not nearly as learned or sophisticated as you, reading CLS stuff, writing papers using it, and having no great difficulty understanding it and none whatever telling it apart from vulgar-Marxist or Populist "law-is-a-ruling-class conspiracy" history. The problem is clearly not the intrinsic difficulty of the material, but what one might call some readers' educated resistance to it.

4. *CLS history is repetitive, narrow, and unimaginative because of its "commitment to polemical dissection of the indeterminacy and contradictions of liberal legalism. . . ." This was a new theme when Roberto Unger wrote* Knowledge and Politics *(1975). "But now the dissection*

has been completed, and application of Unger's insight to the American legal past requires little imagination or insight." *Traditional historians do not simply dissect: they aspire to "identify the dominant principles of our law or to analyze how and why they changed" (274).*

This assertion is worth some discussion because it is the only one in your essay that touches—although still without giving *any* authentic examples of the work it criticizes—on ideas CLS people have actually held. And you are quite right to perceive some of the CLS histories[21] as explorations of the "antinomies" of liberalism discussed by Unger (although quite wrong to suppose they merely reiterate Unger's insights, since it is one thing to expound a contradiction abstractly, and another entirely to write the history of its appearances in the nineteenth-century law of, for example, mortgages or running covenants). The impression you convey here is of writers who, having identified two aims in tension with each other that a body of law was trying to serve at once (e.g. nineteenth-century family law was concerned to promote both family cohesion and the equality/individuality of all family members),[22] immediately start shrieking that this tension shows how rotten and vacuous liberal legalism must be. You say that such tensions inhere in all social life or in "human nature" (274); exposing them is not news.

Here as so often in your essay one must pause to wonder whether you can possibly have read any of the work you are attacking. The CLS historians would probably agree that in one form or another such "fundamental contradictions" as that between the self and others (we need others to realize common projects and a social identity, but fear that they will enslave or engulf us) may be permanent aspects of the social life of human beings. The subject of these CLS histories is a successive set of modern Western claims to have *mediated* these contradictions—to have made them go away, or at least to have made them less painful and terrifying—through law. These mediating devices are inherently unstable: over time they tend to collapse and to be replaced with new ones. One way of writing the story of the "dominant principles of our law [and] how or why they have changed" is therefore as the rise and fall of successive mediating devices.

Let me do what you should have done, and mention some examples. 1) Elizabeth Mensch has applied CLS methods to the study of property disputes in colonial New York.[23] She reveals eighteenth-century conceptions of property rights to be rooted in contradictory models of voluntarism (e.g., use and occupancy; local community distribution) and hierarchy (e.g., deriving from Crown right; security of accumulation). She shows how these conflicts were played out in lawsuits between claimants to property; how the legal system could not embrace either model fully without jeopardizing the legitimacy of the entire structure of property ownership in the colony; how lawyers struggled to find mediating positions such as *selective* assertion of (hierarchical) Crown right and of (voluntarist) Crown policy that would resolve the tension and how these mediators eventually broke down in the Revolution. 2) At about the same time, Joseph Singer published an article about how lawyers in the nineteenth and early twentieth centuries tried to develop a workable scheme for separating the boundaries of one individual's rights from another's on a different, more abstract plane, that of analytical jurisprudence.[24] He shows how legal thinkers hoped to mediate social conflict through rights by establishing that rights generally entailed correlative duties in others to respect the rights. This project required the jurists to push aside the troublesome area of *damnum absque injuria*—activities causing real but legally unrecognized injury—to marginal status. Singer patiently traces through dozens of treatises the growing recognition that *damnum absque injuria* actually encompassed vast and important areas of legally regulated social life (competition, uncompensated spillovers, most family relations, much labor capital conflict, etc.); and that the legal system, so far from generally establishing duties to respect property rights, frequently legislated regimes of privileges in which people were encouraged to demolish one another's property. Holmes developed, and Hohfeld ultimately formalized this insight, which at least at the level of theory put an end to the long supposition that to have a property right necessarily meant to have something whose value the legal system could and would protect from exercises of social and economic power. 3) Gregory Alexander recently wrote a long article[25] in the CLS mode on how nineteenth-century trust lawyers dealt with the contradiction inherent in "dead hand" transfers of property: that the law cannot protect the freedom of donors to tie up uses without restricting the freedom of donees, and vice versa. It was important for lawyers to avoid any sense of contradiction because a large part of the meaning of freedom for them consisted in the emancipation of free disposition of property from feudal restraints on alienation. Alexander shows how contradiction was mediated through such devices as "repugnancy" (the concept that some restrictions were incompatible with the "nature" of the estate granted) and the separation between law and equity. With the growing effort to rationalize trust law on scientific principles, however, the devices were discredited, and the contradiction starkly revealed in debates over the legality of late-nineteenth-century spendthrift trusts. Finally, twentieth-century lawyers invented new mediating devices (balancing tests, economic efficiency, and other social welfare criteria) that do not promise to be much more successful.

If one actually reads these articles and many others like them, your caricature becomes simply incredible. These are not mindless polemics against legalism from a position of rigid ideological dogmatism, but rather careful, thorough, almost lovingly detailed, histories of the development of legal ideas and practices. All of them are based on original research. If their arguments are as stale and familiar as your assert, I wish you'd say where you have heard them before. You may not have learned anything new from the CLS historians, but others have. It is particularly reassuring to find so many of the CLS insights into legal history being confirmed and expanded by non-CLS-affiliated historians.[26] Nobody in CLS has ever claimed that theirs is the only way to write history, or that they are producing more than a tiny fraction of the good history that's coming out. But to take the opposite position, that there's nothing interesting to be learned from CLS work, as you have, seems ungenerous in the extreme, especially considering that you don't even *try* to document it.

4. *Trad. historians stand tall for America, law, and capitalism; CLS historians have a bad attitude toward all these things.* Ultimately, this seems to be what your review comes down to. It's not really a critique of CLS at all (which would explain why you don't deal with any CLS work) but of a bunch of negative attitudes that CLS only vaguely symbolizes for you and that are actually exemplified in a heterogeneous group of writers whose only common fault is that they don't reaffirm basic American values, in particular the value of complacency about our legal and economic institutions and their historical role. This concern seems to be much higher on your agenda than the other concerns for "objective" historiography or "autonomous" law. It turns out in the end that you actually have no objection to overtly partisan history as long as it registers politically correct attitudes, or to instrumentalist explanations as long as they conclude that in the long run law has served *benign* social purposes and interests. The choice between Critics (meaning here simply scholars with bad attitudes) and the Trads. is between "whether one wants to preserve the existing American political order designed to enhance individual autonomy and freedom or to participate in imposing some new collective vision of the good on the polity" (302).[27]

Both your complaints about what you casually label CLS perspectives[28] and your notions about what the correct attitudes are for historians are so incredibly miscellaneous that it's hard to get a grip on them. The heart of the matter seems to be at 287, which tells us flat out that we just can't write any kind of constitutional history, good or bad, unless we're committed to the liberal premises 1) that there can be such a thing as a body of fixed, objective, neutral, determinate legal principles, beyond the reach of political forces, protecting individual rights, *and* 2) that historical study can help to identify what at least some if not all (296) of these principles are, presumably because they have been realized in the historical practices of our institutions and will thus reveal themselves to objective researchers of those practices. Some comments on this set of premises:

(a) I must say that I would be reluctant to equip a young legal historian just setting out on his or her travels with this methodological and ideological baggage, which seems bound to land him or her in unnecessary mischief. Your prescription, unless I misread it, is one for a very "traditional" form of history indeed: a Whig legal history in which the fundamental principles of Anglo-Saxon liberty realize themselves progressively—albeit with regrettable lapses, distortions,and deviations—through time, peaking more or less optimally in our own time. To modern readers—such as the Reid and Nelson who wrote most of the essays in this volume—the besetting weakness of such history is its tendency to anachronism, its insensitivity to the contingency of legal and political language, to the realization that law, politics, equality, property, rights, were embedded in, for example, Marshall's time in a network of interpretive conventions quite different from our own, so that finding functional equivalents in our own time to Marshall's constitutional principles is necessarily a highly problematic and delicate task and one hardly likely to be performable "objectively," beyond the possibility of reasonable dispute: these are, in W. B. Gallie's phrase, "essentially contested concepts." On the whole I think CLS writers have made pretty good historians of legal concepts precisely because they work out of a theory of the social and cultural contingency of legal practices (that apparently identical practices, transposed to different social or ideological contexts, can acquire radically divergent meanings), which leads them to a proper respect for the historicity, the "local meaning," of their materials. I don't mean that there haven't been good histories by Whiggish-minded historians and bad histories by CLS-types: talent or the lack of it can always transcend theory. But I would think it rather more helpful to advise someone just starting to look into past legal practices to expect to find discourses somewhat *alien* to our own, and to see as a first job trying to understand them on their own terms, than to urge that person to search for the genetic ancestors to our legal principles as we understand them: as an initial matter, at least, he or she should be looking for differences, not identities. (This was Maitland's advice, and it still sounds good.)

(b) Your prescription seems also, completely arbitrarily, to rule out certain kinds of conclusions that even a committed liberal might want to advance: the conclusion, for example, that American practices have *not* lived up to our fundamental, recoverable-through-history principles, and would require radical reformation to do so (the kind of conclusion that radical antislavery agitators extracted from the Declaration, in the teeth of the Constitutional entrenchment of slavery). Poor Judith Baer, whose *Equality under the Constitution* would have seemed exactly to fit your specifications for liberal-principles-extracting historiography, is denied "traditional" status and tossed onto the garbage heap with the rest of us CLS bums (264) because she thinks America *hasn't* kept faith with its egalitarian promises. (Also possibly because you don't care for her *Grundnorm*, equality, as much as you do for individual autonomy?) Many historians have lamented the sinking of America's communitarian republican ideology, with its stress on participatory politics, public virtue, and an equal distribution of property as preconditions to freedom-understood-as-self-realization-through-membership-in-a-polis, into the more atomistic ideology of liberalism. You used to be one of the historians yourself (*Americanization of the Common Law*), but now darkly perceive their work as "part of the critical legal studies effort to undermine the individualistic tenor of the American legal order."[29] Have we gone completely back to the 1950s, when anyone who tried to state the claims for democracy, community, and equality risked being labelled a subversive? Radical legalism, as well as radical anti-legalism, is an apple-pie *American* tradition. The individualism that now seems to lie at the center of your commitments was once itself a radical creed: until quite late in the nineteenth century, many highly respectable lawyers and judges reared in the Jacksonian anti-charter ideology continued to believe that the existence of large business corporations was absolutely incompatible with individual autonomy and freedom. I think I would have more respect for your ringing affirmation of individualist values if you were also to adopt their radical, history-approved, corollaries. The radicalism of our legal past, it seems, is acceptable only if it remains safely *in* the past.

(c) Your methodological instructions finally seem to me to rest on a confusion between the self-understandings of the members of a legal community (their motives, their conceptions of their work, etc.) and how an outside observer (a historian, a sociologist) might regard them. You repeatedly answer what you believe to be CLS charges of a legal conspiracy (lawyers and judges deliberately manipulating legal form to the disadvantage of poor, excluded, disfavored, or deviant groups) by pointing to studies affirming the integrity and internal consistency of bodies of law and the high-minded intentions of those who administered that law to do so fairly, apolitically, neutrally. As I said under #3, above, CLS people have no quarrel with that (although they also think it useful occasionally to remind readers of the myriad ways in which the powerful do deploy law instrumentally against the powerless): they have written a lot of that kind of rehabilitative history themselves, especially on the late-nineteenth-century judges who have been saddled (not by CLS but by traditional Progressive historians) with a bum rap as lackeys of the robber barons. That's what a political ideology is all about: people who hold it sincerely believe that it is natural and neutral and based on science or common-sense and best for everybody in the society. But their belief doesn't make it so, or deprive historians of occasions for critical judgment.

Take the classical legal regulation of labor relations. By post-NLRA liberal standards, of course, that legal regime looks piggy beyond belief (except to very right-wing libertarian individualists such as Richard Epstein). But once you enter with provisional sympathy into that judicial mind-set (as a CLS historian would),[30] you can understand what makes it tick: (i) a principle of mutuality: employers are free to hire or not to hire, employees to work at employers' terms or not to work; employees are free to join unions, employers to make nonmembership a condition of employment; neither employers nor employees may conspire to combine with others to restrain trade; neither may cause or threaten harm to the property of others; (ii) a principle of correlative rights-and-duties: a property right gives rise to correlative duties in others to respect the right; (iii) a principle of interpretation: the Constitution is designed to protect property and liberty as those terms have been historically understood at common law (a very Nelsonian proposition). The whole scheme hangs together, and it's wonderfully general, neutral, and apolitical in its formulation. To be sure, in practice it always seemed to result in any potentially effective labor action's being immediately subjected to an injunction, but that was just the break of the cards. You don't have to suppose the judges were consciously biased to explain that result; it flows, in some sense, directly from the premises. But you surely can "deconstruct" the premises, as Holmes[31] and Walter Wheeler Cook[32] did, for example, to show that their apparent neutrality is illusory, and that they can't be applied to concrete cases without "inarticulate" judgments of policy regarding such issues as whether an employer's inchoate property in expected future profits is to be treated as a Hohfeldian privilege defeasible by competition or a labor boycott, or as like a contract right, infringeable if damages are paid, or (the way the U.S. Supreme Court treated it) as a property right protectible by injunction; or whether labor's rights to organize shouldn't also be protectible by injunction; or whether violence at the plant site should be considered criminally unlawful or a privileged defense of (either management's or labor's) property.

This kind of demonstration, the stock-in-trade of both legal realism and CLS, seems to me very valuable. Surely one of the things that historians ought to do is to try to discover the sunken codes of shared inarticulate assumptions that underlie apparently neutral decision systems. Wouldn't that be a lot more interesting project than simply celebrating the system's neutrality and the noble motives of the judges? The only objection seriously put forward is that such deconstructive work, finding the subtext, will "undermine respect for the rule of law," because if people don't believe that general propositions *can* always decide concrete cases, individual liberties will be finished, washed up. I think this is nuts. A commitment to general, neutral legal principles has never of itself precluded political tyranny (has been in fact an instrument of political tyrannies), and can, notoriously, be an extremely serviceable handmaiden to the tyranny of wealth. On the other hand, a commitment to the legal-realist belief in the historical contingency and contextual variability of legal rules does not mean that one doesn't support legal rules and institutions attempting to restrain repressive coercion: a strong commitment, especially on the part of influential elites, to certain ways of interpreting such rules over others that are plausibly advanced, can do a lot to avoid or mitigate political persecution. All the legal-realist or CLS perspective says is that you need the cultural-social commitment to the rule-interpretation and the willingness to engage in politics to back it up, in order to give the rule meaningful content; without that back-up, the legal rule is an empty shell, "reified rights-rhetoric," as the jargon expresses it.

The reason your essay is upsetting, and perhaps worth writing against at this length, is that it shows an intelligent and usually conscientious scholar falling victim to an unhappily common syndrome of reactions to intellectual work originating on the Left: a combination of paranoia and carelessness. The paranoia shows up in the remarkable attribution of every critical sentiment of post-1960s historical scholarship relating to law to this tiny band of CLS scholars, and the still more remarkable conclusion, in the Age of Reagan, that this band—most of whose members are in fact struggling to find and hold on to teaching jobs in environments growing ever more hostile to them—poses a potent current threat to civil liberties. The carelessness is exhibited in your confidence—which is unfortunately probably well founded—that in reviewing work from the Left you don't have to read it, quote it, or engage with any of its arguments in order to trash it. You can just assume you know what it's about, and assume most readers will share your disdain for it. One sees, these days, signs of the syndrome everywhere. The head of the appointments committee of a major law school said recently that his committee would not even interview graduates of law schools with significant numbers of CLS faculty because of the risk that those graduates might have been contaminated by CLS ideas, and that hiring one might cause his school to be taken over by Them. Such a person would presumably think it an absurd imposition on his time and patience to be expected before passing this judgment to learn anything about Their ideas. What really gets to me is that these are often exactly the same people who uphold as against CLS the virtues of "civility" and "the liberal value of respect for the rights of others" (296 n. 186). We really are back to the 1950s, without even the consolations of early rock-and-roll.

NOTES

1. William Nelson and John Phillip Reid, *The Literature of American Legal History* (1985).

2. Chapter 16 (Report for 1981-84).

3. To summarize some of these briefly: 1) Your account seems to blur together several propositions that should be kept distinct. (a) Commitment to the study of law in its political-economic-social context does not have to entail the belief that law is determined by that context. (b) The beliefs, however sincerely held, of judges or lawyers that their practices are autonomous does not make them so, or preclude historians from concluding otherwise. It does not even follow *pace* your Japanese-internment example that, as an empirical matter, judges committed to a formalist-idealist conception of professional autonomy are more likely to resist the pressures of the power politics of their time than judges who think law is mostly the product of social forces. On the contrary, as the Legal Realists were fond of pointing out, legal formalisms certain of their autonomous, neutral, apolitical character are peculiarly prone to permeation with unconscious bias; only a jurisprudence capable of recognizing, rather than committed to denying, the political pressures imprinted on legal doctrines, is likely to be able to transcend such pressures. It was skeptical judges like Holmes, Brandeis, and Hand, not their formalist colleagues, who expanded free speech protections in this century. (c) The opposition seems too stark (as indeed you recognize at 200) between legally maintained "traditions" and the "preferences of politically dominant groups," since the traditions could not become "essential" or even "traditions" to begin with unless the "dominant groups" had adopted and promoted them. 2) Even if a historical method is capable of identifying the "essential traditions" (such as "individualism") of our society, I can't share your confidence that once identified they could or should have the constraining force you want them to have over our legal decisions. (a) The traditions of our culture are plural, not unitary: there is "republicanism" as well as "liberalism," the Puritan commonwealth as well as the rugged individual, the artisanal fraternity as well as the free enterpriser, Eugene Debs and W. E. B. Du Bois (as Mark Tushnet has recently pointed out) as well

as Thomas Jefferson and Andrew Carnegie. (b) Even within liberalism, as critical legal studies historians are fond of pointing out, the traditions point toward opposite goals: an abstract commitment to the traditions of "private property" or "freedom of contract" can perfectly consistently generate completely contradictory regimes of concrete legal rules. (More on this theme later.) At different points in our history, for instance, tradition-minded conservatives have supposed that "individualism" logically *required* prohibiting all corporations, allowing everyone to form corporations, precluding state regulation of corporations, permitting virtually unrestricted corporate combination, and breaking up all large corporations into small ones. It is hard to believe on such evidence that "tradition" is able to inform our policy options in the constraining manner you hope from it. (c) Some of our deeply embedded traditions—racism, nativist xenophobia, repression of dissidence, glorification of the more violent and dominating forms of male sexuality, ecological carelessness, obsession with money making, etc.—are ones we should be rediscovering in order to try to grow out of, not to endow with renewed normative authority.

4. See, e.g., Richard A. Posner, "A Theory of Negligence," 1 J. Legal Studies (1972); Richard Epstein *Takings* (1985).

5. See, e.g., Bruce Ackerman, "Discovering the Constitution," 93 Yale L. J. 1013 (1984).

6. Robert W. Gordon, "Critical Legal Histories," 36 Stanford L. Rev. 57 (1984).

7. Duncan Kennedy, "The Structure of Blackstone's Commentaries," 28 Buffalo L. Rev. 205 (1979).

8. "A Bibliography of Critical Legal Studies," 94 Yale L. J. 464 (1984).

9. Mark Tushnet, *The American Law of Slavery, 1810-1860* (1981).

10. James L. Kainen, "Nineteenth Century Interpretations of the Federal Contract Clause: The Transformation from Vested to Substantive Rights against the State," 31 Buffalo L. Rev. 381 (1983).

11. Jerold S. Auerbach, *Justice without Law?* (1983).

12. William C. Chase, *The American Law School and the Rise of Administrative Government* (1982).

13. Judith Baer, *Equality under the Constitution: Reclaiming the Fourteenth Amendment* (1983).

14. You link Auerbach to CLS thus: "Since Auerbach makes clear his own dissatisfaction with the legal system, it seems clear that Auerbach's work should be perceived as part of the critical legal studies effort to undermine the individualistic tenor of the American legal order."

15. And only two in the footnote (262 n. 7), one of which is co-authored by Schlegel himself.

16. Duncan Kennedy, "Toward an Historical Understanding of Legal Consciousness: The Case of Classical Legal Thought in America, 1850-1940," in 3 Research in Law and Sociology 3 (ed. Spitzer 1980).

17. Robert W. Gordon, "Law and Lawyers in the Age of Enterprise," in *Professions and Professional Ideologies in America* 70 (Geison ed., 1984).

18. See Kennedy, supra note 16.

19. A most peculiar aspect of your article is that one of the few works of a CLS-affiliated historian that actually does set forth instrumentalist (among other) interpretations is a work you don't mention at all, though you seem secretly to be using it as proxy for CLS work generally: Morton Horwitz's *Transformation of American Law*. And while in its instrumentalist mode, as I pointed out in my article, Horwitz's book is entirely within the *mainstream* of social-legal historiography, as politically it is within

the mainstream of Progressive historiography. It is a wonderful book in many ways, but it is not in *those respects* (though it is in others) typical of recent CLS history.

20. See Philip Johnson, "Do You Sincerely Want to Be Radical?", 36 Stan. L. Rev. 247 (1984); Louis B. Schwartz, "With Gun and Camera through Darkest CLS-Land," id. at 413; Paul Carrington, "Of Law and the River," 34 J. Legal Education 222 (1984).

21. Especially those in the "Kennedy School": see supra at note 16.

22. The example is yours (274), suggested by Stanley N. Katz, "Legal History and Family History: The Child, the Family, and the State," 21 Boston College L. Rev. 1025 (1980).

23. Elizabeth Mensch, "The Colonial Origins of Liberal Property Rights," 31 Buffalo L. Rev. 635 (1983).

24. Joseph Singer, "The Legal Rights Debate in Analytical Jurisprudence from Bentham to Hohfeld," Wisconsin L. Rev. 975 (1982).

25. Gregory Alexander, "The Dead Hand and the Law of Trusts in the Nineteenth Century," 37 Stanford L. Rev. 1189 (1985).

26. Hendrik Hartog's book (which you praise) on New York City fits beautifully into the CLS account of the history of the public-private distinction (prefigured by Louis Hartz's great book on Pennsylvania, years ago), as do Scheiber's work on the history of public rights and Steven Diamond's on taxation; Charles McCurdy's articles on Justice Field and on corporation law, Patrick Atiyah's history of contract law, Thomas Grey's article on Langdell (which you also praise, and which is heavily indebted to Kennedy) all dovetail neatly with Kennedy's, Horwitz's, and my material on late-nineteenth-century law; Charles Donahue's and Tom Grey's synthetic histories of property confirm Vandevelde's CLS article on property, and so forth.

27. Observe the rhetorical oppostions in this sentence: You gently and consensually "preserve"; we forcefully and conflictually "impose." Your order promotes "individual autonomy and freedom," ours a "collective" vision of the good. Yours is sanctioned by tradition; ours is "new."

28. Some of your views of CLS are totally wacky—like the identification of CLS with Austinian positivism (290); where did *that* come from, I wonder? Or the notion that CLSers think "Americans are a violent people" (268), especially since later Edward Ayers is praised for his "nondogmatic" explanation of southern crime as the outcome of the "cultural glorification of violence" (275 76). Or that CLS "ignores . . . the persistence of basic social values and social structures even in the face of just demands for reform" (279 n. 99). All these seem to be the purest invention.

29. You say this of Jerold Auerbach's *Justice without Law*, which you proceed to summarize so as to make it sound uncannily like your (apparently now disowned) early work.

30. See, e.g., Ellen Kelman, "American Labor Law and Legal Formalism," 58 St. Johns. Univ. L. Rev. 1 (1983); Kenneth Casebeer, "Coppage v. Kansas and At-Will Employment Revisited," 6 Cardozo L. Rev 765 (1985).

31. Oliver Wendell Holmes, Jr., "Privilege, Malice and Intent," in *Collected Legal Papers* 117 (1920).

32. Walter Wheeler Cook, "Privileges of Labor Unions in the Struggle for Life," 27 Yale L.J. 779 (1918).

Gordon's Response to Nelson

Let me respond to what seem to me to be the its essential points of your letter.

I. Your Characterizations of CLS Historical Work

Specific writers. 1) Tushnet on slavery. I don't at all understand your response here. In the book you say that uninformed readers will be misled to think that Tushnet's history is "objective," since it's actually "Marxist." Now you say you don't believe there's such a thing as objective history. It must follow that uninformed readers of any history will be misled if they suppose it to be objective. So why single out Tushnet's? Of course Tushnet thought his interpretation was a better one than rival ones, or he wouldn't have written it. He drew on Marxist (and even more on structuralist) traditions of explanation because, like his teacher Genovese, he believes with good reason that, judiciously used, these help powerfully to illuminate the historical problem. 2) Kennedy on Blackstone: You say (Nelson's letter, text accompanying note 10) that Kennedy's piece is neither history nor legal argument because it neither locates Blackstone's thought uniquely in the past nor helps lawyers argue for just results in the present. The first charge is just wrong: the entire essay is devoted to situating Blackstone's thought at a historical moment between mediaeval-feudal and modern-liberal, in order to clarify our own categories and assumptions by showing how Blackstone's formulations anticipate, but also differ from our own. The second's validity depends on how one assesses the present utility to lawyers of perspectives—such as (real) legal history, anthropology, or sociology—that study the legal order from the outside, rather than directly engaging in its ongoing arguments and activities, and treat as problematic all the premises (the "common-sense" of the system) that ordinary legal arguments take for granted. How but through such distancing can lawyers achieve reflective self-knowledge about their premises, and change them if they are misguided? Finally, even if CLS histories happened to fall into neither genre you mention (though in fact I think they contribute to both), but into a third genre such as, let us say, historically supported political theory, what would be wrong with that? Legal theory needs jusification in political theory, so why shouldn't we work on the basics?

Instrumentalism. You are "baffled" (see Nelson's letter, text accom-

Law and History Review Spring 1988, Vol. 6, No. 1

panying note 7) by my claim that CLS historians have rejected instrumentalist accounts of law, and respond with a counterclaim of your own that on close inspection the CLS historians "again emerge as rather standard realist/instrumentalists," your evidence for this being the conclusions of Kennedy and others that they have revealed the "apologetic motives" underlying legal structures. [Incidentally, you can't maintain both that CLS departs radically from traditional legal history, much of whose best work (e.g., Hurst and Friedman) is far more overtly instrumentalist that CLS's, and that CLS merely iterates old themes.] Now an "instrumentalist" view of law, as I was using the term, is the view that you attributed to CLS in your book: that the rules, doctrines, arguments, processes of the legal system are best explained as deliberately manufactured in their own interests by (dominant) interest groups or classes. A historian who took this view seriously wouldn't waste much time on the content of law or of legal reasoning or rhetoric or argument, because by his hypothesis these would be nothing but whipped cream, "superstructure," rationalization of naked interest or preference. The historian would be looking for the real dirt, the ruling-class or entrepreneurial interest behind the scenes. But this is clearly neither the method nor the goal of the CLS historians we're discussing because they evidently take the content of law very seriously indeed. "Traditional" historians with good reason usually criticize them for neglecting contexts.

I think the problem you're having grasping what CLS historians are up to ultimately derives from your implicit acceptance of one of the basic dualisms of liberal legalism itself: If law is not objective and determinate, then it must be the product of unconstrained desire or power or arbitrary whim. So if someone undertakes to show that a body of legal doctrine is contradictory or otherwise indeterminate, she must, in your view, believe that it's totally open to manipulation by powerholders or just the whim of the decider. Your response constantly reverts to what Unger in *Knowledge and Politics* has called the "antinomy of reason and desire" in liberal thought: Throughout you keep opposing Reason, represented by law, traditional values, "liberal and humane legalism," to Desire (or Will or Interest), conceived of as the "passions of most Americans," the interests of the middle class majority or of the powerful, and even as "the government" (except the courts).

CLS work has very largely been directed to assaulting this very dualism and to trying to excavate, in one doctrinal field after another, the "deep structures" of legal consciousness that constrain the way legal actors (and often extra-legal actors too) talk and think and act respecting law. Law may not constrain decisions in the way that legal formalism claims:

the lessons of Realism are pretty clearly that it doesn't. But this doesn't mean that legal decisions are unconstrained.[1] On the contrary, decision makers are, usually without being aware of it, prisoners of their conventional categories of discourse. The categories organize and make sense of reality for them; make them see some things as similar and others as different or unrelated; highlight some forms of coercion as intolerable and completely fail to notice (or dismiss as resulting from natural necessity) others; incorporate basic assumptions about nature, history, morality, efficiency, obligation, representation, legitimacy. Almost the entire body of the CLS historical work we've been discussing has been devoted to elaborating such frameworks of constraint on legal thought, or "sunken codes of inarticulate assumptions," as I've been calling them. Law is neither pure power or pure reason, in this view: it's what some writers call "ideology," or a "cultural code," or "social text," or "political language," or "set of discursive practices." And the discourses of law connect with other social discourses to form complex overlapping systems of ideology that help to constitute and shape the desires and powers of interest groups themselves. Interest groups partly are what they are because of legal definitions; they claim from one another and the state (among other goods) things they believe they are legally entitled to (people will die to preserve a "right" to things they would never miss if they hadn't come to think themselves entitled); and they possess power or authority in part because the law confers legitimacy on its exercise. If you start looking at the world this way, the dichotomous model of desire constrained by reason disappears: both "interests" and "law" are seen as social practices that flow in the channels cut for them by complexly structured frameworks of consciousness.

This much CLS scholars have simply borrowed from the many other disciplines—including of course history itself—that have challenged the liberal-positivist tradition in social science with the "interpretive turn." In writing the history of legal doctrine, CLSers have added the insight that the understanding of these doctrinal clusters is illuminated by considering them as successive attempts to mediate—to find rational and stable solutions to—the dilemma of the self's simultaneous need for and fear of others. Now the lawyers who have built these doctrinal systems have usually been powerful people with some stake in the status quo, so that they have generally tried to argue that some (considerably idealized) version of the current legal arrangements provides near-optimal solutions to the dilemma. They are in this sense apologetic (as are your own affirmations of faith in the current legal system as representing for all its flaws about the best we can hope for, with perhaps some room for gradual improvement). CLS historians are indeed concerned to show up the apologetic nature of legal ideology. But they also frequently point out that apology for the status quo is not at all a necessary feature of legal thought; and that because of its contradictions legal thought always contains liberating and emancipatory possibilities as well as conservative ones. Unmasking apology is thus a byproduct of the central purpose of these histories, which is simply to begin to describe—a sufficiently difficult task in itself—the structures, the sunken codes, underlying our commonplace modes of thought.

The task is "obvious" and "trivial." At this point you interject your judgment that the sunken codes are "obvious" and that trying to describe them is therefore "trivial." "I find," you say with breathtaking insouciance, "the unarticulated assumptions and passions of most Americans obvious and rather uneasy to unearth" (Nelson's letter, text accompanying note 23). This certainly simplifies things: We can dispense with social-legal history, the sociology and anthropology of law, the political economy of regulation—forget about literature, psychoanalysis, and every other exploration of the mysteries of the human heart. Struggling hard here to rescue some sense out of this, the best I can do is to guess that your view that CLS's project is obvious derives from your confusing it with that of standard instrumentalist histories.

Your point is perhaps that if all historians do is to uncover the selfish motives of interest groups behind legal enactments, to prove over and over again that law is just a mask for power and self-interest, this will become a boring truth indeed. Even this would be a slander on the instrumentalist histories. It's always valuable to do research exposing the line-ups of interest behind some legal decision or enactment, always interesting and useful to learn such things as that railroad executives were among the lobbyists for railroad regulation and worker's compensation—things that weren't at all obvious and familiar when first written about. In fact I think you'd get rather more insight for your own project of trying to preserve the benefits such as free speech you see in the rule of law from the historical sociology of political action—from the study of how repressive movements arise, and resistance to them succeeds or fails—than from the nuances of First Amendment doctrine. The doctrine is nothing if political will is lacking to back it up: the conditions for nurturing dissident speech have to be pursued through politics. Plenty of respectable legal arguments were available to protect "subversives" from persecution in the 1950s; but on the whole these didn't operate to restrain the persecutors. Yet if this is what you mean, shouldn't you be polemicizing against the Chicago economists who are the prime specialists these days in reductionist economistic accounts of law?

CLS has not been primarily interested in uncovering motives of wealth and interest and power, but in describing latent structures of consciousness. And there's nothing in the least obvious about these: Kennedy does not try to show that classical legal thought was devised to protect capitalists, but that its categories were organized around the master principle of "powers absolute within their spheres," which structured decision making in such disparate areas as federalism, separation of power, the boundaries between public power and private right, and contract and tort. As one who has been working in the period, I find Kennedy's classical legal thought article to be a major advance in the historiography of late nineteenth-century legal thought. If you think it wrongheaded, I think you should engage with it on its own terms. You've also said that Joseph Singer's history of *damnum absue injuria* in analytic jurisprudence was "quite familiar." I don't know of other work that mines the sources as he does, or even looks at many of those sources, or anticipates his interpretations.

II. Your Claim that CLS Histories Are Bad Politically Because They Undermine the Rule of Law

Before addressing this contention, could I ask querulously why it seems such a struggle to get critics of CLS to address the substance of the work? Most of these critics complain about how CLS goes around politicizing everything and undermining scholarly objectivity and all the rest of it, and yet most of their critiques of CLS are pure political polemics, accusations of nihilism or totalitarianism, or that "this perspective is bad because if people came to believe it they would undermine the rule of law." One is reminded of the right-wing lawyers who keep asserting that there just has to be a correct reading of the Constitutional text or the intentions of the Founders because if there isn't we will have nothing fixed to steer by. But the assertion doesn't do a thing to show the skeptical anti-originalists are wrong, or to produce a plausible conservative interpretation of the original understanding.

I can't help contrasting CLS's own trashing projects, such as those directed against law-and-economics, which take the body of work being criticized on its own terms, however alien the terms and the world view behind them may seem to the trasher. There are significant and honorable exceptions, of course; for example, Kornhauser's critique of CLS's legal economics[2] which really tried to get inside the mind set of the work.

But to discuss the politics:

A. *CLS suppresses the Individual.* You don't like our history chiefly because of our politics, and yet your notions about our politics are if possible even more obscure than your notions about our history: CLS "seems part of the new left and presents a puzzling program which is said to be non-Marxist but which, to the best of my understanding, regards minority rights as an issue of secondary importance [secondary to what, one wonders?] and individual rights possibly with hostility" (Nelson's letter, text accompanying note 22). In your book and response you hammer on this theme of CLS's hostility to "the individual," darkly implying some plot to submerge the poor creature in some horrid new collective, perhaps the State. But where do these impressions come from? Certainly not from CLS political writings, which are acutely sensitive to the terrors and constraints of group life. CLS people (and hardly they alone—the basic critiques are as old as liberalism itself and still vital) do criticize many of the conventional liberal ways of thinking about individuals such as the common liberal opposition of the individual *to* the collective, which neglects all the ways in which personality, desires, interests are formed and influenced through collectives; or the classical-liberal claim to have satisfactorily mediated the conflicts between individual and group life by means of such notions as that individuals' consent to workplace hierarchies or domestic violence or political regimes can be presumed to express their desires so long as they don't leave. (Folks have what they want and want what they've got.) People committed to those emaciated forms of liberalism concerned only to protect very abstractly defined negative-liberty rights-to-be-let-alone against formal infringement have not only permitted but also justified as realizations of individual freedom the most appalling social constrictions of personality—in local communities, in small businesses, in big bureaucratic hierarchies, in families.

There are of course varieties of liberalism that fully recognize the indebtedness of the self and its projects to social inheritance and environment; that realize how often "consent" can result from submission to domination; and that see the job for law and politics as one of improving the communal conditions for the fuller and richer development of both individual and social personality. Feminist studies have been perhaps the most copious recent sources of insight into how formal-legal rights can operate both to expand and constrict practical freedom. CLSers identify completely with these varieties of liberalism in seeking to expand the range of individual freedom—by which is meant practical freedom and phenomenological freedom, that is, freedom experienced as freedom—in social life. The politics of liberal rights has undeniably helped expand real freedom in the past and sometimes still does; but sometimes it just produces fancy apologies for unfreedom. It's important to cultivate the ability to discriminate.

B. *CLS histories, by exposing indeterminacies and injustices of legal rule systems, help to undermine the current system of the rule of law and all the good things it protects without proposing anything concrete to replace it.* This is your major complaint.

First just a couple of preliminary points. I'm tired of hearing that CLS never comes up with any constructive ideas, because anyone who takes the trouble to read the work, including even some of the history, can find in it plenty of concrete strategies for trying to change legal doctrines and institution. Anyway, it's a very odd complaint to bring against historians, especially critical ones, that they don't have concrete programmatic suggestions for the reformation of society: they might reasonably think that supplying such proposals wasn't their function; that simply helping us to understand our situation might be a useful foundation for an intelligent politics; and that this might be especially true if—as CLS people believe—some of our ordinary modes of understanding our situation so badly misconceive it that it is difficult even to imagine, much less sensibly discuss, radical reform proposals within the prevailing terms of everyday political discourse. The demand for "practical proposals" is often just a demand that the critic stay inside the boundaries of the very liberal discourse she or he is trying to transcend.

At the core of your response lies the assumption that the currently prevailing liberal notions of the rule of law constitute a system, something that has to be taken (subject to minor adjustments) as a whole, or rejected as a whole and another system installed in its place. The system has faults, even grave faults, but has proved itself superior to rival systems in its ability to protect individual autonomy. Radical criticism (trashing) of the system erodes its legitimacy, throws out the baby with the bathwater, and is thus irresponsible unless it has previously prepared blueprints for a replacement system (and even then, the costs of abandoning the proven present for an untried future might seem unacceptably high). The position thus articulated even by a committed left-liberal such as yourself arrives at a tragically conservative conclusion: "Deep injustices remain in American life . . . [One] way the injustices might be eliminated is through a fundamental restructuring of law and society. I agree, but for me a trip to utopia is just not worth the price" (Nelson's letter, text accompanying note 22.) One of the concrete political benefits of critical historiography—some of the CLS type, and some not—is that it quite directly addresses the presuppositions of this tragic frame of mind in the hope of persuading its possessors to think that fundamental change might be possible without sacrificing every accomplishment of civilized legalism. Here are some quick suggestions about how history might help to do that:

1. *History can help expose the reifications of categories that often underlie claims that babies and bathwater, the good things and the evils resulting from the rule of law, are indissolubly linked together in a system so that the evils are all necessary evils.* For example, "If you let the OSHA inspectors on the factory premises without a warrant, then you'll have to let the police batter down your door at 3 in the morning. There are costs (to workers) to foregoing surprise inspections, but these are surely justified by the benefits we all enjoy from the law's protection against the state's invasion of individual privacy and property." Legal and political argument are of course full of conflations of this kind: histories describing past ones that we now all feel to be absurd and showing how their plausibility depended upon (now exploded) reifications sharpen the ability to recognize such categorizations in our own time. My example is one that is fairly easy for most 1980s liberals to shoot down (although it was not easy for 1880s liberals and is still difficult for their libertarian descendants). One point of history, not just CLS history but any history, is to show how although we can't help thinking through the categories we know, by becoming self-conscious about them we may escape victimization through false ideas of the necessary relations of things included within them.

2. *History can induce skepticism about the corrosive force of skepticism.* As a liberal who has tasted the bitter fruit of legal realism, you find it difficult to pin too much of your faith on the formalist position that liberty depends upon the reality of determinate, nonmanipulable, legal doctrine—predictable neutral rule-applications—and so adopt the common fallback position that liberty depends on at least the appearance of rules beyond politics: "OK, OK, we all know that legal doctrine is indeterminate and full of apologetic nonsense, but if you go around saying so the fascists (or the mob) will take over and minorities and dissidents will be left with no shelter from the furious blast." One hears this all the time, yet can't help but feel suspicious of the claim that juristic skepticism about rule formalism leads to Caesarism or mob rule—or that the appearance of doctrinal consistency does much of anything to prevent them—and would like for once to see the point argued carefully as a historian should argue it. It was fashionable once to argue that Weimar Germany proved the point; but if anything the example tends to show the opposite—even those members of the legal elite who despised the Nazis were so determined to think purely "legally" and not "politically" about what was going on that they allowed them-

selves to be neutralized by the party's perfunctory compliance with legal forms. I might add that the current crop of conservative judges in this country is committed to removing protections for minorities and dissidents in the name not of "indeterminacy" but of legal literalism and fixed constitutional meanings.

3. *History teaches that both the rulers and the ruled are given to identifying and defending as the essential elements of the rule of law what is really only the social-contract-in-force at the time.* This is the usual point of attack of instrumentalist rather than of CLS critical-historians and is charmingly illustrated through your own very instrumentalist parable of the weak persona and the strong person. In the parable—which is in fact the standard liberal parable about the origins of law and the state—the version I like best is Adam Smith's: "Laws and government may be considered . . . in every case as a combination of the rich to oppress the poor . . ."[3]—the strong propose to the weak that if the weak will confirm their domination and rulership the strong will protect the weak in their smallholdings and in some "rights" essential to their identity. This deal continues, not without friction, for a few centuries, when suddenly the weak people (or perhaps some of the more sensitive and guilt-tripped souls among the strong) say: "Hey, it isn't fair that your strong guys should be dominating us like this. We propose that we accede to an equal share in your wealth and power." The strong hire a lawyer, who says indignantly: "What about the sacred tradition of the rule of law?"—(i.e., the original deal)—meaning: "If you folks keep pushing for a revision of the deal, we'll see to it that you risk losing everything. We'll stop protecting the rights you have and stop contributing to the production of wealth for you share in." Now this is a scary threat: it has been made, frequently, against labor and women, for example. It's an effective display of power. It certainly invokes traditions. But I can't say it strikes me very forcibly as a claim of justice, or for that matter as a claim of social necessity (i.e., that the rule-of-law system, the deal *as it stands,* is essential to the well-being of both weak and strong). The strong always argue that the deal in force is optimally—or at least so in this second best world—free and efficient. The weak often grudgingly believe them, although not always; sometimes push for revisions of the deal; and sometimes actually win, if not an equal share of power, then some more extensive "rights." Then lawyers and jurists (who have often played no role in bringing about the resulting compromise except to resist it) turn to justifying the new deal as the essence of sacred legality. It is possible to appreciate such practical protections as established "rights" afford without mystifying

them, that is, without supposing that the fact of having been encoded in law makes of any going deal the best-attainable deal.

4. *History liberates the political imagination by revealing suppressed alternatives.* This needs little elaboration; it's a familiar agenda of social history and has been adopted by some CLS historians, notably those of labor law. For example, it is exceedingly useful to be reminded that the present consensus, if it is one, that fundamental decisions about investment, production technologies, and the organization of work are for management to make is a very recent artifact of the post–World War II period, that it can hardly be explained simply as what American workers "want," because it was disputed for most of our history and has only (unstably) come to prevail after long and violent struggle.

5. *History helps to teach that the rule of law "system" is fundamentally misdescribed, that inspected at close range it's not really a system at all, but a complex mass of competing and contradictory systems.* This is the main point that I want to urge here about the utility of critical history.

Take as a starting point the account you give of the rule of law: as a body of more-or-less definite rules, more-or-less regularly enforced, protecting individual autonomy against infringement, particularly infringement by the actions of state officials. Take—because so much interesting historical work has been done on this aspect of the subject—the most traditional form of the account, which stresses the centrality of the legal protection of private property rights in promoting individual autonomy. What can be learned from history?

A first cut at the account points out simply that property only protects one's autonomy to the extent that one has any. Many people have nothing but a property in their own labor, which practical necessity requires them to contract away immediately and some people (slaves, to some extent married women, often native Americans, etc.) have not even that. So for most of our history we're talking about the "individual autonomy" of propertied white adult males, a fairly small minority of the population. "The rights of property!" is therefore an ideological slogan in the narrow sense of ideology as a partial, interested view of the world that parades as a universal, disinterested vision. By our time all this really is obvious and familiar (although it wasn't so at all, to respectable opinion, until recently), so there's no need to labor the point.

Second: even within this minority, there have been from the first settlements fundamental, irreconcilable disputes about what kinds of uses-and-acquisitions, what sort of "autonomy," the law of property ought to protect. Over and over different groups (tenants versus landlords, squatters versus speculators, craft laborers versus entrepreneurs, open-field grazers versus enclosers, etc.) assert conflicting rights to property founded in opposing visions of how property rights originate and what they are for—labor-theory visions, "republican" visions, "craft-communitarian" visions, as well as classic liberal (Hume-Bentham) visions, etc. The content of the law of property has thus been inescapably shaped by these intense political-ideological struggles to establish the constantly contested and thus unstable and shifting core meanings of the concept itself. (CLS scholars or affiliates—Mensch, Forbath, Hartog, Alexander, Bone, come specially to mind—have added to the growing pile of historical elaborations of this point, but of course this tradition of work has long been established in social history.) And this hasn't simply been a struggle among groups, but within groups and even within individuals, most of whom on close inspection will be found to subscribe to several competing and irreconcilable views of property rights all at once.

Third: When you look closely even at the way that the minority-within-the-minority of Americans who subscribed to the classical-liberal theory of property (and it's doubtful that more than a handful can be found in any period who ever took the theory neat, unadulterated with conflicting theories) actually pursued that theory through the legal system, you still don't find some definite, determinate, agreed-upon notion of property rights. Once more you turn up a nest of multiple, various, contradictory, controversial legal forms.

Your response to my letter, for instance, lays stress on that aspect of the "rule of law" that protects "individual autonomy" through restraints on official power. In the case of liberal property law, this translates into "negative liberty"—the set of rules protecting owners against the interference of others, particularly the state, with the owner's freedom to dispose of (enjoy, exploit, alienate) his or her property. But this is a very partial, one-sided, and ultimately very misleading description of liberal property rights.

(a) Your account stresses the ways in which law restrains power and coercion, but not the ways in which it confers power—in the case of property, the power to exclude or expel from the property people who are not behaving as the owner wishes, or to condition access to the property on obedience to the owner's will—and indeed power backed up by the coercive force of the state.

(b) Likewise, it stresses the benefits law confers on the right-holder but not the burdens it imposes on everybody else, which may be of several kinds: duties not to infringe on the right, obligations to pay damages if one does infringe and most important of all, vulnerability to the arbitrary and uncontrolled discretion of the right-holder within his or her sphere of right. Protecting the freedom and security of some through property rights therefore inevitably means limiting the freedom and increasing the insecurity of others. (Alexander's article on the history of the law of spendthrift trusts elegantly illustrates the point: the law cannot promote the freedom of disposition of both the donor who wants to restrict the freedom of donees and of the donees: it must choose between the two.) As historians like Hurst, Scheiber, Friedman, Horwitz, and a fellow named Nelson have been pointing out for some time, the nineteenth-century American legal system devoted a good deal of effort to destabilizing and destroying traditional rights of some people's property in order to create predictable legal expectations in others. I would love to see you explaining to the thousands of renters who every day are thrown out of their homes so that the owners can abandon the buildings or convert them to condos how the "rule of law" protects their "individual autonomy."

(c) Your account (like the two points just made) stresses one peculiar form of liberal rights, by no means the most prevalent form at that, out of the great variety of historical and possible forms. Your form is of course that of the rights-bundle agglomerated in the hands of an individual owner, and such a bundle as entails duties in others not to interfere with the right. But of course many, perhaps most, actual property rights in our society haven't at all been designed to protect the right-holders from interference. Many property rights are rights in common—riparian rights to "reasonable use," "profits a prendre" in fishing grounds, etc.—whose exercise can leave any individual right holder high and dry with nothing. Or they are "privileges," subject to diminution or total destruction by others exercising like privileges—as for example the rights of competitors to the profits of their businesses, or intra-family immunities. (The Singer article we've discussed relates the gradual dawning of the importance of these distinctions in analytical jurisprudence.)

(d) Finally, you stress such aspects of the rule-of-law as involve rights against the state to the neglect of the rights of the state, "public rights" as the nineteenth-century lawyers liked to call them, and before which, they were wont to insist, individual rights must give way. For lawyers operating in this mode, the core meaning of the "rule of law" was that the community must be legally empowered to override private interest for the common good.

The point is that the legal history of this society hardly reveals anything as simple as a tradition that the law has been designed to protect individual autonomy against the coercive and arbitrary interference of officials. That has been a purpose of the law, of course, but it is no less (although also no more) accurate to say that the purpose of law has been to endow both individuals and collectives (governments, corporations, in more recent times labor unions) with the capacity to exercise arbitrary power over the lives and fortunes of others, backed up by official coercion. Property is a set of limits on sovereignty, but it also *is* sovereignty, a means of facilitating as well as of containing domination. Legal rights in action are experienced by some as confirming their freedom and security; by others as enhancing their vulnerability to being bossed around or to accidents of fortune, or simply as random violence. It's vital to emphasize that these negative effects, the vulnerability and violence, don't happen because of some failure of legality, some imperfection or shortfall in the realization of the rule of law: They are consequences of a particular version of the rule of law. How you evaluate such negative effects on individual autonomy as people invoking the rule of law have helped to bring about is a totally separate project. Some people on the right adopt a Darwinian-utilitarian point of view that, at least until excessive regulation came along and fouled everything up, legal rights gravitated to their most efficient exploiters, the losers all deserved to lose, and even the losers profited in the long run. Others, to put it mildly, suppose that view is excessively complacent or simply contentless because of the incoherence of the efficiency concept. But whatever one's politics as a legal historian, one should be not blind to the realities of how rights work, and why people are always fighting over their content.

The relevance of all this to your position is pretty obvious: It makes hash out of the question constantly posed to critics of legal liberalism: "If you tear down the existing order—the system founded on the tradition of the rule of law—what will you replace it with?" The point of the critique is that there isn't, and has never been, an existing order or system of the type supposed, one that has to be swallowed whole (or almost whole with a few changes) or else replaced wholesale by "utopia." The existing order, like past orders, is a teeming jungle of plural, contradictory, orders struggling for recognition and dominance. Radical reformation of this vast miscellany of contingent practices isn't likely to come about through drawing blueprints to replace one fictitiously described abstract order with another (liberal fantasies about the existing order are often just as vague and utopian as any projection of postrevolutionary communism), but by pressing against thousands of local situations of constraint for the fuller realization of the liberating possibilities that are already immanent in this jungle of orders. The role of history in this politics is the extremely modest but perhaps still useful one of trying to describe as concretely as possible how constraints upon freedom get socially manufactured and how people acting collectively through politics sometimes succeed and sometimes fail in breaking through the constraints. It is a little struggle all in itself to strive to be realistic about how we construct our images of our situation, the current system.

A Postscript on Hegemony

Your response at one point makes striking use of one of the terms of the critical vocabulary: CLS and other new forms of legal thought have "destroy[ed] the hegemony" of "traditional" legal scholarship. As it turns out, you mean traditional scholarship no longer occupies the pages of the law reviews alone, but has to share them with law-and-economics, neo-Kantian moral philosophy, law-and-society empiricism, and a bunch of other approaches. Your usage is a curious one—a Hegemon doesn't live alone in the world, but among others whom he or she dominates—but revealing. Hegemony in critical theory describes the power of a world view so dominant that it has passed into the marrow even of those who could benefit most from overcoming it: even the dominated accept its terms as those of practical realism and common sense. In fact your response provides dramatic proof (if more proof were needed) of the continued hegemony of the liberal-legalist paradigm. For I assume that as a knowledgeable legal intellectual, you are already basically familiar with the main elements of the CLS critique of the paradigm, apparently to the point of conceding that much of it may be true, even trivially true and obvious; more: that you have absorbed and processed the main insights of legal realism, structuralism and poststructuralism, phenomenology, hermeneutics, the "new" social history, and history of political languages, and all the other currents that have fed the work of CLS. Yet—I don't think I'm deceived to infer from your book and response—none of this exposure to the work and its sources has affected even slightly your ordinary way of thinking about law. Your defense of the "rule of law" relies for its force upon virtually every structural feature of liberal-legal thought that CLS has been concerned to assault: the oppositions of law to politics, reason to desire, public to private power, practical reform within the system to utopian revolution outside the system, rational-internal coherence of doctrine to total vulnerability to external manipulation by power or whim, etc. Nor is there any sign of your having grappled with the critiques and found them, at the last, all wanting. The critiques have simply left no traces at all. That's hegemony: the embedding of an ideology so deeply that even one of its sophisticated historians treats it as unproblematic common sense or else (your alternative move) as a political faith beyond alteration altogether by critical examination—"Here I stand, I cannot do otherwise."

The fact that law reviews now carry some critiques as well as endless exemplifications of liberal legalism, that there's some real diversity of political views, a broadening of the ideological spectrum, is evidently progress of a kind, certainly a lot better than the old genteel consensus that—in the names of good sense and reason—supressed everything but the liberal center. But tolerance for diversity is hardly a sufficient condition for the advancement of understanding, which demands that at some point we all be willing to put our most basic premises at risk instead of batting away any challenges to them that threaten our comfort. "It's all obvious," "it's all familiar," "it's dangerous even if true," "it's your thing, not my thing," "it's baffling and obscure"—are the noises made by a system trying to repel disruption to its normal functioning. It's time to get beyond all that.

NOTES

1. Karl Klare argues this point eloquently and precisely in "Traditional Labor Law Scholarship and the Crisis of Collective Bargaining Law: A Reply to Professor Finkin," 44 Md. L. Rev. 731, 748-52 (1985).

2. Lewis Kornhauser, "The Great Image of Authority," 36 Stan. L. Rev. 349 (1984).

3. Adam Smith, *An Inquiry into the Nature and Causes of the Wealth of Nations*, ed. R. H. Campbell (Oxford, 1976) II:715 n. 21.

[11]

William Nelson Replies to Robert Gordon

I did not write chapter 16 of *The Literature of American Legal History* out of hostility to critical legal studies, nor am I now replying to Bob Gordon's review of the chapter for that reason. I have learned a great deal from members of the movement in the past, and I hope to learn more from them in the future. But recently I have grown puzzled about what the message of the movement is, and my puzzlement has led to concern that critical legal studies, having accomplished many of its early objectives and spawned a second generation of scholars, may be at a crossroads. When I read Bob Gordon's invitation to join in a debate about CLS,[1] I concluded that it might be useful to explain why I and perhaps others were finding CLS puzzling, and that my explanation, viewed as a piece of data in the world, might help CLS members decide what they wanted their scholarly message to be.

At bottom, the issue that Gordon's review of my chapter raises is whether I correctly understand the CLS message. Because that message is nowhere stated clearly and concisely, I may well misunderstand. There is no other option, however, but to restate my understanding, in the hope that if it is wrong, Gordon will also restate the CLS position clearly and concisely enough for me to comprehend it.

I shall proceed in the following fashion. First, I shall offer two interpretations of what CLS may be that would, however, trivialize and therefore misinterpret the movement. Even though I therefore reject both of them, I find it necessary to explicate them so that they can serve as guideposts revealing where not to search for the essence of CLS. Second, I shall identify briefly what I understand to be the objects of traditional historical writing and traditional legal analysis. I assume that scholars in the critical legal studies movement are doing something other than or in addition to what traditional scholars do, and accordingly section 3 will try to identify what the difference is. Finally, in part 4, I shall restate my puzzlement with CLS.

I. Preliminary Interpretations of Critical Legal Studies

Let me begin by identifying two possible interpretations of what critical legal studies might be, neither of which I accept as accurate.

The first possibility is that CLS scholars may be, as Gordon says, "a ragtag army" for whom no one person can speak because all its members share no minimal set of coherent ideas. But to treat the critical scholars

Law and History Review Spring 1988, Vol. 6, No. 1

simply as a group of friends who like to attend conferences together without sharing common ideas or common attitudes is to trivialize the CLS movement and to dismiss it too lightly. A movement without an intellectual content at its core is not an academic movement at all and would not deserve the serious treatment that other academics have rightly given it. Accordingly, I shall continue my efforts to ascertain the movement's core intellectual content.

A second interpretation of CLS would identify its core content as negative and critical rather than affirmative and constructive. As I understand the history of CLS's origins, those who first coalesced as founders of the movement were brought together largely by their shared sense that traditional legal scholarship was narrow and stultifying. CLS's founders hoped to expose the narrowness of existing scholarly ways and thereby open the legal academy to new forms of scholarship. But the founders did not agree, and indeed, they never thought it worthwhile to try to agree, about the directions future legal scholarship should take.

This second interpretation sees critical legal studies as an intellectual movement of potentially revolutionary dimension dedicated to dismembering established hegemonic structures without any clear idea about how to replace them. There are two difficulties, however, in understanding CLS as a typical revolutionary movement with only a critical and not a constructive program.

For the first difficulty, I rely on a point made by Thomas Kuhn: old, traditional paradigms typically are not abandoned simply because they fail to serve adequately the ends they are designed to serve; old paradigms fail because newer ones appear to serve the same ends better.[2] Kuhn's argument leads me to infer that, insofar as CLS has successfully carried off its revolutionary effort against traditional scholarship, its victory should be attributed largely to the power of its alternative vision and not simply to its critical force. Even a brief glance at the pages of law journals confirms this inference. Traditional scholarship has not collapsed under the weight of some critical onslaught, but is, if anything, more vibrant than ever. All that has come to an end is its old hegemony, as it now coexists with newer scholarly forms—a coexistence that suggests not that traditional scholarship has been shown by its critics to have no worth, but that newer, alternative scholarly forms such as CLS also have significant constructive value.

But there is also a second, more serious obstacle to interpreting CLS as a purely critical movement with no constructive goals. Such an interpretation would place the critical legal studies movement past its prime. As I survey the product of legal scholarship today, it appears that critical legal studies has accomplished its goal of destroying the hegemony of old-fashioned legal scholarship and thereby enabling others who pursue different scholarly techniques to enter what CLS has helped to make an increasingly pluralistic academic mainstream. Of course, the critical scholars have not been alone in devising new scholarly forms. Only a few other names need be mentioned—Bruce Ackerman, Ronald Dworkin, George Fletcher, Lawrence Friedman, Richard Lempert, Frank Michelman, John Noonan, and Cass Sunstein—to make the point that many other scholars, who fit under neither the CLS nor the law and economics rubric, have contributed to the growing freshness of the law reviews, which now publish a wide variety of work. To mention these names is not to deny the significance of CLS, but only to note that it is part of a larger movement that has brought much needed diversity to the legal academy.

If destroying the hegemony of traditional scholarship is understood as the only objective of CLS, however, then nothing differentiates CLS writers from the liberal scholars whose names are mentioned above. Moreover, nothing else remains for CLS thinkers to do but rest on their accomplishments and turn to other work. But two facts are plain. The first is that an intellectual gulf separates the work of Ackerman, Dworkin et al. from that of Gordon, Kennedy et al. The second is that the critical legal studies movement shows no sign of disappearing. These two facts suggest that members of the CLS movement do have a constructive, affirmative program beyond simply broadening the forms of legal scholarship. However, before outlining my interpretation of what that program appears to be, I wish to note both that I may be wrong about its existence and that, if I am wrong, my error will explain much of what may be a simple misunderstanding between Bob Gordon and myself.

Let me return to Mark Tushnet's book on the law of slavery, toward which I did not mean to take any "dig." As chapter 16 observed, Tushnet offers a striking hypothesis that the law of slavery reflected "a self-contradictory world" grounded, on the one hand, in "bourgeois social relations" and, on the other, in "the total relationships of slave society."[3] If the only point of Tushnet's book were to undercut the scholarly monopoly of traditional historians like A. E. Keir Nash, whose concern was to determine whether southern judges treated blacks fairly in antebellum criminal cases,[4] I have only one minor quibble with it. Tushnet is quite right that slave law can be understood from what he labels a Marxist as well as from a traditional liberal perspective; my only quibble is whether he needs the full documentation of a book rather than simply his stimulating first chapter plus a few illustrations to make such an obvious point.

The fact that Tushnet wrote a book rather than an article, together with his failure to limit himself explicitly to the narrow goal of merely establishing the plausibility of a Marxist interpretation, inevitably will lead readers to suspect that Tushnet wanted to do something more. Readers will suspect that the purpose of his fulsome documentation is to establish the superiority of the Marxist interpretation. If Tushnet's readers possess the attitudes of the reference librarian in my local library system who put Tushnet's book on reserve, they will assume that Tushnet has documented his book in full so as to establish that, in some neutral and objective sense, it is true. Readers like Bob Gordon and I, who doubt the existence of a final neutral and objective truth, will, of course, find this assumption absurd; we will conclude that Tushnet means to establish the political superiority of his interpretation.

This brings me again to a point in the analysis that bears repetition. If CLS historians mean only to discredit hegemonic claims of traditional historians and legal scholars to be the only neutral and objective writers in their fields, they are clearly right.Those who are not part of the movement should thank early CLS scholars for making the useful point that many scholarly approaches exist. But continued reiteration of this message, if nothing else is added to it, becomes tedious. I am convinced, however, that the critical legal studies movement has a more powerful message: that its historians claim not that their syntheses are as good as liberal syntheses but that their syntheses are better.

II. The Goals of Traditional Historical and Legal Scholarship

In order to identify the distinctive message of CLS, it is necessary first to set out briefly what more traditional scholars in history and law do. Regrettably lack of space makes it impossible to justify why traditional scholars ought to do what they are doing.

There are, of course, many views about what historians do. Nonetheless, nearly all traditional historical scholarship, as I understand it, is characterized by sensitivity to the unique character of something in the past. Historians, at a minimum, try to show that the past was different from the present. They may also try to do more. They may, for example, portray relationships between two or more characteristics of a past society. Or they may describe how the characteristics of a society changed over time. In whatever fashion they approach their subject, however, the foundation on which traditional history rests is the identification of some previously unknown way in which the past differed from the present.

Traditional legal scholars, in contrast, are concerned about the future.

Whether they are arguing about cases or statutes, their underlying object is to persuade a decision maker that one out of two or more possible rules of law is the best rule for future governance of the issues at hand. Legal scholars, of course, make many sorts of arguments: some argue, for example, that one rule is superior to others because it more efficiently promotes an important social goal; others may argue that one rule fits best with a particular conception of justice; still others may urge the adoption of one rule over another on the ground it is more consistent with cases decided by courts in the past. All of these forms of argument are perfectly appropriate ones for legal scholars to make.

The hybrid discipline denominated legal history can take the form of either historical or legal scholarship. A historian, that is, can undertake to show the unique characteristics of law at some point in time in the past; indeed, a historian can undertake to study past law in any of the ways he or she can undertake to study anything else in the past. Alternatively, a legal scholar can attempt to use data from the past to make a legal argument that a decision maker should choose one rule in preference to alternatives because of the superior rule's greater consistency with past decisions. Both sorts of scholarship tend to carry the label of legal history, and scholarship of the latter sort can, incidentally to its main purpose, contribute to our knowledge of the law's past. But it is important to remember that only the first sort of scholarship is truly scholarship in the history of law; the latter is a form of legal argument. At the same time, it is also important to remember that both history and legal scholarship are appropriate forms of academic endeavor. The two scholarly forms are quite different, but neither is intrinsically superior.

III. The Goal of Critical Legal Studies Scholarship

I assume that critical legal studies historians are trying to do something other than or in addition to what traditional historians or traditional legal scholars do. Their goal, I think, it not merely to portray the uniqueness of the past or to make a legal argument, but to teach a lesson in political theory. The lesson is that law is politics: that legal institutions adopt rules which serve the dominant interest groups in society.

This, of course, is what I wrote in my original chapter 16. At least one member of the CLS conference, writing what he called an "affectionate" history of the movement, so stated the CLS position,[5] and the other CLS writings that I had examined appeared to support his statement. Even Bob Gordon seems to agree with the statement in his review, when he writes that "surely one of the things that historians ought to do is to try to discover the sunken codes of shared inarticulate assumptions that underlie apparently-neutral decisions systems"—codes that, if Gordon's example from labor law is typical, will reveal how dominant interest groups use law to promote their ends.

But, the main argument in Gordon's review, which frankly puzzles me, is that CLS historians have rejected this familiar instrumentalist/realist approach. Unlike the realists, CLS historians, according to Gordon, study doctrine seriously in an effort to address "a successive set of modern Western claims to have *mediated* . . . contradictions [such as the "fundamental contradiction" between the self and others][6]—to have made them go away, or at least to have made them less painful and terrifying—through law."[7] Gordon is correct about the CLS study of doctrine as a device for mediating contradiction, and I ought to have taken note of this doctrinal character of most CLS history in my original chapter 16. But, as I shall try to show below, once the purpose of CLS doctrinal analysis is appreciated, CLS scholars again emerge as realist/instrumentalists, though with a special twist: whereas at least some realists believed that policy entered the judicial process on an ad hoc basis, as judges responded to policy considerations in individual cases, CLS contends that policy enters the law in a more systematic fashion, as entire bodies of doctrine are pulled and tugged in inconsistent directions by conflicting interest groups. But the ultimate conclusion for both groups is that the outcomes produced by the legal process result from the impact of political and social forces on law, not from any neutral content in the law.

Duncan Kennedy's essay on Blackstone's *Commentaries*, together with the three articles that Gordon cites as examples of good CLS history, are illuminating. Kennedy differentiates his scholarship from traditional liberal writing. He says that the traditional "approach practiced in most law school classrooms" consists "of analyzing the rationale of a decision to see if it 'makes sense.' " He agrees that this traditional method is comparative, for he notes that if the rationale does not make sense, then the law teacher has two choices: either "to formulate an alternative rationale that satisfies us of the rationality and justice of the outcome" or to "propose a different outcome, and explain why it would be better."[8] Kennedy notes that his CLS method is similar, "in that it requires the analysis of the coherence of judicial explanations of outcomes"—that is, it focuses on doctrine. But Kennedy's method is also different, since his "goal is neither an alternative rationale nor a criticism of the outcome." His goal "is to discover not what should have been done, but . . . the apologetic motive that the formal rationale was designed to disguise."[9]

Kennedy is thereby striving to show not how the doctrinal enterprise can be carried on more justly or effectively, but rather that all efforts at doctrinal coherence are "charades"[10] and apologies that "judges could not admit and still retain their legitimacy."[11] His aim is not what I believe the ultimate aim of legal scholarship must be: to show lawyers how to achieve just results or, at least, how to achieve the best results they can in the necessarily imperfect world we inhabit. Nor does he pursue the historian's goal of showing how Blackstone or other people in the past were special and different from people of today. Instead, CLS work such as Kennedy's analyzes doctrine to show that, at least in recent centuries, Anglo-American lawyers have struggled ultimately without success to mediate the contradictions of liberal legalism.

The three articles to which Bob Gordon points in his review as good examples of critical legal history are not significantly different from Kennedy's essay on Blackstone. Because Gordon made special reference to them, each will be examined in some depth.

Because she draws on primary source materials, especially the legal papers of an eighteenth-century New York lawyer that previous historians have not examined in detail, and because those sources reveal a body of legal doctrine vastly different from property law as we know it today, Elizabeth Mensch's article on "The Colonial Origins of Liberal Property Rights"[12] does accomplish the historian's familiar goal of portraying the distinctive character of past doctrine. But that is not her stated objective. Mensch sees eighteenth-century doctrine not as a unique body of law whose uniqueness requires explanation, but as "*representative* of a conceptual dilemma well recognized by the most sophisticated of early liberal theorists," who devoted their efforts "to the creation of mediating concepts which served to mask the inevitable irreconcilability of hierarchy and voluntarism."[13] Her main aim is to show that provincial New York lawyers created their mediating concepts, according to Mensch, by incorporating "elements of both conceptual models [hierarchy and voluntarism] into a vaguely conceived combination, never fully articulated, . . . [that] was inherently unstable, however, and seemed always on the verge of unravelling into its two contradictory elements."[14]

As Gordon promises, Joseph Singer's article, "The Legal Rights Debate in Analytical Jurisprudence from Bentham to Hohfeld,"[15] is a detailed exegesis on the jurisprudential writings of Mill, Bentham, Austin, Holmes, Salmond, Hohfeld, and other lesser figures. It appears that the point of Singer's 80-page-long exercise is not to explicate his quite familiar material but to critique it.[16] Singer's own conclusion speaks best for itself. He urges that his analysis, especially of Hohfeld's writing,

> demonstrates that legal rights are justified by a fundamentally contradictory political and legal theory. Legal decisions are not determined, compelled, or rationally justified by the inherent logic of rights, since rights encompass the contradictory principles of freedom of action and security. Since every legal decision reverts to the fundamental contradiction, we have no alternative but to decide each case in the light of competing goals and interests. To make these decisions, nothing can aid us except the same moral and political arguments we use in other areas of ethical discourse. *It is an illusion to think that legal reasoning is any less political and subjective than the reasoning used by legislators, voters and other political actors.*[17]

Gregory Alexander's article on nineteenth-century trust doctrine likewise "discusses a basic paradox at the core of liberal property law."[18] He explains how, when "the mediating features of pre-Classical legal analysis" failed to resolve the paradox effectively, "legal writers of the late nineteenth century attempted . . . to replace its fragmentary approach to dead hand issues with an integrated conceptual scheme. . . ." But, Alexander notes, their "grand design failed even as it was being articulated by such well-known writers as John Chipman Gray."[19] The ultimate point of this "historical account" is not the traditional historical goal of portraying nineteenth-century trust law for its own sake or the traditional legal goal of arguing about the form that twentieth-century trust law should assume; Alexander's object is to suggest "that within the individualistic regime of consolidated property there is no objective basis for choosing between the autonomy of the donor and that of the donee, the dead hand dilemma; any resolution of that problem is a 'naked preference.' "[20]

The message I take from these four studies of the incoherence and contradiction in legal doctrine and from their refusal to suggest how lawyers could have engaged in better doctrinal analysis is as follows: There are no good or bad, better or worse, approaches to legal analysis. All legal analysis is suspect, and every legal outcome results not from the excellence of lawyers' analysis but from the realities of political power. The point of studying doctrine is not to show that good doctrine leads to better and bad doctrine to worse results, but that all doctrine will be manipulated to attain results favored by those who possess power. Thus the CLS study of doctrine seems merely to point me back to the classic realist/instrumentalist insight that power, not law, determines the outcomes that legal institutions will produce.

IV. The Trouble with Critical Legal Studies

I have two objections to scholarship that reiterates this realist/instrumentalist theme. First, I find it dull and familiar. Although I agree with Gordon that we must never forget how sunken codes of inarticulate assumptions control the application of doctrine to cases, we do not need to read lengthy new books and articles to remember. Nothing teaches this lesson better than some of Holmes's classic, and brief, essays and opinions.[21]

It bears emphasis that my objection is not that political values have no place in scholarship. I agree with CLS writers that a scholar's political views should find a place in his or her writing and that, consciously or unconsciously, they probably will. What I find tedious about CLS is its continual repetition and excessive documentation of this obvious point.

I also have a second objection to CLS work reiterating that law is politics—an objection that goes, I believe, to the heart of my dispute with Gordon. Let me note preliminarily that our division is a political and not an intellectual one, which means that I make no claim that CLS scholarship is bad history or incoherent law or is in any way intellectually inferior to traditional scholarship. My claim is that CLS writers are using their substantial mental capabilities to point American legal scholarship in the wrong direction politically. Let me also note that our division is not a typical Left-Right split, and, indeed, I resent Gordon's imputation of some reactionary bias that allegedly produces "a combination of paranoia and carelessness" on my part to "work originating on the Left."[22] Gordon and I both stand well within the American Left, although we have different visions of the causes the left should support. Mine is the left of John Kennedy's New Frontier, Lyndon Johnson's Great Society, and Jimmy Carter's Justice Department, which all stood for racial and religious equality and individual autonomy. Critical legal studies, in contrast, seems part of the New Left and presents a puzzling program which is said to be non-Marxist but which, to the best of my understanding, regards minority rights as an issue of secondary importance and individual rights possibly with hostility.

I can state my objection to the political direction of CLS most effectively by imagining a simple, two-person society in which one person, A, possesses extensive but not unlimited power over a second person, B. Should A govern B through naked power, or should A and B agree to a government under law, even though they both appreciate the realist/instrumentalist insight that their law will be manipulated largely to serve the interests of A rather than B? As I have observed the efforts of the

United States to coerce the people of Vietnam, of the Soviet Union to coerce the people of Afghanistan, of Protestant Irish to rule Ulster Catholics, of American whites to govern American blacks, etc., I remain convinced of the efficacy of law. Both the governors and the governed seem to be better off if the governors rule not through naked power but through power restrained by law. Put differently, it appears that both the strong and the weak are better off if the weak accede to government by the strong and the strong adopt rules permitting the weak to participate in society while simultaneously retaining rights under law to be different in respect to matters fundamental to their identity.

Law can have efficacy and serve as a restraint on power, however, only if lawyers strive to give it determinate meaning that will point toward specific results in at least some cases. Aware as I am of the strength of the realist/instrumentalist insight, I do not expect that law can ever attain perfect objectivity and neutrality. Nevertheless lawyers must continue trying to make doctrine as consistent as possible with a collective sense of right and justice that transcends the narrow concerns of competing interest groups. Legal scholars must, furthermore, heed an elemental truth—that some legal doctrines, no matter how imperfect they may be, fit better with that collective sense of right and justice than others. Racial equality, even in its half-hearted American style, is better than *apartheid.*

This, in turn, sets an agenda for legal scholars. The aim of legal scholarship must be to analyze the preferability of competing doctrinal formulations: to debate whether one particular doctrinal configuration is better or worse than the alternatives. The debate can range in many directions. Some scholars can usefully argue that doctrine is best when it is internally consistent; others can urge that sound doctrine conforms to some abstract conception of justice; still others can contend that good doctrine is that which historically has served some societal need. And, of course, the debate will never end. But through hard work, effective thought, and an intuitive appreciation of society's values, some scholars will enjoy temporary and partial victory in the debate, and occasionally their victories will become law and thereby constrain the powerwielders.

What is most troubling about CLS scholarship is the failure of its adherents to engage in the debate and thus to assist in the process of making law that can serve as a limitation on power. If CLS scholars were advocating programs to use law affirmatively to redistribute wealth and power to the poor and underprivileged, I and many other liberals would support their program. But CLS does not advocate any such program of affirmative legal reform. On the contrary, it appears that CLS scholars are seeking to undermine law rather than use it to better society. My surmise is that they hope, through revealing the false consciousness underlying liberal legalism, to cause the American people to rise up, to marshall their collective power, to overthrow the current system, and to replace it with some utopian alternative. I do not believe, in contrast, that either American lawyers or the American people suffer from any false consciousness. I think the government we have now is precisely the government that the majority of Americans want and the government that best promotes the majority's interests and well-being. The communities of Middle America that periodically coalesce into a majority are the ultimate source of political power in the nation as we know it, and I fear government in accordance with the naked political preferences of this majority. I can think of no way to restrain this majority other than by appeals to law.

None of what I have said is intended to indicate disagreement with the root CLS claim: that deep injustices remain in American life and that one way the injustices might be eliminated is through a fundamental restructuring of law and society. I agree, but for me a trip to utopia is not worth the price. I am not prepared to throw away one of the more just legal systems the world knows, simply because the system is imperfect and a better system *might* be obtained. What I believe separates me from the scholars of CLS is their willingness to take the risk rather than try to improve the law through less thoroughgoing, meliorative approaches.

Perhaps I misunderstand CLS, and perhaps my disagreement with Bob Gordon is little more than a matter of attitude and emphasis. After all, I agree with Gordon about the need for awareness of "the sunken codes of shared inarticulate assumptions that underlie apparently-neutral decision systems," and Gordon agrees with me that "a strong commitment, especially on the part of influential elites, to certain ways of interpreting . . . rules over others that are plausibly advanced, can do a lot to avoid or mitigate political persecution."[23] But I find the unarticulated assumptions and passions of most Americans obvious and rather easy to unearth, and the liberal and humane legalisms that restrain those passions rather fragile. Thus, I find the CLS program of uncovering the assumptions and unmasking the rules trivial and its challenge to law potentially subversive.

I use this strong language not out of hostility to CLS but with a purpose. My purpose is not to keep CLS members from joining law faculties or from writing whatever they wish; my commitment to liberal and humane legalism and my appreciation for what I have learned from

CLS in the past preclude that. My purpose is to induce CLS scholars, in the long run if not in response to this essay, to elaborate and articulate a constructive program of scholarship that will help make our shared law, however imperfect it is, "the best it can be."[24]

NOTES

1. Robert W. Gordon, "Critical Legal Histories," 36 Stan. L. Rev. 57, 116 (1984).
2. See Thomas S. Kuhn, *The Structure of Scientific Revolutions* 77-91 (2d ed. 1970).
3. Mark V. Tushnet, *The American Law of Slavery, 1810-1860*, at 32-33, 36 (1981).
4. See A. E. Keir Nash, "A More Equitable Past? Southern Supreme Courts and the Protection of the Antebellum Negro," 48 N. C. L. Rev. 197 (1970); A. E. Keir Nash, "Fairness and Formalism in the Trials of Blacks in the State Supreme Courts of the Old South," 56 Va. L. Rev. 64 (1970).
5. See John Henry Schlegel, "Notes Toward an Intimate, Opinionated, and Affectionate History of the Conference on Critical Legal Studies," 36 Stan. L. Rev. 391, 411 (1984).
6. The quote is from Duncan Kennedy, "The Structure of Blackstone's Commentaries," 28 Buffalo L. Rev. 209, 211-13 (1979).
7. Gordon letter at 147.
8. Duncan Kennedy, (supra) note 6. 11. Id. at 219.
9. Ibid.
10. Id. at 372.
11. Id. at 219.
12. 31 (Buffalo L. Rev.) 635 (1982).
13. Id. at 636 (emphasis added).
14. Id. at 660.
15. Joseph William Singer, "The Legal Rights Debate in Analytical Jurisprudence from Bentham to Hohfeld," (1982) Wisconsin L. Rev. 975.
16. *See e.g.*, id. at 997, where, after quoting an argument of Mill, Singer observes that the argument "begs the question." Frequent comments of this nature suggest that criticism rather than explication is Singer's goal.
17. Id. at 1058-59 (emphasis added).
18. Gregory S. Alexander, "The Dead Hand and the Law of Trusts in the Nineteenth Century," 37 Stanford L. Rev. 1189 (1985).
19. Id. at 1228.
20. Id. at 1193.
21. *See, e.g.*, *Lochner v. New York*, 198 U.S. 45, 74-76 (1905) (dissenting opinion of Justice Holmes); Oliver Wendell Holmes, "The Path of the Law," 10 (Harv. L. Rev.) 457 (1897).
22. Gordon letter at 153.
23. Id.
24. The quoted language from my colleague Ronald Dworkin, *Law's Empire* 229 (1986), strikes me as particularly apt here.

Nelson's Second Reply to Gordon

I. Understanding Critical Legal Studies

Let me turn first to the historical value of CLS work, where I now think I can identify what divides me from Gordon. I agree with Gordon that CLS histories fit within the genre of "historically supported political theory." I also agree that "legal theory needs justification in political theory" and that some scholars should "work on the basics." Finally, I agree that scholars who turn to history to elaborate political premises will at times gain new insight into the past; much valuable work comes to mind.[1] Obviously, I am one of the last people who would doubt the utility to lawyers of perspectives "that study the legal order from outside."

But ultimately the value of the contributions that historically supported political theory makes to history and law depends upon the quality of the political theory. It is here that I have difficulties with CLS. At the time I wrote chapter 16, I had come to the conclusion that what CLS "historians do is to uncover the selfish motives of interest-groups behind legal enactments, to prove over and over again that law is just a mask for power and self-interest," and I found this "a boring truth indeed."[2] Although Gordon has shown me subtleties and complexities in CLS theory to which I had not previously paid attention, I remain convinced that the main goal of CLS history is to show that "all doctrine will be manipulated to attain results favored by those who possess power." Perhaps I have misread the many CLS pieces I have examined; perhaps they emphasize what I take to be their subtleties rather than what I see as their main premise. Those who read the pieces I have discussed both in chapter 16 and in my initial response must make their own judgment.

II. The Error in CLS Politics

My other complaint, as Gordon rightly observes, was that "*CLS histories, by exposing indeterminancies and injustices of legal rule systems, help to undermine the current system of the rule of law and all the good things it protects, without proposing anything concrete to replace it.*" This complaint, in turn, was related to my acceptance, in part, of "one of the basic dualisms of liberal legalism"—a recognition of a tension in law between "objective and determinate" principles, on the one hand, and policy values that are a "product of unconstrained desire

Law and History Review Spring 1988, Vol. 6, No. 1

or power," on the other. While I believe, as do the critical scholars, that law as a total system rests both on determinate principles and on arbitrary policy choices, I do not understand that the mixture between the two is fixed. On the contrary, I understand that, if jurists and scholars treat law as arbitrary, it will become more arbitrary, and that, if they emphasize its objectivity, it will move in the direction of becoming more determinate.[3] Thus, when I observe CLS historians urging that law is simply politics, I fear that they will point the legal system as a whole toward greater arbitrariness.

At this point, Gordon accuses me of making a polemical attack on the Left, and he asks why I do not do my "polemicizing" against the Right instead. My response is that it is precisely with the Right that I am concerned. My concern is not that leftist intellectuals will obtain political power and use it to tyrannize others. My fear is that the religious right may come to power in the United States and use its power to suppress what it finds sinful. If that should happen, I want to be able to appeal to law to protect the autonomy of people who have differing visions of good and evil.

To the extent that law has a determinate content directed toward the maintenance of the status quo, the appeal will have the desired effect. But what if critical legal scholars have demonstrated that law is simply political expediency both to the liberal lawyers who would advance the appeal and to the conservative judges who would decide it—judges such as Morris Arnold, Richard Posner, Kenneth Ripple, and Ralph Winter, who continue to proclaim their adherence to the rule of law? Will the appeal to law be as likely to restrain the religious tyrants?

In my judgment, legal scholars should be striving to strengthen the capacity of law to restrain tyranny by building as much objective and determinate content into it as possible. Gordon obviously disagrees. My guess is that three underlying reasons account for his disagreement. First, he finds the status quo more objectionable than I do, and hence he is less willing to see it translated into determinate legal rules.[4] Second, Gordon may be less fearful than I of tyranny by the religious right. Third, Gordon has accepted the CLS emphasis on law as a mask for power and self-interest and thus is less confident than I am of the capacity of legal scholars to give it a more objective content.

Gordon's position is neither incoherent, irrational, nor unworthy of respect. I claim equal coherence, respectability, and rationality for my own liberal legalist position, and, in addition, make one further claim on its behalf: that it is superior to CLS as an instrument for preserving the liberal constitutional structure under which we currently live.

NOTES

1. See, e.g., 1 Michel Foucault, *The History of Sexuality* (Robert Hurley trans. 1978); Louis Hartz, *Economic Policy and Democratic Thought: Pennsylvania, 1776-1860* (1948); Herbert Storing, *What the Anti Federalists Were For* (1981); E. P. Thompson, "The Moral Economy of the English Crowd in the Eighteenth Century," 50 Past and Present 76 (1971).

2. Unlike Gordon, I do not understand my conclusion to be an attack on instrumentalist legal history. Instrumentalist work does not argue that interest is the basis of law; it assumes the importance of interest and then goes on to illustrate how particular interests affected particular rules in particular ways. For example, when Lawrence Friedman, the leading instrumentalist legal historian, analyzes prosecutions for petty crime in the late nineteenth century, the point of his analysis is not to show that these crimes were prosecuted at the behest of interest groups, but to identify what the groups were and what they had to gain from prosecution. See Lawrence M. Friedman and Robert V. Percival, *The Roots of Justice: Crime and Punishment in Alameda County, California, 1870-1910*, 311-13 (1981). It is precisely this attention to contextual detail that makes the work of Friedman and other instrumentalist historians interesting and valuable. In contrast, as Gordon himself notes, "traditional" historians with good reason usually criticize' CLS historians "for *neglecting* context."

3. One of the subtleties I have picked up from Gordon is his thesis that intellectuals should be more skeptical about their ability to influence law so fundamentally as to make it either more objective or more arbitrary. This thesis is sufficiently interesting and important to warrant further research, but until that research shows that law professors lack all such power, it would be irresponsible to act as if what we say has no practical significance.

4. I agree with Gordon that the current maldistribution of wealth in the United States is a troubling element of the status quo. I also agree with one of his main themes that law has often been used to defend this maldistribution. It is not necessary, however, to undermine the rule of law in order to rectify the maldistribution. All that is needed is the political will, which currently is completely lacking, to impose high taxes through progressive rate structures and to use tax revenues to fund social programs that would redistribute wealth to the poor.

[12]

Review Essay

The Critical Tradition in the Writing of American Legal History

The Transformation of American Law, 1870-1960: The Crisis of Legal Orthodoxy. By Morton J. Horwitz.* *New York: Oxford University Press,* 1992. Pp. xii, 361. $30.00.

Daniel R. Ernst†

In early 1914 John Henry Wigmore, dean of the Northwestern University Law School, was invited to join the American Academy of Jurisprudence, founded by a group of elite lawyers to reform the law by settling the "small" number of doctrinal issues left confused and uncertain by conflicting judicial opinions.[1] Wigmore responded with a long circular to the charter members attacking the project. In part, Wigmore opposed the Academy because he wanted to reserve "the scientific statement of the law" for that "specialist in legal

---

* Charles Warren Professor of American Legal History, Harvard Law School. B.A. 1959, City College of New York; Ph.D. 1964, Harvard University; L.L.B. 1967, Harvard Law School.

† Associate Professor of Law, Georgetown University.

The author would like to acknowledge the generous assistance of William Eskridge, James Goodman, Gary Peller, Andrew Ringel, Christopher Tomlins, Mark Tushnet, Joan Williams, and the participants in the Georgetown University Law School Faculty Research Workshop.

1. Letter from John Henry Wigmore to William Howard Taft, enclosed in letter from John Henry Wigmore to Elihu Root (Jan. 28, 1914) (Box 117, Elihu Root Papers, Library of Congress); Letter from James D. Andrews to William Howard Taft (Oct. 7, 1914) enclosed in letter from James D. Andrews to Elihu Root (Oct. 17, 1914) (Box 117, Elihu Root Papers, Library of Congress).

science," the full-time law professor.[2] He also objected to the Academy's mission. "The present decade (or even generation) is precisely the time when a formal statement of the law is inappropriate," Wigmore wrote. "The law is so obviously in a seething change that one might as well expect to analyze a chemical reaction while the test tube is over the flame."[3] "Take any branch of law you like," Wigmore continued. Torts? "The old-time doctrines of liability are changing so fast that it is difficult to keep up with them." Criminal Law? "All along the line a radical re-casting is going on." Evidence? "Nobody knows how many rules are on the point of crumbling away in the next twenty years." Constitutional law? "A prophet would be needed to tell us what its complexion will be as soon as the present unrest has subsided; certainly many existing books may be sold for old paper."[4]

Wigmore stood at the midpoint of the ninety years chronicled by Morton Horwitz in his new book, *The Transformation of American Law, 1870-1960: The Crisis of the Legal Orthodoxy* ("*Crisis*").[5] Many American historians, looking no further than great constitutional cases, have treated the early twentieth century as a relatively static period in American legal thought, a long dark age in which most jurists embraced outdated notions of natural rights and Lockean political philosophy. Often the whole period passes under the label "the *Lochner* era," in honor of the 1905 decision of the United States Supreme Court that most notably defended "liberty of contract" from the intrusions of social legislation.[6] In contrast, Horwitz ranges across American law and discovers sweeping change in legal doctrine, legal thought, and social vision. He has produced the most intellectually ambitious, closely argued, comprehensive, and engaging study of American legal history from Reconstruction through the New Deal that has yet appeared.

Horwitz' grand theme is the inherently political nature of law. Following Duncan Kennedy and his "history-of-doctrinal-contradictions-and-their-mediation school,"[7] Horwitz views American legal history in terms of the rise and fall of dominant structures of legal thought. He begins with late-Victorian jurists and their system of abstract, general principles, "Classical Legal Thought." Classical legal theorists claimed they could deduce from fundamental legal principles certain outcomes in concrete cases. In fact, classical legal thought was rife with

2. Letter from John Henry Wigmore to William Howard Taft, *supra* note 1; *see* John Henry Schlegel, *Between the Harvard Founders and the American Legal Realists: The Professionalization of the American Law Professor*, 35 J. LEGAL EDUC. 311, 315 (1985).

3. Letter from John Henry Wigmore to William Howard Taft, *supra* note 1.

4. *Id; see* WILLIAM R. ROALFE, JOHN HENRY WIGMORE: SCHOLAR AND REFORMER 226 (1977). *See generally* N.E.H. Hull, *Restatement and Reform: A New Perspective on the Origins of the American Law Institute*, LAW & HIST. REV. 55, 57 (1990).

5. MORTON J. HORWITZ, THE TRANSFORMATION OF AMERICAN LAW, 1870-1960: THE CRISIS OF LEGAL ORTHODOXY (1992) [hereinafter cited by page number only].

6. Lochner v. New York, 198 U.S. 45 (1905).

7. *See* Robert W. Gordon, *An Exchange on Critical Legal Studies between Robert W. Gordon and William Nelson*, 6 LAW & HIST. REV. 139, 142 (1988). See *infra* notes 59-64 and accompanying text.

internal contradictions, which the great industrial and social changes of *fin de siècle* America made increasingly apparent. In studies of contracts, torts, corporate law, property, and the figure of Oliver Wendell Holmes, Jr., Horwitz charts the growing perception of contradictions within classical legal thought, the collapse of the structure, and the evolution of law in the following generation to a consequentialist, policy-oriented alternative, "Progressive Legal Thought."

Some members of the new generation of legal thinkers attempted to reconstruct a neutral rule of law on the basis of social science. Others—in particular the "critical realists" who are Horwitz' heroes—rejected this new form of legal positivism and insisted that law was inescapably moral and political. The work of "critical realists" would be revived by the Critical Legal Studies (CLS) movement after 1960,[8] but it had little influence in the intervening years, to judge from *Crisis'* overview of post-realist legal thought. Instead, the social scientific strand of legal realists, working to expand and legitimate the bureaucratic structures of the New Deal, was opposed by "legalist" critics of the regulatory state. Particularly in the 1950's, doubts about the ability of experts to produce "scientific, neutral, and apolitical solutions to social and legal questions" led to the reemergence of a full-blown proceduralist approach to law in the so-called legal process school. Once again, legal thinkers refused to acknowledge the political nature of law, this time by envisioning law as a content-neutral set of procedural rules and guarantees.

Horwitz ends his book just as his generation of legal radicals appear on the scene. As a result, the reader will have to look elsewhere to understand Horwitz' own encounters with the mainstream of legal thought. In Part I of this Review Essay I try to complete the story by placing *Crisis* in the context of the two great traditions of twentieth-century American historiography which Horwitz encountered as a graduate student at Harvard University in the early 1960's. I briefly describe legal process theory in law and history, which Horwitz confronted at the Harvard Law School later in the decade and which he attacked in his award-winning first book, *The Transformation of American Law, 1780-1860* ("*Transformation*"), published in 1977.[9] The founding of the CLS movement in that year provided the most important context for Horwitz' subsequent work. Horwitz' general embrace of structuralism, especially as employed in the early work of the CLS scholar Duncan Kennedy, accounts for *Crisis'* trenchant reading of formal law writing on a variety of doctrinal subjects. It also accounts for the book's most significant shortcoming, an overly schematic view of legal thought and legal change.

In Part II, I turn to *Crisis* itself, which I evaluate by focusing on three topics: (1) classical legal thought and its demise; (2) the jurisprudence of Oliver Wendell

8. Pp. 270-71.

9. MORTON J. HORWITZ, THE TRANSFORMATION OF AMERICAN LAW, 1780-1860 (1977) [hereinafter HORWITZ, TRANSFORMATION].

Holmes, Jr.; and (3) legal realism and the "turn" to social science. Horwitz' identification of an anti-corporation, "old conservatism" among the Gilded Age judges is a welcome addition to a literature that still commonly depicts the late-Victorian bench as the willing instrument of corporate wealth. Rather than develop this revisionist insight into an imaginative reconstruction of the diverse mental universe of late-Victorian judges, Horwitz reverts to a schematic and consensual interpretation of their jurisprudence. His chapter on Holmes shows how historical jurisprudence helped elite jurists navigate between potentially subversive claims of natural right and potentially redistributive acts of unconstrained legislatures—a brilliant point. It also inflates a minor shift in Holmes' theory of torts in the 1890's into a full-blown jurisprudential crisis based on an unconvincing reading of Holmes' most familiar writings. Finally, Horwitz joins Natalie E. H. Hull in rescuing the law professors of the progressive era from the condescension of the legal realists and their heirs,[10] and he insists that the two groups be understood as active participants in the same, broad reform movement. Yet he never systematically discusses his legal academics' stand on the political questions of their day, and he ultimately imposes a dichotomous framework on the realists that obscures the conundrums they faced. One would never suspect from *Crisis* that many enthusiasts of the new critical legal methods—like Wigmore—insisted on the regulation of organized labor and fiercely denounced dissenters during World War I.[11]

In short, Horwitz has written a maddening book, much like his first. Fifteen years after *Transformation* was published, some legal scholars and historians still compulsively frame their research to refute Horwitz' claims.[12] Some critics have gone beyond disagreement over fact and interpretation to charge that Horwitz was so blinded by his radical political convictions that he was incapable of producing trustworthy historical work. These critics did not bother to investigate, articulate and engage Horwitz' particular vision of historical utility, and they wrote as if their own understanding of the uses of history was incontrovertible and value-free.

Although *Crisis*, too, provides readers of many methodological persuasions with ample grounds for sharp dissent, it would be a shame if the appearance of the book set off another round of "Morty-bashing." I, for one, have no desire to pillory Horwitz for harboring biases or lacking "objectivity," as if any historian could reproduce the past *wie es eigentlich gewesen ist*. Yet once one

10. Hull, *supra* note 4.

11. On Wigmore, see ROALFE, *supra* note 4, at 226; Stephen Botein, *John Henry Wigmore*, *in* DICTIONARY OF AMERICAN BIOGRAPHY 821-22 (3d Supp. 1973); John Henry Wigmore, *A New Field for Systematic Justice*, 10 ILL. L. REV. 592 (1916).

12. Much of this literature is reviewed in Wythe Holt, *Morton Horwitz and the Transformation of American Legal History*, 23 WM. & MARY L. REV. 663 (1982). Later examples include Peter Karsten, *Explaining the Fight over the Attractive Nuisance Doctrine: A Kinder, Gentler Instrumentalism in the "Age of Formalism,"* 10 LAW & HIST. REV. 45 (1992); Gary T. Schwartz, *The Character of Early American Tort Law*, 36 UCLA L. REV. 641 (1989).

puts away "that noble dream," historiographic criticism can still be meaningful to the extent the critic applies standards that have gained significant support among professional historians.[13] Judged against those standards, *Crisis* sometimes comes up short, but it also goes a long way toward effecting a major revision of American legal history, one which finally uncouples the history of legal thought from political history and joins it to broad developments in American intellectual life. Any historian who would complete this project and finally comprehend the revolutionary change apparent even to Wigmore, an outspoken opponent of radicalism in the midst of the *Lochner* era, will owe Horwitz an enormous debt.

I. *Crisis* in Context

One of the most important measures of a historian is the relative importance she attributes to conflict or consensus in the society she studies. By the time Horwitz commenced his graduate education at Harvard in the early 1960's, the poles of the "conflict-consensus" continuum had been clearly marked out by two great historical traditions: the "progressive history" of the interwar period, most closely identified with Charles A. Beard (1874-1948), Carl L. Becker (1873-1945), and Vernon Parrington (1871-1929), and the "consensus history" of the 1940's and 1950's, whose most prominent practitioners were Daniel Boorstin (b. 1914), Richard Hofstadter (1916-1970), and Louis Hartz (1919-1986).

Each tradition has interpreted the judiciary of the *Lochner* era in light of an overarching thesis of social conflict or social consensus. The progressive historians, as their name implies, were contemporaries of the war over the *Lochner* Court. They shared Wigmore's belief that the liberty-of-contract cases had produced a remarkable degree of social unrest, and they easily assimilated these decisions into their interpretation of American history as a great struggle between the people and the interests.[14] In *The Rise of American Civilization* (1927), for example, Charles A. and Mary R. Beard treated the judiciary's war on progressive legislation as an incident in the "long and varied campaign to force *noblesse oblige* upon the third estate." Though the judges "confessed to no emotional bias," acted "with sober mien," and spoke "with tongues of logic," their "personal dislike for reformers and all their works" and their economic interests ultimately explained their decisions.[15] This attack on the judiciary continued the debunking of constitutional law that Charles Beard inaugurated with his muckraking expose of the Federal Convention, *Economic Interpretation*

13. *See generally* PETER A. NOVICK, THAT NOBLE DREAM: THE "OBJECTIVITY QUESTION" AND THE AMERICAN HISTORICAL PROFESSION (1988).

14. For a discussion of the concept of "interests" in progressive thought, see DANIEL RODGERS, CONTESTED TRUTHS: KEYWORDS IN AMERICAN POLITICS SINCE INDEPENDENCE 176-211 (1987)..

15. 2 CHARLES A. BEARD & MARY R. BEARD, THE RISE OF AMERICAN CIVILIZATION 587 (1927).

of the Constitution (1913), which revealed that America had never known a true "government of the people."[16] As Horwitz writes, Beard's book implied "that the Constitution itself was conceived in earthly sin, the sin of self-interest and bitter group struggle."[17]

The progressive historians remained enormously influential until 1940.[18] But with the outbreak of the Second World War and the nation's confrontation with Nazism and Stalinism, the mainstream of American history shifted away from the progressives. If the progressives had stressed political conflict, the consensus-school historians of the late 1940's and 1950's thought that "the common climate of American opinion" was more important.[19] Some historians, like Daniel Boorstin, running hard from his 1930's enthusiasm for radical politics, celebrated what he perceived as the enduring American consensus.[20] The most compelling interpretation of American history as "a colossal liberal absolutism," however, was produced by a dissenter, Louis Hartz. His *Liberal Tradition in America* (1955)[21] was (in Daniel Rodgers' words) "a brilliant, scorchingly critical portrait of a political culture without exits, without critics, imprisoned in one dimensionality."[22]

America, in Hartz' telling, was a "'petit-bourgeois' giant" whose "Lockianism was absolute and irrational."[23] The Supreme Court was not the bulwark of the wealthy but "the Hebraic expositor of the American general will, building on the irrational acceptance of Locke the Talmudic rationality involved in [its] application to specific cases."[24] The maximum-hour law struck down in *Lochner* was not done in by the machinations of Big Business. Its fatal flaw was its premise: the existence of permanent classes of workers and employers, monstrosities in the Horatio Alger world of the jurists.[25] Judges were not the only people trapped in that world. The progressive reformer, as well, "spoke of achieving a Horatio Alger world himself by smashing trusts and bosses."[26] Even Charles Beard was a child of "the American absolutism" who built his histories around "a titanic struggle between 'conservative' and 'radical' which had little relevance to Western politics as a whole."[27]

16. CHARLES A. BEARD, AN ECONOMIC INTERPRETATION OF THE CONSTITUTION OF THE UNITED STATES (1913); *see* NOVICK, *supra* note 13, at 96, 98.

17. Morton J. Horwitz, *Progressive Legal Historiography*, 63 OR. L. REV. 679, 679-80 (1984) [hereinafter Horwitz, *Progressive Historiography*].

18. *See* NOVICK, *supra* note 13, at 240.

19. RICHARD HOFSTADTER, AMERICAN POLITICAL TRADITION AND THE MEN WHO MADE IT xxix (2d ed. 1973).

20. *See* NOVICK, *supra* note 13, at 327-28, 333-34.

21. LOUIS HARTZ, THE LIBERAL TRADITION IN AMERICA: AN INTERPRETATION OF AMERICAN POLITICAL THOUGHT SINCE THE REVOLUTION 285 (1955).

22. RODGERS, *supra* note 14, at 8.

23. HARTZ, *supra* note 21, at 204-05.

24. *Id.* at 208-09.

25. *Id.* at 242-43.

26. *Id.* at 205.

27. *Id.* at 205, 236.

As consensualism rose to dominance among historians, it also attained hegemony over legal scholarship. The most important center for the new legal consensualism was the Harvard Law School, where in the 1950's Henry M. Hart, Jr. (1904-1969) and Albert Sacks (1920-1991) articulated an impressively systematic and comprehensive model of the "legal process."[28] Hart and Sacks insisted that judicial decisionmaking, properly conducted, distinguished between "substantive" and "procedural" realms. The substance of the law was a matter for legislators and other popularly elected officials, who were subject to interest-group politics and presumed to represent the entire social order. Questions of "process"— about which governmental body should decide and how—could be objectively and neutrally determined. They were the proper domain of law and the courts.

Legal process theorists had a significant impact on the writing of constitutional history and judicial biography. The *Lochner* Court was the target of much obloquy, but more for its usurpation of the legislative function than for the social consequences of its decisions. Justice Louis Brandeis became a hero for his judicial restraint and insistence on following neutral principles when exercising the power of judicial review.[29] The antebellum bench was scoured for common-law judges who arrived at their decisions through a craftsmanlike process of "reasoned elaboration."[30] Roscoe Pound, dean of the Harvard Law School from 1916 to 1936, provided an influential example with his *Formative Era of American Law* (1938), in which he praised Lemuel Shaw, John Bannister Gibson, and Thomas Ruffin for defending the "taught legal tradition" against "the most powerful political and economic forces of time and place."[31] When the legal realist Walter Nelles argued that Shaw had decided a case in favor of a trade union in order to defuse working-class radicalism, Pound rushed to defend his hero (and the legal process). "It would have been quite impossible for American judges trained in the common-law tradition, acting in the light of the received ideals of the times, to come to any other conclusion," Pound declared. He then counterattacked: "It seems to be impossible for a Marxian economic determinist to comprehend an honest man."[32]

Consensual approaches in history and law were still very much alive at Harvard University when Morton Horwitz (b. 1938) arrived in Cambridge after

---

28. My summary of the legal process school follows Gary Peller, *Neutral Principles in the 1950's*, 21 MICH. J.L. & SOC. REFORM 561 (1988); *see also* William W. Fisher III, *The Development of Modern American Legal Theory and the Judicial Interpretation of the Bill of Rights*, *in* A CULTURE OF RIGHTS 266, 297-301 (Michael J. Lacey & Knud Haakonssen eds., 1991); G. Edward White, *The Evolution of Reasoned Elaboration: Jurisprudential Criticism and Social Change*, 59 VA. L. REV. 279, 286 (1973).

29. *See* Clyde Spillenger, *Reading the Judicial Canon: Alexander Bickel and the Book of Brandeis*, 79 J. AM. HIST. 125 (1992).

30. HENRY M. HART, JR. & ALBERT M. SACKS, THE LEGAL PROCESS 165 (tent. ed. 1958).

31. ROSCOE POUND, THE FORMATIVE ERA OF AMERICAN LAW 82, 84 (1938).

32. *Id.* at 87, 88. On Nelles, who was not a Marxist, see Daniel R. Ernst, *Common Laborers? Industrial Pluralists, Legal Realists, and the Law of Industrial Disputes, 1915-1943*, 11 LAW & HIST. REV. (1993) (forthcoming).

receiving his A.B. in 1959 from the City College of New York. He commenced his graduate training in the Government Department and obtained his Ph.D. in 1964. He wrote his dissertation, *The Problem of Tyranny of the Majority in American Thought*, under the direction of Louis Hartz.[33] He then attended the Harvard Law School, receiving his J.D. in 1967. After a year clerking for Judge Spottswood Robinson of the United States Court of Appeals for the District of Columbia Circuit, he returned to the Harvard Law School as a Charles Warren Fellow and commenced work on his first book. Appointed to the Harvard law faculty in 1970, he published *Transformation* in 1977, for which he received the prestigious Bancroft Prize in American History the following year.[34]

Horwitz' work up to and including his first book is a remarkable deposit of the academic era in which it was written. *Transformation*'s first chapter, which was the first part of the book to be published (in 1971),[35] was reminiscent of the consensualism of his teacher, and, in particular, of Hartz' contribution to the "Commonwealth" studies of the late 1940's and 1950's.[36] Financed by the Rockefeller Foundation, these studies took aim at critics of the New Deal by arguing that, far from being "un-American," governmental promotion of economic development and regulation of economic activity dated from the birth of the republic. The lesson of these works, as Horwitz observed in *Transformation*, "was that there was no norm of laissez-faire and that, if anything, laissez-faire ideology itself represented an aberrational strand in defining the legitimate relationship between government and economy."[37] To provide the New Deal with "its own historical pedigree,"[38] Hartz and his colleagues showed how antebellum legislators advanced the broad, consensual goal of maximum economic growth by means of a program of regulation and the granting of franchises and monopolies. They devoted little attention to the distributive consequences of these policies, an inquiry which might have led them to incidents of sharp social conflict.

33. Morton J. Horwitz, The Problem of Tyranny of the Majority in American Thought (1964) (unpublished Ph.D. dissertation, Harvard University) [hereinafter Horwitz, *Dissertation*].

34. Richard B. Bernstein, *Horwitz Wins 1978 Bancroft Prize for Law History Book*, HARV. L. REC., Mar. 17, 1978, at 8. Alfred D. Chandler, Jr., author of *The Visible Hand: The Managerial Revolution in American Business* (1977) and professor at the Harvard Business School, was co-recipient of the Bancroft Prize.

35. Morton J. Horwitz, *The Emergence of an Instrumental Conception of American Law, 1780-1820*, 5 PERSP. AM. HIST. 287 (1971).

36. *See* LOUIS HARTZ, ECONOMIC POLICY AND DEMOCRATIC THOUGHT: PENNSYLVANIA, 1776-1860 (1948). The school was named after a book by Oscar Handlin & Mary F. Handlin, *Commonwealth: A Study of the Role of Government in the American Economy: Massachusetts, 1774-1861* (1947). *See* Arthur H. Cole, *The Committee on Research in Economic History: An Historical Sketch*, 30 J. ECON. HIST. 723 (1970); Harry N. Scheiber, *Government and the Economy: Studies of the "Commonwealth" Policy in Nineteenth Century America*, 3 J. INTERDISCIPLINARY HIST. 135 (1972).

37. HORWITZ, TRANSFORMATION, *supra* note 9, at xiii. Horwitz was specifically referring to HARTZ, *supra* note 36, and HANDLIN & HANDLIN, *supra* note 36.

38. HORWITZ, TRANSFORMATION, *supra* note 9, at xiii.

Read apart from the rest of *Transformation*—as it was by those who came upon it in an historical periodical edited in Harvard's history department—Horwitz' first chapter seemed more like a *contribution* to the project of fashioning a legacy for liberal reform than a challenge to consensus history from the left.[39] Horwitz argued that the emergence of an "instrumental" style of legal reasoning by common-law judges was just as important as legislation in "underwriting and channeling economic development."[40] He attributed the rise of instrumentalism to the widely-shared experience of framing state constitutions in the revolutionary and early national periods. Even with Charles Beard's example, Horwitz did not look for conflict in the constitution-making process, and he did not investigate whether the disintegration of "the original natural law foundation of common law rules" resulted in clearly discernible groups of winners and losers.[41] Indeed, as Herbert Hovenkamp has noted, to read the article alone "is virtually to conclude that the emergence of an 'instrumental' conception of American law was a good thing."[42]

When the article reappeared in *Transformation*, it was as the first chapter of a neo-Beardian revision of the consensus history of the 1950's. The remainder of the book stressed social conflict; its author had seemingly escaped "the dogmatic business orientation of a nation 'born equal'" that Hartz had found omnipresent in America.[43] While admitting some doubt, and (like Charles Beard) never identifying winners and losers with much precision, Horwitz ultimately concluded that "the tendency of subsidy through legal change during this period was dramatically to throw the burden of economic development on the weakest and least active elements in the population."[44]

None of this struck professional historians as outrageous, as Horwitz' receipt of the Bancroft Prize suggests. In fact, a book that used previously underutilized sources to address a major scholarly debate was precisely the kind of work most likely to impress professional historians. Among legal historians, however, the reaction was, as Robert Gordon put it, one of "horror."[45] In 1977 most of them still believed that legal history should be written to produce something which

39. This may explain why a critic of Horwitz once commended the article to me as having been written during "one of that madman at Harvard's lucid moments."

40. HORWITZ, TRANSFORMATION, *supra* note 9, at 1, 288.

41. HORWITZ, TRANSFORMATION, *supra* note 9, at 17. The article was a better fit with Gordon Wood's *Creation of the American Republic, 1776-1787* (1969), which argued that Americans came to embrace the modern tenets of liberalism in the course of adopting and revising the first state constitutions. *See* Daniel T. Rodgers, *Republicanism: the Career of a Concept*, 79 J. AM. HIST. 11, 15-16, 18-19 (1992).

42. Herbert Hovenkamp, *The Economics of Legal History*, 67 MINN. L. REV. 645, 674 n.123 (1983).

43. HARTZ, *supra* note 21, at 205; *see* NOVICK, *supra* note 13, at 415-68.

44. HORWITZ, TRANSFORMATION, *supra* note 9, at 100-01.

45. Robert W. Gordon, *Critical Legal Histories*, 36 STAN. L. REV. 57, 97 (1984). An exception was Willard Hurst, who lauded the book as "a first-rate monograph," but who preferred a more consensual interpretation. "Along with sharp interest conflicts," Hurst wrote, "consensus, too, was part of the legal history of 1780 to 1860." Willard Hurst, Book Review, 21 AM. J. LEGAL HIST. 175, 175, 179 (1977); *see* Aviam Soifer, *Willard Hurst, Consensus History, and the Growth of American Law*, 20 REVS. AM. HIST. 124 (1992).

a future court may need or use, or to be of other service to the legal profession.[46] Given the difficulty of the subject—and the viciousness with which the amateurs repulsed interlopers[47]—few historians were hardy enough to work in the field and divert it from its premises in legal process theory.

In *Transformation* Horwitz mounted a frontal assault on this orthodoxy. Even before the book appeared, Horwitz delivered a scathing attack on Pound's history at an annual meeting of the American Society for Legal History.[48] As the first step in his demolition of the historical pedigree of the *Lochner* Court, Beard had scoffed at George Bancroft for seeing "the movement of the divine power" in the adoption of the Federal Constitution.[49] Sixty years later, Horwitz scored Pound and his epigones as the opening salvo of a full-scale attack on the liberal-pluralist jurisprudence of the legal process school. Pound's lionizing of judges who stood apart from political and economic strife overlooked the fact that the "taught legal tradition" was itself a product of politics. Pound should have acknowledged "the ideological character of professionalization," Horwitz declared. Instead Pound offered his audience of lawyers the "special anti-Marxist medicine" of an autonomous craft tradition to alleviate their anxiety over the politics of law. He "pervert[ed] the real function of history by reducing it to the pathetic role of justifying the world as it is."[50]

In *Transformation* Horwitz warned that the relative autonomy of law should not be confused with "the self-justificatory claims of lawyers to mediate between social forces in the interest of a politically neutral law."[51] To the contrary, behind the legal change that Pound had attributed to the taught legal tradition Horwitz saw an "alliance between intellect and power," that is, between elite lawyers and "newly powerful commercial and entrepreneurial interests."[52] Reviewers charged Horwitz with unsuccessfully advancing a "conspiracy thesis" and, in Poundian fashion, questioned whether his radical commitments prevented him from accurately observing the past.[53]

With *Transformation* behind him, Horwitz set out to write "a very different kind of book, . . . much less technical and much more directed at changes in

46. *See* JULIUS GOEBEL, JR. & T. RAYMOND NAUGHTON, LAW ENFORCEMENT IN COLONIAL NEW YORK: A STUDY IN CRIMINAL PROCEDURE (1664-1776) xxxiii-iv (1944); WILLIAM E. NELSON & JOHN P. REID, THE LITERATURE OF AMERICAN LEGAL HISTORY 1-2 (1985).

47. *See* Stephen Botein, *Scientific Mind and Legal Matter: The Long Shadow of Richard B. Morris's Studies in the History of Law*, 13 REVS. AM. HIST. 303 (1985).

48. Morton J. Horwitz, *The Conservative Tradition in the Writing of American Legal History*, 17 AM. J. LEGAL HIST. 275 (1973) [hereinafter Horwitz, *Conservative Tradition*].

49. BEARD, *supra* note 16, at 1 (quoting 2 GEORGE BANCROFT, THE HISTORY OF THE CONSTITUTION OF THE UNITED STATES 284 (1882)); *see* Horwitz, *Progressive Historiography*, *supra* note 17, at 679-80.

50. Horwitz, *Conservative Tradition*, *supra* note 48, at 281.

51. HORWITZ, TRANSFORMATION, *supra* note 9, at viii.

52. *Id.* at 266, 258-59.

53. *See, e.g.*, Randall Bridwell, *Theme v. Reality in American Legal History: A Commentary on Horwitz,* The Transformation of American Law, 1790-1860 *and on the Common Law in America*, 53 IND. L.J. 449, 472 (1978) (book review); John P. Reid, *A Plot Too Doctrinaire*, 55 TEX. L. REV. 1307, 1311, 1321 (1977) (book review). For defenses of Horwitz, see Holt, *supra* note 12; Gordon, *supra* note 45, at 97.

legal theory."[54] *Crisis* is such a work. Horwitz has by no means forsaken legal doctrine; in fact, one of its best chapters reinterprets *Santa Clara Co. v. Southern Pacific Railroad*,[55] a landmark decision in corporation law. But *Crisis* is less a history of American law than a history of highbrow legal thought; Horwitz' focus has shifted from judicial chambers to the offices of law professors and treatise writers. This change in setting is not the only reason why *Crisis* is (in the words of Stanley Katz' blurb) "a surprisingly different" book than *Transformation*. Horwitz' first book appeared in early 1977, the same year as the first meeting of the Conference on Critical Legal Studies, held in the spring in Madison, Wisconsin. This event, which Horwitz helped organize, is particularly important for understanding *Crisis*, for it marked the start of a lasting and effective organization of radical legal academics.[56] *Crisis* is as much the product of Horwitz' engagement with other law professors on the left as it is a continuation of an attack on liberal or centrist variants of legal process theory. In particular, the rise and fall of structuralism as the dominant methodology in CLS histories of American legal thought is vital to understanding his new book.

Transformation was not, of course, a work of doctrinaire, "scientific" Marxism; it did not dismiss law as epiphenomenal or endow only material forces with causal significance. "Law is autonomous to the extent that ideas are autonomous, at least in the short run," Horwitz wrote in the introduction; elsewhere in the book he occasionally referred to "structure[s] of thought."[57] Moreover, in an essay published in 1977, he applauded Douglas Hay and Eugene Genovese for bringing to legal history notions of hegemony and legitimation borrowed from neo-Marxists in Western Europe.[58] Yet in the eyes of other, somewhat younger CLS scholars, *Transformation* still underestimated the causal role of ideas. These CLS scholars thought in terms borrowed from the structuralist anthropology of Claude Levi-Strauss and the phenomenological Marxism of Jean-Paul Sartre. Thus, in announcing the founding of the Conference on CLS to readers of Genovese's *Marxist Perspectives*, Mark Tushnet (b. 1945) contrasted the instrumentalism of *Transformation* with the early structuralist legal scholarship of Peter Gabel (b. 1947), Duncan Kennedy (b. 1942) and Roberto Unger (b. 1947).[59]

54. Bernstein, *supra* note 34, at 8.

55. 118 U.S. 394 (1886).

56. John Henry Schlegel, *Notes Toward an Intimate, Opinionated, and Affectionate History of the Conference on Critical Legal Studies*, 36 STAN. L. REV. 391, 395-96 (1984).

57. HORWITZ, TRANSFORMATION, *supra* note 9, at xiii, 30, 35.

58. "As the dogmatic shadows cast by Stalinism and the Cold War have gradually dissipated," Horwitz wrote, "Marxists have finally begun to move away from those simplistic slogans by which thought was dismissed as mere 'ideology' and by which law was treated contemptuously as a mere 'superstructure' that simply 'reflected' class relations." Morton J. Horwitz, *The Rule of Law: An Unqualified Human Good?* 86 YALE L.J. 561, 563 (1977).

59. Mark Tushnet, *A Marxist Analysis of American Law*, 1 MARXIST PERSP. 96 (Spring 1978). On *Marxist Perspectives*, see NOVICK, *supra* note 13, at 460.

Kennedy's historical writings in the middle and late 1970's exerted the most influence on Horwitz. As Joan Williams made clear in her lucid account of the shifting epistemological claims of CLS scholars, Kennedy applied to legal texts the aggressive interpretive methods that Levi-Strauss used to analyze myths.[60] He billed his article on Blackstone's *Commentaries* as the first installment of a history of American legal thought in terms of "the fundamental contradiction" of the human condition—"that relations with others are both necessary to and incompatible with our freedom."[61] Not only was that contradiction an aspect of every legal problem, Kennedy declared, it was "the very *essence* of every problem."[62] Every legal epoch erected a "structure of legal thought"[63] to mediate the fundamental contradiction. Because the contradiction was unresolvable, the structures contained internal inconsistencies that became increasingly apparent as time went on. Eventually, the entire structure gave way, and a new one arose to take its place.[64]

As Williams writes, "[j]ust as Levi-Strauss claimed to have uncovered the deep structure of all myths," in this passage Kennedy "claimed to have uncovered the deep structure of all law."[65] To be sure, Kennedy hedged his bets. He referred to his argument as "a shockingly crude model" and a "hypothesis"; he included the "disclaimers" that his work was simply descriptive and ignored "the question of what brings a legal consciousness into being, what causes it to change, and what effect it has on the actions of those who live it."[66] Still, the main implication of his argument, like those of the less deterministic variants of structuralism sweeping American intellectual history, was that structures of legal thought had enormous causal force.[67]

A second installment of Kennedy's history was the immediate inspiration for *Crisis*' account of Victorian legal thought.[68] The essay, part of a much longer manuscript, described a classical "legal consciousness" that reigned between 1885 and 1935. Classical jurists held: (1) that private individuals and the various branches of government were the basic actors in the legal system; (2) that each legal actor possessed power delegated from the sovereign to carry out its will; (3) that an actor's will was "absolute within but void outside" the actor's sphere of authority; (4) that the role of judges was to police the

60. Joan C. Williams, *Critical Legal Studies: The Death of Transcendence and the Rise of the New Langdells*, 62 N.Y.U. L. REV. 429, 464-69, 472-79 (1987); *see also* Gordon, *supra* note 45, at 114-16, 118-20.

61. Duncan Kennedy, *The Structure of Blackstone's Commentaries*, 28 BUFF. L. REV. 209, 213 (1979).

62. *Id.*

63. *Id.* at 221.

64. *Id.* at 213-17.

65. Williams, *supra* note 60, at 473.

66. Kennedy, *supra* note 61, at 213, 216, 220.

67. On intellectual historians and structuralism, see Rodgers, *supra* note 41, at 22.

68. Horwitz credits Kennedy with being "the first scholar to attempt to elaborate a structure of late nineteenth-century legal thought" and to identify "the history of American legal thought as a coherent scholarly field separate from constitutional history." P. 273 n.1. Horwitz acknowledges that he has borrowed extensively from Kennedy's work. *Id.*

boundaries between these spheres; and (5) that judges could be trusted not to usurp the authority of other legal actors so long as they arrived at their decisions through a formal process of deduction from *a priori* principles of great generality and abstraction.[69] Kennedy then turned to Rufus Peckham's majority and John Marshall Harlan's dissenting opinions in *Lochner* for an illustration. With long quotations but no discussion of Peckham's and Harlan's education, legal careers, or political experiences, Kennedy argued that both men shared a common legal consciousness that was more important to the case's outcome than was the Beards' war between the people and the interests.[70]

Even before Kennedy's historical articles appeared, Tushnet had objected to Kennedy's tendency to "reify structures of legal thought" and endow them with "a life of their own that resisted transformation."[71] In the 1970's and 1980's historians outside of CLS published a number of studies of late-Victorian legal thought premised on less idealistic and more eclectic intellectual constructs, such as the "free labor ideology" of Eric Foner's influential study of the Republican Party.[72] Nevertheless, a band of critical legal historians launched an ambitious voyage across late-Victorian law and jurisprudence and laid claim to the entire field in the name of classical legal thought. With some variation (including greater or lesser degrees of attention to "the fundamental contradiction"), Gregory Alexander, Robert Gordon, Wythe Holt, Elizabeth Mensch, Rudolph Peritz, and Kenneth Vandevelde used Kennedy's formulation in studies of corporate law, the Wall Street bar, judicial review of labor legislation, property, trusts and estates, antitrust, and labor law.[73] In addition, Mensch

---

69. Duncan Kennedy, *Toward an Historical Understanding of Legal Consciousness: The Case of Classical Legal Thought in America, 1850-1940*, 3 RES. L. & SOC'Y 3, 7-8 (1980).

70. *Id.* at 9-14.

71. Tushnet, *supra* note 59, at 107.

72. ERIC FONER, FREE SOIL, FREE LABOR, FREE MEN: THE IDEOLOGY OF THE REPUBLICAN PARTY BEFORE THE CIVIL WAR (1970). Foner was heavily indebted to the anthropologist Clifford Geertz for his understanding of ideology, not as "a rigid, doctrinaire, black-and-white understanding of the world, but, rather, as the system of beliefs, values, fears, prejudices, reflexes, and commitments—in sum, the social consciousness—of a social group." *Id.* at 4. Studies of late-Victorian legal thought in this tradition include Michael L. Benedict, *Laissez-Faire and Liberty: A Re-Evaluation of the Meaning and Origins of Laissez-Faire Constitutionalism*, 3 LAW & HIST. REV. 293 (1985); William E. Forbath, *The Ambiguities of Free Labor: Labor and the Law in the Gilded Age*, 1985 WIS. L. REV. 767; James May, *Antitrust in the Formative Era: Political and Economic Theory in Constitutional and Antitrust Analysis, 1880-1918*, 50 OHIO ST. L.J. 257 (1989); Charles W. McCurdy, *Justice Field and the Jurisprudence of Government-Business Relations: Some Parameters of Laissez-Faire Constitutionalism, 1863-1897*, 61 J. AM. HIST. 970 (1975); Charles W. McCurdy, *The Roots of "Liberty of Contract" Reconsidered: Major Premises in the Law of Employment, 1867-1937*, 1984 SUP. CT. HIST. SOC'Y Y.B. 20 [hereinafter McCurdy, *Liberty of Contract*]; Aviam Soifer, *The Paradox of Paternalism and Laissez-Faire Constitutionalism: United States Supreme Court, 1888-1921*, 5 LAW & HIST. REV. 249 (1987); Kenneth J. Vandevelde, *The New Property of the Nineteenth Century: The Development of the Modern Concept of Property*, 29 BUFF. L. REV. 325 (1980).

73. Gregory S. Alexander, *The Transformation of Trusts as a Legal Category, 1800-1914*, 5 LAW & HIST. REV. 303 (1987); Robert W. Gordon, *Legal Thought and Legal Practice in the Age of American Enterprise, 1870-1920*, *in* PROFESSIONS AND PROFESSIONAL IDEOLOGIES IN AMERICA 70 (Gerald L. Geison ed., 1983); Robert W. Gordon, *"The Ideal and the Actual in the Law": Fantasies and Practices of New York City Lawyers, 1870-1910*, *in* THE NEW HIGH PRIESTS: LAWYERS IN POST-CIVIL WAR AMERICA 51 (Gerard W. Gawalt ed., 1984); Wythe Holt, *Recovery by the Worker Who Quits: A Comparison of the Mainstream, Legal Realist, and Critical Legal Studies Approaches to a Problem of Nineteenth Century*

performed the invaluable service of producing a succinct and accessible survey of "the history of mainstream legal thought" in Kennedyesque terms.[74]

As the structuralist enterprise steamed ahead, however, its captain jumped ship. By 1983, Kennedy decided that structuralism had lost the destabilizing value it once possessed, and he dropped it for a post-modern stance.[75] As late as 1980 Kennedy still maintained that legal structures integrated the diverse elements of legal consciousness into fixed, formal arrangements that mediated the contradictions of everyday life.[76] Now he and a smaller circle of associates argued that legal concepts were far too open-ended and plastic to be corralled into structures. Having demolished the notion of logical necessity within legal thought, they turned to social theory, arguing that its terms and concepts were ambiguous and implied contradictory conclusions.[77] All of this might have opened Kennedy to the charge of anti-intellectualism (which Peter Gabel in fact mockingly leveled at Kennedy in a published dialogue).[78] Fortunately, an imposing scholarly apparatus was at hand in post-modern literary and social theory, and this provided the necessary cover for Kennedy and his compatriots as they set out on a new search for the grail of authentic, unmediated human connection.

Post-structuralist CLS has produced a legal history of its own, most successfully in the work of Gary Peller (b. 1955).[79] A full treatment of the "critical tradition" in American legal historiography would have to study this history in its own right. To understand *Crisis*, however, it is enough to know that Horwitz considered post-structuralism and, like most professional historians, rejected it. As early as 1984 John Henry Schlegel could adopt a nostalgic tone in describing CLS gatherings at which "the balding, almost elfin, Morty Horwitz" defended "his limited version of the socioeconomic determinism of legal ideas from the onslaught of his neighbor in Langdell Hall, Mr. Kennedy."[80] And in 1985 Horwitz published a study of corporation law in the *Lochner* era (now the third chapter of *Crisis*) that committed his response to the post-structuralists to print.[81]

Contract Law, 1986 WIS. L. REV. 677; Elizabeth Mensch, *The History of Mainstream Legal Thought*, *in* THE POLITICS OF LAW 286-87 (David Kairys ed. 1982); Rudolph J. Peritz, *A Counter-History of Antitrust Law*, 1990 DUKE L.J. 263. In Holt's case, the use of Kennedy's structuralism was for illustrative purposes only; Holt preferred a less idealist account of the labor contract cases. Holt, *supra*, at 716-25.

74. Mensch, *supra* note 73.

75. Peter Gabel & Duncan Kennedy, *Roll Over Beethoven*, 36 STAN. L. REV. 1, 14-16 (1986); *see also* Williams, *supra* note 60, at 474-75; Fisher, *supra* note 28, at 289-90.

76. Kennedy, *supra* note 69, at 23-24.

77. Mark V. Tushnet, *Critical Legal Studies: An Introduction to Its Origins and Underpinnings*, 26 J. LEGAL EDUC. 505, 510 (1986).

78. Gabel & Kennedy, *supra* note 75, at 5.

79. Gary Peller, *The Metaphysics of American Law*, 73 CAL. L. REV. 1151 (1985); Peller, *supra* note 28.

80. Schlegel, *supra* note 56, at 402-03.

81. Morton J. Horwitz, *Santa Clara Revisited: The Development of Corporate Theory*, 88 W. VA. L. REV. 173, 175 (1985) [hereinafter Horwitz, *Corporate Theory*].

Although he conceded the post-structuralists a realist antecedent in the form of an article on corporate personality by the pragmatic philosopher John Dewey, Horwitz nevertheless dissented from the position that abstract conceptions have no "entailment in terms of more concrete legal doctrines or rules."[82] Rather, Horwitz argued, "most important controversial legal abstractions do have determinate legal or political significance. In the jargon of the current Critical Legal Studies debate, I wish to deny that legal conceptions are infinitely 'flippable' and instead to insist that they do have 'tilt' or influence in determining outcomes."[83] As "a matter of legal *logic*," the attack on formal legal concepts was correct.[84] But in attempting to discredit orthodox claims to "a non-political, non-discretionary mode of legal *reasoning*," the post-structuralist approach, as Horwitz saw it, ignored

> the obvious fact that when abstract conceptions are used in specific historical contexts they have more limited meanings and more specific argumentative functions. We have spent too much effort repeating the demonstrations of the indeterminacy of concepts in a logical vacuum; but not enough time trying to show that in particular contexts the choice of one theory over another is not random or accidental because history and usage have limited their deepest meanings and applications.[85]

In the field of corporation law, for example, each of the two main conceptions of corporate personality (the "partnership" and "natural entity" theories) "carried with them considerable legal and intellectual baggage that did not permit random deployment or infinite manipulability."[86] Horwitz concluded with a call to make history speak to legal theory by "uncover[ing] the specific historical possibilities of legal conceptions—to 'decode' their true concrete meanings in real historical situations."[87]

Horwitz maintains this position in *Crisis*. He notes the view among "scholars in all fields of social thought" that claims to objectivity are in fact "contests over the appropriate generality of discourse" and that "categories, theories, and frames of reference" are contingent. He wisely observes that historians need to be aware of such theoretical debates "without either solving the problems or being paralyzed by them." Is the book "just my story, with all the connotations of skepticism and subjectivity that the word 'story' implies?" Horwitz asks. "No; I still aspire to give the best possible explanation, but without the wish

82. *Id.* at 175-76 (referring to John Dewey, *The Historical Background of Corporate Legal Personality*, 35 YALE L.J. 655 (1926)).

83. *Id.* at 175-76.

84. *Id.* at 176.

85. *Id.*

86. Pp. 106-07.

87. *Id.*; *cf.* p. 202 ("Yet it should be emphasized that this [Realist] critique of deductive reasoning does not question the necessity of using concepts to bring order to experience. Rather, it is critical of concepts only to the extent that they are so general as to be inherently random in their application.").

to suppress all difficulties by intoning pieties about what a terrible place the world would be without an objective account."[88]

With this aspiration, Horwitz has come to rest well within the outer limits of the conventions of professional historians, who have overwhelmingly rejected French structuralist and post-structuralist methods for a position that "allowed for contingency, stressed human agency, [and] was expressed in an 'empirical idiom.'"[89] To use terms suggested by Joan Williams, Horwitz' limited endorsement of the indeterminacy thesis simply acknowledges the "implication of modernism . . . that all histories are either presentist or boring" given "that every interpretation reflects a particular viewpoint," and that all compelling historical interpretations persuade "because they speak to current concerns."[90] On the other hand, Horwitz' insistence on the existence of "tilt" and of "intellectual and legal baggage"[91] saves his undeniably politically engaged work from embracing "bad" presentism—from producing a history that "cares so much about the present that it ceases to concern itself with a conscientious respect for the pastness of the past."[92]

For my part, I tend to evaluate history in terms that are consistent with those of Williams, if more metaphoric. Good historians, it seems to me, write to learn something from the past about an abiding aspect of the human condition. The historian strikes up a conversation with the past, just as the anthropologist in the Geertzian tradition does her job by "plaguing subtle people with obtuse questions."[93] Properly conducted, the conversation is two-sided and respectful. The historian finds that much of what the past has to say is of little or no immediate use. The past, like a person with whom we converse, has other things on its mind, events transpiring well before we arrived on the scene. The historian should be sensitive to this context, because it gives meaning to what the past has to say. By ignoring context the historian might overlook meaning that is important for her own purposes. Moreover, if critics conclude that the missed meaning was a vital part of the message of the past, they will feel free to attack her history in absolute terms (even though at best they pronounce judgment according to the reigning conventions of the historical profession). The historian was not respectful of the past but rude, the critics will charge. She got her facts wrong; what she produced may not be "nonsense, but neither is it history."[94]

---

88. P. viii.

89. NOVICK, *supra* note 13, at 461, 598-605. Novick observes that at the influential Wingspread Conference on New Directions in American Intellectual History, "Levi-Strauss was mentioned only to be put down" and Foucault, Derrida and other post-structuralists were, with few exceptions, either disparaged or ignored altogether. *Id.* at 605-06.

90. Joan C. Williams, *Culture and Certainty: Legal History and the Reconstructive Project*, 76 VA. L. REV. 713, 720, 744 (1990).

91. *See* Horwitz, *Corporate Theory*, *supra* note 81, at 173.

92. Williams, *supra* note 90, at 720.

93. CLIFFORD GEERTZ, THE INTERPRETATION OF CULTURES 29 (1973).

94. Williams, *supra* note 90, at 720; *see* NOVICK, *supra* note 13, at 625-28.

Just what questions the historian asks the past turns in some measure on her own sense of what is most pressing in the world around her.[95] Kennedy's structuralist legal history, for example, addressed the radical concern that most people took too much of the world for granted, that (in Gabel's words) people experienced "falsely mediated forms of unity" which had to be called to mind and then "broken through before people can in fact experience what's going on between them in a real, honest, experiential way."[96] By revealing the determining force of structures in the past, Kennedy meant to flush out and reveal as contingent comparable structures in the present.[97] Given that purpose, he felt no need to provide anything beyond the most cursory "background information" on Blackstone in his study of the *Commentaries*. His reading paid so little attention to context that he violated professional historians' sense of fair play with the past. As a result, his study was attacked as bad history, "interesting but wrong."[98]

Structuralist historians sometimes sense that traditional narrative histories—ones that follow the choices of individual actors in particular contexts and therefore escape the anathemas pronounced on Kennedy—are the products of historians located to their right on the political spectrum. That structuralist historians want to call structures of thought to their readers' minds as the first step in overthrowing them is, after all, what makes many of them radicals. In fact, the past that many narrative historians recover is intended for use in a very different present than the one radical structuralists inhabit, a present in which people do the best they can in a world they can improve or worsen but not remake.[99] To the extent such narrative historians address a broad audience, they write to provide their readers with useful analogies for the commonplace world in which they live. They resist the implication that structures of thought determine individual conduct or render individual variation essentially uninteresting. What good is it to provide readers with thought-provoking examples if they lack the freedom to act on them? If narrative historians grant the structuralist point that what their subjects took as given was in fact historically contingent, they do not make the demonstration of that fact the central point of their accounts. They are more interested in chronicling the diversity of human thought and action under constraint, which is how they imagine their own social world.

95. If only her need to have a nice day. *See* J. H. HEXTER, *The Historian and His Day*, *in* REAPPRAISALS IN HISTORY 1 (1961).

96. Gabel & Kennedy, *supra* note 75, at 17-18; *see also* Robert W. Gordon, *New Developments in Legal Theory*, *in* THE POLITICS OF LAW, *supra* note 73, at 286-87.

97. Robert W. Gordon described this process as making clear "the menace of historicity." Robert W. Gordon, *Summary of Discussion of* Historicism in Legal Scholarship, 90 YALE L.J. 1060, 1061 (1981).

98. Alan Watson, *The Structure of Blackstone's Commentaries*, 97 YALE L.J. 795, 795 (1988).

99. *Cf.* NOVICK, *supra* note 13, at 622. For a revealing exchange on structure and contingency in the context of early twentieth-century history of the regulatory state, see Gerald Berk, *Corporate Liberalism Reconsidered: A Review Essay*, 3 J. POL'Y HIST. 70 (1991); James Livingston, *A Reply to Gerald Berk*, 3 J. POL'Y HIST. 85 (1991).

II. *CRISIS* CRITIQUED

In *Crisis*, then, Horwitz continues his neo-Beardian, post-legal-process history of American law, but he does so with a greater emphasis on revealing structures of legal thought than he displayed in *Transformation*. "Every complex legal system presents a structure of classification and categorization that reveals many of its dominant concerns and points of tension and contradiction," Horwitz explains in a section headed "Legal Architecture."[100] He investigates those structures for the same reason Kennedy did, to reveal the analogous assumptions of the "legal orthodoxy" of the present. In particular, Horwitz has targeted "the core of ideas that constitute the 'rule of law'—the conviction that there existed a structure of impartial and self-executing norms suggested by the phrase 'a government of laws, not of men.'"[101] This is, as we have seen, an abiding focus of his scholarship stretching back through *Transformation* and his essay on Pound[102] to his dissertation on the problem of tyranny of the majority.[103]

Crisis commences its study of law as politics with a description of the "structure of Classical Legal Thought." Horwitz presents the beliefs of late-Victorian jurists in as reified and abstract terms as any work in the "Kennedy school." His structure even comes complete with a Kennedyesque set of "points of tension and contradiction," which will in time give way under the pressure of social unrest.[104] With the stage set, Horwitz then proceeds to set forth the first of the two main conflicts in the book. In the introduction he describes this conflict as a clash between rival structures: on the one hand, "Classical Legal Thought"; on the other, "Progressive Legal Thought," which originated in Holmes' essays in the 1890's and culminated in the legal realist movement of the 1920's.[105] It turns out in the remainder of the book, however, that heterodox legal scholars enjoy much more independence of mind than their orthodox counterparts. The progressives' beliefs appear in nothing like the structured idea-systems of the classical thinkers; unlike their opponents, they are free to pursue political ends unconstrained by a coherent, integrated structure of thought.[106] This allowance for human agency permits Horwitz to present his second principal

100. P. 10; *see also* Morton J. Horwitz, *History and Theory*, 96 YALE L.J. 1825, 1835 (1987) ("All legal systems have a legal architecture that categorizes and classifies legal phenomena. And every system of legal architecture incorporates deep into that structure a set of normative premises about the proper way to talk about law.").

101. P. 4.

102. Horwitz, *Conservative Tradition*, *supra* note 48.

103. Horwitz, *Dissertation*, *supra* note 33, at 9; *see also* Horwitz, *The Meaning of the Bork Nomination in American Constitutional History*, 50 U. PITT. L. REV. 655 (1989).

104. P. 10.

105. P. 3. For a caveat on Horwitz' use of the term "progressive," see *infra* note 300.

106. Horwitz is silent on this methodological double standard—structuralism and homogeneity for the legal orthodoxy; contingency and diversity for the legal heterodoxy—but it seems to be an artifact of his present concerns. In critical legal histories, it would appear that structuralism is the preferred methodology for describing an orthodoxy to be debunked. The heterodox enjoy a measure of the author's Olympian freedom of movement.

conflict: a fundamental disagreement within legal realism over whether the ideal of a neutral and apolitical rule of law could be salvaged from the wreckage of classical legal thought and placed on the sounder foundation of modern social science.

A. *Victorian Legal Thought*

"Although in every other field of American history," Horwitz writes, "Progressive historiography, premised on a conflict between the 'people' and the 'interests,' has been overthrown as simplistic, in the constitutional history of the *Lochner* era it has continued to be the standard mode of explanation."[107] *Crisis* revises the progressive historians in two ways. First, Horwitz ties the jurisprudence of the *Lochner* era to a particular social vision, one which bears a striking resemblance to the "Horatio Alger world" of Hartz' nineteenth-century America. Second, Horwitz attributes much more causal significance to ideas than Charles Beard allowed.

In Horwitz' account, classical legal thought grew out of a coherent understanding of American society and politics, which he dubs the "'old conservative' world view."[108] Old conservatives believed that decentralized economic and political institutions—a "self-regulating, competitive market economy presided over by a neutral, impartial, and decentralized 'night-watchman' state"—were the fundamental conditions of American freedom.[109] As old conservatives, the Classical legal thinkers on the *Lochner* Court were just as appalled as any progressive reformer by the rise of the giant business corporation in the great merger wave of 1895-1904. They were not the willing servants of corporate wealth that the progressive historians made them out to be.[110]

Once it took shape, classical legal thought became relatively autonomous from society and politics. Indeed, it powerfully influenced how lawyers and judges interpreted the world around them. In setting out "the essential structure of Classical Legal Thought," Horwitz follows Kennedy closely.[111] Classical thinkers (1) sharply distinguished between "what was thought to be a coercive public law—mainly criminal and regulatory law—and a non-coercive private law of tort, contract, property, and commercial law";[112] (2) believed that a judge's only concern in a private law dispute was to vindicate the "pre-political natural rights" of individuals;[113] (3) tried to make legal reasoning "self-

107. P. 7.
108. P. 4.
109. *Id.*
110. *Id.*
111. *See* p. 16.
112. Pp. 10-11.
113. P. 11.

executing and non-discretionary" through abstract and general classifications that turned on clear, distinct, bright-line distinctions;[114] (4) assumed that economic markets "reflected natural and impartial economic laws that needed to remain uncorrupted by political interference";[115] and (5) insisted that the state must be "neutral" and "non-redistributive" in its conduct.[116]

Two examples illustrate the value of Horwitz' approach. His account of *Lochner* shows how late-Victorian jurists used the common law of nuisance and constitutional doctrine on the police power to construct a bright line between the rights of private individuals and the larger public against which legislation could be judged. This resort to lines of cases previously treated as distinct shows the classical jurists' penchant for systematizing large areas of the law. Furthermore, justifying public regulation by reference to the law of nuisance allowed for the growth of modest administrative structures without upsetting the classical commitment to a nonredistributive state. It even permitted classical jurists to argue in *Mugler v. Kansas*[117] that the legislative prohibition of alcohol did not redistribute wealth from saloon keepers to their opponents. Because saloon keeping could be considered an offense against the public interest in health, safety, and morals, prohibition simply corrected an unjust state of affairs—the liquor-sellers' trespass on the rights of the public. In contrast, the ten-hours law in *Lochner* could only be a redistributive act. The public-oriented justifications offered on its behalf were merely a pretence for interfering in the essentially private dealings of employers and employees. Horwitz thus provides a more compelling political and moral explanation of *Lochner* than did Kennedy, and he better relates the decision to the late-Victorian jurists' style of legal reasoning than did earlier historians of judicial review in the *Lochner* era.[118]

Even more original is *Crisis*' treatment of tort, contract, and property. Perhaps the most striking illustration is found in Horwitz' discussion of classical thinking about objective causation in tort. A progressive historian might be forgiven for deciding that the question of how to assign causal responsibility for the commission of a tort was too arcane to reveal much about the war between the people and the interests. Horwitz, however, shows how the idea of objective causation played "a central role in preventing the infusion of politics into law."[119] He commences by reminding the reader that the aim of private law in classical jurisprudence was to do corrective justice to private individuals possessed of natural, pre-political rights. In tort law this would be possible only if a court could objectively identify which person caused another's injury. Otherwise, ordering someone to compensate another would be a redistributive

114. *Id.*
115. *Id.*
116. P. 4.
117. 123 U.S. 623 (1887).
118. For example, Forbath, *supra* note 72; McCurdy, *Liberty of Contract*, *supra* note 72.
119. P. 51.

act. The problem, as Holmes' friend Nicholas St. John Green recognized, was that accidents commonly result from multiple causes. "If the question of which of several acts caused the plaintiff's injury was open to judicial discretion," Horwitz asks, "how could private law stay clear of the dangers of the political uses of law for purposes of redistribution?"[120]

Horwitz finds an answer in Francis Wharton's *Treatise on the Law of Negligence* (1878). While conceding the ambiguity of causation in the physical world, Wharton argued that courts should distinguish between "physical and moral forces."[121] Wharton held that only the latter counted as causes for legal purposes, and that jurists could distinguish moral causes from "merely consecutive" ones, thanks to the determinate nature of moral law. Treating all antecedents as causal, Wharton claimed, would lead to the ruin of the free market system. Because one could always locate a capitalist who was in some way responsible for an accident, he reasoned, actors with shallow pockets would learn to act negligently, confident that they would be passed over "to reach the capitalist who is a remoter condition."[122] Rather than be held liable for all disasters, capitalists would stop conducting business. "No factory would be built," and in time there would be "no capitalist to be found to be sued."[123] Horwitz' comment seems apt: "This seemingly sudden leap that Wharton makes from the technical question of legal causation to his warning of the destruction of capitalism is startling only if one fails to understand the systemic character of legal thought in the late nineteenth century."[124]

If a structuralist approach to legal thought can produce insights such as these, no further evidence of its value as a historical methodology is necessary. The shortcomings of Horwitz' approach are worth noting, however. They suggest the kind of insights to be gained from historians who are more willing than is Horwitz to pursue the origins and limits of classical legal thought—or even to concede that the thought of late-Victorian jurists was too diverse and contradictory to be captured in anything as rigid and precise as a structure. Approached in this spirit, late-Victorian jurisprudence looks significantly different from what we see in *Crisis*. It appears better grounded in moral and religious thought and more the project of a particular segment of Victorian society than a consensual construct. Finally, a less structural approach to legal thought can produce a more convincing account of the decline of late-Victorian legal thought than Horwitz has provided.

Where *did* classical legal thought come from, anyway? As compellingly as Kennedy's and Horwitz' structure accounts for much of the law between the Civil War and the Great Depression, classical legal thought is, after all, an

120. P. 52.
121. P. 54 (quoting FRANCIS WHARTON, A SUGGESTION AS TO CAUSATION 11 (1874)).
122. P. 55.
123. *Id.*
124. *Id.*

historian's artifact and not an historical phenomenon. Late-Victorian lawyers and judges never learned its tenets in the static and systematic form they take in critical legal histories. No single mind produced the cultural universe in which these figures moved; no coherent, neatly-organized system of thought lay in wait until the moment it could leap undisturbed into their minds.[125] Yet once one sets out to investigate where late-Victorian jurists found their ideas and why they thought them useful, one quickly leaves behind the sweeping prospect structuralism affords and descends into a jungle of contingency and detail.

A jungle, but not a chaos. Regularities and generalities await the historian, but only if she is willing to think of late-Victorian legal thought in less consensual and structured terms than does Horwitz. For Horwitz' account of the late-nineteenth century *is* consensual: classical legal thought enjoys the seemingly universal allegiance of the Victorian bench and bar.[126] We would have a more dynamic understanding of classical legal thought if we investigated the breadth of support for its tenets rather than assumed its omnipresence. The result of our investigations might not upset *Crisis'* premise that classical jurisprudence obtained a hegemony over its rivals, any more than R. Kent Newmyer's remarkable essay made the "New England legal culture" of Joseph Story and the Harvard Law School appear any less influential during the antebellum period.[127] The advantages of viewing late-Victorian legal thought as the dynamic project of jurists from a particular class, region, and ethnicity are important nonetheless.[128]

Consider the example of Daniel Davenport, a lawyer born to well-to-do parents in small-town Connecticut in 1852, educated at Yale College between 1869 and 1873, active in Democratic Party politics from before Grover Cleveland's first presidency down to the triumph of the Silver Democrats in 1896, and lawyer to private individuals in their personal and commercial affairs until the turn of the twentieth century. In 1902 he gave up his regular practice to assume the leadership of the American Anti-Boycott Association (AABA), a group formed by proprietary capitalists to bring test cases against organized labor. A Horwitz-inspired historian who stumbled upon Davenport's speeches for the AABA could easily mine them to show how the law of industrial disputes instantiated the structure of classical legal thought. When those speeches are

125. For historians' growing doubts about structuralism in the historiography of the "republican ideology," see James T. Kloppenberg, *The Virtues of Liberalism: Christianity, Republicanism, and Ethics in Early American Political Discourse*, 74 J. AM. HIST. 9 (1987); *see also* RODGERS, *supra* note 14.

126. This is analogous to Horwitz' account of eighteenth-century jurisprudence in *Transformation*, which even a friendly reviewer felt he presented in overly consensual terms. Holt, *supra* note 12, at 704-07.

127. R. Kent Newmyer, *Harvard Law School, New England Legal Culture, and the Antebellum Origins of American Jurisprudence*, 74 J. AM. HIST. 814 (1987); *see also* DANIEL W. HOWE, *Victorian Culture in America*, *in* VICTORIAN AMERICA 3, 6 (1976).

128. One advantage of this approach is that it invites inquiry into how legal thought varied across regions. Harry Scheiber faulted *Transformation* for not taking regional differences into account. Harry N. Scheiber, *Back to "The Legal Mind"? Doctrinal Analysis and the History of Law*, 5 REVS. AM. HIST. 458, 462 (1977) (book review). The same criticism holds for *Crisis*.

placed in biographical context, however, one can account for much content that is ignored by or rests uneasily within structuralist histories. One can also develop accounts of causal change that are more convincing and that better relate our legal past to other branches of American history.

In a forthcoming book, I have tried to do this by putting Davenport's legal thought in the context of developments in gender, politics and industry at the turn of the twentieth century. If Davenport was representative of the college-educated lawyers who dominated the bar associations and law schools of the industrial Northeast and Midwest, his example calls for significant revisions of the critical history of late-Victorian legal thought. What Davenport encountered as he prepared for the bar was nothing so coherent as a structure. In his preparatory academy and at Yale he read the classics of civic humanism, discovering in them the ideas we now know of as the "republican ideology."[129] Under the guidance of William Graham Sumner, Davenport also read works in the liberal tradition, such as textbooks on classical economics and Francis Lieber's *On Civil Liberty* (1856). He learned of the natural rights tradition through his avid interest in the revolutionary era. He also encountered, but apparently failed to appreciate, the historicist learning his teachers had either brought back from their studies in Germany, discovered in Lieber's book, or found in Herbert Spencer's sociology. Finally, Davenport was still taught the rudiments of common sense moral philosophy, in his case from Yale President Noah Porter. Believing with Porter that God had endowed all human beings with the same capacity for knowing right and wrong, Davenport did not hesitate to measure human conduct against universal and immutable standards, to judge public officials less by the consequences of their actions than the morality of their intentions, and to treat social ills as the product of moral shortcomings and human sinfulness.[130]

If this or something like it was the diverse and potentially conflicting cultural inheritance that late-Victorians brought to the law, then some of the anomalies left unexplained by Horwitz can be explained. Take, for example, the unabashed moralism of Wharton's discussion of causation in his 1873 treatise on negligence. Horwitz recognizes this as a problem, given his premise that classical jurists distinguished sharply between objective law and subjective politics. If politics could not produce determinate legal rules, then why in the world did Wharton think morality could? Horwitz tells us that by the end of the century jurists would downplay the "moral element in causation," thereby revealing "their own skepticism about the objectivity of moral categories." He does not convincingly

129. *See* Daniel W. Howe, *Classical Education and Political Culture in Nineteenth-Century America*, 5 INTELL. HIST. GROUP NEWSL. (Intell. Hist. Group, New York, N.Y.), Spring 1983, at 9.

130. *See* Daniel R. Ernst, Davenport (June 25, 1992) (unpublished manuscript, on file with author) the text: [subsequently published as Chapter Two of DANIEL R. ERNST, *Lawyers against Labor: From Individual Rights to Corporate Liberalism* (1995)] The greater attention to formal education that I advocate here is similar to the approach employed in HERBERT HOVENKAMP, ENTERPRISE AND AMERICAN LAW, 1836-1937 (1991), although I would not confine myself to highbrow economic thought and would admit to more contingency and diversity.

explain why, well into the twentieth century, James Barr Ames—a classical jurist if ever there was one—continued to believe that law should follow moral precepts.[131]

Once we look for the influence of moral philosophy, however, we can account for the certainty of Wharton and Ames, as well as judges like Stephen J. Field.[132] We can understand that a system of morality grounded in Protestant Christianity was at least as important a source of their belief in the justice of a priori rules as the notion that legal outcomes could (in Holmes' words) "be worked out like mathematics from some general axioms of conduct." As Holmes' *The Path of the Law* suggests, the "confusion between morality and law" was the more widespread error, at least among Holmes' brethren on the Supreme Judicial Court. "[T]he notion that the only force at work in the development of the law is logic" was merely "the natural error of the schools,"[133] notably the Harvard Law School of Christopher Columbus Langdell.

Another unexplained anomaly in *Crisis* is the coexistence in Victorian thought of natural rights and historicist jurisprudence. At times Horwitz states without qualification that classical jurists considered rights "natural" and "pre-political."[134] Yet his chapter on Holmes acknowledges that Victorian legal writers "as distinguished as Sir Henry Maine and as pedestrian as James Coolidge Carter deified custom" and deployed it "as a conservative intellectual construct . . . to neutralize or delegitimize legislative authority and to defend the slow process of common law decision making under the guidance of judges."[135] Since Horwitz first gave the chapter as the Rosenthal Lectures at the Northwestern University Law School in 1981, a flurry of articles have demonstrated the influence of historicist thought on such important late nineteenth-century treatise writers as Christopher Tiedeman, Thomas Cooley, and John Norton Pomeroy.[136] Read with Dorothy Ross' landmark history of

131. *See* James Barr Ames, *Law and Morals*, 22 HARV. L. REV. 97 (1908). Horwitz attempts an answer by discovering "a return to an individualistic morality" in the early twentieth century and argues that Ames "revived a moralistic attack upon strict liability." Pp. 125-26. He offers no authority for the proposition that orthodox legal thought in general or Ames in particular ever categorically rejected the moral underpinnings of jurisprudence. Randall Bridwell accused Horwitz of inventing about-faces to explain the course of antebellum commercial law in *Transformation*. Bridwell, *supra* note 53, at 493 n.121. I regard the "revival" of moralistic jurisprudence as another such invention.

132. RALPH H. GABRIEL, THE COURSE OF AMERICAN DEMOCRATIC THOUGHT: AN INTELLECTUAL HISTORY SINCE 1815, at 216-27 (1940) (describing the philosophy of Judge Field).

133. OLIVER WENDELL HOLMES, JR., *The Path of the Law* (1897), *in* COLLECTED LEGAL PAPERS 167, 180 (1920) [hereinafter HOLMES, COLLECTED LEGAL PAPERS]. Thus, Horwitz' claim that, above all, "late-nineteenth-century orthodox legal thinkers" tried to "represent legal reasoning as fundamentally different from political or moral reasoning" needs qualification. Pp. 198-99. Both middlebrow jurists and highbrow legal scientists agreed that legal reasoning was fundamentally different from partisan politics. Many judges and some legal academics would deny that legal and moral reasoning was "fundamentally different." Pp. 198-99.

134. P. 155.

135. P. 121.

136. RODGERS, *supra* note 14, at 152-55; Louise A. Halper, *Christopher G. Tiedeman, "Laissez-Faire Constitutionalism" and the Dilemmas of Small-Scale Property in the Gilded Age*, 51 OHIO ST. L.J. 1349, 1363-65 (1990); William P. LaPiana, *The Legal Culture of the Formative Period in Sherman Act Juris-*

American social science and other works,[137] these articles suggest that historicist thought sprang from more diverse and diffuse sources than Darwin's *Origin of the Species* or Herbert Spencer's *Social Statics*.

The recent studies leave many questions unclear. We do not know how many Victorian lawyers and judges joined the academicians in sensing a conflict between a Lockean view of rights originating in a pre-political state of nature and a historicist understanding of rights as "created for the individual by laws and institutions."[138] We do not know how many believed, with Noah Porter, that the state could defend not only "the so-called natural rights of life, liberty, and property" but also "the traditions of the past, the habits of the present, and, above all . . . the intelligence, the self-reliance, and the moral worth of the people."[139] We do not understand what circumstances led some late-Victorians—notably Supreme Court Justices Stephen Field, David Brewer, and Rufus Peckham—to prefer natural rights arguments and others to prefer an historicist jurisprudence.

Finally, we have no good idea what difference the two jurisprudential approaches made in concrete cases. Some evidence suggests that historicist jurists were more tolerant of new claims of authority for the state. Cooley, for example, could easily bring himself to serve as the first chairman of the Interstate Commerce Commission, which Brewer considered an abomination.[140] The historicist Holmes considered eugenics one of the demands the state could legitimately make on its citizens.[141] In contrast, Daniel Davenport, a believer in natural rights, opposed compulsory sterilization of the criminally insane.[142] Yet even historicist thinkers could oppose novel uses of state power because they believed the laws of history followed a certain, divine logic. This was true of Sumner. He saw the United States developing teleologically toward the "more

prudence, 35 N.Y.L. SCH. L. REV. 827 (1990); David N. Mayer, *The Jurisprudence of Christopher G. Tiedeman: A Study in the Failure of Laissez-Faire Constitutionalism*, 55 MO. L. REV. 93 (1990); Stephan A. Siegel, *Historicism in Late Nineteenth-Century Constitutional Thought*, 1990 WIS. L. REV. 1431. As early as 1967, Alan Jones objected to treating Cooley as a natural rights jurist, but Jones' work was overlooked by the historians of classical legal thought. Alan Jones, *Thomas M. Cooley and "Laissez-Faire Constitutionalism": A Reconsideration*, 53 J. AM. HIST. 751, 762-63 (1967).

137. DOROTHY ROSS, THE ORIGINS OF AMERICAN SOCIAL SCIENCE 106, 112, 153-54 (1991); LOUISE L. STEVENSON, SCHOLARLY MEANS TO EVANGELICAL ENDS: THE NEW HAVEN SCHOLARS AND THE TRANSFORMATION OF HIGHER LEARNING IN AMERICA, 1830-1890 (1986).

138. WILLIAM GRAHAM SUMNER, WHAT SOCIAL CLASSES OWE TO EACH OTHER 30 (New York, Harper & Bros. 1883).

139. NOAH PORTER, THE ELEMENTS OF MORAL SCIENCE 490-92 (New York, Charles Scribner's Sons 1885). Novack's recent work suggests that Porter's view enjoyed broad support. WILLIAM J. NOVACK, INTELLECTUAL ORIGINS OF THE STATE POLICE POWER: THE COMMON LAW VISION OF A WELL-REGULATED SOCIETY (Institute for Legal Studies, University of Wisconsin at Madison, Legal History Program Working Papers Series No. 2, 1989).

140. Jones, *supra* note 136, at 767-77; SIDNEY FINE, LAISSEZ FAIRE AND THE GENERAL-WELFARE STATE: A STUDY OF CONFLICT IN AMERICAN THOUGHT, 1865-1901, at 128-29 (1956).

141. Buck v. Bell, 274 U.S. 200, 207 (1927); *see also* Mary L. Dudziak, *Oliver Wendell Holmes as a Eugenic Reformer: Rhetoric in the Writing of Constitutional Law*, 71 IOWA L. REV. 833 (1986).

142. Letter from Daniel Davenport to W. O. Burr (Dec. 6, 1909) (on file with Yale University Archives).

complete realization of a society of free men united by contract."[143] Any social practices incompatible with that ideal ran counter to the mainstream of historical development and were illegitimate.

Crisis does not help us much with these matters. Horwitz offers a shrewd and convincing assessment of the strategic value of historicism; for example, he calls custom "a Rorschach blot onto which conservative social thinkers could project their fantasies of a naturally harmonious society free from the twin dangers of anarchy and coercion, yet capable of organic change and growth."[144] But his premise that classical legal thought existed as a coherent structure keeps Horwitz from pursuing the diversity of Victorian jurisprudence. A narrative historian might think that exploring this diversity could turn up crucial context for the drawing of sensible analogies from the past. Horwitz apparently has concluded that more context would simply obscure the "essential structure" of thought and hamper the debunking force of his history.[145]

One aspect of *Crisis*' treatment of Victorian jurisprudence makes matters worse: Horwitz' somewhat vague and schematic explanation of the fall of classical legal thought. His basic strategy is to argue that sweeping economic or social development aggravated the internal contradictions of the structure until a triggering event (the *Lochner* decision, according to the Introduction) precipitated a sustained, political, and progressive critique of the old order.[146] In *Crisis*, Horwitz advances a cataclysmic model of legal change. Like geologic epochs, his legal eras begin and end in catastrophic events.

In *Crisis*, Horwitz identifies several different aggravating socioeconomic forces. One candidate is the rise of the "business" or "large national" corporation.[147] "The large national corporation not only drew into question the orthodox separation of public and private law," he writes at one point, "but it also challenged the notion that modern property could continue to be represented as a pre-political right and not as a creature of social choice."[148] Another is "the emergence of organizational society," a related but more general development suggested in the work of Robert Wiebe, Ellis Hawley and others.[149] Finally, and most emphatically, Horwitz argues in his chapter on

143. SUMNER, *supra* note 138, at 24; *see* FINE, *supra* note 140, at 84.

144. P. 123.

145. This is how I account for Horwitz' complaint that "the ratio of interesting theoretical generality to undigested historical detail is too small" in E. P. Thompson's *Whigs and Hunters*. Horwitz, *supra* note 58, at 564.

146. P. 3.

147. Pp. 145, 167. The distinction may make a difference. The "business corporation" that in Chapter Five generated valuable but "non-physical" property, flushing into the open "all of the contradictions that had been barely suppressed in traditional doctrine," has been in existence since the antebellum period. P. 151. The large, nationally organized corporation with significant market power, which Horwitz seems more frequently to have in mind, only became a regular feature of the industrial landscape after 1895.

148. P. 167.

149. Pp. 5, 66. The "organizational synthesis" posits that the example of the large business corporation encouraged a broad section of the American populace to pursue social order and stability through bureaucratic structures and administrative expertise. *See* ELLIS W. HAWLEY, THE GREAT WAR AND THE SEARCH FOR

Holmes that the "radical social and economic conflicts of the 1890's" permanently changed the course of American legal thought in two ways. First, the appearance of great social unrest belied the existence of "widely shared customary norms" (thus destroying a premise of historicist jurisprudence).[150] Second, the "emergence of fundamentally new problems" such as economic concentration, labor strife, and "the shift from landed to intangible property" highlighted "the internal inconsistency of natural rights conceptions."[151] The "widespread experience of Americans during the 1890s that the country was falling apart," Horwitz concludes, "is perhaps the most important key to understanding the shift in thought not only in law but in virtually every field of intellectual inquiry."[152]

None of this is unambiguously wrong. It might even be sufficient if experience translated itself into thought uniformly and without the mediation of culture and circumstance. The difficulty is that far too many lawyers and judges ignored these great social events or found that they could account for them without discarding their basic assumptions about law and life. Horwitz rightly notes the appearance in the 1890's of the belief that society was to some extent amenable to self-conscious attempts at social control. To the extent that historicist jurisprudence assumed society developed organically, in response to natural or divine laws, it lost adherents in the first decades of the twentieth century.[153] What survived into the 1920's and beyond was the belief that social processes had a life of their own and that they sometimes produced widely-shared norms. If the mores of early twentieth-century social science lost the *gemeinschaftlich* quality of their counterparts in German historicism, social process and social consensus continued to function as mediating forces between natural rights individualism and democratic statism long after the triumph of the corporation, the advent of organizational society, and the social upheavals of the 1890's.[154]

Rather than trace the persistence of consensualism in American legal thought, Horwitz retains conflict as his main engine of historical change. Horwitz forsakes Hartz and joins Charles Beard in seeing the progressive era as a period of fundamental political struggle between progressive legal thinkers and anti-corporate "old conservatives" and pro-corporate "new conservatives." Horwitz'

A MODERN ORDER 6-9 (1979); RICHARD L. MCCORMICK, THE PARTY PERIOD AND PUBLIC POLICY: AMERICAN POLITICS FROM THE AGE OF JACKSON TO THE PROGRESSIVE ERA 313-15 (1986); ROBERT H. WIEBE, THE SEARCH FOR ORDER, 1877-1920 (1967); Daniel T. Rodgers, *In Search of Progressivism*, 10 REVS. AM. HIST. 113, 119-21 (1982).

150. P. 138.

151. Pp. 138-39.

152. P. 142.

153. Note, however, that James Coolidge Carter wrote Horwitz' exemplar of customary jurisprudence in the twentieth century. JAMES COOLIDGE CARTER, LAW: ITS ORIGIN, GROWTH AND FUNCTION: BEING A COURSE OF LECTURES PREPARED FOR DELIVERY BEFORE THE LAW SCHOOL OF HARVARD UNIVERSITY (1907).

154. *See* Ernst, *supra* note 32.

use of the Beardian terms "conservative" and "progressive" succeeds in underlining the political content of legal thought, but in light of later works of cultural and political history the terms seem terribly blunt and somewhat idiosyncratic. For example, Henry May's interpretation of the prewar era as the end of American innocence is called by Horwitz the last days of a "Victorian world view" before the skepticism and doubt of the 1920's.[155] Yet he never shows us what was "conservative" or "progressive" in the thought of, say, James Barr Ames or Roscoe Pound; what if anything they shared with Lyman Abbott, a leader of the Social Gospel movement; or where either law professor differed from a younger figure like Walter Lippmann. Horwitz' abstract approach raises the specter of legal historians miring themselves in a parochial debate over the content of old conservative, new conservative, progressive, and realist legal thought—a repeat, if you will, of the quarrels over instrumentalism and formalism Horwitz helped provoke with his first article.[156]

Horwitz, of course, breaks no historical conventions in choosing to privilege conflict over consensus. Historical eras are not innately conflictual or consensual. They can be characterized as either, depending upon where the historian looks. As we shall see, Horwitz' attempts to connect legal realism to political conflict produce enormously valuable insights. One drawback of Horwitz' choice, however, is that he leaves to other historians the work of sorting out the common and the contested elements in early twentieth-century legal thought. Only when someone turns to the period without Horwitz' limiting assumptions, with more interest in studying thinkers in their social and political contexts, and with a greater desire to relate developments in legal thought to the history of social thought and social science, will we understand how a progressive academician like Pound and an outspoken conservative like Wigmore could differ so sharply on political matters and still reject Langdell's legal science as hopelessly unrealistic.

B. *Holmes Misplaced*

It happens that Horwitz himself provides an excellent argument for jettisoning the labels "conservative" and "progressive" in his extraordinary chapter on Oliver Wendell Holmes, Jr.[157] By pointing out the similarities in

155. P. 170; *see* HENRY F. MAY, *The Rebellion of the Intellectuals, 1912-1917*, *in* IDEAS, FAITHS, AND FEELINGS: ESSAYS ON AMERICAN INTELLECTUAL AND RELIGIOUS HISTORY 1952-1982, at 3, 11 (1983); HENRY F. MAY, THE END OF AMERICAN INNOCENCE: A STUDY OF THE FIRST YEARS OF OUR OWN TIME, 1912-1917 (1959).

156. *See* William E. Nelson, *The Impact of the Antislavery Movement upon Styles of Judicial Reasoning in Nineteenth Century America*, 87 HARV. L. REV. 513 (1974); Lynda Sharp Paine, *Instrumentalism v. Formalism: Dissolving the Dichotomy*, 1978 WIS. L. REV. 997; Harry N. Scheiber, *Instrumentalism and Property Rights: A Reconsideration of American "Styles of Judicial Reasoning" in the 19th Century*, 1975 WIS. L. REV. 1.

157. Pp. 125-42.

Holmes' thought to the customary jurisprudence of the Wall Street lawyer James Coolidge Carter,[158] Horwitz shows that the longstanding debate about whether Holmes was a "liberal" or a "conservative" was beside the point.[159] He was neither, as those terms have come to be understood over the course of the twentieth century, but something quite different: an elite believer in historicist jurisprudence. This insight, combined with Horwitz' shrewd sense of the politics of legal thought and his years of teaching torts at Harvard, has produced a brilliant analysis of Holmes' *The Common Law*.[160]

Horwitz offers this account of Holmes' great book as the first step in a larger interpretation of the jurist's thought: "I believe it has never been argued that in reality there is an early and a late Holmes," Horwitz writes, "and that his own intellectual journey from *The Common Law* in 1881 to 'The Path of the Law' in 1897 parallels a major change in American social, economic, and legal thought and in the structures of legitimacy in the two periods."[161] In Horwitz' interpretation, *The Common Law* represents the "early" Holmes, the Holmes for whom consensual customs still mediated between law as "pre-political natural right" and law as "the arbitrary command of the sovereign."[162] The "late" Holmes makes his appearance after 1890 in the essays *Privilege, Malice, and Intent*[163] (1894), *The Path of the Law*[164] (1897), and *Law in Science and Science in Law*[165] (1899), and in his famous dissents in the labor cases *Vegelahn v. Guntner*[166] and *Plant v. Woods*.[167]

In Horwitz' telling, the dramatic changes in Holmes' thought can be seen in the jurist's loss of faith both in custom as a standard for judging and in the existence of "external standards" in the law of torts. Holmes came to doubt his earlier positions on these two issues as he reflected on the alarming rise of industrial concentration and industrial strife in the mid-1890's.[168] Well before *Lochner* prompted a full-blown assault on classical legal thought, Holmes could no longer ignore the contradictions inherent in that structure. Holmes' response to his predicament was twofold. First, he dropped the belief in the existence of stable, certain, and consensual customs and urged judges to acknowledge the existence of interest groups and to engage in "direct policy analysis."[169]

158. P. 123.
159. *See* G. Edward White, *The Rise and Fall of Justice Holmes*, 39 U. CHI. L. REV. 51 (1971).
160. OLIVER WENDELL HOLMES, JR., THE COMMON LAW 123-25 (Boston, Little, Brown & Co. 1881).
161. P. 110.
162. P. 116.
163. HOLMES, *Privilege, Malice, and Intent*, *in* COLLECTED LEGAL PAPERS, *supra* note 133, at 117.
164. *See* HOLMES, *The Path of the Law*, *in* COLLECTED LEGAL PAPERS, *supra* note 133, at 167.
165. HOLMES, *Law in Science and Science in Law*, *in* COLLECTED LEGAL PAPERS, *supra* note 133, at 210.
166. 44 N.E. 1077, 1079 (1896) (Holmes, J., dissenting).
167. 57 N.E. 1011, 1015 (1900) (Holmes, C.J., dissenting).
168. Pp. 130-31.
169. P. 127.

In so doing, Horwitz argues, Holmes "pushed American legal thought into the twentieth century."[170]

At the same time, according to Horwitz, Holmes made "a complete about-face"[171] in his thinking about the standards judges should apply in resolving cases of intentional torts, such as the harm labor unions inflicted upon employers in their strikes and boycotts. In *The Common Law* Holmes had argued that judges should consult objective, external, customary norms rather than the moral blameworthiness of the defendant's conduct. In *Privilege, Malice, and Intent*, as well as in *Vegelahn*, and *Plant*, Holmes returned to "the traditional common law subjective tests of 'malice' and 'intent'" he had attacked in his earlier work.[172] In Horwitz' view, Holmes' insistence that malice was material to both the prima facie case in tort and to the defense of privilege marked "a major retreat from the idea of the external objective standard that Holmes had always regarded as his major contribution to legal theory."[173]

This account of Holmes' renunciation of customary jurisprudence and external standards in tort misdescribes Holmes' historicism and overlooks evidence that the jurist remained a historicist throughout his career. Horwitz also misstates the role Holmes envisioned for social science in legal education, which was much less prescriptive than Horwitz suggests. Holmes' thinking about external standards did change after the start of his judicial career, but the shift was nothing like the dramatic *volte-face* Horwitz sees. It commenced earlier than Horwitz allows and is evident in cases having nothing to do with labor strife. Holmes never treated the subjective intent of the defendant as an element in the prima facie case for intentional torts, although as a judge he treated it as one factor to be considered in determining whether the defendant's conduct was justified. Holmes' own characterization of this position as a "supplement"[174] to his chapters on torts in *The Common Law* seems more accurate than Horwitz' description of a "complete about-face."[175]

Holmes wrote the essays of the 1890's not to abandon the historical jurisprudence of his early legal scholarship but to correct his brethren on the Anglo-American bench when they attempted to evade their responsibility as historical jurists by invoking an abstract proposition they claimed to have derived from—of all things—Holmes' own work. The dictum that malicious intent could never make a lawful act unlawful was, to the Holmes of the 1890's, just as wrongheaded as the view he attacked in *The Common Law*—that moral culpability was the sole test of liability. Both approaches were poor substitutes

170. P. 142.
171. P. 133.
172. P. 135.
173. P. 133.
174. Letter from Oliver Wendell Holmes, Jr., to Frederick Pollock (June 26, 1894), *in* 1 HOLMES-POLLOCK LETTERS 54 (Mark D. Howe ed., 1946).
175. P. 133.

for the proper inquiry: determining which litigant represented the preponderant social force in the great historical struggles of the day. If this inquiry sometimes led Holmes to a posture of "judicial self-restraint,"[176] the philosophy behind it was very different from that behind the legal process school's deference to the bargaining of interest groups.

The difference between Holmes' historicism and the judicial restraint of legal process scholars is worth noting, if only because of the continuing importance of many decisions Holmes wrote while on the Supreme Court. This seems particularly true in the field of regulatory takings, where as recently as last term Justice Scalia cited Holmes' opinion in *Pennsylvania Coal Company v. Mahon*[177] in support of aggressive judicial review of land-use regulation.[178] Horwitz' willingness to attribute to Holmes the liberal pluralism of mid-century jurisprudence suggests that Justice Scalia was right to treat *Mahon* as consistent with the work of the legal process theorists who taught him at the Harvard Law School in the late 1950's.[179] In fact, it was the product of a judge who thought he could strike down legislation when, in his independent estimation, it ran counter to the forces of history.

1. *Holmes' Historicism*

Horwitz commences his chapter on Holmes by characterizing the jurist's predicament in *The Common Law* as "a two-front war." On one front, Holmes "challenged orthodox legal theory for its moralism and individualism, qualities that . . . unrealistically ignored the actual regulatory functions of law."[180] On the other, Holmes opposed unbridled, Austinian legislative supremacy, because this would produce "a redistribution of wealth in the interest of the general welfare."[181] Horwitz then turns to Carter and convincingly shows how custom addressed both concerns in his work. "[C]ustom served both to defeat the democratic impulse for legislative supremacy," Horwitz writes, "and, at the same time, to avoid the potential anarchy of a common law based solely on individual natural rights."[182] *The Common Law*, Horwitz writes, was a similar attempt to find "a middle position through the mediating notion of custom."[183] In support of this claim Horwitz cites passages that certainly suggest Holmes believed the law to be the product of a natural evolutionary process rather than a system of morality or the command of an all-powerful state. Horwitz offers

176. P. 142.
177. 260 U.S. 393 (1922).
178. Lucas v. South Carolina Coastal Council, 112 S.Ct. 2886, 2892 (1992).
179. *See* Peter B. Edelman, *Justice Scalia's Jurisprudence and the Good Society: Shades of Felix Frankfurter and the Harvard Hit Parade of the 1950's*, 12 CARDOZO L. REV. 1799, 1799-1801 (1991).
180. Pp. 112-13.
181. P. 113.
182. P. 121.
183. P. 123.

no quotation, however, in which Holmes describes that process as Carter did, in consensual terms.

Having established to his satisfaction that the early Holmes believed law to be grounded in widely-observed custom, Horwitz turns to some of the most familiar passages in the Holmes *oeuvre* to argue for a dramatic change in the judge's thought. They fall into two categories: (1) acknowledgements of social conflict; and (2) calls for lawyers to study not only history but also statistics and economics.

Horwitz' first example of Holmes' recognition of social conflict is the famous rebuke in *The Path of the Law* to lawyers who believe that questions such as whether to imply a contractual term could be settled through a process of logical deduction. "Such matters are really battle grounds where the means do not exist for determinations that shall be good for all time," Holmes wrote, "and where the decision can do no more than embody the preference of a given body in a given time."[184] Horwitz comments: "For Holmes the customary theory of law had collapsed. Law is the product of social struggle. Nothing stands between the state and the individual."[185] Several pages later Horwitz quotes Holmes' remark in *Privilege, Malice, and Intent* that the issue in labor cases "really comes down to a proposition of policy of rather a delicate nature concerning the merit of the particular benefit to themselves intended by the defendants," a question which judges with "different economic sympathies" might well decide differently.[186] Horwitz observes: "Here, for the first time, Holmes suggests that there may be no neutral way of deciding between the claims of labor and of capital."[187] Finally, Horwitz repeats Holmes' position in his *Vegelahn* dissent that the harm workers inflict upon employers in simple, "mine-run" labor disputes was privileged for the same reason as loss incurred in business competition. According to Holmes, both were part of the "free struggle for life."[188]

Horwitz also relies on Holmes' comments on legal education. The Holmes of *The Common Law*, Horwitz points out, was convinced that a historical survey of the development of various legal doctrines would reveal fundamental legal principles, yet in *The Path of the Law* Holmes accorded history a critical place only in "the rational study of law." "It is the first step toward an enlightened scepticism, that is, towards a deliberate reconsideration of the worth of . . . rules." Once historical analysis drew the jurist's attention to the existence of a particular rule, he needed to bring other skills to bear to reach the proper conclusion. "For the rational study of the law the black-letter man may be the man of the present," Holmes wrote, "but the man of the future is the man of

184. HOLMES, *The Path of the Law*, *in* COLLECTED LEGAL PAPERS, *supra* note 133, at 181.
185. P. 130.
186. Holmes, *Privilege, Malice, and Intent*, *in* COLLECTED LEGAL PAPERS, *supra* note 133, at 128.
187. P. 132.
188. Vegelahn v. Guntner, 44 N.E. 1077, 1080-81 (1896) (Holmes, J. dissenting).

statistics and the master of economics."[189] With this comment, Horwitz argues, "the source of experience has shifted from custom to policy" in Holmes' thought.[190] Henceforth the only ground of judicial decisionmaking he would consider was "direct policy analysis."[191]

The Path of the Law, in Horwitz' estimation, "marks the first clear articulation of legal positivism—that is, an insistence on a sharp distinction between law and morals—by any American legal thinker."[192] Convinced that "law is merely politics," forswearing his "search for immanent rationality in customary law," Holmes took up "the mantle of judicial self-restraint for which he became famous eight years later in *Lochner v. New York*."[193] Once "interest group conflict had replaced historical evolution as the key to understanding the law," it was for the legislature to weigh and measure the various competing interests.[194] Horwitz thus paints the late Holmes much as a legal-process theorist would, as a liberal pluralist who deferred to the political bargains worked out in legislative settings.[195] Horwitz completes this portrait of Holmes by citing Arthur Bentley's *Process of Government* (1908), the work commonly considered the first full-length study of pluralism in American political thought.[196]

One problem with Horwitz' account is that he equates Carter's consensual, custom-centered jurisprudence with Holmes' more conflictual and nonteleological historicism when he should have treated the two as species of the larger category of late-Victorian historical jurisprudence. Both men believed that natural historical processes mediated between natural rights and legislative absolutism, but Carter understood that process to be the consensual production of custom, while Holmes understood it as a fierce, Darwinian struggle. Holmes conceived of social conflict not as a lesson of the 1890's but as a conviction dating from the start of his professional career. This thrice-wounded veteran of the Civil War never believed that society could fairly be understood in consensual terms.

Most historicist legal thinkers, as Stephen Siegel notes, believed that "societies, social norms and institutions evolve according to moral ordering principles that are discoverable through historical studies."[197] Without this premise of an immanent morality in history, evolutionary models of social development would have accorded too small a role for divine will to make much headway among the Protestant elite. They would also have provided Victorian

---

189. HOLMES, *Privilege, Malice, and Intent*, *in* COLLECTED LEGAL PAPERS, *supra* note 133, at 187.
190. P. 141.
191. P. 127.
192. P. 140. This claim is in some tension with Horwitz' earlier argument that classical jurists sought to separate law and morals.
193. P. 142.
194. *Id.*
195. *Cf.* HARRY H. WELLINGTON, LABOR AND THE LEGAL PROCESS 24-25 (1968) (noting Holmes' belief that courts should privilege labor activities in pursuit of self-interest).
196. P. 142 n.242.
197. Siegel, *supra* note 136, at 1438.

thinkers with no basis for condemning novel social practices, for any such practice could be justified as an adaptation to novel social circumstances. Herbert Spencer's writings would never have enjoyed the enthusiastic reception they received in the United States had Spencer not declared his laws of social evolution to be the will of God.[198]

In contrast, as Siegel suggests, Holmes rejected the divine teleology which most of his fellow Victorian jurists needed to square evolutionary thought with Protestant theology.[199] Holmes' history was a blind, amoral process, much like war. He studied the legal past not to detect the hand of God, whose existence he doubted, but as a naturalist, with "a harshness in his judgments upon men of good will, a contempt for humanitarianism as an ingredient of public policy, and an expressed preference for the predatory type of individual that his friends usually managed to overlook with embarrassed silence."[200] Thus, while Holmes admired Spencer, he thought the Englishman's insistence upon a divine first principle was "a singular anomaly" in a theory of "the natural development of institutions by successive adaptations to the environment."[201]

As a judge, Holmes considered his sole job to be determining whether one side or the other represented the dominant social force of the day. He once proposed as his epitaph, "Here lies the supple tool of power."[202] When Holmes detected no deep-rooted controversy on a particular issue he spoke of that social force in consensual terms. As early as 1873, however, Holmes clearly acknowledged that judges sometimes confronted the task of determining whether legislation actually represented the dominant of two or more conflicting social tendencies.

This discussion of judging amidst social conflict came in a comment on proposals to revise the English law of conspiracy following a successful prosecution of London "gas stokers" in 1872.[203] American judges had long condemned legislation that favored one social group at the expense of another as a violation of the natural and equal rights of citizens.[204] Holmes felt that this "class legislation" doctrine was premised on a false assumption, "the solidarity of the interests of society."[205] All one could require was "that legislation should easily and quickly, yet not too quickly, modify itself in accordance with the will of the *de facto* supreme power in the community, and

198. *See* FINE, *supra* note 140, at 32-46.

199. Siegel, *supra* note 136, at 1546-47.

200. STOW PERSONS, AMERICAN MINDS: A HISTORY OF IDEAS 285 (1958).

201. Oliver Wendell Holmes, Jr., *Herbert Spencer: Legislation and Empiricism*, *in* JUSTICE OLIVER WENDELL HOLMES: HIS BOOK NOTICES AND UNCOLLECTED LETTERS AND PAPERS 106-07 (Harry C. Shriver ed., 1936) [hereinafter *Legislation and Empiricism*].

202. MERLO J. PUSEY, 1 CHARLES EVANS HUGHES 287 (1951) (quoting Charles Evans Hughes, Biographical Notes).

203. *See* MARK D. HOWE, JUSTICE OLIVER WENDELL HOLMES: THE PROVING YEARS, 1870-1882, at 42-47 (1963).

204. *See* Benedict, *supra* note 72, at 327-31.

205. Holmes, *Legislation and Empiricism*, *supra* note 201, at 107-08.

that the spread of an educated sympathy should reduce the sacrifice of minorities to a minimum."[206] Legislation would inevitably serve the "more powerful interests" which triumphed over their unsuccessful competitors. "[L]ike every other device of man or beast," Holmes concluded, "[legislation] must tend in the long run to aid the survival of the fittest."[207]

How should judges do their job given the fact of social conflict? In common law cases, courts should give effect to the greater of the historical forces implicated in the dispute. Thus, in *Law in Science* Holmes explained that doubtful cases presented judges with "a conflict between two social desires, each of which seeks to extend its dominion over the case, and which cannot both have their way."[208] Judges may defer to precedent in such cases "because one or the other desire may have been expressed in previous decisions to such an extent that logic requires us to assume it to preponderate in the one before" them. Where the precedent is doubtful, "judges are called on to exercise the sovereign prerogative of choice."[209]

Here, and in *Vegelahn*,[210] Holmes was doing nothing so banal as urging deference to the bargains of interest groups. Rather, he was calling upon judges to defer to history, to "the organization of the world, now going on so fast," a tendency plain from "the most superficial reading of industrial history," one which would be "futile to set our faces against."[211] In the field of labor disputes, this fatalism generally implied that courts should refrain from intervening in nonviolent labor disputes, although Holmes did believe judges could act to defend some overriding social interest. "[W]hen the power of either capital or labor is exerted in such a way as to attack the life of the community," Holmes once wrote, "those who seek their private interest at such cost are public enemies and should be dealt with as such."[212]

In passing on the constitutionality of a statute, judges normally could assume that the legislation was an authentic expression of a dominant social force, but it was always open to them to resolve this "empirical" question against the legislature. "I always say that I regard legislation like buying a ticket to the theatre," he wrote Franklin Ford in 1911. "If you're sure you want to go to the

206. *Id.*

207. *Id.*

208. HOLMES, *Law in Science and Science in Law*, *in* COLLECTED LEGAL PAPERS, *supra* note 133, at 239.

209. *Id.*

210. Vegelahn v. Guntner, 44 N.E. 1077 (1896) (Holmes, J., dissenting).

211. *Id.* at 1081.

212. Holmes made this remark in a draft opinion in Hitchman Coal & Coke Co. v. Mitchell, 245 U.S. 229 (1917). Writing Sir Frederick Pollock two years later in the midst of a postwar strike wave, he regretted he never published the sentiment, although he also thought steel magnate Elbert Gary should recognize the unions in his industry. Letter from Oliver Wendell Holmes, Jr., to Frederick Pollock (Oct. 26, 1919) *in* 2 HOLMES-POLLOCK LETTERS, *supra* note 174, at 28.

show and have money to pay for it there is an end of the matter. I may think you foolish to want to go, but that has nothing to do with my duty."[213]

To see what Holmes meant by a judge determining whether a legislative majority in fact "had the money to pay for" a statute, consider his decisions under the Takings Clause while on the Supreme Court. Decided long after Horwitz' "late Holmes" should have taken the stage, the cases show the Justice deferring to custom, traditions, and history. In *Laurel Hill Cemetery v. San Francisco*,[214] for example, Holmes upheld a statute forbidding burials within the city and county of San Francisco. How far a legislature could go in restricting the use of property consistent with the Constitution was not, Holmes observed, "a question for pure abstract theory alone. Tradition and the habits of the community count for more than logic." Long before "the making of constitutions, regulation of burial and prohibition of it in certain spots" were common in the Western world. Holmes concluded, "The plaintiff must wait until there is a change of practice or at least an established consensus of civilized opinion before it can expect this court to overthrow the rules that the lawmakers and the court of his own State uphold."[215]

Holmes made a similar argument in *Jackman v. Rosenbaum Co.*[216] in upholding a Pennsylvania statute that empowered one landowner to place half of a party wall on the land of a neighbor. Holmes noted that the statute was based on a "custom" that dated from the first settlement of the state and had prevailed ever since.[217] "If a thing has been practised for two hundred years by common consent," Holmes wrote, "it will need a strong case for the Fourteenth Amendment to affect it."[218] Were the statute an innovation, he suggested, he might have found it to have effected a taking of the neighbor's land. "But if, from what we may call time immemorial, it has been the understanding that the burden exists, the land owner does not have the right to that part of his land except as so qualified."[219]

In contrast, Holmes struck down a statute in *Pennsylvania Coal Co. v. Mahon*[220] that transferred a well-recognized property interest (the right of support) from the owners of mineral rights and to the holder of the surface estate. Holmes decided that the statute in question *was* an innovation. Was it nonetheless valid as a defense of an overriding common interest, such as the public safety that justifies tearing down a house to stop the spread of fire? That, Holmes

213. Letter from Oliver Wendell Holmes, Jr., to Franklin Ford (Apr. 6, 1911), *in id.* at 44 n. 38. Holmes claimed that his thinking on the subject had not changed since his days as an editor of the *American Law Review*. Letter from Oliver Wendell Holmes, Jr., to Felix Frankfurter (Mar. 24, 1914), *in id.*, at 44 n.38.

214. 216 U.S. 358, 366 (1910).

215. *Id.*

216. 260 U.S. 22 (1922).

217. *Id.* at 31.

218. *Id.*

219. *Id.*

220. 260 U.S. 393 (1922).

wrote, was a "question of degree—and therefore cannot be disposed of by general propositions."[221] Horwitz argued that similar language in *Privilege, Malice, and Intent* signalled Holmes' loss of faith in the possibility of objective or external standards.[222] In *Mahon*, however, Holmes was quite confident of his ability to divine in tradition, custom, and existing social practices the line beyond which "regulation goes too far" and becomes a taking.[223] A year earlier, after upholding a rent control statute in *Block v. Hirsch*,[224] Holmes scoffed at Justice McKenna, who had filed a vigorous dissent: "[H]e not infrequently recurs to the tyro's question: Where are you going to draw the line?—as if all life were not the marking of grades between black and white."[225] No tyro, Holmes decided that the rent control statute in *Block* "went to the verge of the law" but fell short.[226] The act in *Mahon*, he concluded, went too far.[227]

With the benefit of hindsight, of course, one can glimpse the origins of interest-group pluralism in Holmes' writings, including those from before the 1890's. But turning Holmes into a pluralist runs counter to the mainstream of the history of American social science, which holds that pluralism did not succeed as a descriptive political model until the 1920's, and as a normative theory until mid-century.[228] It also leaves the *Mahon* case a mystery. If Holmes was a pluralist, why did he not uphold the statute, as the pluralists Louis Brandeis, Felix Frankfurter, and Dean Acheson believed he should have?[229] If we understand Holmes' opinion as belonging to an older jurisprudential tradition then perhaps *Mahon* would be less valuable than it is to today's opponents of land-use regulation, for whom it remains an important precedent.[230] In sum, Horwitz' depiction of the late Holmes as a liberal pluralist is an anachronism. Horwitz would not have tricked himself into making it but for his assumption that the 1890's had immediate, cataclysmic consequences for American legal thought.

Horwitz' attempt to turn Holmes into a proponent of "direct policy analysis"[231] similarly rushes the jurist too quickly into modern times. As Dorothy Ross has shown, historicism was a transitional phase in American social thought. It rejected claims to the timelessness and divine origin of the social

221. *Id.* at 416.

222. P. 132.

223. *Mahon*, 260 U.S. at 415.

224. 256 U.S. 135 (1921).

225. Letter from Oliver Wendell Holmes, Jr., to Harold Laski (May 8, 1921), *in* 1 HOLMES-LASKI LETTERS 331-32 (Mark D. Howe ed., 1953).

226. *See Mahon*, 260 U.S. at 416.

227. *Id.*

228. RODGERS, *supra* note 14, at 176-211; ROSS, *supra* note 137, at 330-39; John Gunnell, The Declination of the State (1992) (unpublished manuscript, on file with author).

229. Brandeis blamed *Mahon* on Holmes' recent prostate operation. *See* Joseph F. Dimento, *Mining the Archives of* Pennsylvania Coal*: Heaps of Constitutional Mischief*, 11 J. LEGAL HIST. 396, 415-18 (1990).

230. *See, e.g.*, Lucas v. South Carolina Coastal Council, 112 S. Ct. 2886, 2892-93 (1992); Carol M. Rose, Mahon *Reconstructed: Why the Takings Issue Is Still a Muddle*, 57 S. CAL. L. REV. 561 (1984).

231. P. 127.

prescriptions of moral philosophers without fully endorsing the ambitious, positivistic claims of twentieth-century social science. It helped reorient social thought from inquiries into human nature to studies of the physical world, but it did not endow humans with much power to change the course of history.[232] For most elite Victorians, social control amounted to (in Sumner's phrase) an "absurd effort to make the world over."[233] In this respect, Holmes recognized Sumner as a kindred spirit. Both men counselled that social circumstance determined human affairs; neither held out much hope that humans could change the course of history.[234]

Holmes' discussion in the 1890's of the relative merits of history and economics in legal education illustrates this point. In general, his essays evidence no waning of interest in historical jurisprudence.[235] In *The Path of the Law*, Holmes did award the legal future to "the man of statistics and the master of economics,"[236] but this remark should be read with Holmes' elaboration two years later in *Law in Science*. Legal rules should only be recognized insofar as they help advance "a social end which the governing power of the community has made up its mind that it wants."[237] History had a real if limited value in revealing the original purpose a legal rule addressed. Lawyers could then independently determine whether the original purpose was still important or, if not, whether the rule advanced some new purpose of equal social significance.[238]

The role Holmes proposes for social science in this passage is not the aggressive social engineering of Horwitz' "late" Holmes. To the Holmes of *Law in Science*, social science was valuable insofar as it helped judges with a descriptive task: discovering what social ends the governing power of the community desires. Without social science, the judges could rely only upon formulaic maxims or their own "often blind and unconscious" estimates of the relative strengths of conflicting social ends.[239] What statistics and economics promised was *not* a basis for judges to impose their own desires upon society. Judges should not "undertake to renovate the law," Holmes insisted. "That is not their province."[240] Rather, "the only way to solve the problem presented

232. ROSS, *supra* note 137, at 91-97.

233. William Graham Sumner, *The Absurd Effort to Make the World Over*, *in* 1 ESSAYS OF WILLIAM GRAHAM SUMNER 91 (Albert G. Keller and Maurice R. Davie eds., 1934).

234. PERSONS, *supra* note 200, at 268-69; *see also* Gary J. Aichele, *Self-Preference, Competition, and the Rule of Force: The Holmesian Legacy*, 1988 S. CT. HIST. SOC'Y Y.B. 11, 15-16 (collecting Holmes quotes).

235. On several occasions he traced the evolution of legal doctrines just as he did in *The Common Law*. HOLMES, THE COMMON LAW, *supra* note 160, at 183-84; HOLMES, *Law in Science and Science in Law*, *in* COLLECTED LEGAL PAPERS, *supra* note 133, at 214-16.

236. HOLMES, *The Path of the Law*, *in* COLLECTED LEGAL PAPERS, *supra* note 133, at 187.

237. HOLMES, *Law in Science and Science in Law*, *in* COLLECTED LEGAL PAPERS, *supra* note 133, at 225.

238. *Id.*

239. *Id.* at 242.

240. *Id.* at 239.

is to weigh the reasons for the particular right claimed and those for the competing right . . . as well as one can, and to decide which set preponderates."[241] We may doubt the possibility of making this decision without permitting our own desires to alter the outcome. Holmes did not.

2. *Holmes and Malice*

One of Horwitz' great strengths as a legal historian has been his insistence on illustrating his "transformations" in American law with examples drawn from the workaday doctrines of lawyers and treatise writers, as well as formal and self-conscious works of jurisprudence. Torts, the field of private law he knows best, provides Horwitz with his most convincing examples.[242] Not surprisingly, then, Horwitz completes his portrait of Holmes as the prescient observer of the crisis of classical legal thought by drawing upon the jurist's writings on standards of liability in tort. This time, however, Horwitz' discussion is much less persuasive. His self-imposed burden of discovering a dramatic change in Holmes' thinking in the 1890's has led him to exaggerate the change in Holmes' theory of torts and to overlook an explanation for this shift that had little to do with the social unrest of the decade. This explanation was Holmes' changing attitude toward "continuous, logical, philosophic exposition"[243] in legal analysis. Systematic argument was extremely important to the young scholar striving to produce a tour de force in *The Common Law*. It was much less important for the sitting judge, forced to make up his mind at his peril on "a living question."[244]

In his lectures on tort in *The Common Law*, Holmes was most concerned with the first of Horwitz' two fronts: the moralism and individualism of Kant, Rousseau, and the Massachusetts Bill of Rights, and of the middlebrow moralists of the Victorian bench.[245] Holmes advanced his famous notion of "external standards" to make two different assaults on this position.[246] First, he took aim at the moralists' claim that in deciding legal issues judges should consult some a priori system of morals grounded in the natural rights tradition. "[T]he law does still and always, in a certain sense, measure legal liability by moral

241. *Id.* at 242.

242. *See, e.g.*, Horwitz' reading of Francis Wharton's views on objective causation, disucussed *supra*, text accompanying notes 121-124.

243. Oliver Wendell Holmes, Jr., *Speech at a Dinner Given to Chief Justice Holmes By the Bar Association of Boston on March 7, 1900*, *in* OCCASIONAL SPEECHES 122, 123 (Mark D. Howe ed., 1962).

244. HOLMES, *Law in Science and Science in Law*, *in* COLLECTED LEGAL PAPERS, *supra* note 133, at 224; *see* William A. Lundquist, Comment, *Oliver Wendell Holmes and External Standards of Criminal and Tort Liability*, 28 BUFF. L. REV. 607, 623 (1979); Mark V. Tushnet, *The Logic of Experience: Oliver Wendell Holmes on the Supreme Judicial Court*, 63 VA. L. REV. 975, 978-79 (1977).

245. HOLMES, THE COMMON LAW, *supra* note 160, at 77-163.

246. I am indebted to Horwitz for the point that Holmes conflated these two meanings of "external standards" in *The Common Law*. P. 136.

standards . . . ," Holmes acknowledged.[247] Yet this moral standard was not some elaborate ethical system, such as Kant's elaborate deductions from the impossible axiom that people must be treated as ends in themselves. Rather, the source of law was an "objective," "external" standard, morality as "generally accepted." as found in the "actual feelings and demands of the community, whether right or wrong."[248] Holmes would restate the point in *The Path of the Law*: "The law is the witness and external deposit of our moral life. Its history is the history of the moral development of the race."[249] But the morality of the community was "not coextensive with any system of morals. For the most part it falls far within the lines of any such system, and in some cases may extend beyond them, for reasons drawn from the habits of a particular people at a particular time."[250]

Holmes also used the term "external standards" to attack the Victorian judges' assumption that the moral blameworthiness of defendants was the ultimate reason why the law held them liable for tortious or contractual wrongs. As a rule, legal liability was only remotely connected to the moral condition of the defendant or his actual state of mind. "[T]he tendency of the law everywhere is to transcend moral and reach external standards" of liability.[251] Thus, Holmes argued that judges punished unintentional acts not because the actor was blameworthy, but because the actor had failed "to comply with fixed and uniform standards of external conduct, which every man is presumed and required to know."[252] Pushing his insight to the limit, Holmes even attempted to argue that subjective intent was immaterial in such intentional torts as fraud, slander, libel, malicious prosecution, and conspiracy.[253] It is important to note, given Horwitz' use of *The Common Law* as the initial position for Holmes' later "about-face," that the jurist conceded that the case law did not bear him out. This was particularly true for conspiracy, the action upon which much of the law of industrial disputes rested before the New Deal.[254] The most Holmes claimed was that "it would be a strong thing if the presence of malice made any difference" in intentional torts.[255]

Horwitz argues that the 1890's cases involving business and labor combinations led Holmes to renounce his notion of "external standards" as a source of law and a test of tortious liability. In *Privilege, Malice, and Intent* and in his labor dissents, Horwitz writes, Holmes returned to "the traditional common law

247. HOLMES, THE COMMON LAW, *supra* note 160, at 38.
248. *Id.* at 44, 41.
249. HOLMES, *The Path of the Law*, *in* COLLECTED LEGAL PAPERS, *supra* note 133, at 170.
250. *Id.* at 172.
251. HOLMES, THE COMMON LAW, *supra* note 160, at 135.
252. *Id.* at 111.
253. *Id.* at 130-63.
254. *Id.* at 142-43.
255. *Id.* at 145.

subjective tests of 'malice' and 'intent.'"[256] Without "empirically determinable customary norms," Horwitz writes, Holmes found it "difficult, if not impossible, to construct external standards to distinguish between legitimate and illegitimate forms of competition."[257] He therefore "sought in the concept of 'malice' a mediating force that custom could no longer provide."[258] Thus, Horwitz believes Holmes urged his judges to adopt a wholly subjective standard in deciding labor cases such as *Vegelahn* and *Plant*: "Allow the privilege to injure whenever the defendant is furthering his own interests through economic struggle, but deny the privilege where harm is inflicted simply for the purpose of injuring the plaintiff."[259] Under this standard, Horwitz argues, trade unions would generally escape liability, because the trier of fact would rarely be able to find the requisite element of personal ill will toward an employer. To this extent, Holmes "was justly a hero to the next generation of Progressive social reformers."[260]

Horwitz' claim that Holmes completely renounced the notion of external standards cannot be reconciled with Holmes' continued use of the concept in *Privilege, Malice, and Intent* and later writings. Horwitz implies that Holmes made subjective intent the sole consideration in determining whether the workers' intentional infliction of harm was justifiable in *Vegelahn* and *Plant*. In fact, the jurist urged his brethren to treat the purpose of labor combinations as one factor in deciding whether the defendants' conduct could be justified in terms of the external and objective requirements of the community. This modest change in Holmes' tort theory was well underway before the social unrest of the 1890's.

Holmes' doubts about the extent to which external standards explained the law of intentional torts grew with his years on the bench. Two cases in particular led him to conclude that the subjective mental state of a defendant was relevant in determining whether to privilege intentionally inflicted harm. One was *Morasse v. Brochu*,[261] in which Holmes joined a decision holding that a physician had a good cause of action against" a priest who had intimated that he would not administer last rites to his parishioners while they were under the same roof as the plaintiff.[262] The other, *Tasker v. Stanley*,[263] was a suit for the alienation of a wife's affections. Holmes upheld the introduction of evidence that the defendant had advised the wife honestly and in good faith. "[I]n order to make a man who has no special influence or authority answerable for mere advice of this kind because it is followed," Holmes wrote, "we think that it ought

256. P. 135.
257. *Id.*
258. P. 132.
259. P. 135.
260. P. 136.
261. 25 N.E. 74 (1890).
262. *Id. See also* letter from Oliver Wendell Holmes, Jr., to Frederick Pollock (Mar. 17, 1898), *in* 1 HOLMES-POLLOCK LETTERS, *supra* note 174, at 82.
263. 26 N.E. 417 (1891).

to appear that the advice was not honestly given, that it did not represent his real opinions, or that it was given from malevolent motives."[264]

A labor dispute seems to have prompted Holmes to prepare a formal statement of his new position on malice and privilege. *Temperton v. Russell*[265] was an English case upholding a damage suit against unions in the construction industry over a secondary boycott. Holmes thought the case should have been governed by *Mogul Steamship Co. v. McGregor, Gow & Co.*,[266] in which the loss inflicted by a combination of businessmen was held to have been privileged. After *Mogul*, Holmes wrote the eminent English jurist Sir Frederick Pollock that only "class sympathy" could explain the result in *Temperton*. To model a sounder, historicist approach to intentional torts, Holmes prepared what he termed "a supplement to the notion of the external standard which I have gradually worked out in a series of decisions."[267]

Holmes commenced *Privilege, Malice and Intent* by restating the greater part of his chapters on torts in *The Common Law*. In determining whether a plaintiff had made out a prima facie case, he wrote, "[t]he standard applied is external, and the words malice, intent, and negligence, as used in this connection, refer to an external standard." Only when the judge reached the issue of justification would Holmes permit him to consider actual malice.[268] As Holmes later wrote in *Aikens v. Wisconsin*,[269] on this issue the defendant could not argue that his motive was immaterial and that "the standards of the law are external. That is true in determining what a man is bound to foresee, but not necessarily in determining the extent to which he can justify harm which he has foreseen."[270]

Furthermore, even in questions of privilege, Holmes never viewed the presence of actual malice as dispositive. In *Privilege Malice, and Intent*, Holmes explained that the extent of a defendant's privilege was "a question of policy" and turned not on "empty general propositions" but on the peculiarities of particular cases. Sometimes, as in disputes over "spite fences," the defendant's conduct was privileged regardless of motive.[271] Sometimes, as in disputes over medical advice, the loss occasioned was actionable if offered out of actual ill-will toward a plaintiff.[272]

264. *Id.* at 150.

265. [1893] 1 Q.B. 715.

266. Mogul Steamship Co. v. McGregor, Gow & Co., [1889] 23 Q.B.D. 598.

267. Letter from Oliver Wendell Holmes, Jr., to Frederick Pollock (June 26, 1894), *in* 1 HOLMES-POLLOCK LETTERS, *supra* note 174, at 54.

268. HOLMES, *Privilege, Malice, and Intent*, *in* COLLECTED LEGAL PAPERS, *supra* note 133, at 119. Holmes consistently followed this protocol in his tort decisions while on the Supreme Judicial Court. Lundquist, *supra* note 244, at 623.

269. 195 U.S. 194 (1904).

270. *Id.* at 204.

271. HOLMES, *Privilege, Malice, and Intent*, *in* COLLECTED LEGAL PAPERS, *supra* note 133, at 120-21.

272. *Id.* at 124-25. "[J]ustifications may vary in extent according to the principle of policy upon which they are founded," Holmes wrote in *Aikens*. 195 U.S. at 204. While some, such as "those affecting the use of land, are absolute . . . others may depend upon the end for which the act is done." *Id.* (citation omitted).

Holmes was troubled by several American cases excusing business combinations from liability under the "abstract proposition" that malice could never make unlawful an otherwise lawful act.[273] This struck Holmes as being as indefensible an evasion of the judge's duty to consult the dominant social forces as the position that malice was always the test of liability, which he attacked in *The Common Law*. Sometimes, "serious legislative considerations" such as "the organization of the world"[274] demanded that judges ignore motive; sometimes they demanded that judges take motive into account.[275] In *Privilege, Malice, and Intent* Holmes thus distinguished between external sources of law and external standards of liability more clearly than he had in his earlier work. He more willingly acknowledged a role for subjective motive in justifying intentional torts than he did in *The Common Law*. He otherwise restated his belief in external standards of liability, and he in no way qualified his belief in external sources of law.

Several years later, another widely noted English labor case prompted Holmes to return to the subject.[276] "[I]n the elaborate, although to my notion inadequate, discussion which took place," Holmes wrote, "eminent judges intimated that anything which a man has a right to do he has a right to do whatever his motives, and this has been hailed as a triumph of the principle of external standards in the law, a principle which I have done my best to advocate as well as name."[277] This development threatened to turn what Holmes had offered as an antidote to a priori reasoning in *The Common Law* into a new "unreal" and "inadequate" generality.[278] The only way to resolve the issue of justification was to weigh the "grounds of policy and . . . histories" on either side of the question and decide which set prevailed.[279]

Holmes followed his own advice while on the Supreme Judicial Court in his two greatest labor cases. In *Vegelahn* he noted that the defendants had picketed their employer in order to win "a victory in the battle of trade" and not to inflict damage for its own sake.[280] Rather than stop there, Holmes went on to weigh other "considerations of policy and of social advantage,"[281] most notably the tendency toward combination, apparent from even "the most superficial reading of industrial history." Given the inevitable fact of combination on the side of capital, he concluded, the organization of labor was necessary if the battle between employers and employees was to be conducted "in a fair

273. HOLMES, *Privilege, Malice, and Intent*, *in* COLLECTED LEGAL PAPERS, *supra* note 133, at 122-23. The cases were Heywood v. Tillson, 75 Me. 225 (1883); Payne v. W. & Atl. R.R., 81 Tenn. 507 (1884).

274. HOLMES, *Privilege, Malice, and Intent*, *in* COLLECTED LEGAL PAPERS, *supra* note 133, at 129.

275. *Id.*

276. Allen v. Flood, [1898] App. Cas. 1; *see* James Barr Ames, *How Far an Act May Be a Tort Because of the Wrongful Motive of the Actor*, 18 HARV. L. REV. 411, 411-12 (1905).

277. HOLMES, THE COMMON LAW, *supra* note 160, at 241.

278. *Id.* at 229.

279. *Id.* at 241.

280. Vegelahn v. Guntner, 44 N.E. 1077, 1081 (1896) (Holmes, J., dissenting).

281. *Id.*

and equal way."[282] In *Plant*, Holmes similarly inquired into the object of the defendants' conduct, but, as in *Vegelahn*, his decision ultimately turned on the industrial conditions of his day.[283]

In his account of Holmes then, as in his account of late-Victorian legal thought, Horwitz went astray because of his assumption that the social conflict of the 1890's doomed all attempts to ground law in consensual norms, and because he did not listen when his subjects attempted to explain why they wrote what they did. After reading *Crisis*, one imagines Holmes wrote *Privilege, Malice, and Intent* Newton-like, after being hit by a striker's brick. Social change provided Holmes with occasions for his essays and opinions in the 1890's, but he intended them to join ongoing debates about the nature of law that were not revolutionized by the Homestead Strike, Coxey's Army, the Pullman Boycott, or the rise of the holding company. Holmes viewed the momentous events of the 1890's in terms of a historicist jurisprudence that he retained with remarkable tenacity throughout his professional career. His example suggests the need for a less schematic understanding of legal change than the structuralist model Horwitz offers in *Crisis*.

C. *Realist Legacies*

"It is a curious phenomenon of American scholarship," writes Joyce Appleby, "that everyone wants Jefferson on their side."[284] The same might almost be said of the legal realists. Edmund Kitch has called law-and-economics scholarship an outgrowth of the realist's research agenda;[285] G. Edward White has awarded the realist legacy to the law-and-society movement;[286] Mark Tushnet has dubbed CLS in its structuralist phase the "direct descendant of American Legal Realism";[287] and Gary Peller believes that when radical legal thinkers take the post-structuralist turn they find themselves face-to-face with Felix Cohen and Robert Hale.[288] Horwitz joins this scramble for the realist aegis with an interpretation that professes to connect the movement to "the real political

---

282. *Id.* at 1083.

283. Plant v. Woods, 57 N.E. 1011, 1015 (1900) (Holmes, C.J., dissenting).

284. Joyce Appleby, *Historians, Community and the Pursuit of Jefferson: Comment on Professor Tomlins*, 4 STUD. AM. POL. DEV. 35, 41 (1990).

285. Edmund W. Kitch, *The Intellectual Foundations of "Law and Economics,"* 33 J. LEGAL EDUC. 184 (1983).

286. G. Edward White, *From Realism to Critical Legal Studies: A Truncated Intellectual History*, 40 SW. L.J. 819 (1986).

287. Tushnet, *supra* note 77, at 505.

288. Peller, *supra* note 79, at 1219-40. Judge Richard Posner is more reluctant than Kitch to claim the legal realists for the law-and-economics movement. The realists' unsystematic, "liberal meliorism," he writes, makes the relation between the two movements equivocal at best. RICHARD A. POSNER, THE PROBLEMS OF JURISPRUDENCE 441-42 (1990).

Critical race and feminist legal scholars sometimes cite the realists in acknowledging that their post-realist position in legal thought. As a rule, however, they have looked elsewhere for inspiration. *See, e.g.*, Anthony E. Cook, *Beyond Critical Legal Studies: The Reconstructive Theology of Dr. Martin Luther King, Jr.*, 103 HARV. L. REV. 985, 988-89 (1990).

struggles"[289] of the day and that casts legal realism as "a continuation of the reformist agenda of early-twentieth-century Progressivism."[290]

Horwitz' creation of a realist legacy for his own position within CLS has produced some of the most exciting and engaging writing in *Crisis*. In these passages we see a historian looking to the past for a conversation about an issue that has fascinated him since his days as a graduate student: how it happened, "in this most democratic country in the world," that Americans came to endorse the ideal of a government of laws and not men.[291] Horwitz is especially intrigued by how many of the same realists who convincingly debunked the apolitical pretensions of late-Victorian jurisprudence thought they could avoid their elders' mistakes simply by making the law conform more closely to social conditions. Horwitz' heroes are legal realists who doubted this positivistic reconstructive project. Espousing some form of epistemological relativism, these figures rejected the distinction between fact and value. They understood "the social and historical contingency of structures of thought,"[292] and they recognized that even the proponents of "sociological jurisprudence" were compelled to acknowledge and defend their political and moral values.[293]

In *Crisis* the epistemological relativists receive ample time to establish the radical potential of their views. With the exception of Karl Llewellyn, legal realists who thought social science could provide a workable and neutral basis have little opportunity to explain themselves. Horwitz believes the latter have already received too much attention in previous studies of the realists. Laura Kalman, Edward Purcell, John Henry Schlegel, and others have so exaggerated the realists' enthusiasm for social science, Horwitz writes, that the "critical thrust of Realism has been virtually smothered."[294] We have been left with a vision of legal realism as an adjunct of "naively behavioralist" social science, while "the most significant legacy of Realism"[295]—that is, "the socially constructed character of frames of reference, categories of thought, and legitimating concepts"[296]—has been largely ignored.

My quarrel with Horwitz' interpretation is less with his presentist aims than with the dogmatic way in which he pursues them. He insists on a dichotomous understanding of the movement, captured in his section heading "Realism:

289. P. 170.
290. P. 169.
291. P. 193.
292. P. 270.
293. *See* pp. 173-74.
294. P. 182; *see* LAURA KALMAN, LEGAL REALISM AT YALE, 1927-1960 (1986); EDWARD A. PURCELL, JR., THE CRISIS OF DEMOCRATIC THEORY: SCIENTIFIC NATURALISM AND THE PROBLEM OF VALUE 74-94, 159-78 (1973); John Henry Schlegel, *American Legal Realism and Empirical Social Science: The Singular Case of Underhill Moore*, 29 BUFF. L. REV. 195 (1980); John Henry Schlegel, *American Legal Realism and Empirical Social Science: From the Yale Experience*, 28 BUFF. L. REV. 459 (1979); G. Edward White, *From Sociological Jurisprudence to Realism: Jurisprudence and Social Change in Early Twentieth-Century America*, 58 VA. L. REV. 999 (1972).
295. P. 181.
296. P. 182.

Critical or Scientific."[297] He etches the two positions in structuralist terms as a rigid framework of inescapably connected concepts. Horwitz has ordered a variety of realist texts into rival formations that bear a striking resemblance to a CLS scholar's understanding of troop alignments in the current warfare between leftist and law-and-economics scholars at the Harvard Law School. In the process, he has downplayed or ignored aspects of legal realist thought that would upset the order he has imposed. In particular, Horwitz underestimates the importance of a third position within legal realism, a continuation of the historicist tradition in American law, albeit updated in light of pluralist theories of society. For all the strengths of his treatment of the realists, Horwitz' assumption that evolutionary theories of law ended with the 1890's obscures the valuable legacy of the realists' pioneering efforts to envision a role for law in a plural world.

Horwitz commences his account of the legal realists generously enough, by insisting that their ranks be broadened beyond those named on Llewellyn's famous list.[298] He argues that we should devote less time to exploring differences between legal realism and Roscoe Pound's "sociological jurisprudence" and more time to envisioning both movements as part of a larger whole, "Progressive legal thought."[299] In Horwitz' usage, "Progressive jurisprudence" denotes not just the legal phase of the reform movement that appeared before World War I. It extends over the first four decades of the twentieth century and includes not only the legal realists of the 1920's and 1930's, but also prewar figures like John Chipman Gray, Pound, and Harlan Fiske Stone; institutional economists like Richard Ely, John Commons, and Thorstein Veblen; the philosophers John Dewey, Morris Cohen, and Felix Cohen; such "sophisticated doctrinal critics" as Francis Bohlen, Jeremiah Smith, and Fleming James; and the administrative lawyers Felix Frankfurter and John Landis.[300]

According to Horwitz, *Lochner* provoked Pound and other reform-minded law professors into firing the first salvoes in a broad assault on late-Victorian jurisprudence. Pound's work in particular set out "the basic consequentialist

297. P. 208. Two CLS scholars who studied legal history with Horwitz at Harvard have previously published accounts of the legal realists that anticipate *Crisis* in important and imperfectly acknowledged respects. Gary Peller distinguished between "Realism as Critique" and "Realism as Science," in an article published in 1985. Peller illustrated the former "strand" of legal thought with selections from Hale and the Cohens; he illustrated the latter with references to Llewellyn's writing. Peller, *supra* note 79, at 1219-59. Three years later Joseph Singer devoted much of his review of Laura Kalman's *Legal Realism at Yale* to stating Hale's and the Cohens' "attack on the public/private distinction or the attack on the idea of the self-regulating market." Joseph W. Singer, *Legal Realism Now*, 76 CAL. L. REV. 465, 475 (1988) (book review). In *Crisis*, Horwitz refers to Singer's essay as the "interpretation whose perspective I most share." P. 308 n.7. He cites Peller's article only in a chapter on postwar legal scholarship. *Id.* at 338 n.47.

298. Karl N. Llewellyn, *Some Realism about Realism—Responding to Dean Pound*, 44 HARV. L. REV. 1222, 1226-27 n.18 (1931); *see* N. E. H. Hull, *Some Realism about the Llewellyn-Pound Exchange over Realism: The Newly Uncovered Private Correspondence, 1927-1931*, 1987 WIS. L. REV. 921.

299. P. 171.

300. Pp. 182-85. I should add that Horwitz does not consistently reserve the term "Progressive legal thought" for the generic category. At times it refers exclusively to work published before the First World War. *See, e.g.*, p. 189.

critique of orthodox legal doctrine," namely, that judicial decisions were lagging behind the needs of industrial America, that "the law in the books" bore only a distant resemblance to the "the law in action."[301] Progressive legal thinkers from Pound through the legal realists agreed that the judges were consulting their own moral and political agendas, when they should have considered how the law they made would function in society. The progressives differed sharply on a remedy.

One set of reformers, Horwitz' "scientific realists," decided that the courts needed "a purer and more neutral system of legal concepts."[302] They proposed a jurisprudence in which "law became the dependent variable, society the independent variable."[303] To know society better, they turned to social science for expert guidance,[304] a disastrous decision in Horwitz' judgment. "Behavioral and value-free social science not only suppressed the moralism of early Progressive social science," he writes; "it was also dependent on a completely naive view of social thought."[305] With the mustering of many legal realists and their students into the New Deal, the scientific strand of legal realism legitimated the rise of the bureaucratic state and pushed social reform "into a starkly technocratic mode."[306]

Horwitz' critical realists, in contrast, believed the legal orthodoxy had erred, not in permitting its morals and politics to infect the law, but in embracing the wrong kind of morals and politics. These realists "[b]arely conceal[ed]" their political commitments as they set about the task of demonstrating the indeterminacy of orthodox legal reasoning.[307] Most were not moral relativists, and in fact drew upon "a reservoir of political and moral outrage at the injustices of the old order."[308] Their writings were above all contributions to the cause of reform.

Horwitz makes a strong case for the radical potential of critical realism by tracing attacks on natural rights jurisprudence from the historicist Holmes to the law professor Wesley Newcomb Hohfeld to the lawyer and institutional economist Robert Hale. Horwitz starts with Holmes' argument in *The Common Law* that "[l]egal duties . . . come before legal rights."[309] By insisting that rights and duties were correlative and by asserting that historically defined duties were the basis for evaluating a priori claims of right, Holmes mounted a sharp challenge to the natural rights tradition.[310] He would also inspire Hohfeld, who

301. P. 195; *see* Roscoe Pound, *Law in Books and Law in Action*, 44 AM. L. REV. 12 (1910).

302. Pp. 208-09.

303. P. 209.

304. *Id.*

305. P. 210.

306. Morton J. Horwitz, Book Review, 75 J. AM. HIST. 299, 299 (1988).

307. P. 209.

308. *Id.*

309. HOLMES, THE COMMON LAW, *supra* note 160, at 173.

310. *Cf.* William P. LaPiana, *Victorian from Beacon Hill: Oliver Wendell Holmes's Early Legal Scholarship*, 90 COLUM. L. REV. 809, 817-26 (1990).

developed the point into his famous taxonomy of "fundamental legal conceptions."[311] Horwitz writes that Hohfeld's dismantling of property into a bundle of rights, privileges, powers, and immunities "seems to have been" motivated by the growing use of injunctions in the labor disputes of the progressive era. In any event, Hohfeld's system won him a job at Yale and the praise of other reform-minded law professors, who eagerly employed it to contest the formal logic of the judges and the notion of property as "a pre-political, Lockean natural right."[312]

After Hohfeld's death in 1918, Hale developed his system into a full-blown attack on the "naturalness of the market."[313] Hale argued that because buyers and sellers took for granted a set of legally created entitlements, no economic exchange was truly voluntary. Public and private were not distinct spheres in American society; rather, the public realm recognized private rights as it saw fit. Ownership was not a natural right but a delegation by public authority to private individuals of "a discretionary power over the rights and duties of others."[314] Economic regulation was not a coercive intrusion by the state into the private sphere of individual rights but the substitution of one form of state-sponsored coercion for another. With Hale's articles and Morris Cohen's "Property and Sovereignty," Horwitz concludes, property law was recast as a species of public law.[315]

The insight that property and markets are human artifacts is of continuing importance, and not simply for CLS scholars in search of a pedigree, but for all defenders of economic regulation against challenges framed in libertarian terms. Perhaps only someone with Horwitz' political commitments could have recovered that legacy and presented it so well. Yet even taken on its own neo-Beardian terms, *Crisis* has its shortcomings. I will note three: Horwitz' failure to detail the positions of his critical realists on the political issues of their day, his equation of enthusiasm for Hohfeld's system with a politically progressive stance, and his refusal to acknowledge that even his favorite realists slid back into empiricism and functionalism in proposing constructive reforms. Each shortcoming results from Horwitz' structuralist indifference to the context that was part of the meaning his subjects attributed to their texts. Leaving that context unexplored permits Horwitz to sidestep aspects of his critical realists' thought that would lessen their value as role models for contemporary legal scholars on the left.

311. Pp. 128-29; *see* WESLEY N. HOHFELD, FUNDAMENTAL LEGAL CONCEPTIONS AS APPLIED IN JUDICIAL REASONING (1919). On Hohfeld's system, see Joseph W. Singer, *The Legal Rights Debate in Analytical Jurisprudence from Bentham to Hohfeld*, 1982 WIS. L. REV. 975, 986-94.

312. Pp. 197, 155.

313. P. 194.

314. P. 164 (quoting ROBERT L. HALE, RATE MAKING AND THE REVISION OF THE PROPERTY CONCEPT 214 (1922)).

315. P. 165; *see* Morris R. Cohen, *Property and Sovereignty*, 13 CORNELL L.Q. 8 (1927).

The first shortcoming goes to the peculiarly abstract and bloodless way in which Horwitz connects legal realism to the "real political struggles" of early twentieth-century America.[316] From his criticism of the existing literature, one might have expected Horwitz to detail the way in which the realists used their legal theories in commenting on or participating in the great reform causes of the day. Surely without such examples we cannot determine whether the realists themselves derived from their work the political positions Horwitz has discovered there. The only figure whose political activities *Crisis* describes at any length, however, is Karl Llewellyn. His vigorous effort in the Sacco-Vanzetti crusade provides little support for Horwitz' claim that realists like Llewellyn "subordinated political and moral passion to social science expertise."[317]

As far as it goes, Horwitz' research supports his claim that the critical realists considered themselves reformers of one sort or another. Some, like Hale, who received hate mail over the "Bolshevick ideas" he published in the *American Bar Association Journal*, were even perceived as dangerous radicals by their contemporaries.[318] But the mantle of reform covered a wide range of political positions in early twentieth-century America. Lumping the critics of legal orthodoxy together as "progressives" obscures distinctions that made a difference. For example, Horwitz dubs Hohfeld a progressive on the basis of his enthusiasm for Woodrow Wilson's New Freedom.[319] Can we infer that Hohfeld supported Wilson in his refusal to exempt organized labor from the Sherman Antitrust Act?[320] If so, then why should he be classed with the realist Leon Green, who made a critical-realist case for the sit-down strike that would have horrified Wilson?[321] In fact, and as I will argue, realists in both of Horwitz' camps were ambivalent about the legal program of the labor movement. Rather than permit the critical realists to voice their misgivings, Horwitz preserves their heroic stature by rendering their politics in abstract and general terms.

For similar reasons, I think, Horwitz does not explore a more narrowly "political" function Hohfeld's system performed in the 1910's and 1920's, that of demarcating the boundary between law professors and the rest of the legal profession. When Hohfeld wrote, full-time law professors were still actively vying with practitioners for control of legal education. Many saw in his system just the kind of elegant and arcane learning that could support the professoriat's claim to a special competence beyond the ken of the judge or practicing lawyer.[322] That Hohfeld himself saw a link between his system and the

316. P. 170.

317. Pp. 209-10.

318. Letter from Lawrence C. Brooks to Robert L. Hale (Jan. 4, 1923), *quoted in* Gerald Fetner, *The Law Teacher as Legal Reformer: 1900-1945*, 28 J. LEGAL EDUC. 508, 528 (1977).

319. P. 152.

320. ARTHUR S. LINK, WILSON: THE NEW FREEDOM 432-33 (1956), Dallas L. Jones, *The Enigma of the Clayton Act*, 10 INDUS. & LAB. REL. REV. 201, 207-14 (1957).

321. Leon Green, *The Case for the Sit-Down Strike*, 90 NEW REPUBLIC, Mar. 24, 1937, at 199.

322. For this reason Schlegel has called Hohfeld's system "the lynch pin of the grand vocation for the

professionalization of law teaching became clear when he outlined his "Vital School of Jurisprudence and Law." This was in 1914, the same year Wigmore, a social conservative, defended the "specialist in legal science" from the academy of the Wall Street bar.[323]

The legal realists seemed at least as interested in demonstrating the superiority of Hohfeld's "professorial jurists" as they were in advancing a reformist political agenda.[324] Thus, as Schlegel has noted, in 1918 Walter Wheeler Cook used Hohfeld's system not only to contest Justice Pitney's reasoning in the anti-union decision *Hitchman Coal & Coke Co. v. Mitchell*,[325] but also to pillory the New York Court of Appeals for pretending that it had decided to uphold a secondary boycott "by the simple process of deductive reasoning."[326] Felix Cohen thought Chief Justice Taft spoke "Transcendental Nonsense" in the *Coronado Coal*[327] case when he declared the United Mine Workers (in Cohen's words) "a quasi-corporation" and therefore suable under the Sherman Act. Cohen also rejected the union's "metaphysical argument" that it was not subject to liability because it was not a person.[328] Horwitz suggests (without supporting authority) that Hohfeld's system was a response to the attack on the labor injunction.[329] If it was, then it gave support to the defenders of the labor injunction and not to its attackers. The trade unionists' strategy for curtailing the injunction was to distinguish between tangible and intangible property and to limit injunctive relief to the protection of the former.[330] As a social scientist friendly to labor pointed out,[331] a critical-realist approach—the "really radical reconceptualization of property"[332]—exploded the very distinction upon which the trade unionists had premised their argument.

Finally, Horwitz is not always sensitive to the rhetorical context in which his critical realists advanced the argument for social construction. He insists that critical realism was a sustained, fully-rounded intellectual position and not just a method to be employed strategically in attacking orthodox legal thought. Yet once his favorites put aside their critique and stated an affirmative program

law professor." John Henry Schlegel, American Legal Realism and Empirical Social Science 41 (1991) (unpublished manuscript, on file with author). I am grateful to Professor Schlegel for permission to quote from his forthcoming book.

323. Wesley N. Hohfeld, *A Vital School of Jurisprudence and Law: Have American Universities Awakened to the Enlarged Opportunities and Responsibilities of the Present Day?* 1914 ASS'N AM. L. SCH. PROC. 76; *see* Schlegel, *supra* note 322, at 39-40.

324. Hohfeld, *supra* note 323, at 110; Schlegel, *supra* note 322, at 39.

325. 245 U.S. 229 (1917); Walter Wheeler Cook, *Privileges of Labor Unions in the Struggle for Life*, 27 YALE L.J. 779 (1918).

326. Walter Wheeler Cook, *Boycotts of "Non-Union Materials*," 27 YALE L.J. 539, 540 (1918); *see* Schlegel, *supra* note 322, at 54-58.

327. United Mine Workers of America v. Coronado Coal Co., 259 U.S. 344 (1922).

328. Felix S. Cohen, *Transcendental Nonsense and the Functional Approach*, 35 COLUM. L. REV. 809, 813 (1935); *see* Peller, *supra* note 79, at 1228.

329. P. 197.

330. WILLIAM E. FORBATH, THE SHAPING OF THE AMERICAN LABOR MOVEMENT 154-62 (1991).

331. EDWIN E. WITTE, THE GOVERNMENT IN LABOR DISPUTES 105-06 (1932).

332. P. 165.

of reform they typically resorted to arguments that were scarcely less functionalist and empiricist than their "naive," scientific counterparts. Felix Cohen, for example, mixed critical debunking with the "scientific" claim that law was "a product of social determinants and an index of social consequences."[333] Hale surely believed that economic analysis could not free lawyers and judges from making normative judgments. Once economic study clarified a problem, he wrote in 1922, "the final judgment on the issues is an ethical one."[334] Even when Hale debunked the public-private distinction in a brilliant analysis of the state action requirement, however, he then advanced a potentially consequentialist standard ("some matter of high public importance") for making discrimination actionable under the Reconstruction amendments.[335]

In short, Horwitz' distinction between critical and scientific realists is overdrawn. We do not know whether or how his two groups divided on the political quarrels of the day. We have good reason to think that they joined politically quiescent or even conservative academics in using Hohfeldian analysis to keep the practitioners at bay. Finally, whatever theoretical differences separate Llewellyn's famous call for a "*temporary* divorce of Is and Ought"[336] from Hale's ultimately ethical policymaking, they scarcely seem substantial enough to justify pillorying the former as a proponent of "austere positivism" and lionizing the latter as an anti-positivist hero.[337]

I think a more satisfying approach to the history of legal realism begins by noting a strand of legal realism not captured in Horwitz' dichotomy.[338] Horwitz himself notes that the social scientists who most influenced the legal realists were institutionalists who adopted neither "the impoverished behavioral methodological apparatus of logical positivism" nor "the sharp distinction between facts and values characteristic of ethical positivism."[339] Horwitz' treatment of this fact in *Crisis* is contradictory. At one point, he insists on broadening the category of progressive legal thinkers to include such institutional economists as Ely and Commons.[340] At another, he writes that legal progressives "never really adopted the historicist mode that was so powerful in turning the social sciences toward relational thinking."[341] This follows from Horwitz' assumption that the "collapse of Darwinism" in the 1890's left legal progressives with no other choice besides moral reform and technocratic social engineering.

333. Cohen, *supra* note 328, at 843; *see* Peller, *supra* note 79, at 1245-48.

334. Robert L. Hale, *Economic Theory and the Statesman*, *in* THE TREND OF ECONOMICS 225 (Rexford G. Tugwell ed., 1924).

335. Robert L. Hale, *Rights Under the Fourteenth and Fifteenth Amendments Against Injuries Inflicted by Private Individuals*, 6 LAW. GUILD REV. 627, 630 (1946).

336. Llewellyn, *supra* note 298, at 1236.

337. P. 5.

338. On the perils of dichotomy in historical writing, see DAVID H. FISCHER, HISTORIANS' FALLACIES: TOWARD A LOGIC OF HISTORICAL THOUGHT 9-12 (1970).

339. P. 270.

340. P. 182.

341. P. 324 n.36.

To use Horwitz' terms, they could no longer believe that social processes might somehow "combine the descriptive and the prescriptive, the Is with the Ought."[342]

In fact, this historicist tenet reached many realists through institutionalist social science.[343] The middle way between anarchic individualism and democratic statism that some late-Victorian jurists found in the moral sense and others in custom or evolution, some realists found in twentieth-century notions of human life as an ongoing, pervasive social process.[344] Early social scientists, like Sumner, tended to think of the process as encompassing all segments of society. Later scholars continued to think of social development as an organic process, but envisioned it as taking place within groups or institutions, where it could create diverse ways of knowing right and truth. By the 1920's, the problem of governing in a plural society was moving to the center of political thought.[345]

Commons' writing on labor law illustrates one form that the confluence of historicism and pluralism could take. In *Legal Foundations of Capitalism* (1924), Commons endorsed Carter's claims that law was the organic product of social exchanges and that the customs emerging from such exchanges were "a highly intractable force [that] even the most powerful state cannot override."[346] He parted company with Carter in insisting that custom developed in the context of particular groups, so that customs might well differ and conflict. In labor relations, for example, Commons found not one, but two, equally legitimate legal systems. One was "the common law of labor," customary work rules and practices developed in particular industries over time. The other was the law of contract and property of the employers. The latter was more generally incorporated into the decisions of common law judges, but it was just as customary in origin and partial in nature as the law of the workers.[347]

Such social theories had critical and constructive implications for legal realists across Horwitz' positivist divide. As a critical matter, realists could now join Holmes' point about the contested nature of the *Lochner* Court's social theory to a pluralist model of the social order. In his historical articles, for example, the Yale realist Walter Nelles debunked the universals of late-Victorian

342. P. 210.

343. For a succinct overview of the intellectual influences on legal realism, see KALMAN, *supra* note 294, at 14-20.

344. Fred Matthews, *Social Scientists and the Culture Concept, 1930-1950: The Conflict Between Processual and Structural Approaches*, 7 SOC. THEORY 87, 88-90 (1989); *see also* ROSS, *supra* note 137, at 242-47.

345. RODGERS, *supra* note 14, at 176-203; Mary O. Furner, *Knowing Capitalism: Public Investigation and the Labor Question in the Long Progressive Era*, *in* THE STATE AND ECONOMIC KNOWLEDGE: THE AMERICAN AND BRITISH EXPERIENCE 241-46 (Mary O. Furner & Barry Supple eds., 1990); Gunnell, *supra* note 228.

346. JOHN R. COMMONS, LEGAL FOUNDATIONS OF CAPITALISM 299-300 (1924) (quoting John R. Commons, *Law and Economics*, 34 YALE L.J. 371, 376 (1925).

347. COMMONS, LEGAL FOUNDATIONS OF CAPITALISM, *supra* note 346, at 304-05.

labor law as the rationalizations of a particular social group.[348] The constructive implications of the new institutionalism were less definite. Realists who believed with Commons that groups and institutions were natural and homogeneous phenomena, and that their lawmaking imposed few burdens on outsiders, might conclude that the law should limit itself to ratifying and enforcing the preexisting arrangements of social groups. Well before the 1950's, then, we should expect to find precursors of the legal process school. Realists who thought of groups as constructed and manipulable, who were concerned about the fate of individuals within groups, and who appreciated the third-party effects of interest-group bargaining would search for some consensual basis to justify more vigorous regulation by the state of its constituent groups.

Perhaps Llewellyn's jurisprudence best illustrates the more deferential approach. Horwitz struggles to comprehend Llewellyn within his dichotomous framework. While noting the realist's eclecticism, his "typically undogmatic generosity,"[349] and his poetic intellect,[350] Horwitz ultimately classifies Llewellyn as an advocate of "austere positivism."[351] Horwitz does not acknowledge the historicist strain in the realist's thought, which Llewellyn acquired from a variety of sources including Holmes, Commons, and Pound.[352] The most important conduit, however, was Llewellyn's undergraduate reading of Sumner's *Folkways*.[353] In this early landmark work of sociology, the self-confident and politically engaged moralist of Daniel Davenport's college days adopted a detached, scientific tone, describing "the modern mass man with the same cool eye with which he would have looked at a Bushman, expecting in truth to find little difference."[354] Sumner's readers learned that the mores of the masses had a determining force on all aspects of society. Elites and outsiders could influence mass society, but only indirectly and with the certainty that their ideas would be debased as they grew in currency.[355]

Llewellyn's principal mentor at the Yale Law School, Arthur L. Corbin, was a great enthusiast of Sumner's mores, which he saw as combining "the Is with the Ought" in just the way Horwitz thinks was impossible after the fall

348. *See, e.g.*, Walter Nelles, *A Strike and Its Legal Consequences—An Examination of the Receivership Precedent for the Labor Injunction*, 40 YALE L.J. 507, 511-12, 526 (1931).

349. P. 179.

350. P. 181.

351. P. 5.

352. Karl N. Llewellyn, *The Effect of Legal Institutions Upon Economics*, 15 AM. ECON. REV. 665, 665 n.1 (1925). Pound discussed historical jurisprudence in the United States in *The Scope and Purpose of Sociological Jurisprudence*, 24 HARV. L. REV. 591, 598-604 (1911).

353. WILLIAM TWINING, KARL LLEWELLYN AND THE REALIST MOVEMENT 92-93, 414 n.25 (1973); *see also* WILLIAM GRAHAM SUMNER, FOLKWAYS: A STUDY OF THE SOCIOLOGICAL IMPORTANCE OF USAGES, MANNERS, CUSTOMS, MORES, AND MORALS (Ayer Co. 1992) (1940). On the similarities between Sumner's and Commons' work, see Jeff E. Biddle, *Purpose and Evolution in Commons's Institutionalism*, 22 HIST. POL. ECON. 19, 38-45 (1990).

354. STOW PERSONS, THE DECLINE OF AMERICAN GENTILITY 244 (1973).

355. *See* ROSS, *supra* note 137, 219-24; Ernst, *supra* note 32, at 36-38.

of "Darwinism."[356] Corbin argued that law represented "the custom and the interest and the average man," and he urged judges to follow "the multitude." "That judge is just and wise," he wrote, "who draws from the weltering mass the principle actually immanent therein and declares it as the law."[357] Corbin frequently referred to *Folkways* during his classes,[358] and Sumner's influence was discernible even in Corbin's technical studies of contract doctrine, as where he opposed applying the doctrine of privity of contract when its application would run contrary to "the mores of the time."[359]

What Llewellyn found in Sumner was not a mandate for technocratic social engineering but a chastening lesson about the possibilities of planned social change. "But for the early and deep-cut influences of Sumner's writings," Llewellyn wrote in 1924, "I should by now hold some obnoxious fighting faith and be stump-speaking a vigorous progress into jail." Attempts to effect social change seemed useless until one discovered "the laws of change—what can be changed, and how, and with what result?"[360] Llewellyn found the same message in Carter's customary jurisprudence, which demonstrated to Llewellyn's satisfaction "the huge scope of extra-official controls in law and the limits set thereby to official action."[361] One need not invent a "Realist turn to social science" to account for Llewellyn's tendency in drafting the Uniform Commercial Code to endow "economically dominant commercial practices with undeserved normativity."[362] The Code's premise that courts should consult "the mores and usages of honest dealers" (Corbin's words) was much older.[363] It belonged to a historicist strand of American jurisprudence that ran back through the 1890's to the mid-century reception of German historicism by American scholars and intellectuals.[364]

In the field of labor relations, in contrast, legal realists were not content to follow Llewellyn's practice of deferring to group custom. "Scientific" and "critical" realists alike were concerned about the fate of the individual worker in well-organized industries. Walter Wheeler Cook, one of Horwitz' scientific

356. P. 210.

357. Arthur L. Corbin, *The Law and the Judges*, 3 YALE REV. 234, 250 (1914); *see also* TWINING, *supra* note 353, at 30-32.

358. Douglas Arant, *Professor Arthur L. Corbin*, 74 YALE L.J. 212, 214 (1964).

359. Arthur L. Corbin, *Contracts for the Benefit of Third Persons*, 27 YALE L.J. 1008 (1918) (italics omitted), *cited* p. 50.

360. Karl N. Llewellyn, Non-Conformist Puzzles over Education (1924) (Karl N. Llewellyn Papers, University of Chicago Law School), *quoted in* TWINING, *supra* note 353, at 93. *Cf.* Pp. 186-87.

361. Karl N. Llewellyn, *James Coolidge Carter*, 3 ENCYCLOPEDIA OF THE SOCIAL SCIENCES 243, 244 (1937). Among the drawbacks of Carter's work Llewellyn identified was his failure to acknowledge the "multiformity and conflict of subgroup 'customs.'" *Id.*

362. Pp. 212, 211.

363. TWINING, *supra* note 353, at 303 (citing Arthur L. Corbin, *The Uniform Commercial Code—Sales; Should It Be Enacted?* 59 YALE L.J. 821, 835 (1950)). *See, e.g.*, U.C.C. §1-102(2)(b) (1990).

364. *See, e.g.*, Thomas M. Cooley, *Labor and Capital before the Law*, 337 N. AM. REV. 503, 503-06 (1884); *cf.* James Whitman, Note, *Commercial Law and the American Volk: A Note on Llewellyn's German Sources for the Uniform Commercial Code*, 97 YALE L.J. 156, 157-58 (1987).

realists, concluded his attack on the *Hitchman* case by noting that if the labor movement were freed from the threat of labor injunctions, the "community" would require legislation to ensure that unions were "open on fair terms to all alike."[365] To do otherwise would be to permit them to exclude reputable workers for "some unsubstantial reason."[366] When Robert Hale testified in favor of the National Labor Relations Act, he attacked the notion that a closed union shop "destroys the freedom of the worker to be independent of a union if he wishes to be." The claim was true but irrelevant: "in a complicated modern society like ours," Hale explained, "nobody is going to be entirely free." Yet even Hale acknowledged that the choice between the coercion of the employer and the coercion of the union was "a choice between evils," and he conceded that unions sometimes oppressed their members.[367]

The realist figure who perhaps most thoroughly confounds Horwitz' dichotomy is Thurman Arnold.[368] While a law professor at Yale he combined quantitative studies of the courts with some of the most gleeful debunking of legal and economic orthodoxies ever produced by a legal realist. Thanks in part to the influence of his colleague and good friend, the institutional economist Walton Hale Hamilton, Arnold attacked neoclassical economics for (among other things) ignoring "the complex character of political institutions."[369] In 1938 he left academia to run the antitrust division of the Department of Justice. In that capacity he prosecuted over one hundred trade unions for labor practices that disadvantaged "the economy as a whole all out of proportion to any transient advantage which they may give to any smaller group."[370] Notwithstanding the presence of economists on his staff, Arnold's prosecutions owed more to his "progressive moralism"[371] than to the abstractions of welfare economics. In particular, "the exploitation of labor by labor" through the high admissions fees of trade unions and the suppression of internal dissent troubled Arnold.[372] "This sort of thing is not democracy," Arnold declared in the pages of the *Reader's Digest*. "It must not be allowed to spread."[373]

365. Cook, *supra* note 325, at 800-01 & n.56.

366. *Id.* at 801 n.56.

367. 1 LEGISLATIVE HISTORY OF THE NATIONAL LABOR RELATIONS ACT, 1935, at 81 (1949). I am grateful to Mark Barenberg of the Columbia University Law School for drawing Hale's testimony to my attention. Barenberg is at work on an important study of the intellectual and political origins of the Wagner Act.

368. *See* Ernst, *supra* note 32, at 42-53.

369. Thurman W. Arnold, *Theories about Economic Theories*, 172 ANNALS AM. ACAD. POL. & SOC. SCI. 26, Mar. 1934, at 28.

370. Thurman W. Arnold, Statement of Thurman W. Arnold, Assistant Attorney General of the United States, before the Temporary National Economic Committee, with Respect to the Application of Antitrust Laws to Labor Unions, February 13, 1941, at 2 (Department of Justice Papers, National Archives, File 60-194-0, Box 641).

371. *See* Douglas Ayer, *In Quest of Efficiency: The Ideological Journey of Thurman Arnold in the Interwar Period*, 23 STAN. L. REV. 1049, 1052-53 (1971) (tracing the strand of "progressive moralism" in Arnold's youth and early career).

372. Thurman W. Arnold, *Labor's Hidden Holdup Men*, 38 READER'S DIG., June 1941, at 136, 138.

373. *Id.* at 139.

Arnold thoroughly appreciated the critical force of legal realism; he became a vigorous agent of the New Deal state; he never lost sight of the need to square the exercise of public power with ethical ideals.[374] We cannot tell from *Crisis* how many of the other legal realists who left the Yale Law School or the Johns Hopkins Institute of Law for the New Deal escaped with their "political and moral passion"[375] intact. These important figures rarely escape *Crisis*' footnotes, where they suffer a kind of historiographic exile for the crime of enthusiasm for quantitative methods.[376] Arnold's cases suggests that Horwitz was too quick to dismiss the larger portion of the realists as naive, technocratic positivists. Horwitz' structuralist linkage of social science and positivism may serve his present political purposes, but it unduly constrains our view of the legal realists. Allowing for more contingency and contradiction in their thought would have preserved the realist legacy of the Yale-educated members of CLS, many of whom will doubtless be surprised to learn that the "greatest and most enduring contribution of Realism" owed little to their positivistic teachers.[377] It would also have permitted all of us to learn more about the other things on the realists' minds, including the dilemmas of governance in a pluralist society.

III. Conclusion

"It is much more important to understand than to criticize."[378] Pound's remark remains good advice long after his quarrel with the legal realists, particularly for scholars engaged in the common project of studying the history of American law. In pointing out some of the missteps and missed opportunities in Horwitz' study of ninety years of American legal thought, I do not wish to minimize his contribution to our understanding of Victorian lawyers and judges and their successors. Read with Horwitz' earlier *Transformation*, *Crisis* successfully completes a legal analogue to Hartz' great survey of American history, one that shares Hartz' dissatisfaction with the liberal tradition, but not his pessimism about the viability of a radical alternative.

Crisis is the summation of the structuralist tradition in American legal history, a tradition launched by CLS scholars intent on unmasking the supposed necessities of everyday life. The book will serve as the capstone of this historical

374. In this Arnold is consistent with recent studies of fiscal and antitrust policy in the New Deal, which date the rise of a technocratic, managerial approach much later than one would expect from *Crisis*. Alan Brinkley, *The New Deal and the Idea of the State*, *in* THE RISE AND FALL OF THE NEW DEAL ORDER, 1930-1980, at 85 (Steve Fraser & Gary Gerstle eds., 1989); Frederick M. Rowe, *The Decline of Antitrust and the Delusions of Models: The Faustian Pact of Law and Economics*, 72 GEO. L.J. 1511, 1520-24 (1984).

375. P. 209.

376. Pp. 312-14 n.85.

377. *Id.* at 270. On the Yale-educated CLS founders, see Charles E. Clark & David M. Trubek, *The Creative Role of the Judge: Restraint and Freedom in the Common Law Tradition*, 71 YALE L.J. 255 (1961); Schlegel, *supra* note 56, at 392-96.

378. Roscoe Pound, *The Call for a Realist Jurisprudence*, 44 HARV. L. REV. 697, 709 (1931), *quoted* p. 173.

edifice, rather than the cornerstone for a new structuralist project. In part, this is because *Crisis*' contribution to American legal thought is not nearly as novel and important as *Transformation*'s assault on legal process theory. The avant-garde among CLS scholars have already left structuralism behind them; to other legal academics Horwitz' insistence on the social construction of law will come as old news.[379]

More importantly, *Crisis* appears just as the structuralist understanding of the uses of history is coming under attack. As intellectual historians attempt to accommodate the diversity Horwitz overlooks, their studies are growing increasingly contingent and openended. In theory, at least, Horwitz' methodology could accommodate many of my objections to *Crisis*. Horwitz could admit that there was some diversity in late-Victorian legal thought, and still insist that it was reducible to a handful of rival structures, perhaps originating in several broad social categories.[380] He could concede that Holmes' historicism weathered the social upheavals of the 1890's, and still maintain that the next generation of legal thinkers required a new belief system to comprehend the unprecedented social realities of the early twentieth century. He could moderate his criticism of the scientific realists and recognize that critical realism advanced the law teachers' project of professionalization, and still argue that most realists worked from fundamentally different premises than the generations of legal thinkers who preceded and followed them.

As a practical matter, however, any study that fully addressed my objections to *Crisis* would be hard to justify in terms of the critical tradition's notion of the use of history. In such a study, ideas would not rise and fall with the triumph or defeat of the structure in which they are embedded. Instead, they would garner support by proving their worth to individuals in the diverse facets of everyday life, where their remote implications are more easily evaded than CLS historians have suggested. Readers would still learn that their ideas are historically contingent, but they would not be asked to search out and renounce the structures that constrain their own thought. Rather, analogies drawn from rounded portrayals of similarly situated people in the past would broaden their appreciation of the consequences of their beliefs and actions.

One can disagree with Horwitz on this historiographic level without denying him a permanent place among scholars of American legal history. Professional historians will always differ on the relative importance of conflict and consensus, structure and contingency, change and continuity, text and context, difference

379. Thus Cass Sunstein commences his review of *Crisis* with the exasperated remark, "Some people think that it is very important to establish that what we consider 'law' is really 'politics.'" Cass R. Sunstein, *Where Politics Ends*, 207 NEW REPUBLIC, Aug. 3, 1992, at 38. Sunstein's readiness to grant the point validates William N. Eskridge and Gary Peller's observation that mainstream scholars of American public law "deradicalize the left's intellectual discourse even as they embrace it." William N. Eskridge, Jr. & Gary Peller, *The New Public Law Movement: Moderation as a Postmodern Cultural Form*, 89 MICH. L. REV. 707, 764 (1991).

380. *Cf.* Gordon, *supra* note 45, at 117-19.

and similarity; and they will always bring political sensibilities to their work. Horwitz has gone to the past for insight into one of the abiding concerns of the CLS movement: how "American jurists since the Revolution have striven to embody 'a government of laws and not men' in a conception of an autonomous system of law untainted by politics."[381] If *Crisis* suggests that its subjects have other insights to offer those who approach them with different concerns and a more generous spirit, the book nevertheless sets a high standard of intelligence and intellectual ambition that all legal historians would do well to emulate.

381. P. 9.

Part III
The New History of Criminal Justice

THE
MODERN LAW REVIEW

Volume 47 January 1984 No. 1

THE CRIMINAL PROSECUTION IN ENGLAND AND ITS HISTORIANS[1]

I

FOR many historians with no particular expertise in the matter, the doctrines of The Law rather resemble an impressive range of mountains. They loom over the social landscape in every period of the past in which historians labour, and they are undeniably important. The Law Mountains are said (by those who claim to know) profoundly to affect the intellectual climate of an age. The frontier between state and civil society apparently runs somewhere along the line of their peaks. Finally, one of the recognised professional duties of historians is to track every movement of a tiny group of very important people. A surprising number turn out to be lawyers, often from an élite climbing club called The Bar. Many of these men have achieved, in past centuries, a spectacular degree of upward mobility (itself of interest to historians) through mastering the peculiar techniques necessary to scale the slopes of the Law Mountains. We watch in astonishment, from the ground, as our subjects make their way up one or another commanding height of Law (and equally, of social station).

But for most historians, that is about as close as we get. We do not know much about the mountains, even less how to climb them ourselves. Occasionally one of us will try to track the route of one of those lawyer-mountaineers whom we usually watch from the ground. It quickly becomes apparent that even a short walk in the Law Mountains may require an intense, if improvised, course in technique.[2] And to get to the objective quickly (the imperative for all legal climbers) one cannot linger *en route* to ponder the origin of the range, or to wonder at curious rock formations and admire the goats. But that is what the historian will want to do: understand the origins of the mountains, their stratification, the forces that shaped

[1] The Chorley Lecture 1983. I was unable to give the lecture on June 8, as scheduled, to my regret; what follows is a slightly revised version of my text. I am grateful for the sympathetic understanding of the Directors of the *Modern Law Review*, in what were for me difficult circumstances. The lecture was written while I held an SSRC post at the School of Law, University of Warwick, and without implicating my hosts in what follows I wish to say how much I learned from them.

[2] Eric Newby, *A Short Walk in the Hindu Kush* (Secker & Warburg, 1958).

them—and, incidentally, to admire the goats. If practising lawyers are competitive climbers at heart, most historians are contemplative geologists.

Historians tell a modern fable about the Law Mountains. It concerns an historian-geologist who asked a lawyer-climber what he knew about them. The lawyer's answer was (of course), "Because they are there."[3] "But," persisted the historian, "how did they get there? Why are some aspects so precipitous, others so gentle? What's *inside* the Law Mountains?" The lawyer missed the point. "We have manuals that show all the feasible routes, graded according to difficulty. (Indeed, even each assault by members of The Bar is assessed by our most distinguished older members.) And our Maitland Club (few of whom actually climb the Mountains) can show you reports on the main routes from past centuries, and incidentally relate some marvellous tales about great men like Coke and Mansfield who pioneered some of the best ones. Things *have* changed a lot recently. Fellow-Servant Chimney, very popular in the nineteenth century, is now impassable. And a whole party was lost in 1924, in a rockslide started by a silly beggar named Campbell. It quite changed this face of Old Felony."[4]

The historian, perhaps unwisely, stopped listening, and many decades ago organised his fellows to tackle the Law Mountains in a less sporting way. We are tunnelling. The computerised MOLE[5] chews through parchment-paper conglomerates like butter, and Old Felony in particular, which is not much bigger than Snowdon, will be thoroughly honeycombed in the next 50 years or so.[6] As the archives are sounded, the patterns found in the records of the hundreds of thousands of past cases for which records survive have called forth two kinds of explanations which, although related, deal with issues of different scale.

The first group of tentative explanations concerns the relationship between the surface prominences of doctrine and the vast bulk of

[3] On a different occasion, he elaborated: "The view is terrific, the altitude intoxicating, the technical problems endlessly fascinating. As a professional climber I also make quite a lot of money."

[4] Law Reform (Personal Injuries) Act 1948; see J. Ll. J. Edwards, *The Law Officers of the Crown* (London, 1964), Chap. 11, for an account of the Campbell case, which led to the defeat of the first Labour Government, and strengthened the quasi-judicial role of the Attorney-General.

[5] *M*ark *O*ne *L*egal *E*xcavator. The computer has made it possible to handle the great bulk of past judicial records, and to relate them to other social facts, in ways not possible before. English criminal records invite such treatment, particularly for the period before the nineteenth century: see Hay, "War, Dearth and Theft: the Record of the English Courts" (May, 1982) 95 *Past & Present*. The Maitland Club was digging long before.

[6] A very rough estimate (and any other is impossible) suggests that for the year 1783 (an average one for the 1780s, a busy but not grossly untypical decade for the courts) there were less than 50 criminal cases reported, most of them settlement and other poor law cases (1–8 *Brown's Parliamentary Cases* (1–3 E.R.); 3 *Douglas* (99 E.R.); *Caldecott's Magistrates Cases*). In the same year there were 500 committals at the Home Circuit assizes alone, and possibly a total of 10,000 prosecutions on indictment, summarily before magistrates, and on certiorari or by criminal information in King's Bench, for the country as a whole. Evidence for perhaps one-third of that bulk of cases (mostly on indictment) probably survives, with comparable evidence for *each year* of the eighteenth century for the later periods, variable but generally lesser amounts for earlier.

actual litigation decided in the past. It runs two ways. In one direction, how far can doctrinal developments be explained in terms of practical imperatives presented in repeated instances before the courts, rather than simply by an evolution of earlier doctrine? In the other, how far are peculiarities of structure in the mass of litigation explicable by purely legal imperatives, whether of doctrine or administration? The detailed research into the mass of past cases has also generated a second group of explanations, directed to answering rather different questions. To continue the metaphor briefly before abandoning it: what relationship do the Law Mountains bear to theories of plate tectonics? What wider, converging social forces (imperatives of the state, religious belief, purposes of different classes) threw up these heaps of parchment and paper, made litigation so much more voluminous in some eras than others, and gave it distinctive structures? For as we tunnel through we find remarkable changes in the origins of cases, in their incidence, and in their disposition, even within the last few centuries. In recent years those patterns have been much considered by historians interested in both wider social forces and the law.

What follows is not a review of that literature, but an attempt to explain (with a few examples) what some historians are about. The examples are taken from the criminal law in the period 1750–1850, and from prosecution in particular, because that is what I know best, and also because Old Felony (and its twin peak Misdemeanour) have been disproportionately the site of work by historians, like myself, who are not lawyers.[7] If I emphasise questions or sources which are less familiar to lawyers, and perhaps also to some historians whose main concern is with doctrine, there is a reason. It is to suggest, first, that the new social and intellectual history of the law

[7] One reason may be the fact that until very recently the bulk of lawyerly legal history, at least in England, has concerned other areas of the law, perhaps reflecting the powerful ordering of priorities within the profession: "Crime has never been the business of lawyers." (S. F. C. Milsom, *Historical Foundations of the Common Law* (Butterworths, 1969), concluding sentence.) It is easier for me to describe the reasons from the historian's side. They include the development of a large body of work on popular protest, in which the criminal law figures importantly as respondent (and precipitant); the importance of the criminal law to the early history of working-class political movements and trade unionism; a growing realisation among historians (in England dating largely from the establishment of County Record Offices after the war) that the very large surviving deposits of criminal court records contained much information about aspects of past daily experience not found in other sources; the layman's greater consciousness of the criminal law (perhaps reflecting its importance in structuring that consciousness in all periods); the legislative bias of the criminal law, a comfort to those acquainted with only that source of law (and historians continue for the most part to shun the others); the relative simplicity of criminal procedure (although many have not appreciated its complexities); and the place of the reform of the substantive criminal law in general histories of ideas, parties, religion and government in the period 1750–1850. For an introductory account of the literature in the social history of the criminal law for this period see Hay, "Crime and Justice in Eighteenth and Nineteenth-Century England," in Norval Morris and Michael Tonrey (eds.), *Crime and Justice: an Annual Review of Research* (Chicago, 1980). That selective bibliography is now spectacularly out of date. For recent work see references in the *Newsletter* of the International Association for the History of Crime and Criminal Justice, the new annual *Criminal Justice History*, and the leading journals in history and social history and law, where most of the work continues to be published.

is not irrelevant to doctrine—rather the opposite. Secondly, some of the larger hypotheses—those about plate tectonics—are of central importance for any intellectually respectable understanding of law itself, and prompt some reflections about why lawyers and historians may have such different views of the Mountains.

II

When Sir James Fitzjames Stephen wrote his *History of the Criminal Law of England* (1883) he based his account of trials on the highly atypical *State Trials*: atypical because they often concerned treason (with different procedural rules from felony), committed very often by powerful people, and tried in circumstances in which counsel, judges, and prisoners felt heavy pressure from government. Until recently we had little sense of the evolution of the ordinary criminal trial from the time of Sir George Jeffries (not to speak of the dark ages before that) until well into the nineteenth century. By greatly expanding the scope of research to printed records of more ordinary criminal trials, and through exploring the manuscript records of the courts and the private papers of J.P.s and others, not only the trial but also the preliminaries to indictment are becoming much better understood. Much is still contentious, but some things are clear. The role of the private prosecutor was overwhelmingly important in practice as well as in theory until well into the nineteenth century, even after the introduction of the "new" police in some areas. Private Associations for the Prosecution of Felons were extremely widespread, numbering perhaps 1,000 in the country as a whole by the mid-nineteenth century, although they seem to have been of particular interest to manufacturers and tradesmen, especially in the period of their first rapid growth in the eighteenth century. Discretion in framing the charge seems to have been widely extended to prosecutors, without much interference by justices in spite of the Marian committal statutes. Eighteenth-century trials are shown to have been extremely rapid by modern standards—10 or 20 serious felonies in a day at times, with verdicts returned quickly by experienced jurymen who worked closely with very active judges, a necessity when so few criminal cases (apart from poaching and a few other offences of largely rural significance) were heard summarily. Moreover, the eighteenth-century trial revolved to a great extent around assessments of character. The subsequent growth of a body of evidentiary rules, almost certainly the direct result of the growth of a defence bar, had significantly changed the nature of the jury trial by the early nineteenth century. A necessarily congruent development, given the enormous increase in indictable offences from 1815 (and probably the increasing time taken by a trial), was the eventual extension of summary hearings on a very wide scale. From being the epitome of English criminal law in the eighteenth century, the jury trial became the little-used symbol of it in the nineteenth.

The role of juries changed too. In the eighteenth century, petty jury verdicts (and prosecutorial activity) underwent significant shifts in response to wider economic conditions and associated changes in the character of crime. Moreover, longer-term changes in the structure of punishments during the period in which the main capital statutes were repealed in the early nineteenth century, and the increasing participation of police and stipendiary magistrates in the period 1750 to 1850, greatly increased the conviction rate (from 50 to 80 per cent.) and reduced the incidence of committals not resulting in trial (from 20 to 10 per cent.). Finally, many of the innovations effected through legislation, such as the Trials for Felony Act (1836) and Sir John Jervis's Act regulating preliminary proceedings (1848)[8] now appear to be legislative endorsements of longer-term developments rather than unexampled innovations. They also appear, like so many other changes in criminal law in the early nineteenth century (and contrasting with its stasis in the eighteenth) to be intimately involved in party differences and wider concerns in English society. Thus the 1836 Act eventuated in part from long debates about the humanity and justice of English law, including the argument about capital punishment. The 1848 Act in part reflected widespread criticism, professional and political, of the rural Tory lay bench. Both Acts also undoubtedly reached the statute book partly as a result of a phenomenal increase in the size of the legal profession, in the 1830s and 1840s. A great increase in legal journalism, often critical of the *status quo,* and expressive of a desire to introduce the values of self-conscious professionalism to every aspect of prosecution and trial, had much influence on Parliament.

The greatest changes in prosecution practice occurred in the period between 1815 and the mid-1850s, when there was both the most spectacular increase in prosecution levels since the seventeenth century, and the sharpest expression of social division in English society since the same period. Both made the wider connotations of criminal law, particularly in the eyes of a nascent working class, of prime concern to the classes represented in Parliament and on the bench. And throughout the period, many significant changes in substantive law and practice were conditioned in large part by the sheer pressure of numbers on the administrative machinery of justice, whether during the interruption of transportation during the American revolutionary war, peace-time explosions of indictment levels, or the rapid secular rise in prosecutions in the first part of the nineteenth century. By the 1860s, in contrast, a long secular decline in prosecution levels to the end of the century settled the main outlines of Victorian criminal justice as solidly as the walls of the new prisons and the newly respectable image of the British bobby.

If changes in the law were closely connected with the incidence of prosecution, both were shaped by much wider social forces. We are led, in other words, from a consideration of the reciprocal relation-

[8] 6 & 7 Wm. 4, c.114; 11 & 12 Vict. c.42.

ships of doctrine and litigation to a consideration of English society in this period. Not all accounts of the history of prosecution, or of the law and crime in general, attempt to describe those larger dimensions of the context of law. I think it essential to do so. A history which does not inquire behind the legal process leads too easily to the doubtful generalization that attitudes to crime, and hence to much of the law, have changed little if at all for centuries. One of the largest questions concerns the different meanings that the criminal law has for the different classes making up the social order, differing interpretations that obtained in even those periods when stability rather than rapid change seemed to characterise the criminal law.

III

Many historians and other scholars have implicitly described the legitimacy and authority of the criminal law as largely unproblematic. To use Stanley Diamond's dichotomy (advanced in a wider argument), this explanation (what I shall call Argument A), portrays law as a double institutionalisation of customary or popular norms, a replication of pre-existing or consubstantial social values, with perhaps a few awkward gaps between the law on the books and social practice and belief.[9] Where gaps exist, they are successively eliminated through "reform." One suspects that for many English writers, this has been especially true of England. Although the process is never quite complete, the criminal law, according to Radzinowicz, "has always been sensitive to the needs and aspirations of the English people, and it has continuously changed under the impact of the predominant opinion of the day."[10] Very few have been inclined to suggest (as did Diamond himself in Argument B) that in many societies state law instead is the imposition of a conquering class or a ruling class on a population that either formerly enjoyed its own customary law, or continued to adhere to customary mores as long as it could. In either of the latter cases state law is an imposition, but a progressively more powerful one, that cannibalises custom, remaking it and redefining it (when not obliterating it) in the process. More recently, Lenman and Parker have argued that something like this happened in Western Europe, including England, over the last thousand years.[11]

The problem with both these views of the criminal law, even if applied only to two centuries, is not simply that they are very large

[9] Stanley Diamond, "The Rule of Law versus the Order of Custom," in Stanley Diamond (ed.), *In Search of the Primitive: A Critique of Civilisation* (New Brunswick N.J., 1974).

[10] Leon Radzinowicz, *A History of English Criminal Law and its Administration from 1750* (London, 1948–68), 4 vols., i, preface.

[11] Bruce Lenman and Geoffrey Parker, "The state, the community and the criminal law in early modern Europe," in V. A. C. Gatrell, Bruce Lenman and Geoffrey Parker (eds.), *Crime and the Law: the Social History of Crime in Western Europe since 1500* (London, 1980), pp.11–48. The argument that the process was substantially complete, and that popular norms and state law largely coincided by the eighteenth or nineteenth centuries, is either a relative statement of the most general kind or needs more demonstration.

arguments about law for which different historians will advance many different standards of proof, kinds of evidence, chronologies. It is that they are very large arguments about not only what was law, but also about its relation to social belief and practice through whole societies over extended periods of time. And the empirical evidence that should be brought to bear to test such generalisations, even for the criminal law alone, does not lie easily to hand. Not only were large parts of the population, including those most subject to prosecutions, not much given to publishing or otherwise recording their thoughts (a problem acknowledged by all historians). There is also the problem that those who did write for posterity (the enlightened agents of legal change in the first view, the imposers of law in the second) left far from unproblematic comments. In dealing with such a highly political issue as law, one so charged with generating and enforcing moral meanings, one so crucial (or so they believed) to the existing social order, they usually gave a limited range of answers about the purposes of the criminal law and admitted to the existence of only a limited range of questions. To frustrate us further, they often, perhaps usually, were not conscious of the fact that they thought within such limits, precisely because they did so.

The result is that beliefs about law in different social classes, and the way those beliefs entered into the relations between those able to create and use law and those largely excluded from doing so, are very difficult to recover. It is easy but highly misleading to construct a version of the first side of Diamond's dichotomy (A: "law expresses social norms") by relying on an imputation of motive and belief (usually borrowed from literate contemporaries, or the political prejudices of the historian) to the great majority of the population for whom evidence is sparse. And it is easy but highly misleading to construct a version of the second argument (B: "ruling classes impose law") by simply citing substantive criminal law without showing how it was used, or what personal, class and societal needs it met or failed to meet.

When we turn to eighteenth-century England, we find widespread popular beliefs that certain customs were the embodiment of legality (in rights over land, in artisanal practice, in wage payment, in the organisation of marketing foodstuffs). All were increasingly under pressure from the law of the state but by no means dead. Parts of state law in all these areas (but always in particular instances) moved from a partial recognition of some custom, often through increasingly narrow judicial definition, to legislative extinction. Often this evolution met with strong popular resistance, in particular cases, at particular times. One must start, I think, with the assumption that state law and popular belief shared important areas of agreement but also important areas of disagreement, and try to chart both. And because those conflicts so often surfaced in the criminal law (for reasons to which I shall return) any account that hopes to explain the history of doctrine or administration cannot ignore the social beliefs and practices that surrounded the law in action.

Broadly, there have been a number of paths by which historians have tried to approach the relationship between state law and the belief of different classes. Three seem to me to be the most important. One has been to examine the records of the courts statistically to find out who was in fact using the law, for what ends, and to what extent. A second has been to study legal proceedings for their wider social meanings for the class that administered the law, and in particular to illuminate the means by which an often intuitive but sometimes overtly conscious orchestration of legal proceedings was addressed to popular perceptions in the inculcation of a common standard of justice. A third has been to try to reconstruct popular attitudes to particular practices on which state law had (or developed) other definitions, and their reciprocal influences. At many points in the development of criminal law and prosecution over this period of two or three centuries, changes will only be fully understood when all three are taken into account.

The most striking first finding from statistical analysis of prosecutions is that for much of this period the total level of activity was very low indeed. Although the court records surviving from the eighteenth century are voluminous enough to present research problems, it appears that rates of prosecution were markedly lower than in either the seventeenth or the nineteenth centuries. Clearly, most Englishmen and women took their disputes to fora other than the courts of the state. In minor civil cases they had a network of local courts (still little understood), including courts of requests, in which lay adjudicators could dispense with most of the procedural problems of the common law. And in both civil and criminal matters they frequently had recourse to other laymen. One such man, a Quaker, recorded in the autobiography he wrote for his family that in over 40 years there had been no formal litigation in his parish, but that he had settled over 600 disputes. We occasionally find scattered references to other occasions when Justices of the Peace, whose mediating role in misdemeanours was well established, exacted public apologies, sometimes on their knees, from transgressors whom the community condemned. Where popular condemnation was less likely (as in game cases) extorted apologies were more likely to be printed in the press. One tentative conclusion, then, is that particularly in the eighteenth century, the costs, uncertainties (given the acquittal rate) and punishments of the criminal law encouraged even more of an abstention from state law than in other periods.

The statistical examination of past criminal prosecutions has also shown, in some areas of the country in the eighteenth century, and in national totals for the nineteenth, that prosecutions for theft (the greatest part of crime) were closely related to larger economic changes, notably the rapid price changes for foodstuffs that were the consequence of dearth, and the effects on employment of export markets, the trade cycle, wars, conscription, and the massive demobilisation of troops. Each of these has been given much greater specificity than before, and one general conclusion that emerges is that the pressure of poverty can be more closely related to the incidence of crime than was suggested in early studies, flawed by considering too few of several simultaneously operating causes. In some periods, however short, it seems likely that large proportions of the labouring poor experienced both sudden destitution, and a suddenly increased possibility of feeling the direct effects of the criminal law. A *dissensus* of popular norms and law seems a likely result. Against such evidence can be constructed a "legitimacy index" based on the social class of prosecutors. Although historians disagree on the reliability of the sources, and on the meaning of the raw figures, as many as a fifth in theft cases in both the eighteenth and nineteenth centuries were what were called "the labouring poor" in the earlier period, "working men, operatives and labourers" in the later. They were underrepresented as prosecutors, however, compared to other classes, and much commonly appeared in court as defendants. The significance of their use of the criminal law, whether as an instrumental recourse for the recovery of stolen goods, the mounting of vexatious proceedings, or for other ends, will not be adequately known until the sociology of more cases is also known to us.

An important issue in the nineteenth century is whether more working-class complainants had recourse to the courts as prosecution increasingly fell into the hands of the police. The difficulty of disentangling the actions of complainants from the actions of the police (who in the first half of the nineteenth century were accused of fomenting many vexatious and malicious prosecutions in some jurisdictions) has yet to be resolved. Our findings about the role of the police in prosecutions in the nineteenth century are still, surprisingly, not very far advanced. Surprising, because there is a new and extensive literature on police organisation, on the creation of new forces between 1829 and the 1850s, and on popular responses to them. There are important differences in response: a smooth transition from the old parish constabulary in some areas, violent working-class resistance in others, especially in the north of England, where it was believed (as was the case) that the new police were meant to implement the harsh aims of the Poor Law Amendment Act of 1834. There are temporal changes as well, including a recurrence of violence against the police in the 1860s and 1870s, probably due to the use of constables in deterring applicants for poor relief, and in tightening up licensing hours. In the early 1870s it was estimated that every Metropolitan police officer would on average be injured once every two years.

The statistics, then, are suggestive rather than conclusive about popular beliefs as reflected in use of the criminal law, both in the eighteenth century and in the nineteenth. The figures may, in the end, tell us more about middle-class fears: analysis of such "moral panics" as the "garrotting" episode of the early 1860s shows the way in which police responsiveness to Press opinion could readily yield an "increase" in serious crime. Some of the other, larger purposes which wealthier citizens saw in the criminal law can be tracked more easily in other sources.

One strongly-held belief was that private prosecution was an essential constitutional safeguard against possible executive tyranny, a belief which served to preserve in England the right of prosecution relatively unimpaired into the twentieth century. It is also clear that those with property and those who administered the criminal law thought the courts most important for the inculcation of moral values, and a belief in English justice, in a working-class which they did not trust. In part this was to be done through attention to the theatre of justice. A judge at all sensitive to the social importance of law is likely to be acutely aware of this aspect of his work. Lord Devlin gave a modern expression of it:

> "The social service which the judge renders to the community is the removal of a sense of injustice. To perform this service the essential quality which he needs is impartiality and next after that the appearance of impartiality. I put impartiality before the appearance of it simply because without the reality the appearance would not endure. In truth, within the context of service to the community *the appearance is the more important of the two*."[12]

That concern with sensitive vulgarisation of professional learning has its own history. The judicial attention to appearance, especially in acting as counsel for the undefended prisoner in this period, in pronouncing sentence of death, and in making proclamations of the justice and mercy of state law, are of central interest to the historian trying to gauge popular responses to the courts. A detailed history of prosecution is important here, particularly for noting contexts of social distress or widespread riot.[13] The chronology of the transition from the bullying which appears often to have been characteristic of the seventeenth-century bench, to the widely remarked benevolent neutrality of the Hanoverian and Victorian judiciary, is another aspect of the history of legal theatre. We must also look to the increasing disposition of cases to lay magistrates in the early nineteenth century, a process which some contemporaries, in the troubled 1830s and 1840s, believed greatly weakened working-class respect for state courts because of the casual moral brutality (literally Dickensian) characterising part of the lay bench. Many stipendiaries, on the other hand, appear to have been acutely aware that they were attempting to rebuild respect for the law, and some went so far

[12] Patrick Devlin, "The Judge as Lawmaker," the fourth Chorley Lecture (1976), 39 M.L.R. 1, reprinted in *The Judge* (Oxford, 1981), p.9, emphasis added.

[13] See below for an instance in 1800–1801.

as to pretend a civil jurisdiction they did not possess, in order to overawe oppressive landlords or employers late with wages. In those areas of the country in which they also committed hundreds of workmen to prison in master and servant prosecutions, their success was still greater than when justices in the trade did so.

While the detailed symbolic histories of magistrates' courts are difficult to recover (although much work is being done), we know more about the importance attributed by upper-class opinion in the late eighteenth and early nineteenth centuries to the assizes and to their use of the death penalty. The repeal of capital punishment, often explained in terms of a disembodied humanitarianism (expressed in parliamentary debates and in the tenderness of juries and of prosecutors), now appears to have had more to do with developments in doctrinal thinking on the one hand, and overt political considerations, closely tied to a class analysis of English society, on the other. In doctrine, the rise of formalism in important areas of private law, remarked by historians on both sides of the Atlantic, was also part of the attack on the discretion which the judges increasingly had to exercise in selecting a few unfortunates among the condemned for actual execution, as death sentences increased with indictable crime but executions clearly could not. It seemed increasingly unacceptable to reformers like Romilly that no known rules, certainly no rules of law, governed the exercise of the pardon, when criminal procedure and a rapidly expanding law of evidence were observed rigorously in capital trials. The larger political conflict, as it is analysed in a recent account of the parliamentary debates on the capital statutes, was between two conceptions of proper authority, matching two distinct views of the dynamics of English society.[14] On the one hand, Tories committed to the *status quo* of the eighteenth-century system deplored attacks on the capital statutes, which they argued were essential for making discriminating use of the necessary terror of the law. On the other hand, their opponents (and for the most part, the political opposition in Parliament) castigated the erratic operation of the Royal Pardon, particularly under the Prince Regent, as a symbol of the arbitrary nature of aristocratic government. They also warned that far from holding a potentially revolutionary working class in awe, capital punishment would harden the moral sentiments of those already depraved: the state which murdered, and so publicly, could expect little allegiance in return. Many of those arguments were recapitulated, briefly, in the debates which led to the effective end of public executions in the 1860's.

Finally, some of the most interesting work on the relationship of criminal law and social beliefs has centred on instances of direct comparisons or reciprocal influences between state law and popular justice. We know relatively little about such ties, but they were ubiquitous. One cause was the degree to which the high visibility of

[14] Randall McGowan, "The Image of Justice" (1983) *32 Buffalo Law Review* 89.

state justice (from the distant past) permeated popular culture as an exemplar of *the* way of doing justice. Some popular justice—notably the rituals of "rough music"—appears to have remained relatively untouched in form until they died out in the nineteenth century. The most striking opposite case, the elaborate aping of state criminal procedure, took place among groups contaminated by very direct contact with the courts—prisoners holding mock trials in gaols, barristers doing the same in their circuit messes. But other reciprocal influences or similarities between state law and extra-legal social enforcement are more interesting. When judges and legislators ceased to believe in the *maleficium* of witchcraft in the early eighteenth century, and repealed the capital statutes on the subject in 1736, their unexampled mercy did not impress a large number of villagers, who in many incidents in the next half-century continued to interrogate and punish suspected witches by dragging them through ponds (with murder charges by the state sometimes the result). On the other hand, the quick justice of the crowd against thieves caught red-handed, usually through ducking in a horse-trough, appears rather similar to the very rapid assessment of character and guilt which we now know was the norm in the courts, even in trials on capital statutes. Finally, a most interesting example of the complex relationship between state law and popular beliefs about law, or popular justice, is that of the food riot. It is interesting in part because it is now one of the best-studied aspects of eighteenth-century popular culture. And the evidence from many hundreds of instances shows that crowd action against bakers and millers suspected of profiting from high food prices was informed by a belief that seizing food and selling it for a "just" price, or punishing the offender more directly, was legitimated by a long tradition of legal sanctions against such suspected exploiters of the community. Magistrates as well as mobs agreed on the value of Tudor and Stuart (and earlier) legislation against middlemen in food enacted to prevent popular disorder of threatening proportions in times of dearth.[15]

It is worth pursuing this example a little further, as an illustration of the differences between social history of law and more doctrinal legal history, even when the latter is written by a lawyer highly sensitive to the need for contextual study of the legal past. It may also illustrate my contention that much doctrine may be explicable only by following litigation to its sources.

In *The Rise and Fall of Freedom of Contract* (Oxford, 1979) Patrick Atiyah is concerned to construct an argument that judges, in the course of the later eighteenth and early nineteenth centuries, sheared equitable protection from the law of contract. They moved from a tradition that sometimes interfered with agreements that were (or had become through circumstances) inequitable to almost invariable insistence on the execution of the expressed intentions of

[15] E. Thompson, "The Moral Economy of the English Crowd" (1971) 50 *Past and Present* 76, is the central title in a large literature.

the parties, however imbalanced the respective benefits. In making this case he draws on a wide range of evidence of changes in administration, attitudes to legislation, but above all the developing ideology of a market of freely contracting individuals, responsible for their actions, understood in the terms of early classical political economy. There are problems with the narrative, however, when judges behave in ways "difficult to interpret from an economic viewpoint." One such hiccup in the judicial imbibing of free market principles appears to be the decision of Lord Kenyon and his brothers in *R.* v. *Rusby* and *R.* v. *Waddington,* in 1800–1801.[16] In those cases they emphasised that the common law crimes of buying and reselling foodstuffs for gain or in speculative quantities, or before they came to open market (engrossing, regrating, forestalling) still remained after the repeal of many of the statutes in 1772.[17] Moreover, Justices Kenyon and Grose not only repudiated the theories of political economy presented by counsel for the defendants: they also invoked older equitable notions (and Christianity, no less). In *Rusby,* Lord Kenyon said,

> "It frequently becomes the duty of juries in this place to decide causes where the interests of individuals are deeply concerned; but a more important duty than is imposed on them today they never fulfilled: this cause presents itself to their notice on behalf of all ranks, rich and poor, but more especially the latter. Though in a state of society some must have greater luxuries and comforts than others, yet all should have the necessaries of life; and if the poor cannot exist, in vain may the rich look for happiness or prosperity. The Legislature is never so well employed as when they look to the interests of those who are at a distance from them in the ranks of society. It is their duty to do so: religion calls for it; humanity calls for it; and if there are hearts who are not awake to either of those feelings, their own interests would dictate it. The law has not been disputed; for though in an evil hour all the statutes which had been existing about a century were at one blow repealed, yet, thank God, the provisions of the common law [against forestalling] were not destroyed . . . Speculation has said that the fear of such an offence is ridiculous; and a very learned man, a good writer, has said you might as well fear witchcraft. I wish Dr. Adam Smith had lived to hear the evidence of today, and then he would have seen whether such an offence exists, and whether it is to be dreaded. If he had been told that cattle and corn were brought to market, and then bought by a man whose purse happened to be longer than his neighbours, so that the poor man who walks the street and earns his daily bread by his daily labour could get none but through his hands, and at the price he chose to demand; that it had been raised 3d., 6d., 9d., 1s.,

[16] Peake Add.Cas. 189, 170 E.R. 241; 1 East 143; 102 E.R. 56. See Atiyah, pp.363-366 (citing *Rusby* as *Ruby*).

[17] 12 George 3, c.71.

2s., and more a quarter on the same day, would he have said there was no danger from such an offence?"[18]

And in *Waddington*, where the prisoner was a large dealer in hops (held to be foodstuffs because they were essential to brewing), Kenyon declared that engrossing large quantities, in hopes of an exorbitant profit, "is a most heinous offence against religion and morality, and against the established law of the country."[19]

For Atiyah, this is a paradoxical survival of an older tradition of benevolent paternalism, especially since Parliament had repealed the statutory provisions almost 30 years before.[20] (It was a paradox that had surfaced before 1800: Kenyon had taken the opportunity in a case in 1795 to remark that the common law was still in effect.) Atiyah concludes, not unreasonably, that judges often get their law, and their prejudices, fixed at an early age, and suggests that Kenyon (who left the bench in 1802 after a long career) was simply behind the times, uninstructed in the truths advanced by the epigoni of Adam Smith (who indeed had compared the laws against forestalling to those against witchcraft).[21] But the judgments, and particularly *Waddington*, involved more than political economy and paternalism.

Atiyah remarks that that context was one of "acute shortage and high prices" for foodstuffs.[22] It was indeed a crisis. Food prices in 1800 and 1801 were far higher than they had been during other periods of dearth: from early 1799 when wheat was about 6s. a bushel it had increased 300 per cent. to over a pound a bushel in March 1801 in most parts of the country. Vertiginously high prices were sustained throughout 1800 and 1801. Since bread made up so much of the average diet, a large part of the population was made destitute: no less than 40 per cent. of the population could not have bought, unassisted, enough bread to survive even if they had spent their entire family incomes on bread alone for the whole of 1801.[23] But it was a crisis not only for the poor. Food riots were widespread throughout the country, with the mob demanding that the authorities enforce the common law penalties against speculators in foodstuffs, in the belief that they were largely responsible for the dearth. Thousands of troops, by early 1801, faced hostile crowds who in some districts conducted a virtual guerrilla warfare against them. Justices of the peace were hastening to make scores of exemplary prosecutions of middlemen in food, and doing so in the most public manner, in order to restore order. And the magistrates were acutely aware (as was the government) that some of the troops were also disaffected, and that some food riots were accompanied by seditious calls to emulate the French (with whom Britain was at war) by

[18] Peake Add.Cas. 192, quoted in Atiyah, p.364.
[19] 1 East 143, 155.
[20] Atiyah, p.366.
[21] R.H. Campbell and A.S. Skinner (eds.) *Wealth of Nations* (1976), Vol. 1, pp.534 *et seq.*
[22] Atiyah, p.363.
[23] Hay (*supra*, note 5), pp.128–135.

establishing a revolutionary republic in England. It was in these circumstances, when the discretionary use of the laws against forestallers, regrators and engrossers of food was being heavily exploited as almost the only effective response to massive riot, that Waddington's counsel suggested to King's Bench that they reflected mere superstition, and pressed on the court the wisdom of Adam Smith. It is perhaps not surprising that the judges preferred the (rediscovered) wisdom of the common law, and in their judgments used the rhetoric of Christianity and humanity, rather than that of the market.

But the perspective of the judges was a more personal one than that, and again it was imposed on their consciousness by events beyond doctrine and beyond general currents of economic theory. In sentencing Waddington to a large fine and imprisonment, Grose J. argued that the laws against speculation in foodstuff were not an unwarranted interference with trade in the light of other facts: "In support of the legal freedom of trade [he said] the law has declared, and that law has repeatedly been acted upon, that to violate the freedom of trade by intercepting commodities on their way to market, taking them from the owner by force . . . or obliging them to accept a less price than he demands, is a capital offence, for which men have forfeited their lives to the law."[24] Women too had been sentenced to death for food riots, which is what Grose was describing, and he and his brethren had pronounced numbers of such sentences, some of them carried out, in 1783, 1795, and 1800. If freedom of trade had been enforced with such rigour, it seemed reasonable that it also should have legal limits to prevent such tragedies. Grose and the other judges were conscious that if riots could be prevented by prosecuting forestallers and regrators and engrossers, fewer rioters would have to hang. Most important of all, they were also aware that in the extremely disturbed circumstances of 1801, the option of exemplary executions was increasingly foreclosed to them because hangings could provoke more riots than they prevented. Five years later, when prices had temporarily declined, the judges were showing much less hostility to engrossers, and by 1819, when the post-war depression had caused a great and prolonged fall in agricultural prices (and when France was defeated), it was the opinion of the best lawyers that the courts would no longer enforce the common law penalties against middlemen in food without proof of specific intent to raise prices.

Waddington and *Rusby* illustrate the value-breeding, ideological functions of the judges, and their sense of the policy requirements of the criminal law, as much as their traditionalism or their benevolence. Such policy considerations permeated the administration of the criminal law, and, in this instance, perhaps shaped (for a brief time) its doctrine. And those considerations rested, in this instance, on the consciousness that a radically different view, both of what was just and what was law, was held by the labouring poor. In

[24] 1 East 143, 163.

1800–1801, they demanded that the courts respond to their belief that the law of England had been properly embodied in that mass of legislation which Parliament had repealed in 1772. Faced with riot, distress, and the threat of revolution, the judges responded.[25] In elucidating such cases we must reconstruct not only the doctrinal history and the wider intellectual currents of the age, not only the class perceptions of the bench and the differences between judges, but also the larger histories of actual litigation and wider social context. Only then will we illuminate the policy considerations and prejudices which are referred to so fleetingly in the reported cases, if at all, and be able to judge the relative autonomy of doctrine from economic theories, class strategies, and imperatives of government.

I have been able to use this example because Atiyah's account of contract is so rich in references to wider influences on doctrine, and because the food riot has attracted much research. On many other points the young disciplines of social and economic history still provide little commentary, in part because historians have been so ignorant of the chronology of legal change. Conversely, when some scholars come to prove the autonomy (or otherwise) of doctrine in the past, too often they have attempted to do so in a peculiarly unconvincing way. Detailed and informed work on fine distinctions of doctrine is placed against highly schematic, impressionistic versions of social, economic, and political "background," derived from secondary sources which are both dated and general. The connections between law and "context" are then remarked—or, more commonly, their absence noted, which one sometimes suspects was the interest of the enterprise. But no historian believes that causal relations work in such general ways, or that there is any interest in trying to show that they do. Without examining the specific mechanisms at the point of decision, and without knowing what the predicted, perceived and intended ends of many decisions (perhaps at a low level of consciousness) actually were, nothing has been demonstrated. In short, in history there is no "background." There are only a host of forces of different strengths, including the beliefs of different social groups, the effects of which must be weighed in each case, and in the aggregate over time.

IV

I began with an image of the different perspectives of the lawyer and the historian to the legal past, that of the climber and the geologist. Their sources and their purposes differ greatly: in the case

[25] The cases were interesting in other ways. Rusby was convicted, but not punished because the bench was divided on whether regrating was an indictable offence at common law, after hearing arguments on a rule to show cause why judgment should not be arrested. Waddington, who was convicted and also punished by fine and imprisonment, was a Jacobin. He had been expelled from the Surrey troop of light horse for his radical politics, and had attacked Burke in print for slandering the French Revolution. The prosecution was begun by other hop-factors, but for the government he was a most convenient target for a criminal information for engrossing at a time when food riots against engrossers had been tinged with Jacobin slogans. I shall publish a fuller account of the case.

of the lawyer, a thin layer (particularly in England) of doctrinal materials used for immediately instrumental ends; for the historian, all surviving records of litigation, which are being searched for temporal and structural patterns of past law. And that is but the beginning, as some of my examples will have made clear. For historians, there can be no privileged sources, because few questions of any wide significance can be answered from materials, such as reports of cases, constructed for limited and specific ends.[26] Social historians in particular have taken their remit to be a wide one: explaining the beliefs and actions of not only legislators, judges, and the police, but of victims of crime, prosecutors, criminals, potential criminals, spectators in court, the public who read trial accounts, the spectators at executions, the children who lisped the oral tradition of criminal and legal folklore. To the lawyer, who asks what possible *use* such an endeavour may be, or even to a legal historian who knows how much doctrinal history is yet unwritten, such projects may appear to confuse the central with the peripheral, to exemplify perverse antiquarianism. Some take the view that what 90 per cent. of the population thought about the law, or did with it, is unproblematic or uninteresting. When those dead men and women are invoked, it is as past "public opinion" or "the people," shades who live in limbo, like those other unfortunate souls, the passengers on the phantom omnibus which never gets to Clapham.

I have argued instead that popular beliefs are important to any convincing history of past criminal law, even in some of its more detailed doctrinal history. Social historians start from an assumption that past societies (and present ones) are complex places in which apparently unrelated social orders on closer inspection may show a remarkable interdependence. The connections may be circuitous, but because they are not immediately evident does not mean that they are not important. Tracing complex chains of causation, finding unsuspected connections, and revealing unspoken (or at least, privileged) values and decisions, in specific detail, is part of the historian's task. Our approach to the courts and their decisions, and to all those involved in the administration of justice is no different, whatever our theoretical perspectives.

Such an approach seems perverse to some lawyers because it contradicts their own working premisses. I would reply that those premisses subvert historical explanation. At the risk of constructing an hypostatised English lawyer who never existed. I want to suggest some characteristics of legal scholarship which, if transposed to study of the past, would generate histories without depth or process. Our lawyer's handicap can be grouped under two heads: thinking like a lawyer, and doing so in England.

[26] As Kahn-Freund observed, in a modern instance, "the law reports are the worst possible mirror of society. They convey to the beholder a distorted image in which that which is marginal appears as typical, and this may be one of the reasons why sometimes the judgments of lawyers on social policy are so surprisingly warped and ill-founded" (1970) 33 M.L.R. 241, 242.

By "thinking like a lawyer" I mean certain intellectual habits which are purposefully honed in the course of most legal education and practice, but which vitiate historical explanation. It is perhaps most convenient to list the errors in historical logic that seem likely to result from each.[27] Five stand out; some are more common to the arts of advocacy, some to doctrinal analysis in the library.

One to which I have made reference already is the fallacy of *moralism*. It is implicit in any unexamined assumption that state law inscribed a moral consensus, perhaps imperfect, but roughly the same in most social classes for most of the recent past. Yet it is instructive to consider why most historians (of at least this century) have been wary of using such assumptions to ground explanation. They are acutely conscious that their own values are highly contingent on culture and epoch, and are no guide to explaining the past. The point is a truism, even if in practice the boundaries between the theory one inevitably brings to research, and the personal reactions to what one finds, have a common plane. But a corollary is that in historical explanation there can be no privileged actors, whose values can be assumed, or dismissed, because they do or do not appear to coincide with one's own, or a postulated consensus.

All this becomes more difficult to remember if the subject is crime, and if the social actors are rioters and burglars as well as judges and victims. An attempt to explain the values and acts of each in equally neutral or sympathetic terms may seem, to a lawyer, presumptuous and wrong, because it entails an *uncommitted* consideration of the meanings and uses of legal institutions. It has been argued that for those trained in the law, the legal order becomes ideology, that "law, and within it jurisprudence, constitutes 'a world of its own'—which the inquirer who takes legal norms, as such, as object of knowledge, cannot but inhabit and *desire to serve*."[28] The assertion is undoubtedly cast in too absolute terms. But when the historian who approaches the criminal law as an object of knowledge encounters the assumption that because state law is an unqualified human good, its victims are self-evidently beneath serious consideration, he suspects the moralistic fallacy on the grand scale.

Presentism, the fallacy of working from present concerns to past origins, is anathema to historians, but necessarily half the lawyer's

[27] The most readable exposition remains David Hackett Fischer, *Historians' Fallacies: Toward a Logic of Historical Thought* (Routledge and Kegan Paul, 1971): working historians may differ on the choice of examples, but will agree in most cases on the classification, and the perniciousness of each *genre*. See pp.78–82 (*moralistic fallacy*), 135–140 (*presentism*), 177 (*identity*), 195–200 (*rationalist*—or idealist in Fischer's terminology), 9–12 (fallacy of *false dichotomous questions*). To name names on an occasion such as this would be invidious rather than gracious, but I have encountered examples of each of these in recent accounts of the past written by lawyers. Historians usually commit different ones: notably, the genetic fallacy.

[28] Iain Stewart, "Sociology in Jurisprudence: the Problem of 'Law' as Object of Knowledge," in Bob Fryer, Alan Hunt, Doreen McBarnet and Bert Moorhouse (eds.), *Law, State and Society* (Croom Helm, 1981), p.120, emphasis added.

method.[29] Whatever its merits in finding supporting arguments for a brief, it has the effect in historical work of writing out of the past any developments which did not survive in much the same form into the present. Since there is little in human affairs that did so, not even sex and hunger, it is disastrous as an intellectual method for recovering the past. In search of origins, it tends to find false analogies which, when stripped of context, can be made to look like their putative descendants. Where the object of knowledge has few recognisable descendants, the search does not even begin. Presumably that may explain (to take one example) why so little has been written about the wider effects of the purposeful extinction, through parliamentary enclosure Acts, of a great corpus of customary law in England over the last three centuries, a change which has changed the meaning in England of law itself.[30]

The *fallacy of identity* appears likely to be a particular affliction of lawyers looking at history. Training to demonstrate legal consequences from legal causes entails the necessary assumption that legal effects usually have legal causes, or at least that those are the main causes worth considering. It is a presumption that must be immensely strengthened by the persuasive evidence for some autonomy of law and legal culture from wider social forces. But the form of doctrinal debate is (to an historian) a pervasive form of mono-causal explanation, in which the question of autonomy and its degree are not even raised because the answer is assumed: new law largely is considered in terms of the working-out of implications of old law, and awkward cases tend to be dismissed as a residual term, rather than explained. Historians are sometimes surprised to see such cases (and legislation) smoothly accommodated in accounts in the doctrinal tradition. It may make them wonder if the best efforts of the other profession are not often put to reconciling differences which in other disciplines would call for explanation rather than reconciliation.

The assumption of legal autonomy is often closely allied to a *rationalist* view of legal decision-making again conditioned by reliance on a narrow range of sources. This, like many of the other points that occur to an historian about legal reasoning, was one of the concerns of the legal realists, but some of their initiatives were doomed to inconclusive results. When they tried to analyse contemporary law the attempt was sure to be only marginally successful, particularly in studies of judicial decision-making, for two good reasons. One (as the reviewer of a recent biography of Frankfurter

[29] J. H. Hexter's explanation (source distinctions) for "tunnel history" (quoted in Fischer, at p.142) is only part of the explanation; when lawyers commit this fallacy it seems equally likely to be a result of assumptions of autonomy, the imperatives of advocacy, and the interest in policy recommendations (below).

[30] But see C. K. Allen, *Law in the Making* (7th ed., Clarendon Press, 1964), pp.67 *et seq.* and Appendix for the doctrine. What is lacking is the social and economic consequences of its application, and the disjunction between custom in popular understanding and practice on the one hand, and what the doctrine came to allow on the other.

has pointed out) was that they were themselves insiders.[31] Too rigorous an application of realist criticism could be construed as unseemly, impertinent personal criticism of colleagues with whom the rest of their professional lives were spent. More important was the fact that they could not read the private papers of their subjects. Short of the confessional (and one suspects that some judges in the confessional are as aware of exclusionary rules there as in their courtrooms), private correspondence, notably correspondence meant to be kept private, is a prime source from which historians (including realists) have considered the levels of overt intention, collective assumptions, class bias, and professional learning (not necessarily in that order) which a bench brings to a case, or an Attorney-General brings to a prosecution.[32] Analysis *begins* there, since the exercise of power is often a profoundly calculated act, and where it is not consciously so calculated it is enacted within a medium of often unspoken but nonetheless powerful assumptions. Those assumptions include implicit judgments about "proper behaviour" resting on class, interest and ethnicity. Such assumptions often remain unexpressed, either because they are unacceptable within the wider political culture, or simply in the belief that knowledge is often best kept back from most people for their own good. (It is very easy to make that rationalisation if that good is equated with the smooth operation of the instruments of government, or the administration of justice.)[33] They are particularly likely to remain unexpressed by the bench, as irrelevant to the issue, if the dominant style of legal judgments is narrowly formalist, as it has been in this country for well over a hundred years. In that case, as Atiyah suggests to us, we may be obliged to watch for instances in which judges "give themselves away" and reveal values, even unconscious influences, which help them to a decision but which are concealed thereafter in the language of pure doctrine.[34]

Finally, much legal reasoning is dichotomous, which in historical work can easily lead to *false dichotomous questions*. It seems a likely

[31] Alan M. Dershowitz, reviewing H. N. Hirsch, *The Enigma of Felix Frankfurter* (1981) in the *New York Times* February 22, 1981. Karl Llewellyn's nearest approach was a foredoomed attempt in the 1930s to assess the wider influences on judicial decision-making by asking some former colleagues, recently appointed to the bench, to keep notes of their methods! See William Twining, *Karl Llewellyn and the Realist Movement* (Weidenfeld and Nicolson, 1973), p.246.

[32] But it seems unlikely that for many judges we will be given the kind of materials that illuminate the wider sources of doctrine (not that they end scholarly debate about it) of the kind connected with Frankfurter's relationship with Brandeis: see B. A. Murphy, *The Brandeis-Frankfurter Connection—the Secret Political Activities of Two Supreme Court Justices* (New York, 1982), and the review by Robert M. Cover, "The Framing of Justice Brandeis," (May 5, 1982) 186 *New Republic* 17–21.

[33] See Twining, *op. cit.*, p.228, for an incident in which an English judge took Llewellyn to task for the more venial sin of advocating a jurisprudence which would expose the "tacit assumptions and subtle nuances" in the working relationship of English bench and bar, assumptions and nuances which the judge insisted should remain unexpressed and unexamined.

[34] Patrick Atiyah, *The Rise and Fall of Freedom of Contract* (Oxford, 1979) pp.374, 660 *et seq*.

consequence of viewing life in terms of what can be litigated, if not in the logic of law itself.[35] David Hume pointed out that to move from arbitration to litigation was to redefine the problem, and the solution:

> "Hence it is, that in references, where the consent of the parties leave the referees entire masters of the subject, they commonly discover so much equity and justice on both sides, as induces them to strike a medium, and divide the difference betwixt the parties. Civil judges, who have not this liberty, but are oblig'd to give a decisive sentence on some one side, are often at a loss how to determine, and are necessitated to proceed on the most frivolous reasons in the world. Half rights and obligations, which seem so natural in common life, are perfect absurdities in their tribunal; for which reason they are often oblig'd to take half arguments for whole ones, in order to terminate the affair one way or another."[36]

Shared rights and obligations—"so natural in common life"—have found little support in English courts in recent centuries (although *divided* ones, of course, have.) The paradigm of litigation has tended to support a strong bias toward an individualist interpretation of what are collective interests.[37] When such conflicts are mediated through criminal law, as they often have been in the English past, then collective responses can appear, in insufficiently sensitive legal accounts, as individual acts of deviation from an already assumed social norm. This configuration of the two assumptions of a societal consensus and individualist actors, orchestrated in the trial, is also a powerful reinforcement (in criminal law) of the moralistic fallacy. Moreover, when carried into an analysis of the social significance of the criminal law, dichotomous reasoning leads to false questions. Was the criminal law a generator of social symbols, or a service institution for the prosecution of crime? Did the criminal law promote specific class interests or was it used by all social classes? Were rules real constraints on judges or were they aspects of an orchestrated ideology of justice? For the eighteenth century, the answer in each case is "both," and it is that multiplicity which constitutes much of the significance of law.[38]

Any scholar from another discipline, particularly those which try to view societies in the round, will compile her own list of what appear (from such a perspective) to be idiosyncrasies of legal reasoning. But I think they will often in the end lead to two central tenets: that state law has both *matched* an unproblematic social

[35] Llewellyn forcefully warned his students in jurisprudence of this point: see Twining, *op. cit.*, pp.115, 516.

[36] David Hume, *A Treatise of Human Nature*, ed. L. A. Selby-Bigge (2nd ed., Oxford, 1978), p.531. Or, more succinctly, "The continuum in which we live [unlike law] is not the kind of place in which middles can be unambiguously excluded" (Reuben Able, quoted in Fischer, p.12, with my addition).

[37] In the Chorley Lecture for 1982, Patrick McAuslan remarked the importance of this perspective of the courts in their acquiescence in the attack on collective provision by the present Government ((1983) 46 M.L.R. 1, esp. pp.11 *et seq.*).

[38] Arthur Leff, "Law and" (1978) 87 Yale L.J. 989.

consensus and has exhibited a logic largely *independent of context*, particularly that of economic and class interest. We are told that it is sensitively autonomous. I suggested earlier that in fact the legitimacy and authority of the criminal law are often inferred from an undemonstrated social consensus, and some accounts of the legal past tend to import equally undemonstrated assumptions of autonomy. Robert Gordon has suggested that that is why traditional legal scholarship tends to be highly suspicious of history in the sense in which historians *tout court* practice it: that is, of history without a prefix, committed to the understanding of the relationships of all social belief and practice. Historians propose to *test* the autonomy of the law in precisely the way they test the autonomy of other social orders, such as religious beliefs, economic organisation, class division—by looking purposefully for interrelations, in specific detail, in the minds and institutions they jointly form. Gordon argues that legal scholarship, at least in America, responds by employing a battery of intellectual stratagems to resist any recognition of the historical contingency of law.[39]

But I suggested earlier that if an ahistorical consciousness might be an expected result of lawyerly habits of thought, it also, at least in this country, has indigenous causes peculiar to England. By that I meant two things.

The first is that the common-law tradition is so broad a part of the constitutional and cultural foundations of this country that there are a host of intimate relations between popular norms and state law, and have been for many centuries. At least in the past, the connections do not amount to anything like the "autonomous but sensitive" criminal law which is often proposed to us. The social history of the criminal law shows that the relationship was instead contradictory, shot through with collective values opposed to state law, popular celebration of old law which the state was bent on purging, and usually a massive avoidance of the state legal apparatus on the grounds that it was both financially rapacious and unpredictable. Nonetheless, when centralised state law is so powerful and so visible, even in limited contexts, from so early a date in the history of the kingdom, it is easy to make a premature identification of state law and popular mores. That kind of oversimplification is less likely when English law is found in a context where élite perceptions cannot be directly identified with national culture, in law or other areas. The extreme case is that of the Third World, where the abrupt intrusion of English and other European law has done much to develop paradigms of imposed law and legal pluralism, and a sensitivity to the concealed and overt class strategies encapsulated in law.[40] But even in countries where the common law inheritance bulked much larger in the foundations of the national culture, the

---

[39] Robert W. Gordon, "Historicism in Legal Scholarship" (1981) 90 Yale L.J. 1017–1056.

[40] See, for example, the work referred to and presented in *The Journal of Legal Pluralism*.

assumption of an identity of state law and social norms is less likely than in England to be an immediate one.

In Canada, the example I know best, encomiums to the tradition of English law are a staple of formal occasions, and have been ever since underemployed English barristers and solicitors, or refugee Loyalist Americans, began reconstructing English criminal law and practice in eighteenth-century Nova Scotia or Upper Canada. But in Quebec, English criminal law was also the imposition of the English conqueror in 1764 (for reasons of state justified in terms of benevolence) on a population which was 96 per cent. French-speaking and accustomed to Colbert's Ordinance of 1670.[41] They also learned, as Lord Devlin pointed out on another occasion, that it was often the "second-rate" and "the blimps" from England who brought the common law to the colonies.[42] More important, when they used legal arguments resting on English and Imperial precedents, in the cause of self-government, the English response was not congratulation but repression: charges of sedition, imprisonment without recourse to *habeas corpus,* and within another generation the bloody military suppression of an armed populist insurrection in which French and Irish nationalist lawyers figured prominently as leaders.

The Canadian public prosecutorial tradition also exhibits an interesting mix of traditions, one of them being the Imperial interest in maintaining direct colonial rule from London.[43] The contribution of Scots law is probably important here too, and perhaps also Dublin Castle's highly centralised prosecutorial system which (like its police) was in Ireland an outcome of the determination of the British state to maintain its rule in the face of a greatly rebellious population.[44] If some of its emigrant lawyers probably helped to found a system of prosecution in Canada with some similarities, other Irishmen and women carried their traditions of resistance with them. Undoubtedly the most notorious criminal episode in Canadian history, that of the Donnellys, had roots in bloodfeud endemic in those parts of Irish society in which the state's courts were avoided like the plague, and perhaps also from the immigrant experience in England, where Irish prisoners got short shrift from judges in the eighteenth century, and where Irishmen were the most prominent group involved in mutual physical violence with the "new" nineteenth-century police.

The American influence (about which we have, typically, ambivalent feelings) is a conflict of influences. While English law and government in Canada for much of the first century after 1776 were devoted to extirpating republican and democratic constitutional

---

[41] Hay, "The Meanings of Criminal Law in Quebec 1764–1774," in L. A. Knafla (ed.), *Crime and Justice in Europe and Canada* (Wilfred Laurier Press, Waterloo, Ontario, 1981).

[42] Patrick Devlin, *supra,* note 12.

[43] Hay, "Controlling the English prosecutor" (1983) 21 *Osgoode Hall Law Journal* 165; J. Ll. J. Edwards, *Ministerial Responsibility for National Security as it Relates to the Offices of Prime Minister, Attorney-General and Solicitor-General of Canada* (Hull, Quebec, 1980), esp. Chaps. 7, 8 and 10.

[44] John McEldowney, "Crown Prosecutions in Nineteenth Century Ireland" (forthcoming).

heresy whenever it raised its head, and respectable opinion commonly attributed crime to contamination from the same source (and sometimes still does), in late years American influence has affected our view of civil liberties. Once it was based squarely enough on principles within the English tradition (although sometimes reflecting a distinct cultural clash between the working assumptions of French and English-speaking justices in the Supreme Court).[45] But now widespread popular views of police and criminal law in Canada owe much to the American mass media, and at a legislative level may have more than a little to do with our recent enthusiasm for Bills of Rights.[46]

Finally, all students of our Supreme Court and our constitution are aware that some very particular (and occasionally peculiar) conceptions of Canadian society, politics, and federalist imperatives were to be found in the Judicial Committee of the Privy Council, before it ceased to be our final court of appeal in 1949. The experience of having a crippled domestic court which was constantly bypassed for recourse to a body in London which decided crucial constitutional issues, often in a single day and without written briefs, is an important constituent of our experience of disjunctions between "law" and "society."[47]

I have trespassed on your hospitality enough, and I shall not sketch the Amerindian, Scandinavian, German, Italian, or Doukhabour cultural memories which might further condition Canadian perceptions. (Nor can I.) But I hope I have said enough to suggest why Canadian historians perhaps are less sure than their English counterparts that the criminal law (or other state law) reflects in an unproblematic way the wider values in the past society. We are more apt to be aware of legal transplants, imposition of law, recourse to martial law, and the slow and contradictory way in which English law became part of our national culture. The Third World experience, while extreme, is not wholly alien to us. But neither am I convinced (and this is the point which prompted my excursion into chauvinist display) that criminal law *in England* has always exhibited quite so simple a relationship with cultural norms as seems sometimes to be supposed by her lawyers.

One reason is the issue of social class, which has been of central interest to social historians. In the New World, social class and race and ethnicity have often been powerful reinforcing identities. But class divisions (and ethnic and racial ones) have not been unknown in England. It seems curious that the subject so rarely has appeared (I shall note a few significant exceptions) in the larger scholarship of English law, when it is (if an outsider may say so) so striking a constituent of everything English from education to health care,

[45] Peter H. Russell, *The Supreme Court of Canada as a Bilingual and Bicultural Institution* (Ottawa, 1969).

[46] *Canadian Bill of Rights* (1959); *Charter of Rights, Canada Act* (1982).

[47] Robert Stevens, *Law and Politics: the House of Lords as a Judicial Body* (Weidenfeld and Nicolson, 1979), 180, 202.

from the national sense of humour to the temper of academic life. The remarkable reticence among lawyers on the subject may not be unrelated to those aspects of legal reasoning which I suggested help sustain professional belief in the apolitical autonomy of law and the dangerous irrelevance of social inquiry to most legal pursuits. But perhaps there are other reasons too, for it was not always thus. A scholar in Great Britain could once address his students in jurisprudence in the following terms without provoking (as it might in the more ideological climate of the early 1980s) loud denunciations of bias in education:

> ". . . when . . . some have great wealth and others nothing, it is necessary that the arm of authority should be continually stretched forth, and permanent laws or regulation made which may protect the property of the rich from the inroads of the poor . . . Laws and governments may be considered in this *and in every case* as a combination of the rich to oppress the poor, and preserve to themselves the inequality of the goods which would otherwise be soon destroyed by the attacks of the poor, who if not hindered by the government would soon reduce the others to an equality with themselves by open violence."[48]

This quotation, well known only since 1978, is from Adam Smith's lectures on jurisprudence in the University of Glasgow in the 1750s and 1760s. It is his principal characterisation of the state of the law in the second, pastoral stage of an evolutionary model of law and society. As Peter Stein and others have argued, Smith's explanation of social and legal change, while related to the natural law tradition, was based in large part on what he believed was an empirical base of observation or informed conjecture about the actions of men and women, spontaneous or modified by custom, habit, culture, education, or vested interest.[49] But at base was economic reality, and, as he made clear in this passage—"in this and in every case"—Smith was convinced that much of the law of his own society was also "a combination of the rich to oppress the poor. . . ." His division of society into those two elements was a staple of eighteenth-century usage—the poor being the labouring poor, which contemporaries estimated to be at least half the population.[50] The social analysis of the larger purposes of law was an equally common element of the

[48] Adam Smith, *Lectures on Jurisprudence*, [Glasgow Edition] ed. by R. L. Meek, D. D. Raphael, P. G. Stein (Oxford, 1978), p.208 (emphasis added), from the version of 1762–63, and quoted in Peter Stein, *Legal Evolution. The Story of an Idea* (Cambridge, 1980), p.34. The passage continues, "The government and laws hinder the poor from ever acquiring the wealth by violence which they would otherwise exert on the rich; they tell them they must either continue poor or acquire wealth in the same manner as they have done." In the report dated 1766 (at p.404 of the Glasgow Edition and first published in 1896), the point is rendered, "Till there be property there can be no government, the very end of which is to secure wealth, and to defend the rich from the poor." (There is no advice about how to become rich.)

[49] *e.g.* Stein, *op. cit.*; Ronald Meek, *Social Science and the Ignoble Savage* (Cambridge, 1976).

[50] Compare the words of Lord Kenyon in *R.* v. *Rusby* (*supra,*), the examples quoted in Robert Malcolmson, *Life and Labour in England 1700–1780* (Hutchinson, 1981), pp.11–19, and Smith (above, note 21) Vol. 2, p.715.

"philosophical historians" of the Scottish enlightenment. If the passage now brings to mind Marx rather than a "sound" British tradition, it may be, if I read Stein correctly, that the indigenous development of a jurisprudence grounded in social observation and analysis of interests and classes was shortlived, at least in part for ideological reasons of a kind not entirely unfamiliar to us today.

For Smith's observation and his larger approach to law could have a different significance in different hands, and in different circumstances. The prime instance was Smith's disciple, James Millar, who took the social and legal theory of the Scottish enlightenment to its most advanced point. Although no radical democrat, being an advanced Whig was enough, by the 1790s, to ensure that his theories would alarm Tories, one of whom once denounced his "democratical principles, and that sceptical philosophy which young noblemen and gentlemen of legislative rank carried into the world with them from his law-class, and . . . displayed with popular zeal, to the no small danger of perversion to all those under their influence."[51] An analysis which distinguished different interests in society, and contested an aristocratic hegemony in government (at a point when that influence was stronger than any time earlier in the century) was uncomfortable. At a time when the ideologues of the status quo fought Jacobinism by emphasising the blindness of English law to social division, having a "sceptical" law professor do the opposite was deeply disturbing.

England's upper-class political culture was profoundly anti-Revolutionary during the French wars and for decades thereafter, and it was in that period that Smith and Millar's project of historical social inquiry in law was abandoned.[52] If there is a connection, we do not yet understand its dimensions. But when an historical school of jurisprudence once again became significant in Britain, it was anodyne in its analysis and conservative in tendency, using history to oppose a reform movement identified with Benthamism. Its inspiration was Savigny, in whose work there is no hint of class, but an evocation of law as the spirit of Nation and People. History was appealed to in the unspecific and comforting terms which Burke had made familiar to Tory English gentlemen, as an *argumentum ad antiquitam*. Savigny's own work was strongly conditioned by its conservative political significance for Germany; it was embraced, with that of Blackstone and Burke, as the instinctive way to think about the history of English law.[53]

I shall take the word of other scholars for the fact that Maine and others swallowed that tradition of universalism, and undifferentiated

[51] Alexander Carlyle of Inveresk, quoted in Duncan Forbes, "'Scientific' Whiggism: Adam Smith and John Millar" (1954) 7 *Cambridge Journal* 669.

[52] I do not mean to imply that that was the only reason: see for example Meek, esp. Chap. 6.

[53] The legal evolutionist corollary that law at a given time meets an undifferentiated social need is still pervasive in legal thought, sometimes disguised as a form of functionalism. I take it that that is the point of the argument in (*e.g.*) Alan Watson, *Society and Legal Change* (Edinburgh, 1977), although many of his examples are hardly contemporary (Chap. 1).

social wisdom of law, outside any social analysis. (For Maine, classes existed perhaps in ancient Rome, but not in England—or, at least, the virtual absence of British references in his work made it unnecessary to consider the issue).[54] The great emphasis on the medieval period which henceforth characterised legal writing on the history of law, and the abandonment of social inquiry in much professional history, also helped to disinfest the history of law of a social analysis.[55] Where it survived, it was as subtext.

An instance was Sir James Fitzjames Stephen. He may hardly be taken as a typical English lawyer, which is perhaps why he was also the one who wrote the last extensive treatment of the history of criminal law in England until the mid-twentieth century.[56] He was an indefatigable propagandist and controversialist, as well as lawyer, historian, and judge. But undoubtedly one thing that attracted him to the study of criminal law was his deep interest in the issue of class politics in England. He was convinced that man's innate capacity for evil had been dangerously inflamed in the working class. They had been absurdly flattered by advanced democratic theorists and corrupted by irresponsible novelists like Dickens. England, in short, faced great danger from an ignorant and levelling democracy, and Stephen thought it only a matter of time before the disaster of the universal franchise became a reality. In such circumstances the criminal law, although so heavy an engine of social ordering that it should never be used lightly, was absolutely indispensable. A strong and enlightened leadership from men of the higher and professional classes (and Stephen undoubtedly saw himself as one such) could be expected to use it with care and discretion and, where necessary, harsh effectiveness. Criminal law was of political significance, in the widest sense.[57]

But Stephen was also writing within the tradition of legal evolutionism shared by his friend Henry Maine, and probably at its height.[58] There was a marked equivocation in Stephen's treatment of the relationship of the criminal law to wider social norms. On the one hand, he argued in defence of legislation for morals that there was a general social consensus on the boundaries of good and evil, for which the criminal law was (where its standard of proof reached) an effective expression: "the *ratio ultima* of the majority against persons who its application assumes to have renounced the common bonds which connect men together."[59] But the highest efficacy of

[54] Stein, p.93, and Chaps. 4, 5. It will be clear that I am less confident than Stein that everyone now "think(s) it absurd to try to describe legal change in isolation from social and economic changes" (p.127).

[55] On the last, see the conclusions of J. C. Wilsher, "Power Follows Property: Social and Economic Interpretations in Historical Writing in the Eighteenth Century and Early Nineteenth Century" (1983) 16 *J. of Social History*, w. 3, 7–26.

[56] Sir Leon Radzinowicz is hardly a typical English lawyer either, but that is another story.

[57] See James A. Colaiaco, *James Fitzjames Stephen and the Crisis of Victorian Thought* (Macmillan, 1983), pp.3–4, 12, 35–36, 50–55, and Chap. 7.

[58] *Ibid.* at p.110.

[59] Quoted *ibid.* at p.145.

the law is not simply that it expresses such moral majoritarian sentiments—that it gives effect to predominant opinion, especially with respect to the most serious crimes—but that it *shapes* that opinion, and can help *create* normative majorities, if used with care: "Even indifferent or virtuous acts will come to be condemned by the moral sentiment of particular times and places, if the law condemns them."[60] At many points in Stephen's treatment, tensions of that kind, arising largely from the possibility of different class perceptions of The Good, lead him to write a more rounded account of the law than any doctrinal exposition could be. He emphasised, for instance, that prosecution conducted in the form of private litigation also immensely strengthened the capacity of the criminal law to teach moral lessons in a theatrical setting. To contemporary suggestions that the English prosecutorial system was inefficient, he replied that that was a necessary price to pay for the legitimacy that the mode of prosecution conferred on the criminal law, and on the constitution, as a whole. An efficient prosecution in the hands of the state could too easily (even if wrongly) be identified with tyranny. The criminal law's great capacity for obtaining consent to the social order should never be sacrificed to lesser goals.[61]

Stephen shared a belief of many social historians now studying the eighteenth and nineteenth century that "the administration of criminal justice is the commonest, the most striking, and the most interesting shape, in which the sovereign power of the state manifests itself to the great bulk of its subjects." If that was one aspect of its importance, for Stephen there was another: English criminal procedure channelled popular passions into safe ends, inculcated virtue, and taught a working class dangerously close to revolution "to regard the Government as their friend. . . ."[62]

V

My purpose here, and throughout, should not be misunderstood. It is not to say that the Scottish philosophical historians, or Stephen, argued that the doctrines and institutions of the criminal law, or all law, could be understood only or even primarily in terms of a wider social analysis. I have mentioned them for two reasons. The passages I have quoted contrast with many nineteenth century (and twentieth century) accounts of law which assumed rather than demonstrated the substantial identity of law and social consensus, an identification which I have suggested may still be one of the larger background ideas of much traditional legal scholarship, if rarely articulated in explicit terms. Secondly, and more important, they may help to explain to lawyers the interests of social historians now studying how the criminal law worked in that same period (roughly 1760 to 1860). Adam Smith and Sir James Fitzjames Stephen were fascinated

[60] Stephen, *A General View of the Criminal Law of England* (1863), pp.99-100.
[61] Colaiaco at pp.87–88.
[62] *General View*, pp.207, 232–233.

observers of their own societies,[63] and they were convinced that the criminal law was a central nexus of its class divisions, and helped to sustain them. Their expression of that conviction, however foreign to the style of much legal scholarship, is abundantly familiar in tone to historians examining popular and élite opinion in that period. And like Smith and Stephen, when we study the place of the criminal law in Hanoverian and early Victorian society in daily life as well as opinion, we encounter the issues of class, contested norms, and their problematic relationship to the coercive power of an undemocratic state. Those issues demand exploration, particularly of a social institution which avows that it transcends substantive social inequality.

In this century, Adam Smith's tradition of social inquiry has been resuscitated in some areas of legal scholarship. Journals devoted to exploring the law with the tools of social science—the inheritors of the realist programme—or from more radical theoretical perspectives, have established beachheads (I am told) in academic law. But I am also told by its practitioners that the enterprise is regarded as one of marginal interest by most of their colleagues. Some even attribute to it sinister purposes.[64] I hope I have explained why social historians think an uncommitted exploration of the social functions of law to be important. But we too are aware of a degree of wariness among the lawyers. In the fable with which I began, there was one last warning given to the historian before he went off to tunnel through the strata of legal manuscripts. In solemn tones, the lawyer gave him formal notice: "Do no environmental damage. We take conservation of the Law Mountains very seriously indeed."

DOUGLAS HAY*

[63] Smith developed his course on jurisprudence in the 1750s, and died in 1790, before the French and English Jacobins helped to make philosophical history on object of suspicion. Stephen first formulated his principal ideas on the moral educative functions of English criminal law (and the importance of historical work) in his *General View of the Criminal Law* (1863).

[64] See Gordon (*supra*, note 39), and Twining (*supra*, note 31) at p.228.

* Associate Professor of Law and History, Osgoode Hall Law School and York University (Toronto).

[14]

ALBION'S FATAL FLAWS*

DOUGLAS HAY'S ESSAY, "PROPERTY, AUTHORITY AND THE CRIMINAL Law", which sounds the opening shot for the collection titled *Albion's Fatal Tree*, has attracted a huge following, especially outside specialist legal history circles.[1] Hay's main thesis is that some of the most characteristic features of eighteenth-century English criminal procedure for cases of serious crime require to be understood as "a ruling-class conspiracy" against the lower orders.[2] In the present article I shall show that when tested against detailed evidence of the work of the felony courts, Hay's thesis appears fundamentally mistaken. (I shall not be discussing the other essays in the *Albion* volume.)

Although the Hay essay has several strands, in its most important dimension it purports to explain a celebrated peculiarity of the criminal justice system of the eighteenth century, namely the large number of offences punishable by death. The list of nominally capital offences grew throughout the century;[3] various authors reckon it at upwards of 200 by the early nineteenth century, although that figure is bloated in ways that I shall discuss later. In the actual administration of the criminal law, however, capital punishment had been on the wane since the sixteenth century, in the sense that a declining proportion of persons convicted of felony were executed. The puzzle is, why did the "penal death rate"[4] decline while the legislature was threatening ever more capital punishment?

The conventional account of this paradox is Radzinowicz's.[5] I have always found it fundamentally persuasive. I still do, and I shall return to it at the end of this article. Hay offers quite a different explanation. The widening gap between the expanding threats of death on one

* An earlier version of this paper was presented to the October 1981 meeting of the American Society for Legal History. Suggestions and references from John Beattie, J. S. Cockburn, G. R. Elton, Owen Fiss, George Fletcher, Lawrence Friedman, Charles Gray, Thomas Green, Douglas Hay, R. H. Helmholz, Dennis Hutchinson, Gareth Jones, P. J. R. King, Mark Kishlansky, David Langum, Norval Morris, Richard Posner, A. W. B. Simpson, Lawrence Stone and John Styles are gratefully acknowledged.

[1] Douglas Hay, "Property, Authority and the Criminal Law", in Douglas Hay, Peter Linebaugh, John G. Rule, E. P. Thompson and Cal Winslow, *Albion's Fatal Tree: Crime and Society in Eighteenth-Century England* (London, 1975), pp. 17-63.

[2] *Ibid.*, p. 52

[3] For various counts, see Leon Radzinowicz, *A History of English Criminal Law and its Administration from 1750*, 4 vols. (London, 1948-68), i, pp. 3-4; but see p. 118 below.

[4] The famous phrase of J. C. Jeaffreson, *Middlesex County Records*, 4 vols. (London, 1886-92), iii, p. xvii.

[5] Discussed on pp. 115-16 below.

hand and relatively infrequent imposition of the death penalty on the other hand enhanced the discretion of the élite to decide whom to execute and whom to spare. It was "a ruling-class conspiracy" to use the criminal law in order to extract deference from the lower orders. Hay detects this self-serving discretion throughout the main phases of the criminal process — prosecution, trial, sentencing and executive clemency.[6]

Hay does not seriously claim to have identified a conspiracy in the conventional sense of the term, that is, an agreement to promote unlawful or wicked ends. Rather, he says, the plot was one in which "the common assumptions of the conspirators lay so deep that they were never questioned, and rarely made explicit".[7] This way of speaking directs attention away from the mechanism of class concert, which the essay hardly clarifies, and towards the supposed object, emphasized incessantly, of class domination and oppression ("the law . . . allowed the rulers of England to make the courts a selective instrument of class justice . . .").[8]

I think that a critic interested in broad questions of Marxist historical method might take a stern view of so ambiguous a notion of conspiracy, but that is not my mission. Still less do I wish to bring the general tenets of Marxist theory into question. It is true that I am criticizing a Marxist work, and that my own predilections are non-Marxist, but my critique would be largely unaffected if I were to assume that Marx and his followers have correctly characterized the main movements in Western social and political history. Even the most dedicated Marxist would concede that there is a variety of subjects on which Marxist historical method does not throw much light — the history of climatic changes, the invention of the flush toilet, or what have you. In this article I shall be saying that the aspects of eighteenth-century English criminal procedure emphasized in the Hay essay belong on that list of subjects. The criminal law and its procedures existed to serve and protect the interests of the people who suffered as victims of crime, people who were overwhelmingly non-élite.

I
SOURCES

I shall develop this view by drawing on data from a group of 171 cases conducted at four sessions of the Old Bailey during the years

[6] *Prosecution*: "it was in the hands of the gentleman who went to law to evoke gratitude as well as fear in the maintenance of deference" (Hay, "Property, Authority and the Criminal Law", p. 41). *Trial*: "The nature of the criminal trial gave enormous discretion to men of property . . . [in addition to] the prosecutor" (*ibid.*, p. 42). *Sentencing*: character evidence from "employers, respectable farmers and neighbouring gentlemen" might "induce the judge to pass a lesser sentence, or recommend a pardon" (*ibid.*, p. 42). *Clemency*: the pardon process "epitomizes the discretionary element of the law . . ." (*ibid.*, p. 43).

[7] *Ibid.*, p. 52

[8] *Ibid.*, p. 48.

from 1754 to 1756. The data comes from a study being published elsewhere, which is devoted to reconstructing and establishing the reliability of a pair of sources that supply narrative accounts of what was happening at these criminal trials.[9] One source is a set of judge's notes — that is, courtroom minutes of evidence and jury instructions — taken down by Sir Dudley Ryder, chief justice of King's Bench, who sat at the Old Bailey for these four sessions and actually presided over the trial of 44 of the 171 cases. Like his brethren on the common law bench, Ryder served intermittently as a trial judge at the Old Bailey. His notes are exceptionally detailed by comparison with others that survive for the period, for the simple reason that Ryder knew shorthand. As a youth he had mastered one of the standard shorthand systems of the day. His Old Bailey notes, as well as a diary of his assize notes that Hay used in his essay[10] and that I shall also draw upon, have been transcribed into typescript by a cipher expert.

The four Old Bailey sessions at which Ryder sat during his brief judicial career were also the subject of a series of contemporary pamphlet reports, now called the Old Bailey Sessions Papers.[11] The pamphlets were prepared for a lay readership and sold on the streets of London immediately after the trials. I have written about their origins and characteristics in an article published a few years ago.[12] The pamphlets continue to be the main source for the detail of the criminal trials that I shall be discussing for the Ryder years. The Ryder notes both confirm the reliability of what the pamphlets report and add detail, especially legal detail, that the pamphlets bleached out.

In emphasizing a two-year period from mid-century I run the usual risk of sampling error, and I shall be unable to correct adequately for developments later in the century. (The Hay essay also relies heavily but not entirely on mid-century sources.) The main objection to basing a critique of Hay's essay on Old Bailey sources is that London was uniquely urban, whereas Hay's essay blends provincial and London sources. To be sure, we do see less sheep-stealing and more shop-lifting in London than we would find in Lancashire. Fortu-

[9] John H. Langbein, "Shaping the Eighteenth-Century Criminal Trial: A View from the Ryder Sources", *Univ. of Chicago Law Rev.*, l (1983). The Ryder Old Bailey Notes appear as Document no. 14 of the transcribed notebooks. The manuscript and a copy of the typescript are deposited in Lincoln's Inn. The manuscript diary (hereafter Ryder Assize Diary) is transcribed as Document no. 19(f), volume 1129 of the Harrowby Manuscripts, Sandon Hall. Copies of both typescripts have also been deposited at the University of Chicago Law School Library.

[10] Hay, "Property, Authority and the Criminal Law", pp. 28-9.

[11] During the Ryder years the pamphlets were published in London eight times a year, usually in two parts, and bear the title *The Proceedings on the King's Commissions of the Peace, Oyer and Terminer, and Gaol Delivery for the City of London; and also the Gaol Delivery for the County of Middlesex, Held at Justice-Hall in the Old-Bailey* (hereafter *Old Bailey Sessions Papers*).

[12] John H. Langbein, "The Criminal Trial before the Lawyers", *Univ. of Chicago Law Rev.*, xlv (1978), pp. 263, 267-72. For further discussion, see Langbein, "Shaping the Eighteenth-Century Criminal Trial".

nately, when such issues arise in this paper, I shall be able to refer to the findings for provincial Essex contained in a splendid paper by P. J. R. King.[13] It should also be observed that English criminal procedure was very much a national system. Although a few details of Old Bailey practice were peculiar,[14] the fundamental principles applied equally in the metropolis and in the provinces. However much the clientele differed, the procedural institutions were shared. So were the royal judges who sat in turns at the Old Bailey and rode the assize circuits. In 1755, for example, Dudley Ryder presided on the Northern Circuit in March, at the Old Bailey in April, on the Home Circuit in August, and back at the Old Bailey in October.

II
OFFENCES AND OFFENDERS

Prosecutions for felony in the eighteenth century were for offences that had been felony for centuries before. The law that the courts had occasion to enforce in the eighteenth century was not for the most part the law that the contemporary legislature was enacting. An itemization of the offences in my sample for 1754-6, representing four months' worth of all the cases of serious crime prosecuted in the metropolis, will provide a convenient illustration of the actual business in the court of capital jurisdiction. (See Table.)

The prosaic nature of these offences will come as a surprise to readers who have taken seriously Hay's preoccupation with such legislation as that against food riots and work-place insurrections.[15] In my data we do not see offences that exemplify the advance of pre-industrial capitalism. Virtually all of the offences had been felonious back into the middle ages, a point Hay has lately acknowledged in another context in an article in this journal.[16] Most of the offences

[13] P. J. R. King, "Decision-Makers and Decision-Making in the 18th Century Criminal Law: The Social Groups Involved in the Punishment of Property Offenders and the Criteria on Which Their Decisions Were Based" (typescript, March 1981). King's paper, still unpublished, was presented to a conference at the University of Kent, Canterbury, in April 1981.

[14] For example, (1) the Old Bailey sat eight times a year, provincial assizes twice; (2) the Old Bailey had a permanent judge, the Recorder of London, as well as rotating common law judges like Ryder; the recorder pronounced sentence and conveyed recommendations for clemency to the monarch on behalf of the court; (3) the pre-trial process that culminated in trial before the Old Bailey was more systematic, on account of the work of the quasi-official "court justice" (J.P.) for Middlesex and the institution of "the sitting Alderman" in the City.

[15] See Hay, "Property, Authority and the Criminal Law", pp. 20-1: "the class that controlled Parliament was using the criminal sanction to enforce two of the radical redefinitions of property which gentlemen were making in their own interests during the eighteenth century".

[16] Douglas Hay, "War, Dearth and Theft in the Eighteenth Century: The Record of the English Courts", *Past and Present*, no. 95 (May 1982), p. 146: "In spite of the flood of new capital statutes that followed the Restoration, most capital prosecutions continued to be made under Tudor legislation. In the years considered here, 1742 to

(cont. on p. 100)

were only nominally capital, as benefit of clergy pertained and reduced the sanction from death to transportation.[17]

TABLE

OFFENCES PROSECUTED AT DUDLEY RYDER'S FOUR OLD BAILEY SESSIONS 1754-1756*

Homicide	3
Burglary, breaking and entering	7
Highway robbery	4
Livestock theft	6
Pocket-picking	13
Shop-lifting	20
Theft from lodgings, inns, pubs	15
Domestic theft	10
Theft from work-places or employers	13
Other theft, 40s. or over	15
Other theft, under 40s.	53
Receiving stolen goods	13
Forging a will	1
Aiding a gaol-break	1
Assault and robbery	2
Perjury and abuse of legal process	3

* Notes and sources: Offences prosecuted October 1754, April and October 1755, and April 1756, the four sessions at which Dudley Ryder was among the trial commissioners. Offences are categorized in the Table in lay terms; each has been tabulated as originally charged, although juries returned lesser offences or acquitted outright in many. When a case involves multiple charges, only the most serious has been tabulated, in order to avoid double counting. In eight cases involving multiple defendants the court tried separate indictments for receiving stolen goods simultaneously with the related larceny cases, which accounts for the discrepancy between 171 trials and 179 offences. Ryder Old Bailey Notes, pp. 1-62; *Old Bailey Sessions Papers* (Oct. 1754, Apr., Oct. 1755, Apr. 1756). See nn. 9, 11 above.

It is very hard to find figures worthy of romance, even social romance, among the shop-lifters, pickpockets, pilfering housemaids and dishonest apprentices who populated the Old Bailey dock. To be sure, most of them were poor, as criminals tend to be. Anatole France made the most of that in a famous utterance. "The law [of France]", he said, "in its majestic equality, forbids the rich as well as the poor to sleep under bridges, to beg in the streets, and to steal bread".[18] Actually, to the extent that our sources let us see anything about the economic circumstances of the persons accused, we can say that the culprits tried at the Old Bailey are seldom destitute. Some plead hunger or say they are unemployed, but in the main we see employed persons who have yielded to temptation rather than necessity. To

n. 16 cont.)
1802, at least 95 per cent of the 450 capital charges tried at Staffordshire assizes were based on statutes enacted before 1742". (The main Tudor legislation that Hay has in mind supplied statutory basis for offences that had been common law felonies from medieval times. Developments in benefit of clergy, discussed on p. 117 below, precipitated much of the Tudor legislation.)

[17] Discussed on p. 117 below.

[18] Anatole France, *Le lys rouge* (Paris, 1894), quoted in John Bartlett, *Familiar Quotations*, 15th edn. (Boston, 1980), p. 655.

turn these little crooks into class warriors one must wear rose-coloured glasses of the deepest hue.

III
PROSECUTION

If the criminals were often poor, their victims (whom we see serving as private prosecutors in the Old Bailey trials) were not much better off — a point that is played down in Hay's essay.[19] In the Old Bailey cases we often cross a class line when we move from the offender to his victim, but not a class gulf. The victim is usually more propertied than the person who victimized him, although often only slightly. I have not hit upon a way of quantifying this, in part because information about the social status of the victim is so haphazard in the Old Bailey sources, but I think that anyone who studies a volume of the Old Bailey Sessions Papers will conclude that the victims seldom come from the propertied élite. They are typically small shopkeepers, artisans, lodging-house keepers, innkeepers and so forth. Included on the list of victim-prosecutors for the first dozen cases in the October 1754 sessions, for example, are a loom maker, a brass founder, a wine merchant, and a pewterer, each prosecuting pilfering employees; a baker's servant and a journeyman tailor prosecuting thieving prostitutes; a lodging-house keeper and a former room-mate prosecuting for the theft of furniture and domestic goods from lodgings; and a calico printer who had been mugged on the street. Only one — a major who prosecuted a stablehand for horse-stealing — fits Hay's image with any ease.

King's data corroborates the Old Bailey sources in a helpful way. He has worked with Essex quarter sessions records, mostly recognizances in which descriptions of the victims appear fairly regularly. I stress, as King does, that there are important differences between cases triable at quarter sessions on the one hand and at assizes or the Old Bailey on the other hand; in particular, the felonies tried at quarter sessions were non-capital, that is, petty larceny. Nevertheless, it is very telling that King's tabulations of the occupational status of prosecutors for the period 1760-1800 show that "Around 90% of these prosecutors came from three groups — the farmers, the tradesmen and artisans, and the labourers".[20] King further points to the works of Brewer and Styles and of David Philips, both published

[19] Hay, "Property, Authority and the Criminal Law", p. 37: "The poor suffer from theft as well as the rich, and in eighteenth-century England probably far more poor men lost goods to thieves, if only because the rich were few and their property more secure".

[20] King, "Decision-Makers and Decision-Making in the 18th Century Criminal Law", p. 9

after the Hay essay, which reach similar conclusions.[21] Prosecution was not a preserve of the ruling class.

Indeed, one of the main themes in the history of the administration of the criminal law in the second half of the eighteenth century was the effort to encourage prosecutorial activity by the lower orders. In one sense this is a development that traces back to the 1690s, when parliament began to enact the statutes that offered rewards for successful prosecution of certain heinous felonies, including highway robbery, burglary, housebreaking and horse-stealing.[22] In the 1750s the campaign waged by Henry Fielding to obtain a subsidy for expenses for poor prosecutors and witnesses came to fruition in legislation of 1752 and 1754,[23] and we know from Dudley Ryder's assize diary that the statutes were being put to use. He tells us that it had become the convention to award five shillings per day in expenses, and in one case he reports that he refused an award to an innkeeper who seemed too prosperous.[24]

In disputing Hay's version of the prosecutorial process — that "it was in the hands of the gentleman who went to law to evoke gratitude as well as fear in the maintenance of deference" — I have been arguing that gentlemen prosecutors were few and far between. I want also to take modest exception to the notion that since prosecution was private, a potential prosecutor had the discretion to threaten it in self-serving ways. In fact, various factors worked to circumscribe the prosecutor's discretion.

The most endemic aspect of what one might call prosecutorial discretion is the phenomenon of non-reporting of crime. We are all familiar with the recent discussion about whether increases in reported instances of rape reflect increased incidence of the offence, or lessened aversion to reporting it. When we deal with grand larceny, which in all its forms was the predominant eighteenth-century felony, we can be sure that a victim who chose to forgive an offender by not reporting the crime could seldom be stopped. But this was hardly a

[21] *Ibid.*, pp. 3, 12, citing John Brewer and John Styles, *An Ungovernable People: The English and their Law in the Seventeenth and Eighteenth Centuries* (London, 1980), Introduction, pp. 18-19; David Philips, *Crime and Authority in Victorian England: The Black Country, 1835-1860* (London, 1977), pp. 123-9.

[22] See the convenient summary in Patrick Colquhoun, *A Treatise on the Police of the Metropolis*, 7th edn. (London, 1806), pp. 390-2.

[23] 25 George II, c. 36, s. 11 (1752); 27 George II, c. 3, s. 3 (1754). Hay has remarked upon these and subsequent acts in his recent article, "War, Dearth and Theft in the Eighteenth Century", pp. 147-8, but without attempt to reconcile the earlier essay.

[24] Ryder Assize Diary, pp. 7, 13. Beattie reports that his "examination of about ten years in the Surrey and Sussex assizes between the 1750s and 1780s reveals a range of awards from about a pound (though one or two were as little as fifteen shillings) to as much as ten pounds. A very large number were between one and two pounds, though most were probably between two and three pounds": John M. Beattie, "Judicial Records and the Measurement of Crime in Eighteenth-Century England", in L. A. Knafla (ed.), *Crime and Criminal Justice in Europe and Canada* (Waterloo, Ont., 1980), pp. 127, 130.

peculiarity of eighteenth-century English social structure. It is true in today's Anglo-American legal systems and, indeed, in contemporary socialist legal systems. The victim of the property crime has a practical monopoly over disclosure of the offence. Every criminal justice system must depend upon the self-interest of owners for the enforcement of the laws protecting property.

Despite the nominally private character of prosecution in English law, there were forces at work that limited prosecutorial discretion. In homicide, of course, the coroner system largely eliminated it, because the coroner investigated every suspicious death. There was no equally comprehensive approach to larceny. As a matter of statutory design, the pre-trial binding-over system administered by the justices of the peace purported to limit prosecutorial discretion by requiring the J.P. to bind over to trial "all such . . . as do declare anything material to prove the . . . Felony . . .".[25] Yet this scheme assumed, in the language of the statute, a victim willing to "bring" the accusation to the attention of the J.P. There is good reason to think that many potential prosecutors did not bring charges. In his famous essay of 1751, Henry Fielding, who was campaigning to increase the levels of prosecution, stresses that potential prosecutors were either too forgiving or else too necessitous to take the time and incur the expense and nuisance of prosecuting.[26] Among his complaints Fielding did not find room for the abuse that Hay treats as central: affluent victims supposedly manipulating the prosecutorial power in a self-serving manner.

There were aspects of the pre-trial system that limited the discretion of a victim in not reporting to the J.P. Whenever the victim needed the J.P. to help him recover stolen goods — for example, by issuing search or arrest warrants, or by granting immunity from prosecution in order to obtain accomplice disclosures — the J.P. had notice and was able to bind over. These pre-trial investigative steps are frequently evidenced in the Old Bailey cases in my sample, although of course I have no way of identifying the dark figure of unreported events.

When the J.P. did bind over, it was usually on pain of a hefty fine for the prosecutor's non-appearance. Such recognizances survive for most of the Old Bailey trials of the mid-1750s; typically the penal sum they impose is twenty pounds. In the London Record Office papers for the April 1754 sessions there is a pitiful deposition from a shopkeeper, Moses Smith, who had been "bound [over] to prosecute and give Evidence" against an accused for feloniously stealing a handkerchief out of Smith's shop. Smith explains "that he was

[25] 2 & 3 Philip & Mary, c. 10 (1555).

[26] Henry Fielding, *An Enquiry into the Causes of the Late Increase of Robbers* (London, 1751), p. 106.

taken ill about a fortnight before the [trial, with] a violent Fever which continued for several weeks". Smith sent two of his sureties to the lord mayor's clerk to report the problem; the clerk replied that Smith should have his wife attend the trial in his place. "But", the deposition continues, "the said Smith being then so dangerously ill and keeping no Servant [n]or having any person to attend his Shop but his Wife, . . . she could not leave her husband at that time without subjecting him to great Danger". The document concludes with a recital that Smith "did not neglect attending the Sessions with any design to let the [accused] escape any punishment which might have been inflicted on him had he been prosecuted . . .".[27] This picture of a wretched little shopkeeper and his wife, too poor to be able to hire someone to relieve them on the day of the trial, and now terrified of the fine for non-prosecution, contrasts strongly with the notion of unbounded prosecutorial discretion.

Finally, I should advert to another dimension of prosecutorial discretion, which concerns the decision not of whether to prosecute, but on what charge. Ordinary grand larceny was subject to benefit of clergy, meaning in practice that first-time offenders would be transported rather than executed. However, many (perhaps most) property offences could be characterized as something more than ordinary grand larceny. A variety of statutes dealing with thefts from the person, from dwelling houses and shops, and on the highway, withdrew benefit of clergy when these larcenies involved goods above particular amounts. The issue that I do not yet understand is how prosecutors arrived at the decision of whether to invoke these special statutes when the facts permitted. In some of the Old Bailey cases it is clear that the indictment itself down-values the goods, or neglects to charge an aggravating circumstance — for example, that the offence was committed in a dwelling house or a shop. In other cases when such matters are charged, or fully charged, we see juries down-valuing the goods or refusing to find the aggravating circumstance, in order to make the offence clergyable and spare the culprit from the capital sanction. The patterns of indictment down-charging seem sufficiently recurrent that we may doubt whether there was much room for prosecutorial caprice. I suspect that the J.P.s and the clerks of assize and their Old Bailey counterparts had an important hand in advising prosecutors how to charge,[28] and that they were guided primarily by their sense of what verdicts juries were customarily prepared to return in various circumstances.

[27] Corporation of London Record Office, Sessions Papers, April 1754 Sessions, loose document, unnumbered, commencing "Moses Smith of Aldersgate . . .".

[28] In the case of Thomas Rolf, discussed on pp. 111-12 below, the prosecutrix testified that she thought the money stolen from her amounted to more than eight shillings, but she valued the sum at five shillings on the advice of the court justice, John Fielding, who told her "Do it rather under than over": Ryder Old Bailey Notes, p. 30.

I concede, although the actual evidence for it is thin, that élite victims must have been treated with greater courtesy, and allowed greater prosecutorial discretion, than victims like Moses Smith who came from lower social orders. Hay points to a single case, evidenced in the diary of a Lancashire squire, in which both the accused thief and the squire-prosecutor behave as though the prosecutor retains a power of non-prosecution, even though the prosecutor had used the J.P.s of Liverpool to obtain a search warrant and to conduct a pre-trial examination of the accused.[29] If we assume that this was not an aberration, it shows us only that the prosecutorial system was not an engine of egalitarianism. Of course, the prosecutorial system of so stratified a society will be sensitive to the patterns of deference that otherwise pervade the society. What I resist is the idea that such practices justify treating the prosecutorial system as having been constructed for the purpose of furthering the class interests of the élite. It is one thing to avoid conflict with the privileged orders, another thing to promote class aims.

The whole of the criminal justice system, especially the prosecutorial system, was primarily designed to protect the people, overwhelmingly non-élite, who suffered from crime. One can argue, as I am prepared to, that it was a great error on the part of the English to attempt to perpetuate a system of private prosecution and private policing from a medieval setting, where it may have made sense, to the changed circumstances of a more urban and impersonal eighteenth-century society. That was part of a set of constitutional convictions that contemporaries held deeply, even though in retrospect their concern looks to have been misplaced. Within the confines of a system that lacked professional prosecution, steps were taken to make the system serve the interests of the non-élite prosecutors who predominated. They were aided and afforced by the J.P.s, and in some cases subsidized and rewarded for prosecutorial efforts. Accordingly, I would venture to predict that when we finally obtain a satisfactory history of the prosecutorial system of the eighteenth century, self-serving gentlemen will be seen to have played an inconsequential role.

IV
JURIES

Whereas Hay has exaggerated the extent of prosecutorial discretion, he has underemphasized the importance of jury discretion. I had occasion above to refer to the role of juries in down-valuing goods or returning what we today call a "lesser included offence". I shall

29 Hay, "Property, Authority and the Criminal Law", p. 41 n. 2, citing *Blundell's Diary and Letter Book, 1702-1728*, ed. M. Blundell (Liverpool, 1952), pp. 109-11.

follow John Beattie in calling both phenomena by the label of "partial verdict". Acquittals and partial verdicts receive short shrift in Hay's essay. I shall dwell on them because I think that his theory of ruling-class conspiracy is impossible to reconcile with the reality of jury discretion.

Beattie has computed for the period 1736-53 that about 10 per cent of the bills submitted to the Surrey grand jury in urban cases of capital crime were dismissed.[30] I am concerned with the second jury, the trial or petty jury. Beattie has computed that the petty juries acquitted in a third of the capital cases in which the Surrey grand juries had indicted; in another 30 per cent the petty juries returned partial verdicts.[31] My figures for the Old Bailey are in accord. The 171 cases produced 203 accused, of whom 84 were acquitted. I have not tabulated the frequency with which juries down-valued or convicted of lesser offences for the whole of my sample; in the October 1754 sessions, for which I do have the figures, of 31 guilty verdicts 14 involved these two types of partial verdict.

Both the acquittals and the partial verdicts follow patterns that are principled and predictable. When our sources give us narrative accounts of the trials we see that acquittals are usually returned in cases in which the evidence falls short of the standard of proof that was understood to be appropriate in criminal cases. Virtually all cases in which there was only a single accusing witness resulted in acquittal, as did cases in which the identification of the accused was put in any serious doubt.

The partial verdicts are especially interesting, because they were in truth sentencing decisions. They usually had the effect of reducing the sentence from death to transportation; in the relatively few cases in which the goods were valued below a shilling, the effect was to reduce the sentence from transportation to whipping. The striking aspect of the partial verdict practice in the cases in my sample is its regularity, hence predictability. In all cases of highway robbery and livestock theft in which juries convicted, they convicted capitally. They returned capital verdicts in most cases of burglary. Otherwise, juries applied what should be called a strong presumption against capital verdicts, a presumption that would be overcome when the circumstances were especially audacious. Old Bailey juries were harsh on professional or gang criminals, which is scarcely surprising in the setting of London's amateurish law enforcement. Capital verdicts for shop-lifting and for theft from a dwelling house usually occurred in cases with gang overtones, often involving multiple offences and requiring the evidence of an accomplice-turned-crown-witness.

[30] John M. Beattie, "Crime and the Courts in Surrey, 1736-1753", in J. S. Cockburn (ed.), *Crime in England, 1550-1800* (Princeton, 1977), pp. 155, 163.

[31] *Ibid.*, p. 176.

If I were going to organize a ruling-class conspiracy to use the criminal law to terrorize the lower orders, I would not interpose autonomous bodies of non-conspirators like the petty juries. If, on the other hand, I were going to reckon the jurors among my conspirators, I would be troubled that they were so predictably humane by the standards of the day.

I find Hay's account of the jury baffling. He wants to make the jurors co-conspirators. He says: "All men of property knew that judges, justices [of the peace] and juries had to be drawn from their own ranks".[32] This is not a considered statement, because it assimilates men of great wealth and station to the same "ranks" as those who satisfied the ten-pound-a-year minimum juror qualification.[33] In the Reverend Martin Madan's *Thoughts on Executive Justice*, a source several times cited by Hay, the author worries that petty jurors at assizes are receiving inadequate instruction from the judge, "as they usually consist of low and ignorant country people!".[34] In his paper on the enforcement of the game laws, Hay points out that the farmers and tradesmen who were the typical jurors had interests different from those of the propertied élite.[35] From an Elizabethan sample Samaha has reported finding "ordinary people in the town — petty tradesmen such as alehouse keepers and occasionally even day labourers" sitting on trial juries at Colchester assizes, and he concludes: "To send a suspect to the gallows . . . required the concurrence of every segment in the community, since they were all represented at various stages of the criminal process . . .".[36] It hardly seems tenable for Hay to align petty jurors with the English social élite.

Hay is also on weak ground when he conjectures: "A panel of the poor would not convict a labourer who stole wood from a lord's park, a sheep from a farmer's fold, or corn from a merchant's yard". Although Hay is careful to say that he does not think that the juries of

[32] Hay, "Property, Authority and the Criminal Law", p. 38.

[33] The act of 4 & 5 William & Mary, c. 24, s. 15 (1692) fixed the juror qualification at ten pounds a year for England, six pounds for Wales; ss. 18-19 set the sum for talesman at five pounds for England and three for Wales. For the city of London the act of 3 George II, c. 25, ss. 19-20 (1730) imposed a hundred-pound qualification. An act of 4 George II, c. 7, s. 3 (1731) qualified for jury service in Middlesex men possessed of leaseholds of fifty pounds per year, apparently in recognition of the prevalence of leasehold conveyancing. These acts are treated as governing in the 1766 edition of Giles Duncomb, *Trials per Pais: or, The Law of England Concerning Juries by Nisi Prius*, 8th edn. (London, 1766), pp. 110, 162-4.

[34] Martin Madan, *Thoughts on Executive Justice, with Respect to the Criminal Laws, Particularly on the Circuits*, 2nd edn. (London, 1785), p. 148. In his recent "War, Dearth and Theft in the Eighteenth Century", p. 154 and n. 100, Hay states the point somewhat more softly, saying that "at quarter sessions and assizes trial jurors were drawn from a much higher social class than most of those indicted for theft".

[35] Douglas Hay, "Poaching and the Game Laws on Cannock Chase", in Hay *et al.*, *Albion's Fatal Tree*, pp. 189, 211.

[36] Joel B. Samaha, "Hanging for Felony: The Rule of Law in Elizabethan Colchester", *Hist. Jl.*, xxi (1978), pp. 763, 781-2.

the day "convicted against the evidence", he speculates that "a more democratic jury might not have convicted at all".[37] I doubt whether the English poor of the eighteenth century generally condoned the theft of livestock and victuals, and Hay does not produce evidence that they did. Empirical study of twentieth-century juries in the United States — juries long since democratized and freed of property qualifications — squarely contradicts the notion that they are hostile to the law of larceny.[38]

We may come close to understanding how Hay went astray if we reflect upon a passage such as this, in which Hay takes it for granted that the criminal law lacked the adherence of the lower orders. To be sure, there were corners of the criminal law that did not command universal regard. The source of Hay's undoing, I suspect, is that the only part of the substantive criminal law with which he was deeply acquainted when he wrote his essay was the uniquely class-based and arbitrary game law. There certainly was popular dissatisfaction with the game law (and not confined to the poor),[39] but to extrapolate from that bizarre scheme (most of it misdemeanour) to the whole of the law of felony would be a grievous error, just as it would be folly in our own day to equate public attitudes towards marijuana offences and, say, automobile theft. When Hay speaks indifferently of stealing wood from a lord's park and sheep from a farmer's fold, he is making that sort of error. The property crimes that were of major consequence in the workload of eighteenth-century criminal courts — in particular the theft of livestock, shop goods, and personal and household belongings — were those about whose blameworthiness there was a moral consensus that knew no class lines. That is why men of the non-élite could predominate (as prosecutors and jurors) in convicting persons who committed property crimes.

V
JUDGES

The royal judges who presided at assize and Old Bailey trials for felony were certainly élite figures. The trial judge had a variety of means of influencing the verdict of the jury, especially through his powers to comment on the evidence and to instruct the jurors on the

37 Hay, "Property, Authority and the Criminal Law", pp. 38-9.

38 Harry Kalven Jr. and Hans Zeisel, *The American Jury* (Boston, 1966), pp. 76-7.

39 It would be a mistake to think that hostility to the game laws followed any line between elite and non-elite. Blackstone, for example, who thought the game laws "of so questionable a nature", implied derisively that the "false grammar" of one of the statutes reflected on those who promoted the cause: William Blackstone, *Commentaries on the Laws of England*, 4 vols. (Oxford, 1765-9), iv, pp. 174-5. See also P. B. Munsche, *Gentlemen and Poachers: The English Game Laws, 1671-1831* (Cambridge, 1981); P. B. Munsche, "The Game Laws in Wiltshire, 1750-1800", in Cockburn (ed.), *Crime in England*, pp. 210-28.

law.[40] The limits on judicial influence must, however, be understood. Since there was as yet virtually no diversion of felony cases away from trial by jury, all those open-and-shut cases went to jury trial that would today be processed in short-form procedures such as plea bargaining or trial "by the bench" (that is, by judges sitting without juries).[41] Accordingly, most cases that went to jury trial in the eighteenth century involved evidence so overwhelming that conviction was a certainty, there was no room for influence. Further, when jurors deferred to judges, it was because jurors understood that judges spoke from wisdom and experience about matters of legal principle. If the jurors had suspected the judges of abusing their authority in order to promote élite interests, jurors would not have been so ready to follow the judges' lead. The history of bitter judge/jury antagonism in the seditious libel cases later in the century should stand as warning enough against the notion that judges could command jury verdicts by fiat.[42] When the sources for the Old Bailey cases permit us to see what the judges were saying to the juries, it seems largely dictated by the state of the facts or the law.

Hay's boldest theme concerns the supposed discretion of the judges in post-verdict proceedings, that is, in sentencing and clemency matters. In the modern world we are accustomed to judges having a broad, explicit discretion to fix sentences, but that was a nineteenth-century development. In the eighteenth century the English judge had no direct power to choose between death and transportation for felony convicts.[43] The jury, however, did — through the power that it exercised so vigorously of returning a partial verdict that reduced a non-clergyable offence to a clergyable one. Hay is correct to stress that the trial judge had considerable influence over the process by which convicts might receive executive clemency after sentencing. The pardon process is best understood as an adjunct to the sentencing system, compensating for the lack of direct judicial discretion. The secretaries of state and the monarch regularly deferred to the judges on pardon matters.[44]

[40] Langbein, "Criminal Trial before the Lawyers", pp. 284-300.

[41] See John H. Langbein, "Understanding the Short History of Plea Bargaining", *Law and Society Rev.*, xiii (1979), p. 261.

[42] See Thomas A. Green, *The Jury, Seditious Libel, and the Criminal Law* (forthcoming William Andrews Clark Memorial Lib. ser., Univ. of California at Los Angeles).

[43] The statute of 4 George I, c. 11 (1717) that had made transportation the regular sanction for clergyable offences did preserve to the judge the option to impose the lesser sanction of branding, and there are a couple of cases in which that happens in the Dudley Ryder sources under discussion. I should say that I do not understand what conventions may have been prevailing in respect of that seldom-used option. I suspect that a larger sample would show that a disproportionate number of these cases involved married women or gainfully employed fathers — cases in which transportation would have worked hardship on the family (and, perhaps, on the ratepayers as well).

[44] When the trial judges initiated pardon requests, the monarch granted them routinely. Chief Baron Macdonald described the long-established practice to a parlia-

(cont. on p. 110)

"Roughly half of those condemned to death during the eighteenth century did not go to the gallows", Hay writes, "but were transported to the colonies or imprisoned".[45] Data published in 1772 by Theodore Stephen Janssen, who had served as mayor of London in 1755, discloses that for the 23 mayoral years 1749-71 some 443 capital convicts were reprieved (or died in gaol) out of a total of 1,121 sentenced to death at the Old Bailey. Of these 443 who escaped execution, 401 were pardoned for transportation. One indication that these pardons were not awarded capriciously, but with a view to considerations of principle, is that pardon rates varied with the gravity of the offence. Of the 81 persons convicted of murder in Janssen's figures, 72 were executed; of 17 for attempted murder, 15 were executed; of 362 for highway robbery, 251 were executed; of 208 for house-breaking, 118 were executed. By contrast, only 6 of the 23 persons convicted of shop-lifting above the clergyable limit were allowed to hang; 22 of 90 for livestock thefts; 27 of 80 for stealing privately (picking pockets); 27 of 63 for stealing from a dwelling house in an amount above the clergyable sum; and neither of the two condemned sodomites.[46]

What factors were motivating the commutations and pardons? Hay notices that "The grounds for mercy were *ostensibly* that the offence was minor, or that the convict was of good character, or that the crime he had committed was not common enough in that county to require

n. 44 cont.) mentary committee in 1819: "The judges send what are called 'circuit letters' to the secretary of state, stating the places where prisoners have been convicted, their offences, and in general the favourable circumstances that have appeared, that would make a case proper to be recommended to His Majesty, for his pardon; and I do not remember any case in which such pardon was refused when recommended": *Report from the Select Committee Appointed to Consider of So Much of the Criminal Law as Relates to Capital Punishment in Felonies*, Parliamentary Papers (1819), viii, p. 48. The Recorder of London prepared an equivalent document for each Old Bailey sessions; for an example from one of the four sessions at which Dudley Ryder sat, see Public Record Office, London (hereafter P.R.O.), S.P. 36/132/296 (Apr. 1755 sessions). When the convict or a supporter petitioned for clemency, as in the case of Richard Tickner discussed on p. 112 and n. 54 below, the secretaries of state and often the monarch reviewed the merits of the case.

[45] Hay, "Property, Authority and the Criminal Law", p. 43.

[46] Stephen Theodore Janssen, *This Sheet Contains Three Tables, from 1749 to 1771* (London, 1772; Guildhall Lib., London, B'side 27.15). The broadside is reprinted as a foldout appendix in the endpapers of John Howard, *An Account of the Principal Lazarettos in Europe*, 2nd edn. (London, 1791).

It is interesting to note that Janssen emphasizes in this compilation the theme to which John Beattie and now Hay, in his "War, Dearth and Theft in the Eighteenth Century", have been directing recent scholarly attention, namely the seeming connection between rising crime rates and demobilization of the forces following periods of war. Janssen says: "It is worth observing that, as a great many idle Men and Lads are taken into the Sea & Land Service during a war; so we then find the Gangs of Robbers soon broken & that the Business at the Old Bailey gradually diminished to half its duration in time of Peace, nor are half the number of Criminals condemned. For in some Years of war they have not amounted to 20, whereas in Peace they have arisen to 70, 80, and 90. It is farther observable that at the conclusion of a War, through very bad Policy, when we turn adrift so many thousand Men, great numbers fall heedlessly to thieving as soon as their Pockets are empty, and are at once brought to the Gallows".

an exemplary hanging",[47] but Hay thinks that these grounds formed a mere smoke-screen. The judges "were not usually willing to antagonize a body of respectable [local] feeling", he writes. The pardon system was "capricious"; indeed, "the claims of class saved far more men who had been left to hang by the assize judge than did the claims of humanity".[48] In support of this view Hay offers the evidence of a few cases in which élite petitioners referred to the previous good character of the accused and especially to the good repute of his family.

Although my main objection to this line of argument is that it is unrepresentative, I want to say in passing that I would not accept the implication that such factors ought to have been extraneous to what were in effect sentencing decisions. In an age before probation and large-scale penal imprisonment, the existence of family and employment relationships was highly relevant to the decision whether or not to release an offender into the community (or, likewise, whether or not to turn him loose on the inhabitants of Virginia and Maryland by transporting him). Even today, if a convict can get respectable people to support him, sentencing officers are inclined to give weight to that evidence on the ground that it has predictive value on the question of the likelihood of successful resocialization.

Hay's account of the clemency system highlights the peripheral issue of social class and neglects to explore the factors that were of central importance. The Ryder notebooks give us a good window on this question, and the picture we see bears no resemblance to Hay's. Ryder is preoccupied with the merits in clemency questions, and he resists recommendations that involve only élite connections.

In the Old Bailey notebook there is one striking example, the case of Thomas Rolf, convicted of highway robbery at the October 1754 sessions and sentenced to death. The evidence indicated that Rolf, who had been apprehended at the scene, had behaved politely and apologetically to his victim as he robbed her. He told her that destitution led him to his crime. He was unable to find work and his wife was about to deliver their third child.[49] Ryder records in his notes that he urged the jury to convict, since "compassion could not justify finding contrary to truth", but after they heeded this instruction and found him guilty, the jurors "desired I would intercede for him. I said the Recorder [of London] would have an opportunity of representing it fully to His Majesty. [This is a reference to the recorder's regular report to the monarch after each Old Bailey sessions.] And indeed I never in all my life met with a robbery on the highway so clearly proved to be the effect of mere necessity and committed for

[47] Hay, "Property, Authority and the Criminal Law", p. 43 (my italics).
[48] *Ibid.*, pp. 43-4.
[49] *Old Bailey Sessions Papers* (Oct. 1754), Case no. 504, p. 326.

want of necessaries to maintain himself, wife big with child, and two infants".[50] Ryder made this notation with a view towards advising the recorder, and Rolf thereafter received a free pardon,[51] that is one not conditioned on transportation or some other sanction, even though the crown had to pay the prosecutrix the statutory forty-pound reward for apprehending and convicting him.[52]

Ryder's assize diary for the summer 1754 sittings on the Home Circuit contains considerable mention of his practice regarding judicial reprieve, reprieve being the decisive first step towards executive commutation. At Guildford assizes he noted that he let two burglars hang because "It was a very plain and bad case", but he reprieved a horsethief "because the evidence doubtful", a sheepthief "because the evidence not clear", and a pickpocket against whom the evidence amounted in Ryder's view "not quite [to] a clear case".[53]

At the same assizes Ryder resisted élite intervention for clemency in two cases of highway robbery. Richard Gilbert "was recommended to reprieve by Creswick and Andrews his master, being but 20 years old, but being for highway [robbery, and Gilbert having been convicted of two offences committed the same day, I] did not reprieve him". In the case of Richard Tickner, Ryder refused to reprieve although requested to do so by Arthur Onslow the Speaker of the House of Commons, Richard Onslow the lord lieutenant of Surrey, and Henry Talbot the high sheriff of Surrey. Arthur Onslow went to the king; Ryder's opinion was sought, and he records it thus: since "there was no reason to doubt [that Tickner had committed the crime] and there were no circumstances of alleviation, I could not take on myself to say he was an object of mercy . . .".[54] The king let him

[50] Ryder Old Bailey Notes, pp. 21-2.

[51] *Old Bailey Sessions Papers* (Jan. 1755), p. 80.

[52] P.R.O., T.53/45, Money Book, p. 353.

[53] Ryder Assize Diary, pp. 17-18.

[54] *Ibid.* Both Onslow's letter and Ryder's reply survive in the State Papers. Onslow wrote that Tickner, condemned "for a Robbery on the highway of some few shillings", was "a young Man of a very honest Family with us, and for the saving of whose life I am so much importuned, that I cannot avoid troubling your Lordship [the secretary of state] with an humble request for your assistance in obtaining a reprieve for him, in order to his transportation for any time, be the length of it what it will": P.R.O., S.P. 36/128/67 (3 Sept. 1754). Ryder's reply recites that a copy of Onslow's letter had been transmitted to him. Ryder reports on the evidence that had been adduced at Tickner's trial, remarking that the victim testified that Tickner "came up to him, presented a Pistol to his Breast & demanded his Money with a Curse, which on the Second like demand he delivered him to the amount of 14 Shillings". Ryder also reports that three pistols were found on Tickner when he was taken, and that he initially refused to identify himself. He concludes: "On the Whole, as I see no Reason to doubt of the Truth of the Fact, & no circumstances appeared to alleviate the guilt of it, I cannot take on my Self to represent him as an object of your Majesty's Mercy. But if your Majesty out of your great clemency shall be graciously pleased to extend your Royal Mercy to him, I humbly Submit it to your Majesty's wisdom whether it may not be on the Terms of Transportation for Life [as opposed to the seven or fourteen year terms otherwise current]": P.R.O., S.P. 36/128/77-8 (7 Sept. 1754).

hang. At Horsham assizes a few days earlier Ryder sentenced to death a man named Millet for horse-stealing. His diary records: "The clerk of assizes pressed me much to transport Millet, the hosteller, but I refused it because it seems to have been his practice [that is, he was a multiple offender], and nobody spoke to his character".[55] Ryder's handling of reprieve and pardon matters was principled. He was trying to take into account factors that ethical sentencing officers still consult.

King faults Hay for using "a small number of quotations from [the judges' reports to the monarch] to illustrate the importance of one particular factor — the role of respectability or respectable connections . . .".[56] To correct for that, King undertook to categorize all the factors mentioned in all the cases in the state papers for the period from 1784 to 1787. He identifies "five broad groups of factors", of which the respectability of the convict turned out to be the *least* important. The most frequent was good character, including previous good conduct. Although men of relatively high social standing supplied some of these references, King found that "the great majority of character witnesses were drawn from the middling sort or from the poorer but respectable sections of the local community".

Next in order of frequency, he found, was the youth of the offender, which reflected both sympathy and a belief in reformability. Third, King says, came the circumstances of the crime, especially whether violent. The fourth most commonly mentioned factor was the poverty of the culprit and his family. A little of this may have had to do with the desire to spare the ratepayers from having to support an executed convict's family, but the more usual concern was to recognize the lesser culpability of someone who acted in distress (and we remember Dudley Ryder's sympathy for the destitute highway robber Thomas Rolf). Furthermore, King says, wealth hurt. Judges were "very hard on prisoners who were relatively well off and could not therefore plead poverty at the time of the crime". He quotes a judge's report from a case in 1764, which says that it is better "that one man in good circumstances should suffer than 20 miserable wretches". Fifth and last in King's sample comes the factor Hay stresses, the respectability of the convict or his parents. King's totals for the five categories: (a) character and previous conduct, 126; (b) youth, old age and infirmity, 61; (c) circumstances of the crime, 56; (d) destitution or family poverty, 33; (e) respectability, 13. Radzinowicz directed attention several decades ago to the prevalence of a broad range of sentencing-type factors in the pardon process,[57] and

[55] Ryder Assize Diary, p. 13.

[56] King, "Decision-Makers and Decision-Making in the 18th Century Criminal Law", p. 22. The data quoted in text is from *ibid.*, pp. 22-8.

[57] Radzinowicz, *History of English Criminal Law*, i, pp. 115-16.

King has now done a great service in bringing new precision to the subject.

VI
LEGITIMATION

A staple of Marxist argumentation for dealing with contrary evidence is what I call the legitimation trick. Evidence that cuts against the thesis is dismissed as part of a sub-plot to make the conspiracy more palatable to its victims, to legitimate it. The Hay essay contains some splendid examples. Hay notices the pervasive legalism of English criminal procedure, including "the extreme solicitude of judges for the rights of the accused, [in which contemporary visitors from Europe saw such] a sharp distinction from the usual practice of continental benches".[58] Hay also mentions the tradition of strict construction against penal statutes and the recurrent quashing of strong prosecution cases for technical flaws. But Hay undertakes to reconcile this attention to safeguard with his thesis by arguing: "When the ruling class acquitted men on technicalities they helped instil a belief in the disembodied justice of the law in the minds of all who watched. In short, its very inefficiency, its absurd formalism, was part of its strength as ideology".[59]

Now the question that comes to mind is, simply, how does one test that proposition? A revealing manner, I think, is to hypothesize the exact opposite facts. Suppose that the rulers of eighteenth-century England had been operating banana-republic courts, coercing confessions or lynching paupers without trial. Obviously, the ruling-class conspiracy would be equally well evidenced. I have to ask, therefore, what kind of thesis it is that can be satisfied by any state of the evidence, and my answer is that it is not a thesis about the evidence, which means that it is not a thesis about history as I understand the discipline.

Consider another example, the celebrated case of Lord Ferrers, who as Hay tells us "killed his steward, was captured by his tenantry, tried in the House of Lords, sentenced to death, executed at Tyburn, and dissected 'like a common criminal' as the publicists never tired of repeating".[60] Hay dismisses such events as "part of the lore of politics that in England social class did not preserve a man even from the extreme sanction of death".[61] But suppose instead that Lord Ferrers had been privileged to slay as many social inferiors as he pleased, suppose, that is, that the English had immunized the élite from capital punishment. Well, of course, that would fit the thesis

[58] Hay, "Property, Authority and the Criminal Law", p. 32.
[59] *Ibid.*, p. 33.
[60] *Ibid.*, p. 34.
[61] *Ibid.*, p. 33.

just as conveniently. Consequently, the thesis is simply not testable. It floats above the evidence, it is self-proving. I am reminded of the way that some adherents of another economic-determinist school, the modern law-and-economics movement, are able to dismiss contrary evidence: the market makes everything efficient, and anything that is not is a consumption choice.

VII

THE STATUTES

Laying aside Hay's ruling-class conspiracy, what does explain the eighteenth-century paradox — the profusion of capital statutes in an era of declining capital punishment? I do not have a full answer, much less a thesis with the elegance of Hay's. I can, however, point to some factors that I believe bear on this great question.

My starting point is volume one of Radzinowicz's *History of English Criminal Law* published in 1948.[62] This work is not in fashion today, for reasons that I do not understand. In my opinion the burst of recent scholarship on eighteenth-century criminal procedure has done little to detract from Radzinowicz's awesome book. Radzinowicz derived his account from the contemporary tracts and legal literature, as well as from the parliamentary materials produced during the course of the reform movement that became prominent in the 1770s and ran into the middle of the nineteenth century. Radzinowicz observes that Eden and Romilly, the legendary proponents of reform, followed the teaching of Beccaria and argued that punishment should be proportioned to the gravity of the crime.[63] (Blackstone advanced similar ideas in the 1760s.[64]) English law was wrong, they said, to invoke the death penalty for offences of vastly different seriousness. Excessive severity was counter-productive, it weakened deterrence by discouraging victims from prosecuting and by encouraging juries to down-charge or acquit. Nevertheless, adherents of what Radzinowicz calls the theory of maximum severity resisted the reformers' manifestly sensible position well into the nineteenth century. These people who supported the heavy English reliance on the threat of capital punishment were preoccupied with the deterrent policy of the criminal law, virtually to the exclusion of competing considerations such as proportionality. Why? They argued — and I think they believed — that England was uniquely dependent upon the deterrent effect of the capital threat because, alone of the great states of the day, England had neither a professional police force nor the system of non-capital sanctions known as penal servitude that had so widely displaced the death penalty on the Continent.

[62] Radzinowicz, *History of English Criminal Law*, i.
[63] *Ibid.*, pp. 231 ff.
[64] Blackstone, *Commentaries on the Laws of England*, iv, pp. 16-19.

A large chapter of English constitutional and administrative history underlies the eighteenth-century aversion to professional police forces and correction systems. Just as the prospect of a standing army evoked shivers in those who thought back to the days of James II, the suggestion that the police power in the localities be turned over to a corps of hirelings raised alarm. A tyrant might use this force to undercut or repress the liberties of the political community. The administrative challenge of organizing police and correction systems was also daunting to contemporaries. The English had scant experience in dealing with the problems of recruiting, training, financing, leading and controlling such forces. Ultimately, of course, as the urban-industrial age unfolded, the English had to abandon their attachment to amateur law enforcement, but that was the work of the next century; scarcely anyone foresaw it in the eighteenth century when the capital legislation was expanding so greatly.

Radzinowicz emphasizes the sense of insecurity that resulted from the want of effective policing.[65] Contemporaries felt that they needed every ounce of deterrence that they could get. They had to put so much weight on deterrence because they had so little chance of catching and convicting the undeterred. If the fear of hanging deterred some potential criminals, as most people thought it did, then the capital threat was worth making. Likewise, the want of any alternative to the capital sanction better than transportation had a great bearing on the extension of capital punishment to offences created in the eighteenth century.

I think that Radzinowicz's account of the explosion of capital statutes in an age of declining capital punishment has two major virtues when contrasted with Hay's.[66] First, Radzinowicz takes seriously the evidence of the people who were near, and in some cases quite influential in, the legislative events. Contemporaries struggled for decades over the relative merits of maximum severity versus proportionality, and I am persuaded that we should listen to them. Second, Radzinowicz has related his explanation to other, fundamental features of the legal system — that is, to the weaknesses in detection and corrections. In that respect the comparative dimension reinforces Radzinowicz. A notable weakness of Hay's account is that he points to ruling-class self-interest to explain a phenomenon that was distinctively English. Other states of the day had comparable ruling classes, yet the burgeoning of capital legislation in the later eighteenth century was an English peculiarity.

[65] Radzinowicz, *History of English Criminal Law*, i, pp. 23-35, 248 ff., 410.

[66] I should say, however, that I prefer Hay to Radzinowicz on the question of whether, as Radzinowicz contends, the declining penal death rate of the later eighteenth century was frustrating a legislative preference for higher levels of enforcement. Cf. Hay, "Property, Authority and the Criminal Law", p. 23, with Radzinowicz, *History of English Criminal Law*, i, pp. 158-64, esp. p. 164. Belief in the deterrent efficacy of capital punishment need not presuppose high levels of actual execution.

I wish to point to two other peculiarities of the English criminal justice system that help explain the burst of eighteenth-century capital legislation — benefit of clergy and the conceptual impoverishment of the substantive law.

From the middle ages into the eighteenth century, the remarkable institution of benefit of clergy underwent an incessant and contorted transmutation.[67] Originally a device for preserving ecclesiastical criminal jurisdiction over clerics, it became by 1706 a privilege that anyone convicted of a common law felony could claim in order to obtain exemption from the imposition of the death penalty. Pursuant to legislation of 1717, almost all convicts who pleaded clergy after that date were transported to the British colonies in America for a seven-year term of indentured servitude. By the eighteenth century, therefore, benefit of clergy had drained most of the blood from the common law of crime. In order to preserve the capital threat for a crime that had been or would have been capital under the common law, special legislation had to be enacted making the offence non-clergyable. Some such statutes date from the sixteenth century, and a group of important ones appeared in the reigns of William and Anne, but most were Georgian.[68] Accordingly, the so-called expansion of the capital sanction in the eighteenth century was to some considerable extent only a restoration. This process of piecemeal restoration was a major force in the transformation of the law of crime from a common law field to a predominantly statutory one.[69]

This movement from common law into statute law occurred in a legal system that was ill-equipped to handle it. Milsom, speaking of the late medieval period, overstates this point, but let me quote him for the flavour of a notion that I think would repay careful study. "The miserable history of [the law of] crime in England can be shortly told. Nothing worthwhile was created".[70] Many aspects of the English medieval heritage had the effect of reducing the legal-scientific dimension of the criminal law by comparison with Continental law — we might mention the heavy use of laymen to decide and to prosecute criminal cases, the virtual absence of lawyers for prosecution and defence, the tiny number of royal judges, the decentralization of the assize system, and the opacity of the general verdict. English criminal law was primitive in matters of offence definition, especially

67 See generally *The Reports of Sir John Spelman*, ed. J. H. Baker, 2 vols. (Selden Soc., xciii-xciv, London, 1977-8), ii, Introduction, pp. 327-34; James F. Stephen, *A History of the Criminal Law of England*, 3 vols. (London, 1883), i, pp. 458 ff. Hay dismisses benefit of clergy in a footnote: Hay, "Property, Authority and the Criminal Law", p. 22 n. 2.

68 See the convenient list of these statutes in Jerome Hall, *Theft, Law and Society*, 2nd edn. (Indianapolis, 1952), pp. 356-63.

69 See John Styles, "Criminal Records", *Hist. Jl.*, xx (1977), pp. 977, 980.

70 S. F. C. Milsom, *Historical Foundations of the Common Law*, 2nd edn. (London, 1981), p. 403.

the general part, that set of notions about criminal responsibility that cuts across all criminal offences (for example, degrees of culpability, the law of attempts, aiding and abetting, capacity, and most of the affirmative defences). This underdevelopment of the scientific side of English law greatly affected the multiplication of capital statutes. The English did not have 200 separate crimes in the modern sense that could be punished with death. Rather, they lacked general definitions, especially for larceny and embezzlement, with the result that they were constantly having to add particulars in order to compensate for the want of generality.[71] The consolidation movement of the nineteenth century illustrates this point well; few offences were repealed, rather definitions were improved so that the number of separate offences could be reduced. Stephen, writing nearly a century ago, made the point that the 160 capital offences that Blackstone complained were in force in the 1760s "might probably be reduced by careful classification to a comparatively small number".[72]

Not only did English criminal law lack scientific sophistication, on the legislative side it had no central direction. No minister of justice oversaw the administration and amendment of the criminal justice system. Most of the capital statutes, like most of the rest of eighteenth-century legislation,[73] originated as members' bills. In such circumstances the extension of capital sanctions to new forms of property was natural enough, by sheer force of analogy. If the capital sanction suited offences against sheep under Elizabeth, then why not factories under George III? "For once the death penalty is established as the most effective instrument of crime-prevention", Radzinowicz remarks, "there can be no valid reason for invoking it to suppress one offence and not another".[74] Some larger reform of principle is needed to interrrupt that process. Legislatures incline to err on the side of severity when considering particular offences. Particulars are inflationary, because there is no counter-constituency to resist the analogy that extends penal sanctions from one thing to the next. Leniency and proportionality are considerations that come to the fore when a legislature has occasion to compare offences and sanctions — when, for example, it produces a penal code, or (as in nineteenth-century England) revises major segments of the law.

[71] See, for example, Radzinowicz's succinct account of the succession of larceny statutes: Radzinowicz, *History of English Criminal Law*, i, pp. 41-9.

[72] Stephen, *History of the Criminal Law of England*, i, p. 470.

[73] "In the eighteenth century, legislation was not . . . especially a matter for the ministers of the Crown. There was little government legislation apart from routine financial measures . . .": P. D. G. Thomas, *The House of Commons in the Eighteenth Century* (Oxford, 1971), p. 45. On the Treasury's oversight of revenue bills, see Sheila Lambert, *Bills and Acts: Legislative Procedure in Eighteenth-Century England* (Cambridge, 1971), pp. 71-4. See also Hugh Amory, "Henry Fielding and the Criminal Legislation of 1751-2", *Philol. Quart.*, l (1971), pp. 175, 191-2.

[74] Radzinowicz, *History of English Criminal Law*, i, p. 49.

We can, of course, trace the hand of commercial interests (who were often more petty bourgeois than élite, as I have said before) in a considerable fraction of the eighteenth-century criminal legislation, both capital and non-capital. I doubt whether anyone would argue with Jerome Hall's assessment that "it is in this century that one comes upon the law of receiving stolen property, larceny by trick, obtaining goods by false pretences, and embezzlement. Here, for the first time, the modern lawyer finds himself in contact with a body of substantive criminal law which he feels is essentially his own".[75] New forms of economic activity and commercial organization gave rise to new issues of definition. Yet the very fact that the solutions that were reached in the eighteenth century strike us as essentially modern (on issues of culpability, that is, rather than sanction) suggests that these measures were enacted because they were reasonable rather than because a ruling class wrested advantage from others. There is no social interest in failing to criminalize receiving stolen property, larceny by trick, obtaining goods by false pretences, and embezzlement. These offences persist with only technical refinement in modern English law, and comparable provisions grace the codes of modern socialist states.[76]

VIII

THE RULERS

In a recent essay Richard Sparks makes a point that helps us understand why the Hay thesis is so improbable.[77] The criminal law, says Sparks, is only important "at the *margins* of social life; . . . in day-to-day affairs it is not all that important to the maintenance of late industrial capitalism's social order . . . give me the law of contracts (including contracts of employment), and you can have all the rest of the statute book . . . the most generally useful laws are likely to be the ones that define . . . ownership and control [of the means of production], and not some ancillary laws that promise to thump individuals for rather trivial kinds of tampering with those means".[78] The criminal law is simply the wrong place to look for the active hand of the ruling classes. From the standpoint of the rulers, I would suggest, the criminal justice system occupies a place not much more central than the garbage collection system. True, if the garbage is not collected the society cannot operate and ruling-class goals will be frustrated, but that does not turn garbage collection into a ruling-

[75] Hall, *Theft, Law and Society*, pp. 34-5.

[76] For example, *Criminal Code of the Hungarian People's Republic*, trans. P. Lamberg (Budapest, 1962), pp. 108, 110, ss. 292 (embezzlement), 293 (criminal fraud), 301 (receiving goods unlawfully obtained).

[77] Richard F. Sparks, "A Critique of Marxist Criminology", *Crime and Justice: An Annual Review of Research*, ii (1980), p. 159.

[78] *Ibid.*, pp. 193-4.

class conspiracy. The Hay thesis, in a similar fashion, confuses necessary and sufficient conditions.

In this paper I have been maintaining two themes about the administration of the criminal law in the eighteenth century. First, most of the discretion was exercised by people not fairly to be described as the ruling class, especially the prosecutors and the jurors. Secondly, the discretion that characterized this system was not arbitrary and self-interested, but rather turned on the good-faith consideration of factors with which ethical decision-makers ought to have been concerned. The historian does not need a conspiracy theory to explain the discretion, and the discretion does not fit the theory. I concede fully that when men of the social élite came into contact with the criminal justice system in any capacity, they were treated with special courtesy and regard, just as they were elsewhere in this stratified society. To seize upon that as the *raison d'être* of the criminal justice system is, however, to mistake the barnacles for the boat.

University of Chicago *John H. Langbein*

[15]

(MARXIST) SOCIAL HISTORY AND (CONSERVATIVE) LEGAL HISTORY: A REPLY TO PROFESSOR LANGBEIN

PETER LINEBAUGH*

In an anthology entitled Albion's Fatal Tree *several social historians examined eighteenth-century English society through its laws and their application. In this article, Professor Linebaugh, one of the book's editors, responds to Professor Langbein's ferocious challenge to the Marxist interpretation of the century's criminal law provided by one of the essayists, Douglas Hay. Labeling Langbein's legal scholarship "ahistorical" elitism, Professor Linebaugh contrasts it with his colleagues' emphasis on customs and attitudes of ordinary people from the "bottom up." He proceeds to illustrate how Langbein's functionalist approach causes him to misconstrue Hay's point and misinterpret the evidence. Professor Linebaugh paints a world in which underpaid workers customarily took goods from their employers and corrupt trial jurors were drawn from propertied elite classes. He argues that Langbein's narrow vision prevents him from appreciating that because law was rooted in community custom, a more democratic jury may have sanctioned such appropriation. Finally, Professor Linebaugh rebuts Langbein's assertion that criminal law was no more central to society than was garbage collection by graphically illustrating eighteenth-century London's preoccupation with waste disposal. He ends by analogizing the century's criminal justice system to the flush toilet.*

INTRODUCTION

In this Article I contrast a legal view of social relations with a social view of legal relations by examining several issues that have emerged recently in a debate about eighteenth-century English law and society. The issues include the narrow and broad use of judicial records, the ambivalent role of the jury, the contrast between custom or common law and statute or Roman law, and the tendency of a superior social class to see the powerless in terms of garbage.

In particular I respond to Professor John Langbein of the University of Chicago, whose recent article, "Albion's Fatal Flaws,"[1] attacks *Albion's Fatal Tree: Crime and Society in Eighteenth-Century England*,[2] an anthology that E.P. Thompson, Douglas Hay, and I edited.

---

* Visiting Associate Professor of History, Tufts University. B.S., 1964, Swarthmore College; M.A., 1969, Columbia University; Ph.D., 1975, Centre for the Study of Social History at the University of Warwick.

[1] Langbein, Albion's Fatal Flaws, 98 Past & Present 96 (1983).

[2] D. Hay, P. Linebaugh, J. Rule, E.P. Thompson & C. Winslow, Albion's Fatal Tree: Crime and Society in Eighteenth-Century England (1975) [hereinafter Albion's Fatal Tree].

I
SOCIAL HISTORY AND THE LAW

"Albion" was the Greek name for England. By the eighteenth century this name became associated with a mythic, generous idea of a peaceful and harmonious society in very much the same way that the place known as "Jerusalem" has in the Christian tradition been associated with peace and salvation. In this respect the word hearkens to an earlier vision of England, which it counterposes to eighteenth-century England's chauvinism, war, and imperialism.[3] "Fatal Tree" refers to the gallows, especially the London gallows called "Tyburn," at the edge of town in Paddington. Many thousands lost their lives upon this "cheat," as it was familiarly known.[4] Our book began with a quotation from William Blake that expressed the contrast, as it was understood at the end of the eighteenth century, between the hopeful potentiality of human freedom and creativity and the actuality of death and destruction:

> What are those golden Builders doing
> Near mournful ever-weeping Paddington
> Standing above that mighty Ruin
> Where Satan the first victory won.
>
> Where Albion slept beneath the Fatal Tree
> And the Druids golden Knife,
> Rioted in human gore,
> In Offerings of Human Life.
>
> They groan'd aloud on London Stone
> They groan'd aloud on Tyburn's Brook
> Albion gave his deadly groan,
> And all the Atlantic Mountains shook.[5]

These lines from the 1790's express in a mixture of history, myth, and revolutionary aspiration real and vast historical forces that initiated the traffic in human beings on an enormous, epic scale: millions of people were thrown thousands of miles across oceans and continents to forced labor in America and Australia;[6] thousands were dispossessed from common land, Gaelic sept, or Scottish Highlands and torn from their roots

---

[3] See generally D. Erdman, Blake, Prophet Against Empire: A Poet's Interpretation of the History of his Own Times 14-16, 312-13, 479-87 (2d ed. 1969); T. Frosch, The Awakening of Albion: The Renovation of the Body in the Poetry of William Blake 60, 85 (1974).

[4] A New Canting Dictionary (London 1725), quoted in Albion's Fatal Tree, supra note 2, at 66.

[5] W. Blake, Jerusalem, in The Poetry and Prose of William Blake 170 (Erdman ed. 1965).

[6] The English people transported to the colonies for the violation of laws were, of course, not the only people forcibly removed from their homelands. One good source on transportation to the American colonies is A.E. Smith, Colonists in Bondage (1947). On the slave trade in African peoples, see, e.g., D. Mannix & M. Cowley, Black Cargoes (1962).

and communities; whole towns and regions were expropriated in a revolutionizing of human labor in the process habitually, if lamely, called "industrialization." *Albion's Fatal Tree* did not analyze these forces directly or upon a world scale. Rather, we used a series of particular case studies of regional episodes to narrate strictly English conflicts between the murderousness of the eighteenth-century law and the people who not only suffered, but sometimes in their own ways struggled to survive and to maintain their own conception of "Albion." This was called "history from below" when the volume was published nine years ago, and it is this history that Professor Langbein attacks "from above."[7]

One American wrote about the Tyburn hangings and their relation to the development of anatomy.[8] Another wrote about the smugglers of southeastern England and their endemic wars against the excisemen.[9] A Cornishman wrote an essay about the practice of wrecking merchant ships upon the rocky coasts of western England.[10] A Canadian investigated the Game Laws and the poaching of rabbits in a midlands county.[11] E.P. Thompson, who from the Centre for the Study of Social History at the University of Warwick had assembled and guided this international group of scholars, contributed an essay on the "crime of anonymity" that summed up the historiographic problems of "history from below." (As a Newcastle collier wrote, "I Wauld Tel you My Name but My Simplicity Will Not Let Mee.")[12] We might have written about other subjects: piracy, clipping, highway robbery, embezzlement, and counterfeiting. However, because the essays included were so extensively researched, the questions they raised stirred activity in several academic disciplines; a more theoretical or abstract work might not have had the same academic versatility. The essays raised questions about property and the differences and relationships between those who created it and those who consumed it, about the diversity of regional and local attitudes towards the new law, about the class backgrounds of those who enforced it and those against whom it was enforced. Such questions were raised, but not completely answered, because we felt our conclusions had to be

---

7 A. Calder, Revolutionary Empire: The Rise of the English Speaking Empires from the Fifteenth Century to the 1780s (1981), is a massive survey of these forces of "industrialization" and is by no means written "from below." On "history from below" see, e.g., Lemish, The American Revolution Seen from the Bottom Up, in Towards a New Past: Dissenting Essays in American History 3 (1968).

8 Linebaugh, The Tyburn Riot Against the Surgeons, in Albion's Fatal Tree, supra note 2, at 65.

9 Winslow, Sussex Smugglers, in Albion's Fatal Tree, supra note 2, at 119.

10 Rule, Wrecking and Coastal Plunder, in Albion's Fatal Tree, supra note 2, at 167.

11 Hay, Poaching and the Game Laws on Cannock Chase, in Albion's Fatal Tree, supra note 2, at 189.

12 Thompson, The Crime of Anonymity, in Albion's Fatal Tree, supra note 2, at 255, 255.

limited by what was shown in the essays. We were aware that issues of great concern to legal, economic, and social historians were at stake, but we felt that practitioners of other disciplines might do this in a way more understandable to their particular discourses.

In the preface, however, E.P. Thompson did attempt to relate the narratives to a distinction commonly proposed in historiographical discussions of illegal behavior:

> It is rather easy, when taking a superficial view of eighteenth-century evidence, to propose two distinct kinds of offence and offenders. There are 'good' criminals, who are premature revolutionaries or reformers, forerunners of popular movements—all kinds of rioters, smugglers, poachers, primitive rebels in industry. This appears as 'social crime'. And there then are those who commit crime without qualification: thieves, robbers, highwaymen, forgers, arsonists, and murderers.[13]

We found no evidence of a sharp line between a "morally endorsed popular culture" and a "deviant subculture"; different communities appear to have opposed, tolerated, or sheltered varying kinds of offenders.[14] Despite our cautious conclusions, the essays became controversial among legal historians, among criminologists, among eighteenth-century specialists, and more generally among those working on both sides of the Atlantic in "popular history" or "social history." The volume also contributed to the revival of political economy, and Marxists of various persuasions found in it a source of disagreement or encouragement.[15]

The historian is affected by the kind of evidence used, and must therefore learn to be critical of its origins, the reasons for its survival, and the precise nature of its limitations. We turned to legal records because they are a prime source of documentation about the lives of people who left few written records of their own and attracted no attention from biographers. Just as Mary and John Leakey must be expert in paleontology and anatomy because their evidence for the early history of human beings is stones and bones, so we had to become interested in law and the judiciary.

Of the contributors to *Albion's Fatal Tree*, Douglas Hay became

[13] Thompson, Preface, in Albion's Fatal Tree, supra note 2, at 13-14.

[14] See id. at 14.

[15] See, e.g., Crime in England, 1550-1800 (J. Cockburn ed. 1977); Crime & Capitalism: Readings in Marxist Criminology (D. Greenberg ed. 1981); M. Ignatieff, A Just Measure of Pain: The Penitentiary in the Industrial Revolution, 1750-1850 (1978); An Ungovernable People: The English and Their Law in the Seventeenth and Eighteenth Centuries (J. Brewer & J. Styles ed. 1980); Horowitz, The Rule of Law: An Unqualified Human Good? (Book Review), 86 Yale L.J. 561 (1977); Pearson, Eighteenth Century English Criminal Law (Book Review), 3 Brit. J.L. & Soc'y 115 (1976); Rudé, Poachers and Protesters (Book Review), Times Literary Supp., Jan. 30, 1976, at 104 (*Albion's Fatal Tree* "open[s] up a rich field for further exploration and it is to be hoped that historians . . . who have in the past been somewhat slow to become engaged in this type of history 'from below', will be ready to take up the challenge.").

most interested in the law and the lawmakers. In the only essay that is entirely interpretive and analytical, he argued that in the eighteenth century the law replaced religion as the dominant form of ruling class ideological hegemony. The law with its costumes, its courtroom theatrics, its specialized jargon, and its internal, closed intellectualism came to dominate the discussion of property and social relationships.[16] The limits of that domination are implied in the other essays, which deal with proscribed behavior and with self-conscious "resistance" to legal norms. In a sense, therefore, Hay became more interested in the stones and bones than in what they might reveal about crime and criminals. Perhaps it is for this reason that Professor Langbein, a distinguished stone-and-bone man himself, has restricted his attack entirely to Hay's essay, an essay that powerfully conjoined the methods of legal and social history. Langbein is not interested in the other questions the volume raised; the stones and bones are ends in themselves: popular culture, social protest, material life, ruling class attitudes, the ownership and distribution of the "earthly treasury" are of no interest to him. Yet, by attacking Hay, Langbein seeks to discredit the volume as a whole, the deeper questions that it raises, and the view of the eighteenth century that our evidence led us to accept.

II

Langbein's Attack

Let us now turn to Langbein's eight-part attack. First, he attempts to controvert Hay's explanation of the essential paradox of eighteenth-century law—that while the statutory sanction of death expanded at an astonishing rate, from fifty to two hundred offenses, the actual numbers of hangings stabilized or declined. Langbein feigns evenhandedness at the Marxist overtones of Hay's essay,[17] but his rejection of Hay's "ruling class conspiracy" view not only takes a phrase out of context, but wholly misinterprets Hay's analysis. Hay argues that the increasing arsenal of death laws provided the Whig rulers of England with a functional combination of threat, terror, and mercy that established their hegemony over the "loose and disorderly" mass of the population.[18] He writes of "the private manipulation of the law by the wealthy and powerful," as a "ruling class conspiracy."[19] But he never confuses such behind-the-scene manipulations with the public operation of law, which he sees not in

16 Hay, Property, Authority and the Criminal Law, in Albion's Fatal Tree, supra note 2, at 17.

17 Langbein, supra note 1, at 97.

18 Hay, supra note 16, at 17-18, 52.

19 Id. at 52.

conspiratorial terms, but hegemonically: "The law was important as gross coercion; it was equally important as ideology. Its majesty, justice and mercy helped to create the spirit of consent and submission, the 'mind-forged manacles', which Blake saw binding the English poor."[20]

After badly mischaracterizing the thrust of Hay's historical analysis, Langbein suggests that the corpus of eighteenth-century death laws is one of those subjects, like the flush toilet, upon which Marxist historical method throws little light.[21] We shall return to Langbein's interest in sanitation.[22] Here we note only Langbein's refusal to consider the death laws in any terms—Marxist, Gramscian or otherwise—that would require him to move beyond the self-enclosed analysis commonly applied to legal and administrative subjects.

In the second section, attacking Hay's analysis of offenses and offenders, Langbein describes evidence from the *Old Bailey Proceedings*[23] of four of the sessions between 1754 and 1756 at which Londoners were tried for felonies. Although he acknowledges that this is not a statistically significant sample, and that the data are exclusively from London, rather than the countryside, where most English people lived and where Hay considered his case strongest, Langbein does not seem to consider his conclusions tentative. In defending his limited evidence, Langbein argues that the procedure of all courts was similar,[24] ignoring the numerous nonprocedural differences and demonstrating the narrowness of his analysis. His description of the offenders, or, as he would have it, the "little crooks,"[25] who were hanged or spared is similarly misleading, ideologically tendentious, and symptomatic of the limitations of narrowly legal inquiries into the history and meaning of law.

The third section analyzes the social class of private prosecutors and

---

20 Id. at 49. Langbein apparently fails to notice that Hay is more influenced by Gramsci's notion of hegemony than by any "crude Marxist" notions of conscious ruling class manipulation of the working classes. See, e.g., Mouffe, Hegemony and Ideology in Gramsci, in Gramsci and Marxist Theory 168 (C. Mouffe ed. 1979). Langbein dramatically displays this misunderstanding when he alleges that "Hay takes it for granted that the criminal law lacked the adherence of the lower orders." Langbein, supra note 1, at 108. In fact, Hay's essay suggests how the criminal law secured the obedience of the working classes with terror and theater.

21 Langbein, supra note 1, at 97.

22 See text accompanying notes 121-40 infra.

23 The Proceedings of the Peace, Oyer and Terminer, and Gaol Delivery in the City of London; and also the Gaol Delivery in the County of Middlesex, Held at Justice Hall in the Old Bailey [hereinafter Old Bailey Proceedings]. The Old Bailey Proceedings were pamphlets, with somewhat varying titles, containing accounts of recent trials. Professor Langbein has written about the Proceedings in several articles, including Langbein, Shaping the Eighteenth Century Criminal Trial: A View from the Ryder Sources, 50 U. Chi. L. Rev. 1 (1983). Though that article provides some useful information, it must be used carefully because it is flawed by some of the same unexamined and mistaken assumptions discussed in this article.

24 Langbein, supra note 1, at 99 & n.14.

25 Id. at 101.

attempts to show that these were rarely "gentlemen" or members of the elite, but were usually small propertied persons. Though Langbein notes that rewards were enacted to encourage prosecutorial activity by the lower orders,[26] he does not permit this system of "blood money" to interfere with his judgment that the system served the interests of crime victims in general rather than "self serving gentlemen" in particular.

The fourth section seeks to show that jurors were independent from influence by the gentry and urban oligarchs, and that their independence was exercised by the practices of undervaluing the goods that were stolen, acquitting defendants of major offenses and finding them guilty of lesser offenses.

The fifth section defends the Bench, arguing that it did not exercise its discretionary powers of sentencing for the purposes Hay suggested, but was entirely upright, compassionate, "firm," and socially responsible.[27]

The sixth section, called "Legitimation," casually dismisses as unverifiable Hay's explanation of the anomaly that occasionally a rich person was hanged—that such occasions lent an appearance of impartiality to the law. Langbein scoffs at what he calls a Marxist "legitimation trick," through which all practices inconsistent with naked class domination are chalked up to legitimation, making "the conspiracy more palatable to its victims."[28] He rejects Hay's argument that technical acquittals helped legitimate the law as ideology by giving the impression of justice, arguing that a system of "banana republic courts" would be equally good evidence of a ruling class conspiracy.[29] By relying on this repetitious and incorrect charge that Hay imagines a crude class conspiracy,[30] Langbein again misconstrues rather than refutes Hay's point. In fact, "banana republic courts" would do nothing to strengthen the ideology of law. Rather than attempt to understand the morality of the upper classes and the responses of the "lower orders" to their condition, Langbein simply writes off a basic part of Hay's analysis, choosing to meet him on exclusively institutional and legal grounds.

In section seven, Langbein considers the profusion of death statutes in an era of declining per capita hangings, the nub of Hay's concern. Langbein rejects Hay's thesis in part because "[o]ther states of the day had comparable ruling classes, yet the burgeoning of capital legislation was an English peculiarity."[31] But, as Langbein himself notes, England

26 Id. at 102.
27 Id. at 108-14.
28 Id. at 114.
29 Id.
30 See text accompanying notes 17-20 supra.
31 Langbein, supra note 1, at 116.

was unique among European nations because it had no police force and no system of noncapital criminal sanctions.[32] This peculiarity grounds Hay's hypothesis that the criminal law, with its growing store of capital statutes, "made it possible to govern eighteenth-century England without a police force and without a large army."[33]

Ignoring this, Langbein accepts the traditional explanation—that it was the want of policing, the weakness of detection, and the insufficiency of "corrections" that accounted for the expansion of the death laws[34]—and adds to it two of his own, involving the confused legal meaning of the doctrine of benefit of clergy[35] and the "conceptual impoverishment of the substantive law."[36] In this discussion his own theory of law is suggested: it shares more with canon law, Roman law, and Benthamite utilitarianism than with the common law and customs of England which, according to Langbein, lacked "scientific sophistication" and "central direction."[37]

Of the many issues raised in Professor Langbein's attack, I will not consider all here. Others may enjoy investigating the probity of eighteenth-century judges, or the interesting and obscure ways in which the big elite paid the little elite to prosecute in court. Here I wish to concentrate on the difference between how a legal historian and a social historian approach courtoom evidence, on Langbein's one-sided and partial interpretation of the jury, on the antidemocratic and ahistorical tendencies of his theory of law, and on his view of garbage.

III

Offenses

Because it is presented in statistical form and derived from a study of trial records, Langbein's analysis of offenses appears to be the most forceful and soundest part of his attack. In fact it is among the weakest. He analyzes the felonies tried at four Old Bailey sessions from 1754 to 1756, classifying the offenses in sixteen "lay" categories ranging from

---

32 Id. at 115.

33 Hay, supra note 16, at 56.

34 See Langbein, supra note 1, at 115-19. Two of the traditional sources are 1 L. Radzinowicz, A History of English Criminal Law and Its Administration from 1750, at 3-40 (1948), and J.F. Stephen, A History of the Criminal Law of England 469-72 (1883).

35 Benefit of clergy originally served to reserve for the ecclesiastical courts jurisdiction over certain defendants. During the eighteenth century, the doctrine permitted noncapital sentences for certain cases involving capital crimes. However, numerous statutes made certain crimes "unclergyable," making a guilty verdict a mandatory sentence of death. See Radzinowicz, supra note 34, at 3 n.2, 631-32.

36 Langbein, supra note 1, at 117.

37 Id. at 117-18.

homicide to perjury.[38] About these offenses Langbein makes two observations. First, they are "prosaic" and therefore surprising to readers who have accepted Hay's preoccupation with food riots and workplace insurrections.[39] Second, Langbein argues that "[v]irtually all of these offenses had been felonious even back into the middle ages."[40] This approach is most surprising, coming as it does from a legal historian, of whom we might expect some historical sensitivity. It is not enough to suggest that taking things that belong to another is and has long been a crime. The varieties of such crime and the way in which they are defined (for example, what does it mean for a thing "to belong to another"?) say much about the society that creates and enforces the criminal law. Consider, for example, Langbein's categories of "pocket-picking" and "shoplifting," which account for one-fifth of the crimes in his sample.[41] "Pocket-picking" requires pockets to be picked; "shop-lifting" requires shops to be lifted from. There is a history of shops and pockets, but neither was much a part of medieval life, when retailing was a matter not of shops, but of markets, peddling, and hawking, and when personal wealth was protected not by pockets, but by purses.[42] The legal historian will search in vain for laws against pocket-picking or shoplifting in the middle ages, because such offenses did not yet exist.[43] Historical sensitiv-

---

[38] The most numerous offenses are "theft under 40s.," "shop-lifting," "other theft 40s. or over," "theft from lodgings, inns, pubs," "theft from work-places or employers," "pocket-picking," and "receiving stolen goods." Id. at 99-101.

[39] In fact Hay writes little about workplaces. Moreover, had Langbein chosen to examine a session from, for example, 1768 or 1769, years of serious food shortages, he might have been less complacent about the "prosaic" nature of such offenses. See generally W. Shelton, English Hunger and Industrial Disorders: A Study of Social Conflict During the First Decade of George III's Reign (1973).

[40] Langbein, supra note 1, at 99 & n.16. Langbein contends that Hay concedes this point, but in fact Hay's "concession" is far more limited than Langbein suggests. Hay acknowledges that most capital prosecutions were brought under Tudor legislation, but it is a long way from the Tudors back to the middle ages. See Hay, War, Dearth, and Theft in the Eighteenth Century, 95 Past & Present 117, 146 (1982).

[41] Langbein, supra note 1, at 100.

[42] See generally D. Davis, A History of Shopping (1966); F. Kelly & R. Schwabe, Historic Costume: A Chronicle of Fashion in Western Europe, 1490-1790 (1925); 2 M. Davenport, The Book of Costume (1948).

[43] During the Renaissance, new statutes criminalized the acts of "cut purses" and "pick purses." An Act to take away the Benefit of Clergy from certain felonious Offenders, 8 Eliz., ch. 4 (1566), repealed by 7 & 8 Geo. 4, ch. 27, § 1 (1827). An Act that no Man robbing any House, Booth, or Tent, shall not [sic] be admitted to the Benefit of his Clergy, 5 & 6 Edw. 6, ch. 9, § 1 (1551), repealed by 7 & 8 Geo. 4, ch. 27, § 1 (1827), set penalties for "burglary in a tent or booth in a fair or market." Shoplifting was criminalized as such at the turn of the seventeenth century. An Act for the better apprehending, prosecuting, and punishing of Felons that commit Burglary, House-breaking, or Robbery in Shops, Warehouses, Coach Houses, or Stables, or that steal Horses, 10 Will. 3, ch. 12, § 1 (1698) (commonly known as the Shoplifting Act), repealed by 7 & 8 Geo. 4, ch. 27, § 1 (1827). An act to take away clergy from some offenders and to bring others to punishment, 3 W. & M., ch. 9, § 1 (1691), repealed by 7

ity should produce a sense of contingency, especially where property is concerned.

By the eighteenth century, the law of larceny had undergone certain changes.[44] Two were especially salient. First, the venue of the larceny assumed new importance: statutes provided different penalties for thefts depending on where they were committed. Such distinctions corresponded to new patterns of material and economic life. The shop, the warehouse, the stables, the workplace, and the home became, from the standpoint of the law of larceny, decisive to the fate of the offender, determining whether he or she would be hanged or transported.[45] The new importance of venue in the law of larceny reflects, in Marxist terms, new forms of commodity-capital whose value is created in production, realized in circulation, and consumed in final purchase.[46]

The second salient change in the law of larceny concerned not the economic environment of the commodity, but its monetary value. The most important consideration in determining whether an offender charged with larceny would live or die was the jury's evaluation of the monetary value of the misappropriated goods. When the larceny occurred from a shop, stable, or warehouse, the offender was spared his life

& 8 Geo. 4, ch. 27, § 1 (1827), addressed "robberies upon mens persons," but did not specifically refer to "pocket-picking."

(Where Statutes At Large (D. Pickering ed. 1762-1807) conflicts with later sources on the correct regnal year or chapter for statutes, citations follow 1 Chronological Table of the Statutes (1984).)

[44] 1 L. Radzinowicz, supra note 34, at 632-37, provides a summary of some major eighteenth-century larceny statutes. See also J.F. Stephen, supra note 34, at 121-76.

[45] Compare, e.g., An Act for the better apprehending, prosecuting, and punishing of Felons that commit Burglary, House-breaking, or Robbery in Shops, Warehouses, Coach Houses, or Stables, or that steal Horses, 10 Will. 3, ch. 12, § 1 (1698) (stealing from shop, warehouse, coach house or stable "not actually broke open by such offender" excluded from benefit of clergy where goods taken valued at more than five shillings), repealed by 7 & 8 Geo. 4, ch. 27, § 1 (1827), with An act for the more effectual preventing and punishing Robberies that shall be committed in Houses, 12 Anne, ch. 7 (1712) (stealing from "dwelling-house or outhouse thereunto belonging, although such house or out-house be not actually broken by such offender" excluded from benefit of clergy where goods taken valued at more than forty shillings), repealed by 7 & 8 Geo. 4, ch. 27, § 1 (1827). See also, e.g., An act for the further preventing robbery, burglary, and other felonies, and for the more effectual transportation of felons, 6 Geo., ch. 23, § 11 (1719) (seven years' transportation for offenders who "willfully and maliciously assault any person . . . in the publick streets and highways . . . and . . . tear, spoil, cut, burn or deface the garments or cloaths of such person"), repealed by 7 Geo. 4, ch. 64, § 32 (1826); An act for the more effectually preventing the stealing of linen, fustain [sic], and cotton goods and wares, in buildings, fields, grounds, and other places used for printing, whitening, bleaching, or drying the same, 18 Geo. 2, ch. 27 (1744) (theft of enumerated fabrics and yarns from specified places punishable by death or, at the judge's discretion, 14 years' transportation), repealed by 30 & 31 Vict., ch. 59 (1867).

[46] The greater care in the definition of venue that these statutes reflect parallels the growth of new centers of manufacture (production), new forms of transportation and the growth of banking (circulation), and the increased number of households containing small hoards of personal valuables (consumption).

if the jurors evaluated the goods at less than five shillings.[47] When the larceny occurred from a dwelling house, the suspect had not broken in or "put [the victim] in fear," and the misappropriated goods were valued at less than forty shillings, then again the offender's life was spared.[48] In the middle ages what had been legally important was not the monetary value of the property stolen, but the fact that theft indicated a violation of the feudal bonds.[49] Theft was a betrayal of the hierarchical personal relationship in a society where everyone was kept in his or her place, but there was a place for everyone. By the 1690's, in contrast, the personal relationship was concealed in and through the commodity-form.[50] Relationships that were formerly personal, such as those of lord and vassal, or master and apprentice, were converted into exchange relationships. These developments in the law of larceny may be understood, therefore, as allowing human sacrifice to the fetishism of commodities. In legally defined circumstances private property became so significant that its violation broke the most important taboo of capitalist society and required the sacrifice of life.

So, far from presenting the classification of felony in meaningful "lay" terms, Professor Langbein presents it ahistorically, suggesting that crime and specific crimes are eternal or inherent in human society. What he has eternalized, however, are only his legal categories which, under the guise of being "lay," are in fact quite ideological. He thus violates two main tenets of the historian's craft: the principle of historical specification, which examines everything, even legal ideas, in relation to the times when they arose, and the principle of historical periodization, which defines epochs, periods, and phases and accounts for changes

47 An Act for the better apprehending, prosecuting, and punishing of Felons that commit Burglary, House-breaking, or Robbery in Shops, Warehouses, Coach Houses, or Stables, or that steal Horses, 10 Will. 3, ch. 12, § 1 (1698), repealed by 7 & 8 Geo. 4, ch. 27, § 1 (1827).

48 An act for the more effecutal preventing and punishing Robberies that shall be committed in Houses, 12 Anne, ch. 7 (1712) (removing benefit of clergy from thefts of goods valued at forty shillings or more from a house), repealed by 7 & 8 Geo. 4, ch. 27, § 1 (1827). The distinction between grand and petty larceny dates from at least the thirteenth century, see Which Prisoners be Mainpernable, and which not, 3 Edw., ch. 15, § 4 (1275) (twelve pence), but by the early eighteenth century additional distinctions were made. See, e.g., An act to take away clergy from some offenders and to bring others to punishment, 3 W.& M., ch. 9, § 1 (1691) (removing benefit of clergy from daytime larceny from an occupied dwelling house, shop, or warehouse, when the goods stolen were valued at more than five shillings), repealed by 7 & 8 Geo. 4, ch. 27, § 1 (1827); P. Linebaugh, The London Hanged: Crime and Civil Society in Eighteenth Century London, ch. 2 (forthcoming in 1985). See also 13 W. Holdsworth, A History of English Law 397-98 (1952).

49 See, e.g., 1 Dictionary of English History 465 (F. Hearnshaw, H. Crew & A. Beales ed. 1928).

50 See generally G. Cohen, Karl Marx's Theory of History: A Defence 119-22 (1978).

among them.[51] The structures of historical periods and the social determinants of historical change are, of course, matters of interpretation, disagreement, and even controversy. But they cannot be analyzed if one's starting point is categories that conceal the problems of historical particularity and change. Had Professor Langbein simply classified offenses as they were classified in law at the time, readers might have been able to judge for themselves the degree to which seventeenth- and eighteenth-century offenses were historically specific.

IV

The Offenders

We now turn to Langbein's reflections upon the offenders. He finds it "hard to find figures worthy of romance, even social romance, among the shop-lifters, pickpockets, pilfering housemaids, and dishonest apprentices who populated the Old Bailey dock."[52] He does not call any of the offenders by name, nor attempt to follow any particular person's case. He does not attempt to recount any of their trials or travails, nor to reconstruct the social determinants of any of their offenses. Nothing could be further from the methods practiced by the authors of *Albion's Fatal Tree* who presented interpretation and analysis through the specific and concrete. For us the naming of names was essential not only for the narrative or the orderly presentation of evidence, but also as an antidote to the "crime of anonymity."

At his most vitriolic, Langbein writes, "to turn these little crooks into class warriors one must wear rose colored glasses of the deepest hue."[53] Neither Hay nor the other authors of *Albion's Fatal Tree* referred to offenders as "class warriors," partly because the authors did not all agree about the theoretical consequences of that phrase, and partly be-

---

51 A good discussion of these principles may be found in M. Bloch, The Historian's Craft 27-35, 181-89 (1953).

52 Langbein, supra note 1, at 100. We need not discuss in detail the differences Langbein chooses to ignore between "romance" and "social history." And if the population of the Old Bailey dock was not "romantic," perhaps there are other qualities that might stimulate our interest, as historians and other writers have recognized. See, e.g., B. Brecht, The Threepenny Opera (D. Vesey & E. Bentley trans. 1964); J. Gay, The Beggar's Opera: A Faithful Reproduction of the 1729 Edition (1961).

53 Langbein, supra note 1, at 101. Langbein's choice of language is additional evidence of his careless, ahistorical approach. It is not until the nineteenth century that "crook" came to mean "criminal"; in the eighteenth century it meant "sixpence." E. Partridge, A Dictionary of the Underworld 163 (3d ed. 1968). See also 2 Oxford English Dictionary 1186-87 (J. Murray ed. 1893) (use of "crook" to refer to a dishonest person or swindler is United States colloquialism dating from 1880's). Langbein's use of language suggests not merely sloppiness, but a tendency to assume that crimes and criminals mean the same things to all people and in all times. This groundless assumption is fundamentally at odds with historical inquiry of a Marxist or any other nature.

cause they knew that to some others it was a red flag that might bait a bull.

But were they "class warriors"? Perhaps so, perhaps not. One cannot tell without actually examining some crimes and their circumstances, which Professor Langbein has chosen not to do. Here we suggest a few lines of inquiry, if only to raise questions about the offenders and to indicate lines of exploration, lines that Professor Langbein shuts off by his conclusory characterizations and by his ahistorical methods of analysis.

During the first part of the October 1754 Sessions at the Old Bailey,[54] forty-two people were indicted and tried. In thirteen of the cases the information is too scanty to suggest much about the social and occupational background of the offender or the circumstances leading him or her to commit the offense. The remaining cases fall easily into groups. Seven offenders were tried for work-related crimes: a journeyman loom-maker who pawned his master's looking-glass, a cellarman who took thirty-two glass bottles and six gallons of white wine he had been entrusted to deliver, a stable boy who stole his master's cropt bay gelding and rode it towards Hounslow, a journeyman pewterer who took three plates from his master, two sailors who took sails and cordage from a vessel moored alongside their own, and a washerwoman's son who said he was returning to his mother's customers the four handkerchiefs he was alleged to have stolen.

Another five offenders at this Session were indicted for residence-related offenses: a waiter who stole his lodging-house neighbor's watch and coins, a husband and wife indicted for stealing linens and other goods from a lodging room let to them by contract, a sixteen- or seventeen-year-old "spinster" who stole some clothes from the keeper of a lodging house, and a lodger who stole a copper stew-pot and some linens from a "lodging room let by contract."

A third group consists of six offenses relating to the ambiguous transactions of sexuality:[55] a spinster who received a silver spoon from a baker's servant who had lain with her in the baker's cellar, a silk-winder who received a silver watch from a journeyman tailor who had lain with her, a scouring maid who took a silver watch from a drunken cabinet-

54 Old Bailey Proceedings, supra note 23, for October 23-28, 1754. Linda Merrill's study of the Old Bailey Proceedings of December 1755 and December 1756 concluded: "The majority of cases in these sessions show that those who were convicted as well as those accused, were working people . . . and that judging by the small amounts stolen it appears that they were selling [the goods] for quick money in an effort to compensate for inadequate wages." (On file at New York University Law Review.)

55 Were these thefts, appropriations, or exchanges? The cases were brought by male prosecutors, some of whom admit that they did or may have "lain with" the female defendants. The offenders assert that the goods were not stolen, but given or taken as compensation for sexual services.

maker who "had stripped [her] naked," a "spinster," alleged to be "one of the most notorious whores in the whole ward," who took a silk handkerchief from a man to lie with him, an army officer's servant girl who took the silver watch of a sergeant in the Chelsea guards in whose bed she had lain, and a woman indicted for stealing silver and linen from a watchman. He said he permitted the offender and her husband to "lie in [his] bed when [he] was out watching." She said the watchman had told her that if her "husband were dead he'd make [her] possess'd of all, and gave her the key of the door," and that he prosecuted her because she "would not leave [her] husband and come and live with him."

Then there is a fourth group of offenders whose crimes took place in the public spaces of London. These include six who were indicted for taking handkerchiefs from people in the streets, two who were said to have stolen from public houses, and three who were alleged to have stolen during a fight in the streets.

Can these offenders be justly characterized as "little crooks" or "class warriors"? A historian, perhaps, is less interested in the labels than in exploring the nature of the offenders and their offenses within their social and historical context. The grouping of the cases—work-related, residence-related, sex-related, and public appropriation—that is suggested by even the most cursory historical investigation suggests a dynamic of class relations that might explain the existence of the offenses as a matter of contingent historical fact. Langbein's ahistorical and tendentious dismissals of the offenses and the offenders as minor, however, obscures any possible historical explanations of the causes of the offenses.

V

Two Offenders in Particular

Examining two cases from the *Old Bailey Proceedings*[56] shows how further investigation might illuminate the circumstances behind the trial records. First is Michael Harris,[57] a shoemaker's apprentice, who was found guilty and sentenced to seven years' transportation for stealing "three pair of callimanco shoes, value 9s., two pair of satten shoes, value 20s., one linen shirt, one lawn neckcloth, and one linen table-cloth." Some of these he allegedly exchanged at a pawnbroker's, and the rest at "Rag Fair." The case suggests several avenues of investigation. We may examine monetary wage rates and discover that these could be below subsistence.[58] English shoemakers fought at least fifteen wage disputes in

[56] Old Bailey Proceedings, supra note 23, for December 4-10, 1755.

[57] See id. at 2 for the record of Harris's trial; id. at 40 for the record of his sentence.

[58] See, e.g., M. George, English Social Life in the Eighteenth Century 19-25 (1923); J. Rule, The Experience of Labour in Eighteenth Century English Industry 61, 124-43 (1981);

the eighteenth century.[59] Employers did not always pay in currency the wages due their employees in this period when little credit was available to small manufacturers and small denominations of coins were often scarce. In many industries workers customarily appropriated certain materials, which were perceived by both worker and master as payments in lieu of monetary wages well into the eighteenth century.[60]

Second, we need to examine the organization of production. In the putting-out system the fabricator could use materials or goods put out to him or her as collateral for raising money or credit for food and fuel until he or she was paid for other, completed work. As the structure of the shoemaking industry changed, this became a serious problem to eighteenth-century London capitalist cordwainers who in 1722 obtained an Act of Parliament to prevent "journeymen shoemakers selling, exchanging or pawning boots, shoes, slippers, cut leather or other materials . . . and for better regulating the said journeymen."[61] Legislation was unsuccessful in blocking this kind of customary appropriation; only the revolutionizing of the mode of production itself, from putting-out to factory production, could remove the physical conditions permitting such customary appropriations.[62]

Third, we might investigate some of the traditions and legends of these "Sons of Crispin." Saints Crispin and Crispinian were brother cobblers, legend ran, who came from Rome. In Paris whence they fled they labored by day as journeyman shoemakers, and by night to make shoes to be given freely to the unshod poor. After their martyrdom, their bones were enshrined in Kent.[63]

This is a single case. On the basis of the trial record we do not know whether Harris was poorly paid or paid at all. It would require other

---

Becker, Property in the Workplace: Labor, Capital, and Crime in the Eighteenth Century British Woolen and Worsted Industry, 69 Va. L. Rev. 1487 (1982). Langbein's readiness to find the defendants "yielding to temptation rather than necessity," Langbein, supra note 1, at 100, is curious but typically ahistorical. He seeks an easy contrast between employed people, who he presumes "yielded to temptation," and the unemployed. Evidence on the customary composition and timing of wages suggests that some working people sometimes earned far less than subsistence wages and that even those who earned living wages may have gone for long periods without income. See, e.g., J. Rule, supra; Becker, supra, at 1494-95.

[59] C. Dobson, Masters and Journeymen: A Prehistory of Industrial Relations 1717-1800, at 24, 154-70 (1980).

[60] Becker, supra note 58, at 1495, 1510. See also M. George, supra note 58; J. Rule, supra note 58.

[61] 9 Geo., ch. 27 (1722). Cf. Becker, supra note 58, at 1496-1500 (criminalization of woolen workers' takings).

[62] See, e.g., Becker, supra note 58, at 1515 (woolen workers); Oppenheim, The Royal Dockyards, in 2 The Victoria History of Counties of England 336, 347, 351, 374 (W. Page ed. 1926) (stockyard workers).

[63] Butler's Lives of the Saints 197-98 (H. Thurston & D. Attwater rev. ed. 1956) (1st ed. London 1756-1759).

types of historical evidence to find out. Edgar Furniss drew a conclusion about this period which suggests that the English laborer may have needed to take goods to survive: "for no considerable period did he receive much more than subsistence wages and for certain stretches of time his money wages were insufficient to supply him with the barest essentials of physical existence."[64] Was Harris's survival at stake? As the historian begins to ask such questions, evidence can accumulate until the "case" is no longer merely an example proving a point, or a datum composing statistics, or even a defendant requiring a judge to apply a statute or rule. With investigation a "case" can, if the historian is willing to listen, take on a life of its own that may, if the historian will explore, illuminate far more than this or that point, statistic, precept, or statute.

Our second case is that of Samuel Boroughs, who was sentenced to seven years' transportation for stealing ten pounds' weight of linen yarn, value twenty shillings, from his master, Josias Deponthien, a partner in a commercial firm which imported linen from Germany and owned three large warehouses.[65] Boroughs was one of the porters who made up bales and loaded them into carts. His case is interesting because it makes the ambiguities of the class relationships more explicit. Boroughs said that several years before the trial his master gave him "a whole fatt [vat] of damaged yarn; it was often troublesome, and the servants used to throw it up on heaps."[66] Boroughs found that by tediously picking through this damaged yarn, he could find yarn good enough to sell at a dye-house. The master said he had given Boroughs fourteen or fifteen hundredweight of yarn that had been so damaged by bad weather that it "stunk like poison, and was rotten, which we tried skain by skain; some by shaking with a jerk, the ends would fly out, and discover them to be rotten; the others we pulled by twenty, thirty, or more threads at a time, and all that broke: we flung the skain down."[67]

As to the yarn Boroughs was accused of "stealing," he first said he had it from Deponthien's footman, and later that he had it from the firm's bookkeeper. Numerous witnesses, including two former employers, attested to Borough's honesty and industry. The trial records do not tell us how the employer paid the footman or the porter.

Boroughs said there were six good bundles of yarn, four of them sold at six shillings each, a figure that might be equivalent to between two or three weeks' wages.[68] Such "gifts" in an age of incomplete monetiza-

[64] E. Furniss, The Position of the Laborer in a System of Nationalism: A Study of the Labor Theorists of the Later English Mercantilists 24 (1920).

[65] Old Bailey Proceedings, supra note 23, for December 4-10, 1755, at 6-9, 40.

[66] Id. at 8.

[67] Id. at 7.

[68] See J. Rule, supra note 58, at 49-70.

tion of material transactions have a way of becoming customary over time. In other trades, we know, they were fundamental: "cabbage" to tailors, "vails" to servants, "birrs" to leather workers, "chips" to shipwrights, "sockings" to tobacco porters, "sweepings" to sugar lumpers, "wastages" to coopers, "thrums" to weavers—the lexicon of appropriation was as extensive as the names of the trades. Today such appropriations are "perquisites" or "shrinkage." Sometimes they are useful to employers, sometimes to employees. In the eighteenth century the evidence mounts suggesting that they were decisive to the class relationships.[69]

The growth of that evidence permits us to search for similar leads in the cases of Harris and Boroughs. What was regarded by the court as a felony may have been regarded by others as "usages of the trade." Even if it were positively discovered that neither Harris nor Boroughs was appropriating in a customary way, as a harvester might her gleanings or a forester his lops and tops, that would still not mean that, objectively or economically, Harris and Boroughs were not "class warriors." Nobody wishes to be a "class warrior" or to have to fight tooth and nail for subsistence. Eighteenth-century society forced millions of people to such positions where they had to fight by every means necessary. The aggregation of such struggles caused employers, legislators, capitalists—in short, the "elite"—to respond and to fight back.

In sum, Langbein's analysis of the offenders and their offenses is moralizing and unsympathetic.[70] His emphasis on "lay" categories causes him to overlook fundamental novelties in the material conditions of production and circulation (wage labor and the commodity-form), and to write about the law in such general terms that he forgets its historical determinants. His method of categorization and statistical presentation lends itself to such omissions, oversights, and errors. He writes, "[i]n my data we do not see offenses that exemplify the advance of pre-industrial capitalism."[71] But he could have seen much more in his "data" had he arranged it in less conclusory categories, or had he actually become interested in the people who were tried.

69 See, e.g., R. Malcolmson, Life and Labour in England, 1700-1780, at 54-58 (1981); Linebaugh, Soc'y for the Study of Lab. Hist. Bull., No. 25, Autumn 1972, at 11, 13. See also authorities cited in note 58 supra.

70 I suspect that this part of Langbein's argument is directed less against Hay than it is the other essays, because Hay actually considers law as a whole, and not in those parts directly affecting the *modus operandi* of such eighteenth-century workshops as Harris or Boroughs worked in.

71 Langbein, supra note 1, at 99.

VI

THE JURY AND JURORS

Langbein charges Hay with underemphasizing the importance of jury discretion, finding that Hay's "theory of ruling class conspiracy is impossible to reconcile with the reality of jury discretion."[72] He describes methods by which London juries rendered "partial verdicts"[73] —by finding defendants guilty of lesser offenses than those charged, or by "down-valuing" the monetary expression of stolen goods.

The introduction of the sentence of transportation[74] and the emphasis on exchange value as the principal legal consideration in sentencing[75] made down-charging a frequent device in the eighteenth century.

The rendering of partial verdicts used to be called "pious perjury." Its ameliorative effects on the harshness of the law are well known.[76] Though there is much that might be learned from an examination of these partial verdicts,[77] Professor Langbein does not analyze them, but instead suggests that the simple use of "pious perjury" refutes Hay's thesis.

> If I were going to organize a ruling-class conspiracy to use the criminal law to terrorize the lower orders, I would not interpose autonomous bodies of non-conspirators like the petty juries. If, on the other hand, I were going to reckon the jurors among my conspirators, I would be troubled that they were so predictably humane by the standards of the day.[78]

This extraordinary passage requires several responses. First, Langbein's implication that jurors were not drawn from the elite classes is clearly inaccurate. Professor Schwarz has shown that less than five percent of eighteenth-century Londoners possessed taxable incomes exceeding two hundred pounds and that at least three-quarters of the popu-

---

72 Id. at 106.

73 On partial verdicts, see, e.g., Beattie, Crime and the Courts in Surrey, 1736-1753, in Crime in England, 1500-1800, supra note 15, at 155, 171-72.

74 An act for the further preventing robbery, burglary, and other felonies, and for the more effectual transportation of felons, and unlawful exporters of wool; and for declaring the law upon some points related to pirates (Piracy Act), 4 Geo., ch. 11, § 1 (1717) (those formerly entitled to benefit of clergy to be transported for seven years; those excluded from benefit of clergy may be transported for fourteen years at the discretion of the monarch), repealed by 7 & 8 Geo. 4, ch. 27, § 1 (1827).

75 See text accompanying notes 47-50 supra.

76 See, e.g., 1 L. Radzinowicz, supra note 34, at 94-97.

77 It would be interesting to know, for example, whether members of particular groups, such as young, female, or first offenders, were more likely to receive partial verdicts, whether their incidence correlated with the use-value of stolen goods, whether the characteristics of the juror, such as age, status, or past jury service, appear to have played any role.

78 Langbein, supra note 1, at 107.

lation had incomes of less than sixty pounds a year.[79] After 1730 only householders who owned estates of more than one hundred pounds were qualified to serve on London juries;[80] a leasehold of more than fifty pounds qualified a man for service on a Middlesex jury.[81] It is clear that at least the London jury pool was drawn from a small portion of the population—small and propertied.[82] On grounds strictly of income and wealth, without considering other evidence, it is misleading to suggest that such a jury was "autonomous."

Second, and more fundamentally, Langbein's strange framing of the issues precludes reasoned analysis. Langbein seems to envision a black-and-white choice: jurors were either "nonconspirators" or "coconspirators," either "autonomous" or possessing interests identical to those of the most elite. Langbein's simplistic dichotomy does not respond to Hay's more subtle analysis. Hay does not argue that the social status of jurors was identical to that of magistrates and judges, but rather that they were on a continuum defined by property whose social relations imposed dependency and clientage upon lesser property holders.[83]

It is symptomatic of Langbein's tendency to ignore or oversimplify the complex conflicts and interrelationships between classes that he finds in the verdicts of these allegedly class-neutral juries evidence that the "property crimes that were of major consequence in the workload of eighteenth century criminal courts . . . were those about whose blameworthiness there was a moral consensus that knew no class lines."[84] Langbein can make this statement only by ignoring the obvious: the jury was composed of a small, propertied portion of the population whose interests were more closely allied with those of the most elite class than

---

79 Schwarz, Social Class and Social Geography: The Middle Classes in London at the End of the Eighteenth Century, 7 Soc. Hist. 167, 167-69 (1982).

80 An Act for the better regulation of juries, 3 Geo. 2, ch. 25, §§ 19-20 (1731) (local statute, date of repeal unclear).

81 An act to explain and amend an act made in the third year of his Majesty's reign, intituled [sic], An act for the better regulation of juries, so far as the same relates to the county of Middlesex, 4 Geo. 2, ch. 7, § 3 (1731), repealed by 6 Geo. 4, ch. 50, § 62 (1825).

82 Property qualifications for jury service survived well into the twentieth century in England. As late as 1956, Sir Patrick Devlin remarked: "[I]t is an odd thing that if you stopped several men in the street or held up the Clapham omnibus while you interrogated the passengers, you would very likely find that only a few of them were qualified to serve as jurors." P. Devlin, Trial By Jury 17 (3d ed. 1966).

83 This pattern of dependency of the lesser propertied classes upon the wealthier, established elite has been demonstrated in areas of credit, taxation, and politics, see, e.g., Schwarz, supra note 79, at 167-69, and it is likely that its effects spilled over into the courtroom as well. See also Rogers, Money, Land and Lineage: The Big Bourgeoise of Hanoverian London, 4 Soc. Hist. 437 (1979) (discussing how the system of clientage united the rich, plutocratic bourgeoisie, whose "fortunes ranged from tens of thousands to perhaps millions of pounds," with the gentry).

84 Langbein, supra note 1, at 108.

with those of the working class that supplied the majority of offenders.[85] Langbein has no evidence on which to judge the participation of the working classes in this "moral consensus."

A third observation about Langbein's imaginary scenario relates to his perception that the jury was "predictably humane." He reports that one-third of the defendants were acquitted, another third or so transported, and only those engaged in truly serious crimes, such as livestock theft, or suspected of group criminality routinely sentenced to death. Was this "humaneness"? Surely we cannot expect any system to convict or execute all of the offenders, and Langbein suggests no other standard against which we might compare his statistics. In addition, we might pause before accepting the assertion that transportation, which subjected often petty offenders to at least seven years of indentured servitude in a disease-ridden colony thousands of miles from their homes and families, was "humane."[86] We might also consider whether the "humane" sentence of transportation served other needs of the elite. Perhaps the death penalty permitted them to do away with those criminals who they thought were most dangerous while transportation allowed them to rid themselves of the less dangerous characters and supply the labor needed to build their colonies across the sea. Without contemplating such possibilities, how can Professor Langbein suggest that the criminal law protected the poor as well as the rich from evils they all agreed upon?

A fourth comment arises from Langbein's style of expression—"if I were going to organize a ruling-class conspiracy"—which connotes a historical perspective that consigns itself to failure by the very narrowness with which it perceives the issue. No single person or group organized eighteenth-century class forces or created the jury, an institution whose development spanned many centuries.

We cannot understand the theory and practice of the eighteenth-century jury or the rhetoric of freedom to which it belonged if we limit ourselves to the terms that Professor Langbein offers us and the incomplete evidence he explores. An understanding of the eighteenth-century jury must be broad enough to handle contradiction, and Professor Langbein's rigid categories are incapable of doing this. On the one hand, the jury was neither democratic nor egalitarian in its social composition and it was manipulated by the ruling class; on the other hand, it was a bulwark of freedom in its potential and in the rhetoric used to defend it.

---

85 See generally Beattie, supra note 73.

86 For many convicts, transportation was a de facto death sentence. Ordinary felons were customarily chained below the deck during the entire voyage. An average of 15% perished on board, with the death rate reaching 30 or 40% on certain voyages. A.E. Smith, supra note 6, at 125-26. Many of those who survived the grueling voyage succumbed to "colonial fever" within days or weeks. Id. at 5-6.

As dependent small property holders—master craftsmen, inn-keepers, grocers, cattle dealers and the like—the jurors were corruptible by those more powerful on the continuum of property.[87] This was recognized in statutes, such as an act of 1730 which stated, "Whereas many evil Practices have been used in corrupting of Jurors . . . and many Neglects and Abuses have happened in making of the Lists of Freeholders."[88] "Special juries"[89] were impaneled for special cases, such as for the trials of the Windsor Blacks[90] and political dissenters,[91] in order to be especially compliant. An act of 1751 stated that "great and extravagant Fees [had been] paid to Jurymen" and prohibited judges from paying jurors more than one pound one shilling.[92] The venality of jurors was an object of spleen in the most popular of English books, *Pilgrim's Progress*. In a trial presided over by "Lord Hate-good," the accused was convicted of violating statutes of Pharaoh, Nebuchadnezzar, and Darius, and condemned to die by a jury consisting of "Mr. Blind-man, Mr. No-good, Mr. Malice, Mr. Love-lust, Mr. Live-loose, Mr. Heady, Mr. High Mind, Mr. Enmity, Mr. Lyar, Mr. Cruelty, Mr. Hate-light, and Mr. Implacable."[93]

The most persuasive advocates of the jury system criticized its corruptions. Sir John Hawles, a prominent seventeenth-century lawyer, wrote *The Englishman's Right: A Dialogue Between a Barrister at Law and a Juryman*,[94] whose plain and gentle style may partly explain its frequent republication. On the problem of jury corruption Hawles observed:

> There are some make a trade of being Jurymen; that seek for the office; use means to be constantly continued in it; will not give a disobliging

[87] Roberts, Jury Vetting in the Seventeenth Century, 32 Hist. Today 25, 26 (1982) (describing rampant corruption of the juries in the century preceding this study).

[88] An Act for the Better Regulation of Juries, 3 Geo. 2, ch. 25, § 1 (1730) (local statute, date of repeal unclear).

[89] The special jury was composed of citizens of a higher social station or of those deemed to have expertise in the subject matter of particular civil cases. W. Cornish, The Jury 31 (1968). Now used only in special kinds of civil cases, it was used during the eighteenth century in criminal trials as well. Id. at 32-33. Nineteenth-century reformers recognized the special jury as a vehicle for abuse and manipulation, see, e.g., J. Bentham, The Elements of the Art of Packing, as applied to special Juries, particularly in Cases of Libel Law (London 1821).

[90] See E.P. Thompson, Whigs and Hunters: The Origins of the Black Act 74, 78 (1975). The Windsor Blacks were a loose confederation of largely laborers and apprentices who defied a 1723 capital statute and continued their customary practice of hunting deer in Windsor Forest. Whenever packed juries failed to convict the Blacks, the trials were moved to London and conducted before "jurys of men of probity and well enclined towards their Kings and country's service and interest." Id. at 151 (quoting letter from D. DeFaye, Secretary to the Lords Justices, to Viscount Townshend, Oct. 1, 1783).

[91] See, e.g., W. Cornish, supra note 89, at 32, 131.

[92] An Act for the Better Regulation of Trials by Jury, 24 Geo. 2, ch. 18, § 2 (1751).

[93] J. Bunyan, Pilgrim's Progress 153 (J. Wharey ed. 1969) (1st ed. London 1678).

[94] J. Hawles, The Englishman's Right: A Dialogue, between a Barrister at Law and a Juryman (London 1793) (1st ed. London 1680).

> verdict, lest they should be discharged, and serve no more: these standing Jurors have certainly some ill game to play. There are others that hope to signalize themselves, to get a better trade, or some preferment by serving a turn.[95]

Such "standing jurors" may have been those who dominated the other jurors and "rashly deliver[ed] their opinions; and all the rest, in respect to their supposed gravity, and experience, or because they ha[d] the biggest estates, or to avoid the trouble of disputing the point, or to prevent the spoiling of dinner by delay, or some such weighty reason, forthwith agree[d] blindfold . . . ."[96]

Other jurors succumbed to the judges' admonitions and instructions. According to Hawles, "slavish fear" induced them "to eccho back, what the bench would have done."[97]

To the statutory evidence and the testimony of Hawles we may add a statistic that should be understood in the context of the other evidence. My study of thirty-eight different jury panels in London between 1714 and 1717 reveals that an average of two jurors on the City panels had served at least once before. On the panel in Middlesex, the county jurisdiction of the London suburbs in which many poor and working-class citizens lived, more than one-half of the "good men and true," an average of 6.6 to be exact, had sat on the jury at least once before.[98] This evidence of the existence of professional jurors is only an indication of the system of clientage and manipulation ("vetting") that operated at the Old Bailey. London jurors were impaneled from a small but propertied portion of the population, and within that propertied portion their selection was neither random nor disinterested, but mercenary, venal, and corrupt.[99]

Yet the jury was a "bank," holding in "an ocean of oppression," as Hawles said.[100] It was, to quote two authorities on the modern jury, "the one institution . . . which stands between the people and abuse of authority by the state."[101] The jurors' honesty, independence, and impartiality were continuously encouraged in the libertarian rhetoric of the eighteenth century. Occasionally the jury's power was exercised with

[95] Id. at 32. See also W. Cornish, supra note 89, at 131-32 ("regular special jurors . . . lived off the guinea which each case brought, and . . . knew that continuance of this stipend depended on bringing in a verdict for the crown").

[96] J. Hawles, supra note 94, at 31.

[97] Id.

[98] The names of the petty jurors were printed in the Old Bailey Proceedings, supra note 23. My study involved comparing lists between the specified years. See also Beattie, supra note 73, at 165 ("any one jury would be likely to contain a few men with some previous experience").

[99] See generally Roberts, supra note 87.

[100] J. Hawles, supra note 94, at 7.

[101] National Jury Project, Jurywork: Systematic Techniques x (E. Krauss & B. Bonora 2d ed. 1984).

courage and fortitude. This rhetoric of freedom flourished especially in the "Wilkes and Liberty" years[102] and in the 1790's.[103] The jury's protection under Magna Carta and the Declaration of Rights, its associations with pre-Norman England, and its centrality to the complex notions of "the Englishman's birthright" distinguished England to the eighteenth-century contemporaries from arbitrary government and despotism.

There is no adequate historical and analytical study of the eighteenth-century English jury, so at this point it would be premature—for me or for Professor Langbein—to draw conclusions; a fuller exploration of the moving contradiction between the limited social basis of the jury and some of the rhetoric of liberty will have to wait.

VII

Sources of Law

Professor Langbein's treatment of law as institution and theory underscores the shortcomings of his brand of narrow legal scholarship. Langbein stresses elements of continuity, suggesting that law in the Middle Ages, in the eighteenth century, and in our own time played the stable role of protecting both rich and poor from a well-defined criminal element. His analysis of law, custom, and the jury's role not only distorts Hay's central arguments, but reveals the limits of his own static, narrowly functionalist approach.

Langbein finds weak and speculative Hay's assertion that eighteenth-century juries, had they been more democratically composed, might have refused to return convictions in certain prosecutions, especially for theft.[104] Ordinary citizens no less than the elite, Langbein asserts, wanted to punish thieves. To prove his point, he cites a study of twentieth-century American juries that demonstrates, in his view, that these juries, "long since democratized and freed of property qualifications," are not "hostile to the law of larceny."[105] In reading back into

102 See G. Rude, Wilkes & Liberty 28, 30 (1962).

103 London juries acquitted numerous political dissenters indicted during periods of oppression, both in the 1790's and the 1810's. See, e.g., E.P. Thompson, The Making of the English Working Class 19, 80, 468, 721-22 (1963). Thompson found the jury system, along with the political opposition led by Lord Fox, the "last defence of English liberties." Id. at 165. See also W. Cornish, supra note 89, at 129-31.

104 See Langbein, supra note 1, at 107-08; Hay, supra note 16, at 38-39.

105 Langbein, supra note 1, at 108 (citing H. Kalven & H. Zeisel, The American Jury 76-77 (1966)). Even apart from its ahistorical application, the Kalven and Zeisel study lends Langbein only tenuous support at best. Kalven and Zeisel remark that "[t]here is no crime category in which the jury is totally at war with the law . . . as it is said to have been in the eighteenth century with respect to prosecutions for seditious libel." H. Kalven & J. Zeisel, supra, at 76. First, this conclusion addresses wholesale nullification, whereas Hay claims only

eighteenth-century England contemporary American conceptions of the jury, Langbein both fails to rebut Hay's point and neglects crucial features of the early modern jury.[106] First, it was true then as it is now that juries had the power to deliver general verdicts, which could not be refused by the court.[107] Because this power requires that the jury draw a conclusion from a legal major premise in conjunction with a factual minor premise,[108] juries have long been said to have the power to decide the law as well as the facts.[109] Under the doctrine of jury nullification, juries are said to have not only the power but the *right* to judge the law as well as the facts. In the modern-day United States the controversy has been whether juries are entitled to an instruction from the judge as to their power to decide the law;[110] it was settled in England that they were not.[111]

No precise analogy to the contemporary debate about jury nullification is available in the context of the eighteenth-century criminal trial.

---

that a more democratic jury might not have convicted. Second, failure to nullify is not the same as wholehearted support. Third, Kalven and Zeisel's ultimate conclusion, that "[w]hat is required is the inspection of the individual case. . . . [T]he approach by way of analyzing crime categories, as such, was a mistake," id. at 76-77, is congenial to the approach of *Albion's Fatal Tree*.

Even without the reference to Kalven and Zeisel, Langbein's quarrel with Hay rests on simple mystification. Langbein gives away the game when he observes that it is not obvious that "the English poor of the eighteenth century generally condoned the theft of livestock and victuals, and Hay does not produce evidence that they did." Langbein, supra note 1, at 108. Hay is of course committed to no such claim. It suffices to show that the definition of *theft* was up for grabs in the eighteenth century because the very concepts of property and possession were in flux. Thus a jury selected democratically, in the absence of property qualifications, would likely take a different view of what constituted theft, see Hay, supra note 16, at 38 (quoting T. Gisbourne, An Enquiry into the Duties of Men in the Higher and Middle Classes of Society in Great Britain 284 n.b (1974)), from jurors selected under actual eighteenth-century property qualifications.

106 Indeed, Langbein's charge that Hay underestimates the power of jury discretion, Langbein, supra note 1, at 105-06, sits ill with his own delvings into the Old Bailey sources in The Criminal Trial before the Lawyers, 45 U. Chi. L. Rev. 263 (1978), which suggest that Hay is, if anything, overenthusiastic about the power of juries during this period to acquit against the judge's will.

107 See, e.g., 1 G. Duncombe, Trials per Pais: or, the Law of England Concerning Juries by Nisi Prius, &c. 283 (8th ed. London 1766) (1st ed. London 1665) (marginal squib); Howe, Juries as Judges of the Criminal Law, 52 Harv. L. Rev. 582, 583 (1939).

108 See, e.g., J. Hawles, supra note 94, at 30-32 & n.*.

109 Thus, for example, Duncombe speaks of juries "tak[ing] upon them the Knowledge of the Law." G. Duncombe, supra note 107, at 230. Cf. An Examination into the Rights and Duties of Jurors 2 (London 1785) (author's view that libel juries should be restricted to factual questions "opposes the general voice" and "carr[ies] an air of novelty").

110 See, e.g., Scheflin, Jury Nullification: The Right to Say No, 45 S. Cal. L. Rev. 168 (1972).

111 See, e.g., Howe, supra note 107, at 583 ("[I]t is probably the sound view, at common law, that this power of the jury in criminal cases does not and did not, in any distinct and modern sense, import a right on their part to determine the law.") (quoting J. Thayer, Preliminary Treatise on Evidence 169, 256 (1898)).

Langbein himself gives the simple reason: jury instructions of any kind were practically nonexistent at the typical Old Bailey trial, so that the question of the jury's right to an instruction about its power to acquit against the law scarcely arose.[112]

But for several reasons there was also no need for any such instruction. First, jury panels at the Old Bailey contained a surprisingly high proportion of repeaters.[113] Such semiprofessional jurors were familiar through repetition with the relevant criminal statutes. What was most needed from jurors was not bookish law, but "first, understanding to know your duty; and, in the next place, courage and resolution to practice it with impartiality and integrity, free from accursed bribery and malice or (what is full as bad in the end) base and servile fear."[114]

Far more importantly, in an age before the transition to a statutory criminal law was complete, the bulk of the law was known to every potential juror.[115] Recent historical scholarship has demonstrated the strong roots eighteenth-century English law had in the community's customs, that is, in recognized patterns of work, compensation, distribution, marriage, and culture.[116] Practices adhered to and honored by common

---

[112] Langbein, supra note 106, at 284. At least one defendant used his opportunity to address the jury to remind the jury of its power:

> [The jurors] I again declare by the law of England, are the conservators and sole judges of my life, having inherent in them alone the judicial power of the law, as well as fact: you judges that sit there being no more, if they please, but cyphers to pronounce the sentence, or their clerks to say Amen to them: being at the best in your original, but the Norman Conqueror's intruders. . . . And therefore I desire you to know your power, and consider your duty both to God, to me, to your ownselves, and to your country.

4 J. Howell, State Trials 1270, 1395 (London 1816) (quoting J. Lilburne, tried for treason in 1642).

[113] See note 98 and accompanying text supra.

[114] J. Hawles, supra note 94, at 2.

[115] Morris Arnold very acutely makes the point for the medieval jury:

> Positive legislation played a very small part in medieval law . . . custom, derived from shared societal assumptions, was the legal norm, not what some sovereign or his agent decreed. Law . . . was less law than life . . . . It would, of course, be a long time before the law of England became a learned law; it was not taught in the universities because as to much of it there was no need. Why teach life when all one had to do was simply to live it? For the same reason that law did not need to be taught it also did not, in the ordinary case, need to be told to jurors; likewise jurors would have no need to inquire of professionals. Custom, or a "logical" extension of custom, only dimly, if at all, perceived as different from a concrete, natural, and inevitable fact, bottomed on the bedrock of universal acceptance, will supply the answer.

Arnold, Law and Fact in the Medieval Jury Trial: Out of Sight, Out of Mind, 18 Am. J. Legal Hist. 267, 279 (1974). Although statutes certainly had gained a significant role by the eighteenth century, Arnold's explanation provides some insight into eighteenth- as well as fourteenth- and fifteenth-century juries.

[116] See, e.g., C. Fisher, Custom, Work and Market Capitalism: the Forest of Dean Colliers, 1788-1888, at vii (1981) ("To study customs, the social and economic relationships in which they have been embedded and the ways in which the body of custom has been altered over time, is to achieve an insight into the fundamental relations of property, production and law in

law courts over centuries gave rise to legal rights with which the sovereign could not interfere. This concept of customary rights had a profound constitutional dimension, lying at the core of the three great documents that embody the principle of parliamentary constraint on royal prerogative: Magna Carta, the Petition of Right and the Bill of Rights.

Against this backdrop the power of the eighteenth-century jury to decide questions of law takes on a significance unappreciated by Langbein. Jurors, more knowledgeable about and sensitive to custom than were judges, were in a superior position to judge the law. Here the existence of the property qualification becomes crucial. Jurors drawn from the limited pool available to the Old Bailey owned property. Unlike many criminal defendants, they had a relatively ample "margin of survival," and were not driven to crime by continual or occasional necessity. Many were employed laborers or servants, and thus had economic interests directly opposed to those of the propertyless. The groups that benefited from new definitions of property were, in short, those who were represented on juries while those who suffered were excluded by property requirements. As such they stood arrayed in their class interests: those on the juries against those in the dock. It would not have been in the interest of such as Deponthien to have vouchsafed legal recognition to the custom of fatting we examined in the case of Boroughs.[117] It is scarcely surprising that in the transition to an industrial economy such customs fell by the wayside. This example illustrates that the law, or rather the question of which customs would become codified, was unsettled. Can it seriously be doubted that jury panels composed of workers such as Boroughs would have found differently in the fatting case, giving legal sanction to the custom of fatting? It would, after all, have been in their own interest to do so. This is the meaning of Hay's point that a more democratic jury might not have convicted: a more democratic jury might not have been worse disposed toward the law of larceny, but would have allotted the law of larceny a different content. It might have interpreted that law, for example, as not containing sanctions against fatting. Or, had such a jury confronted a statute that on its face forbade

---

a society."). In the case of the coal miners of the Forest of Dean, a customary right to title over coal was taken away by statute in the nineteenth century. For other discussion of the importance of customary appropriations and their transformation into criminal offenses, see generally Becker, supra note 58, at 1514-15:

> While labor's takings were transformed from a customary right (or, at most, a private harm) into a public wrong, dismissal of workers in disregard of standard terms and reduction of their wages or rates below established minimums were transformed from public harms into accepted practices. A transformation of what were deemed protected rights reflected and hastened the development of a capitalist society and economy.

117 See text accompanying notes 65-69 supra.

fatting, it might have recognized the customary status of ambiguous transactions such as the one we have described, in effect shifting the burden of proof to the propertied party that the transaction was indeed a statutory offense against property rather than, for example, a gift.

Langbein writes of "the conceptual impoverishment of the substantive [criminal] law."[118] He bemoans the "underdevelopment of the scientific side of English law," which helped make it "ill-equipped" to handle the transition from common law to statute law.[119] English law, he complains, lacked generality and "scientific sophistication."[120] These remarks clearly indicate a preference for laws that are clear commands serving the values of certainty and predictability. Langbein's is an elite, hermetic theory of law, masked as "professionalism." It makes few, if any, allowances for procedures, ideas, or judgments that do not spring from the "legal mind." It ignores the source of law most central to eighteenth-century English society.

Inasmuch as custom was fundamental at all levels of the debate about eighteenth-century society, whether about the law, production, or the family, it cannot be surprising that Langbein's narrow view of historical inquiry is incapable of leading him to other subjects of social life. As a consequence, Langbein ignores the most significant aspect of the jury: it was—at least potentially—a profound democratic check upon the arbitrary authority of the state, which could be exercised either capriciously or in the name of "scientific sophistication."

VIII
Garbage

The conclusion of Langbein's attack reverts to the question of sanitation with which, in his expressed doubts about the possibility of a Marxist interpretation of the flush toilet, it began. He may intend a kind of retentive wit by raising this question, but because it is among the most revealing and interesting parts of his essay, we may treat it seriously. He writes:

> The criminal law is simply the wrong place to look for the active hand of the ruling classes. From the standpoint of the rulers, I would suggest, the criminal justice system occupies a place not much more central than the garbage collection system. True, if the garbage is not collected the society cannot operate and ruling class goals will be frustrated, but that does not turn garbage collection into a ruling-class

118 Langbein, supra note 1, at 117.

119 Id.

120 Id. at 118.

conspiracy.[121]

Just how central was the garbage collection system? Were we to bisect a map of eighteenth-century London[122] on both its axes, we would find ourselves in a location that was indeed central to both the criminal justice and the garbage collection systems. The main workhouse, the Bridewell, and the largest debtors' prison, the Fleet, were near the Fleet "River" (as it once had been) or "Ditch" (as it had become), which carried garbage and sewage through the center of the city to the River Thames.[123] The Old Bailey lay close by the slaughterhouses and meat markets, which were a huge and constant source of entrails and offal or "pudding."[124] These wastes were carted down Pudding Lane which, at the midpoint of London, fed Dung Wharf and Puddle Dock, two stinking, insalubrious places, with the human and animal wastes of London.[125] The intimate proximity of the prisons and courts to dung and "pudding" in the literal center of London supports Langbein's comparison.

The garbage collection system was also a central concern of municipal policy. An ordinance "For Preserving and Ordering the Streets of London Against Annoyances" described in elaborate detail the urban regulation of sewage and waste.[126]

---

121 Id. at 119. Langbein argues that the criminal law is only important "at the *margins* of social life." Id. (quoting Sparks, A Critique of Marxist Criminology, in 2 Crime and Justice: An Annual Review of Research 159, 193 (1980)). In fact, Langbein takes this quotation out of context. Though Sparks does disagree with *Albion's Fatal Tree* on some points, he explicitly finds "Hay's and Thompson's arguments as to the ideological importance of the criminal law in England in the early eighteenth century . . . convincing." Sparks, supra, at 192.

122 See, e.g., Jean Rocques's mid-eighteenth-century map, reprinted in J. Rocque, The A to Z of Georgian London (1982).

123 M. George, supra note 58, at 86; P. Jones, The Butchers of London 78 (1976). Indeed, during the sixteenth-century reconstruction of the Old Bailey, the headquarters of the criminal justice system, it was decided to cover the Fleet Ditch, making it one of the first modern underground sewers. T. McLaughlin, Dirt: A Social History As Seen Through the Uses and Abuses of Dirt 60 (1971).

124 P. Jones, supra note 123, at 83-99.

125 In a seventeenth-century poem, Ben Jonson observed that these parts of the Thames were so thick that a boat's oars could not stir the slime that

> Belch'd forth an ayre, as hot,
> as at a muster
> Of all your night-tubs, when the
> carts doe cluster,
> Who shall discharge first his
> merd-urinous load.

B. Jonson, On the Famous Voyage (Epigramme 133), quoted in T. McLaughlin, supra note 123, at 61.

126 For example:

> Goung-Fermour shall not carry any Ordure till after Nine of the clock in the Night.
> No Goung-Fermour shall spill any Ordure in the Street.
> The Pudding Cart of the Shambles shall not go afore the Hour of Nine in the Night.

Eighteenth-century Londoners lived close to animals, which were essential to their diet and transportation; sewage clogged their streets and rivers; the disposal of human and animal wastes was a central problem. Amid this picture of filth and stench, however, we should consider the observation of a historian of dirt: "Dirt is evidence of the imperfections of life, a constant reminder of change and decay. It is the dark side of all human activities—human, because it is only in our judgements that things are dirty: there is no such material as *absolute* dirt."[127] The eighteenth-century London elite sought to avoid some of these imperfections by using perfume, living indoors, riding in coaches and chairs, and wearing high patterns, all devices designed in part to elevate the elite from urban "wastes" or conceal wastes from them. For the mass of the people, however, these devices were unaffordable luxuries, so dirt was very much a part of their lives. For many working class people, wastes were essential. Nightsoil men and dung farmers earned their livings recycling London's animal and human wastes by removing them to Pimlico and Victoria to replenish the vegetable garden and orchard soils.[128] The mudlarks derived their livings from coal wastes.[129] Recall the case of Boroughs:[130] what was waste to Deponthien was life to Boroughs. As one author has written, "Nature admits no waste. Nothing is left over; everything is joined in the spiral of life."[131]

In the eighteenth century, that spiral became the source of satire directed against refined society. Swift's Yahoos shitting from the tree tops[132] are perhaps the central picture in his "excremental vision." Hogarth's "The Four Times of Day" depicts Sir Thomas DeVeil, a police magistrate, wincing as a urine bowl is emptied on his head from a window above.[133] It is tempting to examine Langbein's analogy in the same spirit: to compare the "Ordure Bole" to the watchman's lock-up, "jakes" (privies) to the magistrate's examining rooms, "laystalls" (dung and refuse piles) to the Old Bailey and the nitrogenuous properties of

> No Man shall cast any Urine-Boles, or Ordure Boles into the Streets by Day or Night, afore . . . Nine in the Night: And also he shall not cast it out, but bring it down, and lay it in the Channel.

Quoted in W. Bohun, Privilegia Londini; Or the Rights, Liberties, Privileges, Laws and Customs of the City of London 108, 109, 111 (3d ed. London 1723). See also P. Jones, supra note 123, at 91-103 (regulation of slaughterhouse and markets).

127 T. McLaughlin, supra note 123, at 1.

128 Id. at 97.

129 Henry Mayhew described this underside of the fuel economy in 2 H. Mayhew, London Labour and the London Poor 173 (1968).

130 See text accompanying notes 65-69 supra.

131 See S. Van der Ryn, The Toilet Papers: Designs to Recycle Human Waste and Water 5 (1978).

132 J. Swift, 11 The Works of Jonathan Swift 272-73 (2d ed. 1883)(1st ed. London 1726).

133 1 R. Paulson, Hogarth: His Life, Art and Times 402 (1971).

excrementa. But satiric treatment of the analogy might belittle other relations implied by Langbein's insight.

The lectures that Adam Smith delivered in Glasgow in the early 1760's, which became a basis for portions of his *Wealth of Nations*, began with a description of the objects of law: justice, police, revenue, and arms. "Police" was not yet a common English word; it was French and associated with despotism, so Smith reminded his listeners of its Greek derivation, meaning "civil government," and divided it into its three "objects":

> cleanliness, security, and cheapness or plenty. The two former, to wit, the proper method of carrying dirt from the streets, and the execution of justice, so far as it regards regulations for preventing crimes or the method of keeping a city guard, though useful, are too mean to be considered in a general discourse of this kind.[134]

Garbage disposal and crime prevention are two of the basic components of civil government, but they are "too mean to be considered." Dirt and crime are both central and mean, inescapable yet not fit for discourse. Professor Langbein apparently seeks to resolve a similar ambivalence by irony. Yet why are dirt and crime "mean" or unfit for a "general discourse"?

Human waste played an important role in the relationship between the classes. Norbert Elias argues that civilization is only a history of increasing the mediations between the necessary productions of the body and interactions with others.[135] The handkerchief, the nightdress, and the fork exemplify the technology of these mediations.[136] Such buffers against bodily activities and other persons were both a form of class differentiation and a means of denying humanity to others, who could be seen in terms of "garbage," "dirt," or "scum." In challenging Marxists to a history of the flush toilet, Professor Langbein may have been joking, but in light of Elias's thesis, we may treat the suggestion more seriously than it perhaps was intended.

We may suggest four stages in the evolution of the water closet.[137] A rudimentary water closet designed in 1547 for Edward VI was covered with velvet and garnished with fringe, quilting, and 2,000 gilt nails. This was the monarchical phase of the water closet. An improved water closet that delivered water with enough force to completely wash the bowl signaled the beginning of the aristocratic or oligarchic phase, but

134 See A. Smith, Lectures on Justice, Police, and Arms 3-4, 154-55 (1896).

135 N. Elias, The Civilizing Process: The Development of Manners: Changes in the Code of Conduct and Feeling in Early Modern Times 134-43 (1978).

136 Id. at 117-22, 148-52, 163-68.

137 The source for the facts in this passage is T. McLaughlin, supra note 123, at 49-52, 110. The analysis of phases is my own.

the need for a ready supply of water prevented its becoming more than a curiosity in the homes of aristocrats. The third stage was bourgeois: numerous mechanical and hydraulic improvements were introduced, and one manufacturer made 6,000 water closets in the last decades of the eighteenth century. The fourth and final stage saw the spread of water closets to the mass of urban houses. It is of this period that a modern author writes: "The flush toilet made one person's waste equal to another's in the great stream of sewage."[138]

Besides relating its evolution to four stages of history and to four classes (monarchy, aristocracy, bourgeoisie, proletariat), can Marxism add anything further to our interpretation of the flush toilet? If we extend Marx's theory of alienation in the direction suggested by Norbert Elias, we may understand the history of the flush toilet as part of "civilization," or the alienation of humans from our bodies. To flush and forget is not to get rid of a problem, but only to remove it to another place. For the flushers and forgetters of eighteenth-century London, that place was the environment of other Londoners. The elite's new luxury was not accompanied by a new system for waste disposal. Instead,

> closets mostly discharged into sewers or even open gutters running through the streets, and ultimately into the rivers. A large amount of sewage that had previously been confined to earth closets or carted away by nightmen for use on the land was now added to the already foul waterways. In London, the Thames became so polluted . . . that the end of the century saw an increase in the number of deaths from typhoid that paralleled the installation of the closets.[139]

Reality in eighteenth-century London thus turned Swift's Yahoo story on its head: the rich defecated, almost literally, on the poor. "[T]he rich had water closets, the poor merely got more sewage in their drinking water."[140]

Professor Langbein may find garbage collection and criminal law of no great importance. To those who lived in fear of the hangman and of typhoid, however, such systems were important indeed. As the capital statutes and hangings kept the mass of English people in its place, so the elite's adoption of the water closet may have served, on a psychological level, to convince the masses that they were nothing more than human garbage. In both areas, the "active hand of the ruling class"—not in Langbein's sense of conscious conspiracy, but in Hay's sense of social control—was apparent and heavy.

---

138 S. Van der Ryn, supra note 131, at 19-20.

139 T. McLaughlin, supra note 123, at 110.

140 Id. at 111.

CONCLUSION

Albion's Fatal Tree opened up new paths of historical investigation that others have followed in other studies,[141] studies that by no means accept all the interpretations of our early work. Our volume showed how legal materials could be used in new ways. We used trial records and statutes to construct narratives of aspects of eighteenth-century society such as smuggling, hanging, poaching, wrecking, and anonymous letter writing. As narratives, the essays attempted to introduce forgotten subjects in such a way that a reader might find evidence of causalities—as well as the casualties—of historical change. To us the law was neither a mere superstructure upon fact nor a closed system of intellectualism; it was a new kind of evidence. But it was, in the eighteenth century, not only that. We found, and this was Douglas Hay's particular contribution, that law had in itself ideological importance as well as functional purposes that largely served the class interests of the elite. Often the law—its practices, rules, precepts, theater, and punishments—was opposed to "custom," and *Albion's Fatal Tree* helped to reintroduce that ancient antagonism between law and custom into current scholarly discussion.

In this "Reply" to Professor Langbein, I have sought to show the limits of his historical approach. In his classification of criminal statutes, in his characterization of offenders, and in his presentation of evidence about the eighteenth-century jury, Langbein has been limited by his excessively intellectualized and self-enclosed view of the law. This view both isolates that discipline from other modes of historical inquiry, such as economic, social, and political history, and stifles any meaningful analysis of historical change. Langbein's is a conservative and self-enclosed theory of law that is both elitist (hence his stress upon "professionalism") and sanitized (hence his hands-off treatment of the flush toilet).

---

141 See authorities cited in note 15 supra.

[16]

7 *Joanna Innes and John Styles*

The crime wave: recent writing on crime and criminal justice in eighteenth-century England[1]

Introduction

One of the most exciting and influential areas of research in eighteenth-century history over the last twenty years has been the study of crime and the criminal law. It is the purpose of this essay to map the subject for the interested non-specialist: to ask why historians have chosen to study it, to explain how they have come to approach it in particular ways, to describe something of what they have found, to evaluate those findings, and to suggest fruitful directions for further research. Like all maps, the one presented here is selective. The essay begins with a general analysis of the ways in which the field has developed and changed in its short life. It then proceeds to consider in more detail four areas of study: criminality, the criminal trial, punishment, and criminal legislation. This selection makes no pretence of providing an exhaustive coverage. A number of important areas have been omitted: for example, public order and policing.[2] However, the areas covered illustrate the range of approaches, problems and possibilities that lie within the field. We conclude with a discussion of the broader implications of the subject.

The development of the field

Before the 1960s, crime was not treated seriously by eighteenth-century historians. Accounts of crime and the criminal law rarely extended beyond a few brief remarks on lawlessness, the Bloody Code and the state of the prisons, often culled from Fielding, Hogarth and Howard. There were exceptions, but they fell outside the mainstream of eighteenth-century history. The multiple volumes of Leon Radzinowicz's monumental *History of the English Criminal Law* were published from 1948 onwards, but Radzinowicz worked in the Cambridge Law Faculty and Institute of Criminology and, as Derek Beales has pointed out, his findings were not quickly assimilated by historians.[3] The Webbs and the Hammonds had discussed various aspects of eighteenth-century disorder, crime and policing, but in this field at least they attracted few disciples.[4] Mainstream academic history of the 1950s and early 1960s characteristically focused on the sort of high politics associated with the work of Namier, or alternatively on the economic origins and characteristics of the Industrial Revolution, with a particular emphasis on the Rostowian problematic of take-off into sustained growth.

Since the late 1960s, by contrast, there has been an explosion of interest in eighteenth-century crime. In part this dramatic change must be understood in terms of wider academic developments. Both Britain and North America witnessed a boom in higher education in the 1960s. History shared in this general upsurge, and there was considerable expansion in the numbers both of professional historians and of history departments. Not surprisingly this expansion was associated with the exploration of new areas of research. The boom in the social sciences during the same period helped to nurture interest in social history in particular. The intellectual and academic success of the social science disciplines contributed to a demand for a 'new' social history that would transcend the antiquarian and anecdotal approach of much previous work.

To understand why crime and criminal justice in particular became a focus of interest, and why research on these subjects initially took the specific forms it did, it is necessary to refer to a number of the specific features which characterized the 'new' English social history as it developed in the 1960s. Three tendencies within the 'new' social history have been especially influential.

First, and most important, history from below. By this we understand an approach which emphasizes the need to explore and imaginatively to reconstruct the experiences of the dispossessed and inarticulate. In the 1960s and 1970s the study of crime and the criminal law came to be seen as a useful means to this end, especially for periods before the emergence of an independent working class politics. Edward Thompson's work was seminal in this regard. Although all his work has been concerned with the culture of the dispossessed, with the transforming impact of capitalism, and with the nature of class relationships, during these years its emphasis shifted. It underwent a chronological shift from the early nineteenth to the early eighteenth century and at the same time reoriented its focus away from popular politics first to popular disorder and then to certain types of criminality. Thompson's *The Making of the English Working Class*, first published in 1963, charted the emergence of a working class politics in the late eighteenth and early nineteenth centuries. Following this, his 1971 article 'The moral economy of the English crowd in the eighteenth century' explored the 'pre-political' ideas and crowd actions associated with eighteenth-century popular resistance to the imposition of a free market in foodstuffs. Finally, in 1975, *Whigs and Hunters* concerned itself with the resistance, by means of a variety of activities defined as 'crimes', of the early eighteenth-century forest communities of south-east England to the elimination of their customary rights, and with the bloody legislation that the Hanoverian state enacted to crush these initiatives.[5] As he changed course, Thompson drew a number of his research students in his wake. He and they collaborated in the collection *Albion's Fatal Tree*, also published in 1975. For all the contributors it was axiomatic that the study of crime and the criminal law 'were central to unlocking the meanings of eighteenth-century social history'.[6]

The second important tendency within the 'new' social history was that which drew on the methods of positivist social science. The social scientific approach emphasized the discovery and explanation of significant patterns, particularly statistical patterns, in social behaviour. This entailed treating crime as a 'social fact' and using aggregate crime statistics to identify and measure continuities and changes. Those who adopted this approach sought explanations for the patterns they found not in the meanings of actions for individual or collective social actors (as in history from below), but instead in correlative (and arguably causal) relationships between a variety of social facts, for example crime and dearth, or crime and political tension, or crime and the Industrial Revolution. Some of John Beattie's early work best illustrates this approach. Thus his 1975 article on the criminality of women in eighteenth-century England set out 'to uncover the patterns of offences charged against women and to suggest what they reveal about the place of women and the nature of crime'.[7]

The third tendency within the 'new' social history which bears on our concerns was one that will be termed here the 'reform perspective'. The reform perspective was to a great extent an inheritance from an older historiographical tradition, but during the 1960s and 1970s it gained a new lease of life from its ready compatibility with other preoccupations of the day. Adopting a reform perspective has traditionally entailed accepting at least a substantial part of the account of eighteenth-century society and its institutions propounded by late-eighteenth- and early-nineteenth-century reformers. It has meant accepting their view that early-eighteenth-century government was grossly corrupt and inefficient, and hailing as a major watershed in English social and political development a set of changes in society, in ideas and in policy thought to have taken place in the late eighteenth and early nineteenth centuries. Both the Webbs' and Radzinowicz's accounts of, for example, policing and punishment are substantially written from a reform perspective.

Historians of the 1960s and 1970s have very frequently taken a more jaundiced view of the content of 'reform' than their predecessors. At the same time, it is striking how commonly they have reproduced a traditional view of the chronology of change, and of the relative significance of institutional developments at different periods. Developments late in the century have remained central to their concerns. The continuing appeal of this view of the basic shape of history in the period is probably partly to be explained in terms of its neat fit with a notion of a late-eighteenth-century industrial revolution effecting a general social transformation. Whether in its Weberian or Marxist variants, the notion of industrialization has often been elevated to a position of central causal significance in the recent history of crime and the law, as in the 'new' social history more generally. Michael Ignatieff is certainly inclined to assign it a major causal role in his study of prison reform, *A Just Measure of Pain* – a study which exemplifies the reform perspective at its most sophisticated.[8]

The distinction between these various tendencies is helpful in as much as it serves to clarify the development of the field. But it must be emphasized that the tendencies do not represent three opposed schools. In particular, it must be stressed that the distinction between history from below and statistical approaches has not corresponded – at least in the history of crime and the criminal law – to a distinction between Marxists and non-Marxists. Thus Douglas Hay has been a student of both John Beattie and Edward Thompson, and his work, though broadly Marxian in emphasis, has involved (amongst other things) both statistical analysis and the study of crime as resistance.[9] In general, scholars working on the history of crime over the last twenty years have been markedly disposed to cooperate with each other, to learn from and adopt each other's ideas and approaches, and to welcome insights from other periods and disciplines. But it is also noteworthy that, for some, the field has not fulfilled its early promise. Eric Hobsbawm, in particular, has not followed up his early contribution on social protest and social crime.[10]

If the field has lost its attraction for some, this may be because the concerns of research have shifted. The first two tendencies outlined above, whatever the differences between them, did at least share a concern with the actions of those who offended against the criminal laws. Both histories from below and positivist histories represented the study of those actions as a key to understanding the wider society. However, during the last decade there has been a shift from the study of offences towards the study of the institutions and more particularly the processes associated with the administration of the criminal law. Indeed much of the work currently being undertaken in the field might justly be called administrative history, despite the fact that few of its practitioners would want to describe themselves as administrative historians. Unlike much traditional administrative history, this new work on the administration of the criminal law is strongly contextual. Its proponents have sought to understand the advantages and shortcomings of eighteenth-century arrangements as these were understood by those who lived with, sustained, or contemporaneously sought to change them. As a result of applying this approach to the earlier eighteenth century, at least some historians have now begun to question the reform perspective. They are beginning to uncover a dense and complex pattern of early-eighteenth-century legal and institutional change.

Why has this shift in emphasis in favour of the study of legal institutions and processes come about? A number of influences seem to have been in play. First, historians of crime have developed an increasingly sophisticated awareness of the limitations, as well as the possibilities, of their sources. This has been a general trend in early modern social history, but has been particularly important in the study of criminality. Early studies that focused on the behaviour of offenders relied heavily on an analysis of court records. It was assumed that those records could be made to tell us about crime and criminal offenders in general. But to use court records to study criminal behaviour in the world at large demands at the very least an understanding of the highly selective ways in which the machinery of criminal justice responded to offences and offenders. Historians were of course quick to recognize the need to study both why and how this machinery was set into motion, but were nonetheless initially oversanguine as to how easy it would be to control for consequent 'distortions'.[11] Subsequently, many have come to doubt that the records can properly be used in the ways they at first envisaged. However, in the meantime institutional studies originally undertaken as a means to an end have come to win acceptance as worthwhile exercises in their own right. As interest in the character and operations of institutions has grown, historians have increasingly come to accept that in the machinery of criminal justice we are dealing with an instrument of state power, but, nonetheless, disputes continue as to how important an instrument this was, and as to which groups or interests participated in its exercise and benefited from it.

Another factor which has encouraged a shift in emphasis towards the study of the administration of criminal justice has been interaction between historians of eighteenth-century crime and British sociologists. Two concerns in recent British sociology have been particularly influential: labelling theory and theories of the state. Labelling theory is associated with the British 'new' criminology of the late 1960s (though the theory's origins are in fact American). Labelling theorists argue that 'deviance is *not* a quality of the act the person commits, but rather a consequence of the application by others of rules and sanctions to an "offender" '.[12] In this view, the records of the courts or the police merely chronicle the activities of the controllers. The controllers' activities have their own momentum and the records they generate bear no relationship to the incidence of 'real' crime.[13] The influence of labelling theory has served to reinforce historians' own scepticism about the court records as a source for the history of crime – and, indeed, about the very possibility of such a history.

An interest in theories of the state, particularly Marxist theories of the state, was one of the most striking developments in British sociology from the late 1960s. It was part of a wider revival of Marxist ideas in British intellectual circles and grew specifically out of a dissatisfaction on the left with pluralist political science. Hence questions about how, why, and whether the state was the tool of a particular class predominated, although the answers offered were extremely diverse. The influence of these developments on historians has been important but diffuse, a matter of sensitizing them to and encouraging their interest in conceptual issues regarding class, ideology, and state power. It should be noted, however, that the flow of ideas has not been only, or even predominantly, from sociology to history. Two powerful interpretations of the character of state power were presented by Edward Thompson in *Whigs and Hunters* and Douglas Hay in *Albion's Fatal Tree*. Both have influenced sociologists.[14]

Finally, a third factor that has prompted a shift towards the study of the administration of criminal justice has been the influence of legal history. Before the mid 1970s there was little work by legal historians on the eighteenth century (Radzinowicz apart). The new work on eighteenth-century crime and the criminal law has been greeted with some suspicion by legal historians, but also with much interest.[15] Legal historians are now coming increasingly to work in the field. Legal history has a long tradition of internalist explanation of legal change: of explaining changes in the law in terms of developments internal to the law and the legal system. The long dominance of this approach to the subject means that all legal historians share an awareness of its importance, although some have recently been moved to challenge it.[16] As legal historians have come to work on eighteenth-century criminal law, social historians have been made increasingly aware of the need to pay serious attention to the legal complexities of the machinery of criminal justice.

The shift of emphasis towards institutions and processes has been regretted by some.[17] It is argued that it involves an undesirable shift away from big historical questions about the relationship between crime and capitalism, or crime and industrialization, questions which give the subject significance in the eyes of non-specialists and undergraduates. It is true that the newer approaches demand much more careful attention to the workings of the criminal justice system, to the meanings of the sources and to the ways in which concepts like capitalism or industrialization are deployed as explanations. However, very often criticisms of the newer approaches amount to little more than an attempt to reinstate a version of the reform perspective, with its glib assumptions about the all-transforming character of an 'industrial revolution' which, it is increasingly clear, is incapable of bearing the explanatory demands placed on it.[18] The newer approaches still seek to address general questions about the relationship between crime, the criminal law, and the broader society and economy, but general questions that are better specified theoretically, better articulated archivally and better grounded in an understanding of the complexities and ambiguities of the administrative process. It is possible to make these accessible to a non-specialist audience.

That is not to say it is easy. The pattern of publication in the field testifies to this. Most work has appeared in the form of articles or essays, despite the existence of a number of long-completed and important doctoral dissertations, in particular Douglas Hay's magnificent 1975 dissertation, a model and inspiration for all students in the field.[19] It was only with the publication in 1986 of John Beattie's *Crime and the Courts in England 1660–1800*, that monographs began to appear.[20] The delay is a measure of the difficulty of opening up a subject that hardly existed twenty years ago. Although a number of provocative interpretations were generated quite rapidly, the process of testing and refining those ideas has been an arduous one. It is that process that is discussed in the rest of this essay, by means of an examination of four areas of study that are particularly important to the past and the future development of the subject.

Crime and criminality

As remarked above, 'criminality', as distinctive social phenomenon, though originally central to the concerns of those who pioneered the new history of crime, has recently ceased to be the focus of the most innovative work in the field. Work has continued to appear, witness the chapters devoted to crime and criminality in John Beattie's largely Surrey-based study *Crime and the Courts in England 1660–1800* and in several recent theses.[21] Nonetheless, neither in terms of sources exploited, nor in terms of categories and analytical techniques employed does this new work mark much of an advance beyond Beattie's own 1974 article 'The pattern of crime in England' and the essays in *Albion's Fatal Tree*. Instead, we see the application of established techniques to new data, or critical reflection on established techniques and categories, or their defence against criticism. Douglas Hay's 1982 article 'War, dearth and theft', an enquiry into the merits and limitations of aggregate statistics – one of the most impressive of these studies – is characteristic in being primarily defensive in purpose.

There are, it will be argued, good reasons why research in this field should have stalled, for there are very real and intractable difficulties associated with both of the main approaches historians have so far adopted to the study of crime: the positivist, statistics-based approach, and the quest for the meanings of criminal behaviour. A number of the problems that have become apparent are outlined in the next few pages. Although it is argued that some lines of enquiry have proved to be dead ends, it is also suggested that there may yet be a way forward.

It is easy to understand what first attracted historians of crime to the study of statistical time series. Criminal indictments – the documents from which time series have most commonly been constructed – are highly standardized in form, and survive in larger numbers than have the other records of the criminal courts. Their terse and formulaic character, which renders them almost useless to historians bent on reconstructing the character of criminal activity, suits them admirably for quantification. Time series founded on indictments hold out the promise of chronological precision, unobtainable by other means. They can readily be correlated with time series measuring other economic and social phenomena. Furthermore, exercises of this kind have a long, albeit controversial, pedigree among criminologists.

Eighteenth-century historians who have adopted a statistical approach have increasingly limited their attention to the study of short-term fluctuations in property crime, fluctuations over say five or ten years. Neither sixteenth- and seventeenth- nor nineteenth- and twentieth-century historians have confined themselves so narrowly: they have dealt with both short- and long-term fluctuations, with offences against the person as well as those against property.[22] Eighteenth-century historians have been well aware that they might address this wider range of topics. If they have held back it is because they have justifiably doubted the value of most of these exercises – at least as a source of insights into the changing character of criminal behaviour.

Long-term changes in the volume of any sort of indictments are formidably difficult to interpret. The influences possibly at work changing the relationship between 'real' levels of crime and levels of crime prosecuted are so numerous, and so resistant to measurement, that it seems impossible to pronounce with any confidence on the meanings of the patterns observed. Where indictments for interpersonal violence are concerned, the significance of both long- and short-term fluctuations has been sharply questioned. Such supplementary evidence as survives to illuminate the nature of the encounters which gave rise to indictments for assault (the principal prosecuted offence in this area) suggests that both the circumstances of assaults and the degree of violence involved varied enormously. In other words, it is not at all clear that the events at issue had enough in common to justify their aggregation. Furthermore, it appears that a strikingly high proportion of indictments for assault arose out of quarrels between men of the 'middling sort' (farmers, tradesmen, artisans).[23] If indictments for assault were, as this suggests, no more than a means by which the middling sort pursued their differences, there is no reason to believe that changes in their number will shed much light on general levels of violence in the society. Finally, even if we accept such changes as an index of changes in the propensity to violence in society at large, it is questionable whether we stand to learn much from correlating them with time series charting, say, the changing cost of living, or levels of political tension. Although there are a number of sociological and psychological theories linking violence to social tension, it seems unlikely that the very crude social and economic indicators available for the eighteenth century could ever serve adequately as even approximate indicators of such tension.[24]

Acts of illegal appropriation, like acts of interpersonal violence, were undoubtedly more various in character than the indictments reveal. However, a much more powerful case can be made for correlating short-term changes in the former with movements in other time series, particularly time series which attempt to chart changing levels of material deprivation. Between one-half and three-quarters of those prosecuted for property crimes were drawn from the 'labouring poor'. Their offences characteristically involved the theft of items of small value in an opportunistic fashion. We know that many of the eighteenth-century 'poorer sort' were recurrently un- or underemployed, that they were vulnerable to short-term increases in the cost of living, and that even at the best of times they might have difficulty obtaining adequate supplies of food and fuel. It is a reasonable hypothesis that fluctuations in the level of indictments for property offences may have been causally related to fluctuations in the cost of living and in the earning capacity of the working population.

Recent studies have identified as points of especial interest two characteristic features of short-term fluctuations in indictments for property offences. First and most strikingly, periods of peace contrast with periods of war, peace being attended with relatively high indictment levels, war with low ones. The transition from war to peace was usually marked by a very steep rise in the number of indictments. Second, in wartime (but not in peacetime) there was a strong positive correlation between annual changes in the numbers of indictments and annual changes in the cost of living.

Historians have tended to interpret these findings in broadly similar ways. Douglas Hay marshals the argument most convincingly.[25] Crucial to his interpretation is a distinction between two kinds of theft: minor thefts, undertaken by the normally law-abiding under pressure of destitution, and more serious and more skilled capital thefts, undertaken by people who stole with some regularity and not merely under pressure of immediate need.

During wars, Hay suggests, the level of indictments was low because the often forced recruitment of tens of thousands of young men removed from the country a large proportion of adult males from among the labouring poor. Those recruited were from the class and age group most likely to face unemployment. Young men suspected by their neighbours of being habitual thieves were especially likely to be recruited. Men engaged in crime both sporadically and habitually must have been among those extracted. Their removal explains the fall in indictments, and, in particular, the observed disproportionate fall in the more skilled and serious forms of offence. In their absence, it was the minor thefts, committed under pressure of immediate need, that predominated, hence the strong positive correlation during wars between fluctuations in the indictments for property offences and fluctuations in the cost of living.

Peace and rapid demobilization not only released on the country men previously suspected or even convicted of offences, but also glutted labour markets. Both habitual offenders and the chronically unemployed might turn to theft, particularly to such serious offences as highway robbery and burglary. Indictments for property offences in general, but especially for serious theft, accordingly registered massive increases with the end of each war, remaining at high levels as long as peace continued. With the reappearance of such offenders, the wartime correlation between property crime and dearth disappeared.

In his 1974 article, John Beattie summed up his reading of the evidence thus: 'The evidence of the indictments seems to point clearly to this conclusion: that crimes against property in the eighteenth century arose primarily from problems of employment, wages and prices.'[26] Although Hay's argument allows some role to habitual offenders, who were not necessarily responding to economic pressures, clearly his interpretation too attaches great weight to material circumstance.

However, there remains a major difficulty here, a difficulty associated with all attempts to interpret criminal statistics. Hay's argument turns on the assumption that the relationship between numbers of indictments and numbers of offences remained fairly constant, such that changes in numbers of indictments can be taken to reflect real changes in the criminal behaviour of the poor. Yet this is a highly questionable assumption.

Hay, once again, has marshalled the most persuasive arguments in its favour. Although his analysis is too rich to summarize here in its entirety, two of its more ingenious features are worth examining in detail. Criminologists have argued that modern crime statistics are distorted by the activities of those who enforce the law, whose own priorities may be idiosyncratic and may change over time. Hay suggests that the absence from eighteenth-century England of any professional police force or prosecution service eliminates this problem. Eighteenth-century prosecutors were usually the victims of the crimes concerned, individually making their thousands of independent decisions.

Hay acknowledges that the propensity of victims to prosecute may have varied collectively as a result of widely-shared prejudices or pressures, which are virtually impossible to measure. He suggests that the same variations should, however, be observable in the well-documented decisions of juries, because they were composed of men from a similar social position. Juries, it emerges, were more likely to be lenient in years of high prices. If prosecutors were moved by similar instincts, then high indictment levels in high price years are more likely to under- than to overstate 'real' levels of crime. The suggested relationship between times of need and crime still holds good.

Despite the elegance and apparent force of Hay's argument, it remains vulnerable, we believe, to certain damning objections. The key difficulty has been well-expressed by Peter King. So long as the ratio of prosecuted crime to all crime was low (and eighteenth-century commentators and modern historians share the belief that it was) even small changes in the behaviour of prosecutors would have had far greater effects on fluctuations in the movement of indictments than quite large changes in the behaviour of offenders.[27] Furthermore, it seems likely that changes in the behaviour of prosecutors were more common and also more difficult to measure than Hay would have us believe.

Consider, for example, the low incidence of indictments for serious offences during wartime. The pressures on local officials to encourage recruitment were intense. It is therefore not surprising that diaries and the newspapers mention (although not in any systematic way) prosecutors giving apprehended offenders the option of enlistment as an alternative to prosecution, often at the behest of the examining magistrate. Thus at Leeds in 1762 an apprehended burglar was taken before a magistrate 'who gave him his choice, whether he would inlist into his Majesty's service, or be committed to York Castle, the former of which he accepted'.[28] Such a procedure had its attractions for magistrate, prosecutor and offender alike. The magistrate secured a recruit; the prosecutor, the removal of the offender from the locality without the trouble or expense of a trial; the offender, relief from a period of pre-trial imprisonment, and perhaps from the threat of a capital sentence. Yet it was a procedure not available on any scale during peacetime. Documentation of this kind of informal arrangement is too unsystematic to allow us to calculate precisely how many were extracted from the criminal process in this way, but they need have constituted no more than a small fraction of the tens of thousands who were recruited to explain a large part of the fall-off in property crimes during wartime.[29] Even a large county like Staffordshire saw no more than forty to fifty fewer indictments a year in war than in peace.[30] The case for interpreting the evidence of the indictments as an index of a fall in 'real' crime consequently seems a shaky one.

Similarly there are difficulties with Hay's interpretation of the effect of high prices on prosecutors. While prosecutors may have shared broadly similar backgrounds and therefore attitudes with jurymen (though even this is debatable), high-price years did not necessarily have the same practical consequences for their behaviour towards criminal offenders. Even if, like jurymen, prosecutors were disposed to be more merciful in years of dearth, at the same time they were more likely to face offenders unable, because of financial hardship, to buy off prosecution. Buying off prosecutors was believed to be very common, and the vast majority of references to it mention cash payments. If the propensity to mercy tilted the balance one way, therefore, a decline in the ability of offenders to buy forgiveness may have tilted it the other – and there is no way of knowing which carried the more weight. In these circumstances once again it is difficult to put much faith in movements in indictment levels as indicators of movements in 'real' crime.

It is doubtful, in sum, whether time series based on indictments can be used as indices of the behaviour of property offenders. But even if those time series were an accurate guide to changes in the level of 'real' crime, doubts would remain concerning the manner in which correlative techniques have been applied in analysing them, and the conclusions that have been drawn from the use of those techniques. Doubts about the way the techniques have been used centre on the questionable consistency of the relationship between fluctuations in prices and in indictments during wartime. If that relationship was very strong in years of exceptionally high prices and very weak in years of moderate or low prices it would be misleading to use, as Hay does, time series compiled without reference to this distinction as the basis for price–indictment correlations. At least one of the county studies, the study of Essex by Peter King, suggests that the relation did vary in this fashion.

King points out that, if the exceptional years of high prices – 1740–1, 1772, and 1800–1 – are removed from the Essex data, the wartime correlation between fluctuations in indictments and fluctuations in the cost of living is reduced to a level that is statistically meaningless. In Hay's Staffordshire it is reduced to a level of significance verging on the marginal.[31] Even if it could be assumed that the indictment series did accurately measure changes in the level of crime, these findings would indicate that it was only in years of exceptional hardship that necessity obliged the poor to turn on any scale to theft.

Also important to bear in mind is a fact that is often overlooked in the excitement when the computer finally declares that the relationship between two time series wrung from intractable historical sources is characterized by a strongly positive coefficient of correlation. These statistical techniques measure the extent to which changes in one variable reflect changes in another. They do not demonstrate that the relationship was one of cause and effect. Even if there are firm grounds for believing that a causal relationship was involved, it extends only to the changes in the two variables. Thus if a strong positive correlation could be established with confidence between changes in annual totals of offences (as opposed to indictments) and changes in prices, it would still not necessarily follow, to paraphrase Beattie, that all crime against property arose primarily from problems of prices. It would merely suggest that changes in the numbers of such crimes were related to such problems, and that, given the precariousness of the budgets of the poor, the relationship was probably a causal one.

This section of the discussion has been developed at some length. The shortcomings of studies based on time series derived from indictments deserve careful attention because, given a longstanding academic and popular obsession with rises and falls in crime, the approach they embody has proved extremely seductive. However, while the valiant efforts of historians to render the statistics intelligible have undoubtedly deepened our knowledge of the processes of prosecution and trial, it has yet to be demonstrated that such studies can contribute very significantly to our understanding of criminal behaviour.

The same complaint might be levelled against the other principal approach thus far adopted to the study of eighteenth-century criminality: that which has attempted to distinguish between different forms of behaviour defined as criminal in terms of popular attitudes towards them and in terms of their implications for broader economic and social conflicts. The approach in question is that which has emphasized distinctions between 'social criminality' and other types of criminality.

Social criminality is not a concept that has been specified very tightly. Thus for Eric Hobsbawm, who first defined the concept for historians, it 'occurs when there is a conflict of laws, e.g. between an official and an unofficial system, or when acts of law-breaking have a distinct element of social protest in them, or when they are closely linked with the development of social and political unrest.'[32] At its weakest, therefore, the notion of 'social crime' amounts to little more than an acknowledgement that in the eighteenth century, as before and since, a large number of activities defined by the law as criminal were not recognized as such by large sections of the population. At its strongest, it implies that at least some of these activities were, either explicitly or implicitly, proto-political forms of protest or resistance by the poor: a form of opposition, perhaps the only possible form of opposition, to their exploitation and subordination by the rich.

It is their fascination with this second, stronger version of 'social crime' that has attracted eighteenth-century social historians to the study of activities like smuggling, poaching, wrecking, and certain types of gleaning, wood gathering, and pilfering in the workplace.[33] Their concern has been to explore the ideas – the legitimizing notions – through which popular sympathy for these activities was expressed, and to relate those ideas to the material conflicts involved. The key point of departure here has been Edward Thompson's study of the moral economy of the English crowd in the eighteenth century. Thompson argued that 'it is possible to detect in almost every eighteenth-century crowd action some legitimizing notion. By the notion of legitimation I mean that the men and women in the crowd were informed by the belief that they were defending traditional rights or customs; and, in general, that they were supported by the wider consensus of the community.'[34] The traditional rights and customs defended in the food riots that were the subject of Thompson's 1972 article were those pre-eighteenth-century regulations concerning the distribution of grain that required that the needs of the poor consumer should have priority in times of scarcity. The enemy against which this moral economy of provision had to be defended was the profit-orientated, unregulated market economy.

For Thompson, this analysis of the food riot was a key which unlocked the meaning of whole areas of eighteenth-century popular culture: a culture which 'resists, in the name of "custom", those economic innovations and rationalizations . . . which the rulers or employers seek to impose. [These are] most often experienced by the plebs in the form of exploitation, or the expropriation of customary use rights, or the violent disruption of valued patterns of work and leisure.' Thus most forms of crowd action, and many of the other kinds of illegal activity which enjoyed widespread popular support, emerge as forms of popular resistance to a specifically eighteenth-century 'innovation of capitalist process'.[35]

The merits of this approach with regard to the study of crowd action need not detain us.[36] Whatever its shortcomings in that context, there can be no doubt that it has immensely enriched our understanding of the eighteenth-century crowd. Its success in illuminating the character of eighteenth-century criminality has been much more qualified. The most obvious difficulty here is the relegation of offences which lack the historiographically attractive, proto-political associations of the 'social crimes' to the status of unintelligible counterpoint. While historians working with this approach have spawned studies of several armies of 'social criminals', we have no detailed studies of the petty larcenists, burglars, horse stealers, and highway robbers who made up the bulk of the business of the courts of Quarter Sessions and Assizes.[37]

Given that within this framework it is the proto-political implications of the 'social crimes' that make them historically interesting, one way to render 'normal' crime intelligible in the same terms has been to downplay the validity of the social crime/normal crime distinction altogether. Instead it is asserted that much property crime, irrespective of whether it involved explicit, collective opposition to capitalist innovation, was a result of such innovation and a challenge to it. Thus, for Peter Linebaugh, the creation of 'a "free" mobile labour force, ready to submit to the discipline of working for hire', required on the one hand the destruction of old, customary forms of work and income, often by transforming customary practices into crimes, and on the other the removal of 'the possibilities of living without "visible means of support" or "living by one's wits" ', by enhancing and enforcing the whole range of laws against theft.[38] In this perspective, most of the crimes of the labouring poor become, implicitly if not explicitly, forms of resistance to the development of capitalism – a development Linebaugh suggests to have been taking place at a particularly marked pace in the eighteenth century.

This approach fails to convince on several counts. It has marked shortcomings conceptually, chronologically, and empirically. It is not at all clear that working for hire was something that had to be forced on people: waged labour was often embraced with enthusiasm. Nor is it evident that the reason people turned to theft was to avoid submitting to the discipline of the wage. Even if it had been necessary to discipline people into waged labour by means of the repression of theft and the use of the law to attack customary work practices, neither these activities nor attempts to suppress them were peculiar to the eighteenth century. It is true that some of the offenders who came before the eighteenth-century courts of Quarter Sessions and Assizes were charged with offences newly created in the eighteenth century to defend new forms of commercial property, but these were a small minority. The bulk of property offenders continued to be charged with offences that could have occasioned similar proceedings in the same courts two hundred years earlier.

Some of these points also bear on the more conventional uses of the notion of social criminality by historians of the eighteenth century. The idea that offences which enjoyed widespread popular support necessarily involved resistance to a capitalist economic order is highly problematic. It is difficult to see smuggling, the greatest illegal business of all, as a form of resistance to commercial capitalism, whatever difficulties it posed for the eighteenth-century fiscal state. Poaching was an attack on one of the landed gentry's most prized marks of status, not on their capacity to profit from a commercialized agriculture. It supplied the commercial trade in game to which it was the gentry that offered resistance.[39] Even in the case of those illegal activities enjoying popular support which can most plausibly be represented as having created difficulties for 'capitalists', it is doubtful whether that support was characteristically a product of resistance to capitalist initiatives peculiar to the eighteenth century. Take pilfering in the outwork industries, for example. It is far from clear that manufacturers in general were more concerned to redefine and restrict the property rights of the labouring poor in the eighteenth century than they had been in the seventeenth.[40]

The fundamental problem here is that we are presented with an oversimplified and overly determinist view of the nature of social and economic change, and of the relationship to it of the criminal law on the one hand and of the poorer section of the population on the other. The development of capitalist relations of production and consumption is presented as a unilinear evolution in which the eighteenth century comprised a distinct stage, with a particular emphasis on the redefinition of property rights,[41] whereas, in fact, such development, insofar as it can be traced, was extremely protracted, remarkably uneven, and remained incomplete. It is assumed that from some logic of capitalist development can be read off discernible 'tasks' or 'needs' which are necessary for its successful realization. The law is one of a number of tools used by the capitalist ruling class to achieve these requirements, as, for example, in the elimination of customary property rights. However, it is highly questionable whether capitalism can be usefully portrayed as having specific 'needs'.[42] On the contrary, it can flourish under a remarkably wide range of social and institutional arrangements. Finally, it is assumed that the attitudes of the poor to capitalist innovation tended to be hostile. In fact, attitudes were ambivalent and contingent, hostile to certain forms of expropriation and impoverishment, but enthusiastic towards some opportunities for new forms of work and consumption.

The argument so far has been that both the main approaches to the study of eighteenth-century crime adopted by historians over the last twenty years – the use of statistical time series and the use of the notion of 'social crime' – are unsatisfactory. In particular, it has been argued that what makes them unsatisfactory are the ways in which they try to provide an understanding of criminality in terms of the social relationships, understandings, and changes which characterized the wider society. Such an understanding certainly remains an admirable goal; the problem, however, is how to achieve it.

Despite the problems that beset existing approaches, it is possible to indicate ways in which they might be further refined. Statistical work has remained largely confined to the study of indictments. This is in contrast to work on modern crime statistics, where an intensive effort has been made to probe behind the official statistics by interviewing both the public at large and offenders about numbers of offences. Interviews are obviously an option that is closed to the eighteenth-century historian, but it is surprising that those pre-prosecution records of crime that do survive, particularly newspaper advertisements and diaries, have not been brought systematically to bear on the debates about fluctuations in the level of crime. More comparative work might be done on the indictments themselves, involving more counties, larger samples, and a move into the late seventeenth and early eighteenth centuries, which remain remarkably underexplored. Even if studies of time series will not reveal for us the pattern of 'real' crime, the compilation of indictment statistics remains a necessary starting point for students wishing to explore other records (such as depositions), or other stages in the machinery of criminal justice (such as trial or sentencing).[43]

Similarly, within a loosely 'social crime' perspective, a great deal of important work remains to be done on the precise constellations of support that characterized the different offences enjoying extensive public sympathy. Not all such offences attracted support from the same social groups, nor, for that matter, were they all justified in terms of custom.[44] Rather than represent such activities as part of a general defence of popular custom and of an undifferentiated popular culture of resistance, we need to explain how it was that different activities, different people, and different legitimizing notions could all be associated with collective opposition to the law.

At the same time it must be recognized that these refinements will not by themselves substantially enhance our understanding of the bulk of the offences against property that came before the criminal courts. At this stage in the development of the subject it is these forms of criminality that cry out for investigation, but it is precisely these forms of criminality that neither the statistical time series approach, nor the 'social crime' approach can adequately illuminate, given the difficulty of rendering the statistics intelligible and the way the analytical purchase of the 'social crime' approach is confined to those offences enjoying wide collective support. In our opinion what is required here is an approach that considers these activities from three points of view.

First, much more attention needs to be paid to the ways different forms of illegal appropriation were undertaken and organized:

what was stolen, how it was stolen, what was done with the stolen property. In other words we need systematically to investigate different forms of illegal appropriation as economic activities with their own histories. Sources for such studies are available not only in the depositions which survive in huge numbers for many Quarter Sessions and Assizes, but also in newspaper reports, diaries, and criminal life histories. Ironically, some of this work is already being done, not by historians of crime, but by historians interested in the economic history of particular commodities, such as Peter Edwards in his work on horse stealing in the seventeenth century.[45] The need for systematic investigation must be stressed. One of the attractions of counting crimes is the precision and the possibility of comparison across time and space that it appears to offer. A systematic qualitative analysis can offer some of the same advantages.[46]

Second, although it must not be assumed that crime is an automatic or even an obvious response to poverty, or that the relationship between the law and the poor was necessarily a hostile one, we need to locate the various forms of illegal appropriation that enjoyed the attention of the courts in relation to the various solidarities, attitudes, and material cultures which characterized the enormous range of people whom the rulers of eighteenth-century society labelled the 'poorer sort' or the 'labouring poor'.[47] Given the difficulty of securing evidence about the behaviour and attitudes of the poor, work like that by Peter King on the age of prosecuted offenders and that by Peter Linebaugh on the life histories of offenders is important here.[48] Useful too would be attempts systematically to analyse depositions and newspapers to establish the willingness or otherwise of different kinds of people to apprehend and provide evidence against different kinds of offenders.[49]

Third, it must be recognized that, in practice, there can be no history of criminality separate from the history of law enforcement. In one sense, this statement amounts simply to a reiteration of the problem of the representativeness of prosecuted offences that was raised in the discussion of the use of time series. To some extent the approaches we have outlined here can get round that problem. Qualitative analyses do not require the sort of statistical precision quantitative analyses demand. Furthermore, in a systematic qualitative analysis, law enforcement will not appear mainly as a distorting factor: a consideration of the risks of apprehension and prosecution will be an integral part of any such analysis. Finally, sources like newspapers and life histories make it possible to penetrate, to some extent, beyond that fraction of offences that was prosecuted.[50]

Problems of evidence may determine that the history of criminality cannot be separated from that of the law and its enforcement, but there are other considerations which suggest that any attempt to separate them would be misdirected. The history of property crime is, to a considerable extent, the history of the control of large sections of the poor. Then, as now, it was their infractions that were legislated against more harshly and their infractions that were prosecuted more rigourosly. To understand how and why the poor were selected for these attentions, it is necessary to look beyond the condition of the poor themselves to the preoccupations of those who shaped the law and set it in motion. At the same time, due consideration must be given to those aspects of the life of the poor which attracted such attentions. It is possible to shift the emphasis of analysis either towards the activities of the poor as law breakers, or towards the activities of the law enforcers and law makers, but the two can never be separated. In this respect Douglas Hay is certainly correct. Although certain aspects of his work on crime have been singled out for criticism in this section, it must be acknowledged that in his unpublished work, he has gone further than most other historians of crime in applying those qualitative techniques which we consider potentially the most fruitful approach to future research on eighteenth-century criminality.[51]

The criminal trial

The history of the eighteenth-century criminal trial is a field which has only recently been opened up by research. This development is symptomatic of the shift in favour of the study of institutions and processes which we have noted as characteristic of the last decade. Douglas Hay's 1975 essay 'Property, authority and the criminal law' must be given a large part of the credit for stimulating interest in trials, but important new lines of investigation have also been initiated by legal historians.[52] Indeed it is undoubtedly in this field that legal historians have made their most important contributions to date.

Hay's essay deals with much more than simply the conduct of trials and some other aspects of his discussion are touched on in subsequent sections. Among the many topics his essay has laid open to enquiry, however, are two that can be conveniently discussed in this connection. First, the essay has provoked research and debate as to the social status of those who participated in criminal trials. Second, it has stimulated interest in the character of the decision-making process which produced verdicts and sentences.

Hay's essay highlights what he himself identifies as a curious paradox at the heart of the eighteenth-century system of criminal justice. At a period when parliament created huge numbers of new capital offences against property and resisted calls for reform of the capital code, the proportion of death sentences actually carried out was small and declining. To explain this apparent discrepancy, Hay points to the enormous discretion available at almost all levels of the judicial process and particularly to prosecutors, juries, and judges. He argues that this discretion was subject to the control of a small eighteenth-century ruling class, who used it to sustain their authority over the common people and to protect their own interests. The combination of capital punishment and extensive discretion enabled them to secure acquiescence of their rule by means of both coercion (the occasional exemplary hanging) and benevolence (the calculated act of mercy in forgoing a prosecution, acquitting on a technicality, or securing a pardon). The criminal law achieved an ideological hegemony over the common people by means of public spectacle, the selective application of the prerogative of mercy, and the reaffirmation of the ideal of justice through the occasional punishment of the mighty on the gallows.

Peter King and (in part on the basis of King's work) John Langbein have both taken issue with several parts of Hay's account and interpretation.[53] Further criticisms have come more recently from Thomas Green.[54] None of Hay's critics has disputed the importance of discretion in the administration of the eighteenth-century criminal law. However, King in particular has questioned whether this power was concentrated in the hands of as narrow a social group as Hay implies and furthermore has argued that considerations other than those Hay details played a significant part in determining the outcome of trials.

On the question of the social distribution of power over the course of the trial and its outcome, King argues against Hay that it was 'possible for individuals or groups of widely differing social and economic status to modify or choose not to modify the severity of the law in line with their needs, beliefs and ideas of justice. These opportunities were not always equally distributed, but wide discretionary powers were available to middling men and in a more limited way to the labouring poor.'[55] By using recognizances and depositions from the court records, he shows that two-thirds of prosecutors in property cases tried at Quarter Sessions were farmers, tradesmen, or artisans. Both he and Langbein argue that petty jurors too were drawn from these middling groups in the population. King also points out that men of this sort formed the largest group among those who petitioned for pardons and enjoyed a success rate as high as that of the gentry.

These are very telling arguments against the Hay thesis because, although Hay is remarkably imprecise about who constituted his ruling class, on most occasions when the phrase is used in his essay it encompasses only the aristocracy, the gentry, and possibly the great merchants.[56] If the middling groups in English society participated in the exercise of discretion in the judicial process to the degree that King suggests, Hay's assertion that this discretion was subject to the control of the ruling class is rendered implausible, and Brewer and Styles's view that the law was 'a limited multiple-use right available to most Englishmen' is reinforced.[57]

Hay and King have worked out their differences most thoroughly in relation to the petty jury.[58] King has subjected evidence relating to Essex juries to detailed analysis while Hay has exploited Northamptonshire and Staffordshire sources. Both agree that, as a consequence of property qualifications established by statute, participation on juries was restricted to a good deal less than half the adult male population. Hay suggests that, at most, only the wealthiest quarter of adult males would have qualified. King is more reluctant to advance a precise percentage, but it is not clear that he would find this figure implausible. However, King's evidence allows him to be more precise than Hay about which elements of the population qualified. He establishes that the qualified minority did not simply represent a top slice from the wealth pyramid. The requirement that qualifying property be held in freehold meant that tradesmen and farmers who were relatively small holders of land might be eligible for jury service, while substantial tenant farmers might be excluded.

This in itself is not incompatible with Hay's findings. The real difference between King and Hay lies in their assessment of the cohesiveness of the qualified group. Hay stresses the common interest of all the qualified that the criminal law should defend their property against propertyless thieves. King, by contrast, emphasizes the presence of fissures and tensions among those who qualified for jury service. The interests of the middling sort (who dominated petty juries) were not identical to those of the gentry (who avoided service); the middling sort were themselves heterogeneous. As a consequence, King argues, the qualified did not always act in concert. His finding that jurors, though propertied, were not necessarily drawn from among the very wealthiest farmers and tradesmen in Essex parishes adds plausibility to this picture of jury behaviour.

King's argument is not, however, based simply on a consideration of the kind of people that exercised discretionary power. He also challenges Hay's view that such discretion was based on 'class favouritism and games of influence' by asking on what principles discretionary decisions were made.[59] To answer this question, he analyses the criteria according to which pardons were granted to capital convicts, and the influence of age on sentencing.[60] His analysis reveals that the most important principles on which both sentencing and pardoning decisions were made consisted of ethical criteria for assessing culpability that were widely-recognized and long-established in English culture, such as the youth or infirmity of offenders, their good character and conduct, their prospects of employment or reform, and the desparateness of their destitution. In combination with King's scepticism about the importance of influential connections for securing a pardon, this evidence renders highly questionable Hay's contention that 'the claims of class saved far more men who had been left to hang . . . than did the claims of humanity'.[61]

Thomas Green's findings echo those of Peter King. Unlike King, Green focuses on only one level of discretionary influence within the machinery of criminal justice – the trial jury – but he is able to bring to bear on the discussion of eighteenth-century juries the fruits of his analysis of the institution across the medieval and early modern periods. Green contends that for many centuries participation by lay jurors in criminal trials had significantly constrained possible trial outcomes. Lay jurors typically shared with the populace at large, Green suggests, a reluctance to see the commission of any but a narrow and particularly abhorrent range of crimes result in the offender's death – except perhaps in cases where the offender's notorious bad character or the felt need for some monitory example removed the usual objections. Over the centuries, Green tells us, juries persistently showed themselves willing to twist or perversely misread the evidence in potentially capital cases in whatever way was necessary to secure what they judged to be a tolerable outcome. Both judges and legislators, unless they wished to attempt to dispense with juries altogether, had to resign themselves to accommodating jury prejudice.

Green's studies have persuaded him that juries were a force to be reckoned with. Hay, he suggests, is inclined to underrate them.[62] It is true that, although juries do figure in the argument of 'Property, authority and the criminal law', much more attention is paid to the role of judges and to the pardoning process. Green's criticisms raise the important issue of the balance of power between the different levels of discretionary influence within the machinery of criminal justice.

This question of balance must be numbered among the many topics thrown up by debate on Hay's essay which stand in need of further research. As has been noted, Hay and King have already carried forward the debate about the social composition of the jury and its implications for our understanding of the part played by that very loose and general category 'the middling sort' in the criminal justice system. Both in his book and in his contribution to the Cockburn and Green collection, John Beattie introduces a new consideration into the debate on the role of the jury.[63] Having demonstrated that most jurymen – in Surrey and the City of London at least – repeatedly served on trial juries, he argues that we must take their probable familiarity with the law and courtroom conventions into account in our speculations as to how much of an independent voice they may have had.

Further research may make Hay's suggestion that the nature of trial and sentencing procedures strengthened the hands of a relatively small ruling elite look more or less plausible. But it must be noted too that, at a certain rarefied level, Hay's original interpretation is scarcely open to falsification. Evidence that broad sectors of the population might participate in the criminal trial process, that jury prejudice constrained judicial (and legislative) options, or that humane criteria were applied in pardoning can in every case, with more or less effort, be incorporated into the original theory – every sign of weakness being read as a strategic concession whose ultimate effect was to strengthen ideological hegemony. Even evidence supplied by both Green and John Brewer that the conduct of criminal trials was frequently the subject of controversy and that critics of government repeatedly seized on issues raised by the conduct of trials to further their cause can carry little weight in the balance.[64] For after all, the ruling class continued to rule. However trials were conducted and however they were regarded, they cannot be assigned a part in its downfall.[65]

Debate stimulated by Hay's provocative essay has not generally been marked by a strong time dimension. Most contributors have been relatively little concerned with change over time, and even Thomas Green, who does take a long view, stresses continuity rather than change. By contrast, questions of change over time are central to the line of enquiry opened by a legal historian, John Langbein.

Langbein's interest in the history of the criminal trial derives essentially from modern controversy over the merits and limitations of Anglo-American trial procedures. He has been particularly concerned to trace the origins of that adversary procedure that he believes to have rendered criminal jury trial, in the United States at least, 'unworkable as a routine dispositive procedure'.[66] Langbein has used judges' notes and the detailed printed reports of the Old Bailey Sessions to argue that it was only from the 1730s that the judges allowed the accused to have the assistance of counsel and that this subsequently led to the silencing of the accused and the development for the first time of a substantial law of evidence.[67] His explanation for this change, though as yet not completely developed, is largely internalist. He points to the judges' concern about the admissibility of the evidence of accomplices and the misuse of the reward system. Unable, because of constitutional scruple, to deal with these problems by professionalizing policing and pre-trial procedure, they responded by importing into the criminal law, in an *ad hoc* manner, practices derived from the civil law, over which they also presided.[68]

These are important arguments in their own right. They also raise questions about the terms in which the debate around the Hay thesis has been conducted. For not only has that debate had relatively little to say about change over time, but also it has taken little account of the professional self-interest of lawyers, of the possibility of relatively autonomous developments in legal procedure, or of the impact either of these may have had on decision making, regardless of continuities in other aspects of the staging of trials.[69] Thus Langbein suggests that the balance of power between the trial judge and the jury was utterly transformed during the eighteenth century, from a situation in which the judge actively shaped the jury's adjudication to one in which he remained passive. Yet this transformation appears to have to have taken place without any significant change in the social composition of the jury.

Langbein has opened up an interesting line of enquiry and at the same time has highlighted some of the blind spots of an alternative approach. This is not to say that his own work is free of difficulties. Indeed several elements of his emerging explanation for the appearance of counsel and the development of the adversary system and the law of evidence fail to convince. It is not at all clear that, under eighteenth-century conditions, the professionalization of policing and pre-trial procedure would have removed the need for the evidence of accomplices of reward seekers.[70] Furthermore, Langbein has not yet been able to produce a chronology which plausibly links supposed cause and effect. Thus, he has made much of the blood money scandal of the 1750s, but has not demonstrated that the mid-century marked a watershed in courtroom procedure. This is not to say that a more plausible chronology, preserving important elements of his explanation, might not yet be worked out.[71] Finally, it has not yet been demonstrated that these procedural changes can adequately be explained in terms of developments entirely internal to the legal process. After all, the introduction of defence counsel in treason cases in 1696 was a political decision, and it appears that in the mid-eighteenth century legal decisions of an explicitly constitutional character, like the general warrants decision of 1763, could have a significant impact on the administration of the more mundane aspects of the criminal law.[72]

The eighteenth-century criminal trial is currently the area of most lively debate in the field of crime and criminal justice. It has also been characterized by particularly fruitful exchanges between scholars emerging from a number of different disciplines. In this section the frontiers of research and the directions in which established researchers are moving have both been indicated. In conclusion it should be noted that substantial parts of the subject still remain underexplored. More research is needed on the steps which led to offenders appearing in court. In particular, more needs to be known about the discretion exercised by prosecutors (touched on in the last section) and by law officers such as constables and magistrates. More needs to be known too about courts other than Quarter Sessions and Assizes. Summary hearings stand in urgent need of investigation – at the moment it is not even certain how they were conducted, let alone how much discretion was available to magistrate and prosecutor. It is far from clear that the image of unconstrained magisterial authority which the very adjective 'summary' so readily evokes is warranted.[73] Finally, there remains to be considered the role of the higher courts in London, particularly the court of King's Bench, which had a supervisory jurisdiction over the inferior courts.[74]

Punishment

In contrast to the history of trial, the history of punishment has long engaged the attention of historians. In this field too, however, it is noticeable how much the pace of research has recently quickened. Whereas for many decades historians contented themselves with building on foundations laid by a few classic early works, supplementing, perhaps in some respects refining their conclusions, more recently new research has gone off in a number of previously underexplored directions, and important features of the conventional wisdom have come under challenge.

Some of the new work on punishment has been undertaken by people more generally concerned to fashion a new history of crime and criminal justice. Thus Peter Linebaugh, Douglas Hay, and John Beattie, all of whom we have already mentioned in other connections, have all produced interesting work on punishment. Important contributions have also been made by scholars emerging from other disciplines, however, most notably from sociology or the social sciences. Scholars who are not historians by profession have been particularly active in reworking the history of prisons. It is easy to see why this subject should have aroused their especial interest, given the centrality of the prison in modern penology, and the by now well established notion that the late eighteenth and early nineteenth centuries constituted a crucial formative period in the shaping of the modern prison.[75]

This section begins with an account of the ways in which the history of eighteenth-century punishment has traditionally been approached. Some of the new directions recent research has taken and some of the new interpretations recent writers have offered are then indicated. Innovative features of recent works are noted, but it will also be remarked that, in certain important respects, recent writers have been inclined rather to echo than to question the habits and assumptions of their precursors. The account of punishment provided in John Beattie's 1986 study, *Crime and the courts in England 1660–1800*, has broken most decisively with older habits and assumptions, both in its approach and in its conclusions. For this reason, we devote most time and care to an exposition of Beattie's work.

The foundations of modern research in the history of eighteenth-century punishment were laid above all by two books which appeared in the first half of this century: Beatrice and Sidney Webb's study of *English Prisons under Local Government* – the first scholarly study to attempt to survey the development of English prisons – and the first volume of Leon Radzinowicz's *History of English Criminal Law and its Administration from 1750*, an account of the eighteenth- and early nineteenth-century history of capital punishment.[76] The Webbs' study has now been superseded, but Radzinowicz's *History* retains much value and significance, both because of the extraordinary amount of information it pulls together and because of the enduring influence of its interpretations.[77]

Two characteristics of these classic studies deserve special emphasis because of the part they appear to have played in shaping the course and character of subsequent work. First, both books adopt what we have termed a 'reform perspective' on their subject matter. Both, that is to say, effectively treat the early eighteenth century as a backdrop, against which they proceed to set a tale of late-eighteenth- and early-nineteenth-century humanitarian reforming endeavour. The end of the eighteenth and beginning of the nineteenth centuries are identified as critical periods of change, and the account of the disadvantages of the old and advantages of 'reformed' practice offered echoes of that which was provided by the reformers themselves.

Not only the basic shape that both the Webbs and Radzinowicz imposed upon their stories, but also their implicit definitions of the boundaries of their subject matter have influenced subsequent research. The Webbs' history of prisons is exclusively a history of prison management. To point to only one of the several topics they pass incuriously over, they show remarkably little interest in the grounds on which people were imprisoned, or in determining what was clearly the prison's changing role within the larger penal system. Radzinowicz's study ranges more widely. He not only surveys the history of capital statutes, and summarizes the substance of relevant parliamentary debates (chiefly those in which penal reformers inveighed against the incessant proliferation of capital statutes), but also investigates judicial interpretations of statutes, which of course affected their courtroom application, and even provides a lengthy account of the changing ways in which executions were actually carried out. However, Radzinowicz too has relatively little to say about sentencing patterns and the various influences bearing upon them, perhaps in part because this is a topic difficult to approach through the printed sources on which he mainly relies. Moreover, Radzinowicz too does relatively little to locate capital punishment in relation to other penal practices of the day.

Two impulses have powered recent work on the history of eighteenth-century punishment. First, the urge to probe more deeply into pre-reform practice, which older works illuminated only in a patchy and uneven fashion. Douglas Hay's essay, 'Property, authority and the criminal law', which has already figured in our discussion of trial, also merits attention in this connection. One of Hay's objects in this essay was to discover why some by no means illiberal or thoughtless eighteenth-century gentlemen (notably Archdeacon Paley), far from enlisting under the banner of penal reform, pronounced themselves substantially satisfied with the status quo. Hay's own account of the indirect contribution made by the drama of terror and mercy to the maintenance of the social order draws heavily on the writings of the Bloody Code's contemporary apologists. Another contributor to *Albion's Fatal Tree*, Peter

Linebaugh, explored some of the social tensions that hedged public execution in his ethnographically rich account of gallows riots against surgeons seeking bodies for their dissecting tables.[78] Roger Ekirch's study of transportation to the American colonies during its mid-century heyday is the first ever full-length study of this form of punishment – by far the most common fate visited upon men and women convicted of felony between the Hanoverian accession and the American war.[79]

Other writers have been happy to reproduce the traditional emphasis on the century's final decades, but have challenged traditional interpretations of reform. The motives and achievements of prison reformers have been subjected to especially searching scrutiny, notably by Rod Morgan in a brief article, and by Michael Ignatieff and Robin Evans in more substantial works.[80] The reformers' ostensible humanitarianism, we are now told, went hand in hand with a formidably severe disciplinary project. As a result of 'reforms', greater numbers of men and women than ever before were channelled into prisons (most of whom would previously not have been hanged, but transported, whipped or fined). Once inside, they were subjected to harsh and coercive systems of prison discipline. Michael Ignatieff, whose study is subtitled, *The Penitentiary in the Industrial Revolution*, argues that industrialization, rather than the rise of some socially inspecific humanitarian urge, provides the crucial context within which these developments must be set if they are to be understood.[81]

The best of these recent books and articles have certain characteristic merits. First, their authors display considerable sensitivity and imagination in their use of sources – especially when they are using these sources to shed light on the attitude and experiences of the punished. Second, by challenging conventional pieties, these writers have frequently been able to open up interesting new topics to enquiry. If reformed practice was not necessarily more humane, or even more effective, how can we explain why some came to champion it, and why their proposals were ultimately implemented, at least in part? If we find that the rhetoric and the reality of reform do not coincide, how should we interpret this discrepancy? Finally, it is a merit of much recent work that it has placed the question of the relationship between social and institutional change very firmly on the agenda. If some of the hypotheses offered as to the nature of that relationship have been overbold, at least they have helped to direct attention to the problem.

Novel features and novel emphases in recent work leap to the eye. Less immediately striking, but nonetheless worthy of note, are respects in which recent writers have tended to reproduce characteristics of older work. It is remarkable, for example, that traditional views of the basic chronology of change have not been more critically scrutinized. New work has more frequently challenged the substance of the older story than its general shape. If anything, 'revisionists' have been inclined to sharpen the traditional contrast between static pre- and dynamic post-reform eras. Thus, whereas older accounts commonly stressed the slow pace of ameliorative action, recently the accent has been placed instead on the speed and extent of change.[82] Similarly, the older notion that histories of punishment should concern themselves chiefly with the organization and application of punishments has persisted. Only rarely have attempts been made to link the history of punishment back into the wider history of crime and criminal justice, as that is now developing: to link punishment back to crime, to the management of prosecution and to the trial process.[83]

The great merit of John Beattie's study of punishment lies in its combination of those characteristics already commended in other recent works, with constructive innovations on several other fronts. Beattie shifts the time boundaries of our knowledge radically backwards. Beginning his study at the Restoration, he uncovers a rich and complex history of penal change and experimentation in the late seventeenth and early eighteenth centuries. He also grasps the nettle others have failed to grasp, and integrates his study of punishment into a broader study of crime and criminal justice. The brief exposition of Beattie's method and conclusions presented here is organized around an account of his approach to the subject and its implications. It will become clear as we proceed that it is in large part because of the approach he has adopted that he has been able so dramatically to expand our knowledge of the earlier years of the century.

Punishment is the subject of only the last third of Beattie's book, the first two-thirds being concerned with crime and trial respectively. Although the studies of crime and trial have their merits, the section which deals with punishment is undoubtedly the most impressive of the three. This is not to suggest that any of the sections could easily be disjoined from the others, however. The strengths of the section on punishment largely derive from the very fact that it is grounded on a careful study of the changing volume and composition of charges brought against offenders (at the Surrey and to a lesser extent Sussex courts of Assizes and Quarter Sessions), and of the ways in which these charges were handled in the courts.

The standard practice of historians of punishment before the publication of Beattie's book was to approach their subject from the other end, from punishment itself. Historians generally placed some instrument of punishment – the gallows, the prison – at the centre of their concerns and worked outwards from there. The shortcoming of this method is that it offers no ready way of relating different punishments to each other. In fact, one of the most striking features of the eighteenth-century English penal regime was what might be called its 'penal pluralism'. A wide variety of different forms of punishment were simultaneously in use: hanging, transportation, imprisonment, whipping, pillorying, and fining. Although the frequency with which different forms of punishment were employed changed over time, no one penal instrument was wholly abandoned in the course of the period, and even trends in use appear to have followed no very straightforward linear pattern. (In these circumstances, let it be noted that it behoves the historian of any single penal form to be modest in his or her claims as to quite how much light any monofocal study of punishment is likely to shed on eighteenth-century attitudes and social relations.)

Approaching the study of punishments, as he does, through a study of sentencing, Beattie, uniquely, encounters 'penal pluralism' not as a problem, but rather as a phenomenon which sets the terms of the problem. The analytical and interpretative task confronting the historian, as it presents itself from this angle, may be resolved into two main parts. First, it has to be established how judges, or others who had the opportunity to influence the outcome of the sentencing process, negotiated their way through the range of available options. What sorts of considerations led them to plump for one form of punishment rather than another? Second, one must clearly go on to ask what patterns of change over time emerge from a diachronic study of trial outcomes and sentencing patterns – and how the patterns of change thus revealed may best be explained.

It might be thought that this agenda is in at least one respect misconceived, that the punishments visited upon eighteenth-century offenders were determined, not by any courtroom or other decision-making process, but rather by the mechanical application of common law or the provisions of penal statutes, with the corollary that explaining change over time is chiefly a matter of explaining changes in the law. However, Beattie convincingly demonstrates (taking up a theme previously aired by Douglas Hay) how substantial were the opportunities for discretionary choice available in the interval between the first bringing of a complaint, and the final disposition of an offender. In some instances, common or statute law straightforwardly offered choices. When it did not, opportunities for the exercise of discretion could usually be manufactured, by manipulating the form of the charge, the precise character of the verdict, the rules determining eligibility for benefit of clergy, or, finally (the matter which particularly preoccupied Hay), the royal prerogative of mercy.

This is not to say the state of the law was irrelevant. Some laws constrained opportunities for the exercise of discretion more narrowly than others (for instance, by clauses disallowing benefit of clergy). The passage of a new law could make new penal options available for use in connection with particular categories of offender, or could make certain forms of punishment more readily available and thus open the way for their more extensive use. However, one of the interesting conclusions that Beattie's account nudges us towards is that it would be a mistake to conceive of eighteenth-century penal statutes as having emerged, in every instance, in an erratic and irrational fashion out of the deliberations of ill-informed legislators. Some statutes, at least, appear to have arisen out of, and very effectively to have addressed, problems encountered in the courtroom. In some instances the judiciary played a part in their drafting and promotion. In particular, the contribution of high court judges and the Attorney- and Solicitor-General to the shaping of eighteenth-century penal legislation merits further enquiry.[84]

Beattie is inclined to argue (with King and against Hay) that the choices made with regard to the disposition of particular offenders were chiefly influenced by such considerations as the offender's age and character. His most interesting findings relate not so much to the distribution of offenders between punishments at any moment, however, as to changes over time in the balance between punishments visited upon particular categories of offender. He is able to provide an elaborate chronology of, for example, the movement in and out of favour of execution, transportation, whipping, and imprisonment as punishments for particular forms of felony, and of fining and imprisonment as punishments for criminal assaults.

The most striking finding that emerges from this exercise undoubtedly concerns the late seventeenth and early eighteenth centuries, which now stand revealed as having witnessed several dramatic shifts in penal practice, as well as a number of interesting small-scale penal experiments – many of which have previously passed almost entirely unnoticed. Beattie has been able to reveal this interesting and generally unsuspected face of early-eighteenth-century penal history largely because of his chosen method of study. The ready availability in print of extensive pamphlet and parliamentary debate relating to possible modes of punishment long since alerted historians to the importance, in penal history, of the later decades of the century. In the absence of comparable earlier material, many scholars felt it safe to conclude that there were no comparable earlier doubts, projects, debates, or shifts in practice. It is clear now that this conclusion was unwarranted. What emerges as novel and distinctive about the later eighteenth century is not the fact of discontent with the penal status quo, or a willingness to experiment with new options, or even the character of the options experimented with (for example, there was also an early eighteenth-century experiment with the more extensive use of imprisonment), but rather the extent to which these questions were aired before and agitated among an extensive, concerned 'public'.

Beattie alerts us to a much longer and more complex history of penal innovation and experimentation than previous historians had led us to expect. What suggestions does he make as to how his revised version of the story should be explained? His treatment of this topic, and in particular his account of who participated, and in what ways, in the shaping of penal policy, is by no means exhaustive. Nonetheless he makes a large number of interesting, thoughtful, and well-documented suggestions.

He suggests first that the immediate stimulus for changes in penal practice was often provided by a surge in the number of cases (in general, or of some particular kind) coming before the courts. He is able to point to such apparent 'crime waves' as precipitants of change, of course, because he has grounded his study of punishments on a study of crime and trial.[85]

To identify a stimulus is not, of course, to explain a response. In order to pursue this question further it is necessary to distinguish between two possible kinds of response. 'Crime waves' sometimes triggered no more than a short-term, crisis response – usually an increase in the ratio of hangings to other lesser forms of corporal punishment. At other times, short-term shifts in favour of severity were accompanied by much more far-reaching attempts to rethink and reshape the conventional tariff of penalties. An innovative response was more likely to emerge in the face of a massive and prolonged 'crime wave', such as commonly occurred at the end of wars. Other features of the general political environment also might affect both the propensity to innovate, and the kinds of innovation discussed and adopted.

Beattie does carefully distinguish between the different character of the different considered responses mounted at different times. However, he also points to important continuities over time in the character of the options and strategies considered and favoured. From the very beginning of his period, he claims, policy makers were already inclined to believe that the most promising way forward lay in extending the range, and increasing the effectiveness of *secondary* punishments: punishments less final than death, more effectively deterrent than whipping or branding in the hand. The main contenders for the role of intermediate punishment were perennially two: transportation and imprisonment. The history of English penal policy from 1660 to 1800 is largely (though not exclusively) a story of the alternation of these two in favour, and of the changing (mainly growing) role assigned to such secondary punishments within the penal system at large. The arguments advanced in favour of intermediate punishments changed relatively little from one end of the period to the other. At all times reference was made to a venerable stock of ideas about the most effective ways to nip incipient delinquency in the bud, involving intervention at the earliest possible stage, and the removal (as far as possible) of all sources of moral contagion.

Finally, Beattie also suggests that lying behind and conditioning more particular and abrupt patterns of change was a long-term and gradual shift in sentiment against the use of physical violence, evident both in society at large and in the criminal justice system in particular. He suggests that the penal reform movement of the later eighteenth century should be seen in part as an outgrowth and expression of this more fundamental shift in attitudes, which (ironically but consistently) also found expression in a shift in favour of the more severe punishment of crimes of violence.

Beattie's work very substantially advances our understanding of the history of eighteenth-century punishment. The lesson other researchers should draw from his work is not that all studies should henceforth proceed along similar lines, however. There is room for *some* more work on similar lines: in particular, it would be interesting to know more about regional variations in penal practice. How typical were Surrey and Sussex? In general, one would expect a high degree of consistency between the sentencing practices of circuit courts in different parts of the country (which is very much what the Surrey/Sussex comparison suggests) but more variation at the level of Quarter Sessions. Beattie himself has now turned his attention to the City of London, a densely packed urban district with its own distinctive problems, where not only the Quarter Sessions, but also sessions of Gaol Delivery might be dominated by 'local' figures.[86] At the same time, other approaches remain not only legitimate, but necessary, to complement the work Beattie has already done. Thus, there is room for more work on the organization of punishment, on popular attitudes to punishment, and on the character of public and parliamentary debate.[87] Beattie has opened up to enquiry the subject of penal policy making (Who influenced the shaping of penal policy? What considerations bore most powerfully upon them?), but has himself only supplied a limited number of tentative answers to his own questions. There is clearly room for further interesting work in this area.

Those wishing to pursue these many alternative lines of enquiry are nonetheless likely to continue to find Beattie's work of great use – for in two, rather different senses, Beattie's study provides a map or a model, that should help future researchers to orient themselves and to direct their research intelligently. First, Beattie's work provides a rich and complex map of patterns of change over time; a map, moreover, which repeatedly highlights moments of crisis and change, of doubt and debate. Second, in the course of the three parts of his book Beattie painstakingly explores the interconnections between different parts of the machinery of criminal justice, suggesting how decisions made or developments set in motion in one sphere affected developments and decisions in other spheres. Armed with the knowledge and understanding of the larger context of their work (in these two senses) which Beattie's study provides, future researchers should be well placed both to home in quickly on topics worthy of study, and to reflect in an informed fashion on the plausibility and larger implications of their conclusions.

For all its merits, John Beattie's account of eighteenth-century punishment inevitably has certain limitations. We will conclude by noting two of these, in order to draw attention to certain topics we believe still to stand in need of investigation.

Beattie's book implicitly issues a major challenge to those who wish to insist on the peculiar and distinctive character of changes in penal practice in the final decades of the eighteenth century. The picture he paints of late-seventeenth- and early-eighteenth-century developments makes it difficult to maintain with as much confidence as once seemed appropriate that changes in the late eighteenth century were either extraordinary in extent or unprecedented in kind. But this is not to say that there was 'nothing new' about developments of the later eighteenth century, still less that the prison and more general penal reform movements had no features of special interest. Beattie himself identifies increasingly wide diffusion of humanitarian views as a distinctive feature of the later eighteenth century. But precisely what was new, in terms either of ideology or of tactics, about the classic penal reform movement needs more pertinacious and extended consideration in the light of Beattie's findings than he himself provides. Very probably this is a task not best approached, or not best approached solely, on the basis of one or two county studies. For while the local response to reform proposals certainly needs to find a place in the larger account (and there are reasons to think late-eighteenth-century local governors may well have taken up reform proposals more enthusiastically than their counterparts earlier in the century) at the same time it increasingly appears, as we have already remarked, that the manner in which the policy debate was carried on may have been one of the most distinctive features of late-eighteenth-century experience.[88]

A second limitation of Beattie's work is by no means peculiar to his study. Beattie's book, like most other recent accounts of eighteenth-century crime, concentrates on indictable offences – and consequently on the punishments attached to indictable crimes. Offences tried summarily in the eighteenth century were conventionally punished by some combination of whipping, fine, and imprisonment, the latter usually at hard labour in a house of correction. Summary offences, and administrative responses to them are not well documented. It is possible, however, to put together some picture of how houses of correction were employed, since calendars of prisoners admitted to them survive in some county record collections. Houses of correction have now begun to attract attention.[89] This attention seems well placed, for two reasons. First, the house of correction – in effect the first reformative prison – represented an interesting penal experiment, pioneered at lower levels within the penal system (from as early as the sixteenth century) before being adapted for more general use. Second, the study of house of correction records provides one of the few ways into the study, not only of punishments attached to summary crime, but also of summary crime itself. In this case it appears that punishment is a promising point of entry to the wider field.[90]

Criminal legislation

In the course of this essay we have expressed our belief that it is important for historians of crime and the law to treat eighteenth-century institutions seriously and to pay careful attention to developments during the first half of the eighteenth century. These considerations loom large in the ensuing discussion of criminal legislation. In this section we offer an assessment of existing work on the subject and a sketch of alternative approaches we ourselves are currently researching.[91]

One of the most striking features of existing accounts of eighteenth-century crime and the law is the amount of attention they have devoted to legislation. It has not been criminal legislation as a whole that has captured this attention, but rather the Bloody Code: the large number of statutes that attached the penalty of death by hanging to a wide variety of offences, both great and small. This body of statute had developed over several centuries and recent commentators have acknowledged that most of those who faced a capital charge during the eighteenth century were accused of offences that had been made capital by a small number of statutes in the sixteenth century. It is, however, the eighteenth-century proliferation of such statutes, irrespective of the extent to which they were applied in the courts, that has excited the interest of historians of crime and the law. The number of capital statutes grew from about fifty in 1689 to over two hundred by 1820. Most of the new statutes were concerned with offences against property. Douglas Hay's opinion that 'this flood of legislation is one of the great facts of the eighteenth century' is an eloquent statement of a widely-held view.[92]

In attempting to account for this 'great fact', historians have focused on the objectives which the capital statutes were designed to fulfil and the characteristics of the legislative system that produced them. The most influential interpretation is that provided by Radzinowicz, who draws heavily on the criticisms of the Bloody Code offered by late-eighteenth- and early-nineteenth-century law reformers.[93] He argues that eighteenth-century legislators were influenced by an exceptionally penal attitude towards property offences. Capital statutes were able to proliferate chiefly because almost any member of parliament, seized by the desire to make some offence capital, could obtain an act to such effect almost automatically. Eighteenth-century capital statutes imposed the death penalty for a wildly disparate range of offences, often taking little account of existing law regarding the offence in question. This, Radzinowicz argues, was because legislators lacked modern notions of 'scientific' legislation, with their general definitions of offences and general rules about the gradation of punishments. In the absence of such notions a particularistic and incoherent method of legislating resulted in a particularistic and incoherent body of capital statutes.

A more elaborate analysis of the objectives of the new laws is offered by Edward Thompson and Douglas Hay.[94] They argue that the new capital statutes were 'the legal instruments which enforced the division of property by terror', legal instruments which served both the personal interests of a handful of members of parliament and the broader needs of a developing capitalism.[95] They acknowledge, of course, that capital statutes were mitigated in practice – that not all those convicted were hanged. Nevertheless, they believe that this legislation retained enormous instrumental force. Thompson argues that the definition of crime was enlarged by means of the new capital statutes in order to crush various forms of appropriation by the poor that had previously been regarded, at most, as violations of trust or community obligation.[96] Hay points to the way the new capital statutes protected new forms of commercial property.[97] Both are agreed that the extent to which the legislation was concerned to defend property by means of the noose was both new and distinctive.

The picture that emerges has been best summarized by Douglas Hay himself in *Albion's Fatal Tree*:

> What is certain is that Parliament did not often enact the new capital statutes as a matter of conscious public policy. Usually there was no debate, and most of the changes were related to specific, limited property interests, hitherto unprotected for one reason or another. Often they were the personal interest of a few members, and the Lords and Commons enacted them for the mere asking.[98]

At the heart of these accounts, then, are three linked propositions: that the numerical increase in capital offences in the eighteenth century was out of all proportion to what had gone before; that this increase was the work of a peculiarly ruthless ruling class, which, in its own interests, extended the scope of the death penalty to enforce radical redefinitions and restrictions on the property rights of the poor, as well as to defend new forms of commercial property; and that in a parliament that was the tool of this ruling class, the process by which new capital offences were created amounted simply to the uncritical rubber-stamping of any and every proposal. These are all highly questionable propositions and the next few paragraphs offer alternatives to each of them.

Consider first the way the proliferation of eighteenth-century capital statutes has been measured. We can approach this issue in two ways: in terms of the appropriate standard of measurement, and in terms of how the individual units to be counted have been defined. Century-by-century comparisons of legislative output have conventionally been handled by a straightforward juxtaposition of total numbers of statutes passed in the course of each century. But for many interpretative purposes such a comparison is much too simple-minded. If the question is whether there was an increase in the propensity of members of parliament to enact capital or other legislation from one century to the next (or between any two periods), surely what is needed is a standard of measurement that takes account of changes in the number, length, and regularity of parliamentary sessions, and hence of changes in opportunities to legislate. An unsophisticated but nevertheless effective way to achieve this would be to adjust century-by-century counts of capital statutes in such a way as to control for century-by-century changes in both the number of parliamentary sessions and the total number of statutes per parliamentary session. On this basis, the eighteenth century does not look as wildly out of step with earlier centuries as the conventional accounts imply, for a decisive change in the opportunities for legislating was brought about by the Glorious Revolution of 1688–9.

Before 1688, parliaments did not necessarily meet every year. When they met, it was often only for a few months at a time, and sessions were liable to be suddenly and unpredictably cut short by prorogations or dissolutions. In these circumstances, not only were opportunities to legislate intermittent, but even when they arose large numbers of bills met sudden death at the end of a session. After 1688, by contrast, parliaments invariably met annually and on a regular pattern, almost never for less than four months and sometimes for as many as six. One effect of this change was to create vast new openings for legislation. Obstacles like those faced by manufacturers promoting a bill against industrial embezzlement in 1621 were largely eliminated. That bill was 'well approved of by the whole House of Parliament, yet by reason of the sudden dissolution of the said session, nothing was done therein'.[99] Parliament met during only four of the subsequent eighteen years and provisions of the kind the manufacturers sought were not enacted until 1703.

However, the problems associated with measuring the expansion of eighteenth-century capital statutes are not simply a matter of the standard by which that expansion should be gauged. The successful employment of any standard of measurement depends on the consistency with which the units to be measured are defined. The way the units employed in measuring the eighteenth-century expansion of the capital sanction have usually been defined is in this respect deficient. The conventional accounts assume that the growth in the number of statutes entailed a meaningful expansion in the number of capital offences. Each statute, or sometimes each capital provision within a statute, is treated as a unit for the purpose of analysis. The growing number of those units is then taken as a reasonable indication of the extending scope of the capital sanction. On this basis, as we have seen, the eighteenth century does on the face of it look wildly out of step with both the seventeenth century and the nineteenth century in its propensity to provide for capital punishment. But did each eighteenth-century capital statute create one or more new capital offences in a sense that allows straightforward numerical comparisons with the proceeding and subsequent centuries? It is our contention that the apparent multiplication of individual capital provisions in the eighteenth century does not provide an unproblematic measure of the expansion in the numbers of capital offences. Studies which simply treat the multiplication of capital provisions as a 'great fact' should take account of the experience hard-won by students of eighteenth-century indictment statistics and pay more attention to how that fact was constituted.

In adopting this line of argument, we follow John Langbein, who has pointed out that to talk, as Radzinowicz does, of the number of capital offences being increased between 1689 and 1800 by perhaps two hundred is misleading. 'The English did not have 200 separate crimes in the modern sense that could be punished with death. Rather they lacked general definitions, especially for larceny and embezzlement, with the result that they were constantly having to add particularity in order to compensate for generality.'[100] Had modern notions of legislative consolidation been applied by eighteenth-century parliaments, the same range of activities could have been rendered subject to the death penalty by means of only a fraction of the number of statutes. There was an increase in the number of capital offences in the eighteenth century, but the conventional account of its size and significance, relative both to what came after and to what had gone before, needs to be reassessed.

Earlier capital legislation had not so commonly been particularistic. This goes a long way to explain why most of the new capital statutes of the period after 1688 were so little used. The capital statutes on which prosecutions were grounded most frequently in the eighteenth century continued to be that handful dating from the sixteenth century that dealt with broad categories of offences: for example, burglary (1547), horse stealing (1548), and pickpocketing (1565).[101] The majority of the new statutes (although by no means all of them) defined the offences concerned in such a narrow way that the number of potential prosecutions was inevitably tiny.[102] Each of the following, for example, was the occasion of a separate capital statute: forging an entry in a North Riding of Yorkshire land register (1735); destroying Fulham Bridge (1725); destroying Westminster Bridge (1736); embezzling notes by servants of the Bank of England (1742); embezzling the effects of the South Sea Company by its officers or servants (1751).[103]

Two conclusions, therefore, emerge from our assessment of the way the eighteenth-century capital statutes have been counted. If, as we have argued, a much larger proportion of the eighteenth-century statutes were particularistic than had been true earlier, then the proposition that eighteenth-century parliaments engineered an increase in the number of capital offences out of all proportion to that undertaken by previous parliaments is considerably weakened. Similarly, if the opportunities for legislating were much greater in the eighteenth century than had been the case before, doubt is also cast on the notion that eighteenth-century members of parliament had a greater propensity to enact capital legislation than had their predecessors.

The conventional accounts, however, propose not merely an expansion in the number of capital offences in the eighteenth century, but also (especially the work of Edward Thompson and Douglas Hay) a change in the sort of activities that were held to merit the death penalty. Even if the significance of the numerical expansion is, as we have argued, much more limited than the conventional accounts suggest, the change in character is not necessarily affected. Indeed it appears very likely that some of the new capital statutes did, as Edward Thompson argues in *Whigs and Hunters*, transform popular customs or their defence into capital crimes. It is important to note, however, that recent research suggests that the Black Act of 1723, which both Thompson and Radzinowicz present as a key index of the legislative sensibility that spawned other eighteenth-century capital statutes, does not easily fit into such a category. Thompson has argued that the act was a characteristically bloody response by the Hanoverian ruling class to episodes of deer killing and other outrages in the forests of Berkshire and Hampshire by the Blacks, who were foresters resisting the assault on their customary rights by 'improving' landlords and the forest authorities. New archival work suggests that the undoubtedly harsh terms of the act can best be explained not in terms of the need to sustain this rationalizing assault on forest custom, but by the fact that the act was first and foremost a political measure in the narrow sense, occasioned by the Blacks' Jacobite connections.[104]

Less open to contention is the claim that eighteenth-century parliaments extended the capital sanction to many new forms of commercial property (some of which may possibly have overridden customary rights). Examples are the forgery of a wide range of commercial paper and malicious damage to major capital investments, such as the destruction of turnpikes (1735), or setting fire to coal mines (1737).[105] Yet we remain sceptical as to whether all this should be interpreted as a specifically eighteenth-century enlargement of basic principles regarding what sort of offences merited death. After all, coining and many serious thefts were already capital offences in the mid sixteenth century. In the eighteenth century, the same basic principles which underlay the infliction of the death penalty in these instances were often simply extended to equivalent forms of property that had subsequently come into existence, or become more prominent. Eighteenth-century England was a commercially and technologically more diverse society than had been the case in the sixteenth century. Many new forms of commercial paper and investment had emerged which could justify the protection of the death penalty on the basis of analogy with activities which had benefited from earlier capital legislation.[106]

Clearly this does not detract from the importance in practice of these extensions for the offenders concerned, nor can meaningful analogies be found in the sixteenth century for every new capital offence created in the eighteenth. It is also true that late-seventeenth- and eighteenth-century parliaments did not much diminish the scope of capital punishment (although it is worth remembering that the capital statutes against the export smuggling of wool and against witchcraft were repealed in 1693 and 1736 respectively). Nevertheless, we remain unconvinced that they greatly extended the fundamental criteria determining the kind of offences that were believed to merit death.

A parliament which unevenly and often hesitatingly extended the capital sanction to offences analogous to those already liable to the death penalty, but which was decidedly reticent about extensions to the basic principles regarding which offences deserved death seems to be a parliament very different from the uncritical ruling class tool that emerges in the conventional accounts of the eighteenth-century legislature's enactment of capital statutes. Such accounts have also misrepresented the process by which parliament enacted capital and other criminal legislation. One of the most striking shortcomings of the picture they commonly offer is the way it wholly ignores the existence of the large numbers of legislative proposals which failed to reach the statute book. Excluding government-backed revenue or military measures (which were almost always enacted), over a third of bills failed in the eighteenth century. If, as the conventional accounts suggest, legislation was rarely the subject of debate, if parliament merely concerned itself with rubber-stamping private members' proposals, it is difficult to understand why so many bills (including many concerned with crime) should have failed. It is our belief that in order to explain the failure of so many proposals for legislation, it is necessary to acknowledge that legislation was often a matter of intense disagreement and debate in eighteenth-century parliaments.

Given the destruction of the manuscript records of the House of Commons and the sparseness, before the 1770s, of diary and newspaper accounts of debates other than those concerned with political or constitutional issues, it is difficult to establish the shape of debate. Insofar as we can reconstruct the parliamentary careers of criminal proposals (capital and non-capital), it appears that they were usually scrutinized with care and routinely subjected to debate, sometimes at great length.[107] A variety of outcomes was possible. A proposal might be introduced and debated in parliamentary session after session, but never enacted.[108] It might fail outright in one session and never reappear.[109] A bill might fail, but then be re-introduced and pass in a drastically modified form.[110] It might pass in the session it was first introduced, but nevertheless undergo significant changes in the course of its passage.[111]

It is only when we are fortunate enough to have copies of the bills and other evidence about their passage through parliament that the extent of the modifications and the reasons for them can be established. Such cases nonetheless alert us to the fact that even when a bill did pass unmolested in its first session, this was at least as likely to be a consequence of its inoffensiveness in terms of prevailing parliamentary criteria, as it was a result of its slipping through in a momentary lapse of parliamentary scrutiny (although this is not to deny that such lapses did occur). The need to avoid stirring up controversy was recognized by those who promoted legislation. The parliamentary manager of the 1749 industrial embezzlement act commented during its passage that 'care should be taken while endeavours are used to make it effectual, to make it so unexceptional as not to hazard the passing of it'.[112]

What forms did criticisms of such proposals take? This is not the place for a comprehensive account, but three sorts of issues were prominent. First, bills had to face practical criticisms as to their desirability, feasibility and scope. Thus William Hay MP spoke against a proposal to increase the penalties for assault with intent to rob in 1734 because he considered 'there was a sufficient punishment already, and a better than was proposed by the bill'.[113] Bills also had to confront competing views of the public interest. Thus the House of Lords' attempt to tack clauses dealing with deer stealing on to the transportation bill of 1717–18 was staunchly opposed in the Commons, with the argument that the offence was imprecisely defined, 'whereby innocent persons may be liable to prosecutions upon frivolous pretences'.[114] Finally, bills had to run the gauntlet of legalistic objections. Sir John Lowther MP, describing the debate in 1752 on a bill to make the unlawful taking of black lead (graphite) from mines a felony, bemoaned the fact that 'the lawyers make such distinctions between taking things before, or after the owner has sever'd them from the freehold, as if the injury was not equal'.[115]

This picture of lively and informed parliamentary debate is so much at odds with the conventional view of criminal legislation that one might well wonder how both can derive from the same set of sources. Part of the explanation lies in the superficial difficulties of the sources. Finding it hard to determine the character of parliamentary discussion, historians have been surprisingly willing to suggest that there was no discussion. When systematic reporting improves in the 1770s, historians begin talking of a new concern with the deficiencies of the criminal law, citing the reports of parliamentary debates as evidence. Interesting new developments were not lacking in the later eighteenth century, but the contrast between the periods before and after 1770 is easily exaggerated.

We have presented in this section some key elements in our reinterpretation of eighteenth-century capital legislation. Our thinking about each of the components of our argument is, as yet, far from complete, but a number of their implications for the broader study of eighteenth-century law and parliament are already clear. If, as we have argued, the significance attached in the existing accounts to the numerical increase in capital statutes has been exaggerated, then the failure of these accounts seriously to consider penal legislation which inflicted less severe punishments is highlighted. Not only was non-capital criminal legislation more important numerically than is commonly allowed, but also there is potentially a great deal to be learnt about the capital statutes themselves from an analysis that locates them alongside their non-capital counterparts. The more historians distance themselves from mere counting, the more possible it becomes to shift the emphasis of analysis towards qualitative distinctions between statutes: distinctions between, on the one hand, legislation of the importance of the transportation act of 1718, which (though not a capital statute) shaped the way all capital statutes were used during the rest of the century, and on the other, those numerous, but little-used capital statutes of the later eighteenth century which dealt with a multitude of narrowly defined acts of forgery.

This section has disputed Edward Thompson and Douglas Hay's proposition that eighteenth-century legislators were more prepared than their predecessors to extend the ways the capital sanction was used, in order to advance their own economic interests and those of other wealthy and powerful groups. Nevertheless, we remain sympathetic to their desire to understand criminal legislation in terms of the concerns of those with property and political influence in eighteenth-century society. What marks their accounts of criminal legislation is a repeated tendency to substitute the conspiratorial hand of an anthropomorphically self-conscious 'ruling class' for an analysis of the impact on criminal law making of those fractions of the adult male population which enjoyed at least some property and political influence. As we have indicated, criminal law making was often a contentious matter. Before we decide that the criminal law was the instrument of any single interest or class, we need to discover more about the individuals and groups who disputed it, the arguments to which they appealed and the legislative machinery available to them.

The picture we have provided of a parliament where debate over criminal legislation was both routine and important is in direct contradiction to that offered by existing accounts of the Bloody Code. But it is also at odds with the image of eighteenth-century parliaments as legislating bodies found in the mainstream political histories, an image which historians of crime and the law have simply reproduced. Even though eighteenth-century parliaments have been the commanding objects of political historians' attentions, their legislative concerns have been largely ignored. This is largely because Lewis Namier, the dominant figure in the study of eighteenth-century parliamentary history, had no interest in what parliament did (as opposed to its function as the crucible in which a ruling elite was fused). Political historians have subsequently been too busy debating the implications of Namier's views for the history of party and political ideas to contest the implications of those views for the study of legislation. Looking at parliament from the vantage point of the criminal law, however, what emerges most strikingly is how sustained and important a role it played in the domestic government of England by means of various kinds of legislation, including that concerned with crime. If work on criminal legislation can help generate new perspectives on the activities of eighteenth-century parliaments, then studies of crime and criminal justice will be contributing to an area that has as yet resisted their influence and, indeed, the influence of social history in general.

Conclusion

The second section of this essay quoted the statement made by the authors of *Albion's Fatal Tree* in 1975 to the effect that the issues addressed in the study of crime and the criminal law are 'central to unlocking the meanings of eighteenth-century social history'.[116] Despite the changes over the last fifteen years which we have outlined, this proposition still retains its force, both as a justification for working in the field and as a statement of the subject's potential. However, it is a proposition that should also alert us to the responsibility borne by historians of eighteenth-century crime and criminal justice to integrate their findings into a broader picture of eighteenth-century English society. Insofar as the field's potential has not yet been fully realized, this is because the ways in which historians have attempted that integration have been deficient.

This is not to suggest that historians in the field have been insensitive to the need to consider the broader implications of their work. The attraction for them of the three social historical approaches outlined in the second section was the distinctive way in which each approach made crime and criminal justice intelligible in terms of broader historical developments. For history from below such intelligibility lay in the transforming impact of capitalism upon the experience of the dispossessed; for social scientific positivism it was to be found in the relationship between crime and other social variables; and for more recent variants of the reform perspective it lay in the social tensions and administrative changes called forth by industrialization. As vehicles for integrating the history of crime and criminal justice into a broader picture of eighteenth-century English society, each of these approaches has had its strengths, but each has also had considerable shortcomings.

Thus although historians adopting a reform perspective have recognized the importance of the way the law was administered – of questions such as who staffed the machinery of criminal justice and how did it work – their emphasis on industrialization as the motor of change has left them incapable of addressing the earlier eighteenth century as anything other than a counterpoint against which the theme of reform is played. The positivist approach, because it involves no necessary assumptions about the trajectory of change, can avoid the teleology implicit in the reform perspective. But its narrow and mechanical comparisons between crime and other social facts cannot alone provide general explanations of the workings of the criminal law. Moreover, even these narrow comparisons have failed to fulfil their limited promise, as a result of the almost insuperable obstacle posed by the doubtful intelligibility of indictment-based time series.

The most fruitful of the attempts to integrate crime and criminal justice into a broader vision of eighteenth-century English society has undoubtedly come from the approach we termed history from below. The great strength of this approach, compared with the other approaches described, has lain in the ambitious efforts its practitioners have made to develop a coherent interpretation of what was distinctive about relationships of power and inequality in the eighteenth century. Armed with a set of ideas on this score, they have been able to provide a stimulating and broadly conceived account of how and why the criminal law was important in eighteenth-century society. In *Albion's Fatal Tree*, the conclusion they offer is that the criminal law was not merely important, but the essential cement which held a highly inegalitarian eighteenth-century social order together. Its preeminent role in this respect rested both on its capacity to discipline and change society, and on its potency as a system of ideas moulding people's understanding of that society.

Whereas historians working within the other two approaches have attempted to give the history of crime and the criminal law a broader significance simply by juxtaposing changes in crime or law enforcement to other historical changes that are considered significant (for example, changes in the cost of living, or the Industrial Revolution), those adopting a history-from-below approach have tried to provide some account of the processes that linked crime and criminal justice to the wider society. Their attention to process marks a considerable advance, but, nonetheless, the results of their work remain unsatisfactory. In particular the suggestion that the eighteenth-century criminal law held a position of overwhelming preeminence in sustaining the social order remains unconvincing. Proponents of this view have exaggerated both the extent to which the law replaced older instruments of control (whether institutionalized, like the poor law, or informal, like the authority exercised by landlords) and the extent to which it was an instrument of economic innovation and rationalization. They have also presented a much exaggerated estimate of the capacity of law to displace religion as the main source of legitimation for authority.[117] These exaggerations stem from a number of misconceptions about eighteenth-century society, misconceptions which touch on many of the issues already raised in this essay and which take us to the heart of the problem of how to integrate the study of crime and the criminal law into a broader picture of eighteenth-century England. These misconceptions are three.

First, a point we have previously noted and taken up, the idea that the eighteenth century witnessed a distinct stage or phase in capitalist innovation, during which the criminal law played a decisive role by enforcing new definitions of property. Insofar as the criminal law has played this role historically, it seems unlikely that it did so only during the eighteenth century. Here historians seem to have been mesmerized by the work of C.B. Macpherson and his account of the rise of the notion of absolute private property in the late seventeenth and early eighteenth centuries, an account that looks increasingly untenable in the light of subsequent work in the history of political thought.[118]

Second, an associated misconception is the notion that the eighteenth-century state was weak. The evidence offered for this proposition is the British state's failure to use force swiftly in episodes of public disorder, its display of ideological tenderness towards the liberties of the subject, and its lack of an effective bureaucracy.[119] As a result of this weakness, it is argued, it was the criminal law that became the principal terrain on which the eighteenth-century ruling class effected control of their social inferiors, a control which required the subtle manipulation of the law's coercive and ideological capacities. Not only is it inherently implausible to characterize as 'weak' a state which in recurrent international conflicts proved itself one of the most powerful in Europe, but also to do so is to overlook the proven capacity of the eighteenth-century state to pursue domestic policies in relation to, for example, taxation or the management of poverty with considerable success. In eighteenth-century terms, a state need not necessarily have been weak simply because it was obliged to affirm certain notions of individual liberty or because it lacked an administrative bureaucracy on the French model.[120]

Third and finally, historians adopting the history from below approach, in their concern to emphasize 'the great gulf between rich and poor', have been curiously blind to the size and importance of the large middling groups in English society and to their influence on the way the criminal law was used.[121] Edward Thompson in *Whigs and Hunters* has indeed argued that wide sections of the population could use the law defensively to hold off the rapacious exactions of the narrow eighteenth-century ruling class, but this fails to take sufficient account of the extent to which people from the middling groups in particular could put the law to use to pursue their own interests. Although the law did facilitate the exercise of authority by those at the apex of the eighteenth-century social hierarchy, it was principally employed by lesser men. Both as a practical instrument and as a system of ideas, 'the law was not the absolute property of patricians, but a limited multiple-use right available to most Englishmen'.[122]

These misconceptions all revolve around questions about the

character of the eighteenth-century British state. Who controlled it? To what ends was its power used? How great was that power? The answers to these questions provided in this essay are different from those offered by historians working with the approach we termed history from below. Nevertheless, like them, we believe the history of crime and the law can best be integrated into a broader picture of eighteenth-century English society by careful attention to its relationship with the history of the eighteenth-century state. We also believe the history of crime and the law can make an enormous contribution to providing better answers to these and other questions concerning the character of the state. The subject has, consequently, a great deal to offer that wider audience of historians and other scholars who are interested in coming to grips with questions of this kind. It is for this last reason in particular that the trend towards a greater emphasis on the study of process and institutions in work on eighteenth-century crime and the criminal law (often in reaction against work informed by the history from below approach, but at the same time stimulated by it) is so promising a development. It promises to enrich our knowledge of eighteenth-century governance by locating the criminal justice system alongside other policy areas like taxation or the poor law as part of the administrative repertoire of what is all too rarely recognized as a domestically active and, by contemporary standards, effective eighteenth-century state.

There is no doubt that much of this work involves a great stress on technicalities. This essay has included some discussion of these, if only because it is important that aspiring research students should be acquainted with some of the difficulties involved in research in the field. Nonetheless, we must remember that the study of such technicalities is a means to an end. That end is an understanding of the way eighteenth-century society was governed. Traditional political historians have offered a picture of eighteenth-century government which isolates a small group of men holding the reins of power and shows them exercising that power in a limited range of contexts (in particular, statesmanship and lining their own pockets). Those writing about eighteenth-century crime and the criminal law from a history from below standpoint have helped expand our view of what constituted the significant parts of the machinery of government and our sense of the problems with which government grappled. They have introduced into the picture the courts and the gallows, theft and public disorder, the use of brutal coercion, and the fostering of public consent.

Nevertheless, perhaps because this *is* history from below, for which the state represents a separate and antagonistic force, its practitioners (like the political historians) leave us with a vision of institutional power concentrated in the hands of an extremely limited group. They take insufficient account of the ways in which the substance of policies and the operation of institutions were shaped by the very extensive range of people who participated at one level or another (and to greater or lesser effect) in the machinery of government. In other words, the many faces and the many levels of institutional power – from parish to parliament – are not sufficiently explored. The history of crime and the criminal law can make a decisive contribution to their exploration. It is the most important task that faces students of eighteenth-century crime and criminal justice today.

Notes

1 This essay was first published in the *Journal of British Studies*, XXV, 1986, and has been updated to take account of subsequent publications. The authors would like to thank the *Journal of British Studies* and the University of Chicago Press for permission to re-publish it here. 0021–9371/86/2504–0002$01.00.

2 For policing, see two important recent publications: D. Hay and F. Snyder, eds., *Policing and Prosecution in Britain, 1750–1850*, Oxford, 1989, and S.H. Palmer, *Police and Protest in England and Ireland, 1780–1850*, Cambridge, 1988.

3 Leon Radzinowicz, *A History of English Criminal Law and its Administration from 1750*, I, London, 1948, II, 1956, III, 1956, IV, 1968, V, with R. Hood, 1986; D. Beales, 'Peel, Russell and reform,' *Historical Journal*, XVII, 1974, p. 879.

4 S. and B. Webb, *English Local Government from the Revolution to the Municipal Corporations Act*, 9 vols., London, 1906–29; J.L. and B. Hammond, *The Village Labourer*, London, 1911, *The Town Labourer*, 1917, *The Skilled Labourer*, 1919. L.A. Knafla, 'Crime and criminal justice: a critical bibliography', in J.S. Cockburn, ed., *Crime in England*, London, 1977, offers an overview of work in the field at a time when the fruits of the new wave of research had scarcely begun to appear.

5 E.P. Thompson, *The Making of the English Working Class*, London, 1963; Thompson, 'The moral economy of the English crowd in the eighteenth century', *Past and Present*, L, 1971, pp. 76–136; Thompson, *Whigs and Hunters: The Origin of the Black Act*, London, 1975.

6 D. Hay, P. Linebaugh and E.P. Thompson, eds., *Albion's Fatal Tree*, London, 1975, p. 13.

7 J.M. Beattie, 'The criminality of women in eighteenth-century England,' *Journal of Sccial History*, VIII, 1975, p. 80. Also see J.M. Beattie, 'The pattern of crime in England, 1660–1800,' *Past and Present*, LXII, 1974, pp. 47–95.

8 M. Ignatieff, *A Just Measure of Pain: The Penitentiary in the Industrial Revolution, 1750–1850*, London, 1978. But see also his autocritique in 'State, civil society and total institutions: a critique of recent social histories of punishment', chapter 4 in S. Cohen and A. Scull, eds., *Social Control and the State*, Oxford, 1983.

9 D. Hay, 'War, dearth and theft in the eighteenth century: the record of the English courts', *Past and Present*, XCV, 1982, pp. 117–160, and 'Poaching and the game laws on Cannock Chase', chapter 5 in D. Hay, *et al.*, *Albion's Fatal Tree.*

10 E.J. Hobsbawm, 'Social Criminality', *Society for the Study of Labour History: Bulletin*, XXV, 1972, pp. 5–6.

11 For example, J.M. Beattie, 'Towards a study of crime in eighteenth-century England: a note on indictments', in P. Fritz and D. Williams, eds., *The Triumph of Culture: Eighteenth Century Perspectives*, Toronto, 1972, pp. 299–314.

12 H.S. Becker, *Outsiders: Studies in the Sociology of Deviance*, New York, 1973, p. 9.

13 For the most ambitious statement of this position, see J. Ditton, *Controlology: Beyond the New Criminology*, London, 1979. For the best discussion of its implications for the historian of crime and the criminal law, see V.A.C. Gatrell, 'The decline of theft and violence in Victorian and Edwardian England', chapter 9 in V.A.C. Gatrell, B. Lenman and G. Parker, eds., *Crime and the Law*, London, 1980.

14 See, for example, P. Corrigan and D. Sayer, *The Great Arch: English State Formation as Cultural Revolution*, Oxford, 1985. In turn, Hay's essay 'Property, authority and the criminal law', chapter 1 in Hay *et al.*, *Albion's Fatal Tree*, seems to draw heavily on Gramscian ideas.

15 J.H. Langbein, 'Albion's Fatal Flaws', *Past and Present*, XCVIII, pp. 96–120.

16 For example, D. Sugarman and G. Rubin, 'Introduction. Towards a new history of law and material society in England, 1750–1914', in

Rubin and Sugarman, eds., *Law, Economy and Society*, Abingdon, Oxon., 1984. For a historian's critical, though by no means unfriendly, assessment of legal historians' legal history, see D. Hay, 'The criminal prosecution in England and its historians', *Modern Law Review*, XLVII, 1984, pp. 1–29.

17 See the fears expressed by D. Philips, 'A just measure of crime, authority, hunters and blue locusts: the revisionist social history of crime and the law in Britain 1780–1950', chapter 3 in Cohen and Scull eds., *Social Control and the State*, pp. 67–8.

18 See M. Fores, 'The myth of a British industrial revolution', *History*, LXVI, 1981, pp. 181–98 and K. Tribe, *Genealogies of Capitalism*, London, 1981, chapter 3.

19 D. Hay, 'Crime, authority and the criminal law: Staffordshire, 1750–1800', University of Warwick Ph.D. dissertation, 1975.

20 J.M. Beattie, *Crime and the Courts in England 1660–1800*, Oxford, 1986.

21 See, in particular, P.J.R. King, 'Crime, law and society in Essex, 1740–1820', University of Cambridge Ph.D. dissertation, 1984, and S. Pole, 'Crime, society and law enforcement in Hanoverian Somerset', University of Cambridge Ph.D. dissertation, 1983. Some new directions have begun to be opened up by P. D'Sena, 'Perquisites and pilfering in the London docks, 1700–1800', Open University, M.Phil. dissertation, 1986, and R. Short, 'Female criminality, 1780–1830', Oxford University, M.Litt. dissertation, 1990.

22 The literature on these subjects is enormous. The following represent significant interventions in the debates and provide wide-ranging bibliographies. For interpersonal violence see T.R. Gurr, 'Historical trends in violent crimes: a critical review of the evidence', in M. Tonry and N. Morris, eds., *Crime and Justice*, III, Chicago, 1983, pp. 295–353; L. Stone, 'Interpersonal violence in English society', *Past and Present*, CI, 1983, pp. 22–33; J.A. Sharpe, 'The history of violence in England: some observations', *Past and Present*, CVIII, 1985, pp. 206–15, J.S. Cockburn, 'Patterns of violence in English society', *Past and Present*, CXXX, 1991, pp. 70–106. For offences against property, see J. Sharpe, *Crime in Early Modern England, 1550–1750*, London, 1984, chapter 3; Gatrell, 'The decline of theft and violence in Victorian and Edwardian England'.

23 Hay, 'Crime, authority and the criminal law: Staffordshire, 1750–1800', pp. 53–4; Pole, 'Crime, society and law enforcement in Hanoverian Somerset', pp. 180–1.

24 The relationship between violence and gender is another conceptual angle which is now attracting considerable interest. For contrasting approaches, see A. Clark, *Women's Silence, Men's Violence: Sexual Assault in England, 1770–1845*, London, 1987, R.

Porter, 'Rape: does it have a historical meaning?', is S. Tomaselli and R. Porter, eds., *Rape*, Oxford, 1987, and Short, 'Female criminality, 1780–1830'.

25 Hay, 'War, dearth and theft in the eighteenth century'.

26 Beattie, 'The pattern of crime in England', p. 95.

27 King, 'Crime, Law and Society in Essex, 1740–1820', p. 30.

28 *Leeds Intelligencer*, 9 February 1762.

29 S.R. Conway, 'The recruitment of criminals into the British army, 1775–1781', *Bulletin of the Institute of Historical Research*, LVIII, 1985, pp. 46–58, points out the many different channels through which offenders could find their way into the armed forces.

30 Hay, 'War, dearth and theft in the eighteenth century', p. 125.

31 King, 'Crime, law and society in Essex, 1740–1820', pp. 61–3.

32 E.J. Hobsbawm, 'Social criminality', p. 5.

33 See, for examples, 'Conference report: distinctions between socio-political and other forms of crime', *Society for the Study of Labour History: Bulletin*, XXV, 1972, pp. 5–21; Hay *et al., Albion's Fatal Tree*; Thompson, *Whigs and Hunters*; J. Rule, 'Social crime in the rural south in the eighteenth and early nineteenth centuries', *Southern History*, I, 1979, pp. 135–53; B. Bushaway, *By Rite: Custom, Ceremony and Community in England, 1700–1880*, London, 1982, chapter 6.

34 Thompson, 'Moral economy', p. 78.

35 E.P. Thompson, 'Eighteenth-century English society: class struggle without class?', *Social History*, III, 1978, p. 154.

36 For a sympathetic but telling critique of Thompson's work on the crowd, see J. Bohstedt, *Riots and Community Politics in England and Wales 1790–1810*, Cambridge, Mass., 1983.

37 Though see D'Sena, 'Perquisites and pilfering in the London docks, 1700–1800', R.A.E. Wells, 'Sheep rustling in Yorkshire in the age of the industrial and agrarian revolutions', *Northern History*, XX, 1984, pp. 127–45, P. Edwards, *The Horse Trade of Tudor and Stuart England*, Cambridge, 1988, chapter 4.

38 P. Linebaugh, 'Eighteenth-century crime, popular movements and social control', *Society for the Study of Labour History: Bulation*, XXV, 1972, p. 12.

39 P.B. Munsche, *Gentlemen and Poachers, Cambridge*, 1981, chapter 3.

40 J. Styles, 'Embezzlement, industry and the law in England, 1500–1800', chapter 7 in M. Berg, P. Hudson and M. Sonenscher, eds., *Manufacture in Town and Country before the Factory*, Cambridge, 1983. For a similar argument in respect to gleaning, see P. King, 'Gleaners, farmers and the failure of legal sanctions in England, 1750–1850', *Past and Present*, CXXV, 1989, pp. 116–50.

41 The influence of C.B. Macpherson's *The Political Theory of Possessive Individualism*, Oxford, 1962 is crucial here.

42 For a critique of this mode of argument, see A. Giddens, *A Contemporary Critique of Historical Materialism*, London, 1981, pp. 18–19.

43 Beattie, *Crime and the Courts* illustrates the benefits of using the indictments as a starting point in this way. See our discussion of his work on pp. 230–40.

44 J. Styles, ' "Our traitorous money makers"; the Yorkshire coiners and the law, 1760–83', chapter 5 in J. Brewer and J. Styles, eds., *An Ungovernable People: The English and Their Law in the Seventeenth and Eighteenth Centuries*, London, 1980.

45 Edwards, *The Horse Trade of Tudor and Stuart England*, chapter 4. Also see B. Lemire, 'The theft of clothes and popular consumerism in early-modern England', *Journal of Social History*, XXIV, 1990, pp. 255–76, D'Sena, 'Perquisites and pilfering in the London docks, 1700–1800', and Wells, 'Sheep rustling in Yorkshire in the age of the industrial and agrarian revolutions'.

46 For a discussion by a modern criminologist of how such an analysis might be undertaken, see A.K. Cohen, 'The Concept of criminal organisation', *British Journal of Criminology*, XVII, 1977, pp. 97–111.

47 These and other eighteenth-century terms of social description require a great deal more investigation. Historians have made much play with the term 'labouring poor', but it is not clear that eighteenth-century usage warrants its by now almost standard employment as a supposedly non-anachronistic substitute for the modern term 'working class'.

48 P.J.R. King, 'Decision-makers and decision-making in the English criminal law, 1750–1800', *Historical Journal*, XXVII, 1984, pp. 25–58; P. Linebaugh, *The London Hanged*, London, 1991.

49 For an exploration of these issues in relation to horse theft, see J. Styles, 'Print and policing: crime advertising in eighteenth-century provincial England', in Hay and Snyder, eds., *Policing and Prosecution*, pp. 91 and 111.

50 See, for the use of such sources, P. King, 'Newspaper reporting prosecuting practice and perceptions of urban crime: the Colchester crime wave of 1765', *Continuity and Change*, II, 1987, pp. 423–54, and L.B. Faller, *Turned to Account: The Forms and Functions of Criminal Biography in Late Seventeenth- and Early Eighteenth-Century England*, Cambridge, 1987.

51 Hay, 'Crime, authority and the criminal law: Staffordshire, 1750–1800', chapters 2 and 3.

52 Hay, 'Property, authority and the criminal law'.

53 Langbein, 'Albion's Fatal Flaws'; King, 'Decision-makers and decision-making in the English criminal law'.
54 T.A. Green, *Verdict According to Conscience: Perspectives on the English Criminal Trial Jury, 1200–1800*, Chicago, 1985.
55 King, 'Decision-makers and decision-making in the English criminal law', p. 26.
56 For two rather different perspectives on who controlled the workings of the criminal law, compare Hay, 'Property, authority and the criminal law', pp. 38–9 and pp. 60–1.
57 Brewer and Styles, eds., *An Ungovernable People*, Introduction, p. 20.
58 P. King, ' "Illiterate plebians, easily misled": jury composition, experience and behaviour in Essex, 1735–1815', and D. Hay, 'The Class composition of the Palladium of Liberty: trial juries in the eighteenth century', in J. Cockburn and T.A. Green, eds., *Twelve Good Men and True: The Criminal Trial Jury in England, 1200–1800*, Princeton, 1988.
59 Hay, 'Property, authority and the criminal law', p. 46.
60 King, 'Decision-makers and decision-making in the English criminal law'.
61 Hay, 'Property, authority and the criminal law', p. 44.
62 Green, *Verdict according to conscience*, chapter 7, esp. footnote 156.
63 Beattie, *Crime and the courts*, chapter eight, and 'London juries in the 1690s', in Cockburn and Green (eds.), *Twelve Good men and True*.
64 Green, *Verdict according to conscience*, chapter 7; J. Brewer, 'The Wilkites and the law 1763–1774: a study of radical notions of governance', in Brewer and Styles, eds. *An Ungovernable People*, pp. 128–71.
65 For a characterisation of this self-confirming aspect of Hay's argument as a peculiarly Marxist shortcoming, see Langbein, 'Albion's Fatal Flaws', pp. 114–15. Note that here is little evidence that Hay himself wishes the argument to be carried on at this 'rarefied' level.
66 J.H. Langbein, 'Shaping the eighteenth-century criminal trial: a view from the Ryder sources', *The University of Chicago Law Review*, L, 1983, p. 134.
67 J.H. Langbein, 'The criminal trial before the lawyers', *The University of Chicago Law Review*, XLV, 1978, pp. 263–316, and Langbein, 'Shaping the eighteenth-century criminal trial'.
68 Langbein, 'Shaping the eighteenth-century criminal trial', p. 133.
69 For an account which stresses one lawyer's flamboyant self-promotion in the role of defence council, see J. Beattie, 'Garrow for the defence', *History Today*, XLI, February 1991, pp. 49–53.
70 It is necessary to ask what improvements in policing could, under

eighteenth-century conditions, have plausibly been made that would have achieved this goal. For a discussion of some of the possibilities an limitations of eighteenth-century police reform, see J. Styles, 'Sir John Fielding and the problem of criminal investigation in eighteenth-century England', *Transactions of the Royal Historical Society*, 5th series, XXXIII, 1983, pp. 127–49.

71 It may be, as John Beattie has tentatively suggested, that more extensive government involvement in criminal prosecutions was a stimulus to change.

72 Styles, 'Our traitorous money makers', p. 208 and footnote 177.

73 See Munsche, *Gentlemen and Poachers*, pp. 93–102 for what is perhaps an over-generous account of magisterial rectitude in these matters, and R.B. Shoemaker, *Prosecution and Punishment: Petty Crime and the Law in London and Rural Middlesex, c.1660–1725*, Cambridge, 1991, chapter 7 for a more sceptical view. For high court and parliamentary attempts to impose constraints on magistrates in the exercise of their summary powers, see N. Landau, *The Justices of the Peace 1679–1760*, Berkeley, 1984, pp. 348–52.

74 Landau, *Justices of the Peace*, pp. 343–59 tackles various aspects of this supervisory relationship. Douglas Hay and Ruth Paley are currently working on a calendar of references to Staffordshire cases in King's Bench archives which, when completed, will appear in the Staffordshire Record Series.

75 Michel Foucault's work – informed as it is by the notion that the prison is in some sense a representative modern institution – has undoubtedly played an especially important part in attracting social scientists to the history of prisons. See especially M. Foucault, *Surveillir et punir. Naissance de la prison*, Paris, 1975, translated into English by A. Sheridan as *Discipline and Punish*, New York, 1978, and also the comments of M. Ignatieff in 'State, civil society and total institutions'.

76 S. and B. Webb, *English Prisons under Local Government*, London, 1922; Radzinowicz, *History of English Criminal Law*, vol. I.

77 See, for example, Langbein, 'Albion's fatal flaws', pp. 115–19, and also pp. 240–50 below.

78 P. Linebaugh, 'The Tyburn riot against the surgeons', chapter 2 in Hay *et al.*, *Albion's Fatal Tree*.

79 R. Ekirch, *Bound for America: Convict Transportation, Crime and Society in the Eighteenth Century*, Oxford, 1987.

80 R. Morgan, 'Divine philanthropy: John Howard reconsidered', *History*, LXII, 1977, pp. 388–410; Ignatieff, *A Just Measure of Pain*; R. Evans, *The Fabrication of Virtue: English Prison Architecture, 1750–1840*, Cambridge, 1982.

81 Though see Ignatieff's second thoughts in his 'State, society and

total institutions'. Thomas Green's recent study of the criminal trial jury incidentally provides material for the reassessment of another set of 'reform' proposals. Green suggests that the campaign for reform of the capital statutes should be seen not primarily as an attempt to change the conventional tariff of penalties, but rather as an attempt to take the power to tailor a decision to fit their assessment of a particular case out of the hands of the jury, Green, *Verdict According to Conscience*, Chapter 7. Green naturally focuses on the jury, but in fact the argument can be given a more general reference. It is clear that many reformers were concerned to reduce the discretionary powers of judges also.

82 Though see Margaret DeLacy's critical comments in M.E. DeLacy, 'Grinding men good? Lancashire's prisons at mid-century', chapter 8 in V. Bailey, ed., *Policing and Punishment in Nineteenth Century Britain*, London, 1981, and also some questioning of the established chronology in her 1980 Princeton Ph.D. dissertation, 'County prison administration in Lancashire, 1690–1850', especially chapters 1 to 4. Michael Ignatieff, in 'State, civil society and total institutions', pp. 82–3, concedes in the face of DeLacy's criticisms that changes came more slowly and were implemented more unevenly than readers of his book may have been led to believe, but remains strikingly uninterested in the possibility that traditional views of the basic shape of change may be more fundamentally flawed.

83 Michael Ignatieff deserves credit for taking up the question of who was sentenced to imprisonment and on what grounds, and of the effect of changes of sentencing policy on penal administration in *A Just Measure of Pain*, especially chapters 2 and 4 – if only in a rather impressionistic fashion.

84 See J. Innes, 'Parliament and the shaping of eighteenth-century English social policy', *Transactions of the Royal Historical Society*, 5th series, XL, 1990 and J. Beattie, 'London crime and the making of the English criminal law, 1689–1718', in L. Davison, *et al.*, eds., *Reform and Regulation: The Debate over Social and Economic Problems in England, 1689–1750*, 1992.

85 We have previously expressed our own reservations about the usefulness of fluctuations in indictments as a guide to changes in the 'real' incidence of crime. However, it is clear that contemporaries did often respond to them on the assumption that they offered such a guide.

86 J. Beattie, 'London crime and the making of the English criminal law, 1689–1718', in L. Davison, *et al.* eds., *Reform and Regulation*.

87 For the most ambitious work in these areas to date, see R. McGowen, 'The body and punishment in eighteenth-century England', *Journal*

of Modern History, 59, 1987, pp. 651–79 and 'The changing face of God's justice: the debates over divine and human punishment in eighteenth-century England', *Criminal Justice History*, 9, 1988, pp. 63–98.

88 Landau, *Justices of the Peace*, chapter 11 and *passim*, supports the Webbs' view that justices of the peace tended to become more active and conscientious as the eighteenth century progressed, a change she describes in terms of a changing vision of the ideal justice. For the Webbs, see *The Parish and the County*, London, 1906, especially pp. 350–73.

89 J.M. Innes, 'Prisons for the poor: English Bridewells, 1555–1800', in F. Snyder and D. Hay eds., *Labour, Law and Crime* (London, 1987), pp. 42–122; R.B. Shoemaker, *Prosecution and Punishment: Petty Crime and the Law in London and Rural Middlesex, c.1660–1725*, Cambridge, 1991.

90 Justices' notebooks are the other indispensable source for the study of petty offences. The virtue of house of correction calendars as a source lies first in their wider chronological and geographical coverage, and second in the fact that they shed more light on the particulars of sentencing.

91 This section draws on our joint research in progress on eighteenth-century legislation in general and criminal legislation in particular, part of which has appeared in Innes, 'Parliament and the shaping of eighteenth-century English social policy'. We should like to express our gratitude to Sheila Lambert for her generosity in sharing with us her notes on failed bills, 1660–1792. Responsibility for the conclusions we have drawn from this material is entirely ours.

92 Hay, 'Property, authority and the criminal law', p. 18.

93 Radzinowicz, *History of the English Criminal Law*, vol. I, chapter 1.

94 Thompson, *Whigs and Hunters*; Hay, 'Property, authority and the criminal law'.

95 Hay, 'Property, authority and the criminal law', p. 21.

96 Thompson, *Whigs and Hunters*, p. 207.

97 Hay, 'Property, authority and the criminal law', pp. 20–1.

98 Hay, 'Property, authority and the criminal law', p. 20.

99 Public Record Office, SP 14/140, f. 82, State Papers James 1, 1622, petition of worsted makers in Norfolk, Suffolk and Essex, n.d. (1622–3).

100 Langbein, 'Albion's fatal flaws', p. 118.

101 1 Edw, VI, c.12; 2/3 Edw. VI, c.33; 8 Eliz., c.4.

102 One of the most important exceptions was 15 Geo. II, c.34, 1741, which made sheep stealing a capital offence. But capital statutes of

this kind, dealing in one statute with an offence that was very common, formed a much smaller proportion of capital statutes in the eighteenth century than they had in the sixteenth century.

103 8 Geo. II, c.6; 12 Geo. I, c.36; 9 Geo. II, c.29; 15 Geo. II, c.13; 24 Geo. II, c.11.

104 E. Cruikshanks and H. Erskine-Hill, 'The Waltham Black Act and Jacobitism', *Journal of British Studies*, XXIV, 1985, pp. 358–65; J. Styles, 'Criminal records', *Historical Journal*, XX, 1977, pp. 977–81.

105 8 Geo. II, c.20; 10 Geo. II, c.32.

106 For the statutes against forgery, see L. Davison, 'Public policy in an age of economic expansion: the search for commercial accountability in England, 1690–1750', Harvard University Ph.D. dissertation, 1990, chapter 8, and work in progress by Randall McGowen.

107 It is extremely difficult to establish precisely the kind of punishment intended in the case of failed bills, since even when the text of a draft bill survives, the specific punishments proposed were, as a matter of form, always left blank.

108 For example the succession of bills 'for the more effectual preventing, and punishing, the stealing, or unlawful killing of cattle', introduced in the sessions of 1714–15, 1715–16 and 1717–18; *Journals of the House of Commons*, XVIII, 1714–18.

109 For example the bill for 'better preventing the malicious burning and destroying houses, buildings, fences, corn, hay, grass and other improvements', introduced in 1698–9; *Journals of the House of Commons*, XII, 1697–9.

110 For example, 25 Geo. II, c.10, an act for the more effectual securing mines of black lead from theft and robbery.

111 For example, 22 Geo. II, c.27, an act for the more effectual preventing frauds and abuses committed by persons employed in various manufactures.

112 British Library, Additional Manuscripts 35590, folios 267–8, Horatio Walpole to the Earl of Hardwicke, 25 March 1749.

113 Northamptonshire Record Office, L(C) 1732, diary of William Hay, entry for 13 March 1733–4.

114 *Journals of the House of Commons*, XVIII, 1714–18, p. 768, 18 March 1717–18.

115 Cumbria Record Office, Carlisle, D/Lons/W/58, Lowther Manuscripts, Sir John Lowther to John Spedding, 11 February 1752.

116 Hay, *et al.*, *Albion's Fatal Tree*, p. 13.

117 For an impassioned, if rather overwrought presentation of the ideological importance of religion in eighteenth-century England, see J.C.D. Clark, *English Society 1688–1832*, Cambridge, 1985, especially pp. 87–90.

118 Macpherson, *The Political Theory of Possessive Individualism*. For work that challenges Macpherson's account see A. Ryan, *Property and Political Theory*, Oxford, 1984, chapter 1, R. Tuck, *Natural Rights Theories*, Cambridge, 1979, especially pp. 2–3, and J. Tully, *A Discourse on Property*, Cambridge, 1980, especially p. 172.

119 E.P. Thompson, 'Patrician society, plebeian culture', *Journal of Social History*, VII, 1974, p. 403. A more nuanced analysis is Thompson, 'Eighteenth-century English society', especially p. 162. For a critique of Thompson's views, see p. Anderson, *Arguments within English Marxism*, London, 1980, pp. 87–94.

120 For a wide-ranging discussion of these issues, see J. Brewer, *The Sinews of Power: War Money and the English State, 1688–1783*, London, 1989.

121 Hay, 'Property, authority and the criminal law', p. 18. For a recent study which emphasises the significance of these groups, see P. Langford, *A Polite and Commercial People: England, 1727–1783*, Oxford, 1989.

122 Brewer and Styles, eds., *An Ungovernable People*, p. 20. It appears that even the labouring poor were able to share, to a greater extent than Brewer and Styles suggested, in this 'multiple-use right'.

Part IV
Writing 'Law and Society' Histories: New Directions

[17]

Hermes, Clio, Themis: Historical Interpretation and Legal Hermeneutics

Donald R. Kelley
University of Rochester

I

The theory of interpretation has enjoyed a considerable revival of interest in recent years, especially in relation to historical methods.[1] Intellectual fashion aside, the main attraction of hermeneutics seems to be its promise of alternatives to intimidating behaviorist, quantitative, or abstract-structuralist approaches to the human sciences. In the pandemonium of "scientific" methods for the study of society and culture the one common feature has been the attempt in one way or another to do away with the thinking subject. In the name of scientific objectivity, psychoanalysts and Marxists have likewise looked for impersonal forces below, or beyond, the level of consciousness; functionalists and structuralist have sought patterns, or codes, which likewise transcend, or subsume, human behavior; "deconstructionist" literary critics have subordinated authorial intention and consciousness to the medium of discourse, whether language or "writing"; and "new" economic and social historians have cast their explanations in statistical and serial terms which make personality, quality, and perhaps values irrelevant. Each of these lines of inquiry undeniably has value and its own insights, but each is also threatened by some sort of reductionism, and none can tell the whole truth. In particular each tends to neglect, or to misconstrue, the role of the observer, which is to say the interpreter, usually by affecting to replace judgment by a technique. Now despite Kierkegaard's urging, subjectivity may not be truth, but neither is technique. What hermeneutics proposes is to accommodate

[1] Besides translations of the works of Gadamer, Habermas, and Ricoeur, recent studies include Karl-Otto Apel, *Transformation der Philosophie* (Frankfurt, 1973); Zygmunt Bauman, *Hermeneutics and Social Science* (New York, 1978); Joseph Bleicher, *Contemporary Hermeneutics* (London, 1980), and *The Hermeneutical Imagination* (London, 1982); David Hoy, *The Critical Circle* (Berkeley, 1978); Erwin Hufnagel, *Einführung in die Hermeneutik* (Stuttgart, 1976); T. K. Seung, *Structuralism and Hermeneutics* (New York, 1982), and *Semiotics and Thematics in Hermeneutics* (New York, 1982); and John B. Thompson, *Critical Hermeneutics* (Cambridge, 1981). For the most part I omit reference to the even larger bibliography from literary criticism.

[*Journal of Modern History* 55 (December 1983): 644–668]

both the inquiring subject and his intransigent object in its interpretive scope, to find a place in the routine of question-and-answer for the questioner-and-answerer, no matter what his perspective or scientific equipment.

"Interpretation" is pre- if not nonscientific, as old as literature, older than philosophy; and the theory of interpretation goes almost as far back. Indeed its origins are mythical, *hermeneia* being associated with the messenger-god Hermes and with the priests of the Delphic oracle, hence with the process of divination. From the beginning the aim of interpretation was to give human expression to superhuman, or general, truth; and philosophically, from Aristotle's *Peri Hermēnias*, it was regarded as the primary function of the intellect, that is, the formulation of statements preliminary to logical reasoning. But almost from the beginning, too, there was interest in finding the general "meaning" of human creations, especially written creations: there was, in other words, a philological as well as a philosophical hermeneutics, starting especially with criticism of the Homeric poems. Here was the first major encounter between Hermes and Clio; and their offspring, the science of philology, played an important part in the development of historical method, although the philosophical and theological varieties of hermeneutics have in large measure come to overshadow their literary cousin.

The classic historical survey remains Wilhelm Dilthey's *Entstehung der Hermeneutik*, which treats its subject as a cornerstone of the human sciences as well as a major dimension of Western history and indeed as an aspect of that "critique of historical reason" which was Dilthey's life task.[2] In Judaeo-Christian tradition, book-bound as it has been, hermeneutics has played a crucial and indeed shaping role. Talmudists and Christian exegetes alike expounded and explicated God's word as expressed in scriptures, and then extended their interpretations into larger earthly and heavenly domains. In the most elementary sense "interpretation" meant literary translation; and as biblical practitioners of this art from Jerome to Erasmus learned, it was a most demanding and even dangerous occupation: what man could presume to give human expression to the diving Logos? Fortunately, there was a hermeneutical dispensation. The old rule that "the letter killeth while the spirit giveth life" licensed not only translators but also more creative patristic and scholastic readers of the "sacred page."[3] The climax of medieval hermeneutics came with

[2] *Gesammelte Schriften* 5 (Munich, 1927): 334 ff.; and cf. Joachim Wach, *Das Verstehen, Grundzüge einer Geschichte der hermeneutischen Theorie im 19. Jahrhundert* (Tübingen, 1926).

[3] See Beryl Smalley, *The Study of the Bible in the Middle Ages* (Oxford, 1952), pp. 94 ff., and cf. Herman Hailperin, *Rashi and the Christian Scholars* (Pittsburgh, 1963), pp. 32 ff.

the famous three- or four-fold theory established by Origen and elaborated by the Victorine school of biblical criticism. History, allegory, tropology, and morality were the four conventional rubrics of the literal and various figurative modes of interpretration which allowed pious men to uncover the different levels of scripture, defined by Hugh of St. Victor as "the letter, the sense and the deeper meaning."[4] Despite protests of fidelity to texts—Latin *sensus historicus, fides historiae*; Greek *kyrios*; Hebrew *peshạt*—biblical hermeneutics developed into a complex "sacred science," a discipline which, by the Middle Ages, admitted the critical subject as well as the divine object into its domain.

Renaissance humanism at once broadened and simplified the theory of interpretation: broadened it by introducing notions of style, cultural context, anachronism, and a varity of critical tools; simplified it by insisting on the "historical sense" and discarding the conventions and apparatus of figurative interpretation. "Grammarians" like Lorenzo Valla and Erasmus had as little use for the etymological speculations of Isidore of Seville and allegorizing fantasies of the Victorines as they did for the metaphysical fictions of the scholastics; and they rejected all on the same grounds, that is, the metahistorical and metalinguistic character of such interpretation. The classic humanist treatment was Leonardo Bruni's *De interpretatione recta*, which inquired into the conceptual resources of Latin and the propriety of translating authors like Aristotle.[5] For Bruni the interpreter's basic skill was not philosophical depth, however, it was literary expertise and mastery of ancient authorities; and this scholarly requirement was even more essential for more complex interpretation, such as Valla's pioneering "higher criticism" of the New Testament and the conjectural emendations and "restitutions" made by classicists like Angelo Poliziano and Ermolao Barbaro.

It was in the sixteenth century, however, that hermeneutics emerged in a recognizably modern form. The philological "science" established by Bruni and Valla and developed by Poliziano, Budé, and Erasmus was perfected by the great generation of "critics," including Casaubon, Lipsius, and above all, the young Scaliger.[6] More famously, perhaps, this age of religious reform saw the emergence of the Protestant school of biblical criticism, which has conventionally been regarded as the point of departure of modern hermeneutics as formulated by Schleiermacher, extended to the world of human culture by Dilthey, and developed by such followers

[4] *Didascalion*, trans. J. Taylor (New York, 1961), p. 147.

[5] "De interpretatione recta," *Humanistisch-Philosophische Schriften*, ed. H. Baron (Leipzig, 1928), pp. 81–96.

[6] See Jean Jehasse, *La renaissance de la critique* (Saint-Etienne, 1976).

as Heidegger and Gadamer. In particular Flacius Illyricus, reacting to the definitions of Christian "tradition" set by the Council of Trent, had devised a "key" to scriptural criticism based on a combination of Renaissance philology and the Lutheran approach to biblical interpretation (which, though also devoted to the "historical sense," was by no means the simplistic fundamentalism some have misjudged it to be).[7] In the eighteenth century another stage was reached when G. F. Meier expanded theological hermeneutics into what (in 1757) he called "The Idea of a General Theory of Interpretation," while in the nineteenth century biblical scholars like Strauss extended their interpretations into the broader fields of mythology and cultural history.[8] From Dilthey's time this complex of intellectual traditions, chronicled with reverent detail in Joachim Wach's *Das Verstehen*, has broadened into a wide range of human sciences; and despite positivist resistance, its offshoots still thrive as special forms of "critical" philosophy. Through the partnership between Clio and Hermes the "thinking subject," *homo interpres* as he might be called, still lives; and so does hermeneutics.[9]

II

Yet if hermeneutics lives, indeed is enjoying a revival, it is not beyond reproach even by its admirers. Two basic criticisms may be suggested (not including the misguided charge of subjectivism), and they correspond neatly to the polarity evident in the theory of interpretation from its Greek beginnings. On the one hand there is the tendency of philological hermeneutics toward hypostasis and idolatry of the written text: Alexandrine *grammatikoi* do not look beyond Homer even when Homer nods; and Michel Foucault, Jacques Derrida, and other textualists have likewise, if more self-consciously, inclined to a fetishism of the printed page, a fixation on the "text-model." There are no doubt grounds on which such attitudes can be justified, and it is difficult to resist Paul Ricoeur's arguments for the "semantic autonomy of the text," if not for its exclusive identification with the "hermeneutical field."[10] The question here, however, is not the conceptual plausibility of textualism even in its extreme

[7] See Wilhelm Preger, *Matthias Flacius Illyricus und seine Zeit* (1859–61), 2: 478 ff.

[8] *Die Idee einer allgemeinen Auslegungslehre*, based on lectures at the University of Halle; and for the historical background of the "higher" criticism, David Friedrich Strauss, *The Life of Jesus Critically Examined*, 2nd ed., trans. George Eliot (London, 1892).

[9] Andres Ortiz-Oses, *Antropologia hermeneutica* (Madrid, 1973), pp. 79, "hombre-interpres," and 84, "animal hermeneuticum."

[10] *Interpretation Theory* (Ft. Worth, Texas, 1976), p. 29.

Derridean forms, but rather its methodological value for historical investigation and interpretation.

A similar reservation must be made about the philosophical school, which from Aristotle to Gadamer inclined toward what E. D. Hirsch deprecates as "metaphysical hermeneutics" or what Ricoeur characterizes more favorably as a shift "from epistemology to ontology," whether the surrogate text is secular or religious, phenomenal or noumenal.[11] In the "transformation of philosophy" pursued by German philosophers the key is also the fundamental "linguisticality" of the human condition; and again we seem to be confronted by an up-to-date version of the Baconian idols of the den, or perhaps the Vichian conceit of scholars. If for French devotees of *l'écriture* the book is seen as a world, for German defenders of *Sprachlichkeit* the world appears as a book; and neither metaphor, generative of so much scholastic debate, seems adequate for historical understanding. The fallacy of the first is the uncritical elevation of the subject above the object of interpretation, that of the second an existential, perhaps irreversible, leap into phenomenology. Perhaps from an aversion to old-fashioned "historicist" attitudes, both seem to have lost Dilthey's vision of a unifying and fructifying science of humanity, one by a literary ploy amounting to a sort of higher fundamentalism, the other by philosophical circumvention which in effect smuggles hermeneutics into metaphysical speculation. For the historian neither will do.

With the language model itself there are certain difficulties and diverting assumptions. "History is, as it were, the great dark book," Gadamer has written, "the collected work of the human spirit, written in the language of the past, the text of which we have to understand."[12] But let us not forget the "as it were," for the historical process is not merely a silent clamor of "intersubjective" thought. Much of its substance—actions, interactions, institutions, social patterns—may well escape the net of interpretive systems which bind themselves to conscious thought and expression, and so fall into the idealist fallacy expressed most famously in the Croce-Collingwood proposition that "all history is the history of thought" and preserved in the "existential subjectivity" of Gadamer. This would seem enough in itself to discredit the thinking subject, and indeed it has been the basis of one of the major complaints registered by positivist and behaviorist critics. It is a view which has implications

[11] Hirsch, *The Aims of Interpretation* (Chicago, 1976), p. 85, and Paul Ricoeur, *Hermeneutics and the Human Sciences*, trans. J. Thompson (Cambridge, 1981), p. 53.

[12] *Truth and Method*, trans. G. Barden and J. Cumming (New York, 1975), p. 156. Even more extreme is George Steiner, *Extraterritoriality* (New York, 1977), p. 62: "History, in the human sense, is a language-net cast backwards."

antisocial as well as antiscientific, and it needs a corrective from beyond the worlds of verbal behavior.

The point is that the "hermeneutical field" must accommodate not only the thinking subject and his medium but also the objects of his attention, which indeed serve to establish and to define his subjectivity. The world of "things," however remote and impenetrable in an ontological sense, needs to be accommodated as sphere of potential experience beyond the horizons of perception—an extension of the hermeneutical field to be explored and analyzed, perhaps civilized and socialized. A common failing of both philological and philosophical hermeneutics has been the general neglect of social and historical context. Gadamer's conviction that "Being that can be understood is language"[13] does not seem adequate to the problem of gaining access to the dimension of inarticulate human action, individual or collective, rational or irrational. Such indeed is the implication of the critique of Gadamer offered by Habermas, who has tried to provide remedies by attending (in Marxist or at least Marxoid fashion) to problems of ideology, to action theory and to "social systems."[14] Gadamer rejects this as in effect a reversion to dualism, while at the same time acknowledging the force of Habermas's concerns. How then can we overcome the subject-object paradox (which may itself be inherent in *Sprachlichkeit*) and at the same time accommodate the process of history without succumbing to reductionism, economic or political, or to the fallacies of "value-free" social science? Gadamer's answer is most provocative, though not systematically followed up. "Legal hermeneutics," he has declared, "is able to point out what the real procedure of the human sciences is."[15] This is the suggestion which, from a historical

[13] *Philosophical Hermeneutics*, trans. D. Linge (Berkeley, 1976), p. 31. It should be understood that the present critique is limited to questions of historical investigation and interpretation and does not confront the problem of Heideggerian "prejudice," which would in effect deny the possibility of historical understanding beyond our present *Kulturkreis*. This sort of epistemological relativism (which itself can be seen "historically" as well as logically and ontologically) is useful in suggesting the philosophical limits of historical knowledge and may even in effect reduce it, strictly speaking, to a form of imagination; but it can hardly be allowed to interfere with historical or anthropological inquiry; and indeed the aim of Gadamer, Ricoeur, et al. is precisely to salvage the philosophical standing of the human sciences.

[14] See Thomas McCarthy, *The Critical Theory of Jürgen Habermas* (Cambridge, Mass., 1981), p. 187, and Bleicher, *Contemporary Hermeneutics*, p. 153; also Martin Jay, "Should Intellectual History Take a Linguistic Turn? Reflections on the Habermas-Gadamer Debate," *Modern Intellectual History*, ed. D. LaCapra and S. Kaplan (Ithaca, New York, 1982), pp. 86–110.

[15] *Truth and Method*, p. 292.

rather than philosophical or literary angle, I propose to pursue here, beginning with a brief sketch of the historical background.

III

Unlike the long-standing relationship which Hermes has maintained with Clio, that with Themis, goddess of justice and social order, has hardly been noticed, except within professional legal scholarship—and that intellectual tradition has been largely cut off from the human sciences and even philosophy in the past century or more. This is a curious and lamentable circumstance, for legal hermeneutics has a history almost as long and colorful as those of the theological, philosophical, and literary varieties. What is more, it has enjoyed some of the same harvest times, most notably in medieval commentaries on civil law (corresponding to biblical exegesis), in Renaissance treatises on the *ars critica* in law, and in romantic theories of interpretation parallel (as well as contemporary) with those of Schleiermacher and Friedrich Ast. It has not, however, enjoyed a comparable revival, or historical appreciation, in the present century.[16] Preoccupied with Schleiermacher, his *Vorläufer* and his epigones, Dilthey did not even deign to mention the almost congruent legal tradition, nor is it touched on in the authoritative survey of Wach or later sketches known to me. Even Emilio Betti, though the law furnished his own intellectual provenance and though he touches on the subject (*interpretazione giuridica*; *juristische Auslegung*) says virtually nothing about the historical background.[17]

The starting point for such an inquiry must be Roman jurisprudence, although the debts to Greek philosophy and rhetoric were extensive and should not be forgotten. The pretension of Roman law to the status of true "science" and beyond that the highest form of human wisdom (*sapientia* as well as *scientia*) was based on two arguments: one that law was rational and universal, explicable in terms of "causes" and in accord with nature; the other that it took into account human values and social

[16] There is extensive literature on legal hermeneutics beginning especially with Savigny (see below, n. 25), but little carries over into historical or social thought. See, however, Manfred Thiel, *Interpretation: Philosophie, Jurisprudenz, Theologie* (Regensburg, 1980), pp. 320–493; Maximilian Herburger, *Dogmatik: Zur Geschichte von Begriff und Methode in Medizin und Jurisprudenz* (Frankfurt, 1981); M. Fuhrman, H. R. Jauss, and W. Panenberg, eds., *Text und Application: Theologie, Jurisprudenz und Literaturwissenschaft im hermeneutischen Gespräch* (Munich, 1981); Franz Wieacker in *Philologie und Hermeneutik im 19. Jahrhundert*, ed. H. Flashar, K. Gründer, and A. Horstmann (Göttingen, 1979), pp. 312–20; and P. Piovani, "Ex Legislatione philosophia," *Studi in onore di Emilio Betti* (Milan, 1962), 1: 392–428.

[17] See below, n. 30.

goals and worked, actively and "practically," to achieve them. It represented, in other words, both *theoria* and *praxis*. The great tradition of expertise in "legal science" began, as Max Weber has argued, with the empirical and theoretical masters called *honoratiores*, whose business was both to judge social reality (the facts of a case or, as legal reformers, the condition of a society) and to apply the reason of the law according to established method, eventually to contribute also to the analysis, conceptualization, and systemization of the law.[18] These professional scholars were at once practitioners (*prudentes*), scientists, and "priests of the law," but they were above all interpreters (*juris interpretes*), whose base was not only the accumulated (and accumulating) experience of civil law and the "law of nations" (*jus gentium*) but also the ill-defined concept of natural law. The legal hermeneutics developed by these forefathers of social science from at least the second century B.C. was the life principle of Roman, Romanist, and Romanoid jurisprudence for two millenia and more.

The great landmark in the history of Roman legal science is the work of legal codification carried out in the sixth century by the Emperor Justinian and his Byzantine editors, who tried to sum up and to systematize more than ten centuries of legal experience and interpretation. One of the premises of this effort was the hope of the Emperor that his law should "prevail forever, " and one corollary was the ban he placed on all "interpretation" whatsoever.[19] But to avoid what Justinian himself called "the vain discord of posterity" was an illusion, not only because of the instability of the human condition but also because of the demise of imperial authority in general. Beginning with the twelfth century revival of civil law, legal hermeneutics found new life and, through the ambitions and controversies of medieval *juris interpretes*, an astonishingly active career. For scholastic jurisprudence, "interpretation" was essential not only to discover the meaning or "spirit of the law" (*mens legum*, *ratio legis*) but also to give applicability to modern society and even to reform and to "correct" laws; and it did not hesitate to treat questions of political

[18] *On Law and Society*, trans. E. Shils and M. Rheinstein (Cambridge, Mass., 1954), pp. 198 ff. Classic discussion by Fritz Schulz, *History of Roman Legal Science* (Oxford, 1953), and for the medieval phase Ennio Cortese, *La norma giuridica* (Milan, 1962–64); more generally Helmut Coing, *Die juristische Auslegungsmethoden und die Lehren der allgemeinen Hermeneutik* (Cologne, 1959). There is a huge literature relevant to hermeneutics and to the cultural sciences more generally.

[19] Constitution *Deo Auctore* prefacing the Digest, on which F. Pringelsheim, "Justinian's Prohibition of Commentaries to the Digest," in his *Gesammelte Abhandlungen* (Heidelberg, 1961), 2: 86–106.

"power." In the course of such discussions there emerged practical awareness both to problems of subjectivity and to the necessity of making judgments in terms of times, places, circumstances, and persons: the science of law had also, in short, psychological, epistemological, and sociological dimensions.[20]

The first great age of modern legal (as of theological) hermeneutics was the sixteenth century. In connection with the widespread search for a proper scientific "method" in various disciplines, legal scholars also began to produce treatises on legal methodology and then specifically on the theory of interpretation (*De interpretatione legis* and *De extensionibus* being the conventional ways of defining the subject).[21] These discussions were informed not only by the issues of scholastic jurisprudence but also by the historical and literary insights of humanist scholars—"grammarians" who approached the legal canon of Justinian, as they approached holy scriptures, as human documents. As Erasmus interpreted the Bible in the light of philology, so his younger friend Andrea Alciato introduced similar critical methods into the study of civil law. This was the age, too, of the great methodological conflict between "legal humanism" and the old-fashioned scholastic jurisprudence, reflected most famously in Alberico Gentili's dialogue of 1582 but more profoundly in contemporary treatises devoted to the problem of legal systematics and its relation to history and philology.[22] This polemical and "scientific"

[20] More detailed treatment in my articles, "Vera Philosophia: the Philosophical Significance of Renaissance Jurisprudence," *Journal of the History of Philosophy* 14 (1976): 267–79; "Civil Science in the Renaissance: Jurisprudence Italian Style," *The Historical Journal* 22 (1979): 777–94; and "Civil Science in the Renaissance: Jurisprudence in the French Manner," *History of European Ideas* 2 (1981): 261–76. See also Pietro Costa, *Iurisdictio. Semantica del potere politico nella pubblicistica medievale 1100–1433* (Milan, 1969), and Pierre Michaud-Quantin, *Etudes sur le vocabulaire philosophique du Moyen Age* (Rome, 1970).

[21] Most essential are V. Piano Mortari, "Il problema dell'interpretatio iuris nei commentatori," *Annali di storia del diritto*, 2 (1958): 29–109, and *Ricerche sulla teoria dell'interpretazione del diritto nel secolo XVI* (Milan, 1956). The connections between the methods of law and history have often been noted, for example by Julian Franklin, *Jean Bodin and the Sixteenth-Century Revolution in the Methodology of Law and History* (New York, 1963).

[22] *De iuris interpretibus* (London, 1582). See also Aldo Mazzacane, *Scienza, logica e ideologia nella giurisprudenza tedesca del sec. XVI* (Milan, 1971); Hans Erich Troje, "Wissenschaftlichkeit und System in der Jurisprudenz des 16. Jahrhunderts," in *Philosophie und Rechtswissenschaft*, ed. J. Blühdorn and J. Ritter (Frankfurt, 1969), pp. 63–97, and "Alciats Methode der Kommentierung des 'Corpus iuris civilis,'" in *Der Kommentar in der Renaissance*, ed. A. Buck and O. Herding (Godesberg, 1975), pp. 47–61; and Piano Mortari, *Diritto, logica, metodo nel secolo XVI* (Naples, 1978).

defense of professional methods constituted a dramatic prelude to a long series of hermeneutical controversies, including that between Savigny and Thibaut in the romantic age and, more recently, those carried on by Gadamer, Apel, Habermas, and Betti.

It is worth noting, too, that the collateral descendant of Roman jurisprudence (that is, canon law) likewise, congruently and dependently, developed a theory of interpretation which was even more "extensive" and socially conscious than that of the civilians.[23] For in their efforts to give social meaning to laws canonists attended not only to doctrinal tradition and professional convention (the *communis opinio* which might also reflect tacit consent) but also to the variables and unpredictables of the human condition—time, place, social condition, and circumstances—basic to what from the twelfth century has been called "positive law." Canonists have had their own peculiarly flexible standards of judgment (*aequitas canonica*) because of their special need to join public and private spheres, and as a result they have had recourse to various interpretive strategies—exceptions, privileges, dispensations—in order to "relax" abstract laws and accommodate them to society as well as to transcendent demands. Most characteristic of all was the canonist technique of "harmonizing interpretation," which was consummated in Gratian's great collection originally entitled "Concord of Discordant Canons" and subject to the same sort of interpretive glosses and commentaries as Justinian's secular canon. It is significant that canonist interpretation came to maturity at just the time of that religious "Reformation" which, besides challenging canonist tradition, formed the context of that seminal phase of modern hermeneutics described by Dilthey.

Since the "golden age" of legal science in the sixteenth century there has been a fairly continuous tradition, or set of traditions, of interpretation theory down to modern times. For theology Dilthey has located some of the major figures between Flacius and Schleiermacher, but for jurisprudence the trail remains largely unexplored, as has the stage since the early nineteenth century. The rise of "historicism," which produced the "higher criticism" of the Bible, gave impetus likewise to controversies over that reincarnation of civil law which was the Code Napoléon of 1804. Like his prototype Justinian, the French emperor tried to forbid

[23] Important discussions by Charles Lefebvre, *Les pouvoirs du juge en droit canonique* (Paris, 1931); J. Salgado, "La méthode d'interprétation du droit en usage chez les canonistes," *Revue de l'Université d'Ottawa* 21 (1951): 201–13; and 22 (1952): 23–35; and Stephan Kuttner, *Harmony from Dissonance* (Latrobe, Pa., 1960); also Pierre Legendre, "L'historie du droit canonique et la science des cultures," *Proceedings of the Second International Congress of Medieval Canon Law* (Rome, 1965), pp. 281–94.

"interpretation" while succeeding in fact only in politicizing the issue and in intensifying the old conflict between legislative authority and judicial discretion.[24] Ensuing debates, especially after the publication of Thibaut's *Theorie der logischen Auslegung des römischen Rechts* (1799) and Savigny's later responses, were addressed not only to professional questions of adapting a purportedly rational system of law to a recalcitrant social reality but more generally to the relationship between human action and historical change.[25] "What is the influence of the past on the present? " as Savigny phrased the question, and "What is the relation of what is now to what will be ?" The effect of the historical school under Savigny's leadership was not only to reinforce ties between historical and legal scholarship but to introduce hermeneutics into the partnership.[26] This new trinity of Hermes, Clio, and Themis was involved, at some points collectively, in efforts of considerable importance for the human sciences.

Until fairly recently the achievements of this partnership have been limited mostly to historical scholarship and to the professional domain. On the one hand we have seen the proliferating offspring of the *historisches Rechtschule* in the form of investigations of legal, institutional, and certain kinds of social history; on the other hand the endless and divergent debates of jurists over the value of historicism, positivism, formalism, naturalism, and various sorts of socialism (not only Communist law but also *droit social* and *Rechtssoziologie*, which is also heavily endebted to Savigny). Less significant has been the theoretical contribution of specifically legal hermeneutics to history and the human sciences, though Weberian sociology certainly owes much to legal categories (Weber himself having been trained in the law) and Gadamer has touched upon "the exemplary significance of legal hermeneutics."[27] Only one philosopher has tried comprehensively to follow up this insight, however; and this is Gadamer's most searching critic, Emilio Betti, a man who has himself been a major figure in contemporary hermeneutics, though little appreciated

[24] *Code Civil*, art. 5, discussion in P. A. Fenet, *Recueil complet des travaux préparatoires du Code Civil* (Paris, 1827), 1: 20. In general see Julian Bonnecase, *La pensée juridique française* (Bordeaux, 1933), and Eugene Gaudemet, *L'interprétation du Code Civil en France depuis 1804* (Basel, 1935).

[25] See J. Stern, *Thibaut und Savigny* (Darmstadt, 1959); also Savigny's own great *System des heutigen römischen Rechts* (Berlin, 1840), 1 (book J., chap. 4); R. von Jhering, *Der Zweck im Recht* (Leipzig, 1893), and François Geny, *Méthode d'interprétation et sources en droit privé positif* (Paris, 1899); and cf. Edouard Lambert, *La fonction du droit civil comparé* (Paris, 1903).

[26] Further discussion in D. R. Kelley, *Historians and the Law in Post-Revolutionary France* (Princeton, forthcoming).

[27] *Truth and Method*, p. 289.

in the Anglophone world (and hardly at all by historians). Since Betti came to hermeneutics from jurisprudence, bringing with him essential juridical ideas and insights, he is ideally suited to appear here as the principal witness for the defense of the partnership of Hermes, Clio, and Themis.

IV

Betti was a center of professional controversy from at least 1927, when he published his Milanese inaugural lecture on Roman law and contemporary legal doctrines.[28] Ostensibly, his aim was to restore the normative value of Roman law (and in this sense, perhaps, to "return to Savigny"); but more importantly his hope was to restore the "autonomy" and neutrality of jurisprudence in a period when it was being threatened by the positivism of jurists like P. De Francisci and especially by the political priorities of Fascism. In this period of a "crisis" both of historicism and of jurisprudence[29] Betti wanted to reconcile historical tradition and legal system (*storia* and *dogma*) in much the same way that Savigny had tried to distill his historical reconstruction of the Roman tradition into an up-to-date "Pandectist" system intended to form the basis for a German Code. In another sense, however, Betti was pursuing, in the crucible of Fascist experience, the age-old goal of reconciling the ideals of justice with social reality, and especially with the intrusions of political power. It was a losing battle for the most part, but it did prepare him for a larger intellectual effort. Betti's transition to philosophy after the war represents a sort of expansion, or sublimation, of his original professional and "technical" goal, culminating in his monumental treatise, published in German as well as in Italian, on "the general theory of interpretation."[30]

It was via legal hermeneutics, then, that Betti passed from Crocean "idealist historicism" to a more concrete and differentiated (though non-

[28] "Diritto romano e dogmatica odierno," *Archivio giuridico* 99 (1928): 26–66; and see the articles of Antonio de Gennaro and Pietro Costa in *Quaderni Fiorentini per la storia del pensiero giuridico moderno* 7 (1978): "Emilio Betti e la scienza giuridica del Novecento," pp. 79–111, and pp. 311–93.

[29] See especially Karl Heussi, *Die Krisis des Historismus* (Tübingen, 1932).

[30] Betti's treatise is cited from both Italian and German versions, *Teoria della interpretazione* (Milan, 1955), and *Allgemeine Auslegungslehre als Methodik der Geisteswissenschaften* (Tübingen, 1967). A brief summary, *Die Hermeneutik als gemeine Methode der Geisteswissenschaften*, has been translated in Bleicher, *Contemporary Hermeneutics*, pp. 51–94. In general see the articles in *Quaderni Fiorentini* (above, n. 28), especially by Gadamer, Franco Bianco, Mario Bretone, Luigi Mengoni, Rudolf Malter, Giuliano Crifo, and Aldo Schiavoni; and those in the first volume of his Festschrift (cited above, n. 16), especially those of G. Funke, A. Heuss, G. Kandler and A. Plachy (vols. 2–5 treat technical legal subjects).

Marxist) theory of interpretation which encompassed a variety of disciplines besides jurisprudence, including art, language, science, law, and social and economic structures. The encyclopedic range of Betti's work opens up a richer historical perspective (as well as philosophical range) than the orthodox tradition. In significant contrast, too, with the existential and phenomenological concerns of Gadamer (and the "ideological" concerns of Habermas) Betti's purpose was to return to the tradition of the human sciences and to the enterprises of philosophers like Dilthey, Cassirer, Erich Rothaker, and Michael Landmann. What is more, Betti's approach was methodological and in this sense prescriptive, being directed (as Gadamer himself acknowledged) to the *quaestio juris* and not merely the *quaestio facti* of interpretation, which is to say to the possibilities rather than the limits of hermeneutics.[31] This may be the main reason, too, that Betti refused to be bound by either the text-model or even the privileged position of language.

Betti's point of departure was epistemology (*gnoseologia*; *Erkenntnistheorie*)—the relation of the thinking subject (*soggetto pensante*; *denkende Subjekt* or *subjectives Bewusstsein*) to a world inferrable through experience, yet identified not with the Kantian *Ding an sich* but rather with an "ideal objectivity" inseparable from subjective judgment. He joined subject and object in a single dialectical process mediated by hermeneutical constructs he called "representative" or "meaning-full forms," through which meaning is communicated and preserved, according to Betti's famous four canons of interpretation which define the whole continuum of understanding.[32] Here the legal connection is clear. Jurists were always supposed to respect the "meaning" of laws, the *mens* in the sense of will or intention of the original lawgiver; and to a large extent Betti preserved this professional "intentionalism." We may be the ones who pose questions of a text, but this text has a will of its own and literally "talks back" to the interpreter (or judge). As Betti put it, "We must assume that the text has something to say which we do not know from ourselves and which exists independently of our act of understanding."[33] This is what Betti meant by his first canon, which asserts "the hermeneutical autonomy of the subject."

Whence Betti's motto, *Sensus non est inferendus sed efferendus*: meanings are not to be imputed to objects of analysis but derived from

[31] See Bleicher, *Contemporary Hermeneutics*, p. 146.

[32] *Teoria*, p. 19, and *Auslegungslehre*, p. 16. Cf. *Teoria*, p. 119, "L'oggettivazione dello spirito in una forma representativa"; and *Auslegungslehre*, p. 78, "Objektivationen des Geistes der sinnhaltigen Formen."

[33] *Teoria*, p. 35; *Auslegungslehre*, p. 49; and see Richard E. Palmer, *Hermeneutics* (Evanston, Ill., 1969), p. 58.

them in their historical context, which in turn involves not only intuition but also an array of historical methods and techniques.[34] In this "objective" sort of interpretation (*Auslegung* as distinguished from *Verstehen*) Betti could hardly confine his view of the "methodology of the cultural sciences" to purely literary reconstruction; for the hermeneutical field was social and—again the legal analogy—concerned with things, actions, and institutions as well as verbal communication. Jurists had to establish the "facts" of a case, and necessarily such facts had to be given legal, which is to say social, meaning in order to be subjected to categorical or equitable judgment on the basis of legal principle. Similarly, the nonverbal materials of the historical process had to be given meaning through selection and interpretation. Like Habermas, in other words, though in a more integral fashion, Betti tried to confront problems of social context, historical tradition, and implicitly ideology. Beyond "philological," "critical," and "psychological" moments of exegesis in which an interpreter tried to recreate a cultural object or pattern there is also what Betti calls a "technical-morphological moment," which seeks particular structural meanings defined in relation to other fields, including economic and social action.[35] Gadamer would have none of this; but though he might seem to have the best of this debate in philosophical terms, Betti's broader, more encyclopedic (and more eclectic) vision seems better suited to the needs of historical understanding.

Historical interpretation is not simply a matter of apprehension and formal judgment, of course; it has also to take into account human volition and values, those of the interpreter as well as the object of study. Interpretation is itself a social process, in other words, depending on a species of "good faith" (*bona fides*) and carried out in a "world of values" (*cosmos di valori*; *Kosmos der Werte*) in which value judgments (*giudizia di valori*; *Werturteil*) were unavoidable.[36] Again the mediating position of the jurist suggests a model, since judgments had to involve not only original intention but also rationality and social values, such as equity or public utility. Historical judgment is not normative in this direct sense; and yet historical interpretation does have its own standards of larger meaning, which depend on the norms and direction of (professional) historical inquiry. Historians, too, must work within a "meaning system," not only to pass judgment but also to formulate meaningful questions. For the epistemological, sociological, and anthropological requirements of history and the human sciences jurisprudence offered benefits which

[34] *Teoria*, p. 100; *Auslegungslehre*, p. 65.
[35] *Teoria*, p. 291; *Auslegungslehre*, p. 204.
[36] *Teoria*, p. 11; *Auslegungslehre*, p. 10.

were wholly lacking in what Betti called the "mathematical" and "mechanical" (*automatica*) "surrogates" of naturalism.[37]

In general, it seems to me, the significance of Betti's work for the study of history is that it addresses itself precisely to the problem of how to accommodate the scholarly inquirer as well as the object of inquiry in discussions of "method" and "truth," and that it posits an object of interpretation(*oggettivazione della spirito in una forma representativa*; *Objektionen des Geistes der sinnhaltigen Formen*) in terms of a multiplicity of texts and testimonies. What he took from the law in particular was its "gnoseological" and "axiological" orientation—that is, its concerns with the problems of knowing and judging, of human will (conscious and, implicitly, unconscious), aspirations and values—in a context of structured social "reality." What he discarded was its formalism and professional estrangement from the human sciences in Dilthey's sense. Betti stands in somewhat the same relation to the tradition of legal hermeneutics as do Gadamer, Habermas, and perhaps Ricoeur to the theologico-philosophical tradition.

V

What does the legal model of hermeneutics have to offer to the study of history? I have suggested that it is superior to, or at least historically richer than, the more familiar philological, philosophical, and theological varieties because it is concerned more directly with social reality, human actions, and collectivities. Like "general" hermeneutics, the legal theory of interpretation further offers an alternative to conceptions of history which look to, or lust after, scientific models of one sort or another, especially Betti's "mathematical surrogate." This point is intended not to revive the old quarrel between "historicism" and "naturalism" (in the words of Ernst Troeltsch, characterizing the famous distinction made by Wilhelm Windelband and Heinrich Rickert between *Kultur*- and *Naturwissenschaften*) but only to avoid the naive fallacies about "objectivity" and "value-free" social science generated in particular by the *Werturteilsdiskussion* opened by Max Weber in 1914.[38] At the very least hermeneutics offers an alternative to this blind alley. Hermeneutics does not presume to ban investigations based on quantitative or behavioral assumptions but only to insist that the meanings attributed to such research are themselves the products of culturally conditioned human effort.

Hermeneutics has implications for the "philosophy of history" in both of the forms it has tended to assume in recent years—the "analytical"

[37] *Teoria*, p. 180; *Auslegungslehre*, p. 120.

[38] Survey of these problems in Pietro Rossi, *Lo storicismo tedesco contemporaneo* (Turin, 1956).

and the "speculative" or (as Arthur Danto calls it) "substantive."[39] Despite a long and distinguished heritage reaching from Toynbee and Spengler through Hegel back to Otto of Freising and Augustine himself, the speculative philosophy of history seems to have fallen on bad times, despite noble efforts by Peter Munz, Haskell Fain, and others to seek "the whole truth about history."[40] Emerging from theology and myth, this genre seems bound to return to its source, at least in its conventional universal (i.e., Judaeo-Christian) form. This is the classic sort of "metahistory" and has ties as well with the classical tradition of hermeneutics. Explicitly or implicitly, it is also tied to beliefs about prehistory, especially myth, and posthistory, especially prophecy. It is hard for critical historians nowadays to take seriously such neo-Augustinian efforts to find the "grand design," whether of God or a mindless, material "law." Yet it may be equally foolish for historians to pretend that they do not operate in effect from metahistorical assumptions, at the very least from those present in language; and one might wonder about the advisability of devoting some critical effort to deciding about some of the larger meaning of history from our perspective. Not to do so may condemn us to the predicament ascribed by Whitehead to those who affect to have no metaphysical presumptions—which is to be disadvantaged by the instinctive metaphysics of the nursery. Legal hermeneutics has long grappled with the question of the need of a large conceptual framework in order to achieve validity and consistency in judgment and interpretation, and the analogy may well hold for historical studies as well.

The "analytical philosophy of history" is something else again. Although it has been represented as a reaction to idealism (especially that of pre-1914 Germany) and uncritical speculative philosophy, it is historically as old as F. H. Bradley's *Presuppositions of Critical History* (1874). Obviously, this "critical" approach had little to do with that of neo-Kantian philosophers like Rickert or Dilthey; it intended, and portended, a recourse to logic and naturalism as a way of making history "scientific" beyond the dreams of Ranke or even J. B. Bury. As a consequence, especially in the past generation or two, the theory of history has been dominated by a new scholasticism whose stock in trade includes prescriptive talk about "holism," "covering laws," action theory, the most naively positivistic notions of research (as "data-gathering"), and the

[39] Arthur C. Danto, *Analytical Philosophy of History* (Cambridge, Mass., 1965). As in the case of hermeneutics this brief critique is offered from the point of view not of philosophy but of historical method and interpretation.

[40] Fain, *Between Philosophy and History* (Princeton, N.J., 1970), and Munz, *The Shapes of Time* (Middletown, Conn., 1978), the most learned and provocative of recent contributions.

most rigid insistence of the primacy of "explanation" in history.[41] Marginally, this literature, which has gained the status of a professional specialty, may have a cleansing effect; but mostly it has been irrelevant because of its tendency to focus on explanatory logic to the exclusion of concrete understanding—to empty form of its content, except as paradigmatic cases (and even then the cracking of a radiator or an automobile accident is often preferred to even a generic historical "event" like a war or a revolution). In such arid discussions one would like to recommend Clifford Geertz's arguments for "thick description" and that sort of evidence jurists would call circumstantial.[42]

The spectre haunting these discussions is that of causal analysis—and lurking behind, perhaps, that minor offspring of La Place's Demon, the "covering law." Here submission to a scientific model is most complete—and seems most inappropriate. No one has shown this more convincingly than the analytical philosophers themselves, notably Karl Popper, who has argued that the purpose and indeed the premise, of causal analysis is prediction. The historical counterpart of this operation can only be (as Isaiah Berlin and Paul Veyne have pointed out) "retrodiction," a process which has little utility and less verifiability.[43] Or rather, it introduces a serious misconception of historical understanding, representing another example of the "tendency among tough-minded philosophers," noted by Leon Goldstein, "to assimilate knowing the historical past to knowing the natural present."[44] The point is not that causal analysis is not useful for special lines of inquiry, only that it does not suffice for many interpretive and synthetic purposes and that it may often be illusory—a mockery of scientific procedure. As Berlin has pointed out, strategic placement of "thus's" and "therefores" does not necessarily constitute demonstration; and as Veyne has suggested, it may be more appropriate to offer some information on the grounds simply that it is "interesting" ("c'est intéressant que . . ."), the precise relevance being either indeterminate or yet to be determined, yet significant for evaluation and judgment. As in jurisprudence, meaning must be established not only through particular

[41] Standard literature collected in William Dray, ed., *Philosophical Analysis and History* (New York, 1966); Patrick Gardiner, ed., *The Philosophy of History* (Oxford, 1974), and *Theories of History* (Glencoe, Ill., 1959); and Sidney Hook, ed., *Philosophy and History* (New York, 1963); while various Beiheften of *History and Theory* have gathered more extensive bibliography.

[42] See Ronald G. Walters, "Signs of the Times: Clifford Geertz and Historians," *Social Research*, 47 (1980): 537–56.

[43] Berlin, "The Concept of Scientific History," in *Philosophical Analysis*, ed., Dray, p. 13, and Veyne, *Comment on écrit l'histoire* (Paris, 1971), p. 182.

[44] *Historical Knowing* (Austin, Texas, 1976), p. 161.

facts, their linkages and their classification, but also through what Geertz has called structures of signification and W. H. Walsh has termed "colligatory concepts," including correlations, coherences, and continuities which cannot be subsumed under the rubric of causation.[45]

"Interest" suggests another school of analytical philosophy, this one identified as "narrativist" (Maurice Mandelbaum calls it "reactionist"),[46] though it is not really concerned with the philosophy of history as commonly understood. Rather it is interest in history as the construction of "story" (the root meaning of "history") and so it has a closer affinity with the rhetorical tradition, which since the time of the sophists has carried on its own running warfare with philosophy. The strength of narrativism is that it has helped to redress the balance upset by the naive realism and naturalism which so often accompany the "normal science" of history. Yet it is also in danger of falling victim to the old "scissors-and-paste" fallacy criticized by Collingwood, to the extent that it tends to neglect or to undervalue the sort of intertextual criticism and controls by which historians try heuristically and imaginatively to restore earlier mental and social contexts. In any case narrativism, which takes its inspiration from literary criticism, tends to be, as Goldstein remarks of W. B. Gallie, "a philosophy of history for readers of history only."[47] This is especially the case with textualists like Hayden White, who focus more or less hermetically on "historical imagination" and its literary expression, and of course critics like Foucault and Derrida, who have thrown off the "burden of history" altogether. Indeed this school seems in the process of declaring its independence of historical scholarship in much the same way that literary criticism has at times (and especially in recent times) separated itself from literature. This would be a pity, for the study of history needs the sort of scrutiny offered by this descendent of philological hermeneutics.

VI

But let us look more closely at the model of hermeneutics suggested by jurisprudence. The point of departure of the legal tradition has always been the conscious, willful, and in some sense "interested" subject. That this subject may be prey to unconscious, natural, or social forces beyond his control or perceptual horizons limits but does not change this

[45] Geetz, *The Interpretation of Cultures* (New York, 1973), 3 ff., and Walsh, "Colligatory Concepts in History," in *The Philosophy of History*, ed., Gardiner, pp. 127–44.

[46] "The Problem of Covering Laws," in *The Philosophy of History*, ed. Gardiner, p. 51.

[47] *Historical Knowing*, p. 164.

premise. In contrast to natural science this human orientation defines an evenly observable field and, in a metaphorical sense, a "perspective." It has been the boast of science that it has overcome subjectivism on several levels—that it removed man from his sovereign position first in the cosmos, then in nature, and finally in his own psyche. Yet this is not a view which can be maintained in the practical business of living, achieving, or even surviving, and certainly not of observing the remoter reaches of the human condition in the past. Social life is necessarily anthropocentric and in many ways, because of linguistic limitations, anthropomorphic; and hermeneutics makes this circumstance an axiom of historical understanding.

The basic structure of conventional law derives from the ubiquitous juridical trinity of person, thing, and action (*persona*, *res*, *actio*), and I would emphasize four suggestive feautures of this arrangement.[48] First is the principle of personality, which is to say that law is subject-centered and, in a variety of ways, concerned with individual will, or at least responsibility, consciousness, and judgment. Secondly, from this anthropocentric point of view, a systematic attempt is made to comprehend the surrounding world of "reality," referring above all to social "things" (ranging from goods, or property, to complex institutions, culminating in the "public thing," the *respublica* itself). Third is the circumstance that legal interpretation must address itself not only to facts and "real" predicaments and to the "letter and spirit" of texts but also to questions of values, which implies problems of partisanship and "ideology" as well as social goals. Finally, like language but more broadly, law implies a large system of meaning in which facts and patterns acquire a significance in terms of location and relationship. In Betti's conception legal interpretation involves a two-fold operation which accommodates subject as well as object—attribution of human significance (*Sinngebung*) as well as determination of objective meaning (*Auslegung*).[49]

The historical observer struggles, then, with a cultural predicament as well as a recalcitrant and sometimes intractable object of study—a context as well as a text. He cannot observe and judge his domain with omniscient objectivity, and perhaps in his writing he should stop posing as the "omniscient observer" of Victorian fiction; for he is limited by cultural horizons, temporal perspective, and a largely impenetrable future.[50] Looking around, the observer sees a natural world challenging

[48] Further discussion in my "Gaius Noster: Substructures of Western Social Thought," *American Historical Review*, 89 (1979): 619–48. According to Betti's distinction this discussion focuses on "technical-juridical" interpretation in "historical" rather than "normative" terms.

[49] *Teoria*, p. 574; *Auslegungslehre*, p. 438.

[50] Cf. Martin Duberman, *The Uncompleted Past* (New York, 1965), pp. 43 ff.

him, relatives and neighbors facing the same challenge, more remote actors competing with and perhaps threatening him; and he sees, or at least feels, the pressures and demands of institutions, political as well as social and economic. Looking back, through various professional aids, he may perceive a tradition, a heritage, which sustains and weighs on—or obstructs—his own actions. Looking forward, he formulates hopes and aspirations, perhaps even programs of action, as well as doubts and fears. In all of these observations ego-centric value judgments and social interpretations must be formulated in a particular cultural and linguistic context. And as it is with the individual, so it must be, on a larger scale, with a society, with a meaningful social science, and with historical understanding in general.

But if the interested, participating, time- , space- , and culture-bound observer must remain content with a limited social science, he also occupies a field of inquiry in which social interaction—"intersubjectivity"—becomes plausible and self-criticism possible (as well as necessary). Habermas's "self-reflection of the cultural sciences" is a built-in condition.[51] Interpretation, involving interaction between subject and object, takes place in an intellectual continuum, and here the legal analogy is clear. Legal interpretation likewise has to give priority to the person (legal "subjectivity") and to judge in terms of times, places, and circumstances, yet within a social and cultural tradition. The task of the juridical *interpres* is not only to determine the "facts" and to apply principles but also to evaluate the appropriateness of principles, themselves derived from earlier experiences, just as the historian must find some standard or resonance—"prejudice" in a nonpejorative hermeneutical sense—in his own experience to give meaning in that of others. He observes and judges within a conventional social field and professional tradition which themselves represent both subject and object. In legal, and analogously historical, terms the interpreter makes transits of what is generally called the "hermeneutical circle."

Such interpretation involves not only a hermeneutical circle connecting alien and familiar experience but also, as Gadamer has argued, a double focus including judge and the observed "reality" to which he is professionally bound to "do justice." Hence it must also involve a double set of values, corresponding as it were to the home and alien territories. Here is one of the dilemmas of the hermeneutical process, familiar to critics through the quandaries involved in translation and historians in the form of anachronism. In methodological terms, for example, should nineteenth-century political, social, or psychological theory—institutional,

[51] *Knowledge and Human Interests*, trans. J. Shapiro (Boston, 1971), p. 161.

class- or psycho-analysis—be projected back into the Old Regime, and if so, how far? Or is it advisable to utilize what have been called "nativist theories," conceptualizations drawn and adapted from the cultural context of the object in question? In any case the past is indeed a "foreign country," and the guide books for which historians are responsible must try to show the ways in which "people do things differently there."[52] Since understanding the past depends in part on appreciating its values, while its significance depends on modern values, the hermeneutical circle involves a most complex axiology. By it are determined the selection and definition of "facts," the patterns inferred and reconstructed from these facts, the "genealogy" of particular generalizations, and the long-range interpretation of the historical process.

What preserves the integrity of the interpretive process, what makes it possible to complete the hermeneutical circle, is above all the medium of language, which like historical facts can only be understood in societal terms. "Everything in a given text which requires fuller interpretation," wrote Schleiermacher, "must be explained and determined exclusively from the linguistic domain common to the author and his original public."[53] One consequence of this premise (much criticized by phenomenologists beginning especially with Heidegger) is that historians must often be content with convention rather than logic in their analyses—with "humanly followed rules," as Peter Winch puts it, rather than with causal laws.[54] The persistence of myth, ritual, and other metalogical behavior must be kept in mind when the historian pursues what E. D. Hirsch and Betti have called "recognitive interpretation."[55] A corollary is that historical interpretation must take notice not only of language in general but of particular languages. It is a curiosity of most American and English work in the human sciences, especially sociology and most especially the analytical philosophy of history, that practitioners seem to assume that a science of society can be adequately formulated in a single brand of technical English devoted to generalized factors (and one may doubt that exclusive recourse to German—or Greek—is much more adequate). Hermeneutical understanding depends on the particularity and "thickness" which only varied linguistic experience can afford.

Yet the language surrogate, like the "mathematical surrogate," is surely insufficient for a hermeneutics of history; for while it makes plausible

[52] L. P. Hartley, *The Go-Between* (London, 1953), p. 1.

[53] Cited by Hirsch, *The Aims of Interpretation*, p. 76.

[54] "Concepts and Actions," in *The Philosophy of History*, ed. Gardiner, pp. 41–59, and cf. "The Idea of a Social Science" in *Rationality*, ed. Bryan R. Wilson (Oxford, 1970), pp. 1–17.

[55] Hirsch, *The Aims of Interpretation*, chap. 2; Betti, *Teoria*, p. 343, and *Auslegungslehre*, p. 255.

the completing of the hermeneutical circle, it suggests the impossibility ever of breaking out of it. According to the Whorfian view and what has been called "Gödel's theorem of language," language can yield no ultimate human meaning.[56] This is where the legal theory of interpretation seems to open up the frontier of historical understanding. Unlike philological hermeneutics, which confines itself to the text, and unlike philosophical hermeneutics, which expands its horizons to existence itself as the text analogue, and unlike theological hermeneutics, which devotes itself to a still higher transcendent object—unlike all of these legal hermeneutics has concentrated, however artificially, on a concrete expression of human society and culture. Unfortunately, while hermeneutical attitudes have made their way into social and cultural science (especially in the work of Gadamer, Habermas, Ricoeur, and especially Betti), with many a glance back at the classical theory of interpretation, little or no attention has been paid to the legal model.[57] By way of conclusion let me suggest some of the points at which the historical study of society and culture may draw (and perhaps inadvertently and uncritically have drawn) insight and inspiration from the tradition of European law.

VII

Contemporary hermeneutics seems to me monopolized by philosophers and literary critics, all of whom invoke the historical tradition but without a comprehensive grasp of it. The larger pattern of development should take into account not only the centuries-long interplay between philosophical and rhetorical interpretations—the debates of Platonism and sophism repeated in changing contexts, complicated by the intrusions of theology—but also the theories and practice of interpretation elaborated by ancient legal (and more recent social) science. Not that normative jurisprudence carrying on its strictly professional functions (any more than Christian theology, carrying on the pursuit of the "historical Jesus") can be imported directly into current hermeneutical discussions. The point is rather that the needs and interests of historians may be better served, their sense of the relevance of hermeneutics enhanced, by bringing into these discussions some of the questions, conventions, and connections made with the—nowadays unfortunately isolated—legal branch of the Western tradition of hermeneutics.

Legal hermeneutics is unrepentently anthropocentric. It starts with a conception of *personalitas*, of the individual and perhaps psychological

[56] Hirsch, pp. 50, 66.

[57] See the collection edited by Paul Rabinow and William M. Sullivan, *Interpretive Social Science* (Berkeley, 1979), and the work of Baumann (above, n. 1).

aspect of the human condition; then goes on to *realitas*, which is to say social reality, based above all on the institutions of property and economic behavior; and finally treats *actio*, action theory, collective as well as individual. Within the framework of this conventional legal-sociological triad legal interpretation confronts a wide range of essential social categories and concepts. Suffice it here to mention just a few types: ideas of social organization (family, kinship structures, corporative groups, subversive groups, administration, nationality), ideas of authority and power (popular and traditional as well as public, political, and administrative), ideas of social interaction (commerce, war, international problems), ideas of social continuity ("wills," succession, inheritance) and discontinuity (the whole range of criminal law), ideas of social change (not only legislation but legal reform and the rise and fall of custom, *consuetudo* and *desuetudo*) and ideas of causation (one of the grounds for the claim of law to be a true "science").[58] Of course modern legal science (since the thirteenth century) has been intensively interpreted and, through historical and comparative as well as philosophical methods, reinterpreted and transformed by these ideas.

Legal science has never been value-free, however, and all of these themes have been interpreted in normative and even teleological terms: social organizations have their own goals (families to ensure their future strategies, corporate groups their "interests," etc.), authority is joined to "public utility," social interaction is supposed to further the common good and continuity, and social change is intended to take place in the direction of legal ideas, especially peace and justice, perhaps prosperity and political expansion as well, while causation has indissoluble ties with "just" and "good" causes.[59] For the jurist these norms represent ideals, or at the very least professional pretexts; but for students of social and cultural structure and change they also reflect a basic dialectic of historical change. The point is not that historians should interject such values into their analyses but rather that the meaning of actions and perceptions should be assessed in terms thereof—and ideology be joined to society. For legal interpretation has always made an effort, according

[58] A sampling of relevant works includes Riccardo Orestano, *Azione, Diritti soggettivi, Persone giuridiche* (Bologna, 1978); Paolo Zatti, *Persona giuridica e soggettivita* (Padua, 1975); Carol Maiorca, *La cosa in senso giuridico* (Turin, 1937); Peter Stein, *Regula Iuris* (Edinburgh, 1966); Pietro Costa, *Iurisdictio* (see above n. 20); and more generally Eugen Ehrlich, *Fundamental Principles of the Sociology of Law*, trans. W. Moll (Cambridge, 1936). See also H. L. A. Hart and A. M. Honoré, *Causation in the Law* (Oxford, 1959), and the criticism of Maurice Mandelbaum, *The Anatomy of Historical Knowledge* (Baltimore, 1977), pp. 199–204.

[59] Cortese, *La norma giuridica*, 1: 179 ff.

to its own lights, to establish what Quentin Skinner has called "social meaning"; and jurisprudence, in its own fashion, represents in general what Clifford Geertz has referred to as a "meaning system," or set of meaning systems, and so potentially the basis for a fuller appreciation of the historical process in all of its social and cultural significance.[60]

In the nineteenth century the "scientific" pretensions of traditional jurisprudence came increasingly under fire, especially from the new disciplines of political economy and sociology, which had even more aggressive claims to universality and explanatory power. Bentham rejected the old legal tradition in favor of simplistic social calculus; Comte rejected it in favor of a naturalistic conception of society amenable to control by "positive" science; and Marx rejected it in favor of a dialectical method joined to economic analysis. For all of these jurisprudence was the ghost of a dead, or dying, culture, scientifically useless because of its freight of ancient conventions and "values"; for Marx, indeed, it was the very embodiment of bourgeois ideology.[61] In the past century and a half these disciplines, since become vast and imposing professions, have been dominated by scientism, especially in France and England, where the legacy of positivism has been intimidating; and in various ways the study of history has fallen under the spell of quantitative and explanatory social science. For anthropology, on the other hand, and for the science of culture and more generally speaking, the inadequacies of economic or sociological reductionism have become increasingly obvious, especially with the passing of old-fashioned ideas of objectivity (*Wertfreiheit*) and naturalistic "explanation." And this, for historical studies, is where hermeneutics comes in. Dilthey and his followers have reached back profitably to older and in some ways richer conceptions of historical change and understanding, drawing in particular upon romantic literary and biblical interpretation. It seems to me that this line of inquiry could be deepened and given a more social orientation by attending as well to the insights and suggestions to be found in the legal tradition, though without neglecting the criticisms of recent philosophers, including Gadamer, Habermas, and Apel, as well as Betti.

And so the old question, "What is history?"—this time in the light of the theory of interpretation associated with legal (and more recently

[60] Geertz, *The Interpretation of Cultures*, and Skinner, " 'Social Meaning' and the Explanation of Social Action," in *The Philosophy of History*, ed. Gardiner, pp. 106–26.

[61] Discussion in D. R. Kelley, "The Metaphysics of Law: An Essay on the Very Young Marx," *American Historical Review*, 83 (1978): 350–67, and "The Science of Anthropology: An Essay on the Very Old Marx," forthcoming in *Journal of the History of Ideas*.

social) science. To this question there have been many prescriptive answers, from the idealizations of Cicero ("the light of truth, the mistress of light," etc.) to those of E. H. Carr ("the study of causes"), from the mystifications of St. Augustine (the working out of God's "grand design") to those of Gadamer ("the great dark book . . . written in the language of the past"), and from the aestheticism of Pliny ("always pleases") to that of Hayden White (a story well told). My own preference lies between the extremes of philosophy, theology, and rhetoric. Like law and hermeneutics history is a human form of apprehension—*prudentia* or *phronesis* rather than *episteme* (or *praxis*, for that matter). And like legal interpretation, historical interpretation had the same ultimate aim, which according to Ricoeur remains "to make one's own what was previously 'foreign.'"[62] According to Johann Huizinga's still useful definition, "History is the intellectual form in which a civilization renders account to itself of its past."[63] Without being too rigid, this formulation seems to provide for the traits of hermeneutics listed above: it is anthropocentric, value-oriented, responsible to tradition, and grounded in a meaning system. Less formally, it envisions the study of history as a human operation aimed at finding answers about the human past. What better way to express the significance of the partnership of Hermes, Clio, and Themis?

[62] *Interpretation Theory*, p. 91; and see Richard Rorty, *Philosophy and the Mirror of Nature* (Princeton, 1979), pp. 315 ff., discussing the transition "from epistemology to hermeneutics."

[63] "A Definition of the Concept of History," in *Philosophy and History*, ed. R. Klibansky and H. Paton (Oxford, 1936), p. 5.

[18]

European Legal History – A New Field of Research in Germany[1]

REINER SCHULZE

1. THE 'EUROPEANISATION' OF LEGAL SCIENCE

What was self-evident for lawyers in most parts of Europe for hundreds of years before the beginning of the modern age is only now slowly becoming familiar again: they work with a common body of law. The *ius commune* united lawyers of the Middle Ages and the early modern period from the origin of their profession onwards; it unified the law from the Iberian peninsula to the Baltic and from southern Italy to Scandinavia. In our century a common European law has come into being in very different circumstances. Particularly in the Member States of the European Community, it increasingly affects the everyday work of the courts, lawyers and the administration. No longer does this constitute a challenge only for comparative law, international law and Community law: what seems to be necessary now is a 'Europeanisation of legal science'[2] encompassing all disciplines in which there is a growing need for intellectual preparation and involvement in the harmonisation of law in Europe.

At present, however, an intellectual context, transcending frontiers, on which a common European jurisprudence could be built is still largely lacking. Since the 'nationalisation' of jurisprudence in the eighteenth and nineteenth centuries the traditions of national legal thinking, the way in which jurisprudence is bound by the national legal culture and the corresponding understanding by lawyers of their own role have prevailed even in continental Europe, and as a legacy of the heyday of the nation-state they continue to mould present-day thinking. Today's European jurisprudence must first bring the older common European traditions up to date, identifying the more subtle interconnections in European legal culture which, even in the heyday of the nation-state, were founded on those traditions and then put that common European history of law to use in cooperation in legal science and the definition of the role of lawyers[3] and perhaps even in the building of a new *ius commune*.

It is neither desirable nor, in any event, likely that Europe in the twenty-first century will still warrant the strictures, still largely true in the

Reiner Schulze, University of Trier

The Journal of Legal History, Vol.13, No.3 (1992), pp.270–295
PUBLISHED BY FRANK CASS, LONDON

twentieth century, of the German jurist Rudolf von Ihering, who said of the nineteenth century in comparison with the great tradition of the *ius commune*: '. . . [legal] science has come down to the level of local law; in law scientific boundaries coincide with political boundaries . . . A humiliating and unworthy state for a science'.[4]

Within the national structure of legal science which still prevails, even that turn towards the European context of the law is of course initially caught up in the web of national academic discussion. After the loss of the common basis of *ius commune*, the national schools of jurisprudence in Europe – despite their common history – are today not only concerned with differing national legal rules and systems but have developed different styles and working methods, different educational processes and separate organisational structures. Moreover, language barriers and the consequent lack of European legal journals all too often force the first steps towards a common legal science in individual European countries back within the bounds of national legal culture. In those circumstances it is a small but necessary step along the way to a European orientation of jurisprudence for lawyers to learn something of the discussions and research in other countries and exchange views on their approaches and perspectives. That is the purpose of the following review of the contribution that the new German research initiatives in European legal history can make to a European legal science.

2. THE ORIGINS OF 'EUROPEAN LEGAL HISTORY' IN GERMANY

During the last few decades legal history, alongside other disciplines such as comparative law and international law, has made some first attempts at a 'Europeanisation' of legal science. An important contribution was made at an early stage by Roman lawyers such as Erich Genzmer[5] and Paul Koschaker.[6]

The way was opened in the 1950s by the development of the relatively new discipline of modern history of private law, which in the 1930s – in very different academic and political circumstances – had taken its place in German study programmes alongside the three existing historical disciplines: Roman law, German law and canon law. The two basic text-books in this new discipline placed the history of German private law in a European context; no longer was its subject-matter an independent 'German legal history' and a 'German private law' viewed in isolation,[7] and no longer was it concerned to reconcile Roman law with a separate 'organic' context of German legal life. The very title of Wesenberg's work placed the history of modern German private law in the 'framework of the development of law in Europe'.[8] And in Franz Wieacker's work the phrase 'history of private law' itself stood no longer for a national but for a European phenomenon: 'Privatrechtsgeschichte der Neuzeit unter besonderer Berücksichtigung der deutschen Entwicklung' [Modern history of private law with particular reference to the development of the law in Germany].[9] The book dealt with the development of the law in Germany – simply 'referring to' it in particular – as an aspect of 'European legal culture' and 'European jurisprudence'.[10] This European orientation of the history of modern private law made it possible in legal education to promote an understanding, from a historical point of view, of common aspects of European legal culture even before the development of European Community law and the resulting expansion in the list of subjects brought additional European features into University syllabuses.

Particular impetus was subsequently given to research by the foundation of the Max Planck Institute for European Legal History in Frankfurt am Main.[11] Very recently, moreover, German universities have devoted increased attention to the challenges of European legal history in research and teaching. An outward indication of this may be seen in the titles of new academic chairs, which include 'European legal history' among other historical disciplines.[12]

If we review the development of German research in European legal history since the 1950s we see an extension and intensification of interest in various directions. The results and future research plans in the following areas merit closer attention: the reconstruction of a body of European private law in our time; the interconnection of national legal cultures in the modern period going beyond the pre-modern *ius commune*; the history of public law, constitutional law and the administration in Europe; and, finally, the historical relationships between continental Europe and England and between western and eastern Europe, which is attracting increasing interest.[13]

3. FROM *IUS COMMUNE* TO EUROPEAN PRIVATE LAW

(a) Since research in Germany has turned its attention to European legal history, the concept of 'European legal culture' has been one of its main focuses. The range stretches from Wieacker's fundamental work[14] to Coing's analysis of 'a series of factors which entitle us to speak of European legal culture'.[15] The law is thus seen as one of the unifying elements of European culture; legal history is viewed as part of European cultural history in a general sense (and the use of the broad term 'cultural history' means that it is not defined narrowly as the history of ideas or as social history).

The present and the past are linked in the concepts of European legal culture and European legal history in two ways: the awakening of interest in research into European legal history is prompted by the experience of the present, namely the present-day efforts towards the development of a body of common European law. The resulting research can in turn influence present-day thinking in that, contrary to another tradition and present-day experience, namely the legal thinking moulded by the nation-state, it contributes from a historical standpoint to a consciousness of a shared European identity. The concept of European legal culture is thus directed at the definition of an identity for the present based on the past whilst research in European legal history is both defined by and directed towards the present.

Something which as a more general problem has for some time given rise to lively discussion in German historical circles is thus of particular importance for European legal history: in historical research there is necessarily a degree of tension between the endeavour to understand the matters under investigation as events from a bygone period on the one hand and the inescapable restrictions of the intellectual context of one's own time on the other.[16] This tension cannot be resolved by complete immersion in the sources, resulting in a pure 'objectivity' unaffected by the experience of the researcher and the interests and assumptions of his time.

Objectivism, which has been developed in varying forms both in idealist and in materialist and positivist doctrines, must in the light of modern theories of knowledge and history be regarded as an illusion. This does not of course relieve historical research of the obligation to seek to achieve some understanding of past thinking, (nor must it go to the other extreme of falling into a subjectivism which regards historical sources simply as resource material for the confirmation of modern views. In particular it does not mean that research need no longer rely on the sources of the period under consideration as a precondition for any *historical* statement and does not free it from the requirement that it discuss these sources in a *scientific* manner *lege artis* – that is to say, according to the rules of the art as these have been recognised in historical disciplines since the time of historicism. On that basis, however, increased understanding is likely to arise not from any decision not to relate research to the present but precisely from the reflection of research criteria in this unavoidable tension between past and present.[17]

Thus European legal history can contribute to the 'Europeanisation' of modern legal thinking not just as any general historical consciousness – reflecting the *Zeitgeist* to a greater or lesser extent – can influence present-day thinking and conduct. Instead, its potential influence is extended when its research results are disseminated, through academic education, to the *lawyers* of different European countries in their capacity as the main vehicles and shapers of present and future legal culture. This contribution of European legal history is crucial for the future development on the part of lawyers from European countries of a new conception of themselves as *European* lawyers and the growth of the future professional class of 'lawyers for Europe'.[18]

(b) Whether European legal history can go beyond this contribution to the 'Europeanisation' of legal thinking and legal education and contribute directly to the reconstruction of a common body of European law for our time is the subject of some dispute. A contrast may be seen between the rather 'contemplative' conception of legal history as a historical discipline in the teaching of Wieacker on the one hand and the endeavour to include European legal history in the practical application of jurisprudence in the work of Helmut Coing on the other.

With his model of legal history as a historical discipline (primarily rooted in the history of ideas), his distinction between the 'contemplative' work of that discipline and 'practical' jurisprudence (drawing on Emilio Betti's[19] hermeneutic ideas in contrast to Hans-Georg Gadamer[20]) and his criticism of the history of legal doctrine,[21] Wieacker had drawn the logical conclusion from the development of history in Germany since the late nineteenth century. Whereas the 'historical school' had previously included legal history to a very large extent in its view of the constructive role of jurisprudence and sought to fashion a private law for its own time on the basis of historical sources, in the course of the last 100 years and particularly since the introduction of the *Bürgerliches Gesetzbuch* in 1900, historical research and the doctrinal discussion of positive law have drawn further and further apart in Germany. It is true that in academic positions legal history is still frequently attached to that of civil law (though not necessarily the reverse), but historical contributions play no decisive role in constructive doctrinal discussion or in judicial argument.

Conversely, Coing's work[22] in European private law is aimed at the incorporation of legal history in the practical role of jurisprudence. His initial work has recently been taken further in different directions by Reinhard Zimmerman[23] (focusing on the modern relevance of the doctrinal analysis of the *ius commune*) and Filippo Ranieri[24] (on the theoretical contribution of legal history to the development of European law 'beyond the illusions of codifications and legislators'. The ideas put forward from the standpoint of comparative law by Hein Kötz[25] are broadly in harmony with the preoccupations of these historical contributions.

There is a long-term prospect of cooperation between legal history and comparative law in the academic (re)construction of a common body of European private law.[26] If one pursues further the approach taken by Coing and Kötz, legal history and comparative law could, in an analysis of the common historical bases and different national manifestations of law in Europe, seek to provide European lawyers with a set of principles and legal concepts that would permit communication despite differences in national styles and codification and so become a unifying element in lawyers' work. Even if different civil codes continue to apply in individual countries, the practice of law in Europe would acquire common academic points of reference. Such a new *ius commune* could not of course eliminate the national fragmentation of private law in Europe, but it could have all the more success in countering it since in continental Europe codification has in any event already lost some of its importance in the development of national law in comparison with other forms of development of the law.[27]

(c) Coing's conception would incorporate legal history on a European scale much more closely in the development of positive law than has yet been the case at the national level in Germany or in other continental European countries in this century. In the German academic context it is perhaps made easier by the fact that some of the present conditions affecting the development of law in Europe are reminiscent of the situation in Germany at the zenith of the historical school in the 19th century. In Europe today, as in Germany between 1815 and 1870, there is an increasing need for harmonisation or unification of the law but a lack not only of common codifications but of political prospects or legal competence for the enactment of unifying legislation. Before the national unification of Germany, jurisprudence, using the means available to it, worked towards the unification and modernisation of the law in a manner which could not be achieved by legislation: the development of the law without regard for state boundaries, more or less independently of political institutions (spurred in particular by Savigny's programmatic tract *Of the Vocation of Our Age for Legislation and Jurisprudence*[28]). Reliance on the (actual or supposed) common legal history of Germany furnished an arsenal of concepts and arguments, supported by a consensus among the lawyers of the various German states. However, the appeal to history in no way prevented legal science from adapting legal institutions and the legal system to cope with the fundamental changes brought about by industrialisation and conceiving a modern legal structure for an industrial society on apparently traditional foundations.

We cannot, of course, expect to solve today's problems with the concepts and methods of the nineteenth century. Just as legal science, since its rebirth in northern Italy in the Middle Ages, has repeatedly but in different ways at different times drawn on older law and older traditions (from the 'discovery' of the *Corpus Iuris* in its inception through the turn towards the *ius patriae* in the early modern period to the pandectism of the nineteenth century) in order to develop law for its time, it must today in a European context develop special methods to draw on the history and theory of law for a common doctrinal approach. For example, it cannot simply adopt the attitudes of the nineteenth century on the continuity and 'organic' growth of the law, culminating in the association of law and *volksgeist*, but must take a new view of the historical context of legal doctrine in a dialogue with modern social science and social history. Thus European legal history cannot simply become a neo-pandectism on the German model of the nineteenth century. Taking into account that and other historical experiences, its aims and methods will be shaped only in a broader discussion between representatives of different approaches and national traditions in the European countries concerned, in accordance with the specific conditions of *modern* legal development.

4. PRE-MODERN FOUNDATIONS OF EUROPEAN LAW AND THE AGE OF THE NATION-STATE

(a) If one reviews the individual areas with which German research has been concerned, it is clearly the pre-modern *ius commune* that is central to historical interest. Its development in northern Italy and its spread throughout much of Europe brought out important characteristics of European legal culture, some of which had, however, already been traced by ancient Roman law and the Christian ecclesiastical tradition. These characteristics included the independence – to a very large degree in comparison with other advanced civilisations – of the legal field in relation to other cultural sectors, particularly religion, and a correspondingly high degree of differentiation between legal rules and other normative systems such as those of theology, morality and ethics.[29] This differentiation between rules systems was associated with the growth of an independent science of law and the specialisation and professionalisation of competence to deal with legal issues through the emergence of the legal profession.

Another specific feature of European legal culture is its differentiation within the legal field: secular law (*ius civile*) and ecclesiastical law (*ius canonicum*) not only developed separately from non-legal normative systems but as early as the Middle Ages developed independently also of each other.[30] As two separate legal systems, they formed the *utrumque ius* whose exegesis united lawyers in most parts of Europe well after the Middle Ages.

In accordance with its particular interest in the history of private law, German research in *ius commune* has been directed above all towards its secular part (*ius civile*). Thus recent work on European legal history[31] has been able to build on a rich tradition of research in the Roman law of the Middle Ages, beginning with the 'antiquarian' work of the eighteenth century[32] and Savigny's *History of Roman Law*.[33]

Despite an equally rich older research tradition, the *ius canonicum* has met with less attention. That is due in part to the excessively narrow orientation of research interest on the basis of the classification and importance of disciplines in the positive law of today (in contrast to the great historical significance of canon law for European legal culture) and also to a historical conception inherited from the nineteenth century which regarded the encounter of Roman and German law as the predominant conflict of legal systems in Europe since the early Middle Ages. In that tradition of German historical writing the dualism of ecclesiastical law and secular law was all the more neglected inasmuch as the influential Prussian Protestant historical writing of the late nineteenth century – in the context of the *Kulturkampf* between Bismarck and the Catholic church – regarded canon law with the greatest disapproval and was inclined to criticise its Christian legitimacy and denigrate its historical significance.[34] However, in the last few decades various proposals have pointed the way towards increased research into canon law in relation to the development of modern secular law in Europe,[35] not only for private law[36] but also for criminal and public law (and for the development of the state and the administration[37]).

(b) In addition to academic *ius commune*, the attention of researchers has been focused recently on other unifying elements of European legal history in the Middle Ages and later. That is to say, from the High Middle Ages onwards academic (or 'taught') law developed in a cultural environment in which the content and direction of the law was still strongly influenced by older patterns of thought and behaviour. In particular, legal culture (and culture generally) in pre-modern European society[38] was only in a stage of transition towards literacy. Legal historical research must thus concern itself with the common structural characteristics of what was at first a primarily oral legal culture in Europe[39] and take into account the long conflict between that culture's legal rules and ways of thinking and academic law during the period in which the law gradually became a written phenomenon. In the context of European legal history such an old research topic of German legal history as customary law takes on new relevance.[40] Again, just as historians and cultural sociologists have recently turned their attention to the courtly life of the Middle Ages as a factor which helped to fashion European civilisation,[41] European legal history must study feudal law[42] and the legal customs of the nobility. Similarly, with regard to the connections between developments in the law in different parts of Europe – to cite only two traditional topics of legal history which are also full of potential for European legal history – attention must be directed towards the adoption of the law of German cities in eastern Europe[43] or the influence of French bodies of customary law (with their medieval origins, their importance for the application of European legal doctrine to local law in the early modern period and finally their continued influence in the models of the *Code Civile* of 1804, particularly in family law – models which with the spread of French law in turn became authoritative well beyond the borders of France).[44]

Particularly in regard to the sixteenth to eighteenth centuries – the period between the Middle ages and the modern age usually referred to by German historians as the early modern period – research is focusing on the question of the concept, manner and extent of the reception of Roman law in various European countries and is also beginning to take a new look at the turn towards the historical legitimacy of the law and the *ius patriae* in various countries in the seventeenth and eighteenth centuries. In contrast to the national historical conceptions of the nineteenth century, from the point of view of European legal history this does not represent an isolated development in individual countries or indeed an assertion of the *Volksgeist*, but a process which took place throughout Europe within a jurisprudence that was still united by the tradition of the *ius commune*, from Scotland to France and to Germany. New research must therefore be devoted in particular to the influence of legal developments in individual parts of Europe (for example the particularly striking development of Roman–Dutch law in the seventeenth and eighteenth centuries[45]) on the further development of the law in other parts of Europe and on the attempts there at a synthesis of *ius commune* and territorial or national law.[46]

With regard to the early modern period, greater attention has also been paid to the role of natural law in European legal history, but it is far from having been exhaustively discussed. While for the history of criminal law and of constitutional and administrative law the decisive influence of the great common European ideas of natural law and the Enlightenment are probably beyond question, there has been far less explanation in German studies of the history of private law in Europe of the extent to which the separate innovations of natural law helped to impel its doctrine and methodology beyond the tradition of the *ius commune* (in its later development through the *usus modernus pandectarum*).[47]

(c) The nineteenth century – somewhat broadly defined as the period between the French Revolution and the First World War – presents a particular challenge for European legal history. During that period most European countries moved from a system of feudal status relationships to modern systems of private and constitutional law and their legal systems acquired the essential features they have today. The beginning of the modern age also brought the age of the nation-state, of national legal systems and national legal cultures. With this rise of the nation-state as an ideal and as the determining political unit in Europe the cohesion of common European jurisprudence in its traditional form was destroyed. The 'nationalisation' of jurisprudence in the countries of Europe resulted in a diversity of approaches. Whether on the basis of a revolutionary national consciousness (as in France) or on the hypothesis that national law grows naturally out of its history as applied by a people (as in Germany under the influence of the historical school); whether by way of an abrupt codification or in a gradual process of scientific unification, almost everywhere the idea of the nation-state was accompanied by the claim that a country should have its 'own' national law. Accordingly the consciousness of a common European legal background rooted in the *ius commune* was overshadowed by the orientation towards national law and immersion in the national legal culture.

Between the pre-modern common European law and today's first steps towards a common body of European law there was thus a period during which the ascendancy of the nation-state makes the European history of law at least much harder to grasp than during the earlier period or today. This intermediate period suppressed the earlier consciousness of the general context of the law and led to the situation described at the beginning of this article, in which the common legal background is only slowly becoming familiar for lawyers in a way in which it was self-evident for centuries. Indeed, it raises the question whether there can really be said to be a European history of law from the Middle Ages to the present, incorporating the nineteenth century.

A positive answer to that question is suggested in particular by two German research initiatives. First, some work is being done on the complex continued influence of the common jurisprudential tradition on the various modern national legal systems. This research is concerned with the continuing effect not only of individual rules, doctrinal constructs and solutions to problems but also methodology and the way in which lawyers are taught to think[48] in spite of increasing diversity in working methods, literary style and training. Secondly, research is beginning to focus, alongside our common legal traditions, on the new ways in which legal knowledge and experience were exchanged in the nineteenth century.[49] It has become apparent that the age of the nation-state, contrary to first impressions – and often also to contemporary conceptions – was a period in which national legal systems in Europe drew on each other to a large extent and in which there were complex transfers of legal knowledge between them. These new connections were prompted above all by the effort to develop the law in response to the demands of industrialisation.[50] They arose largely from the fact that different European countries faced comparable problems – although frequently at different times – and the continued influence of the older common academic tradition also favoured them. Under these new conditions the place of the unifying common jurisprudence was largely taken by comparative law, which covered wide areas of the legal systems and at the same time became a special discipline within legal science.[51]

For this age not only of the nation-state but also of comparative law, not only of the loss of older common features but also of the emergence of new connections in Europe, the mutual awareness of legal systems and the way in which they drew on each other merits particular attention from researchers.[52] In that respect it is indispensable, though not easy (from the linguistic point of view if nothing else), to go beyond bilateral relationships and examine the complex multilateral connections between national legal cultures in the nineteenth century.[53] If we pursue such connections between several national legal cultures we will in many cases find an 'international dissemination and circulation of concepts and theories'.[54] Moreover, researchers cannot restrict themselves to the developments in the centres of the principal legal systems as these are usually distinguished in historical and comparative legal literature: the German or central European system, the French or Roman system, the English or common law system and so on[55]). They must instead turn their attention to the zones of contact and overlap, the peripheries, and examine the mutual influences, the mixing of systems and the resulting stimulation of new thinking in the centres. Areas which from the point of view of the national legal history of France or Germany are on the fringes, such as Belgium and the Netherlands, or the Rhine provinces in western Germany (where throughout the nineteenth century German lawyers applied French law),[56] lie at the centre of *European* legal history.

That example of French law in the Rhine provinces thus prompts German researchers to analyse the question to what extent, in the heyday of the nation-state, two great national legal systems in Europe were compatible. Study of the administration of justice in the Rhine provinces reveals something which for many German or French lawyers of today is scarcely imaginable but is encouraging for the European lawyers of the future: for a long period German lawyers were able to deal as a matter of course with French law in many areas of activity and at all levels of the judiciary (as far, finally, as the German *Reichsgericht*). At the same time such zones of overlap of different national legal systems may be regarded as 'bridges' for the development of relations between those legal systems as a whole. The adaptation of one body of law to another and the experience thus gained by lawyers make those areas a natural focus for the transmission of legal attitudes, rules and institutions from one country to the other. The French law adapted to German conditions in the Rhine provinces thus influenced the development of the law in Germany[57] and also in France (although the latter influence has received less attention from French as well as German researchers). That influence[58] resulted not only from the translation into French[59] of the well-known work of Karl Salomo Zachariae[60] but also from the work in France of influential lawyers who through their training, their work as teachers or their practice had become familiar with the contact between the French and German legal systems in the Rhine provinces.[61]

To take Italy as a further example, recent Italo-German research has confirmed that the development of the law in Europe can in no way be regarded as a product of the centres of the great legal systems, other countries essentially being mere recipients of their innovations. Strong as the reliance on German constitutional and legal theory was in Italy, in the encounter between the two legal cultures Germany was in no way solely the example and Italy the passive recipient. Instead, Italian legal culture – favoured precisely by its relative openness towards ideas from abroad – was able to offer valuable ideas in various areas to other countries, including Germany. Those ideas – which have not yet been fully investigated – range from the development of comparative law and private international law[62] to the stimulus given by Italy to the discussions on the reform of criminal law through its *scuola positiva* and its criminal code of 1890, the *Codice Zanardelli*.[63] In general these studies show how important it is not to view the peripheries and zones of overlap simply as passive areas to which developments in the centres subsequently spread but to look there for innovations arising out of the contact between differing national legal cultures.

(d) Finally, the heyday of the nation-state was followed in our century in Europe by various efforts at international and supranational integration. The study of the re-emergence of a common body of European law through these developments is just as much a task for European legal history as the investigation of legal developments in the pre-modern period and in the age of the nation-state (although German researchers have so far devoted little attention to this area). The work of political scientists and historians[64] cannot adequately deal with the legal conditions and developments, just as the historical process – and thus the character of the development of European law[65] – is not sufficiently taken into account by the legal disciplines of European Community law or international law. In so far as these disciplines have recourse to historical arguments in relation to the positive law with regard to a concrete situation or in relation to a necessary further development in the law, they do not as a rule go in detail into more complex historical circumstances and are thus no substitute for research by legal historians.

For research in legal history these developments of our century constitute the nexus between the rich historical experience of community in Europe and the present-day experience of lawyers. In this broader historical context, European legal history must incorporate the developments of the second half of our century – such as the emergence and development of the institutions and law of the European Community – as *historical* processes in the consciousness of the present. European legal history faces essentially the same task as that which has recently been the subject of discussion in other areas of legal history in Germany – the problem of 'legal history as contemporary history'.[66] European legal history too must be aware in particular of the possibilities of 'current event research' such as interviews of contemporary witnesses and at the same time communicate to a new generation historical events and processes which lie outside their own experience. For most lawyers working today their present experience of European institutions and European law is no longer linked to a personal experience of their genesis and early development. That task is particularly important in respect of the law students of today and tomorrow, for whom the legal developments of the 1950s and 1960s are already outside the framework of contemporary history and form part of an 'early' period of European legal history.

5. HISTORY OF PUBLIC LAW, THE CONSTITUTION AND THE ADMINISTRATION

(a) The special role played by private law in the development of European legal culture in the pre-modern period[67] only partly explains why German research in European legal history has initially been devoted mainly to this area. A more important reason was the traditional orientation of legal history towards private law, rooted in the nineteenth century.[68] In recent years that orientation has frequently been criticised.[69] For European legal history in particular it is inadequate. Alongside the history of private law (and linked to it in some respects), common traditions of constitutional law (in particular the development of fundamental rights), together with common views and international discussions on the administration and administrative law, social welfare and the social responsibility of the individual have contributed to the emergence of common principles of democracy, the rule of law and the welfare state in Europe. Beginning in the Middle Ages, unifying European foundations for these central components of modern European legal culture may be found in the development of jurisprudence and – often related to it – political thought. In particular, the rediscovery in the High Middle Ages of the teaching of Aristotle gave rise to a European debate which has taken many forms but has continued into the modern period, concerning the organising principles of society – a debate in which discussions of the ethics of princes, reason of state, natural duties and freedoms, human rights and citizens' rights, the constitution and the rule of law became linking factors in political and legal thought in Europe.

For European legal history increasing importance is thus attached to an area of research which has brought together lawyers from the disciplines of public law and legal history and historians. The term 'constitutional history' has been current as a research concept in Germany since the nineteenth century,[70] today's prevailing ideas are influenced above all by the teaching of Otto Brunner[71] and the discussions prompted by them.[72] In European comparison and debate some thought must be given to whether these traditional ideas of constitutional history provide a suitable foundation for research into European constitutional history. Dietmar Willoweit has recently shown that until now German conceptions have usually been oriented towards the treatment of specific historical phenomena, in the framework of an idiographic model of history, and cannot provide an adequate basis for a comparative constitutional history of Europe.[73] He has proposed a contrasting model of a European constitutional history in which historical comparison is aimed at laying the conceptual foundations for legal and political organisation in the Europe of today. The idea of an 'applied' legal history in relation to private law outlined above is thus joined by a proposal for a constitutional history which can be developed as an 'applied' science, albeit in a very different way.

(b) In recent years the European context has aroused increased interest also in the history of the administration and administrative law. To some degree German research has regarded constitutional history and the history of the administration as a single research area.[74] For some time the expansion of the activity of the administration and the increased responsibility of the state under the concept of the welfare state (*Sozialstaat*, which under Articles 20 and 28 of the Basic Law is one of the central principles of German constitutional law) have led to considerable preoccupation in Germany with the theoretical foundations and legal problems of the modern administration[75] – having regard, for example, to the relationship between public law and private law, the relationship between the rule of law and the welfare state and thus the foundations and limits of the benefit system, the legal restraints on the authorities and their discretionary freedom. This modern development has also directed attention towards the history of the administration and administrative law and in recent years has begun to establish a counterweight to the previous concentration of historical research on private law. Attention has focused in particular on the traditions of 'good administration' in the early modern period, as they were affected by the conflicting forces of jurisprudence, politics, ethics and economics, on the basis of the older Aristotelianism, together with the related question of the economic and social history of mercantilism (or of cameralism, the version of mercantilism which prevailed in Germany).[76]

In Germany this interest in the history of the administration has turned towards the European context from various starting points. Two examples of this – prompted for example by Hans Maier's pioneering work[77] – are the comparison of Germany and western Europe from the point of view of German peculiarities, or indeed a special German approach, and the more detailed study of the French influence on the emergence of administrative law as a separate legal discipline in Germany.[78] This European orientation of research into administrative history has recently received particular impetus from the discussions concerning a 'European administrative law' for our time. As in the case of constitutional history, we are faced here with the problem that today 'administration' means different things in different European countries[79] and as a historical concept denotes a subject-matter which goes far beyond the use of the term 'administration' in the historical sources themselves.[80] In spite of that problem research in the field of administrative history has already distinguished itself in international co-operation, as the recent comparative accounts[81] and the new *Jahrbuch für europäische Verwaltungsgeschichte*[82] show.

6. 'EUROPE' – THE EXTENT OF THE RESEARCH AREA

(a) In recent years, not only has research interest in European legal history been turned to new questions, periods and areas of the law, but the scope of interest has also broadened from the geographical point of view. In particular, during the last decade much more attention has been devoted to the historical connections between continental and English law.[83] While the differences, largely determined by historical circumstances, between English (and American) common law and continental European law ('civil law', in English terminology) are well known, it is now clear that their historical relationships and common structural features are much greater than was previously assumed by most people. Recent work has of course been able to build on some earlier basic research in the field, for example the work of Heinrich Brunner[84] and F.W. Maitland[85] (to which Helmut Coing and Knut Wolfgang Noerr referred in the inauguration of their new series of publications[86]), or on studies such as those of Pringsheim,[87] which had pointed out at an early stage the common features of Roman law (and thus the roots of continental civil law) on the one hand and the English common law on the other.

The series founded by Coing and Noerr in particular has brought to light a great many historically based common features of English and continental law, so that we can no longer think in terms of the isolated, wholly separate development of the law in the continental and English (or Anglo-American) areas respectively. The aspects that divide them are obvious, but there are also a wealth of historical connections. Among them, as several recent studies have shown, are not only the fact that the tradition of the older academic law had a much greater influence on England than has been assumed, but also the fact that in the modern period the different systems have drawn on each other to a very large extent in virtually all areas of the law, from private law[88] through criminal law,[89] procedural law and judicial organisation[90] to constitutional law.[91] Further information on structural similarities and the compatibility of juridical approaches to solutions in the – only apparently so incompatible – legal systems of England and the continent is likely also to be provided by studies of the zones of contact and overlap of the two legal areas, such as Zimmerman's work in relation to South Africa.[92]

(b) Much less German research in European legal history has been devoted to eastern Europe, on the other hand. In so far as obstacles had arisen as a result of the circumstances of our time – that is to say, the political division of western and eastern Europe and the related cultural estrangement, with all its consequences, including inadequate linguistic knowledge – the changes of the last few years certainly open up new possibilities for scientific cooperation. More to the point, they also provide an incentive to overcome the narrowing of historical perspectives which had arisen out of the recent past and to place what it is hoped will become the new European sense of community in the context of the common history of Europe before the political split of the 20th century.

For a broad area from the Baltic through Poland and Hungary into the Balkans, sometimes referred to generally as east central Europe, some recent work has already paved the way for further research, since it has shown that this area belongs to the zone of influence of the *ius commune*.[93] Other connections betwen the east and the rest of Europe must also be studied, for example the intensive contacts in the area of the Baltic Sea (including Scandinavia) and their consequences far into the east of the continent since the Middle Ages; links with the development of the law in Germany, for instance through the adoption of the law of German cities[94] (from the perspective of European legal history, of course, not from that of national history, as in the older tradition of German research); the emergence and continued influence of an international sense of community under the Habsburg monarchy,[95] and so on.

There is some controversy, however, concerning the position of the large part of Europe which in the Middle Ages was moulded not by the Latin church and language but by the Greek and Byzantine tradition. Until now the prevailing notion of Europe in German research in legal history has been restricted essentially to the Latin area, excluding the Greek and Byzantine east and south-east.[96] This point of view may, however, excessively neglect the unifying elements of common European culture in favour of the – highly developed, it is true – common features of 'Latin Europe' (perhaps because of the experience of the recent past, in which Russia, for example, had not yet opened up to the European idea and the European Community, before the accession of Greece, had not yet been extended to the south-east).

It is true that as historiographical concepts 'Europe' and 'European legal culture' need not necessarily cover the whole of the geographical entity or indeed be restricted to it. They should instead be defined in accordance with the cultural and historical source material and the field of interest. From that point of view the common historical origins of the development of the law in Latin Europe and in Greek-Byzantine Europe in antiquity – that is to say, the Christian tradition and Roman law – provides a substantial common foundation in a cultural area encompassing western and eastern Europe; they are what set the cultural development of Europe as a whole apart from non-European legal cultures. For example, in respect of Russia in the Middle Ages and the early modern period research might be undertaken into common features which were perhaps transmitted through canon law, despite the schism in the church, or resulted from the connections with Scandinavia and central Europe. On the basis of these older inter-relationships, the abundance of new connections between eastern and western Europe (in respect of Russia, above all during the reforms of the eighteenth and nineteenth centuries[97]) may be regarded, despite the differences in their previous development, not simply as the encounter of two entirely foreign legal cultures but rather the far-reaching renewal – moving essentially from the west – of cultural relationships founded in antiquity.

(c) Moreover, in the light of the universal spread of European legal systems in the modern age (including, for instance, the combination of the law of the former colonial power with customary law in large parts of Africa), European legal history is not necessarily restricted to Europe. However, for two reasons its field of interest is primarily the geographical area of Europe, and it is distinguished at least in that respect from a universal history of modern law. It is exclusively in Europe that the early foundations of European legal culture were laid and there that it developed until well into the modern age. In particular, however, it is in respect of Europe that the needs of today have, in the last few decades, made European legal culture the focus of historical interest and research. That does not of course mean that problems and connections going beyond this geographical area may not become relevant, such as the mixed system of Roman–Dutch and common law in South Africa (from the point of view of the compatibility of continental and English law or the 'modernity' of the *ius commune*). It would go far beyond our topic, however, thoroughly to examine the development of European legal cultures outside Europe in former colonies such as America or Australia (and in Germany such an interest does not appear to have been pursued in the context of European legal history). The various processes of reception of European legal systems in non-European legal cultures with their own history and the emergence of mixed systems of European and indigenous law deserve separate investigation and analysis, distinct from the research tasks of European legal history (partly, of course, in order to avoid the importation of narrowly Eurocentric perspectives into the study of such universal processes of reception and integration).

7. CONCLUSION

As the above summary has shown, the change in outlook from the national historical conceptions of the nineteenth century to the integration of German legal history in European legal history has affected the issues and areas of interest of current German research in legal history. Legal historians are engaged in research into such areas as *ius commune* and *ius naturale*, the mediaeval *consuetudines* and the *ius patriae* of the early modern period, not only as the historical foundations of German law but increasingly as components of a common European legal culture which developed in pre-modern European society. The new focus on the history of this European legal culture places legal developments in Germany (and in other countries which became nation-states in the modern period) in the context of European history. It thus runs counter to the nineteenth century concept of a 'German legal history' (or the 'national' legal history of any other country) which was to be examined in its own 'organic' context and could be described in isolation.

The approaches and themes of this research into European legal history in Germany are extremely diverse: investigations into the history of legal science and the development of individual concepts of legal theory; work on the history of legislation and the case law of the courts; research into the social history of the legal profession. Historical/genetic, structural and historical/comparative approaches each open different avenues and give rise to debate on methodology. Moreover, the research interests of legal historians overlap to some degree with legal anthropology and historical ethnology in so far as common fundamental features of European legal culture – such as, for example, the separation of law from religion and ethics or the independence of secular from ecclesiastical law as early as the Middle Ages – show themselves to be features specific to that legal culture only in comparison with other cultures (for example Islamic culture).

In respect of the Middle Ages and the early modern period (the sixteenth to eighteenth centuries) research has since the 1950s been directed towards the common foundations of private law in Europe. Attention has been directed in particular at the *ius commune* as the common historical point of departure for the development of national law.

More recently, however, the interests of researchers have expanded far beyond that area. They extend now to the history of criminal law (in which the *ius commune*, the Enlightenment and ideas of natural law in the eighteenth century and the reform debates of the nineteenth century provide a broad basis for the whole of Europe) and above all to the history of public law (*ius publicum*) and the related common traditions of political thought in Europe. The German term '*Verfassungsgeschichte*' [constitutional history] in this context incorporates not only the development of constitutional law but also the history of political institutions, the administration and political thought in the new research area of European constitutional history. Finally, the analysis of common structural features and the international transfer of legal knowledge in Europe in the nineteenth century is coming to constitute a new focus of research, concerned with the link between the common European legal culture of the pre-modern period and the present-day rebirth of a common body of European law, the continuation of the *European* history of law even in the heyday of the nation-state.

This new interest in European legal history can make a significant contribution to contemporary developments in national law in Europe from the point of view of the harmonisation of laws and the continuing development of European Community law by giving lawyers, in their capacity as the creators of this modern European law, some awareness of the historical common elements of the law and the legal profession, which transcend all national differences. European legal history is thus a foundation for European-oriented legal studies and the training of 'lawyers for Europe'. The manner in which this is to be taken into account in the curricula of law faculties is now beginning to be as earnestly discussed in Germany as the question whether European legal history can make a direct contribution – perhaps even one comparable, despite its different theoretical and methodological bases, to that of the historical school in the development of German law in the nineteenth century – to the development of European legal theory today. These questions cannot be answered in Germany alone, but call for Europe-wide discussion of the perspectives of European legal history.

NOTES

1. The following article is based on lectures by the author at the Universities of Stockholm, Freiburg (Switzerland) and Cologne and on his paper 'Vom *Ius commune* bis zum Gemeinschaftsrecht – das Forschungsfeld der Europaäischen Rechtsgeschitchte', in Reiner Schulze, ed. *Europäische Rechts-und Verfassungsgeschichte – Ergebnisse und Perspektiver*, Berlin 1991.
2. Cf. Helmut Coing, 'Europäisierung der Rechtswissenschaft', *Neue Juristische Wochenschrift* 1990, 937; see most recently Peter Ulmer, 'Vom deutschen zum europäischen Privatrecht?', *Juristenzeitung* 1992, 1; Reinhard Zimmermann, 'Das römisch-kanonische ius commune als Grundlage eruopäischer Rechtseinheit, *Juristenzeitung*, 1992, 8; and Hein Kötz, 'Was erwartet die Rechtsvergleichung von der Rechtsgeschichte?', *Juristenzeitung* 1992, 20.
3. Dietmar Willoweit and Bernhard Grossfeld, 'Juristen für Europa', *Juristenzeitung* 1990, 605; François Ost and Mark van Hoecke, 'Für eine europäische Juristenausbildung', *Juristenzeitung* 1990, 911; Filippo Ranieri, 'Der europäische Jurist', *Ius commune* 17, 1990, 9, esp. at 15.
4. Rudolf von Ihering, *Geist des römischen Rechts auf den verschiedenen Stufen seiner Entwicklung*, vol. 1 (1st edn. Leipzig, 1852; quoted here from the 6th edn. Leipzig, 1907, reprint Darmstadt, 1968), 15.
5. See most recently Helmut Coing, 'Erich Genzmer' in *Juristen an der Universität Frankfurt am Main*, Bernhard Diestelkamp and Michael Stolleis, eds., Baden-Baden, 1989, 200, and Filippo Ranieri, 'Eine Dogmengeschichte des europäischen Zivilrechts?' in Schulze, note 1, 89.
6. Paul Koschaker, *Europa und das römische Recht*, (1st edn 1947) 4th edn, Munich, 1966.

As examples of further literature the following may be singled out: for canon law, Hans Liermann, 'Das kanonische Recht als Grundlage europäischen Rechtsdenkens', *Zeitschrift für evangelisches Kirchenrecht* 6 1957–58, 37; for German law, Hans Thieme, *Das Naturrecht und die europäische Privatrechtsgeschichte*, 2nd ed Basel, 1954.

7. For example, in the tradition of Germanic studies, from Karl-Friedrich Eichhorn to Heinrich Mitteis; cf. Eichhorn, *Einleitung in das deutsche Privatrecht: mit Einschluß des Lehenrechts* 1st edn Göttingen, 1823, reprint of the 5th edn 1845, Frankfurt am Main, 1983: Eichhorn, *Deutsche Staats- und Rechtsgeschichte*, 2 vols., 1st edn Göttingen, 1808, reprint of the 5th edn 1843–44, Frankfurt am Main, 1983; Mitteis, *Deutsche Rechtsgeschichte: ein Studienbuch* 1st ed Munich, 1949, 18th edn Munich, 1988 (revised by Heinz Lieberich): *Deutsches Privatrecht: ein Studienbuch*, 1st edn Munich, 1950, 10th edn Munich, 1988 (revised by Heinz Lieberich).
8. Gerhard Wesenberg, *Neuere deutsche Privatrechtsgeschichte im Rahmen der europäischen Rechtsentwicklung*, 1st edn Lahr (Baden), 1954 (4th edn Vienna, 1985), continued by Gunter Wesener.
9. Franz Wieacker, *Privatrechtsgeschichte der Neuzeit unter besonderer Berücksichtigung der deutschen Entwicklung*, 1st edn Göttingen, 1952 (2nd edn 1967).
10. Wieacker, note 9, 1st edn, s.3, 'The origins of European legal culture', and Part 2 'The reception of European jurisprudence in Germany'; see at p.8, 'The history of European private law is, like European history generally, a single entity; the history of German private law is simply a particular instance, and its great eras can without exception be understood only in that European context', (in the second edition the corresponding ideas are to be found in the headings to section 2 *et seq.* and at p.18).
11. See in particular *Handbuch der Quellen und Literatur der Neueren Europäischen Privatrechtsgeschichte* (Helmut Coing, ed.), Munich, 1973–88; *Ius commune* (vols.1–9 edited by Helmut Coing, vols.10–13 by Dieter Simon and Walter Wilhelm, and from vol.14 (1987), as *Zeitschrift für Europäische Rechtssgeschichte* by Dieter Simon) and special issues of *Ius commune*.
12. Initially at the universities of Regensburg and Trier, and now also in Giessen. It is also interesting to observe that the 28th Conference of German Legal Historians (*Deutsch Rechtshistorikertag*) (1990) was held for the first time in a European country outside the German-speaking area: in Nijmegen in the Netherlands.
13. See below, section 6.
14. Wieacker, note 9.
15. Helmut Coing, 'Das Recht als Element der europäischen Kultur', *HZ* 238, 1984, 1.
16. Otto Gerhard Oexle, 'Die Geschichtswissenschaft im Zeichen des Historismus', *HZ* 238, 1984, 17.
17. Reiner Schulze, 'Das Recht fremder Kulturen – Vom Nutzen der Rechtsetnologie für die Rechtsgeschichte', *Historisches Jahrbuch* 1990, 446, at 451 et seq.
18. Willoweit and Grossfeld, note 3.
19. Emilio Betti, *Die Hermeneutik als allgemeine Methodik der Geisteswissenschaften*, 2nd edn Tübingen, 1972.
20. Hans Georg Gadamer, *Wahrheit und Methode, Grundzüge einer philosophischen Hermeneutik*, 5th edn Tübingen, 1986, esp. at p.xviii.
21. Wieacker, note 9, 2nd edn at 15 et seq., 416 et seq. and 425 et seq.; Wieacker, 'Der gegenwartige Stand der Disziplin der neuren Privatrechtsgeschichte'. in *Eranion Maridakis I*, Athens, 1963, 339; Wieacker, 'Art. Methode der Rechtsgeschichte', *HRG*, vol.3, Berlin, 1984, col.518 et seq.
22. Helmut Coing, 'Die europäische Privatrechtsgeschichte der neueren Zeit als einheitliches Forschungsgebeit', *Ius commune* 1, 1967, 1, and in Coing, *Gesammelte Aufsätze* II, Frankfurt am Main, 1982, 67; see in addition Coing, *Europäisches Privatrecht*, 2 vols., Munich, 1985/89, and most recently 'Europäisierung der Rechtswissenschaft', note 2.
23. Reinhard Zimmermann, 'Usus hodiernus pandectarum', in Schulze, note 1, 61.
24. Ranieri, note 5.
25. Hein Kötz, 'Gemeineuropäisches Zivilrecht', in *Festschrift für Konrad Zweigert*,

Tübingen, 1981, 481.
26. Cf. Ranieri, note 5.
27. Cf. Wieacker, note 9, 2nd edn at 539 et seq.
28. Friedrich Carl von Savigny, *Vom Beruf unserer Zeit für Gesetzgebung und Rechtswissenschaft*, Heidelberg, 1814.
29. See Coing, note 15; on the differentiation of law from other disciplines from the sociological point of view see Niklas Luhmann, *Rechtssoziologie*, 3rd edn Opladen, 1987, esp. at 217 et seq.
30. Peter Landau, 'Der Einfluss des kanonischen Rechts auf die europäische Rechtskultur', in Schulze, note 1, 39; see also Harold J. Berman, *Law and Revolution. The Formation of the Western Legal Tradition*, Cambridge Mass. & London, 1983.
31. See for example, *Handbuch der Quellen und der Literatur*, note 11; Coing, *Europäisches Privatrecht*, note 22; and, most recently, the work in English of the German legal historian Reinhard Zimmermann, *The Law of Obligations*, Johannesburg, 1990.
32. See Roderich von Stinzing and Ernst Landsberg, *Geschichte der deutschen Rechtswissenschaft*, 3rd part, 1st half-volume, Munich and Leipzig, 1898 (reprinted Aalen, 1957) p.228 et seq.; Wieacker, note 9, at 168 et seq., 222 et seq.
33. Friedrich Carl von Savigny, *Geschichte des römischen Rechts im Mittelalter*, vols. 1–7, Heidelberg 1815–31; reprint of the 2nd edition (1834–50), Bad Homburg, 1961.
34. A typical remark is that of Rudolph Sohm: 'The nature of ecclesiastical law is at variance with the nature of the church', in *Kirchenrecht*, vol. 1, 'Die geschichtliche Grundlagen', Leipzig, 1892; on this see Landau, note 30.
35. For example Liermann, note 6.
36. From a programmatic point of view, see Coing, *Handbuch*, note 11, I/1, foreword; see also Udo Wolter, *Ius Canonicum in Iure Civili*, Cologne, 1975.
37. Cf. summary in Landau, note 30. The centre of research in this aspect of European legal history is now on the other side of the Atlantic, at the Institute of Medieval Canon Law, Berkeley, California.
38. On this concept cf. Otto Brunner, *Land und Herrschaft* Baden bei Wien, 1939, 5th edn Vienna, 1965 (reprint Darmstadt, 1973); Brunner, *Neue Wege der Verfassungs- und Sozialgeschichte. Vorträge und Aufsätze*, 3rd edn Göttingen, 1980; Dietrich Gerhard, 'Periodization in European History' AHR 61, 1956, 900 (German version in Dietrich Gerhard, *Alte und Neue Welt in vergleichender Geschichtsbetrachtung*, Göttingen, 1962, 40).
39. Just as historians enquire into 'The Middle Ages in the Typology of Oral Societies' ('Das Mittelalter in der Typik der oralen Gesellschaften', the title of an article by Hanna Vollrath in *HZ* 233, 1981, 571, with further references).
40. See Gerhard Dilcher et al., *Mittelalterliches Gewohnheitsrecht* (Schriften zur Europäischen Rechts- und Verfassungsgeschichte, Berlin, prob. 1992).
41. See Nobert Elias, *Über den Prozeß der Zivilisation*, vol. 1, 'Wandlungen des Verhaltens in den westlichen Oberschichten des Abendlandes', 15th edn Frankfurt am Main, 1990.
42. Including its academic treatment on the basis of the *libri feudorum*.
43. Cf. Dietmar Willoweit and Winfried Schich (eds.), *Studien zur Geschichte des sächsisch-magdeburgischen Rechts in Deutschland und Polen*, Frankfurt am Main, 1980; and most recently Irena Kwiatkowska, 'Das sächsische Recht in der polnischen juristischen Literatur des 17. Jahrhunderts', in *Deutsches Recht zwischen Saschsenspiegel und Aufklärung, Festschrift für Rolf Lieberwirth zum 70. Geburtstag*, Gerhard Lingelbach and Heiner Lück, eds, Frankfurt am Main, 1991, 119.
44. See *inter alia* Konrad Zweigert and Hein Kötz, *Einführung in die Rechtsvergleichung*, vol. 1, 2nd edn Tübingen, 1984, 101 et seq., 113 et seq.; Hans Schlosser, *Grundzüge der neueren Privatrechtsgeschichte*, 6th edition Heidelberg, 1988, 107.
45. Cf. Reinhard Zimmermann, 'Das römisch-holländische Recht und seine Bedeutung für Europa' *Juristenzeitung* 1990, 825, at 837. Shortly to appear on the same subject, Robert Feenstra and Reinhard Zimmermann, *Die Fortschritte des Zivilrechts im 17. und 18. Jahrhundert – Das römisch-holländische Recht* (Schriften zur Europäischen Rechts- und Verfassungsgeschichte), Berlin, 1992.

46. The work of Klaus Luig in particular has shed more light on the various reciprocal influences in this general European turn towards territorial and national law. See Luig, 'Institutionenlehrbücher des nationalen Rechts im 17. und 18. Jahrhundert', *Ius commune* 3, 1970, 64.
47. While the Prussian Allgemeine Landrecht of 1794 is of prime importance in this respect for German legal history, recent work has been devoted to the contribution of natural law to the development of private law in the European context. See for example Klaus Luig, 'Natürliches Privatrecht – Die Rolle des Privatrechts in den naturrechtlichen Gesellschafsentwürfen des 17 and 18. Jahrhunderts', in Schulze (ed), note 1, or on the international character of codifications based on natural law, Wilhelm Brauneder, 'Vernünftiges Recht als überregionales Recht: Die Rechtsvereinheitlichung der österreichischen Zivilrechtskodifikationen 1786–1797–1811', in Schulze, note 1.
48. See *inter alia*, Coing, *Europäisches Privatrecht*, note 24, vol.2; Zimmermann, note 31; Zimmermann, note 23.
49. Cf. Reiner Schulze, Introduction, in Schulze, (ed.), *Deutsche Rechtswissenschaft und Staatslehre im Spiegel der italienischen Rechtskultur während der zweiten Hälfte des 19. Jahrhunderts*, Berlin, 1990, 3, esp at 8.
50. Cf. Coing, note 15, 1–5.
51. On the development and importance of comparative law, cf. Bernhard Grossfeld, *Macht und Ohnmacht der Rechtsvergleichung*, Tübingen, 1984, esp. at 37 et seq.; Hein Kötz, 'Neue Aufgaben der Rechtsvergleichung', Juristische Blätter 104, 1982, 355; Léontin-Jean Constantinesco, *Rechtsvergleichung*, vol.1, *Einführung in die Rechtsvergleichung*, Cologne, 1971, 69 et seq.; Helmut Coing, 'Rechtsvergleichung als Grundlage von Gesetzebung im 19. Jahrhundert, *Ius commune* 7, 1978, 168.
52. In this respect it is necessary also to consider to what extent modern terms such as 'reception', 'influence', 'model' or 'follow' adequately express the cultural relationship between two countries, and in particular whether they adequately reflect the manner in which legal rules and structures may be changed in the context of the other law, and the concomitant evolution in Europe through the linking of components of different national legal cultures. Cf. Aldo Mazzacane, 'Die Rechtskultur in Deutschland und Italien nach der nationalen Einigung – Anmerkungen zu einem Forschungsprojekt', in Schul'e, note 49, at p.55, and Erk Volkmar Heyen, 'Zur Einflussfrage in der Staats- und Rechtswissenschaftsgeschichte', ibid., 75.
53. To cite just one example, the concepts of the German pandects reached Italy not only directly from north to south but also after a detour to the west: in France the methodological and theoretical stimulation of German jurisprudence in the first half of the nineteenth century prompted the 'germanisme' movement, and this in turn was one of the sources of the 'germanesimo' of late nineteenth century Italy. Cf. Pasquale Beneduce, 'Germanisme, la terrible accusation. Fremde Lehrsysteme und Argumentationsweisen in de italienischen Privatrechtswissenschaft während der zweiten Hälfte des 19. Jahrhunderts', in Schulze, note 49, 105.
54. As recently proposed in relation to developments in labour law in the late nineteenth century by Cristina Vano, 'Hypothesen zur Interpretation der "vergleichenden Methoden" im Arbeitsrecht an der Wende zum 20. Jahrhundert', in Schulze, note 49, 225. at p.242.
55. Schlosser, note 44; Zweigert and Kötz, note 44.
56. Summaries of the history of French law in Germany in the nineteenth century may be found in Werner Schubert, *Französisches Recht in Deutschland zu Beginn des 19. Jahrhunderts*, Cologne and Vienna, 1977, and in Hans-Jürgen Becker, 'Das Rheinische Recht und seine Bedeutung für die Rechtsentwicklung in Deutschland', *JuS* 1985, 338.
57. Numerous examples in Elmar Wadle, 'Französisches Recht und deutsche Gesetzgebung im 19. Jahrhundert', in Schulze, note 1, 210.
58. More on the German influence on France is now to be found in Alfons Bürge, 'Das französische Privatrecht im 19. Jahrhundert', *Ius commune* special issue no.52, Frankfurt am Main 1991. In view of the role of French jurisprudence as an intermediary between Germany and Italy (above, note 53), it is hardly surprising that a translation of

Zachariae's work from French into Italian was a contributing factor in the transmission of methodology and theory developed by German jurisprudence, through the intermediate step of their application to French law in the Rhine Provinces, to Italian legal thinking; see Pasquale Beneduce, note 53.

59. Charles Aubry and Charles Rau, *Cours de droit civil français dáprès la méthode de Zachariä*, 8 vols., 5th edn Paris, 1869–83.
60. *Handbuch des französischen Civilrechts*, 1st edn, 2 vols, Heidelberg, 1808; 2d edn, 4 vols, Heidelberg, 1811–12; 8th edn by Carl Crome, Freiburg im Breisgau, 1894–95.
61. In particular François Auguste Dufrayer and Johann Kasper Foelix; cf Ludwig Mallmann, *Französische Juristenausbildung im Rheinland 1794–1814, Die Rechtsschule von Koblenz*, Cologne and Vienna, 1987, 165 et esq., esp. 167 et seq.; Alfons Bürge, 'Der Einfluss der Pandektenwissenschaft auf das französischen Privatrecht im 19. Jahrhundert: Vom Vermögen zum patrimoine', in Schulze, note 1, 221, in particular section 6, with further references.
62. See Heinz-Peter Mansel, 'Mancini, von Savigny und die Kodifikationen des deutschen internationalen Privatrechts von 1896', in Schulze, note 49, 245; Erik Jayme, 'Dionisio Anzilotti und das Internationale Privatrecht', ibid., 297.
63. Further details in Reiner Schulze, 'Il contributo italiano al diritto penale nel tardo Ottocento', to be published in the papers of the conference on 'Problemi istituzionali e reforme nell' età Crispina' (LV Congresso di Storia del Risorgimento), Sorrento, 1990.
64. An introductory selection of the voluminous literature may be found in Werner Weidenfeld ed., *Die Identität Europas*, Bonn, 1985, 279. Taking into account present developments, see also Peter Haungs ed. *Europäisierung Europas*, Baden-Baden, 1989; Jens Hacker and Siegfried Mampel, *Europäische Integration und deutsche Frage*, Berlin, 1989. For one of the few German contributions to the history of European integration from the point of view of legal history see Markus Göldner, *Politische Symbole der europäische Integration* (dissertation, Kiel), Frankfurt am Main etc., 1988.
65. Increasingly discussed, from various perspectives, in recent writing: see for example Roland Bieber and Jürgen Schwarze, *Verfassungsentwicklung in der Europäischen Gemeinschaft*, Baden-Baden, 1984; Schwarze, 'Entwicklungsstufen des Europäischen Gemeinschaftstechts', in *Festschrift für Karl Carstens*, Cologne etc, 1984, vol. 1, 259; Schwarze, Introduction, in J. Schwarze and R. Bieber eds., *Das europäische Wirtschaftsrecht vor den Herausforderungen der Zukunft*, Baden-Baden, 1985, 9; Ulrich Everling ed, *Das europäische Gemeinschaftsrecht im Spannungsverhältnis von Politik und Wirtschaft*, Baden-Baden, 1985; Roland Bieber and Georg Ress eds., *Die Dynamik des Europäischen Gemeinschaftsrechts*, Baden-Baden, 1987.
66. See especially Bernhard Diestelkamp, 'Rechtsgeschichte als Zeitgeschichte', *ZNR* 1985, 191.
67. Cf. Luig, note 47.
68. Public law, more closely linked to political conditions, was not lost from sight, particularly by Germanists such as Eichhorn, Beseler and Gierke, but in the teaching of general methodology and the training of lawyers, for example, it did usually take second place to private law. That tradition was reinforced by the fact that legal history was attached to chairs of private law in German law faculties.
69. Michael Stolleis, *Geschichte des öffentlichen Rechts in Deutschland*, vol. 1, Munich, 1988, 50; Stolleis, 'Aufgaben der neueren Rechtsgeschichte, oder: Hic sunt leones', in *RJ* 4, 1985, 251.
70. Ernst-Wolfgang Böckenförde, 'Die Einheit von nationaler und konstituioneller politischer Bewegung im deutschen Frühliberalismus', in Böckenförde ed, *Moderne deutsche Verfassungsgeschichte (1815–1914)*, 2nd edn, Königstein, 1981.
71. Brunner, note 38; Brunner, 'Der Historiker und die Geschichte von Verfassung und Recht', *HZ*, 1969, 1.
72. There is a particular need for consideration of the relationship between this research area and areas of study which in other European countries cover some of the same ground, for example 'history of institutions' and 'history of political thought' in France, Italy and other countries in the Roman tradition.

73. Dietmar Willoweit, 'Probleme und Aufgaben einer europäischen Verfassungsgeschichte', in Schulze, note 1, 141.
74. On the close connection between constitutional and administrative history (which allows administrative history to be discussed as part of constitutional history), see Reiner Schulze and Robert Mizia, 'Verwaltungsgeschichtsschreibung in Deutschland und Österreich', *Die Verwaltung* 1985, 351.
75. See the summaries in Peter Badura, *Das Verwaltungsrecht des liberalen Rechtstaates*, Göttingen, 1967.
76. See Reiner Schulze, *Policey und Gesetzgebungslehre im 18. Jahrhundert*, Berlin, 1982, at p.115 et seq., 179 et seq.
77. Hans Maier, *Die ältere deutsche Staats- und Verwaltungslehre*, 2nd edn, Munich, 1980 (1st edn, Neuwied 1966); Maier, *Ältere deutsche Staatslehre und westliche politische Tradition*, Tübingen, 1966.
78. An influence exerted in particular through the work of the German lawyer Otto Mayer; cf. Erk Volkmar Heyen, 'Otto Mayer: Frankfurt und das Deutsche Reich', *Der Staat* 19, 1980, 444; Heyen, *Otto Mayer: Studien zu der geistige Grundlagen seiner Verwaltungsrechtswissenschaft* (Publications of the Hochschule Speyer), Berlin, 1981; Alfons Hueber, *Otto Mayer. Die 'juristische Methode' im Verwaltungsrecht* (Schriften zum öffentlichen Recht), Berlin, 1982.
79. For the States of the European Community see Jürgen Schwarze, *Europäisches Verwaltungsrecht*, Vol.1, Wiesbaden, 1988, at 13.
80. Cf. on the definition of the subject-matter of constitutional history, the articles by Reinhard Koselleck, Karl Kroeschell and Rolf Sprandel in 'Gegenstand und Begriffe der Verfassungsgeschichtsschreibung', *Der Staat*, special issue 6, 1983.
81. See in particular Erk Volkmar Heyen (ed.), 'Geschichte der Verwaltungswissenschaft in Europa', *Ius commune* special issue No.18, Frankfurt am Main 1982; further examples in the Italian literature (with international contributions): *Filosofia politica*, Vol.1988/II; *ISAP Archivio: L'amministrazione nella storia moderna*, 3, Milan, 1985; and in the publications of the Institut International des Sciences Administratives, Brussels.
82. Erk Volkmar Heyen, Guido Melis, Jean-Louis Mestre, Vincent Wright, Bernd Wunder (eds.), *Jahrbuch für euorpäische Verwaltungsgeschichte*, Baden-Baden since 1989.
83. Several detailed articles on legal connections between England and the continent in Mauro Cappelletti (ed.), *New Perspectives for a Common Law of Europe*, London etc., 1978. The research topic of the connections between England and the continent requires separate consideration at some length; this review of European legal history can do no more than give a few references.
84. Heinrich Brunner, *Überblick über die Geschichte der französischen, normannischen und englischen Rechtsquellen*, Leipzig, 1882; Brunner, *Geschichte der englischen Rechtsquellen im Grundriss. Mit einem Anhang über die normannischen Rechtsquellen*, Leipzig, 1909.
85. Cf. F.W. Maitland, *Roman Canon Law in England*, London, 1898.
86. Helmut Coing and Knut Wolfgang Nörr, foreword to *Englische und kontinentale Rechtsgeschichte: ein Forschungsprojekt*, Berlin, 1985, 5. This is the first volume in the series Comparative Studies in Continental and Anglo-American Legal History.
87. Fritz Pringsheim, 'The Inner Relationship between English and Roman Law', 1935, 5 *CLJ* 347.
88. Cf. Nörr, 'The European Side of the English Law. A Few Comments from a Continental Historian', in Coing and Nörr, note 86, 15; John Barton (ed.), *Towards a General Law of Contract*, Berlin, 1990.
89. See for example Schulze, note 63.
90. Cf. Vito Pier-giovanni (ed.), *The Courts and the Development of Commercial Law*, Berlin, 1987; Antonio Pādoa Schioppa (ed.), *The Trial Jury in England, France, Germany 1700–1900*, Berlin, 1987; John H. Baker (ed.), *Judicial Record, Law Reports and the Growth of Case Law*, Berlin, 1989; Charles Donahue (ed.), *The Records of the*

Medieval Ecclesiastical Courts, Berlin, 1989.

91. Cf. most recently Eckhart Hellmuth (ed.), *The Transformation of Political Culture. England and Germany in the late Eighteenth Century*, London and Oxford, 1990; Roland Kleinhenz, *Königtum und parlamentarische Vertrauensfrage in England 1689–1841*, (dissertation, Würzburg) Berlin, prob. 1991.
92. Reinhard Zimmermann, *Das römisch-hollandische Recht in Südafrika. Einführung in die Grundlagen und usus hodiernus*, Darmstadt, 1983; Zimmermann, 'Usus hodiernus pandectarum', note 23.
93. See the summaries in Coing, *Handbuch*, note 11, for the Baltic area by Werner Kundert and Barbara Dölemeyer, Vol.III/2, 2071; for Poland by Leslaw Pauli, 2099; for Hungary by Janas Zlinsky, 2141; for Romania by Valentin A. Georgescu, Vol.III/5, 1; and for Yugoslavia by Sergij Vilfan, 325.
94. Cf. Willoweit and Schich (eds.), note 43; Kwiatkowska, note 43; on the law of Magdeburg in Kiev, see most recently Heiner Lück, 'Magdeburger Recht in der Ukraine', in *ZNR* 1990, 113; Lück, 'Das Denkmal des Magdeburger Rechts in Kiew', in *Forschungen zur Rechtsarchäologie und rechtlichen Volkskunde* (Louis Carlen, ed.), Zurich, 1990, Vol.12, 109.
95. See Wilhelm Brauneder, note 47.
96. See Coing, note 15, at p.4: 'This *Ius commune* and the learning devoted to it is thus a component of what has been called the Latin culture of the Middle Ages. Its area is that of the Latin Church . . . The east European countries beyond the borders of Italy, Hungary and Poland form a different area which rests on the same foundations of Roman law and Christianity but belongs to the Greek culture of Byzantium and not to the West. When I speak here of Europe, it is in this narrower sense.'
97. See for example Claes Peterson, *Peter the Great's Administrative and Judicial Reforms. Swedish Antecedents and the Progress of Reception*, Stockholm, 1979; Marc Raeff, *The Well-ordered Police State. Social and Institutional Change through Law in the Germanies and Russia 1600–1800*, New Haven and London, 1983.
98. See Reinhard Zimmermann, note 23; Zimmermann, note 45; with regard to America, see for example Cappelletti, note 83.

[19]

'SUPERIOR KNOWLEDGE OR REVELATION': AN APPROACH TO MODERN LEGAL HISTORY

By STEVE HEDLEY *

> I have had three clients who, whilst expressing the fullest confidence in my opinion, have submitted them through a medium for the consideration of dear ones departed. It puts one at a disadvantage. One simply cannot argue legal points with the blessed dead, and one has the uneasy feeling that, from their superior knowledge or revelation, they are more likely to be right.[1]

The history of the English legal system since the Judicature Acts cannot take the same form as that for earlier periods. There is no call for weighty tomes on 'the law of contract in the 1890s'; anyone who wishes to know about it can consult the weighty tomes written at the time. Of course, there is always scope for differences of approach and differences of interpretation. Nonetheless it would be a brave individual indeed who took issue with an Anson or a Pollock. No amount of scholarship can get over the point that the people who lived in the 1890s knew a great deal more about it than do subsequent historians. However watertight the arguments for supposing Victorian textbook writers were wrong on a particular point, you should always be left with the uneasy feeling that they are, after all, more likely to be right. So it is no surprise that, to the extent that a modern legal history has been written at all, it has retreated from the black-letter tradition. Legal historians have for the most part either turned away from the Law Reports altogether, or attempted something more challenging within them: the search for values in legal reasoning.

This search for values is so far a somewhat under-researched area. Yet to a great extent the problem is not the absence of writing, but the preponderance of writing of the wrong sort. There is already a large body of literature purporting to explicate Victorian legal materials, and which is increasingly paying attention to the values embodied in them. But this great scholarly effort is turned to expounding the *modern* law of contract. I say nothing against the view that the modern law of contract is a battle-ground between a 'classical', laissez-faire conception of the subject and a 'modern', corporatist conception;[2] if the law of contract is to be studied as a unit at all, there is a lot to be said for this view. But the continual innuendo that the 'classical' model is an accurate summation of the Victorian law of contract would be hard to justify. This innuendo is a comfortable one for both conservative and radical commentators, for the conservatives can claim to be appealing to a valuable tradition, whereas

* Fellow in Law, Christ's College Cambridge. I would like to thank the following, who made helpful comments on an earlier draft: David Johnston, Ian Kirk, Stephen Livingstone, Paul Matthews, Frank Rose, Geoffrey Samuel, David Sugarman and David Yale.

1. Reginald L. Hine, *Confessions of an un-common attorney* (1946) p. 34.
2. eg Hugh Collins, *The law of contract* (1986).

the radicals can say that they are attacking ideas which are a century out of date. But considered as history, this approach depends upon a rather naive view of the history of private law: that the simple view of contract promoted by Anson and his colleagues was, to their contemporaries, unanswerably correct; that they were able to promote a simple view of contract not because they *over*simplified but because the law actually was that simple; that the amazing coherence of the 'classical' view of contract reflects a feature of the Victorian law, and not of the single-minded approach of Victorian text writers.

On top of this, there is a problem which lawyers like to think of as uniquely theirs, but in fact affects all decision-makers. Unlike a kadi under a palm-tree or the writer of a political manifesto, it is said, Judges cannot say what they like. So it would not be right to read reported judgments as if they were statements of personal values and commitments. Judges must say what the law is, and their personal opinions may well be different. The flaw in this reasoning lies in supposing that anyone, anywhere can simply 'say what they like'. The manifesto-writer plainly cannot, being constrained by the need to persuade and encourage listeners to some political action. And the stereotyped view of the kadi is a misunderstanding of the Islamic tradition; kadis are entitled to develop their own interpretations of the Koran, just as Western Judges are entitled to develop their own view of the law; but in neither case can they simply 'say anything they like'.[3] The upshot of all of this is that a full intellectual history of the judiciary will have much to say about the social pressures which determine what Judges are allowed to say, *as well as* analyzing the use they have made of the freedom they have.

In this essay, then, I will discuss generally the limits within which Judges are free to promote their own values, and the use they make of this freedom. After this analysis, I will take a concrete example of a Victorian judgment, to show what we can and what we cannot establish about judicial values on this sort of evidence. As I hope to show, an analysis of this sort calls into question the usual characterization of the Victorian judiciary as pro-laissez-faire; even in that most laissez-faire-ish of tasks, the determination of the intentions of the parties, other values keep creeping in.

The Bar

Rules constrain barristers at every turn. Some rules prescribe a particular course of conduct, leaving no choice in the matter; others leave a range of choices, still others simply specify how a particular result is to be achieved, but say nothing on whether it should. I do not mean to confine myself to 'rules of law' strictly so called. The rules on what barristers must wear in court are as much in issue as the doctrine of consideration.

3. On kadis see Martin Shapiro, *Courts - A comparative and political analysis* (1981) ch. 5.

The enforcement of these rules is through social pressure. How does a new barrister become aware of this pressure? Much of it is part of the wider culture: 'common sense' will tell barristers not to insult the Judge, and not to cite the latest Labour manifesto as an authoritative source of law. Other aspects will be picked up from law books and formal instruction. Colleagues will instill yet others. And much will be learned the hard way, from a Judge or colleague aggrieved by infringement of the rule - notoriously, the rule against expressing a personal opinion in court is learned this way.

For any particular rule it ought to be possible to define its source - by which I mean not its historical origin but the authority that makes it a recognized rule - whether a particular document, a particular official or just a vague 'everybody says ...' Identifying the source of a rule is often not very important, but when its detail is in issue or there are other, apparently conflicting rules, sources can be all-important. So for most purposes it makes little difference that the bar's ethics were not expressed in a single authoritative document until 1980, but this change will have transformed any argument on the finer points. To take another example, the old law of larceny was scrapped in 1968 and replaced by a (conceptually very different) law of theft; the foundations of the economic order did not noticeably shake, but the detail of the subject was rendered unrecognizable.

The social isolation of the bar, and its high social density, together ensure a great homogeneity in the rules.[4] Yet the rules do not apply equally to all - at least, not in the pedantic sense that the same conduct would be equally condemned whoever did it. Rules can designate roles (eg Prosecuting Counsel, Judge), and prescribe conduct making roles *complementary,* rather than prescribing the same rules for all. So Judge and counsel are all bound to participate in the legal argument in court, but this 'participation' involves very different things from the Judge than it does from counsel. Moreover, the prestige conferred by these roles influences the degree of pressure that can be brought to bear on an infringer. Judges who invite their dogs to join them on the bench[5] might be 'frowned on' by the bar, but the pressure involved would be far weaker than on counsel who tried the same thing. And similarly with precedent: the higher the rank of the Judge, the fewer binding precedents. To say that there are different rules for different roles is true but only half the truth; the other half being that the greater the prestige attached to the role, the easier it is for that role-player to resist pressure to conform.[6]

But in some respects high rank involves greater restriction. A Judge in

4. See Maureen Cain, 'Necessarily out of touch - thoughts on the social organization of the bar' (1976) 23 *Sociological Review Monographs* 226.
5. eg Hawkins J.: see *The reminiscences of Sir Henry Hawkins (Baron Brampton)* (1904) volume II, p. 45. No doubt the bar frowned even more when 'Jack' disrupted argument by barking (p. 57).
6. And see 'The beginner who thought he would do it himself' in *Forensic Fables* by 'O' (pseudonym of Theo Mathew) (1961) pp. 267-8.

a provincial town, from whom an appeal is rarely taken, is probably freer from rules than an appeal Judge in London, in the full glare of legal publicity, who is only ever confronted by the most able of counsel. This is probably the main feature distinguishing the sorts of argument you find in reported cases from the general run of cases. There is much less need for argument about facts, and so any freedom the Judges have derives from their considerable skills in technical legal argument. You get a better class of argument in the Court of Appeal.

I have so far run together rules on legal argument and other rules. This is quite deliberate, to emphasize that rules on argument are part and parcel of the bar's culture. There are rules defining what barristers may argue just as there are rules on what they may wear. Rules limiting legal argument only appear distinct if ripped from their context, on the ground that what is ripped out is 'law' and what is left is 'practice'.[7] This essay, however, concentrates on the courts, in particular the appeal courts, and so it is irrelevant for present purposes that 'law' 'exists' outside the court.[8] So, consider rules restricting legal argument. In what follows I will be emphasizing diversity, rather than uniformity, in the restrictions on argument; this does not, however, represent a difference in kind from other restrictions, but a difference in the degree of attention they have been paid. Judges differ considerably in their tolerance of long-winded rhetoric from counsel, but little has been written on this, whereas much has been written on their differing attitudes to precedent. The diversity of the latter is therefore better documented.

Though pressure to conform to the rules is all-pervasive, their sources are various. 'Common sense' will tell barristers that some arguments are just 'not legal'; other restrictions will only be learned with experience.[9] It is by no means always true that an argument is 'not legal' if it plainly has a source 'outside' the legal professions, but many types of argument have been rejected on pretty much that ground: for example, arguments from sociological considerations have been rejected purely and simply because they are sociological.[10] The acceptability and weight of arguments from different sources has varied considerably. Even the acceptability of textbook statements has been doubted, surprising as this may seem.[11] The only staples of legal argument are case law and statute law, though the

7. This is a general feature of 'academic' legal argument, but is particularly noticeable in discussions of precedent.
8. This is a statement of what this essay is about; it is not a jurisprudential manifesto, nor is it approval of the 'appellate-courtitis' of mainstream legal scholarship.
9. See for example Fitzmaurice and Pease, *The psychology of judicial sentencing* (1986) pp. 133-4, noting the limited range of matters referred to in pleas of mitigation, even though 'in theory' counsel could refer to anything they wish.
10. eg Scrutton L.J., *Place v. Searle* (1932) 48 T.L.R. 428, 429-30.
11. There is sometimes said to have been a rule that textbooks may only be cited in court if the author is dead: eg R.J.Walker, *The English Legal System* (5th edition 1980) p. 163. However, I cannot confirm this; practice seem to have varied from Judge to Judge. See also H. Kay Jones, *Butterworths - History of a publishing house* (1980) pp. 40-2 (early difficulties in allowing citation of *Halsbury's Laws*).

precise arguments that might be based on this material have fluctuated (eg there have been differences in whether counsel may refer to the purpose of legislation as a guide to determining its legal meaning). Positivistic legal philosophers who try to define an ideal notion of "sources" are thus always on the verge of ahistoricality: if they claim to define sources for all time, they in fact speak for no time in particular.

There are other, more general rules on argument, though some are spasmodic in their appearance. At some points, for example, there seems to be a requirement of 'generalizability', that is to say that counsel may not argue about what would be a reasonable result in the case before them, but must argue about what would be a reasonable *rule*. Yet at other times this is ignored.[12] Sometimes Judges justify the result of the case as reasonable, sometimes the rule; and sometimes they do one to avoid having to attempt the other.

It is a commonplace of legal philosophy that, on many issues, legal argument is not completely constrained by rules (or, to put it another way, 'the law' is often indeterminate). But we can expect barristers to find this less so than academic lawyers. A good sense of what is a 'legal' argument cannot be acquired *simply* by an academic study of precedent and statutory interpretation; there is also a significant sense of 'what you can get away with', on which books alone give few clues.[13]

A final point is that these rules restricting legal argument, taken together, are likely to produce considerable ignorance at the bar. If Judges forbid themselves to listen to arguments based on (say) economics, then counsel have no reason to learn economics, and when in turn new Judges are selected from counsels' ranks they will simply re-affirm the restriction on economic arguments, perhaps without serious thought to whether it is appropriate. What may originally have been a principled rejection becomes in time simple ignorance.[14] Indeed, with the increasing compartmentalization of knowledge over the last century, the legal professions have become less and less knowledgeable. Permitted knowledge of matters 'outside' the legal system has failed to expand, and in some respects has contracted; pride in legal professionalism has often led to contempt of other disciplines. One important facet of the 'rule of law' consists of taking pride in not listening to highly relevant arguments. Being unrealistic is part of the job. *How* unrealistic Judges are supposed to be, and in fact are, is a proper matter for legal historians.

12. There are examples of both approaches in the *Fearon* case, discussed below.
13. On this point see generally Barry Barnes, 'On authority and its relationship to power', in *Power, Action and Belief - A new sociology of knowledge?*, edited by John Law, 32 *Sociological Review Monographs* 180 especially at 192-3.
14. It seems that some Judges knew a little classical economics, but later developments seem have passed them by completely: see P.S. Atiyah, *The rise and fall of freedom of contract* (1979) pp. 666-669.

The Bar v. The Bench

Litigants do not appear at court unannounced and tell their tales of woe to the Judge direct. Rather, their tales are processed and packaged for judicial consumption, in a set of documents called the 'pleadings'. Rule-based restrictions only permit a certain limited number of stories to be told. Tenants wishing to complain of their landlord's perfidy cannot sling mud at random; they must usually find a way of saying that the landlord has broken the contract between them. This is not however as limiting as it may at first sight appear.

A skilfully drawn set of pleadings will be a subtle blend of fact and supposition, showing that the litigant's complaint is recognized by law and (if necessary) hinting at enough of the real facts ('the merits') to excite the sympathy of the Judge, to show that the claim is technically correct but no mere technicality either.[15] The truth is both added to and subtracted from. It is necessarily added to, for the rules of the court will often require litigants to give yes/no answers where they could only truthfully say 'I don't know'; the pleadings will say what 'the plaintiff will contend' is the case, and this allegation will only later be vindicated as true, discarded as false, shunned as irrelevant, or traded away as a nuisance the other party will pay to avoid.[16] And, by the very nature of the business, the truth is subtracted from: the demands of conciseness, and the rules prohibiting 'legally irrelevant' material, will cut out much of what would be said if the story were being told for fun, or merely to inform. It is not a question of the lawyers *failing* to give an objective picture of the facts; they will not have been *attempting* to do so. There is even a legal maxim for this, though it is not generally mentioned in this context. *Supressio veri suggestio falsi:* 'Hiding the truth is one way of lying'.

Others have commented on this process of simplified story-telling, noting that the process necessarily changes the story in the course of telling it, calling it an example of 'conceptualism' or 'reification'. There are two points here. The first is that it is a mistake to regard legal categories as any more abstract than non-legal categories. This point should be elementary, since (from one point of view) language consists of abstract terms. Yet if a court rules for a defendant on the ground that 'the plaintiff signed a contract', many would think this more abstract than a by-stander's observation that the plaintiff should have won 'because the defendant is obviously a crook' - even though 'contract' is not obviously more abstract than 'crook'. Legal terms are *not* unusually abstract; they are however unusually precise, pictures drawn with them are unusually colourless. A quite spurious clarity is given to the picture by leaving out much of the

15. See for example Harvey's description of 'the merits': C.P. Harvey, *The advocate's devil* pp. 51-2.

16. And see *In re Morgan, Owen v. Morgan* (1887) 35 Ch. D. 492, where the defence pleaded eight separate incompatible grounds in answer to the plaintiff's claim. The plaintiff's attempt to have four of them struck out failed, on the defendant's plea that he was an executor and could not fairly be expected to choose between the various defences until discovery.

detail.

My second point is that much 'conceptualism' is borrowed by the lawyers from the wider culture. Take, for example, the tendency to reify 'property', to speak of things 'belonging to' particular individuals when a more realistic picture would be of legal regulation between individuals in respect of things. Whether or not people in general think of this as a peculiarly 'legal' way of discussing issues, the young barrister will have learned it from the culture at large.

This leads me to the point that to talk of arguments being constrained by rules, or to make accusations of 'formalism', is to make an implicit assertion of what *un*restrained argument would take into account, what form the argument would take if there were no rules restricting it.[17] Thus a Marxist would regard property law as highly formalistic - for do not its rules postulate non-existing entities and then elaborate upon their 'properties' and the ways they can be 'changed' or 'transferred'?[18] A Libertarian, by contrast, would regard them as highly un-formalistic, if vitiated by occasional, misguided attempts to talk of 'fairness'. And there would be many other views between and beyond these. The point is that many political theories seem to their opponents to be not wholly wrong but as under- or over-formalistic versions of a more defensible theory; a defensible theory plus or minus a few elements, a half-truth treated as a whole. Western political theories can be very different from one another, but their constituent conceptual building blocks may not be very different.[19]

Accordingly, talk of 'formalism' is almost invariably the language of dissent. Someone completely satisfied with every aspect of the legal system would see no formalism anywhere, for while the legal system excludes many factors from consideration, such an individual would say that they

17. This point is implicit in the analysis of P.S. Atiyah and R. Summers, *Form and Substance in Anglo-American Law* (1987), though they do not bring it out as clearly as I would wish, even where failure to do so takes them close to apparent paradox. Thus the everyday activities of the courts can be seen as thoroughly formalistic and rule-bound from some angles but as perfectly sensible, substantively justifiable activity from others (p. 24). Indeed, their entire thesis may be summed up as a claim about the standard of comparison appropriate when evaluating legal systems.

18. See for example I.D. Balbus, 'Commodity form and legal form: an essay on the "relative autonomy" of the law' (1977) 11 *Law and Society Review* 571 especially 573-580; R. Cotterell, *The Sociology of Law* (1984) 124-5.

19. 'It is perhaps worth remembering that, in spite of their long history of animosity and vilification, Marxists, Christians and the bourgeoisie have a common value system. This value system, which is taken for granted in the western world today, is certainly *not* universal. For example, the idea that all men are born equal and are endowed with unalienable rights is obviously no self-evident truth in societies with a caste system - Ideas of equality and of inherent human rights arose out of the bourgeoisie's struggle against feudalism and were the progressive achievement of capitalism. The schism only developed when capitalists, having attained their coveted objective, had no wish to let these ideas go further than what suited their own purposes. It was at this stage that they were given a purely legalistic interpretation, and it was against this restriction, not against the ideas themselves, that the socialists objected and continue to object': Y.S. Brenner, *Capitalism, Competition and Economic Crisis* (1984) pp. 32-3.

truly are irrelevant, and *ought* to be left out of consideration.[20]

This shows one way in which a particular body of law can have a noticeably political tilt to it, quite regardless of the views of those who administer it. This is particularly noteworthy where the political tilt is present implicitly, through the concepts with which the lawyers are required to discuss it. So left-wing labour lawyers have opposed the 'individualism' of the common law,[21] by which they mean the cluster of rules which force discussion of employment issues in 'individualistic' terms, involving individual workers and individual employers. This obscures the difference in power between individual workers and 'individual' employers (usually companies), presents individual contracts of employment as the 'natural' basis for workers' rights, and all-too-often portrays individual unions as 'interfering' in the 'freely negotiated' contracts between individual workers and 'individual' employers. I trust I am not indulging in fairy-stories here, when I say that this 'individualism' exists regardless of the views of the lawyers involved. *Of course* this aspect of common law reasoning was introduced by Judges who mistrusted unions, and *of course* Judges are drawn from social classes with more sympathy for employers than for unions. My point is that we are not dealing with some special ideological trick brought out to confound the unions, but with a quite general feature of legal reasoning in this jurisdiction.

The legal battle, then, will be fought on the basis of a thoroughly processed view of the facts - an over-simplified, distorted vision of the case.[22] Counsel on either side will each try to place their own label on the facts, their own version of which general legal category the case falls into; and oral argument at trial will be a continuation of this. So far as oral argument goes, the real advantage seems to be with the first lawyer to speak; once a label has been applied, it tends to stick. This is illustrated by the anecdote of RA Wright Q.C., who expressed his chagrin on hearing that his junior had won an important case in the Court of Appeal while

20. Atiyah and Summers (above, note 17) are the exception that test the rule, for they decline to treat 'formalism' as a pejorative term (pp. 29 *et seq.)*, yet think it needs a careful and well-reasoned defence.

21. eg Wedderburn, 'Labour Law: From here to autonomy?' (1987) 16 I.L.J. 1. But compare David Howarth, 'The autonomy of labour law: A response to Professor Wedderburn' (1988) 17 I.L.J. 11. Compare also Bennett and Feldman's account of how criminal courts may effectively be biased against defendants from particular ethnic backgrounds, simply because the accounts these defendants give of their actions make no sense to Judges and jurors drawn from other ethnic backgrounds: W. Lance Bennett and Martha S. Feldman, *Reconstructing reality in the courtroom* (1981) ch. 8.

22. And compare Patrick Devlin, *Easing the passing* (1986) at p. 79: 'Is it then true that the cases that come into court are cooked by the lawyers? Of course they are, or most of them. It is the nature faddists who have forced a sinister meaning on the verb 'to cook'. There are indeed delicious fruits and vegetables that are best eaten in their natural state and the good cook does not try to improve them. But in general uncooked food is indigestable as well as unpalatable. This is as true of unprocessed evidence'.

Wright had been occupied elsewhere: 'Well, it's a pity - I wanted to open that case in the Lords'.[23]

The relationship between Judge and counsel is a rather close one. Each is peculiarly vulnerable to the other. 'I am in your lordships' hands', say counsel when they mean that the Judges may act as they think fit - and they are right. Counsel spend their lives in their lordships' hands, and so take care not only to provide a sufficient legal justification for the result they want, but also to make it sound palatable. After all, unless the other advocate is incompetent, the Judge will soon have an acceptable legal justification for deciding the case *either* way. It must be stressed that counsel do not *argue* with the Judge, but seek to persuade.[24] The appeal to law, the argument that the Judge *must* decide the case the way counsel says, is a powerful instrument, but it is also a notoriously double-edged one, likely to produce a mulish reaction from a Judge who does not like being pushed around. Manuals on advocacy speak more warmly of appealing to the sympathies of the Judge and then 'showing him/her the way home': that is, providing an acceptable justification for the result counsel has convinced the court is correct.[25] Persuading the Judges is easier than pushing them in a direction in which they do not wish to go.

Yet the Judge, too, is peculiarly in counsel's hands. The Judge usually knows nothing of the facts but what counsel choose to say;[26] the Judge's powers to demand further facts are sharply limited, and in any event it is usually futile to demand more facts without a pretty good idea of what one is looking for. So far as points of law are concerned, the Judge might be in a better position; perhaps the Judge already knows a little of the law in question, and in any event counsel are under a broad duty to inform the Judge of all relevant legal materials.[27] But the Judge has no personal

23. Harvey, *op. cit.* p. 22. Harvey attributes it to Wright, but adds that '[t]he same remark has been attributed to many other leaders'. Cognitive psychologists call this an 'anchoring effect', showing that 'supplying a starting-point (anchor) for consideration of an issue changes the range within which that judgment will be made': Fitzmaurice and Pease, *op. cit.* pp. 21-22.

24. Indeed, counsel who actually *argue* with the Judge are well on the way to losing the case. As David Pannick points out with only slight overstatement, 'it is only in fiction that the conventions of politeness to Judges are defied' *(Judges* (1987) p. 106). Biographies of famous counsel make much of disagreements with the Judges, presumably because it takes a really superb counsel to emerge the victor of such an argument. See Harvey *op. cit.* pp. 38-9, 41-2 and 52-3; 'Ephesian' (pseudonym of Bechhofer Roberts), *Lord Birkenhead* (1926) pp. 104-5; JA Strahan, *The Bench and Bar of England* (1919) pp. 9-11 and 21-25.

25. eg Keith Evans, *Advocacy at the bar - a beginner's guide* (1983) pp. 79-83. For an example see Simon's defence of Douglas Malcolm on a charge of murder, in reality on the plea that his victim had been having an affair with Malcolm's wife, but 'showing the jury the way home' through a plea of self-defence: Bechhofer Roberts, *Sir John Simon* (1938) pp. 129-146.

26. And compare Harvey, *op. cit.* p. 39: 'There are few more difficult tribunals to deal with than the Judge who ... has taken the trouble to read all the papers in the case ... before it is opened'.

27. *Code of Conduct for the Bar of England and Wales* (1980) para. 136. See also Alfred Phillips, *The Lawyer and Society* (1987) pp. 195-6, arguing that this rule is in counsel's own interests.

researcher to call on;[28] apart from what may be hurriedly jotted down from the library while writing the judgment, the Judge must rely entirely on counsel, who (for all the Judge can tell) may be stating precisely the converse of the view they really hold. No doubt many Judges have thought, or even said, to counsel 'I wish I could ask what you really think'[29] and wished they could get a straight answer. Even (or perhaps especially) when the Judge takes an apparently independent line in argument, there is a lurking suspicion that counsel may subtly have lead the argument that way.

> Interviewer (Hugo Young): Barristers are not vessels, though, of pure wisdom and pure reason ..
>
> Sir Nicholas Browne-Wilkinson VC: No.
>
> Interviewer: .. they've got their own devices, they've got their client to satisfy. You were a barrister, you must have had a lot of tricks of the trade. Do you find, sitting back on the other side of the court, [that] you can spot it? What do you feel about [it], when you can see the artifice?
>
> Browne-Wilkinson: Well, you only see the artifice with a bad barrister, that's the trouble. The good advocate, the first rule of a good advocacy, is to study your Judge; and you find his little vanities, and his little weaknesses, and you dangle them in front of his nose. And the essence of it is that he doesn't see that the fly's being dangled, and so he goes for it. There's no point like the Judge's own point, as a Judge [if] you think you've had a good idea, it's the devil's own job for counsel to get it out of your mind. And that sort of advocacy is extremely difficult to spot.[30]

Some might say that I have it the wrong way round about relations between the bench and the bar. Paeans of praise for the legal profession talk of the great camaraderie of the bar and its high moral and professional standards, and the great level of trust between bar and bench.[31] This objection puts the cart before the horse. These great protestations of mutual trust would be incomprehensible but for the background against which they arise: the enormous opportunities for deception, and the obvious temptations they offer. Judges have no way of

28. See especially Lord Denning's rather sheepish admission that he sometimes looked at material to which counsel had not referred him: *The discipline of law* (1979) p. 289.
29. Judge Owen Thompson, asking the question of Henry Leon, in argument: Henry Cecil (pseudonym of Henry Leon), *Just within the law* (1975) p. 55.
30. 'The Judges', BBC Radio 4, March 30, 1988. The rule 'Know your Judge' is often cited as being the First Rule of Advocacy: eg Harvey *op. cit.* pp. 21-22; and see generally pp. 45-51.
31. eg Strahan *op. cit.* pp. 30-31.

knowing when the wool is being pulled over their eyes.[32] Putting the case into shape for the Judge, squeezing it within the legal forms, *necessarily* means that things are said which one would not have said when describing the case to a trusted friend, and that much is left out. *The Judge is necessarily kept in the dark, and this is an important part of what is meant by saying that the Judges must decide cases by law.* Exploiting the dark and the various shades of grey is the work of the advocate, who indeed has precious little else to work with.

The Judgment

So, counsel have done their work. What of the decision and the judgment, the detailed justification of the decision?

The difficult position of the Judges must be appreciated. In their earlier lives as barristers, they will have absorbed a complex picture of the respective roles of counsel and Judge, and presumably have become adept at playing counsel's role. Yet the role of the Judge is not merely complementary to counsel's but often involves doing quite the opposite. There are three intertwined problems: Sincerity, Persuasion and Free-will.

Sincerity is a problem because the new Judge will have had no practice in it. Counsel are forbidden to be sincere by their code of ethics: 'A barrister must not, when conducting his case, assert his personal opinion of the facts or the law to the Court'.[33] Lying is prohibited[34] but so is honesty. Moreover, many take a professional pride in this, claiming as one of the glories of the bar the 'taxi-cab principle' that members of the bar must accept any brief they are offered, and be prepared to argue for either side with equal conviction.[35] This surely puts an enormous strain on the Judges, who *are* supposed to be sincere, rather than simply mouthing sentiments they do not necessarily believe. It would be quite wrong, and indeed a negation of the judicial role, to start with the desired conclusion and 'work backwards' to an acceptable legal justification. Yet this 'working backwards' will be precisely what the Judges are skilled in, what they have spent a large proportion of their lives doing.

A related problem is that of Persuasion. For decades, the Judges-to-be have spent most of their working hours preparing legal arguments and then making them. In time, they have learned what sort of arguments are

32. The anecdote is usually told in relation to juries, not Judges (eg Strahan *op. cit.* pp. 86-7), of counsel who win cases not by brilliant displays of advocacy but by giving the impression that they are dull, barely competent hacks with the luck to be fighting a case where their client is plainly in the right.
33. *Code of Conduct* (above) para. 132. The problem of sincerity in advocacy is a much-discussed one; the *locus classicus* is Dr Johnson's brazenly inaccurate reply to the question of how a barrister can defend a case known to be a bad one: 'Sir, you do not know it to be good or bad till the Judge determines it'. For general discussions see Harvey, *op. cit.* pp. 6-19, 108 and 113, and Maureen Cain, *loc. cit.* p. 234; and compare 'Ephesian' (pseudonym of Bechhofer Roberts), *Lord Birkenhead* (1926) pp. 99-106 and 212-3.
34. *Code of Conduct* (above) para. 130.
35. On which see Harvey *op. cit.* pp. 155-7.

accepted and what sort are not. They will not have had time to sort out whether they get accepted because they are in some sense 'good' arguments or because they successfully exploit the Judges' foibles. Nor do they have any need to decide. But when they become Judges themselves, this becomes an acute problem. It becomes vital to know whether arguments made are actually good ones, or whether counsel is exploiting the Judges' known foibles. This problem is posed to the Judge by the very nature of the job, yet the Judge's training will not have included the means to decide it. Perhaps the Judge evolves a satisfactory solution to this; perhaps the confusion remains. But either way the problem is the same: yet again it is the Judge's very training that make the job so difficult.

Finally, the problem of Free-will. Are Judges really passive instruments, listening to the arguments on either side and deciding in favour of the stronger one? Or do they play a more active part in the process? If you want clues on this, you can always read what they say about this themselves. You will find some Judges who say decision-making is always a matter of technique, of listening to the arguments and deciding which is the stronger; and you will find others who say it is inevitably a matter of judgment, that the Judge has no choice but to decide personally which argument *should* win.[36] Then all you have to do is decide which group of Judges is telling the truth! Is it that the first group are simply mouthing sentiments they know to be untrue, as a thread-bare cloak to conceal their exercise of unbridled power? Or is it the second group that we should ignore, as an embittered bunch of cynics, engaged in a subtly malicious campaign to denigrate their own colleagues? (And of course, having resolved that question, you will of course be able to state whether you reached this conclusion because the facts constrained you to do so, or whether it was simply some quirk of your personality that pre-disposed you to take that view ...) These questions are not unimportant ones, nor are the answers obvious. Yet for present purposes it seems best to assume that Judges do indeed have free-will, that their choices and judgments are real ones, if constrained by social pressures. The facts of the case, the relevant legal materials, and the ethical environment are all given; I propose to study what the Judges do within these constraints.

I have already indicated the confused mental apparatus that the Judge will bring to bear on the judgment. People who have spent 30 years or more presenting legal arguments in court are the last people you should expect to give a clear account of what they are doing, or why they want to do it. They will have been trained, not to give their actual reason, but to give their *justification;* they will have been trained to throw dust in the eyes of those who wish to see whether they are really presenting a case they believe to be true, or whether they would have been quite happy to argue

36. See for example the (private) disagreement between Haldane and Sankey on this point: *Holmes-Laski letters* vol. II, p. 1052. Contrary to the impression I would otherwise have formed, it is Haldane who defends a 'declaratory' theory and Sankey who insists that 'Judges inevitably legislate'.

the other way (with equal conviction). It is unrealistic to suppose that people trained this way will, on promotion to the bench, drop the habits of a lifetime, and give a clear account of their reasons. They presumably continue in much the same way as before: explaining why they might be thought justified, indeed constrained to act the way they do. Observers who think they can tell when this is true and when a sham simply do not know when they are outclassed.[37]

The judgment, then, will not be a statement of the actual reasons why the Judge feels one side should win; a judgment cannot possibly do this and still conform to law. Yet unless the Judge is both a hardened cynic and a practised hypocrite it will not be completely unrelated to them either. The judgment will be a statement of how the decision conforms to law and (almost necessarily) how the Judge views the case. Yet to whom, if anyone, is it addressed?

Various analysts have suggested that a legal judgment must have an *addressee*, a person or group of persons at whom its argument is aimed. This is usually based on the part sociological, part semantic claim that judgments are messages and messages have addressees.[38] Yet who is the addressee of a judgment? The litigants? On the more technical points, the litigants will not have the slightest idea of what it means - yet you can imagine the outrage that would follow if one of the litigants broke in to say 'This is a pointless exercise, because I can't understand a word of what you're saying ...' Perhaps the judgment is aimed at the lawyers involved? But while they will often be there to hear the judgment, they surely have better things to do with their time, and would surely pass up the occasion if given a choice. Perhaps it is so that the lawyers of the losing party may consider whether they should appeal? But if so, no judgment would be delivered in a case where no appeal lies from the decision. Is it for the guidance of future lawyers? Perhaps it is sometimes, in some respects, though the pedantry with which Judges insist that they are deciding only the issues in front of them, and not other related issues, suggests that this concern is not uppermost in their minds.

The moral is surely that while there is a lot to be gained from asking who the Judge's 'audience' is, it is a mistake to seek too precise an answer. Just like an actor, the Judge must get used to the idea of a mixed audience, shrouded in darkness, with varying tastes and with considerable diversity in its understanding of the niceties. Attempts to define the ideal 'legal audience',[39] the people the Judge *ought* to be worried about, are of strictly limited relevance to the empirical question of which people the Judges are in fact worried about.[40] The modern judgment is in some ways

37. Compare A.G.D. Bradney, 'Facade: The Poplar case' (1983) 34 N.I.L.Q. 1.
38. eg Alan Paterson, *The Law Lords* (1982) pp. 9-11.
39. John Bell, 'The acceptability of legal arguments' in MacCormick and Birks, *The Legal Mind* (1986) p. 45 at 53 *et seq*.
40. Compare Alfred Philips, *op. cit.* at p. 224 on 'the other lawyer' as comprising at least part of the 'audience' in legal drafting generally; and see pp. 226-9 on drafting and obsessional neuroses.

a puzzling institution, the more baffling because of the philosophical problems that surround it, and the fact that most legal systems do not require their Judges to deliver anything so detailed. The important point, however, is that Judges manage to write and deliver these judgments day in day out, oblivious to the theoretical difficulties. Giving judgment is part of the job of a Judge.

The judgment, then, will demonstrate the conformity of the decision to law, by presenting the facts and the law in such a way that one couples neatly with the other. Yet this contrast between general rules and particular facts is misleading. Appeals to generalities need not be appeals to specifically *legal* materials. The point may seem a small one, but it is a vital one for the legal history of the last two centuries. Reliance on general rules (in the face of plain injustice on the particular facts) may be seen as needing no justification beyond a reference to the rule itself, or may be accompanied by general observations that general rules are necessary even though some injustice inevitably results. Yet there is a certain type of *moral* argument that takes a similar form, and this form was particularly common in the nineteenth century. When writers discussed questions of morality they were as often as not discussing which moral *rules* should be instilled; some writers, for example, would claim that it was *always* morally necessary to keep to your promises, even though the results of so doing might be regarded as unjust if seen in themselves.

I do not intend to unravel all the various strands on this issue, but simply to point to the problem.[41] A rule is a device for narrowing inquiry, for stating precise criteria to govern an issue instead of allowing a more general inquiry. But the reasons for doing this are various. You may believe that all decisions should be taken this way, or that legal ones should, or that legal decisions should be taken this way where the alternative is a policy analysis the court is ill-equipped to perform, or whatever. Each supposed example of blind adherence to rules must therefore be taken on its own merits. To take the example of a broad and general approach to the law of contract, we may speculate that some Judges adopted this out of a deep ideological commitment to laissez-faire, others out of ignorance that there was any other approach, and others still on the ground that the more abstract and legalistic the principles with which the Judges work the less open they are to criticism.

So it does not follow that, simply because Judges appeal to general legal rules, they are therefore not bringing moral, economic or sociological principles to bear. Indeed, in many cases law and its 'purpose' - moral, economic, or whatever - are thoroughly bound together. Yet in the application the two often come apart. A moral philosopher and an amoral lawyer may agree on some such formulation as 'people should keep their promises'; yet when they come to apply this simple rule to concrete circumstances they will find that they have not been agreeing at all - each

41. Compare P.S. Atiyah, *The rise and fall of freedom of contract* (1979) pp. 388-397.

will say in many cases 'Yes, there was a promise, and yes, it was broken, but that is not particularly important here ...'; and they will not always be the same cases. This is, of course, a non-problem so long as we do not feel the need to place neat labels on judicial actions, to say when they are acting to uphold the law and when to uphold morality. There is no necessary incompatibility.

The Case of the Annoyed Husband

To illustrate the themes I have just discussed, I will now consider a case from the 1880s. Many issues in contract depended, then as now, on determining the "intention of the parties"; in other words counsel were bound, up to a point, to justify their arguments not by appeals to morality or legal principles generally but to norms to which the parties have expressed agreement. I hope to show the inadequacy of an approach which takes this commitment at face value, rather than asking how much freedom the legal actors had to smuggle in other values. The point is not to dispute the Victorian Judges' commitment to laissez-faire, but to investigate what that commitment meant in practice.

Fearon v. The Earl of Aylesford[42] was one stage in a ferocious legal battle. We can only guess the fuller history from the law report, and telling how important the action was to the parties themselves is well-nigh impossible. As ever, the stark legal issues reduce a complex series of interactions to a simple story with one hero and one villain, the only mystery being which is which. The story told on behalf of the trustee for the wife[43] was simple enough: the wife and husband had agreed to separate, and executed a separation deed; one term of which was that the husband should pay the wife maintenance. However, he subsequently failed to do so. An open-and-shut case, surely? The husband's case was equally clear in its factual allegations: he said that his wife was now living with another man, and had given birth to a child by this other man.

Simple though the husband's factual allegations were, their legal status was more problematical. Often a separation deed would have included a promise to pay maintenance *dum casta manet:* while the wife remained 'chaste'.[44] Yet this *dum casta* clause was missing from the deed these parties had executed. Counsel for the husband had three arguments to explain why, despite this, he could nonetheless bring up her behaviour to discredit her claim; all relied heavily on the assumption that the (male) Judges and jury would think her conduct wicked, immoral and therefore a

42. (1884) 12 Q.B.D. 539 (Queen's Bench Division), (1884) 14 Q.B.D. 792 (Court of Appeal). For subsequent litigation see *The Aylesford Peerage* (House of Lords Committee for Privileges, November 6, 1885) 11 App. Cas. 1; *in re Earl of Aylesford's Settled Estates* (Bacon V.-C., February 20, 1886), 32 Ch.D. 162.

43. The trustee was suing on behalf of the wife, as trustee of the settlement into which the husband should have paid the money.

44. The deed was in English, not Latin. But the lawyers in the case consistently refer to it as a *dum casta* clause.

complete answer to her claim for maintenance. First, counsel argued, the *dum casta* clause was implied in the agreement. Secondly, (an argument never clearly separated from the first), public decency demanded that she lose; for if the omission of the *dum casta* clause was deliberate then she must have been trying to free herself from the legal consequences of adultery; surely something the law could not countenance. Thirdly, the wife had undertaker in the deed not to 'molest' her husband, and yet had done so in various respects: the most serious of which was that she had claimed that her latest child was legitimate, and therefore heir to her husband's estates.

At the trial, the jurymen had accepted the husband's argument that he had been 'molested', and ruled in his favour. On appeal, this order was varied: Denman and Manisty JJ. held that the various undertakings in the deed were 'independent covenants', that is to say the husband might have damages for the 'molestation' (which they assessed at £100) but could not plead it as a defence to the claim for maintenance.[45] Both parties appealed from this verdict.

The official law reports do not contain verbatim accounts of counsels' arguments, but only a summary. Argument took place over two days, and was not the impossibly brisk affair you would see if actors recited the report of the argument. Almost certainly the Judges had to be informed on each detail of the case as the argument went along,[46] and the argument would have proceeded slowly enough for them to take notes. Brief references to cases would no doubt have been extended readings and discussions on them:[47] the apparent high degree of legal erudition is by-and-large an artifact of the report. The reporter would have summarized in one line what may have been a variety of contentions on a similar theme. Counsel for the husband may well have been expecting a rough ride; Brett M.R. was notorious for his brisk and searching interventions in argument,[48] and the other members of the court had been parties to the decision in *Gandy v. Gandy,* which while dealing with technically very different considerations, had rejected arguments which to the non-technical eye would have been very similar to the ones the husband now wished to raise.[49] Counsel begin by complaining about the quality of the

45. March 29, 1884, 12 Q.B.D. 539. The wife was claiming £475, though of course the suit effectively decided not only this but also the question of future liability as well. Manisty J. did not accept that there was 'molestation' here, but as there was no majority on that point the jury's verdict stood.
46. Attempts to speed up appellate hearings by allowing the Judges to preview counsel's argument were not seriously made until 1983: see *Practice Note* [1983] 2 *All England Reports* 34.
47. And see anecdote of Brett (Lord Esher), Strahan *op. cit.* pp. 26-8.
48. See for example 'The late Lord Esher' 43 *Solicitors Journal* 505-6 (May 27, 1899).
49. *Gandy v. Gandy* (1882) 7 P.D. 77, March 21, 1882 Hannen P., April 18, 1882 Jessel M.R., Cotton and Lindley L.JJ. Factually and as a matter of morality the case is hard to distinguish from *Fearon*, but the legal arguments take a very different course.

evidence. Yet soon they reach the nub of the case:[50]

> ... But even upon the facts as they stand, the defendant as the husband is relieved from liability under the deed of separation by his wife's unchaste conduct, although no *dum casta* clause was inserted: he is bound to pay the annuity only so long as she is chaste: that term is implied in the covenant to pay; and to hold otherwise would be contrary to public policy and even decency, for it must be assumed to have been contemplated that the wife should live chastely. It may be that the *dum casta* clause is not a 'usual covenant' in a separation deed: *Hart v. Hart* 18 Ch.D. 670;[51] but in that case the decision is perhaps inconsistent with other authorities, and at all events is not binding upon this Court. The deed of separation is not to be considered as a letter of licence to the Countess of Aylesford to commit adultery: *Sullivan v. Sullivan* 2 Addams, 299 at p. 303;[52] and the *dum casta* clause is to be implied and is to be read into the deed as one of its provisions.
>
> Brett, M.R.: If the *dum casta* clause is to be read into the deed as one of its clauses, upon one act of unchastity by the wife the right to the payment of the annuity will be gone for ever.

A cautious comment. Counsel have been making a quite general proposition, which if true would apply to all separation deeds. Brett uses this against them, implying that there would be *some* cases where this argument could lead to an unfair result. Thus he is able to stigmatize the husband's argument as unfair, despite that point that (as everyone in court knew) the wife had committed considerably more than 'one act of unchastity'. Counsel press their point, hinting that the wife deliberately arranged for the clause to be left out, so that the deed is immoral even though it doesn't look immoral 'on its face':

> If any part of the consideration of a deed is immoral, even although the immorality does not appear on the face of it, the deed is void or at least not enforceable: *Willyams v. Bullmore* 33 L.J.(Ch.) 461.

50. The argument here is quoted verbatim from the official law report (14 Q.B.D. 794-797), except that the original footnotes (all case references) are brought up into the text. Footnotes appearing here are my own commentary.

51. June 24, 1881, before Kay J. A suit for divorce was settled out of court, one term being 'Deed of separation with usual covenants'. On the wife's application for specific performance of this agreement, it was held that a *dum casta* clause was not appropriate. Kay treated the husband's argument as being that *he* had understood it to include a *dum casta* clause, which of course ruled out his claim, under the 'parol evidence' rule (pp. 674-5).

52. 162 *English Reports* 303, Arches Court, 1824. The issue was whether a deed of separation operated as a waiver of the husband's right to divorce the wife for adultery, a claim which Sir John Nicholl rejected.

Lindley, L.J.: That was a case of the sale of a daughter's chastity.[53]

Cotton, L.J.: This is not a case of immoral consideration; and the deed is good, unless it is against public policy that a deed of separation should be drawn without inserting the *dum casta* clause.

Brett, M.R.: There is no evidence that at the time of the execution of the deed the Countess of Aylesford intended to commit adultery, and that the deed was executed in furtherance of that purpose.

Cotton, L.J.: In that case the deed of separation might have been invalid: *Evans v. Carrington* 2 De G.F. & J. 481.[54]

Counsel for the defence: A husband, when he separates from his wife, must be assumed to contemplate that she will live chastely; because if she is unchaste and has a bastard child, he will be prima facie held to be the father of an offspring that is really spurious. A deed of separation is merely an arrangement for living apart, and when a state of things arises which was not in contemplation when the deed was executed, it is no longer binding: *Morrall v. Morrall* 6 P.D. 98.[55]

Cotton, L.J.: It seems to have been assumed by the Court of Appeal in *Gandy v. Gandy* 7 P.D. 77, 168 that a deed of separation will hold good, notwithstanding the parties to it may commit adultery.[56]

Counsel for the defence: No doubt *Gandy v. Gandy* is the strongest case against the defendant ...

By now it is plain that the Judges think little of the husband's first two arguments. Counsel take them through a few case reports but make little headway. Their proposition is not going to be accepted, either because it is too broad, or because the Judges have not yet been sufficiently impressed by how wicked the wife has been. Moreover, they are not going to accept that 'a single act of adultery' alone is enough to avoid liability to pay, and the husband's argument seems to entail that consequence: Brett's 'generalization' comment has taken root. The husband's third argument gets around these difficulties, however, as it gives counsel a chance to show that there is something worse here. '[M]olestation may be of

53. March 17, 1863, Romilly M.R. A rather tangled domestic dispute, involving a loan on mortgagee apparently intended to facilitate the mortgagee's seduction of the mortgagor's daughter. Romilly refused to enforce the mortgage, leaving the mortgage to his remedies at law, if any.

54. 45 *English Reports* 707, December 10, 1860, Campbell L.C. A deed of separation was held invalid on the ground that 'the wife, having before the marriage had illicit intercourse with [another man], induced the [husband] to execute the deed in contemplation of a renewal of that illicit intercourse, and that she might carry it on with more facility' (p. 712).

55. March 8, 1881, Hannen P. Deed of separation, including a covenant by the wife not to claim more from her husband than the sum provided for in the deed; she subsequently discovered that he had committed incestuous adultery, and divorced him; the deed was held no defence to her claim for maintenance.

56. See note 49 above.

different kinds', say counsel, and so give themselves a broad licence to review the wife's behaviour, and to ram home the charge of immorality:

> [A]dultery and the birth of an illegitimate child as a consequence of that adultery are sufficient evidence of molestation; so also is open and notorious adultery; and, further, adultery accompanied by the birth of a spurious child and by the holding out of that spurious child as legitimate, is sufficient evidence of molestation. Surely profligacy in a wife amounting almost to open prostitution[57] is molestation within the meaning of the covenant, although there may be no personal or bodily interference with the husband. There is evidence that the lady's-maid to the Countess of Aylesford had stated that she and other servants had been directed by the Countess to address the spurious child as 'Lord Guernsey', which would be the courtesy title of the eldest legitimate son of the defendant.
>
> Brett, M.R.: That evidence was mere hearsay ...

There is a brief wrangle over this point; and counsel briefly attack the 'independent covenant' argument, saying that 'it would be most unreasonable that a husband should be compelled to contribute to his wife's support, if she continued to annoy him'. Then they return to the meaning of 'molestation':

> A mere threat to do something of an annoying nature may amount to a breach of a covenant against molestation in a separation deed: *Sanders v. Rodway* 22 L.J.(Ch.) 230.[58] Any act which annoys or injures another, 'molests' him: *Reg. v. Duffield* 5 Cox, C.C. 404. Adultery is molestation, because the injured husband must be annoyed; and a wife who commits adultery must be taken to have contemplated the consequence of her act; she must be taken to have intended to annoy her husband.
>
> Brett, M.R.: A woman commits adultery in order to gratify her own unlawful passion: she does not think about the annoyance to her husband when she abandons herself to her lover.
>
> Counsel for the defence: The gratification of her unlawful passion does not exclude the intention to annoy her husband. The Countess of Aylesford was receiving the wages of prostitution[59] from her paramour, who had settled an income upon her.

57. Reference to 'prostitution' as denoting any female participation in extra-marital sex are not uncommon in judgments. Compare Bucknill J. in *Upfill v. Wright* [1911] 1 K.B. 506 at 512-3: 'It was urged that prostitution is one thing, and living as one man's mistress is quite a different thing. They may differ in degree, but they both stand upon the same plane'.
58. November 11, 1852, Romilly M.R. Husband assumed to have 'molested' his father-in-law by threatening legal proceedings over a separation deed he had executed.
59. See above, note 57.

The Court of Appeal then decided it was unnecessary to call opposing counsel; they immediately delivered their judgments.[60] Their general tenor will be obvious from what has gone before, so I will simply call attention to a few points.

First, what does the decision tell us about Victorian judicial attitudes to separation and divorce? It tells us remarkably little about the individual Judges in the case but speaks volumes on the formal restrictions within which they worked. The Judges agreed with the husband's counsel that the wife had committed a very grave offence. They did not ask why or in what circumstances she did it. They did not even begin to inquire whether the husband's own behaviour was as bad or worse.[61] They did not question the husband's order of moral priorities, which seemed to be that committing adultery was serious, having a child as a result more serious, but using that child to claim the husband's estates was by far the most serious. Yet despite all this the Judges strive mightily to find for the wife. Why? Perhaps they secretly *did* feel that the husband's own behaviour was relevant, and at least as bad as his wife's. Perhaps judicial boredom had driven them to a weary appreciation that common-or-garden adultery didn't merit a condemnatory response from the courts. Perhaps the case would have been different if the parties had been plain Mr and Mrs Aylesford. We don't know, and can't know. The Judges' rejection of the morality urged on them by the husband is clear enough, but they do not say what is wrong with it; by analyzing the argument in the context of doctrine generally we can see which way the Judges were pushing, but not why.

Secondly, consider the treatment of the husband's 'public policy' argument. In form, the Judges were simply rejecting the husband's plea that they should depart from what the deed said, in favour of what it ought to have said on his view of policy. This is a common figure in Victorian appellate rhetoric and it is important not to misunderstand it. The view the Judges were taking was by no means a 'neutral' one; they were not saying that the husband's argument was wrong because the courts should not consider public policy at all, but that it was wrong because public policy was in favour of the wife. They made no attempt to conceal which way public policy took them on this particular issue:

> I am at a loss to see how public policy requires that when a woman commits adultery she shall at once be made destitute and be entirely stripped of all those means which her husband provided for her when they separated, so as to prevent her from falling into a state of

60. This was not uncommon in reported cases at this period, or indeed (I presume) in appeal cases generally. Judges are of course bound to listen to parties before deciding *against* them.

61. Brett notes that the husband's attempt to get a divorce fell through, but ostentatiously adds 'I inquire not why - it signifies not' (p. 798).

indigence and want.[62]

If this point were now for the first time to be decided, I myself should absolutely refuse to say that owing to the mere fact of a woman falling into this grave offence under any circumstances of neglect by her husband, or after any effluxion of time, public policy requires that - whatever may have been the temptation under which the woman has succumbed - the husband shall not be obliged to pay her the annuity, which he has undertaken to pay her without any such condition being expressed.[63]

It is only if we make the neat assumption that we can rigorously divide 'what the document said' from 'what is reasonable' that the Judges appear to be confusing the two; the flexibility of 'interpretation' blurs the two irremediably. Victorian Judges routinely adhered to the strict meaning of contracts largely because they seemed sensible in their provisions; but this apparent complacency on the Judges' part would be displaced in an appropriate case. Victorian denials that the intentions of the parties should be modified to avoid an inconvenient result should be read *alongside*, not *against*, their insistence that documents be given a reasonable construction. Where, as here, they reject views based on public policy, it is usually quite explicitly on the ground that public policy requires no such thing. Public policy came in not only expressly but also through what would now be regarded as the back-door, namely as a pointer towards the most reasonable construction to give to the contract. It is a mistake, therefore, to view the Victorian commitment to laissez-faire as a commitment made *at the expense of* their other value-commitments.

This point also emerges in the legal argument on the meaning of the deed. In discussing its meaning, the Judges' sympathies emerge quite clearly, both in what they say and in what they do not say. They evidently felt constrained from saying that the husband's claim was a trivial one. Yet there is none of the passion of the husband's condemnatory rhetoric. Brett's view of how important the 'grave offence' is emerges implicitly in his withering comment on the husband's 'implied term' argument. To say that the *dum casta* clause was implied by law was, he hints, to insult the generations of lawyers who had inserted it expressly, an offence in comparison with which mere adultery fades into insignificance:

If that argument be true, the clause, which is often put into such deeds by the most expert conveyancers, was an absolutely futile and senseless clause ...[64]

More difficult to deal with was the husband's final argument. This had a

62. Cotton, p. 808.
63. Brett, p. 799. Note that Brett is generalizing again, hinting at all sorts of injustices that could arise in other circumstances, without accusing the husband of anything specific.
64. Brett, p. 799.

wicked simplicity about it. 'Molesting' the husband meant annoying him; the husband was undoubtedly annoyed as a result of his wife's conduct; therefore she had 'molested' him in breach of her covenant. We do not know whether the Judges truly thought that he had no business being annoyed, on the ground that her conduct was trivial, or no worse than his own, or simply none of his business. They did not say any of these things, and it is hard to see how they could have done without openly defying the moral restrictions within which they were working. Rather, they put enormous efforts into showing that she had not *intentionally* annoyed him. Brett delivers a short lecture on why women commit adultery, postulating that they do it not to annoy their husbands but 'from other motives'.[65] Yet, as any neophyte bold enough to challenge the court could have said, the covenant said 'molest', not 'intentionally molest'; and besides, it was a general principle that people are to be taken to have intended the natural consequences of their actions.

Here the 'generalization' approach, hitherto so much against the husband, is substantially in his favour; the general principle seems to bring the case within the covenant. Cotton simply ignores the point, claiming that 'molestation' demands not only knowledge of the possibility of annoyance but also a *wish* to annoy.[66] Lindley acknowledges the difficulty but blandly concludes that 'I cannot understand that conduct to be a breach of the covenant ... It seems to me that so to hold would be to stretch language, and would be to put a forced construction upon the words which they would not bear in ordinary parlance'.[67] (As if 'ordinary parlance' would usually be any guide to the way the courts interpret words in formal documents!)[68] Only Brett grasps the nettle, in a sustained display of mental gymnastics that shows his legal abilities to the full:

> Then can adultery come within the principle, that the wife is doing an act with knowledge that what she is doing must of itself without more annoy her husband? Certainly not. The utmost that can be said, is that she must know that if it comes to the knowledge of her husband it will annoy him; but that is to introduce another circumstance which does not come within the proposition, that circumstance being that her

65. 14 Q.B.D. p. 802.
66. 14 Q.B.D. pp. 805-6.
67. 14 Q.B.D. p. 810.
68. Compare Cotton in *Ralph v. Carrick* (1879) 11 Ch.D. 873 at 878: 'As regards our duty when wills come before us for construction, it is obvious to say that it is in each case to consider the words of the will. I say that, for the purpose of calling attention to the argument that in the absence of any rule of law laid down or established by cases, we are at liberty to construe wills as ordinary intelligent persons would do. There is a fallacy in this. We are bound to have regard to any rules of construction which have been established by the Courts, and subject to that we are bound to construe the will as trained legal minds would do. Even very intelligent persons whose minds are not so trained are accustomed to jump at a conclusion as to what a person means by considering what they, under similar circumstances, think they would have done. That is conjecture only, and conjecture on an imperfect knowledge of the circumstances of the case ...'

adultery shall be brought to his knowledge; and therefore the mere fact of the adultery does not come within either proposition, and something else must be relied upon to constitute molestation. If that is not within either proposition, the mere fact of having a child afterwards is not. Then it has been urged that, however great her distance may be from her husband, if she commits adultery publicly so that people know that she is doing it, that must molest him. But again the molestation will depend upon whether the people who know it, will go and tell her husband. Another and a particular circumstance must be introduced, for which the wife is not responsible, and which does not necessarily follow, and therefore in no view can it be molestation.[69]

See these brave individualists, fearlessly upholding the values of the common law! As abstract propositions they maintain that adultery is wrong and that all people shall be taken to intend the natural consequences of their actions. Yet when the point is actually put to them, they do everything in their power to avoid the implications of this. It is not that the apparent individualism of the Victorian Judges was a sham; far from it. The structure of the legal argument was shot through with individualistic assumptions. But other values make their appearance, often running sharply counter to individualism. The Victorian Judges were individualists, yes, but they were many other things as well.

Conclusion

There is much more that could be extracted from the *Fearon* case. Yet research in this area has to proceed in a crab-wise fashion. I do not doubt that Victorian legal reasoning has a distinctively 'individualistic' cast; but we are only at the beginning of the process of working out what that 'individualism' meant in practice, what things it was possible to say in the language of individualism, and what the Judges in fact wanted to say. Plainly the Judges were *not* individualistic in any sense that connotes a reluctance to judge other people by values they do not necessarily share. Perhaps the relevant sense is the judging of people by standards they intended to be judged by? *Fearon* shows how problematical this is. Theory, law and the brute facts of human psychology combine to limit the circumstances in which we can truly know what others intend. It is not an *accident* when other values creep in. The Victorian commitment to respecting 'the intention of the parties' cannot be taken as an established fact. It is a black box, the contents of which we cannot observe directly. One way forward is perhaps to formulate meanings for 'individualism' that

69. 14 Q.B.D. pp. 802-3. 'The business of a Judge is to find a good legal reason for the conclusions of common sense': attributed to Brett (Lord Esher), 'Builders of our law: Lord Esher' (1902) 36 *American Law Review* 526 at 523-3 (copied from article of same title, 113 *Law Times* 38, May 10, 1902); though note that this attitude (in the abstract) is said to have scandalized Cotton.

are compatible with what the Judges did - never forgetting that the Judges themselves did no such thing.

In doing so we do not, of course, build up a picture of what the Judges 'really thought' about the case in front of them. Perhaps they 'really thought' no one thing. Perhaps the plaintiff reminded one of them of Aunt Mabel. Perhaps the Judges had only a vague yet powerful sense of how the case should go; perhaps they were as much strangers to themselves as they are to us. I do not see that it is possible, on such a point, to go beyond informed guesswork. But we can hope that our guesses will become more and more informed as we proceed.

[20]

OPENING THE TIME CAPSULE: A PROGRESS REPORT ON STUDIES OF COURTS OVER TIME

LAWRENCE M. FRIEDMAN

This essay traces the rise of longitudinal studies of courts. In the United States, the rise of a sociolegal school of history (the "Wisconsin school") was the immediate stimulus. Longitudinal studies, in Europe and the United States, explored the relationship between law and the economy; they tended to find an inverse relationship. But more recent findings suggest some reversal of this trend. Changes in the nature of business relationships have stimulated increases in some forms of major business litigation. Moreover, in modern legal culture, freedom is conceived of in substantive terms; and the courts appear more and more to be the place where true justice can be found.

A small number of law and society scholars—a dozen or two at the most—have tried their hand at longitudinal court studies. This term means nothing more than the empirical analysis of data from some court or courts over time rather than at a single point in history. The majority of the scholars have studied trial courts. There has also been at least one fairly large-scale study of state appellate courts (Kagan *et al.*, 1977, 1978; Friedman *et al.*, 1981; Wheeler *et al.*, 1987). Most of the researchers have looked at American courts, but certain European jurists have studied their own systems; in fact, some of the seminal work has been done abroad.

The basic idea of these studies is disarmingly simple—so simple that one is tempted to ask why the work began so late and why it continues to be so rare. Among the dozens and dozens of law reviews and related journals, and in the jungle of literally thousands of books, articles, and treatises about courts, judges, and their work, only a handful have elected to use longitudinal technique. But, after all, many simple ideas are not socially simple; that is, they seem to require a certain context, a background, before they can flourish. For example, the idea of studying the lives of ordinary people, including housewives, in the eighteenth century is hardly the stuff of which Nobel prizes are made; yet apparently the idea did not occur to most historians until the recent upsurge of interest in women's history and in social history in general. Similarly, the social conditions for longitudinal court studies were not ripe before a certain small, dignified revolution took place in legal history and in legal studies generally: the rise of the "Wisconsin School," associated with Professor J. Willard Hurst at the University of Wisconsin.[1]

Before Hurst, American legal history was an arid, stunted field primarily concerned with the evolution and development of legal doctrine; it was in some ways a colonial lapdog of English legal history; and like legal scholarship in general, it centered almost exclusively on appellate courts.

Hurst decisively reversed the emphasis. He was primarily interested in the relationship between law and the economy. He rejected the "internalist" view of law—the view of law as "autonomous," to use the currently fashionable term—and treated it as a social product, in essence instrumental. In American society at least, law was a tool, an implement, which concrete interest groups and individuals manipulated for whatever ends they had in mind.

Law was therefore, by and large, a dependent rather than an independent variable, shaped by events and ideas from outside. Since law was an instrument, doctrine and legal theory were less important than law as actually used and experienced. This meant that legal historians should turn to or return to a study of "living law"; this in turn meant that they could not and should not neglect the trial courts. It would be wrong to concentrate on flashy events at the appellate level. There were valid, even vital reasons to emphasize the modal, the average, rather than the extraordinary, the piquant, the dramatic. Hurst himself did not study any particular court longitudinally, but the pioneer example of this art form was a book—pretty much forgotten or neglected today—on the trial courts of Chippewa County, Wisconsin, published in 1959 by Francis Laurent, under the direct influence of Hurst, who wrote the introduction.[2] For the first time, there were data on the number and kind of cases a particular court actually handled, and on how these had changed over time.

After Laurent, there came a period of comparative silence. A new start was made in the 1970s, and it began in what American legal scholars—on the whole a provincial lot—would consider an unlikely source: Spain. A young Spanish scholar, José Juan

[1] The opening shot in the Hurst revolution was the publication of his *Growth of American Law: The Lawmakers* in 1950. Perhaps the most influential of his many books was *Law and the Conditions of Freedom in the Nineteenth-Century United States* (1956). For a brief overview of the history of legal history see Friedman (1984); for a different slant, see Gordon (1984b). For another view of the influence of Hurst on longitudinal studies and on law and society theory in general, see Munger (1988).

[2] Hurst in Laurent (1959: xvii) reminds us that the data are relevant "not only to the history of the legal system itself, but also to the story of the law's living relation to general values and processes of the society." In fairness to the neglecters and forgetters of Laurent's book, it should be pointed out that the book consists mostly of tables and not much analysis or explanation.

Toharia (1974),[3] published a remarkable book in which he tried to examine the relationship between law and social change in Spain between 1900 and 1970, using statistics on the work of the Spanish courts over time. Toharia found that the caseload of the courts had not kept pace with economic growth. Indeed, stagnation and decline were most marked in those parts of Spain that had most advanced industrially; the courts had held their own in rural backwaters.

This somewhat surprising result did not mean that "law" in the broad sense was irrelevant to economic growth, or that "legal activity" did not reflect changes in the pace and nature of commercial and industrial life. Quite the contrary: Toharia also looked at other indicators—notarial acts, including the formation of corporations—that were equally "legal," although not judicial. Here he found the expected correlations: dramatic increases in quantity followed strong economic growth; and the correlations were most dramatic in the urban and industrial centers of Spanish life (*ibid.*, ch. 5, pp. 149–67).

Two of the themes of Toharia's book resonated with themes of the Hurst school: first, the (relative) irrelevance of formal courts and litigation in society and within the legal system; and, second, the intimate connection between the legal system *as a whole* and economic life. The declining function of the courts could thus be explained either externally (that is, in terms of characteristics of social behavior), internally (that is, in terms of some institutional defects), or through some combination of the two.

At the time, a number of commentators stressed the internal issues. The courts seemed too slow, too expensive, too formalistic, too hidebound and impervious to change.[4] The engines of economic life, as they grew monstrously great, would either crush the court system, trapped in its prison of Weberian formal rationality, or find ways around it. The courts themselves were instruments much too blunt to handle the *general* job of conflict resolution within society, for a variety of reasons.[5]

---

[3] Toharia had been trained in law in Madrid and then earned a Ph.D. in sociology at Yale University.

[4] This seemed at the time not only plausible but also a general phenomenon in the modernizing Western world. Industrialization would at first bring about an increase in litigation, but this would be followed by a period of stagnation and decline. The reasons were simple: A mature industrial society should disfavor litigation, which interferes with a vigorous, ongoing economic life; hence in such a society, slow, hidebound, expensive courts are actually functional. See Friedman (1976: 25, 33).

Gutiérrez (1979: 240–41), studying the courts of Costa Rica longitudinally for the period 1945–70, found an increase in litigation rates, but he predicted, on the basis of the theories just mentioned, that litigation was likely to decline as the country modernized.

[5] See the discussion of the Macaulay thesis below. One might also mention the work of the Civil Litigation Research Project (CLRP), which also operated out of the University of Wisconsin, as an example of the general attitude in the law and society community toward litigation as such. CLRP tried

Other European scholars took up Toharia's theme (see Rottleuthner, 1985),[6] and a new wave of American longitudinal studies also began (Friedman and Percival, 1976a; McIntosh, 1980–81; Daniels, 1985). The American studies had various purposes, methods, and agendas. Although it would be too strong to say that they confirmed Toharia's thesis at all points, they were in the main consistent with his findings. These studies did not document an actual *decline* in litigation at the trial court level. The most that could be said is that they did not find positive evidence of any startling rise in litigation. Thus, in the 1970s, longitudinal researchers found themselves caught up in the controversy over whether there was in fact a "litigation explosion." Most of the discussion of this subject was empty talk; judicial statistics in the United States were woefully inadequate, and the "explosion" was a matter of impressions and anecdotes.[7]

In theory, longitudinal studies should have been able to answer the question definitively: Were litigation rates rising or not? In practice, however, they could not and did not solve the puzzle. This was in part because of problems of definition: What *is* a litigation explosion? What is litigation? What are we measuring when we count the number of cases filed in court (Friedman and Percival, 1976a)? Nonetheless, there had been such wild talk about litigation in the United States that it was quite proper to cite the longitudinal studies on one side of the issue. The historical evidence, ambiguous and difficult to read as it was, did not support the thesis of a terrible "explosion."[8]

Longitudinal and historical studies did not find, of course, that courts had been abandoned, that courtrooms were deserted and covered with cobwebs, that judges were snoring on the bench. They did find that disputes, and especially *economic* disputes, made up a declining portion of the caseload. They found that the docket, over the last century or so, had shifted in the direction of more "personal" matters, particularly those that did not involve an actual contest in court. For example, if the modal case in a trial court in 1870 was a dispute over title to land or an attempt to make sureties pay up on a promissory note, the modal case in 1970 was an uncontested divorce. Friedman and Percival (1976a: 296)

---

to study the life cycle of disputes, that is, the way in which disputes arise and are dealt with in "real life"; only a few such disputes ever turn into lawsuits, of course, which was one of the issues that the project examined. On CLRP, see Trubek (1980–81a). One should mention as well the great research interest in what is known as "alternative dispute resolution."

[6] Some material on Scandinavian litigation rates had also appeared in Blegvad *et al.* (1973: 105–9).

[7] Newspapers and magazines regularly reported various horror stories about the litigation explosion, and scholars wrote articles denouncing "hyperlexis" and similar atrocities. See, e.g., Manning (1977).

[8] For a summary of the literature on this point see Galanter (1983a); Friedman (1985: ch. 2); see also Galanter (1986b).

spoke of a shift from trials of disputed matters to what they called "routine administration." Other studies too found the courts spending more of their effort on administrative work and spending less on actual litigation, although there was some dispute over details.[9] There were parallel trends in the appellate courts as well (see Kagan *et al.*, 1977); and in criminal actions, the percentage of felony cases that went to trial had also declined between the mid-nineteenth century and the present, as plea bargaining—a much more administrative mode of handling such cases—came to occupy a pervasive role in the system.[10]

The findings of these studies, like Toharia's, concerned the work of particular courts in a particular culture at one point in history; they were not evidence of laws about the behavior of courts, or about the relationship between courts and economic growth.[11] They did isolate and attempt to explain how courts operated under one special set of social circumstances. They were, in some ways, methodologically crude; in part this was unavoidable because the materials of study were in poor condition and hard to use. Moreover, the studies were primarily historical and only secondarily aimed at modern policy issues. Of course, they had to begin and end their data gathering at some point, and that point was never yesterday. Friedman and Percival (1976a), for example, carried their data only to 1970; and so did Toharia (1974).

The research continues, of course; and it not only revises and reinterprets the older studies, it also gathers more recent data. The new research has turned up some surprising facts; surprising, that is, in the light of the earlier longitudinal studies. Is it possible that the courts of the 1980s have come to occupy a position in soci-

---

[9] The Family and Commercial Disputes Study, sponsored by the U.S. Justice Department and conducted by Arthur Young & Co., and Public Sector Research, Inc., attempted to "replicate on a national scale" the study by Friedman and Percival by examining state trial courts in five counties scattered about the country. Some of the data from this study are summarized in Lieberman (1984: 48 ff.). A memorandum by J.J. Perlstein dated January 21, 1981, also sums up the findings. The two main foci of the study were "changes in the frequency of filings in selected categories of cases" and "the courts' formal involvement in the disposition of particular actions," that is, its actual role in dispute resolution. The findings were "mixed." Some of the trial courts behaved very much like the two California courts studied by Friedman and Percival, but in certain regards others did not. See also McIntosh (1980–81).

Daniels (1985) found that only a small percentage of filed matters led to contested hearings on trials but that this pattern had held firm over time, which puts the findings for the Illinois counties he examined somewhat out of step with those in the other studies.

[10] There is of course a large literature on plea bargaining; see, e.g., Mather (1979a). On the history of plea bargaining, see Friedman (1979); Heumann (1975).

[11] In the late 1970s, the findings of Toharia's study and of the American studies seemed to justify more sweeping generalizations than those findings do today; see Toharia (1987: 70) and McIntosh (1980–81: 846–47), who states that the rate of civil litigation in the St. Louis Circuit Court "exhibits a nonlinear relationship with socioeconomic development."

ety somewhat different from the position of the courts of the 1960s? Toharia himself returned to the study of Spanish legal culture and examined what happened in his country's courts between 1970 and 1980 (Toharia, 1987). He found an astonishing reversal of some earlier trends. Civil litigation rose dramatically during the decade; indeed, it more than doubled. Toharia also cited figures indicating rising rates in other European countries as well.[12]

There are signs too of important changes in the United States. Federal caseloads continue to rise (Clark, 1981), and there is evidence of increasing litigation in some states, for example, Florida (Gifford and Nye, 1987; see also Marvell, 1987). More significant are certain qualitative changes. For example, the amount of money and effort spent on litigation has apparently risen dramatically over the last decades (Galanter and Rogers, 1988). It seems likely that a small number of very large, very significant lawsuits are responsible for the lion's share of this money and effort. These "megacases"—giant class actions, huge private antitrust suits, enormous trademark and patent marathons—enlist literally hundreds of lawyers, cost millions of dollars, and greedily absorb judge and courtroom time (Chayes, 1976).

There may be something of a pattern here. The "liability crisis" is often discussed in the same breath as the "litigation explosion." And, as with civil suits in general, there does seem to be objective evidence of increases in the amount and consequences of tort liability. Certainly, insurance premiums have risen, tort litigation has driven the asbestos industry to the wall, and individual lawsuits have bankrupted small businesses here and there. We hear about closed playgrounds and abandoned ski lifts, all as a consequence of litigation; and the threat of malpractice suits has apparently led some doctors to change their branch of practice or to engage in "defensive medicine" (Zuckerman *et al.*, 1986; Tancredi and Barondess, 1978). But here, too, important longitudinal evidence suggests that average tort recoveries have not been rising as rapidly as all the noise and hullabaloo would suggest. Rather, a few very large recoveries distort the overall picture.[13]

There are more surprises in recent research as well. For example, one hears now talk about the rebirth of contract litigation and an upsurge in lawsuits between businesses. This, if true, would flatly reverse the strongest trend of the first wave of longitudinal studies, trial and appellate alike—the decline of commer-

---

[12] The Spanish figures were, however, the most dramatic. There were very modest increases in England and Wales, and striking increases in Belgium and France. In the Federal Republic of German, however, there was a slight decrease.

[13] The evidence for post-World War II jury behavior and the size of awards comes most notably from studies sponsored by the Rand Corporation; see Shanley and Peterson (1983). On the late nineteenth-century situation, see Friedman (1987); another longitudinal study of tort actions is Munger (1987a).

cial litigation. But why should there be a revival of purely business or commercial lawsuits?

Perhaps one place to begin is with Macaulay's famous article of 1963, which examined the "living law" of contract among Wisconsin businessmen. On one level, Macaulay was interested in the relationship between the contractual behavior of his subjects and the demands and postulates of the formal law of contract. What he found was an unbridgeable disparity. Business people showed a marked disinclination to *use* their rights under contract law. When contracting parties stand in a valuable continuing relationship—as is true quite generally in the business world—they will avoid litigation over breaches of contract; they will instead find ways to accommodate each other. Business people are generally anxious to deal with each other again; highly formal negotiated contracts and a willingness to resort too quickly to litigation stand in the way of smooth relations. The Macaulay thesis harmonized neatly with the dominant ethos in the sociology of law of the 1960s, and it fit in beautifully with the postulates of the Hurst school (Macaulay himself was a professor of law at the University of Wisconsin and was closely associated with Willard Hurst). The impulse to pursue Macaulay's line of research was Hurstian to the core (classical legal scholars had better things to do than sit around and chat with minor officials of Milwaukee paper companies), as were his essential findings, which assumed an instrumental approach to law and debunked the centrality of formal legal doctrine, appellate courts, and litigation.

The Macaulay thesis had two sides to it; but later scholars rarely discussed or even noted the second side: why people *do* behave "contractually" and even litigate, and when. After all, there is and always has been a certain amount of business litigation, and Macaulay attempted to explain exactly what circumstances might (or might not) lead to carefully planned contracts and ultimately to litigation. Put most simply, contractualism and litigation could arise out of certain rare but highly complex business situations; or out of ruptured or one-time transactions in which long-term relationships were not of any particular value; or circumstances in which conventional business norms and customs simply did not govern.

Macaulay's business people avoided litigation because their business world *was* a world of long-term, continuing relations. In an important recent paper, Galanter and Rogers (1988: 3) argue that the "environment of American business practice" has altered, in a way that affects the Macaulay thesis, since the early 1970s: "[m]arkets have fissured, products have become more specialized, competition has increased, and business dealings are in general marked by greater instability." These factors of course describe a business environment that is less likely to foster the conditions that led to the "noncontractual" side of the Macaulay thesis. The new competitiveness, for example, creates an atmosphere in which short-run "bottom-line" concerns predominate; it increases the "relative stakes in individual transactions," which each become "more 'all or nothing' " (*ibid.*, p. 6). Because of these factors, Galanter and Rogers predict a rise in business litigation; and they claim corroboration in a surge of contract filings in federal courts.[14]

The Galanter and Rogers thesis also gains a bit of support from research, some of which they discuss, that look at the phenomenon in another setting: the large law firm. Here too abservers have described a tremendous increase in volatility since the 1970s. The "Wall Street" lawyer—the big-firm, corporate attorney—traditionally avoided litigation and enjoyed long-term stable relationships with the businesses the firm represented. Recent trends have shattered these cozy arrangements. The relationship between business and law firm has become more "transactional," that is, more ad hoc and confined to a single (often enormous) matter (Nelson, 1988a; Friedman, 1989a). The resulting environment is shaky, unstable. Law firms merge, unmerge, branch out, split, and in general show the same volatility as the business community that employs them.

These changes, as we have said, demand the rejection of neither the Macaulay thesis nor the first Toharia thesis, nor its reflections in Friedman and Percival and other American longitudinal studies. They do, however, call for a certain amount of reformulation and fine-tuning. No doubt business firms tended to avoid the courts in part because of failures in the court system itself: its stiffness, expense, and formality—in short, factors which led litigants to think of courts as costly and irrelevant. But the megacases are less troubled by factors of costs and delay. A rhinoceros laughs at a barrier that holds back gazelles.

However, there are undoubtedly other, deeper factors that led to avoidance of courts. The latest trends, if real, invite us to explore some of the social conditions that affected and still affect the courts. First of all, in this (and in most societies) there are by-pass systems, or alternatives to courts—ways of dealing with disputes—that function well among those who share some sort of norm system or sense of community. To deal with disputes, businesses have always used arbitration—or simply learned to work things out, as Macaulay (1963) so well described.

The business people in Macaulay's study were in many regards ordinary maximizers: They had their eyes on profitable business relations, and their behavior was rational enough to satisfy any economist of the classical school. These business people had sim-

---

[14] They admit that the evidence for such a surge in contract cases is much weaker in state courts; however, see the data on Florida in Gifford and Nye (1987).

ply learned that nothing was maximized but trouble if they behaved crudely and legalistically, offended their colleagues, and ruined all their comfortable—and profitable—relationships. It is richer and more realistic, however, to analyze Macaulay's findings in broader terms as well, that is, in terms of legal culture, and to speak of business norms and of a culture of "getting along" and avoiding courts. We should not view this culture of court avoidance as a mere quirk of the American business personality (similarly, one should be very careful about describing Americans as "litigious"). Rather, three factors interacted to produce the described behavior.

The first factor was the business environment, as explained by Macaulay: a web of continuing relationships, governed by informal norms, in which litigation was reserved only for extraordinary, rare, intrusive cases of "marital breakdown," as it were. The second factor was the court system itself, which betrayed certain repellent and "archaic" characteristics; these had survived because the system was insulated from the actual world of business, not to mention other worlds even more remote from the courtroom. The court system thus came to handle, in the main, two kinds of cases: routine administrative matters, and, more rarely, pathological and borderline cases—cases growing out of freak, unusual, or one-time situations.[15] Third, there was the legal culture itself, a general cluster of attitudes largely produced by the two other factors but which also influenced and interacted with them, insofar as the attitudes determined when and to what extent individuals, businesses, and groups would actually turn to law. A divorce rate—to take a nonbusiness example—reflects (1) the marital environment within which men and women interact; (2) the legal rules about divorce and the court system (how much does a divorce cost? how long does it take?); and, (3) last but not least, *attitudes* toward divorce within the culture (do neighbors, friends, and family support or stigmatize those who divorce?).

Legal culture is an elusive subject, which I have tried to deal with elsewhere (1990a, 1985). It seems plausible that general attitudes toward law in modern Western society differ strikingly from those that prevailed a century or more ago. One aspect of legal culture of the nineteenth century was a more sharply defined sense of the *limits* of law. There is, in general, an inverse relationship between the use of law (in the formal sense) and the strength of custom, traditional authority, and norms that are applied in face-to-face situations. Another, related aspect of the older legal culture was the view that there was a specifically "legal" domain, that is, certain types of dispute were appropriate for legal process, while others were outside this domain.

15 See also Friedman (1965) on the appellate caseload of the Wisconsin Supreme Court in three historical periods.

In the twentieth century, for one reason or another, traditional authority has continued to weaken in Western countries. The nuclear family is not what it used to be, and the authority of teachers, the clergy, employers, and, generally speaking, the state also seems a bit shakier. In these societies, urban life, industrialization, and the increasing division of labor have vastly expanded the domain of interactions with strangers—the people who jostle us on the street, who produce the goods we eat, wear, and use, the experts who examine our bodies, souls, and portfolios. These relationships are the domain of "law," and the more ad hoc and impersonal, the more "legalized" they become. This is true for individuals and for Macaulay's business people as well.

In modern legal culture, populations consume and demand more law; this places increasing pressure on legal institutions, including the courts. The response in the United States and in many other countries has been such that, for better or worse, these institutions became or seemed to become more relevant than in the past. Social change has opened a door to expanded use of courts and to an expanded *conception* of courts. Viewed from this aspect, the findings in Toharia's 1974 book, and in the American longitudinal studies, although presumably accurate, were misleading insofar as they tempted law and society scholars to think in terms of very long-term trends. They were in fact only temporary phenomena.[16] At least this is a possibility—a starting point for theory and research.

To be sure, longitudinal and other historical studies have uncovered other periods with massive use of courts, although "litigation" may not be exactly the right word. The American colonial period is one example. A researcher who examined the court records of a tiny Virginia county during a three-year period in the seventeenth century (1633–36) found that the names of almost all the adult residents of the county appeared in the records as litigants, witnesses, or in some other capacity (Curtis, 1977: 274, 277). But the courts then served a rather different function than they do today. They reflected neither a minimalist nor an expansive conception of law; rather, the courts were general organs of government, at a time when the line between state and private was not clearly drawn; the courts operated paternalistically, as extensions of traditional authority, rather than as institutions that affirmed and protected rights, as places to which people went to demand redress for essentially private grievances (Hartog, 1976). Once again,

[16] Toharia (1987: 137) himself, on the contrary, thinks of the findings of his second study as the temporary phenomenon. He feels that the best explanation for the rise in Spanish litigation in the 1970s is the "important and sustained economic crisis" of that decade. Thus, the "litigation explosion" in Spain in that decade is best looked at as "a transitory phenomenon"; when the crisis abates, the level of litigation will return to the patterns that had been established for almost a century.

we must be careful not to speak of "courts" as if the term had some eternal, abiding meaning, isolated from social and historical context.

When all is said and done, longitudinal research on courts is obscure, scholarly stuff. It does not have much resonance in popular legal culture. It is good, honest research, and it looks for truth in a corner of life where propaganda and hysteria abound. But the hysteria is itself an important social fact. One cannot help wondering what impact the hysteria has on public attitudes and therefore, indirectly, on the use people make of the courts.

Public attitudes have been curiously ambivalent. The public is deeply suspicious of law, lawyers, and courts, and yet at the same time grossly exaggerates their power and efficacy and learns to lean on them inordinately. Modern American society is amazingly legalized;[17] it places a great deal of emphasis on law, legal process, and—yes—litigation. This does not mean, of course, that people are "litigious" or that everybody is suing everybody else. As noted, changes in legal culture and in social conditions generally may have consequences for litigation that on the whole are more qualitative than quantitative, at least so far; at any rate, the results are not all in.

One form of litigation that has grown tremendously in this century is constitutional litigation. Civil rights and civil liberties hardly figured in nineteenth-century dockets, even appellate dockets. By the 1970s, however, the constitutional rights of criminal defendants were a major element in such dockets (Kagan *et al.*, 1977).[18] Congress passed a series of important civil rights laws in the 1960s, and the number of suits brought under these acts has been high and continues to grow.

Why the great surge in constitutional litigation? There are surely many reasons, but in part it occurred because of the way in which the average person now conceives of freedom, rights, and entitlements. Lawyers on the whole have a procedural theory of

---

[17] I use this term rather than "legalistic," which has pejorative overtones and in any event is quite misleading. "Legalistic" implies some kind of wooden, bureaucratic sticklerism, which in my view is absolutely false to American legal culture. By "legalized" I mean two things: First, relationships are subject to law or legal processes in various senses rather than defined as completely beyond the reach of such process; students' or prisoners' rights thus represent a higher stage of legalization than leaving students or prisoners absolutely to the tender mercies of authorities. Second, a process is "legalized" to the extent that it takes on some of the aspects of judicial process. For example, tenure decisions today are more "legalized" than they were two generations ago. There has been considerable national and international discussion of legalization. See, e.g., Werle (1982).

[18] There is surprisingly little empirical study of civil rights litigation, but see Eisenberg (1982).

justice; the layperson's theory is, to the contrary, substantive.[19] Concepts of freedom of choice, personal privacy; the right to work, quit work, and change work; the right to travel: substantive claims. The absence of discrimination, fair treatment in all settings, and decent opportunities—these are the essence of "law." And if we ask, what modern *institution* is concerned with enforcing substantive rights, particularly against government and large organizations? the answer is the courts, for all their limitations. The courts—not the legislatures, not the bureaucracy, not the executive branch—are where "justice" can be found. In this cultural climate, the whole social meaning of litigation gets redefined, and the use of litigation, one expects, changes accordingly.

Longitudinal research—and I include here not only the historical studies but also ongoing, longitudinal research—is of particular value, because it is sensitive to changes in legal culture, and in the functions of the courts. The existing research on this rather murky subject has accomplished a good deal. It has even greater possibilities for future contributions: to policy analysis and to legal theory. The studies, defective and scattered as they are, provide baseline data, against which to measure and monitor what is happening in our own turbulent times.

REFERENCES

BLEGVAD, Britt-Mari, P.O. BOLDING, and Ole LANDO, in cooperation with Kirsten GAMST-NIELSEN (1973) *Arbitration as a Means of Solving Conflicts.* Copenhagen: New Social Science Monographs.

CHAYES, Abram (1976) "The Role of the Judge in Public Law Litigation," 89 *Harvard Law Review* 1281.

CLARK, David S. (1981) "Adjudication to Administration: A Statistical Analysis of Federal District Courts in the Twentieth Century," 55 *Southern California Law* 65.

CURTIS, George B. (1977) "The Colonial County Court, Social Forum and Legislative Precedent, Accomack County Virginia, 1663-1636." 85 *Virginia Magazine of History and Biology* 274.

DANIELS, Stephen (1985) "Continuity and Change in Patterns of Case Handling: A Case Study of Two Rural Counties," 19 *Law & Society Review* 381.

EISENBERG, Theodore (1982) "Section 1983: Doctrinal Foundations and an Empirical Study," 67 *Cornell Law Review* 482.

FRIEDMAN, Lawrence M. (1989a) "Litigation and Its Discontents," 40 *Mercer Law Review* 973.

(1987) "Civil Wrongs: Personal Injury Law in the Late 19th Century," 1987 *American Bar Foundation Research Journal* 351.

(1985) *Total Justice*. New York: Russell Sage Foundation.

(1984) "American Legal History: Past and Present," 34 *Journal of Legal Education* 563.

(1979) "Plea Bargaining in Historical Perspective," 13 *Law & Society Review* 247.

(1976) "Trial Courts and Their Work in the Modern World," 4 *Jahrbuch fur Rechtssoziologie and Rechtstheorie* 25.

(1965) *Contract Law in America: A Social and Economic Case Study*. Madison: University of Wisconsin Press.

---

19 This is a surmise, a hypothesis, if you will. I do not mean to suggest, of course, that procedural justice is not a matter of importance to people; it most surely is, and there is a body of research on what people think of as procedural justice. See, e.g., Tyler (1988).

FRIEDMAN, Lawrence M., and Robert PERCIVAL (1981) *The Roots of Justice: Crime and Punishment in Alameda County, California, 1870-1910*. Chapel Hill: University of North Carolina Press.

(1976a) "A Tale of Two Courts: Litigation in Alameda and San Benito Counties," 10 *Law & Society Review* 267.

GALANTER, Marc (1986b) "The Day After the Litigation Explosion," 46 *Maryland Law Review* 3.

(1983a) "Reading the Landscape of Disputes: What We Know and Don't Know (and Think We Know) About Our Allegedly Contentious and Litigious Society," 31 *UCLA Law Review* 4.

GALANTER, Marc and Joel ROGERS (1988) "The Transformation of American Business Disputing: Some Preliminary Observations." Presented at the Annual Meeting of the Law and Society Association, Vail, CO.

GIFFORD, Donald G., and David J. NYE (1987) "Litigation Trends in Florida: Saga of a Growth State," 39 *University of Florida Law Review* 829.

GORDON, Robert (1984b) "Critical Legal Histories," 36 *Stanford Law Review* 57.

GUTIERREZ, Carlos José (1979) *El Funcionamiento del Sistema Juridico*. San José, Costa Rica: Editorial Juricentro.

HARTOG, Hendrik (1976) "The Public Law of a County Court: Judicial Government in Eighteenth Century Massachusetts," 20 *American Journal of Legal History* 282.

HEUMANN, Milton (1975) "A Note on Plea Bargaining and Case Pressure," 9 *Law & Society Review* 515.

HURST, James Willard (1959) "Introduction," in Francis W. Laurent, *The Business of a State Trial Court*. Madison: University of Wisconsin Press.

(1956) *Law and the Conditions of Freedom in the Nineteenth Century United States*. Madison: University of Wisconsin Press.

(1950) *The Growth of American Law: The Law Makers*. Boston: Little, Brown.

KAGAN, Robert, Bliss CARTWRIGHT, Lawrence FRIEDMAN, and Stanton

(1978) "The Evolution of State Supreme Courts ," 76 *Michigan Law Review* 961.

(1977) "The Business of State Supreme Courts 1870-1970," 30 *Stanford Law Review* 121.

LAURENT, Francis W. (1959) *The Business of a Trial Court: 100 Years of Cases*. Madison: University of Wisconsin Press.

LIEBERMAN, Jethro K. (ed.) (1984) *The Role of Courts in American Society: The Final Report of the Council on the Role of Courts*. St. Paul, MN: West Publishing Co.

MACAULAY, Stewart (1963) "Non-contractual Relations in Business: A Preliminary Study," 28 *American Sociological Review* 55.

MANNING, Bayless (1977) "Hyperlexis: Our National Disease," 71 *Northwestern University Law Review* 767.

MARVELL, Thomas B. (1987) "Caseload Growth - Past and Future Trends," 71 *Judicature* 151.

MATHER, Lynn (1979a) *Plea Bargaining or Trial? The Process of Criminal-Case Disposition*. Lexington, MA: Lexington Books.

McINTOSH, Wayne V. (1980-81) "150 Years of Litigation and Dispute Settlement: A Court Tale," 15 *Law & Society Review* 823.

MUNGER, Frank (1988) "Law, Change and Litigation: A Critical Examination of an Empirical Research Tradition," 22 *Law & Society Review* 57.

(1987a) "Social Change and Tort Litigation: Industrialization, Accidents, and Trial Courts in Southern West Virginia, 1872 to 1940," 36 *Buffalo Law Review* 75.

NELSON, Robert (1988a) *Partners with Power: Social Transformation of the Large Law Firm*. Berkeley: University of California Press.

ROTTLEUTHNER, H. (1985) "Aspekte der Rechtsentwicklung in Deutschland. Ein soziologisher Vergleich Deutscher Rechtskulturen," 6 *Zeitschrift für Rechtssoziologie* 206.

SHANLEY, M.G., and M.A. PETERSON (1983) *Comparative Justice: Civil and Jury Verdicts in San Francisco and Cook Counties, 1959-1980.* Santa Monica, CA: Institute for Civil Justice.

TANCREDI, L.R., and J.A. BARONDESS (1978) "The Problem of Defensive Medicine," 200 *Science* 879.

TOHARIA, Jose Juan (1987) *"Pleitos Tengas!" Introduccion a la cultura legal espanola.* Madrid: Siglo XXI de Espana.

(1974) *Cambio Social y Vida Juridica en Espana.* Madrid: Edicusa.

TRUBEK, David (1980-81b) "The Construction and Deconstruction of a Disputes-focused Approach: An Afterword," 15 *Law & Society Review* 727.

TYLER, Tom R. (1988) "What is Procedural Justice? Criteria Used by Citizens to Assess the Fairness of Legal Procedures," 22 *Law & Society Review* 103.

WERLE, Raymond (1982) "Aspekte der Verrechtlichung," 3 *Jahrbuch für Rechtssoziologie und Rechtstheorie* 2.

WHEELER, Stanton, Bliss CARTWRIGHT, Robert A. KAGAN, and Lawrence M. FRIEDMAN (1987) "Do the 'Haves' Come Out Ahead? Winning and Losing in State Supreme Courts, 1870-1970," 21 *Law & Society Review* 403.

ZUCKERMAN, S., C.R. KOLLER, and R.R. BORBJERG (1986) "Information on Malpractice: A Review of Empirical Research on Major Policy Issues," 49 (no. 2) *Law and Contemporary Problems* 85.

[21]

Text, Translation, Context, Conversation,

Preliminary Notes for Decoding the Deliberations of the Advisory Committee that Wrote the Federal Rules of Civil Procedure

by PETER CHARLES HOFFER*

Once upon a time, when history had newly established itself in our universities and its professors likened their labors to a science,[1] historians assumed that objectivity was the first canon of their craft. Documentary evidence spoke for itself; the historian need only train himself to understand what the document said.[2] We are still trained in that canon, but in it there is a trap for the unwary—the siren's call of scholarly omniscience. The danger then as now is that such "graphireadings" of historical texts flattens them,[3] silencing the author's voice and replacing it with the omniscient scholar's printed account. Lively speech becomes dead writing.

This need not be so. If we abandon the conceit that our goal should be a single, objective, authoritative "history" that recovers truth about the past, and accept instead that there are many histories—many competing stories that people tell themselves and others—we can begin to hear the stories that our subjects told. Then will the scholar become a bricoleur, a fabricator of materials at hand,[4] and history "fundamentally an interpretive exercise, a sorting out of conflicting perceptions and an appreciation

---

*Research Professor of History and Adjunct Professor of Law, University of Georgia. I thank the members of the N.Y.U. School of Law Legal History Seminar, in particular William Nelson, N.E.H. Hull, of Rutgers Law School-Camden, and David Schoenbrun and Alan Watson, of the University of Georgia, for their comments upon earlier versions of this paper, and Stephen Burbank, of the University of Pennsylvania Law School, who shared the fruits of his research with me.

1. A deductive science, in the manner of Leopold Von Ranke's famous admonition to tell it "wie es eigentlich gewesen." See Peter Novick, *That Noble Dream: The Objectivity Question and the American Historical Profession* (Cambridge, 1988), 21-46.

2. Ibid., 61-85. From that dream there are some who do not want to waken. See, e.g., C. Beham McCullagh, *Justifying Historical Descriptions* (Cambridge, 1984), arguing that there is a "then" which we can know; historical truth is attainable. McCullagh does not call this history scientific—it is positivist and empirical. He does not grant, however, that positivism is a pose and empiricism has to carry its own heavy baggage of assumptions about knowing.

3. Denis Donoghue, *Ferocious Alphabets* (Boston, 1981), 151-52

4. See N.E.H. Hull, "Networks & *Bricolage*: A Prolegomenon to a History of Twentieth-Century American Academic Jurisprudence" 35 *American Journal of Legal History* 307 (1991). After reading a copy of the essay, Bernard Bailyn, arguably one of our greatest living historians, wrote Professor Hull: "now I know what I am—a bricoleur." N.E.H. Hull communication to the author, December 4, 1992.

of the narratives that humans have always invented to make sense out of their lives."[5]

This historical sensibility can profoundly reshape our approach to legal texts. A new narrative style of legal writing on constitutions[6] has already sought to go beyond the one voice of authority to find the many, diverse voices of people who bring their claims to the courts. The stories in this new genre of legal writing are contemporary; often they recount the author's own experiences.[7] A comparable view of law seeks "the way that law is understood, promulgated, argued about, experienced, and assimulated."[8]

I believe that post-modernist legal history—to coin a phrase—can assist us to recover the original voices of those who prepared our basic legal texts. In this essay, I want to consider one of these—the Federal Rules of Civil Procedure. No text is more essential to the way litigants, litigators, and judges function in our federal courts, and none seems a less likely candidate for the post-modernist project. The Rules have been flattened into dry as dust formality in the classroom and the law review. Yet behind them is a dramatic and exciting human story, people speaking to each other. The historian's job is to listen for those voices behind the text; to make the text live. This essay is a musing on the method by which we might begin that process of recovery. I am still far closer to the beginning of my labors than their completion, and offer these reflections on a work in progress in the hope of stirring further conversation among legal historians.

TEXT

Legal history remains terra incognita to the ordinary reader of history and is shunned by the average historian. There is little legal history in our textbooks or our classrooms. The reason for indifference to legal history cannot be the inherent dullness or mystery of legal institutions, laws, and litigation. They affect the world we live in profoundly, fill the morning news programs, and daily shape our expectations of others' conduct. On television, courts and lawyers appear regularly. Legal history should be very popular, but quite the reverse is true.

If law concerns everyday life, the language of legal texts is foreign to most of us, including most historians. Consider the average lawsuit. The story that the plaintiff tells is one of good faith violated, or of pain and suffering and harm, and the plaintiff's words are in the vernacular. In law, these claims sound different, abstracted, rarefied, clothed in mysteri-

5. T.H. Breen, *Imaging the Past: East Hampton Histories* (Reading, Mass., 1989), 14.

6. See, e.g., "Legal Storytelling" 87 *Michigan Law Review* 2073 (1989).

7. See, e.g., Mari J. Matsuda, "Legal Storytelling: Public Response to Racist Speech: Considering the Victim's Story" 87 *Michigan Law Review* 2320 (1989).

8. Jack M. Balkin, "What is a Postmodernist Constitutionalism?" 90 *Michigan Law Review* 1966, 1978 (1992).

ous terms of art. Pleading is a translation of the words and emphases and accents and idioms of parties by specially trained and certified court functionaries and lawyers "far removed from the language of ordinary people. . . . Official legal discourse tends to transform or simply to ignore the discourse of the disputants whose problems are the law's very reason for being."[9]

To be sure, American legal text has steadily moved away from the extreme artificiality of the forms of action in common-law writ pleading[10] but not necessarily always in the direction of the vernacular tongue. In the nineteenth century, a period which saw the rise of legal professionalism, by which I mean the introduction and inculcation of a language that professionals spoke to each other,[11] the most common mark of the texts of law remained their abstraction from ordinary discourse. The idiom of lawyers—the words and phrases uttered in the formal steps of law—now surrounded itself with a new incantanabula: "doctrines" of "contributory negligence" and the "fellow servant rule," a distinctive vocabulary impenetrable to all but an initiated few.[12] Insofar as law school education (and

9. John M. Conley and William M. O'Barr, *Rules Versus Relationships: The Ethnography of Legal Discourses* (Chicago, 1990), 9. Seen from within its own boundaries, legal discourse possesses a beauty and order which are not so censurable. Consider James Boyd White, *Justice As Translation* (Chicago, 1990), 240-241: "an argument that the law should be regarded as creating a distinct discourse of its own, in which words are given their meaning by reference to the purposes and contexts of the law, not to the shifting usages of ordinary speech. To us this seems obvious, for we have long lived with a technical legal language. . . The reading of legal texts requires a kind of judgment that is in fact a form of law-making, entailed in the very act of interpretation itself." Translation of law is the application of legal texts created at one time and place to new and altered contexts. But how impenetrable these can be to the uninitiated!

10. The writ was purchased from the English crown and used to begin or continue a lawsuit in the royal courts. "The principles of the common law were not laid down in the abstract, but grew around the forms through which justice was centralised and administered by the king's courts. There was a law of writs before there was a law of property, or of contract, or of tort. . . . Once a writ had been issued it became a precedent for the future, and there was a reluctance to change the formula if it was found serviceable. A plaintiff did not, therefore, concoct his own writ . . . he had either to find a known formula to fit his case, or apply for a new one to be invented. [After 1258, this became very difficult.] If a would-be plaintiff could not find a writ in the register he was without remedy as far as the two benches [of Kings Bench and Common Pleas] were concerned." In this way rights and remedies came to be conflated with an administrative implement. J. H. Baker, *An Introduction to English Legal History* (3rd ed. London, 1990), 63, 65, 66.

11. The point is mine, but it was suggested by Robert W. Gordon, "'The Ideal and the Actual in the Law': Fantasies and Practices of New York City Lawyers, 1870-1910" in Gerard W. Gewalt, ed., *The New High Priests: Lawyers in Post Civil-War America* (Westport, Ct., 1984), 51-74, and Gordon, "Legal Thought and Legal Practice in the Age of American Enterprise, 1870-1920" in Gerald L. Geison, ed., *Profession and Professional Ideologies in America* (Chapel Hill, 1983), 70-110. I do not find the lawyers making ideologies, however, but borrowing key words and phrases from ideologies to restructure the language of law.

12. William Nelson, *The Americanization of the Common Law: The Impact of Legal Change on Massachusetts Society, 1760-1830* (Cambridge, Mass., 1975), 77-88; Morton Horwitz, *The Transformation of American Law, 1780-1860* (Cambridge, Mass., 1977), 160-210.

certification of lawyers) replaced reading law in a practitioner's office,[13] the grip of this arcane idiom grew complete and more compelling within the profession.

Nowhere was the grip of argot upon text more apparent than in civil procedure, where successive attempts by democratic state legislatures to make courts more accessible to ordinary men and women had led only to more detailed instructions and complex formalities. The Field Code in New York (1848), a model for the merger of law and equity forms that abolished the writ system,[14] was soon cluttered with such additions, all in the vocabulary of the lawyers who quickly turned the apparent simplicity of fact pleading into arcane understandings of "ultimate facts."[15] As George Wickersham, a New York practitioner and incumbent U.S. Attorney General wryly told the New York Bar Association in 1911, "The New York Bar may well command the intellectual respect of the nation. Any bar that have been able to practice law under the Code of Civil Procedure in the State of New York with a degree of success which enables them still to receive comfortable emoluments from their clients have earned no mere distinction."[16] When the Progressive legal academics announced their agenda for reform of law early in our century, they zeroed in their guns on the deadliness of civil procedure.[17]

One of these academics was Charles E. Clark of Yale Law School, the Reporter (chief draftsman) of the Federal Rules of Civil Procedure

13. Robert Stevens, *Law School: Legal Education in America from the 1850s to the 1980s* (Chapel Hill, 1983), 51-111.

14. New York Laws 1848 c. 379 sec 62: "The distinction between actions at law and suits in equity, and the forms of all such actions and suits heretofore existing are abolished." The reform was based on the Report of the Commissioners on Practice and Pleading, 1847, which David Dudley Field led. On the Code, see Charles M. Cook, *The American Codification Movement: A Study of Antebellum Legal Reform* (Westport, Ct., 1981), 158-191. On Field, see Daun Van Ee, *David Dudley Field and the Reconstruction of the Law* (New York, 1986) and Stephen N. Subrin, "David Dudley Field and the Field Code: A Historical Analysis of an Earlier Procedural Vision" *Law and History Review* 6 (1988), 311-374.

15. "Fact pleading" required ultimate facts—only those facts upon which the court was to rely. Thus fact pleading limited what juries had to decide. Fact pleading also meant that the plaintiff had to decide in advance that theory of law which was most likely to be a winning theory. On the fate of the Code, see Charles E. Clark, *Handbook of the Law of Code Pleading* (2nd ed. St. Paul, 1947), 47-50. Clark argued that successive legislative attempts to maintain Field's original concept were diluted by the New York State courts' persistence in separating legal and equitable causes. Robert Bone brilliantly has traced the concern for precise distinctions in pleading in his "Mapping the Boundaries of a Dispute: Conceptions of Ideal Law Suit Structure from the Field Code to the Federal Rules" 89 *Columbia Law Review* 1011 (1989) without, I think, realizing the extent of his debt to the strictures of nineteenth-century legal grammar.

16. George Wickersham, address at the banquet of the New York State Bar Association, reported in *The Green Bag* 23 (July 1911), 335.

17. See, *e.g.*, Roscoe Pound, "Is Equity Decadent?" 5 *Columbia Law Review* 20 (1905) and "Mechanical Jurisprudence" 8 *Columbia Law Review* 605 (1908); Walter Wheeler Cook, "The Place of Equity in Our Legal System" 3 *American Law School Review* 173 (1912), and Wesley N. Hohfeld, "The Relations Between Law and Equity" 11 *Michigan Law Review* 537 (1913).

(1935-1938). He believed that efficiency and justice would both be served by making pleading hear the voices of the parties to a lawsuit.[18] During and after his service on the Advisory Committee that rewrote the rules, Clark strove to change legal pleading in that direction.[19] But there is more to his story, and mine, than that.

It is a story about Clark I want to tell in this essay, but not as the authoritative spokesman, not at all. Over the past decade, other legal scholars and lawyers have turned their attention to Clark and the framing of the Federal Rules, believing that "the evidence of history is, in many respects, compelling."[20] They argue that their reading of original sources like Clark's correspondence,[21] and the verbatim record of the deliberations of the Advisory Committee that drafted the Rules,[22] reveals the heretofore hidden but true story about the writing of the Rules.

---

18. An early goal of some conservative would-be reformers of pleading in the federal courts was "uniformity." These critics of separate law and equity dockets, notably former President William Howard Taft and ABA leader Thomas Shelton, spearheaded the first movement for a code of federal procedure merging law and equity. See Stephen N. Subrin, "How Equity Conquered Common Law: the Federal Rules of Civil Procedure in Historical Perspective" 135 *University of Pennsylvania Law Review* 909 (1987). Subrin finds that Clark made the corporatist motives of Taft and his cohorts acceptable to New Deal political leaders. Ibid., 969. Clark is clever and less obvious, and also less political, in Stephen B. Burbank, "The Rules Enabling Act of 1834" 132 *University of Pennsylvania Law Review* 1015, 1132-1137 (1982).

19. My story of this effort, "Translations of Pleading; Charles Clark and the Federal Rules of Civil Procedure" is forthcoming. Clark told the story himself. See, e.g., Clark, *Handbook of the Law of Code Pleading* (St. Paul, 1928), 23-38 (code pleading in need of reform, particularly at federal level); "The Challenge for a New Federal Civil Procedure" 19 *Journal of the American Judicature Society* 8 (1935) ("stimulated thereto by the intelligent leaders of the bar and even more by the enlightened pressure exerted by the lay public" the Supreme Court and Congress have agreed to long-awaited reforms); "The Proposed Federal Rules of Civil Procedure" 22 *A.B.A.J.* 447 (1936); "The Federal Rules of Civil Procedure" 23 *A.B.A.J.* 976 (1937) (progress reports to the American Bar Association on the activities of the Advisory Committee); *Handbook of the Law of Code Pleading* (2nd ed. St. Paul, 1947), 31-71 (celebrating the achievement of the Advisory Committee).

20. Burbank, "Rules Enabling Act," 1025. Burbank finds that the Advisory Committee that wrote the rules did not pay sufficient regard, indeed, either cavalierly ignored or deliberately transgressed, the boundaries of procedural codification laid down by the Enabling Act of 1934. "Rules Enabling Act," 1132-1137. But Burbank does not wish to be read as an omniscient narrator of historical events. *Ibid.*, 1185. He is instead concerned with the "legal interpretation" of an historical document, on which enterprise historical research throws some light. Burbank to the author, December 9, 1992. It might be rejoined that this sort of legal interpretation, above and beyond the historical events, is the very sort of graphireading that post-modernist legal history seeks to avoid. For Burbank's further comments, see "Of Rules and Discretion" 63 *Notre Dame Law Review* 693 (1988) and "The Transformation of American Civil Procedure: The Example of Rule 11" 137 *University of Pennsylvania Law Review* 915 (1989).

21. The Charles E. Clark Papers at the Sterling Library, Yale University. I am grateful to Judith Schiff and William Massa, Jr., archivists, for giving me permission to use the papers and for guiding me through them.

22. A full transcription of the deliberations of the Committee from 1935 to 1937 was deposited by Edgar B. Tolman, secretary of the Committee, with the Supreme Court. These were archived at the Suitland, Maryland facility of the National Archives. Stephen Burbank

I demur. I present here pieces of three extended narratives, all based on or arising out of the same set of primary sources, that compete for credence. The first is the story Clark told at the time to the public in his many talks and articles. The second is crafted by Clark's critics from his letters and a reading of portions of the deliberations of the Advisory Committee on which he sat. The third story is one Clark revealed late in his life, which still remains untested. "Which of these stories in true?" is the wrong question; it is rooted in a delusion of scholarly omniscience and a longing for definitive accounts that can only mislead. Instead we should ask what the multiplicity of stories reveals about human actions, about Clark and his comrades on the Advisory Committee. We want to listen to the voices in the text, rather than reading it aloud in our own.

Clark told his story in public over and over, creating a thickly textured if repetitive text. For the most part he wrote for and spoke to professional audiences, although he did his best to avoid technical terms. His story's plot was simple: before the Advisory Committee changed the rules, the separation of law and equity on federal dockets caused confusion, injustice, and delay. According to Clark, "Until 1938, federal procedure was one of the most difficult in the country, requiring the skill of trained specialists for the application of its esoteric principles."[23] A model existed for the more efficient, just, and flexible adjudication of civil cases—the Supreme Court's rules for proceedings in equity.[24] Clark opined that "equity practice was affording a convincing demonstration of the great advantage of a single uniform system under the rule-making power as granted by the Supreme Court by express statute."[25] The Court, in a wise exercise of its rule-making power, gave great latitude to the Advisory Committee. In turn, the Committee crafted rules that conferred great discretion on trial court judges. When the Committee's job was done

---

kindly directed me to this source. Through the good offices of James Macklin and Ann Gardner of the Administrative Office of United States Courts, Washington, D.C., I have been able to obtain a duplication of the transcription, all the drafts of the rules prepared by Clark and his staff, and the comments of members of the bench and bar in the various judicial circuits to those drafts, along with permission to quote from the various documents. These materials comprise over 5000 typescript pages.

23. Clark, *Code Pleading*, 31.

24. See 226 U.S. appendix 1 (1912).

25. Clark, *Code Pleading*, 32-33. The U.S. Constitution gives to the Congress the power to "constitute Tribunals inferior to the supreme Court" (Art. 1, sec. 8), which comprehends fashioning rules of procedure for inferior federal courts. Over the course of years, Congress had done just that—but it had left the Supreme Court free to lay down the rules for the equity cases it would hear. See Peter Charles Hoffer, *The Law's Conscience: Equitable Constitutionalism in America* (Chapel Hill, 1990), 94-106. In 1934, the Congress gave to the Court the authority to write rules for procedure in law. The new rules were to be reported to Congress. The second section of the Act permitted the Court to unify the two systems of law and equity. Chief Justice Charles Evans Hughes, after some hesitation, argued publicly for merger of the two systems. For Hughes' speech at the American Law Institute on May 9, 1935, see 21 *A.B.A.J.* 340 (1935). On the 1934 Act, see Burbank, "Rules Enabling Act."

the Rules were clear and simple. The bench and bar were delighted, and the new Rules quickly gained their approval.[26]

Clark's story was simultaneously self-effacing and self-congratulatory. It had the virtues of animation and intimacy, if not of drama or heroism. He never took credit he deserved, but left no doubt in his readers' minds that when the Committee's work was done, his vision was triumphant. As he had planned, the Federal Rules fundamentally shifted the process from a common-law model to an equity model. Celebrants and critics[27] of the Rules agree that under the Rules the judge gained the wide discretion once given the chancellor sitting in equity.[28] The old language on common-law pleading was gone.[29] Equitable joinder of parties, consolidation of claims, class action, and wide latitude for discovery were made central to the new Rules, giving them a thoroughly equitable cast.[30] The discretion of judges to intervene in suits, in effect managing them, was materially increased by the rules, and continues to grow today.[31]

Clark's story was just that, his story, and the impression he intended to leave with his audience was that the drafting of the rules was done by the Committee as a whole, a faceless entity faced with dire circumstances,

---

26. Clark was quite consistent in his story, from the first time he told it, *e.g.*, in Clark, "Fundamental Changes Effected by the New Federal Rules, I" 15 *Tennessee Law Review* 551 (1938) to the last, in Clark, "The Role of the Supreme Court in Federal Rule-Making" 46 *Journal of the American Judicature Society* 250 (1963). I do not want to trash Clark's tale, and many leading proceduralists still agree with it. See, *e.g.*, Geoffrey Hazard, "Discovery Vices and Trans-Substantive Virtues in the Federal Rules of Civil Procedure" 137 *University of Pennsylvania Law Review* 2237 (1989).

27. The extent and growing incivility of the quarrel over how much "reform" the Rules need to make them either fulfill the intentions of the framers or, alternatively, work today is apparent in the recent flood of literature accompanying the fiftieth anniversary of the Rules. See, *e.g.*, Jack B. Weinstein, "After Fifty Years of the Federal Rules of Civil Procedure: Are the Barriers to Justice Being Raised" 137 *University of Pennsylvania Law Review* 1901 (1989) ("reform" of the Rules movement may conceal an animus to the open access program of the framers).

28. For example, today federal courts are permitted to allow amendment of pleading "at any time in its discretion and upon such terms as it deems just" (Fed. R. Civ. P. 4 [h]), enlarge the time limit on pleading (6 [b]), and encourage "a short and plain statement of the claim showing the pleader is entitled to relief" (8 [a] [2]) for "no technical forms of pleading or motions are required." (8 [e] [1]).

29. The last vestige of the banished litany: Fed. R. Civ. P. 7 (c) (demurrer is explicitly abandoned).

30. Fed. R. Civ. P. 13 (cross claim and counterclaim); 15 (amendments); 18 (joinder of claims); 19 (joinder of parties); 20 (permissive joinder of parties); 21 (misjoinder); 22 (interpleader); 23 (class actions); 26-37 (discovery).

31. See, e.g., Steven Flanders, "Blind Umpires—A Response to Professor Resnik" 35 *Hastings Law Journal* 505 (1987) and Marc Galanter, "The Emergence of the Judge as a Mediator in Civil Cases" 69 *Judicature* 257 (1986). More recently, Title I of the Judicial Improvements Act of 1990, Pub. L. 101-650, 104 Stat. 5089; 28 U.S.C. 471, commonly called the Civil Justice Reform Act, has provided for increased judicial discretion in the management of civil litigation. A number of "early implementation districts" have been authorized to plan and deploy their own programs to place different kinds of litigation on fast, and complex tracks. Clark would have been delighted.

motivated by public spiritedness, and tutored by practical wisdom. There were problems; the Committee worked long and heard to solve them; and it succeeded. Clark's underlying assumptions—that men of good faith working toward a common purpose could lift themselves above special interests—would have struck a responsive chord with his audience, or so he had reason to believe. He presumed that there was such a thing as the common good, and this powerful ideograph[32] was widely shared by the audience most important to him—the faculty of elite law schools during the New Deal Era.[33]

Modern critics of the Rules have found flaws in this story, and replaced it with their own. They accuse Clark of misreading or disobeying the command of Congress,[34] giving too much discretion to federal judges,[35] or willfully subordinating law to equity.[36] They have revealed Clark's machinations to foist upon the Committee a highly personal vision of reform.[37] The sources for the critics' tale include Clark's correspondence with a number of his future co-workers and with the men who would in one way or another supervise the work, as well as materials produced by and for the Advisory Committee that drafted the Rules.[38] Crucial are Clark's exchanges with former Attorney General William Mitchell, whom Chief Justice Charles Evans Hughes named chairman of

32. An ideograph is a cluster of ideas pulled together and represented by a single word or phrase. "The common good" is an ideograph. See Michael Calvin McGee, "The 'Ideograph': A Link Between Rhetoric and Ideology" *Quarterly Journal of Speech* 66 (1980), 1-16. I am grateful to Marouf Hasian for calling the concept and this reference to my attention.

33. Such assumptions, of good men and good faith, were common among the elite law professors. John Henry Schlegel, "The Ten Thousand Dollar Question: Review of Laura Kalman, *Legal Realism at Yale, 1927-1960*" 41 *Stanford Law Review* 435, 463 (1989).

34. Burbank, "Rules Enabling Act," 1136.

35. Judith Resnik, "Failing Faith: Adjudicatory Procedure in Decline" 53 *University of Chicago Law Review* 494 (1986).

36. Subrin, "How Equity Conquered Common Law," 961-973.

37. Subrin, "How Equity Conquered Common Law," 973; Subrin, "Charles E. Clark and His Procedural Outlook: The Disciplined Champion of Undisciplined Rules" in Peninah Petrack, ed., *Judge Charles Edward Clark* (New York, 1991), 115-152.

38. See, e.g., the manuscripts consulted by Burbank, "Rules Enabling Act" 1132-1133, n. 529. Burbank cites the copies of the transcripts retained by Clark, now archived at the Sterling Library, Yale University, Edmund M. Morgan's copies of the materials, including drafts of the Rules and the comments of judges and lawyers from various judicial circuits, on deposit at the Langdell Library, Harvard Law School, and the Edgar Tolman typescript of the draft materials and transcript, at the University of Chicago Law School Library, subsequently reclassified as a rare book. I have found and copied all the extant materials from the official records, housed at the National Archives. See note 23 *supra*. My copies have notes in Tolman's handwriting. He was the secretary of the Advisory Committee, representing the department of justice on it, and his copies were the official ones. As far as I can tell from comparison of them with the Clark and Morgan materials, and examination of Tolman's notes about the missing portions of the transcript, the official documentary collection has everything in the Clark and Morgan collections as well as materials neither Clark nor Morgan retained.

the Advisory Committee,[39] and with Edson Sunderland of the University of Michigan Law School, arguably the foremost proceduralist of his day and one of the academics that Clark sought to place on the Advisory Committee.[40] In support of these critical revelations I found further evidence from Clark's correspondence with Homer Cummings of Connecticut, named Attorney general by President Franklin D. Roosevelt in 1933[41] and the architect of the Rules Enabling Act.[42]

Clark's private writings seem to undermine the guileless plot line of the story he told in public. They supply abundant evidence that he tried to manipulate others, to bend them to his will with bluff and brilliance. In using his own letters to prove a case against him, however, one must not claim that the letters speak for themselves—no more than one ought to be believe that his addresses and lectures spoke for themselves. Some of Clark's modern critics have looked at his correspondence and concluded that Clark's motives were as suspect as his methods. Just now, I lean toward a somewhat different conclusion, not because my investigation of additional pieces of correspondence allows me to be more objective, but

---

39. On Mitchell, see *New York Times*, August 25, 1955, p. 23; American Law Institute, *Minutes in Remembrance, 1925-1975* (Philadelphia, 1976), 78-79.

40. On Sunderland, see 58 *Michigan Law Review* 1 (1959) (articles by Charles Clark and Charles H. King, and a bibliography of Sunderland's work); AALS *Directory of Teachers in Member Schools* (1937), 145; *New York Times* March 30, 1959, p. 31; Elizabeth Gaspar Brown, *Legal Education at Michigan, 1859-1959* (Ann Arbor, 1959), 81, 210, 236-237, 342, 346. Sunderland had spent his career at Michigan, becoming a research professor there and the director of legal research. He was a certainty for inclusion on the Advisory Committee, but Clark recommended him to Edgar Tolman, secretary of the American Bar Association and the Attorney General's representative on the Committee. See Clark to Tolman, January 4, 1935, Clark Papers, folder 39, box 108. The Sunderland correspondence is to be found in the Bentley Historical Library, The University of Michigan, Ann Arbor. I am grateful to Becky Fogel, Research Assistant, and Francis X. Blouin, Jr., Director, for copies of letters regarding the Federal Rules.

41. On Cummings, see 24 *A.B.A.J.* 998 (1930); *DAB* (6th supp.) 136-138; *New York Times* September 11, 1956, p. 317, and Carl B. Swisher, ed., *Selected Papers of Homer Cummings* (New York, 1939).

42. See, e.g., Clark Howell to Homer Cummings, June 20, 1934, Cummings Papers, University of Virginia Library, box 103: "you have done a wonderful piece of work in this, and the whole country is indebted to you for the masterly manner in which you secured congressional action." Howell's paper, *The Atlanta Constitution*, said much the same in an editorial two days before—a not quite spontaneous outpouring of admiration, for Howell admitted on the 20th that Cummings had suggested the editorial on the 16th. Clark and Cummings worked closely in accord, during and after the Rules project. See, e.g., Clark to Cummings, September 5, 1934: "May I therefore tender my services to you and your department in any way you may find useful in your plans for the suggestion of forms of the new rules." Cummings to Clark, September 11, 1934: "The whole matter is in a formative stage and I would be greatly pleased if we could have the benefit of your judgment . . . I would be greatly pleased if you would call in and talk over the subject with me." Cummings Papers, University of Virginia Library, box. 86. I am grateful to Gregory A. Johnson, Senior Public Services Assistant, for allowing me to use these papers. Clark and Cummings dined together on October 4, and met the next day. Thereafter they worked as a team. Clark praised Cummings in print for promoting passage of the Rules Enabling Act, see e.g., "The Proposed Federal Rules of Civil Procedure," 447.

because I am not seduced by the dream of objectivity. To put the matter crudely, Clark's critics believe that by mining his private letters they can arrive at some quantum of absolute fact—"the real Clark." I disagree with their conclusions not because I may have read materials that they missed, but because I see his letters as I see his speeches, as part of Clark's effort to tell a story, only this time to insiders, by making the semantic moves necessary to persuade and bargain with equally powerful players in the game.[43]

The third story of Clark and the Rules is one that Clark took some pains to hide until the last decade of his life. In a 1955 talk to the New York City bar eight years before his death he submitted that his advocacy of equitable forms of pleading, his belief in judicial discretion, his support for Edson Sunderland's faith in extensive pre-trial discovery and summary judgement, were all an attempt to minimize the role of lawyers in pleading. Clark told the New York City Bar that he wanted the words of the real parties, the common language of harms and broken promises, to control the outcome of cases, not the formalities of pleading or the tricks of counsel. "Instead of pressing for more pleading detail [Clark's long-standing quarrel with "fact pleading"] we should turn to the modern devices of pretrial discovery, and summary judgement; for by their processes of reaching at once to the party himself, rather than to his lawyer, they may actually obtain further clarification of what did happen with respect to the concrete issues dividing the parties."[44]

How are we to make sense of these three completing stories? We must begin once again with primary sources, and ask ourselves how historical texts can be translated for modern readers. The most important source for understanding Clark's efforts to mold the new Rules comes directly from the fifteen men who wrote the Federal Rules of Civil Procedure.[45] Known to a few, read in their entirety by fewer still, the stenographic transcription of the deliberations of the men who wrote the Federal Rules is a marvelous repository of the words of the draftsmen. Under the terms of the Congressional Rules Enabling Act of 1934,[46] the Supreme Court was to promulgate new rules of pleading for federal trial courts. The Advisory Committee the Supreme Court appointed to write these Rules sat from 1935 until 1938. A final draft was submitted to the

43. Clark could be curt and abusive. He could also be warm, generous, and thoughtful. He was contentious and occasionally pedantic, but not selfish or uncaring. In short, a complex person. Interview with Elias Clark, July 10, 1991; Elias Clark, "Memories of My Father" in Petrack, ed., *Clark*, 153-164.

44. Clark, "A Modern Procedure for New York" 30 *New York University Law Review* 1194, 1199 (1955).

45. William D. Mitchell, Chairman, Scott M. Loftin, George W. Wickersham (replaced after his death in February, 1936 by George Wharton Pepper), Wilbur H. Cherry, Charles E. Clark, Reporter, Armistead M. Dobie, Robert G. Dodge, George Donworth, Joseph G. Gamble, Monte M. Lemann, Edmund M. Morgan, Warren Olney, Jr., Edson R. Sunderland, and Edgar B. Tolman.

46. Act of June 19, 1934; 48 Stat. 1064; 28 U.S.C. secs. 723b, 723c.

Court in the Fall of 1937, approved, and thence sent to Congress, which had the power to demur, but did not.[47]

The full stenographic record of those three years of deliberation runs over 5000 typescript pages, and with two short gaps (the stenographer was absent), travels from the first gathering, in June 1935, to the final meetings early in 1937. I have arrayed alongside it the various drafts of the Rules prepared by Clark and his staff, comments from lawyers and judges in the various judicial circuits, and the three published versions of the rules, in May 1936, April 1937, and 1938, with the Advisory Committee's footnotes and comments.

At first blush, the transcript seems less a learned forum than a distant cousin of the FBI transcription of the John Gotti tapes one can find in airport bookstores.[48] If one expected leading legal practitioners and professors to speak in complete paragraphs, one would be disappointed with this transcription. Recorded verbatim, the conversation meandered forward in fragments, bits of thought carried in awkward sentences. Unlike Gotti and his cohorts, the Advisory Committee members did not use the La Cosa Nostra system of never mentioning precise names, places, or dates (developed to prevent wiretappers from positively identifying any particular event or person), but the Committee exchanges were encoded nonetheless. The members alluded to cases by an abbreviation of their captions or particular facts, made oblique references to this or that judge, and told stories without beginnings or ends. And this is the delight of the transcription: these deliberations are not the glossy, finished product, the printed, formal Rules. They are alive—contentious, thoughtful, and humorous by turns.

TRANSLATION

In trying to make sense of this often oblique and occasionally opaque argot one must translate. All historians are translators. We take words and sentences from then and there and render them into the language of here and now. To our readers we offer glosses on meaning, deci-

47. A near thing, some on the committee feared. William Mitchell, Charles Clark, and Edgar Tolman all appeared before the House and Senate judiciary committee hearings to allay some Congressmen's concerns about the new rules. The original sources are House Judiciary Committee, *Hearings on Rules of Civil Procedure*, 75th Cong. March 1-2, 1938; Senate Judiciary Committee, [Hearings on] *Rules of Civil Procedure for the U.S. District Courts*, April 18, 1938. The testimony is discussed in Burbank, "Rules Enabling Act" 1178 (acceptance in House was easy, but some Senators wanted more time to study the Rules). In fact, there was powerful interest groups that worried about the rules—particularly the labor unions. See House Hearings, 13-14, 21, 66; Senate Hearings, 24-25. The key issue was the injunction, so often used against labor union activity in federal courts and barred by the Norris LaGuardia Act of 1932. 47 U.S. Stats. 70 (1932); 29 U.S.C. secs 101-115. Labor union leaders and Congressmen who spoke for the unions were afraid that the Rules section on injunctions might be construed to allow return to the older practice. But the Committee had specifically provided in Rule 70 (e) that nothing in it might alter the provisions of Norris-LaGuardia with respect to "employer and employee."

48. Ralph Blumenthal and John Miller, eds., *The Gotti Tapes* (New York, 1992).

phering what the speakers wished to convey to each other.[49] Such messages in a setting like the Advisory Committee meeting are really quite complicated strings of signs and symbols, often stretching through more than one burst of words. The meaning of any single statement or exchange or dialogue must be understood in the context of exchanges of longer duration. The conversation over time—long periods of time—structures a discourse.

But how exactly do we render their words into our words? We might conclude that the process of translation is quite simple. The Advisory Committee members carried on their conversations in English. Would it not be sufficient to recover their shared body of experiences, reread the cases and rules that they cited to one another, and then summarize what they said? They certainly acted as though they understood the same things about those experiences. They might refer to cases in shorthand, but I can find the full text of the opinions and supply these. When they disagreed, as they often did, or asked for clarification, or talked right past each other, they still tried to communicate. Such slippage is common in all extemporaneous speech. A speaker may assume that his audience is familiar with his subject and understands his words as he does, but we know that "commonly a speaker cannot explicate with precision what he meant to get across, and on these occasions if hearers think they know precisely, they will likely be at least a little off. ("If speaker and hearer were to file a report on what they assumed to be the full meaning of an extended utterance, those glosses would differ, at least in detail.")[50] Nevertheless, historians are prepared to translate such texts, for "we are a professionally text-oriented people in a text-oriented society."[51]

The obvious dictionary for such a translation of the deliberations is the lexicon of highly formalized terms of art developed over many years in English and American courts and legislatures. Unfortunately, the meaning of these terms is not quite fixed with precision. The Committee spent hours arguing over the meaning of commonly used words like "motion" and "necessary party."[52] Such language is still susceptible of multiple meanings, and is regularly contested by bench and bar. Terms of art structure times and places of pleading, but do not translate themselves. Recognizing this, the framers of the Federal Rules added an appendix of forms to the text of the rules to aid the lawyers get the filing, pleading, and motions right.[53] Even were all the contested, variant definitions of

49. See, e.g., Joseph F. Graham, *Difference in Translation* (Ithaca, N.Y., 1985), 13-30.

50. Erving Goffman, *Forms of Talk* (Philadelphia, 1981), 10.

51. Inga Clendinnen, *Aztecs: An Interpretation* (Cambridge, 1991), 281.

52. See Federal Rules of Civil Procedure, Rule 7 note 1, *Report of the Advisory Committee on Rules for Civil Procedure* (Washington, D.C., April 1937), 21. In fact, the members of the Committee spent much of the afternoon of November 15, 1935 arguing about what was a pleading and what was a motion. See Transcript of the Deliberations of the Advisory Committee, Edgar Tolman copy, National Archives [hereafter Transcript], 331-357.

53. *Report of the Advisory Committee* (1937), Fed. R. Civ. P. 86 note 1.

terms of art included in this expanded dictionary of pleading, it would contain all the words and phrases a translator of the transcription would need. The conversation among the Committee men—the text of the deliberations—featured a far larger vocabulary than employed in the Rules of Civil Procedure itself.

These irreducible problems notwithstanding, a knowledgeable "insider"—say a professor of civil procedure today—might claim to be able to translate the language of the deliberations without much difficulty. Indeed, the insider as interpreter of legal texts is a familiar and trusted figure in modern juristic theory. Owen Fiss has argued that control of judicial discretion lies in the restraint of insiders' expectations.[54] James Boyd White agrees that the insider knows what and what not to say in the discourse that is law. "One of the central characteristics of law, then, is that it works on the principle of the separation of powers: each actor, private or public [including judges I presume] inhabits a world in which some issues, some questions, are reserved for him, at least in the first instance, while others are remitted to others. To live sensibly and effectively in this world requires respect for the choices made by others within their respective spheres of competence."[55] Alan Watson has traced the grip that these insiders have upon the elucidation of legal texts. Their interpretations become law, for their authority is "self-sustaining: a good jurist is one regarded as such by his fellow jurists; a good judge is one acknowledged as such by other judges and leaders of the bar. They establish this position by skill in applying a particular method of reasoning, which varies from place to place, to the legal issues. . . . Law develops on this basis, and is, to a considerable extent, autonomous from the society in which it operates."[56]

Fiss, White, and Watson remind us that there is a continuity to the texts of law that does not float in a world of Cartesian certainties or Platonic forms, but is imbedded in an ongoing discourse among legal scholars and jurists over time. A knowledgeable insider-translator would immediately recognize the shape of the discourse. In law school one learns to read, write and converse in a jargon rooted in long standing usages. Many of the basic concepts of contracts, property, torts, and other required law school subjects did not change much between 1935 and 1992. The structure of the first year's course work at Harvard Law School today is substantially the same, despite periodic curriculum review committees' recommendations, as it was in 1935—and 1900.[57]

---

54. Owen Fiss, "Objectivity and Interpretation" 34 *Stanford Law Review*, 739, (1982).

55. White, *Justice as Translation*, 96.

56. Alan Watson, *Joseph Story and the Comity of Errors: A Case Study in Conflict of Laws* (Athens, Ga., 1992), 77.

57. I have read all the Harvard Law School catalogues from 1900 to 1960 in the Red Set in the basement of Langdell Library and last year compared them to the one the Law School sent my son, Williamjames, when he applied for admission. It is striking how little has changed in the first-year curriculum.

The translator of old legal texts who is an insider thus may claim to tap into a fund of shared learning and writing reaching back to the early twentieth century. To be sure, the claim rests upon the assumption that this conceptual framework is diachronic as well as synchronic. The argument for synchronic ties is incontestable. At any one time, networks of law professors stretch out from the centers of legal study and from the bar to overlap, like many spider webs in a cavernous old barn.[58]

Are such networks diachronic as well? If they are not, the ability of the insider-translator to render the words of past generations of legal writers may be challenged. It is certainly true that in the past master networkers like Felix Frankfurter tried to help younger scholars begin their careers in teaching, government and practice, just as they had been helped by patron-mentors (in Frankfurter's case Henry L. Stimson, Roscoe Pound, Oliver Wendell Holmes Jr., and Louis Brandeis). Younger clients repaid their patron-mentors with information and loyal service. Insider-translators like Charles Alan Wright could claim Clark as patron.[59]

Most would-be insider translators, that is, most legal scholars who cite or quote in their work portions of the transcription of the deliberations—even those who are members of current synchronic networks (for example members of the current Advisory Committee)—cannot claim to be part of the diachronic network reaching back to Clark. Nevertheless, even these scholars act as though they are non-participant observers at the meetings of the Advisory Committee, omnisciently rendering the conversation into modern words.

I am not in sympathy with this form of translation. Its practitioners assume that behind the language of the members of the Committee are forms of pleading, veritable platonic entities, which do not change with time—words that are pale reflectors of the things to which they correspond. Such translations silently presume that words do not alter their meaning over time or place, or change in meaning from one individual to another. We must avoid assuming that a "hermeneutic community" speaks with one voice, clearly and truthfully. Such an "imperialistic hermeneutics"[60] is seductive in its promise of a definitive account, but the promise of such finality is invariably left unfulfilled.

Worse still, such translations de-contextualize historical occasions, producing the "graphireading" which supplants the voices of real historical actors with the omniscience of the scholar. The resulting account is almost invariably presentist, using bits of the historical record to support a criticism or reform proposal of the author. The historian cannot accept such readings of texts—we demand context.

58. See Hull, "Networks and *Bricolage*," 307-322.

59. See *Felix Frankfurter Reminisces* (New York, 1960), 41-49, 105-112, 165-177, 235-250, 263-269; Charles Alan Wright, "Charles E. Clark and the *Spector* Case" in Petrack, ed., *Clark*, 193-198.

60. Susan Mann, "The Universe and the Library: A Critique of James Boyd White as Writer and Reader" 41 *Stanford Law Review* 959, 960 (1989).

CONTEXT

The smallest circumference of context is what John Henry Schlegel has recently termed a "hermeneutic circle."[61] This is a metaphor of course, but it is a strong one. The circle is drawn around a group of people who share the same intellectual outlook and experience. Such magic circles have always captivated western minds and law schools are in many ways the inheritors of the agon—the contested circle of the Ancient Greeks. The law schools are continual testing grounds, with formal rules for victory and defeat. The keepers of the magic are the law faculties, and leading lights in these at a school like Yale or Harvard carry on extended conversations with each other about internal matters of law, theory, and pedagogy.

At critical moments—particularly the selection of deans and the tenuring and appointment of faculty—circles of allies and enemies converge and overlap to debate those rules. Leading practitioners enter the circle throughout their careers; first as students, later as patrons or even part-time teachers. One such circle, Schlegel suggests, engirded the legal realists at Yale in the 1930s. Clark, a superb networker, extended this circle by recruiting leading younger scholars to Yale,[62] regularly attending meetings of the American Association of Law Schools in Chicago,[63] and even recommending a number of those in his extended circle—Armistead Dobie of the University of Virginia, Edmund M. Morgan of Harvard Law School, and Sunderland—for places on the Advisory Committee.[64]

Despite the utility and elegance of Schlegel's metaphor, it only begins our study of context, for not all the members of the Committee were Clark's cronies. With some he had crossed swords. Others were acquaintances. For some, like Edgar Tolman, Clark had barely concealed contempt.[65] At the same time, the members of the Advisory Committee knew each other. In effect, there was a larger, concentric circle beyond Schlegel's hermeneutic orbit, enclosing a broader segment of the elite legal community within which the members moved. They had served together on government commissions, boards of private institutions, and professional committees, and worked sided by side on the American Law Institute and on the Association of American Law Schools' projects. Some had held official positions in government and still advised judges, legislators, and presidents. All had ties to powerful political and economic interests, but they were not named to the Committee to represent these interests.

All the members were chosen on the basis of professional connections and achievements by Chief Justice Charles Evans Hughes. There

61. John Henry Schlegel, "The Ten Thousand Dollar Question," 460.

62. Kalman, *Legal Realism at Yale, 1927-1960* (Chapel Hill, 1986), 115-144.

63. Elias Clark, "Memories," 162.

64. Clark to Edgar Tolman, January 4, 1935, Clark Papers, folder 39, box 108.

65. Subrin, "Clark and his Procedural Outlook," 122.

was little overt attempt to represent powerful economic or political interests outside of the legal profession despite the force these interests exerted in New Deal policy making.[66] In effect, Hughes regarded adjective law as the autonomous domain of the elite of the bar and the academy, subject to the supervision of the Court, and selected men whose prior service in government, legal education, and legal practice made them obvious candidates.[67]

George Wickersham, the senior member of the Committee in age and public prestige, was a former attorney general under President William Howard Taft and led one of New York City's leading corporate law firms. He was also the serving president of the American Law Institute and had recently stepped down as chairman of the National Commission on Law Observance and Enforcement.[68] He represented a professional group within the legal world—the corporate bar—and he vocally advocated what he took to be the requirements of New York lawyers unused to the new Rules. Scott Loftin was current president of the ABA.[69] Edgar Tolman was secretary of the ABA, editor of its Journal, and represented the Department of Justice (that is, the government's lawyers).[70] Armistead Dobie of the University of Virginia Law School was the author of the foremost casebook on federal jurisdiction.[71] Charles Clark was the author of the standard treatise on code pleading and dean at Yale. Edson Sunderland of the University of Michigan Law School was an acknowledged expert on discovery and summary pleading.[72]

The context of the deliberations cannot however be confined within a circle of legal practitioners and academics. Any adequate contextualization of the words of the members of the Committee must account for the outside pressures on the Committee, for these pressures shaped the outermost circle within which the framers of the Rules operated. The Committee met in troubled times for lawyers and lawmakers. At home, the Great Depression called into question the wisdom of the corporate bar.

---

66. The interests of the majority came to Washington, D.C. encoded in farmers' lobbies and union lobbies. New Deal policy mobilized and empowered such interest groups. Alan Dawley, *Struggles for Justice, Social Responsibility and the Liberal State* (Cambridge, Mass., 1991), 371-408.

67. Charles Evans Hughes to Harlan Fiske Stone, copy in Charles Clark Papers, folder 41, box 108. On Hughes' view of the Court and the law, see Samuel Hendel, *Charles Evans Hughes and the Supreme Court* (New York, 1950), 91-136, and Merlo J. Pusey, *Charles Evans Hughes* (New York, 1951), 2:683-748.

68. On Wickersham, see 20 *A.B.A.J.*, 624-625 (1934); *New York Times*, Jan 26, 1936; *DAB* (2nd supp), 713-715; *Minutes in Remembrance*, 19-22. The NCLOE was colloquially referred to as the Wickersham Commission. See *Wickersham Commission Reports* (Wash, D.C. 1931), of which there were 14.

69. 20 *A.B.A.J.* 610 (1934); 39 *A.B.A.J.* 982-983 (1953).

70. 7 *A.B.A.J.* 3 (1921); 25 *A.B.A.J.* 700-702 (1939); 33 *A.B.A.J.* 1188 (1947).

71. *New York Times* August 8, 1962, p. 32. Dobie's volume was *Handbook of Federal Jurisdiction and Procedure* (St. Paul, Minn., 1928).

72. Brown, *Legal Education at Michigan, 1859-1959*, 338-339.

Asked about the causes of the depression, John W. Davis, a leader of that bar, admitted that he had no clue.[73] Conservative lawyers accused the new Deal of undermining the Constitution.[74] Young law professors rushed to Washington, D.C. to save the country from itself, and manned the levers and switches of the new regulatory machinery. Often, they found that their adversaries were lawyers representing corporations, insurance companies, and banks.[75]

The Advisory Committee knew that powerful interest groups watched the Committee to insure that legal benefits they had obtained through statutes and Supreme Court rulings would not be diluted. Insurance companies were frightened that new provisions for discovery would lead to damaging fishing expeditions through company files.[76] Labor union leaders and their lawyers were expected to object that rules on injunctions would take back what the unions had won at great cost in the Norris-LaGuardia Act.[77] Government lawyers protested through Tolman that the United States as plaintiff or defendant should not be held to the Rules designed for private litigants.[78]

The Committee responded to these pressures by informing important segments of the legal community about the progress of the Rules. The typescript of the verbatim deliberations was circulated to all the members and the substance of the deliberations was shared in both informal and formal ways with other members of the legal community.[79] All drafts of the Rules, starting with the preliminary typescript draft prepared by Clark and his aides for the November 1935 meeting, were circulated to bench and bar in the federal districts. The second draft and the third draft of the Rules were printed and widely distributed "for the purpose of inviting suggestions and criticisms."[80] The comments of various bar associations, prominent practitioners and leading judges were not only read by members of the Committee, but were referred to and quoted in the course of their deliberations. The deliberations became the basis for a series of footnotes in the latter drafts, on occasion expressing the dissent of one or another of the members of the Committee.

---

73. Davis quoted in Arthur M. Schlesinger, Jr., *The Age of Roosevelt, Volume I: The Crisis of the Old Order* (Cambridge, Mass., 1957), 4-5.

74. Michael Kammen, *A Machine That Would Go of Itself* (New York, 1986), 269-279.

75. See, e.g., William O. Douglas, *Go East Young Man: The Early Years: The Autobiography of William O. Douglas* (New York, 1974), 257-376; Laura Kalman, *Abe Fortas: A Biography* (New Haven, 1990), 65-101; Peter Irons, *The New Deal Lawyers* (Princeton, 1982), *passim*.

76. Clark to Jerome Frank, December 14, 1944, Clark Papers, folder 321, box 63.

77. Transcript, November 20, 1935, 2215, 2216, 2218, 2221, 2223, February 25, 1936, 1415, 1419.

78. Advisory Committee Memo, January 30, 1937, Clark Papers, box 106.

79. William Mitchell, June 20, 1935, Transcript, 2-9 (describing plans for the dissemination of the drafts and the comments to bench and bar in the federal judicial districts).

80. *Report of the Advisory Committee* (1937), i.

Clark himself lobbied judges and law professors for support.[81] In turn, other law professors, leading members of the bar, and judges made their interest known to the Committee.[82] Foremost among these observers were the members of the Supreme Court. Throughout its lifespan, the Committee worked for and reported to the Supreme Court. The Court had named the Committee and the Committee reported to the Court. When the Committee reported, it included notes for the Court's information in addition to citations of relevant statutes and earlier rules.[83] Individual members of the Court supported individual members of the Committee and discussed their progress with them. Chief Justice Hughes was a strong supporter,[84] but one member of the Court, Justice Louis Brandeis, carried on a quiet campaign against the Rules and in the end refused to agree to them.[85]

After the third draft of the Rules was approved by the High Court with minor modifications and both houses of Congress decided not to interpose objections, Clark, Mitchell, and other members of the Committee met with practitioners in special conferences in Washington, D.C., New York City, and elsewhere to explain the new rules.[86] Close reading of the speeches and answers of these members of the Committee indicates that they had rehearsed for these conferences over the two years of Committee deliberations. That is, the exchanges within the Committee prepared Clark and Mitchell to pitch the new rules to the legal community.

---

81. Actually, Clark began his campaign, characteristically, before the Committee even met. See, e.g., Clark to [leading judges and law professors], February 1, 1935, Clark Papers, folder 40, box 108 (seeking support for complete merger of law and equity and enclosing a copy of his January 1935 *Yale Law Journal* article with James William Moore). Clark continued to promote the project in a series of reports in the *American Bar Association Journal* (22 *A.B.A.J.* 447 [1936], 22 *A.B.A.J.* 787 [1936], and 23 *A.B.A.J.* 976 [1937]).

82. See, e.g., John Henry Wigmore to Clark, January 1, 1936, Clark Papers, folder 45, box 109 (Wigmore complaining about the evidence provisions of the new Rules).

83. Supreme Court, October 1934 Term (June 3, 1935) (named committee and laid out rules for reports of its drafts to the Supreme Court) printed in *Report of the Advisory Committee* (1937), iii-iv.

84. Charles Evans Hughes, "Address to the American Law Institute" *The American Law Institute Proceedings* (Philadelphia, 1935) 12: 54-60; Hughes to Attorney General Homer Cummings, December 20, 1937, Swisher, ed., *Selected Papers of Homer Cummings*, 192. For more, see Subrin, "Clark and his Procedural Outlook."

85. Louis Brandeis to Felix Frankfurter, December 28, 1937: "As you know doubtless, our Court will send (or has) to the A.G. 'The Rules of Civil Procedure' adopted pursuant to Act of July 19, 1934, ch. 651. I asked the C.J. to advise A.G. that I do not approve of their adoption. I am sure several others feel as I do, but thought they must be silent as the Court was committed. Will anything be done in Congress to prevent them becoming operative?" Melvin I. Urofsky and David W. Levy, eds., *'Half Brother, Half Son': The Letters of Louis D. Brandeis to Felix Frankfurter* (Norman, Okla., 1991), 606.

86. See, *Rules of Civil Procedure* House Judiciary Committee Hearings, 75th Cong. March 1, 1938; *Federal Rules of Civil Procedure, Proceedings of the Institute At Washington D.C., October 6, 7, 8, 1938, and of the Symposium at New York City , October 17, 18, 19, 1938*, ed. Edward H. Hammond (Chicago, 1939), 39-79.

Within the Committee, individual members gave different weight to the various segments of this audience. Clark continued to seek aid from legal academics.[87] Robert Dodge, of Boston, George Donworth of Seattle, Monte Lemann of New Orleans, Wickersham, and Warren Olney of San Francisco, all practitioners, continued to worry how their peers would receive specific rule changes. When a new rule diverged from established practice, one or another of these men protested explicitly on the grounds of expected resistance from the practitioners. For example, in the discussions on the initial version of what is now Rule 11 (signing of pleadings, motions, and other papers, sanctions)—Rule 20 in Clark's October 1935 first draft of the Rules—Donworth and others were worried that sanctions for signing arguable pleadings were too harsh on working lawyers. Donworth remarked: "There is one thought in this connection; it is going to be hard on the lawyer, and I think on his conscience. When you find these things in your complaint and go over things you find certain things that are true and you find certain things that you can safely deny. Then there is a middle ground, where you say, 'That is dangerous ground'; we do not know; we are not sure that is so. Let them prove that. Now, if you deny that, the lawyer must certify in effect that he believes the allegations false, and some of the may be true. . . . I do not see how lawyers can get along without denying things in the doubtful ground, although they may be true."[88]

In the process of trying to predict and then explain outside response to their efforts, members of the Committee fell back upon the division between academics and practitioners. Wickersham, Dodge, Olney, Donworth, and Lemann began to divide up the Committee into the working lawyers and the "law school men." Loftin, who rarely spoke, nevertheless insisted that the Committee approach its work "from the lawyer's standpoint."[89] This was somewhat unfair—Clark, Morgan and the other law professors had all practiced law—but Clark had to fend off implications that he and Sunderland, Morgan, Dobie, and Wilbur Cherry, Dean of the University of Minnesota Law School, were dreamers and perfectionists, out of touch with real world of practice. Dobie protested and Clark squirmed.[90] Wickersham had a point, not because of the vast difference in

87. See, *e.g.*, Charles Clark to Zechariah Chafee, Jr., November 9, 1935, Clark Papers, folder 42, box 108 (mollifying Chafee, who thought that the merger of law and equity in the Rules would doom equity courses like those he taught at Harvard Law School).

88. George Donworth, November 15, 1935, Transcript, 403-404. On the later fate of Rule 11, see Burbank, "The Example of Rule 11."

89. Scott Loftin, November 14, 1935, Transcript, 245.

90. At the very first meeting of the Committee, Dobie pleaded: "being a law school man myself, and not imposing too much confidence in the law school men, I think it would be extremely unfortunate if in any way it gets out to the Bar of the United States that this is a law school project . . . ." Dobie, June 20, 1935, Transcript, 29. Later, Clark, backed to the wall by Loftin and Wickersham's recitation of their experience, retorted, "When I was in practice I remember one case where the judge held up the decision for over a year." November 14, 1935, Transcript, 250. Clark had practiced in New Haven for almost seven years, but preferred to cite law review pieces and his own treatise on code pleading.

the experience of the members, but because Clark and his allies wanted the approbation of other law professors more than did Wickersham and his cohorts.

The discovery of circles of "legal context" demonstrates the weakness of the claims of insider-translators, but has its own inherent flaw. Just as the insider's translation is centripetal, collapsing the story into the dense formality of the framers' technical concerns, contextualization is centrifugal, flying off into the void.

We need to think one more time about how to fully and faithfully tell the story embedded in a long, rich and complex document. Since the arrival on our shores of the deconstructionist movement, prioritizing the text, many historians have become much more sensitive to the distinctness of their sources.[91] One immediate result has been leading historians' frank avowal of the problems posed by their sources. Unlike the deconstructionist, the historian wants to return to the voices that the text imperfectly records. The historian wants to hear and see; reading text is a means to that end.

In the past decade, four prize-winning historians have tackled the problem of full decoding of hitherto intractable long primary sources, and their achievement suggests the inadequacy of a simple translation *cum* context approach. In *Voyages to the West*, Bernard Bailyn unravels the many meanings of an emigration Register—a comprehensive record of persons who left British ports for the North American colonies between December 1773 and the Spring of 1776. Bailyn's Register has a history of its own, a history that gave it shape and made it so useful to later scholars. By the end of 1773, with justification, British authorities were afraid that emigration would soon depopulate the British Isles. Treasury officials instructed customs collectors to compile lists by asking emigrants about their age, origin, occupation, gender, status, and destination. "The result is a documentary collection that illuminates as does no other source, literary or statistical, essential characteristics of the most mobile elements in British society; the process by which British North America was peopled in the years before the Revolution; and a major segment of the immigrant population in pre-revolutionary America."[92]

Bailyn was not the first to use the document, but he was the first to make it the focus of an extended account. He recognized the weakness of the Register as a source: "The British Register of Emigration is thus far from a perfect statistical source. It was produced in a pre-statistical age to provide a general indication of what kinds of people were emigrating from the British Isles, why they were leaving, and where they were going. Though many of the listings can be proved to be generally accurate, the

91. John H. Towes, "Intellectual History After the Linguistic Turn" *American Historical Review* 92 (1987), 879-907; David Harlan, "Intellectual History and the Return of Literature" *American Historical Review* 94 (1989), 581-609.

92. Bernard Bailyn, *Voyagers to the West: A Passage in the Peopling of America on the Eve of the Revolution* (New York, 1986), 69-70.

Register as a whole was not compiled according to modern information-gathering methods. The quantities that can be derived from it can only be the product of many decisions of classification and interpretation made by the analyst, some of them invariably arbitrary, which are buried in the solid-seeming tables that result [here]. They provide not rigorously precise information, but windows, insights, into the past, when used in some sensible conjunction with non-quantitative historical sources."[93] Bailyn then subjects the list to detailed quantitative analysis: grouping, regrouping, and describing. He makes the list speak; we can hear the questions that the customs officials asked and the answers that the passengers gave.[94]

Laurel Thatcher Ulrich's prize winning *A Midwife's Tale, The Life of Martha Ballard, Based on her Diary, 1785-1812* transforms a slender and terse diary of midwife, mother, and businesswoman Martha Ballard into a source for the entire range of women's activities in early modern New England. "The structure of the diary forces us to consider midwifery in the broadest possible context, as one specialty in a larger neighborhood economy, as the most visible feature of a comprehensive and little known system of early health care, as a mechanism of social control, a strategy for family support, and a deeply personal calling. One might wish for more detail, for more open expressions of opinion, fuller accounts of medical remedies or obstetrical complications, more candor in describing physicians or judges, and less circumspection in recording scandal, yet for all its reticence, Martha's diary is an unparalleled document in early American history. It is powerful in part because it is so difficult to use, so unyielding in its dailiness."[95] From the diary, Ulrich magnifies the echoes of a world in which women bonded through work and family; reached out to the world of their menfolks and within to the worlds of their children.

In his magnificent recreation of the sounds and sights of the eighteenth-century Virginia countryside, Rhys Isaac seeks the contextualized translation: "translation is the fundamental task of ethnographers, and in its inherent perplexities lies their greatest challenge. . . . Through a process of elucidating [historical] contexts, structures and meanings, we can learn to reconstruct something of the participants' worlds as they experienced them."[96] The relative size and perspective of house, church, and public building, the idioms of common speech and common commerce, the dramas of religion and court day, these come alive because Isaac makes us see and hear the words.

Inga Clendinnen is less comfortable with her central primary source than Bailyn, Thatcher, and Isaac, but she strives for the same goal: to make us see and hear what survives only in bare written form. In her

93. Ibid., 83-84.

94. Ibid., 89-239.

95. Laurel Thacher Ulrich, *A Midwife's Tale, The Life of Martha Ballard, Based on Her Diary, 1785-1812* (New York, 1990), 33.

96. Rhys Isaac, *The Transformation of Virginia, 1740-1790* (Chapel Hill, 1982), 324-325.

account of the Mexica (Aztec) before Tenochtitlan was conquered by the Spanish, she was dependent upon the Franciscan Missionary Bernardino de Sáhàgun's *General History of the Things of New Spain*. Between his arrival in 1529 and his completion of the volumes in 1568, the missionary worked closely with surviving Mexica elders. His scribes wrote in Nahuatl, the native tongue of the Mexica, and he later added a Spanish commentary. The books, names the "Florentine Codex" for their eventual home, "remain the major source for Mexica life in the decades before the conquest. With all its defects—produced by survivors of the erstwhile ruling group; exclusively male; further distanced from the actuality we seek to glimpse by its idealizing tendency and its Spanish eliciting and editing; abducted into English [that Clendinnen used] it is nonetheless the best source we have for Mexica views, and for accounts of Mexica actions as described by Mexica voices."[97]

From the *General History* and other sources, Clendinnen set out to "discover how ordinary people understood 'human sacrifice: their inescapable intimacy with victims' bodies, living and dead, how that intimacy was rendered tolerable; what meanings were attached to it. . . . My interest is . . . in sensibility; the emotional, moral, and aesthetic nexus through which thought comes to be expressed in action, and so made public, visible, and accessible to our observation."[98] The Florentine Codex does not address emotions and sensibilities, but it does give full descriptions of rituals. Clendinnen assumes that because the elders who were Sáhàgun's sources emphasized ritual, ritual must have been a key event in the life of the Mexica. Ritual was "for the Mexica a highly elastic and dynamic expressive mode, more street theatre than museum piece. A great warrior sedately turns in the dance, the detail of his military biography inscribed in his glittering insignia; his wealth, his prestige and his power manifested in the respectful space left around him."[99] Ritual captured and expressed the social distance between groups and genders, between Mexica and their neighbors. Ritual bound god and human into complex wholes. Ritual dramatized tension and gave release from it.

In ritual Clendinnen has found the key to language. That is, she decides that the words have meaning not in themselves, but in the actions that they portray. From mere words Clendinnen tries to retrieve what people saw and did. Her reconstruction is highly imaginative, filled with psychological stops and starts. True, her recreations are only as potent as her own words. *Aztecs*, a book filled with colorful images of birds, fruits, and animals, or richly costumed and intricately choreographed dances, of feigned and deadly combats, of the visual spaces that set off people's lives and gave those lives meaning, has no pictures. The Mexica not only decorated their murals with pictures; every design was filled with meaning. Costume was richly patterned because each pattern told a story. Hemmed

97. Clendinnen, *Aztecs*, 279.

98. Ibid., 4-5.

99. Ibid.

in by mountains, living on a city on a lake, the Mexica created a culture of vivid hues. If Clendinnen's prose, poetic, richly hued, does justice to the ritual and the color of the Mexica, it is because she persuades us, not because she has brought the past to life. The Mexica have inspired her and she has gripped our imaginations.

CONVERSATION

Bailyn, Thatcher, Isaac, and Clendinnen bid the historian make leaps of imagination—not back into the past, but from past sources into the present. Their example empowers us to make sense of our transcription by regarding texts as exchanges of words and signs within cultural structures. The exchange of legal signs and symbols, whether in the courtroom[100] or the conference room of the Supreme Court[101] is activity. As Rhys Isaac has said of such text, "we must run it through the talking-picture projector of the mind."[102]

The conversion of conversation to action was pioneered by Kenneth Burke, when he promoted the idea that "spontaneous speech is not a naming [of objects independent of the speaker] at all, but a system of attitudes, or implicit exhortations. . . . These emotional and moral weightings inherent in spontaneous speech tend to reinforce the act itself, hence making the communicative and active aspects of speech identical. Such speech is profoundly *partisan* [author's italics]."[104] Any translation of the Advisory Committee transcript will be inadequate if it regards the deliberations as the mere exchange of ideas, instead of a study in group dynamics.

The efforts of the Advisory Committee have appeared opaque and lifeless to historians because we have focused upon the terse and technical published drafts, instead of the conversation of the men who crafted those rules. There we will find the human drama of lawmaking. We can easily visualize the activity leading up to the meeting—the members alighting from their trains at Union Station in the chill of early Autumn, and walking briskly downhill along Second Street to the new Supreme Court building, and then finding their way to the conference room, the hearty greetings, the flurry of motion as briefcases landed on the long table, the scrapping of chairs and the rustling of papers.

100. For example, see Peter Charles Hoffer, *Law and People in Colonial America* (Baltimore, 1992), 2-3 (visualizing the royal courts at Westminster on the eve of colonization of the New World).

101. G. Edward White, *History of the Supreme Court, Volumes III-IV: The Marshall Court and Cultural Change, 1815-1835* (New York, 1988), 157-200 (description of the court's meeting places and everyday travails), and Mark Tushnet and Katya Lezin, "What Really Happened in *Brown v. Board of Education*" 91 *Columbia Law Review* 1867 (1991) (the use of sources in understanding how Supreme Court justices reached their decision).

102. Isaac, *Transformation*, 337.

103. Kenneth Burke, *Permanence and Change* ([1935] 2nd rev. ed. Indianapolis, 1954), 177.

104. Donoghue, *Ferocious Alphabets*, 101.

The conversation is a continuation of this study in movement. The order of speech, the swift riposte and earnest entreaty, the punctuated bursts of conversation, the solemn reading of pieces of the draft, are actions. The members of the Committee interacted in words and gestures and silences that were pregnant with meaning. Their words and sentences are part of this pattern of action, not disembodied symbols floating in the ether of pure legal discourse. To decode the transcription, we must be "epireaders" of their conversation, "transposing the written words on the page into a somehow corresponding human situation of persons, voices, characters, conflicts, conciliations."[105] The epireader "moves swiftly from print and language to speech and voice and the absent person. Prolific in narrative, the epireader construes reading as translation. . . . And the use of words may be translated into corresponding acts and gestures . . . "[105]

We can begin to translate words into actions—to see and hear the conversation of the Committee members—by bearing in mind the following five general guidelines. First, conversation in the Committee was relational.[106] There was no absolute meaning to words apart from the relationship between the speaker and the audience.[107] "When a word is spoken, all those who happen to be in perceptual range of the event will have some sort of participation status relative to it. The codification of these various positions and the normative specification of appropriate conduct within each provide an essential background for interaction analysis ...."[108] Meaning depended upon who spoke to whom. The personalities of the speaker and the listener; their relative status; and their past shared experiences all gave meaning to their exchanges. Meaning also depended upon spatial relations; what speaker and audience saw. The social distance between the performers is no more important than the real space in which they performed.

We see the importance of relationships in the Wickersham-Clark exchanges that dominated the first two sittings of the Committee, in June and November 1935. Fresh from his chairmanship of the National Commission on Law Enforcement (called the Wickersham Commission in the press), Wickersham expected to dominate the group. His seniority and experience at the bar and in government certainly entitled him to respect in that setting, but Clark had already tangled with Wickersham over Clark's report on the business of the Federal Courts.[109] Clark also

105. Ibid., 146-147.

106. Synchronic, cross-sectional, spatially referenced.

107. I do not wish to be mistaken for a defender of the "no audience, no text" theories of literary criticism. There is a text without an audience. The meaning of the text, however, is not transparent on its face. Audience reactions give meaning; so does authorial intent. The historian has to be aware of both of these processes because the historian adds to them: the historian is also an author and an audience. We do not read text for itself; we read to engage the author.

108. Goffman, *Forms of Talk*, 3

109. In 1930, Clark had lobbied the ALI, of which Wickersham was president, and the Wickersham Commission to prepare a detailed summary of the civil and criminal business

discovered that Wickersham did not want wholesale revisions of the rules. At the second working meeting of the Committee, on November 14, 1935, Wickersham expressed doubts about the value of merging law and equity,[110] Clark's guiding principle. Wickersham preferred the New York Rules and fact pleading.

At first, Clark let Mitchell, whose public status was nearly equal to Wickersham's, handle the conflict. Mitchell deferred to Wickersham's age and experience, and mollified the older man by recasting the idea of merger as one growing out of the Field Code. Mitchell insisted that Clark's efforts were nothing more than an attempt to fully realize Field's ideal, and how could Wickersham, who defended New York's Procedure Revisions, object to such a plan. Wickersham conceded (for in fact he had little choice, given that Chief Justice Hughes had already come out for full merger).

What did Wickersham, in his eighties, tired (he would die in February 1936), badgered, see across the table? Clark was impressive visually as well as intellectually. A shade under six feet tall, thick shouldered, with a large head, full features and a wide mouth, he could dominate a conversation by his presence alone. His " bullfrog smile" and resonant voice conveyed the immense energy of the man. His workaholic habits and strict moral standards were already well known and his ernest manner was almost intimidating.[111] Sitting across a conference table from Clark must have been a real treat, particularly if he had decided you were wrong about something he wrote or said.

Second, conversation in these face to face conferences was situational.[112] The retorts and statements and stories were situated in time. Their meaning depended upon what was said before. Almost always a statement was composed as an answer. Without knowing the previous situation, a reader might wholly mistake the latent content of any comment. Often, even after the chairman, Mitchell, moved the group on to its next topic, individual members went back to bits and pieces of the draft rules already

---

of the federal courts. Both organizations agreed to fund such a study. The latter, once underway, proved that the enforcement of prohibition was dominating federal trial court dockets. Wickersham's Commission had already determined that national enforcement of prohibition was not working, but opined that enforcement ought to continue. Thus Clark's findings were a direct embarrassment to Wickersham. Wickersham could not suppress Clark's project, but he did pressure Clark to omit any analysis of the data that called the Wickersham Commission report into question. Clark resented the intrusion and Wickersham was annoyed by Clark's aggressiveness. See Hoffer, "Review of Peninah Petrack, ed., *Judge Charles Edward Clark*" forthcoming Cardozo *Law Review*.

110. November 14, 1935, Transcript, 54 et seq. In notice pleading, plaintiff's complaint merely informs defendant of the general nature of the claim, not the ultimate facts on which plaintiff will rely. See Clark, "Ancient Writs and Modern Causes of Action" 34 *Yale Law Journal* 879 (1924).

111. See, e.g., the discussion of Clark in Kalman, *Legal Realism at Yale, 1927-1960*, 115-144.

112. Sequential, diachronic, longitudinal, chronologically contexted.

discussed to pick up threads of the prior discussion. The discussion thus circled upon itself.

Situational sequences might stretch back for months or years. Clark's running battle with New York procedure influenced directly much of his confrontation with Wickersham. Wickersham had to be aware of Clark's articles and the feeling of the New York City bar about Clark. Thus the exchanges between the two men were situated in a much larger context of Clark's long standing and much publicized animus for New York lawyers and their forms of action.

A second set of communications stretched back in time, crossed over the boundaries of the academic/practitioner gulf, and held the Committee together. Over the course of the year before the Committee first met, Clark had forged a personal bond with Mitchell. Clark had built the foundations of this relationship soon after Mitchell was named Chairman of the Committee. In a series of letters to Mitchell, Clark had intrigued to get himself named Reporter instead of Sunderland, in the process seeding Mitchell's mind with the principles Clark wanted the Rules to effectuate. Mitchell did not always grasp the point, but Clark's patient tutoring eventually paid dividends. Mitchell supported Clark for the post of Reporter and thereafter worked closely with Clark on the project. Clark had become, in one way, the older Mitchell's protege, in another way Mitchell's teacher. During the deliberations, Mitchell often asked Clark directly what the reason for or consequences of a new rule might be. Clark would patiently explain. Mitchell would then thank Clark, and use the carefully structured exchange to build consensus, while Clark sat quietly.[113]

Third, conversation of this type was dramaturgic, almost scripted in its twists and turns. Personal confrontations were lightened by moments of teasing and expressions of mutual respect. There were personal statements, like George Donworth's soliloquies in praise of the hardworking lawyer and Mitchell's pleas for thoroughgoing reform while the opportunity was there. Clark's contributions were as calculated as his tone. Sometimes he was self-effacing, pleading with the Committee to instruct him and his staff, and on other occasions he bullied other members into silence. If we were to conceptualize the deliberations as ensemble acting and each contribution as performance: then "Neatly bounded interchanges are produced, well formed to prevent at least one of the participants from establishing a tenable position."[114]

In one sense, Clark was the playwright of this talky drama, for the drafts of the Rules he and Sunderland and their staff prepared were plot

113. For example, early in the deliberations Lemann, Dodge, and others questioned the full merger of law and equity; Mitchell stepped in, Clark abased himself, and Mitchell reminded the lawyers that Clark had merely adopted the language, and the pure motives, of the Field Code. Wickersham, persuaded, defended the Reporter. Opposition subsided. See November 14, 1935, Transcript, 54-61.

114. Goffman, *Talk*, 27.

outlines for the deliberations. Their first draft, with its novel provisions for joinder, discovery, and summary judgment, was destined to provoke dramatic confrontations. When the group turned to Sunderland's proposals on discovery, for example, Clark welcomed Sunderland "to the arena" and Sunderland admitted ruefully, "If the Reporter [Clark] thinks that he has had trouble about these rules, he does not know anything about it."[115] In fact, Clark had given the assignment to Sunderland only in part to acknowledge the latter's expertise. Clark was also manipulating Sunderland, rewarding him with the right hand for bumping him out in the competition to be the Reporter of the Rules with the left, thus scripting even this scene in the drama.[116]

Clark was an experienced plotter of group scenarios. As dean at Yale Law School, he presided over one of the most intellectually alive—even raucous—faculties of law ever assembled. At his faculty meetings (and his table at Yale Commons) in the early 1930s were Thurman Arnold, William O. Douglas, and others equally brilliant, petulant, and whimsical.[117]

There was comic relief in the script as well, for example moments in the deliberations when it appeared than more than one of the members of the Committee did not understand what their comrades had said. Wickersham toyed with a running joke about the "cause of action"—a term that Clark despised and Wickersham preferred. The discussion would then stop, recoil, switch back upon itself, sometimes retracting its steps, as individuals played with each other's words. The Committee had before it both Clark's *Code Pleading* and Dobie's *Federal Jurisdiction*, and late in the afternoon of the 16th of November, 1935, the Committee members began to trade quotes from the books. Clark had his own words cited against one of his positions, and quipped "what page?" to general laughter.[118] Such respectful bantering relieved tension and created bonds within the Committee.

115. November 17, 1935, Transcript, 1000.

116. In May, 1935, Mitchell was still trying to decide whether Clark or Sunderland should be Reporter. Clark did not let his opportunity slip away, but undermined Sunderland's views to Mitchell. When Mitchell agreed that Clark ought to have the job, Clark wrote to Sunderland and offered him the task of preparing the rules on discovery, just as dear to Sunderland as merger of law and equity was to Clark. Sunderland asked to prepare the rules for summary judgment, and Clark sweetened the pot with that concession—and $125 per week or $500 per month—to Sunderland. Thereafter, Sunderland supported Clark consistently. See Clark to Mitchell, May 11, 1935; Mitchell to Clark, May 16, 1935; Sunderland to Clark, May 22, 1935; Clark to Sunderland, May 25, 1935; Mitchell to Clark, May 22, 1935; Clark to Mitchell, May 23, 1935; Mitchell to Sunderland, May 23, 1935; Clark to Mitchell, May 25, 1935; Clark to Sunderland, June 22, 1935; Sunderland to Clark, June 25, 1935; Clark to Sunderland, June 28, 1935. Clark Papers, folders 40, 41, 42, box 108.

117. On Clark as dean, see Kalman, *Legal Realism at Yale, 1927-1960*, 115-154. Arnold's version is given in *Fair Fights and Foul. A Dissenting Lawyer's Life* (New York, 1965), 63-68. Douglas chips in his recollections in *Go East Young Man*, 170-172.

118. November 16, 1935, Transcript, 741a.

Fourth, the conversation was filled with silences. Every face to face conversation is a mixture of sounds and silences, like electricity, electrons flowing in one direction, holes in the other. "We have, for example, a special way of knotting up the face to convey the fact that we do not understand what it is a speaker seems to be trying to convey, and that a rerun is in order. And gestures obviously can also be freighted with ritual significance."[119] The Committee members' gestures are now lost. What is more, the stenographers gave us a concordance. The ums and uhs were not recorded. There is no indication of lapse of time between speakers, of hesitations or moments of common silence.

The pattern of silences in speech, what is left out, nevertheless can be as important as what is actually said. Are the silences in any given discussion the result of lack of prescience or because everyone silently understood the unenunciated points? Was the missing text—the text we expected to read and do not find—reserved for later inclusion by speakers or conveyed by some other means, a gesture perhaps. Typically, votes on contested issues ended up unanimous. This too is part of a pattern of silences. Opponents of the particular phrasing of a passage in a draft made their opposition known, lobbied for a small change, announced that they were satisfied with it, or simply said nothing further, and then acquiesced in the final formulation by voting for it.

Law is inherently wordy and the Advisory Committee was a wordy group. The tradition of great legal addresses to juries remained strong in the conference room, as did the newer but equally powerful model of law school lecturing. Nevertheless, the pattern of alternating silence and speech, or overlapping speech, is important, because it established relationships. The stenographers used the word "interposing" in parentheses to indicate when one member of the committee interrupted another. (This choice of word itself indicates the attitude of the stenographers toward the speakers—one of deference. Members of the advisory Committee did not interrupt--they interposed.) Certain members interposed quite often—Morgan, for example—and thereby put the impress of their personality upon the deliberations. He was often the last person to speak on an issue; quipped or spoke ironically, and was greeted with friendly laughter (so the transcription says). In effect, he had the last word. I am sure that Morgan's style of "interposition," part realist and part cynic, altered the meaning of what he said and its effect upon the group, at the same time as it gave a structure to the discussion of this or that particular.[120]

119. Goffman, *Talk*, 36.

120. There is one silence in the record which was palpable. It was contrived by the Committee itself when it (I cannot tell who) instructed the stenographer to stop recording a brief exchange between Wickersham and Dobie over contempt citations for witnesses or parties who refused to answer material questions during oral depositions. The exchange had become personal and bitter when the stenographer was told not to reproduce the rest of it in the transcript. The transcript proceeds: "There was an informal discussion which the stenographer was directed not to record." The next speaker on record was Sunderland, whose

Fifth and finally, conversation within the Committee could be ironic. The dynamics of the meeting led to unexpected reversals and twists of fortune. Both Wickersham and Clark came in with plans—Wickersham to use the New York State rules as a model, Clark to use the Equity Rules of 1912 as guide. Both men gave in to a series of trade-offs. It sometimes appears that no one got exactly what they wanted, a variant of legislative decision theory. On other occasions, it appears that individuals really did change their minds. Not only did they say so, but one can see their stated positions shifting under the weight of the entire Committee's views. The push and pull of opinions around some small point of language in the draft (for example the exact role of the clerk in the filing of claims or the exact wording of the rules on parties required for adjudication of a suit) developed tremendous torque and moved members from one position to another.

For example, the Advisory Committee introduced the "pre-trial conference" into the practice of the federal courts. In its present form, as Rule 16, the trial judge may summon the parties to appear to expedite or manage the suit, discourage timewasting, and facilitate the statement of the case.[121] These conferences, in which judges may control complex litigation, are hotly defended and hotly attacked today, but the original intention of the Committee was different. The modern Rule 16 was an ironic by-product of discussion of a draft rule with a very different spin. True, the notion that judges might order a hearing at which the parties to a suit would be asked to formulate their differences[122] was indeed one of the Advisory Committees' great innovations. At the time, Clark said "it is quite new," though later, in print, both Clark and Sunderland argued that it had precedent in state courts and English practice.[123]

In fact, Rule 38, as drafted by Clark and his staff for the November, 16, 1935 gathering of the Committee, did not contemplate a conference at all, but a hearing on the written briefs or memoranda submitted by counsel. The committee then spent about a half an hour trying to determine what kinds of written matter counsel should prepare for such hearings.[124] The voice in favor of oral meetings came not from the Committee, but from a federal circuit judge in Kansas. A letter from Judge George T. McDermott, dated July 1, 1935, included in the written matter sent to each member, related that he regularly and successfully allowed either party to come to his chambers to confer with their opposite number and the judge

comments were bland and conciliatory to both Dobie and Wickersham. November 17, 1935, Transcript, 1070.

121. Fed. R. Civ. P. 16.

122. Rule 38, Tentative Draft of Federal Rules, October 15, 1935. Tolman deposit, Administrative Office of United States Courts, Washington D.C., [hereafter Draft, October 15, 1935].

123. Charles E. Clark, "Objectives of Pre-Trial Procedure" 17 *Ohio State University Law Journal* 163 (1956); Edson Sunderland, "The Theory and Practice of Pre-Trial Procedure" 36 *University of Michigan Law Review* 215 (1937).

124. November 16, 1935, Transcript, 801-811.

on the facts in dispute, the issues of law, and the appropriate judicial orders to get "at the nub of the controversy at the outset of the litigation." McDermott reported that this jawboning process, a forerunner, if not quite the same as modern case management, led to a "prompt trial."[125] McDermott's letter was read by Clark to the Committee (although they all had copies of it already) and McDermott had made his views public in the American Judicature Society Journal.[126] The Committee then recalled that local courts in Boston and Detroit permitted similar pre-trial conferences. Momentum gathered for amendment of Clark's Rule 38 to specifically permit oral hearings, an ironic inversion of the original draft's thrust. The result was Rule 20 in the second draft of the Rules Clark prepared—a rule that resembled McDermott's letter—the true ancestor of Rule 16.[127]

A final irony merged with silence: there were three members of this blue-ribbon Committee who seem to have been intellectually bowled over. Scott Loftin, a Florida practitioner and past President of the ABA, Joseph Gamble, a Des Moines lawyer, and Wilbur Cherry, a Professor at the University of Minnesota, rarely spoke. For them, the irony was that after distinguished careers filled with arguments and briefs and lectures, they found so little to say at all.

CONVERSATION DECODED

By regarding the conversation of the members as action, and by stressing relationships, situations, scripts, silences, and ironies, the historian runs the risk of trivializing the precise technical content of the deliberations—even if one does not believe that such precise detailed technical matters are fixed, certain, and external to the conversation (my position in this essay). For the historian of law, indifference to technical correctness is inexcusable, but mindless obeisance to technical nuance returns the historian to the problem of selection and emphasis. We have to let some detail go, or we cannot craft an intelligible story.

125. George T. McDermott to Edgar Tolman, July 1, 1935, attached to local suggestions on Rule 38, Draft.

126. George T. McDermott, "Just What is Your Defense?" 18 *Journal of the American Judicature Society* 100 (1935). Clark had strong ties to the executive director of the Society, Herbert Harley, had lectured to the Society on the proposal for new rules, was a member of the editorial board of the Journal, and no doubt either solicited or heartily approved Judge McDermott's article. See Michal Belknap, *To Improve the Administrative of Justice: A History of the American Judicature Society* (Washington D.C., 1992) , 74, 84, 87. Clark was not the only advocate of such a procedure on the Committee. Sunderland, from his post in Ann Arbor, was fully in touch with and had praise for the pre-trial hearing introduced in Detroit. See Sunderland to Harry D. Nims, November 1, 1935, Sunderland Papers, University of Michigan.

127. Tentative Draft No. 2, December 23, 1935, Rule 20. The Rule was debated by the Committee in its February 21, 1936 meeting, Transcript, 506-515. It became Rule 16. *Report of the Advisory Committee* (1937), 44-46.

For the legal scholar, missing a detailed point can be far more debilitating than for the historian, particularly if that point is central to the story the law professor wants to tell. The law professor has her own story, and although recovery of some portion of past records—legal text—may be a part of the narrative, often the moral of that story is not understanding of the past, but improvement of the operation of law in the future. This is not my concern, however my own labors may contribute to the construction of such a story.

We return at the end to the starting place, the source, and to T.H. Breen's cautious optimism that history is an "interpretive exercise." The product of such exercise is not incontrovertible truth, but a conversation, part of an ongoing scholarly enterprise. Such historical narratives cannot invent, but are themselves inventions. They are successful if, like the best translations, they turn words into actions and allow readers to see and hear as they read.

[22]

Moving Beyond the Canon of Traditional Constitutional History: Anti-Federalists, the Bill of Rights, and the Promise of Post-Modern Historiography

SAUL CORNELL

Few aspects of post-structuralist literary criticism have garnered as much attention and provoked as much controversy as the move to challenge the idea of a fixed literary canon of great texts. The implications of deconstructing the canon extend well beyond the study of fiction. All fields of scholarship have a canon of established texts, methodologies, and questions.[1] Critiques of the literary canon resemble the challenge to conventional history posed by the new social history and its efforts to write a history from the bottom up that would supplant traditional historical scholarship.[2] A similar revisionist effort is now only just beginning to emerge in constitutional historiography. Proponents of "a new constitutional history" are seeking to challenge the canon of tra-

1. John Guillory, "Canon," in *Critical Terms for Literary Study*, ed. Frank Lentricchia and Thomas McLaughlin (Chicago: University of Chicago, 1990), 1233–49; for other studies of canonization, see Nina Baym, "Melodramas of Beset Manhood: How Theories of American Fiction Exclude Women Authors," *American Quarterly* 33 (1981): 1233–49; Bruce Kuklick, "Seven Thinkers and How They Grew: Descartes, Spinoza, Leibniz; Locke, Berkeley, Hume; Kant," in *Philosophy in History: Essays in the Historiography of Philosophy*, ed. Richard Rorty, Jerome Schneewind, and Quentin Skinner (Cambridge: Cambridge University Press, 1984), 125–39.

2. Alice Kessler Harris, "Social History," in *The New American History*, ed. Eric Foner (Philadelphia: Temple University Press, 1990), 179.

Saul Cornell is assistant professor of history at The Ohio State University.
Michael Les Benedict, Hendrik Hartog, Stanley Katz, Bruce Mann, John Murrin, and the members of The Ohio State University History Department Workshop/Colloquium read and commented on earlier drafts of this article.

Law and History Review Spring 1994, Vol. 12, No. 1

ditional constitutional history.[3] While this revisionist project has not been cast in post-structuralist terms, the perspective provided by recent critical theory can refine the practice of the new constitutional history.[4]

A number of historians have expressed skepticism, and in some cases hostility, toward the claims of post-modern history.[5] Not all recent theory can be of use to historians. The techniques of deconstruction associated with Jacques Derrida, the theorist most often attacked by historians, do pose serious epistemological problems for historians. In particular, deconstruction's claims that history is composed solely of texts and that context cannot fix the meaning of texts challenge the notion of contextualizing past events and documents.[6] A more appealing alternative to deconstruction is provided by another approach to textuality that presents a less radical challenge to contextualism—hermeneutics. Several types of hermeneutic strategies are available to scholars interested in exploring post-modern history. One approach, pragmatic hermeneu-

3. Kermit Hall, "American Legal History as Science and Applied Politics," *Benchmark* 4 (1990): 236.

4. On post-structuralism in general and deconstruction in particular, see Pauline Marie Rosenau, *Post-Modernism and the Social Sciences: Insights, Inroads, and Intrusions* (Princeton: Princeton University Press, 1992); Peter Dews, *Logics of Disintegration: Post-Structuralist Thought and the Claims of Critical Theory* (London: Verso, 1987); Jonathan D. Culler, *On Deconstruction: Theory and Criticism After Structuralism* (Ithaca: Cornell University Press, 1982); Christopher Norris, *Deconstruction, Theory and Practice* (London: Methuen, 1982); idem, *The Contest of Faculties: Philosophy and Theory after Deconstruction* (London, 1985); Terry Eagleton, *Literary Theory: An Introduction* (Minneapolis: University of Minnesota Press, 1983); Quentin Skinner, *The Return of Grand Theory in the Human Sciences* (Cambridge: Cambridge University Press, 1985); J. M. Balkin, "Deconstructive Practice and Legal Theory," *Yale Law Journal* 96 (1987): 743–86. On the new historicism within literary study and its debt to deconstruction, see H. Aram Veeser, ed., *The New Historicism* (New York: Routledge, 1989).

5. Lawrence Stone, "History and Post-Modernism," *Past and Present* 131 (1991): 217–18; idem, "History and Post-Modernism," *Past and Present* 135 (1992): 189–208; Steven Watts, "The Idiocy of American Studies: Poststructuralism, Language, and Politics in the Age of Self-Fulfillment," *American Quarterly* 43 (1991): 625–60; Bryan D. Palmer, *Descent into Discourse: The Reification of Language and the Writing of Social History* (Philadelphia: Temple University Press, 1990); Gertrude Himmelfarb, "Telling it as You Like it: Post-Modernist History and the Flight From Fact," *Times Literary Supplement*, Oct. 16, 1992.

6. On contextualism see R. H. Collingwood, *The Idea of History* (Oxford: Oxford University Press, 1946); Quentin Skinner, "Meaning and Understanding in the History of Ideas," *History and Theory* 8 (1969): 3–53. For another discussion of this theory, see Murray G. Murphy, *Our Knowledge of the Historical Past* (Indianapolis: Bobbs-Merrill, 1973). For a critique of contextualism from the perspective of post-structuralism, see Dominick LaCapra, *History and Criticism* (Ithaca: Cornell University Press, 1985) and idem, *Rethinking Intellectual History: Texts, Contexts, and Language* (Ithaca, N.Y.: Cornell University Press, 1983).

tics, acknowledges that all historical evidence may in certain contexts be treated as texts and that the meaning of texts depends not just on what an author intended, but is also a product of the diverse responses of particular readers of a text.[7]

Applying a pragmatic hermeneutics to the subject of canon formation involves a number of interpretive strategies. First, it is important to examine the way in which the existing canon excludes certain types of evidence and certain groups from serious scrutiny. Next, it is important to examine the perspective of those marginal groups responsible for producing non-canonical texts. The circulation of canonical and non-canonical texts and the interaction of elite and non-elite readers are empirical problems central to a pragmatic hermeneutics. Like most forms of post-modernism, such an approach pays especially close attention to the contradictions within particular discourses and the tensions arising from the effort to combine different discursive traditions.

The historiography on the origins of the Bill of Rights provides an excellent illustration of the way in which the construction of a set of canonical texts influences the way scholars interpret a particular historical problem. The *Founders' Constitution*, an authoritative reference work, provides a good way of identifying what is included in the canon.[8] Currently, the canon in constitutional history includes *The Federalist*, the state ratification debates, and the legislative debates during the First Congress. The canon also includes some essays drawn from the popular press that contemporary scholars believe represent the most thoughtful expressions of Federalist and Anti-Federalist writing. Other works by Anti-Federalist writers deemed less theoretical have generally been ignored, even when those works may have been more representative of popular thought. Nor have the actions of Anti-Federalists in state politics during the constitutional period been examined in a systematic fashion. Taken together these non-canonical sources provide a set of alternative texts that can help illuminate more traditional sources.[9]

The existing scholarly literature on the origins of the Bill of Rights contains a host of contradictions. One of the most conspicuous failures

7. Saul Cornell, "Early American History in a Post-Modern Age," *William and Mary Quarterly* 50, no. 2 (April 1993): 329–41.

8. Philip B. Kurland and Ralph Lerner, eds., *The Founders' Constitution* 5 vols. (Chicago: University of Chicago Press, 1987).

9. A good case in point is Herbert Storing's edited collection of Anti-Federalist writings, *The Complete Anti-Federalist* 6 vols. (Chicago, 1981). Historians have generally been critical of the criteria Storing used to assemble his collection of documents, on this point see Saul A. Cornell, "The Changing Historical Fortunes of the Anti-Federalists," *Northwestern University Law Review* 84 (1989): 56.

of the existing historiography on the Constitution is its inability to explain the paradoxical relationship between Anti-Federalism and the Bill of Rights. Standard constitutional histories credit the Anti-Federalists for initiating the campaign to secure a bill of rights.[10] The absence of a bill of rights was among the most frequently voiced objections made by the Anti-Federalists. Yet, when the First Congress met to consider amendments to the Constitution, a number of prominent Anti-Federalists serving in Congress opposed Madison's draft of the Bill of Rights.

Some constitutional scholars have been puzzled by the discrepancy between the rhetoric of leading Anti-Federalists and their behavior regarding a variety of constitutional issues. In particular, it has been difficult to reconcile Anti-Federalist calls for explicit protection of the core freedoms that were eventually incorporated in the First Amendment and their behavior in state politics during the constitutional era. Passionate defenses of individual liberty seem difficult to reconcile with calls for religious tests for public office holders. These actions have led some to conclude that the opponents of the Constitution were "men of little faith," who cared little for individual liberty or democracy.[11] Still other scholars have argued that these actions demonstrate that Anti-Federalist support for a bill of rights was a rhetorical device designed to conceal their true political agenda. According to this view it was states' rights, not individual rights, that motivated Anti-Federalist opposition to the Constitution.[12]

This article builds on the efforts of the new constitutional history and post-structuralism and seeks to expand the existing constitutional canon. A post-modern approach to constitutional history must explore a wider variety of texts and the diverse communities of readers who interpreted those texts. Adopting this perspective will avoid the homogenizing tendency of traditional scholarship and restore some of the complexity that previous scholars have ignored.

---

10. See, for instance, Daniel A. Farber and Suzanna Sherry, *A History of the American Constitution* (Saint Paul: West Publishing, 1990).

11. Cecelia M. Kenyon, "Men of Little Faith: The Anti-Federalists on the Nature of Representative Government," *William and Mary Quarterly*, 3d ser., 12 (1955): 3–43.

12. Leonard Levy's views on the origins of the Bill of Rights are developed in *Legacy of Suppression: Freedom of Speech and Press in Early America* (Cambridge: Harvard University Press, 1960); *Emergence of a Free Press* (New York: Oxford University Press, 1985); *Essays on the Making of the Constitution*, 2d ed. (New York: Oxford University Press, 1987); and *Original Intent and the Framers' Constitution* (New York: Macmillan, 1988). For another view of the Anti-Federalists, stressing their commitment to states' rights, see Alpheus Thomas Mason, *The States Rights Debate: Antifederalism and the Constitution* (Englewood Cliffs, N.J.: Prentice Hall, 1964).

Beyond the Canon 5

Whigs and Anti-Whigs: A Heritage of Liberty or a Legacy of Suppression?

Traditional constitutional historians have portrayed Anti-Federalism in monolithic terms. Anti-Federalist texts have been read as though they were the product of a single intelligence, an Anti-Federalist alternative to the *Federalist*.[13] One consequence of this approach is a tendency to treat the opponents of the Constitution as though they were impelled by a single ideology or political agenda. While some scholars have viewed the Anti-Federalists as uniformly liberal, others have portrayed them as uniformly anti-liberal. Much of the existing scholarship has been cast in terms of a dialectic between these two opposing points of view.

In *The Birth of the Bill of Rights*, Robert Rutland, a distinguished political historian of the constitutional era, chronicles Anti-Federalist demands that explicit guarantees for basic rights be included in the text of the Constitution. Rutland's discussion of the debates in the First Congress over the Bill of Rights devotes little attention to the apparent shift in Anti-Federalist attitudes toward the utility of a bill of rights. As a result of this decision, his larger story of an unfolding tradition of liberty is unchanged by Anti-Federalist grumbling during the First Congress. He closes his account with this observation: "The great men of the Revolution . . . risked their lives for the principle that individual freedom was the sine qua non of good government."[14]

In his influential narrative history of the Bill of Rights, legal scholar Bernard Schwartz does not see Anti-Federalist opposition to Madison's draft of the Bill of Rights during the First Congress as a contradiction. Nor does Schwartz see the reluctance of some Anti-Federalists to accept Madison's draft of the Bill of Rights as a significant shift in ideology. Neither of these factors causes Schwartz to question his claim that American constitutionalism has been continuously evolving toward an ever-expanding respect for individual liberty. At the end of *The Great Rights of Mankind*, Schwartz contrasts this movement with the views of modern legal theorist John Rawls. For Schwartz, Rawls's contractarian doctrines and distributive theory of social justice mark a departure from mainstream constitutional thought. As Schwartz observes, Rawls's

13. Of course, commentators on the *Federalist* have also exaggerated the coherence of Publius. For a discussion of this problem, see Alpheus T. Mason, "The Federalist—A Split Personality," *American Historical Review* 57 (1952): 625–43.

14. Robert Rutland, *The Birth of the Bill of Rights, 1776–1791* (Chapel Hill: University of North Carolina Press, 1955), 232.

theory "tends toward a bloc view of life rather than an individual one; it reverses the historic movement toward respect for the individual." Schwartz depicts American constitutionalism in organic terms, continuously evolving toward greater individual liberty.[15]

Both Rutland and Schwartz organize their histories around meta-narratives, models of history that unfold in an inexorable process of progressive development.[16] These studies are classic examples of Whig history. In his study, *The Whig Interpretation of History*, Herbert Butterfield noted that this approach glorifies the principle of progress and presents a story in which history appears to flow inevitably toward the present.[17] Whiggish accounts of the Bill of Rights present American constitutionalism as an inexorable process. As the title of one popular constitutional history suggests, American consitutionalism can be seen as "a march of liberty."[18]

No historian would dispute the claim that the concept of liberty figured prominently in the rhetoric of the American Revolution and the discourse of American constitutionalism in the late eighteenth century. Invoking liberty as the sine qua non of Revolutionary principles, however, ignores the degree to which liberty was itself an essentially contested concept.[19] While American patriot leaders would have agreed that the Revolution was fought to preserve liberty, it is also true that Americans disagreed bitterly over what liberty meant in both theory and practice. Nor were these disagreements narrow instrumental questions about the best way to secure a common libertarian ideal. Within the ranks of American society there were distinctly different views of what sort of social order would best promote liberty. Conflicts over public funding for religion and over paper money acts were only two of the most notable instances in which radically different conceptions

15. Bernard Schwartz, *The Great Rights of Mankind: A History of the American Bill of Rights* (New York: Oxford University Press, 1977), 230.

16. On the tropes of historical writing and the notion of meta-narrative, see Hayden White, *Metahistory: The Historical Imagination in Nineteenth-Century Europe* (Baltimore: Johns Hopkins University Press, 1973).

17. Herbert Butterfield, *The Whig Interpretation of History* (New York: Norton, 1965); and David Hackett Fischer, *Historians' Fallacies: Toward a Logic of Historical Thought* (New York: Harper and Row, 1970), 139.

18. Melvin I. Urofsky, *A March of Liberty: A Constitutional History of the United States* (New York: Knopf, 1988).

19. On the relevance of the notion of "essentially contested concepts," see Terrence Ball and J. G. A. Pocock, eds., *Conceptual Change and the Constitution* (Lawrence: University Press of Kansas, 1988). For one effort to distinguish between diverse libertarian traditions in America, see David Hackett Fischer, *Albion's Seed: Four British Folkways in America* (New York: Oxford University Press, 1989).

of liberty were articulated by different groups within Revolutionary America.[20]

Eager to discover a viable libertarian heritage, narrative histories of the Bill of Rights have ignored the presence of alternative ideological traditions in American life. Rather than seeking a single intellectual tradition, it makes far more sense for scholars to acknowledge the plurality of competing discourses available to American citizens in the late eighteenth century.[21] Indeed, many of these discourses contained tensions and contradictions that had profound consequences for American constitutionalism.

One of the most important countervailing forces arrayed against the libertarian tradition was the constellation of ideas that historians have grouped together under the rubric of civic republicanism. While liberalism stressed the centrality of liberty, civic republicanism stressed the good of the commonweal.[22] One of the leading historians contributing to the revival of interest in republicanism, Bernard Bailyn, drew attention to the tension between liberty and authority in Revolutionary thought. Bailyn, J. G. A. Pocock, Gordon Wood, and the other writers associated with the "republican synthesis" provided a useful corrective to the idea that American political culture in the eighteenth century was dominated by a liberal political philosophy and a libertarian ethos.[23]

Recasting American constitutionalism in terms of a dialectical struggle between liberty and authority has profound consequences for how we

---

20. For useful narrative accounts of this period see Richard B. Morris, *The Forging of the Union, 1781–1789* (New York: Harper and Row, 1987); and Edward Countryman, *The American Revolution* (New York: Hill and Wang, 1985).

21. Isaac Kramnick, " 'The Great National Discussion': The Discourse of Politics in 1787," *William and Mary Quarterly*, 3d ser., 45 (1988): 3–32; Forrest McDonald, *Novus Ordo Seclorum: The Intellectual Origins of the Constitution* (Lawrence: University Press of Kansas, 1985).

22. Bernard Bailyn, *The Ideological Origins of the American Revolution* (Cambridge: Harvard University Press, 1967); J. G. A. Pocock, *The Machiavellian Moment: Florentine Political Thought and the Atlantic Republican Tradition* (Princeton: Princeton University Press, 1975); Gordon Wood, *The Creation of the American Republic, 1776–1787* (Chapel Hill: University of North Carolina Press, 1969). On liberalism, see Joyce Appleby, *Capitalism and the New Social Order: The Republican Vision of the 1790s* (New York: New York University Press, 1984); and John Diggins, *The Lost Soul of American Politics: Virtue, Self-Interest, and the Foundations of Liberalism* (New York: Basic Books, 1984).

23. On the notion of a republican synthesis, see Robert Shalhope, "Toward a Republican Synthesis: The Emergence of an Understanding of Republicanism in American Historiography," *William and Mary Quarterly*, 3d ser., 29 (1972): 49–80; idem, "Republicanism and Early American Historiography," *William and Mary Quarterly*, 3d ser., 39 (1982): 334–56.

understand attitudes toward the state in this period. Within the commonwealth tradition of republican thought, there was an important anti-statist libertarian tradition, one hostile to centralized authority. There was also a decidedly statist tradition that accorded tremendous power to government to legislate on behalf of the public good. Yet another way of conceptualizing this problem has been suggested by constitutional historian Herman Belz who invokes Isaiah Berlin's notion of negative and positive liberty. The former was central to a liberal libertarian tradition of individual rights that defended freedom from arbitrary power. The latter was associated with a republican tradition that stressed the rights of self-governing communities to regulate their own conduct to promote public virtue. Revolutionary constitutionalism contained both negative and positive views of liberty.[24]

The point of calling attention to the weakness of Whiggish accounts of the Bill of Rights is not to deny that there was a viable and vibrant libertarian heritage in eighteenth-century America. The problem with the liberal thesis is not that it is untrue but that it is at best a partial truth.

The excessively Whiggish tone of so much constitutional scholarship has provided the basis for an aggressively revisionist anti-Whig position. For anti-Whigs, the legacy bequeathed to us by the Founders was not one of liberty, but rather a legacy of suppression. The most notable attempt to mount an anti-Whig counteroffensive is evidenced in the writings of Leonard Levy, which argue that there is a noticeable divergence between modern jurisprudence's libertarian impulses and the original understanding of various constitutional provisions of the Bill of Rights.[25]

Levy's thesis about the origins of the Bill of Rights contains two interrelated suppositions. First, Levy argues that Federalists did not seriously believe their own arguments against the necessity of a bill of rights. Secondly, Anti-Federalists, he claims, were equally disingenuous in their demands for a bill of rights. According to this interpretation, the Anti-Federalists used the issue of the bill of rights as a rhetorical device to block ratification. Levy argues that Anti-Federalists "sought

24. Alfred H. Kelly, Winfred A. Harbison, and Herman Belz, *The American Constitution: Its Origins and Development*, 6th ed. (New York: Norton, 1983), chap. 5.

25. For an overview of this literature see James Hutson, "The Birth of the Bill of Rights: The State of Current Scholarship," *Prologue* 20 (Fall 1988): 150. Levy's interpretation has been subjected to a number of withering attacks: Fischer, *Historians' Fallacies*, 132–33; David M. Rabban, "The Ahistorical Historian: Leonard Levy on Freedom of Expression in Early American History," *Stanford Law Review* 37 (1985): 795–856.

to prevent ratification and exaggerated the bill of rights issue because it was one with which they could enlist public support. Their prime loyalty belonged to states' rights, not civil rights."[26]

To buttress his claim that Anti-Federalists were concerned with states' rights and not civil rights, Levy relies quite heavily on the actions of the two Virginia Anti-Federalists who served in the First Congress, Richard Henry Lee and William Grayson. For Levy "the private correspondence of Senators Lee and Grayson of Virginia reveals the explanation for the attitude of their party toward a bill of rights."[27] Grayson confided to Patrick Henry that amendments being considered in Congress "shall effect [sic] personal liberty alone, leaving the great points of the Judiciary, direct taxation, &c, to stand as they are." Grayson later observed that the proposed amendments "are good for nothing, and I believe, as many others do, that they will do more harm than benefit."[28]

Levy approaches the Anti-Federalists as though they constituted a coherent party with a single intellectual and political agenda, a highly problematic assumption given the evidence of considerable diversity within the ranks of opponents of the Constitution.[29] Levy never articulates a coherent explanation to justify his choice of which Anti-Federalist voices are to be taken as representative of Anti-Federalism. Nor does he explain why William Grayson's views can be taken as a full and fair representation of Anti-Federalist ideas in other states.

It is not necessary to move beyond Virginia to challenge Levy's argument. There is good reason to wonder if Grayson's views are entirely representative of the full spectrum of Anti-Federalist attitudes within the Old Dominion. After all, it was Grayson's fellow Virginian and Anti-Federalist George Mason, who wrote the Virginia Declaration of Rights. Mason had even gone so far as to offer his services at the end of the Federal Convention, arguing that a draft of a bill of rights could easily be produced in a short interval. Yet, Levy never explains why Grayson's view of a bill of rights is more representative than Mason's views. When Levy discusses Mason he notes "the sincerity of Mason's desire for a bill of rights is beyond question, but he had many other

26. Levy, *Emergence of a Free Press*, 221.
27. Levy, *Original Intent*, 169.
28. Ibid., 170.
29. On the inadequacy of the notion of party during this period, see Ronald P. Formisano, "Deferential-Participant Politics: The Early Republic's Political Culture, 1789–1840," *American Political Science Review* 68 (1974): 473–87. Jackson Turner Main, *The Antifederalists: Critics of the Constitution, 1781–1788* (Chapel Hill: University of North Carolina Press, 1961) provides ample evidence of the divisions within the ranks of the Anti-Federalists on a variety of issues.

reasons for opposing the Constitution."[30] Levy's one-dimensional account of Anti-Federalist motivations leaves no room to consider the possibility that other opponents of the Constitution might have had more than a single animus against the new government. Even more problematic is Levy's failure to explore the possibility that Anti-Federalists like Lee, Grayson, and Mason might have seen the protection of states' rights as inextricably linked to the protection of individual rights.

A close examination of Levy's evidence about Grayson's views casts further doubt on the charge that Anti-Federalist thought was hostile to liberty. Consider Grayson's dismissal of the version of the Bill of Rights being debated in Congress. He explicitly faulted Congress for failing to address Anti-Federalist concerns about the judiciary and taxation. Both the issue of taxation and the structure of the judiciary were crucial to the constitutional arguments that Revolutionary leaders enunciated in the struggle against Britain. If there was any liberty interest at stake during the Revolution, it was the right not to be taxed without consent and the right to have access to an impartial administration of justice. By stressing these issues, Grayson adhered to a view of liberty and rights that was closely akin to the one patriot leaders espoused in 1776.[31]

Levy's distinction between states' rights and individual rights is anachronistic. Anti-Federalists affirmed a traditional variant of republican ideology that was distinctly localistic. Federalists broke with the logic of Revolutionary republicanism by arguing that it was local governments, particularly the overbearing democratic majorities in the state legislatures, that constituted the greatest threat to republican government.[32] Anti-Federalists rejected this departure from traditional constitutionalism, clinging to an older view rooted in Revolutionary thought. In their view, the greatest threat to liberty came not from the state legislatures, but rather from a distant central government.[33]

Yet another problem with Whiggish and anti-Whiggish accounts of

30. Levy, *Original Intent*, 148.

31. Here the work of legal scholar John Philip Reid is crucial, especially his *Constitutional History of the American Revolution: The Authority of Rights* (Madison: University of Wisconsin Press, 1986) and idem, *The Concept of Liberty in the Age of the American Revolution* (Chicago: University of Chicago Press, 1988).

32. For a discussion of Levy that shows how his analysis has failed to respond to the challenge posed by Wood's *Creation of the American Republic*, see Rabban, "The Ahistorical Historian."

33. Kermit L. Hall and James W. Ely, Jr., "The South and the American Constitution," in *An Uncertain Tradition: Constitutionalism and the History of the South*, ed. Hall and Ely (Athens: University of Georgia Press, 1989), 3–16.

the origins of the Bill of Rights is their dismissal of popular traditions of constitutionalism. There is a marked elitist bias in both Whig and anti-Whig history. Popular ratification ensured that questions about the nature of American constitutionalism were subjected to an unusually wide scrutiny by the public. The popular press published a staggering array of commentaries, some quite learned and others decidedly unlettered. Dismissals of Anti-Federalist appeals to the people as mere rhetorical hyperbole are typical of Whig and anti-Whig approaches to constitutional history.[34] "The history of the framing and ratification of the Bill of Rights indicates slight passion on the part of anyone," Levy writes, "except perhaps 'the people,' to enshrine personal liberties in the fundamental law of the land."[35] This sarcastic rejection of the invocation of the people as a mere rhetorical ploy seems misguided. It was precisely these sorts of fictive appeals that provided the legitimacy for so many ideas and institutions within Anglo-American political culture. To be sure, every appeal to the people did not signal a popular mandate. Nor did every pamphleteer who signed his name "One of the Common People" actually represent the views of the vast majority of Americans. Although no comprehensive social history of ratification exists, there is evidence to suggest that some of the essayists who published in the popular press were more in tune with grassroots sentiments than were many members of the Anti-Federalist elite. Rather than dismiss popular constitutionalism, it makes more sense to try and explore how "the people" understood the rhetoric of ratification.[36] Establishing the character of popular constitutionalism during the struggle over the Bill of Rights is particularly important to modern constitutional theory. Constitutional theorists as diverse as Bruce Ackerman, Robert Bork, and John Hart Ely all ground their approaches to constitutionalism in the fact that the Constitution was ratified by popular majorities in the states. Appeals to the people carry a special resonance in American constitutionalism because the legitimacy of the Constitution depends on the "super majorities" in the various state-ratification conventions that adopted the new frame of government.[37]

---

34. Rutland's *Birth of the Bill of Rights* cites evidence of popular belief but does not explore the distinctive popular vision of these Anti-Federalists.

35. Levy, *The Emergence of a Free Press,* 266.

36. On this point, see Saul Cornell, "Aristocracy Assailed: The Ideology of Backcountry Anti-Federalism," *Journal of American History* 76 (1990): 1148–72.

37. On the idea of political fictions, see Edmund S. Morgan, *Inventing the People: The Rise of Popular Sovereignty in England and America* (New York: Norton, 1988), 209–39. On the importance of democratic theory to original-intent jurisprudence, see Daniel Farber, "The Originalism Debate: A Guide for the Perplexed," *Ohio State Law*

Whig and anti-Whig approaches to constitutional history fail to explore the diversity within the ranks of the Anti-Federalism and instead posit a monolithic Anti-Federalist ideology. In particular, these approaches ignore the popular voices within the ranks of the opposition to the Constitution. Exploring the connections between canonical and non-canonical sources challenges the homogenizing tendency of traditional constitutional scholarship. Another advantage of a post-modern approach is that it calls attention to the tensions within particular discourses and the conflicts between different discursive traditions. Anti-Federalist attitudes toward liberty are a good illustration of this problem. Only by appreciating the tension between liberal and republican conceptions of liberty can historians understand the nature of Anti-Federalist constitutionalism.

Intentionalists and Straussians: The Search for Timeless Truths

Legal scholars have not been troubled with apparent inconsistencies in the Anti-Federalists' attitudes toward the Bill of Rights because they have not been interested in the political motivations of the Anti-Federalists. The jurisprudential search for original intent eschews questions about the subjective intent of historical actors. It is the professed values of the Anti-Federalists, not their political behavior, that concerns lawyers. Intentionalist scholarship focuses on a fairly narrow range of constitutional texts and has not sought to link these texts to broader patterns of thought and behavior in the post-Revolutionary period. Some constitutional historians have simply ignored the actions of Anti-Federalists in state politics and have not recognized any tension between their professed beliefs and actions. Others have taken Anti-Federalist actions as a sign of hypocrisy and have used behavior as a way of discrediting Anti-Federalist ideas as empty rhetoric. Both of these approaches have presented a distorted image of the Anti-Federalists.

One particularly good example of intentionalist scholarship is Russell

---

Journal 49 (1988–89): 1085–1106. For additional discussion of original-intent jurisprudence, see the essays in Jack Rakove, ed., *Interpreting the Constitution* (Boston: Northeastern University Press, 1990). The theories of John Hart Ely, *Democracy and Distrust: A Theory of Judicial Review* (Cambridge: Harvard University Press, 1980); Robert Bork, *The Tempting of America: The Political Seduction of the Law* (New York: Free Press, 1990); Bruce A. Ackerman, *We the People: Foundations* (Cambridge: Harvard University Press, 1991) all depend on variants of democratic theory to support their models of constitutional interpretation.

Caplan's influential study of the original meaning of the Ninth Amendment. In Caplan's view "the provision which ultimately became the ninth amendment," was designed by Madison "to assure the antifederalists that the Constitution would leave intact those individuals rights contained in the state constitutions, statutes, and common law."[38] Like many recent scholars writing about the Founders' era, Caplan believes that Anti-Federalists and Federalists should be consulted when seeking the intent of the Founders.[39] His reading of the Ninth Amendment directly challenges the expansive view of this provision of the Bill of Rights developed by Justice Arthur J. Goldberg in his controversial opinion in *Griswold* v. *Connecticut*.

Like much intentionalist scholarship, Caplan assumes that there was a single Anti-Federalist ideology and that it can be assembled by weaving together various statements by diverse Anti-Federalists. Homogenizing the Anti-Federalists ignores the fact that there was significant ideological diversity within the ranks of the opponents of the Constitution. It is hard to reconcile Caplan's reading of the original intent of Anti-Federalist attitudes toward the Bill of Rights with the ideas expressed by New York Anti-Federalists. The New York State Constitution did not include a bill of rights. The views of New York Anti-Federalists toward their constitution were developed by a writer who assumed the venerable republican pen-name of "Sydney." Federalists in New York exploited the absence of a state bill of rights to attack Anti-Federalists who criticized the federal constitution for failing to include a declaration of rights. "Sydney" responded by arguing that the Revolution had returned New Yorkers to a state of nature. Since New Yorkers were in a state of nature, the state constitution they drafted was a document of strictly limited powers: a constitution in which all powers not delegated by the

38. Russell L. Caplan, "The History and Meaning of the Ninth Amendment," in *The Rights Retained by the People: The History and Meaning of the Ninth Amendment*, ed. Randy E. Barnett (Fairfax: George Mason University Press, 1989), 281. Caplan's work was cited by Robert Bork during his confirmation hearings when he was questioned about the meaning of the Ninth Amendment. On this point, see Roy M. Mersky and J. Myron Jacobstein, ed., *The Supreme Court of the United States: Hearings and Reports on the Successful and Unsuccessful Nominations of Supreme Court Justices by the Senate Judiciary Committee, 1916–1987*, vol. 14 (Buffalo: William S. Hein, 1990), 428, 999.

39. For a discussion of this transformation, see Saul A. Cornell, "The Changing Historical Fortunes of the Anti-Federalists," *Northwestern University Law Review* 84 (1989): 39–73. For two recent examples of the Anti-Federalist intent of the Ninth Amendment, see Calvin R. Massey, "The Anti-Federalist Ninth Amendment and Its Implications for State Constitutional Law," *Wisconsin Law Review* (1990): 1229–66; and Thomas McAfee, "The Original Meaning of the Ninth Amendment," *Columbia Law Review* 90 (1990): 1215–1320.

constitution were retained by the people. The unique situation of New York meant that a bill of rights was not needed. A government of delegated authority, like the New York Constitution, functioned as a bill of rights. The most important safeguard for liberty was the structure of the legislative branch. With a relatively weak executive and a legislature tied to the people by a policy of frequent rotation in office, there could be no serious threats to liberty. "Sydney's" argument that state constitutionalism was governed by a different logic than that of the federal constitution calls into question Caplan's analysis of the function of the Ninth Amendment.[40] For New York Anti-Federalists, a federal bill of rights had to protect natural rights broadly defined and affirm that all power not explicitly delegated to the new government would be retained by the people.[41]

Supporters of Goldberg's view of the Ninth Amendment might take considerable comfort from the writings of New York Anti-Federalists. Melancton Smith, an influential New York Anti-Federalist, favored a broad statement of natural rights in the amendments he proposed for the federal constitution because he believed that the authority of the new central government, unlike the authority of the State of New York, was not strictly one of enumerated or delegated authority. To curb the broad elastic clauses of the Constitution, Smith turned to George Mason's language in the Virginia Declaration of Rights. Smith argued that the federal constitution should declare that "all freemen have certain essential inherent Rights of which they can not by any Compact deprive or divest their posterity."[42] Although Smith believed that this language

40. On this dimension of the state bills of rights, see James H. Hutson, "The Bill of Rights and the American Revolutionary Experience," in *A Culture of Rights: The Bill of Rights in Philosophy, Politics, and Law—1791 and 1991*, ed. Michael J. Lacey and Knud Haakonssen (Cambridge, England: Cambridge University Press, 1991), 94.

41. "Sydney," [Abraham Yates?] ed., *The Complete Anti-Federalist*, ed. Herbert J. Storing, 7 vols. (Chicago: University of Chicago Press), 6:109–10. On New York politics in this period, see Edward Countryman, *A People in Revolution: The American Revolution and Political Society in New York, 1760–1790* (Baltimore, 1981). For a discussion of the character of New York Anti-Federalism, see Saul Cornell, "Politics of the Middling Sort: The Bourgeois Radicalism of Abraham Yates, Melancton Smith, and the New York Anti-Federalists," in *New York in the Age of the Constitution, 1775–1800*, ed. William Pencak and Paul Gilje (Rutherford, N.J.: Associated University Presses, 1992), 151–75.

42. Melancton Smith, "Amendments Proposed to the New Constitution of Government," draft manuscript, Melancton Smith Papers, New York State Library, Albany, New York. For a general discussion of natural rights theory during this period, see Knud Haakonssen, "From Natural Law to the Rights of Man: A European Perspective on American Debates," in *A Culture of Rights*, 19–61 and Suzanna Sherry, "The Founders' Unwritten Constitution," *University of Chicago Law Review* 54 (1987): 1127–77.

should be included in the federal constitution, he did not think it was necessary to include such language in the New York State Constitution. Neither Smith nor "Sydney" fit Caplan's understanding of how Anti-Federalists understood a federal bill of rights would function to protect liberty.

One of the most eloquent statements of Anti-Federalist views on natural rights was produced by "Brutus," who attacked the expansive powers ceded to the new government in the following terms:

> This power, exercised without limitation, will introduce itself into every corner of the city, and country—It will wait upon the ladies at their toilett, and will not leave them in any of their domestic concerns . . . it will enter the house of every gentlemen, watch over his cellar . . . note down all he eats or drinks; it will attend him to his bed chamber, and watch him while he sleeps. . . it will follow the mechanic to his shop . . . and will haunt him in his family, and in his bed.[43]

The view of liberty defended by Brutus hardly resembles Caplan's description of Anti-Federalist intent. Modern libertarians eager to defend Justice Goldberg's view that the Constitution protects privacy would be heartened to learn that Brutus seems to agree with their position. The problem with such a reading is that it conveniently ignores the tensions within the discourse of Anti-Federalists like Brutus. There are serious problems with trying to cast him as a modern liberal, since he ardently supported the New York State Constitution. Although that document was one of enumerated authority, Brutus would have recognized that the legislature enjoyed broad powers to enact laws to promote the common good. While "Brutus" would have expected legislators to respect a right of privacy, he would not have looked to the courts to guard this right.

Brutus believed that the judiciary contained "a very extensive influence for preserving or destroying liberty, and for changing the nature of government." In particular, he feared that Americans were insufficiently attentive to the dangers posed by the judicial branch. Americans schooled in republican precepts were apt to be "jealous of the legislature, and especially the executive; but not always the judiciary." Brutus concluded that failure to properly limit judicial power left Americans "in danger of sowing the seeds of arbitrary government."[44]

43. "Brutus," in Storing, *Complete Anti-Federalist* 2:396.

44. "Brutus," ibid. 2:315–16. On Brutus, see William Jeffrey, Jr., "The Letters of 'Brutus'—A Neglected Element in the Ratification Campaign," *University of Cincinnati Law Review* 40 (1971): 643–63; and Anne Stuart Diamond, "The Anti-Federalist 'Brutus,' " *The Political Science Reviewer* 6 (1976): 249–81.

While Brutus acknowledged that the legislature might overstep its bounds occasionally, he framed his criticism of the legislature in terms that echoed the democratic ethos characteristic of so many Anti-Federalist writings. "The measures of popular legislatures naturally settle down in time, and gradually approach a mild and just medium," he wrote, "while the rigid system of the law courts naturally become more severe and arbitrary."[45] Brutus expected the popularly elected legislators to defend natural rights, not the courts. It would have been almost unimaginable to Brutus that the federal judiciary could protect the liberties of the people by declaring the actions of a popularly elected state legislature unconstitutional. Brutus fused a liberal view of natural rights with a republican belief in the supremacy of the legislative branch. Modern categories like liberal or conservative, communitarian or libertarian, cannot easily accommodate the thought of Brutus. The process of eliciting an original intent from his thought that might support or refute Goldberg's view of the Ninth Amendment invariably homogenizes what was an extremely complex and distinctly eighteenth-century constitutional vision.[46]

Political theorist Herbert Storing's edited collection, *The Complete Anti-Federalist,* has played an indispensable role in rescuing the Anti-Federalists from the margins of the American political tradition and restoring them to an honored place within the canon of our constitutional heritage.[47] "If, however, the foundation of the American polity was laid by the Federalists," Storing wrote, "the Anti-Federalist reservations echo through American history."[48] In Storing's account, the Anti-Federalists are properly thought of as the true progenitors of the Bill of Rights. "While the Federalists gave us the Constitution," Storing noted, "the legacy of the Anti-Federalists was the Bill of Rights."[49] Yet, if Storing's work is indisputably a major contribution to recent American constitutional theory, it is less successful as a work of history. Part of the problem with Storing's approach stems from a failure to examine the relationship between Anti-Federalist rhetoric and action. Instead, he concentrates on the debate between Anti-Federalists and leading Federalists over the necessity of a bill of rights and thus casts the Anti-

45. "Brutus," in Storing, *Complete Anti-Federalist* 2:315–16.

46. For a study that uses Brutus in this fashion, see Gary McDowell, "Were the Anti-Federalists Right: Judicial Activism and the Problem of Consolidated Government," *Publius* 12 (1982): 99–108.

47. On Storing's place in recent scholarship on Anti-Federalism, see Cornell, "The Changing Historical Fortunes of the Anti-Federalists," 56.

48. Storing, *Complete Anti-Federalist* 1:72.

49. Ibid. 1:65

Federalists as political philosophers, removed from the immediate political context of the Revolutionary era. In his account, contradictions are rendered invisible because actions are not treated as though they provide clues to understanding the Anti-Federalists' political philosophy.

Storing's treatment of the Anti-Federalists is more attuned to the role of liberal and republican ideals in the Founders' era. Still, like so many political theorists influenced by the teachings of Leo Strauss, Storing casts the debate over the Constitution within the larger context of a battle between ancient republicanism and modern liberalism.[50] Storing admitted that he had turned to the study of the Anti-Federalists expecting to find "that they defended . . . residual principles of premodern, preindustrial, preliberal" thought. In Storing's view, these ideas were, however, "strikingly absent" from Anti-Federalist thought. "The Anti-Federalists are," in his account, liberals "in the decisive sense that they see the end of government as the security of individual liberty, not the promotion of virtue or the fostering of some organic common good."[51] Part of the problem with casting this debate in these terms is that it wrenches Anti-Federalism out of the context of the political struggle of the Revolutionary era. While Anti-Federalists routinely employed pseudonyms that suggest classical influence, the evidence for sustained borrowing from classical sources is extremely limited. As political theorist Donald Lutz has demonstrated, classical sources accounted for less than ten percent of Anti-Federalist citations. (Federalists by contrast cited classical sources thirty-three percent of the time.)[52] Storing's attempt to place Anti-Federalist ideas within the larger context of classical political philosophy ignores the most important context in which Anti-Federalist thought must be situated.[53] The grand tradition of western philosophy

50. An excellent introduction to Straussian scholarship is Leo Strauss and Joseph Cropsey, eds., *History of Political Philosophy*, 3d ed. (Chicago, 1987). A critical assessment of the Straussian paradigm can be found in Gordon S. Wood, "The Fundamentalists and the Constitution," *New York Review of Books* 35 (1988).

51. Storing, *Complete Anti-Federalist* 1:83.

52. Donald S. Lutz, "The Relative Influence of European Writers on Late Eighteenth-Century American Political Thought," *American Political Science Review* 78 (1984): 189–97. In many cases Anti-Federalist ideas about Locke or Brutus were obtained from the popular press and did not necessarily reflect a direct knowledge of classical texts either in the original or in translation.

53. For discussions about the difference between modern and ancient approaches to the meaning of virtue, see Lance Banning, "Second Thoughts on Virtue and Revolutionary Thinking," in *Conceptual Change and the Constitution*, 194–212, and Jean Yarbrough, "Republicanism Reconsidered: Some Thoughts on the Foundation and Preservation of the American Republic," *Review of Politics* 41 (1979): 61–95.

was less significant than the emerging tradition of American constitutionalism.

Like Whigs, anti-Whigs and intentionalists, Storing does not adequately contextualize concepts like liberty. Storing recognizes that "the security of liberty does require, in the Anti-Federalist view, the promotion of civic virtue and the subordination . . . of individual interest to [the] common good." Yet, having made this claim, he then contradicts this statement by affirming that "virtue and the common good are instrumental to individual liberty."[54] Storing seeks to settle the question of what is instrumental and fundamental in Anti-Federalism by a close reading of the texts he judges to be the most thoughtful expressions of Anti-Federalist ideas. Storing's hostility to contextualism is evident in his criteria for analyzing Anti-Federalist texts. He eschewed a search for the most representative or influential texts, in favor of a search for those texts that captured the essence of the Anti-Federalist ideal. "In searching for the underlying unity in the Anti-Federalist position," Storing admitted, "we are not tabulating the frequency of different arguments. We are looking not for what is *common* so much as for what is *fundamental*."[55] The criteria used by Storing for selecting various Anti-Federalist texts invariably contributes to the homogenization of Anti-Federalist thought. Another problem with this approach is that it makes it difficult to contextualize liberty and other key concepts. Storing's refusal to examine Anti-Federalist actions makes it difficult to evaluate what liberty actually meant in practice. Was the Anti-Federalist conception of liberty compatible with loyalty oaths and religious tests? A more useful way of evaluating what was fundamental and what was instrumental in Anti-Federalist thought would be to identify those instances in which Anti-Federalists adjudicated or legislated on complex constitutional questions that required defining the scope of liberty permissible under constitutional government.

While no single example can serve to illuminate the entire range of Anti-Federalist belief, the Pennsylvania Test Acts provide one occasion to examine the meaning of liberty in practice. The effort of Pennsylvanian Anti-Federalists to force loyalty oaths on Quakers and Germans who sympathized with the loyalist cause has been cited as an example

54. Storing, *Complete Anti-Federalist* 1:83. Forrest McDonald is one of the few critics to note this contradiction in Storing's work: *Novus Ordo Seclorum*, 285. For another effort to view the Anti-Federalists as liberals, see Richard C. Sinopoli, *The Foundations of American Citizenship: Liberalism, the Constitution and Civic Virtue* (New York, Oxford, 1992).

55. After acknowledging the heterogeneity of the Anti-Federalists, Storing proceeds with the task of seeking their underlying unity. *Complete Anti-Federalist* 1:6.

of Anti-Federalist hostility to liberty. In the view of constitutional historian James Hutson, the Anti-Federalists' "advocacy of a bill of rights in the ratification debates of 1787 seems hollow" in light of their support of loyalty oaths.[56] Hutson's analysis raises serious questions about Storing's claim that the Anti-Federalists were liberals. Ultimately, it is not necessary to choose between Storing and Hutson's approaches to Anti-Federalism. Just as the choice between Whig accounts and anti-Whig accounts presented a false dichotomy, so too do the approaches of Storing and Hutson create a spurious choice for historians. One need not cast the problem in terms of the liberal or anti-liberal character of Anti-Federalists. There is another way of understanding the Anti-Federalist conception of liberty that avoids either of these alternatives. The actions of Pennsylvania Anti-Federalists must be placed within a civic republican framework. By failing to support the Revolutionary cause, the individuals excluded by the test acts were placed outside of the republican polity. Like women and other excluded groups, such individuals still enjoyed some basic legal rights even if they would not have enjoyed all the rights of citizenship. Only individuals capable of demonstrating their capacity for republican virtue were entitled to full citizenship. The right of the community to legislate for the public welfare took precedence over the liberties of the disenfranchised Quakers and Germans. Seeking to identify Pennsylvania Anti-Federalists with a monolithic republican or liberal constitutional philosophy obscures the complex ways in which both of these traditions informed Anti-Federalist constitutionalism.

By refusing to look at Anti-Federalist actions or policies, particularly on constitutional questions, Straussians have constructed an ideal type that only faintly resembles the complex realities of Anti-Federalism. The approach of traditional constitutional historians is equally problematic. Positing a sharp division between philosophy and action makes little sense when studying a group like the Anti-Federalists. One of the most important consequences of a post-modern approach to constitutionalism is that it recognizes that behavior and rhetoric are both shaped by discourse. Actions are best approached as social texts that can be read in much the same way that one might read a supreme court decision. By exploring the inter-textual connections between these social texts and other more conventional sources, it is possible to see how Anti-Federalist ideas and behavior were part of a continuum of

56. Hutson, "The Birth of the Bill of Rights," 150. On the debate over the test acts in Pennsylvania, see Douglas M. Arnold, *A Republican Revolution: Ideology and Politics in Pennsylvania, 1776–1790* (New York: Garland, 1989), 103–19.

belief. When set within the context of civic republicanism, the actions of the Anti-Federalists need not be interpreted as hypocritical. The test acts can be interpreted as an effort to arrive at a balance between the competing values of liberal and republican constitutionalism.

Constitutional History as Discourse

Neither Whigs nor anti-Whigs, Straussians nor intentionalists have been willing to acknowledge the diversity within the ranks of the Anti-Federalists. All of these approaches have sought a monolithic original intent for each side in the ratification debate. Another conceptual scheme is required if we are to move beyond the limits of these approaches. Here methodological insights derived from other avenues of historical inquiry can be extremely useful. Traditional legal and constitutional history resembles the impressionistic intellectual history of an earlier generation. More recent work in intellectual and cultural history has abandoned the idea of a single American mind and has been concerned with exploring diverse communities of discourse. Increasingly, intellectual historians have endeavored to expand the range of ideas, individuals, and groups included in studies of the American Revolution. By contrast, scholars working on the Bill of Rights have remained interested in a fairly narrow range of thinkers who espoused "serious" legal and constitutional ideas.[57]

The recent efforts of intellectual historians to move beyond canonical texts closely resembles the approach of legal scholars associated with the "new constitutional history."[58] Hendrik Hartog, a leading practitioner of the "new constitutional history," rejects the "search for the single meaning of law," choosing instead to focus on the law as an arena of social conflict in which different groups seek to articulate their own

57. Michael Ermarth, "Mindful Matters: The Empire's New Codes and the Plight of Modern European Intellectual History," *Journal of Modern History* 57 (1985): 506–27; John E. Toews, "Intellectual History After the Linguistic Turn: The Autonomy of Meaning and the Irreducibility of Experience," *American Historical Review* 92 (1987): 879–907; David Hollinger, *In the American Province: Studies in the History and Historiography of Ideas* (Bloomington: Indiana University Press, 1985). Artisan republicanism is treated by Sean Wilentz in *Chants Democratic: New York City and the Rise of the American Working Class, 1788–1850* (New York: Oxford University Press, 1984). Gendered meanings of republicanism are treated in Linda Kerber, *Women of the Republic: Intellect and Ideology in Revolutionary America* (Chapel Hill: University of North Carolina Press, 1980).

58. Kermit Hall, "American Legal History as Science and Applied Politics," *Benchmark* 4 (1990): 236.

distinctive conceptions of law, rights, and justice. The guiding assumption of this approach is a belief that the meaning of legal rules and texts for elites "could differ significantly from the meaning constructed by a group of people having different class status, race, or gender."[59] This approach has restored a voice to groups in American society who had been "banished from the domain of constitutional history" because their vision of law was not accorded the same status as those who were empowered to be "official interpreters" of the law. The "new constitutional history" has provided the prospect of writing a constitutional history from the bottom up to complement traditional constitutional historiography. By exploring the intersection between an elite tradition of constitutional thought and popular traditions of constitutionalism, it is possible to see how the thinking of James Wilson, a formally trained jurist, existed on a continuum with the legal and constitutional thought of farmers and artisans.

The new constitutional history has begun the process of expanding the canon in legal history. Insights gleaned from post-structuralism can help refine the process of revision. In addition to exposing the limits of the existing historiography, it is important to expand the canon to include new non-elite sources. Post-structuralist efforts to read behavior as a form of social text closely resemble the efforts of social and cultural historians to explore ritual as a means of restoring a voice to groups once deemed to be "inarticulate." Social texts provide one source for illuminating popular constitutionalism. Political behavior, after all, is an extremely elaborate form of symbolic action. It is possible to read constitutional ideas about rights in the social behavior of individuals or groups who did not produce traditional texts.

Moving beyond the monolithic character of earlier accounts of Anti-Federalism requires a new model for relating social reality and ideology. The pragmatic hermeneutic strategy adopted by a number of intellectual historians provides one way of analyzing this type of problem. The concept of discourse and discursive community seems well suited to the concerns of the new constitutional history. From the point of view of historical inquiry, discourse can be treated as a set of rules governing the way knowledge is produced, interpreted, and organized in society. In effect, discourse guides the way texts are interpreted. Another hallmark of post-structuralist theory is the belief that no discourse is ever completely successful at limiting alternative modes of thought.

Discourse theory can be extremely helpful when confronting a com-

59. William E. Forbath, Hendrik Hartog, and Martha Minow, "Legal Histories from Below," *Wisconsin Law Review* (1985): 764.

plex text like the Declaration of Independence. Understanding this text involves locating the various discourses that Jefferson might have drawn upon when drafting his document: republicanism, liberalism, Scottish moralism, natural rights theory, common law. Each of these discourses contributed to Jefferson's own distinctive political vision. It is also important to locate the conflicts and tensions within particular discourses and the conflicts arising from the effort to reconcile different discursive traditions. It is precisely these nodes of contradiction that provide the cultural space for resistance and contestation. Jeffersonian thought, for example, sought to balance the concepts of equality and natural aristocracy in ways that were often irreconcilable. Various groups within American society were able to exploit these nodes of contradiction and use them as the basis for legitimating their own alternate readings of particular discourses or texts. One important consequence of focusing on the interactions between discourses and discursive communities is that it draws our attention to the dynamic interactions between authors and readers. The post-structuralist emphasis on the process of reading provides an important corrective to earlier approaches to texts that focused entirely on authorial intent. While historians ought not abandon the concept of intent, they must recognize that in many instances it is the varied response of diverse communities of readers, not the intent of particular authors that establishes the most important reading of a text. Once published, texts circulate in a public sphere in which an author's intent may not always control the way a text is interpreted. The Declaration of Independence is a classic illustration of this quality of textuality. The notion of equality articulated in the Declaration of Independence was interpreted in quite different ways by various groups within American society. Southern planters, African-American slaves, women, and laborers all approached Jefferson's text in a distinctive fashion.

The post-structuralist concept of discourse resembles the more familiar historical concept of ideology. Two distinctive theoretical traditions have informed recent historical use of the term ideology. In materialist approaches to history, the concept of ideology is closely related to social class. According to materialists, ideologies are determined by underlying social and economic structures. A variety of materialist approaches to early American history including those of Progressives, Neo-Progressives, and Marxists have influenced writing about the Constitution. For these historians, the struggle over the Constitution was essentially a battle between competing socio-economic factions.[60]

60. For an excellent discussion of materialist approaches to ideology, see Terry Eag-

A quite different approach to ideology can be found in the work of historians influenced by anthropologist Clifford Geertz's cultural or semiotic approach to ideology. For Geertz, ideology provides a "problematic map of social reality," an effort to construct a coherent symbolic system to comprehend the world. According to this view, economic interest is itself a cultural construction. The approach of the "ideological school" of early American history has had a profound impact on recent writing about the Constitution. For these scholars, the struggle over the Constitution was a battle between competing world views.[61]

While both of these approaches to ideology have greatly expanded our understanding of the origins of the Constitution, there are problems with each of these analytical frameworks. Materialists have been criticized for failing to acknowledge the role of cultural beliefs in shaping action, while cultural approaches to ideology have been charged with ignoring social conflict. A different model is needed to move beyond these two paradigms. An analysis of discourse and discursive community avoids many of the problems associated with previous approaches to ideology.

The notion of discursive community includes groups organized around traditional materialist categories such as social class, but also includes groups organized around cultural constructions such as gender or discursive categories such as common law jurisprudence. The flexibility

---

leton, *Ideology: An Introduction* (London: Verso, 1991). The classic Progressive interpretation of the Constitutional struggle is Charles Beard, *An Economic Interpretation of the Constitution* (New York: Macmillan, 1913); the most influential neo-progressive account is Jackson Turner Main, *The Anti-Federalists*. For a neo-Marxist account, see Gary B. Nash, "Also There at the Creation: Going beyond Gordon S. Wood," *William and Mary Quarterly,* 3d ser., 44 (1987): 602–11.

61. Clifford Geertz, *The Interpretation of Cultures* (New York: Basic, 1973). The ideological school's debt to Geertz was more readily apparent in the methodological statements that followed their earlier monographic historical contributions. See, in particular, Bernard Bailyn, "The Central Themes of the Revolution," in *Essays on the American Revolution,* ed. Stephen G. Kurtz and James Hutson (Chapel Hill: University of North Carolina Press, 1973), 10–12, 23; Gordon S. Wood, "Intellectual History and the Social Sciences," in *New Directions in American Intellectual History,* ed. John Higham and Paul K. Conkin (Baltimore: Johns Hopkins University Press, 1979), 27–41; and idem, "Ideology and Origins of Liberal America," *William and Mary Quarterly,* 3d ser., 44 (1987): 628–40. Geertz's framework was developed in the context of detailed ethnographic field work that helped him establish the boundary of the ideological community he analyzed. Historical scholarship invoking Geertz has assumed that America was a single ideological community. This has introduced a strong homogenizing tendency in works inspired by Geertz. For a critique of Geertz, see Ronald G. Walters, "Signs of the Times: Clifford Geertz and the Historians," *Social Research* 47 (1980): 537–56.

provided by the concept of discourse seems well suited to the study of constitutionalism. In many cases the interpretive communities studied by constitutional scholars are organized around an intellectual tradition or a reaction to a particular text. Anti-Federalism is a good case in point, since the one thing all Anti-Federalists held in common was a hostility to the Constitution. Indeed, from a hermeneutic perspective, one would have to argue that the one thing that held Anti-Federalists in common was the text of the Constitution, since different Anti-Federalists interpreted that text in a number of distinctive ways that reflected their cultural and social position in American society.

The Varieties of Anti-Federalist Discourse: Amending, Swearing, and Rioting

In a brief article it would be impossible to provide a complete survey of the various discursive communities within the ranks of the Anti-Federalists. Still, if we consider just one of the most salient divisions among Anti-Federalists, the tension between popular and elite variants of constitutionalism, it is possible to see the utility of a post-modern approach.[62]

One influential discursive community within the ranks of the Anti-Federalists included members of the southern gentry elite. Arthur Lee, a prominent Virginian, wrote the letters of "Cincinnatus," consciously choosing a pen name linked to a classical patrician image of republican statesmanship. Lee's essays provided one of the most articulate Anti-Federalist defenses of religious freedom and closely resembles the thought of another influential Anti-Federalist leader from Virginia, George Mason. Both men were spokesmen for one strand of elite Anti-Federalist thought that was committed to a liberal view of individual rights.

After attacking the new government for failing to protect freedom of the press, "Cincinnatus" wrote that people were left "in equal insecurity," regarding the "liberty of conscience."[63] Lee believed the Constitution's prohibition on religious tests vindicated the common Anti-Federalist claim that the new government would operate directly on individuals and would pose a threat to personal liberty. Why else, Lee wondered, was it necessary to include a ban on religious tests unless

62. For a more detailed discussion of the variety of discursive communities within the ranks of the Anti-Federalists, see Saul A. Cornell, "The Political Thought and Culture of the Anti-Federalists," (Ph.D. diss., University of Pennsylvania, 1989).

63. "Cincinnatus," [Arthur Lee?], in Storing, *The Complete Anti-Federalist* 6:14.

the powers ceded to the new government would have authorized Congress to impose religious tests? Lee echoed common Anti-Federalist concerns about the elastic nature of certain clauses within the body of the Constitution and believed that the new frame of government threatened to absorb all power within its orbit. Lee clearly disapproved of religious tests. Contrary to the image of the Anti-Federalists presented by anti-Whig historians, Lee favored greater written safeguards for individual rights.

If Lee and Mason can be viewed as spokesmen for one particular discursive community, then Massachusetts Anti-Federalist Amos Singletary can be taken as a spokesman for a more popular constitutional discourse.[64] In addition to articulating one of the most self-consciously populist critiques of the new frame of government, Singletary also attacked the Constitution for failing to include a religious test to prevent "Papists or Infidels" from holding office under the Constitution.[65] A similar discourse informed the writing of the Massachusetts Anti-Federalist who took the name "A Watchman," who contrasted the proposed constitution with the "democratical" character of American constitutionalism, which he described as a system in which "power is in the people." "We are," he went on to observe, "allowed to choose our rulers, make our laws, and perform religious worship according to the dictates of our conscience." Tolerance for religious diversity was not, however, the same as genuine religious pluralism. After attacking the new Constitution for failing to include a bill of rights that would protect the rights of conscience, Watchman went on to attack the new government for leaving the "door opened for the Jews, Turks, and Heathen to enter into publick office, and be seated at the head of government of the United States."[66]

The actions of Anti-Federalists in the town of Carlisle, Pennsylvania, provides additional evidence of popular Anti-Federalist constitutionalism.[67] The behavior of the Carlisle rioters can be read as a social text that can be related to other Anti-Federalist discursive practices. The Carlisle riot erupted when Federalists staged a parade to celebrate their victory in the state ratification convention. The Anti-Federalist majority

64. Cornell, "Aristocracy Assailed."

65. Cecelia Kenyon, *The Anti-Federalists* (Indianapolis: Bobbs-Merrill, 1966), lxviii. See also Richard Hofstadter, *Anti-Intellectualism in American Life* (New York: Knopf, 1962), 151.

66. "A Watchman," in Storing, *The Complete Anti-Federalist* 4:232.

67. Cornell, "Aristocracy Assailed." For a similar effort to recover popular legal thought, see Hendrik Hartog, "Pigs and Positivism," *Wisconsin Law Review* (1985): 899–935.

in Carlisle warned their enemies that "their conduct was contrary to the minds of three-fourths of the inhabitants, and must therefore produce bad consequences if they persisted."[68] When Federalists disregarded the Anti-Federalist warnings, the opponents of the Constitution sought to enforce the will of the community with extra-legal crowd action and blocked the Federalist celebration. Interestingly, Anti-Federalists viewed themselves as "friends of liberty," consciously linking their actions to the traditions of crowd activity associated with the Revolution.[69] From the perspective of modern civil libertarians, the actions of the Carlisle rioters seem anything but liberty enhancing. The author of a "A Watchman," Amos Singletary, and the Carlisle rioters, all supported a popular variant of republican constitutionalism that willingly compromised individual liberty in those instances when the good of the community demanded such sacrifices.

Clearly there was no single voice that spoke for all Anti-Federalists. There were considerable differences between Anti-Federalists in different states, and in some cases there could be important differences among Anti-Federalists within individual states arising from class loyalties or regional identities. Depending on which voice we take to be the true spirit of Anti-Federalism, it is possible to construct quite different interpretations of the character of Anti-Federalist thought. If Arthur Lee is our model of Anti-Federalism, then it might make sense to see Anti-Federalists in much the same way as Whiggish historians do, as libertarians. Taking the Carlisle rioters as representative spokesmen for the Anti-Federalists lends some credence to the anti-Whig view that Anti-Federalists were not genuine liberals. Part of the paradox of Anti-Federalism can be resolved by simply dis-aggregating the opposition to the Constitution into several distinctive discursive communities. This sort of solution would accept that Whigs, anti-Whigs, intentionalists, and Straussians have all been partially correct.

Exposing the diversity of the opposition to the Constitution, however, solves only part of the riddle of Anti-Federalism. Merely accepting a greater degree of ideological pluralism does not explain the tensions within particular discursive communities. Consider the case of George Mason, the author of the Virginia Declaration of Rights and the most insistent spokesman during the Constitutional Convention for a Declaration of Rights. Both of these actions suggest a libertarian cast to Mason's thought. Yet Mason also proposed that the Constitution enact

68. Merrill Jensen et al., eds., *The Documentary History of the Ratification of the Constitution* (Madison, Wis.: State Historical Society, 1976–), 2:675.

69. Ibid. 2:685.

sumptuary legislation designed to discourage luxury and vice.[70] How can we reconcile a libertarian ideology with an expression of a classical republican policy like sumptuary laws? Like so many Anti-Federalists, Mason embraced liberal and republican values.

Within other discursive communities the balance between liberal and republican values might be struck differently. The case of "A Watchman" is a good illustration of how this dilemma was handled in one strand of popular Anti-Federalist constitutionalism. The author of this essay sought to protect religious freedom and prevent non-Protestants from holding office. From the perspective of modern constitutional theory, there appears to be a clear contradiction between a liberal defense of freedom of religion and republican efforts to define citizenship in terms of a religious conception of virtue. To understand this variant of Anti-Federalist belief, we must acknowledge that it also contained both liberal and republican elements. There was no contradiction between advocating greater protection for religious conscience and arguing for religious tests for public office holders. The inalienable rights of conscience were distinct from the alienable political rights of citizens. Without virtue, free government would perish. The liberties of the people required that a certain amount of individual liberty be sacrificed to promote virtue. There was nothing cynical about this dimension of Anti-Federalist thought; it reflected commonplace republican precepts.

The case of the Carlisle rioters is a more dramatic example of the same logic. Within a republican understanding of liberty, the good of the community and the protection of the commonwealth provided a reasonable justification for the Anti-Federalist suppression of their opponents. Legitimate dissent did protect criticism that threatened the survival of republican government. Rather than view these Anti-Federalists as hypocrites, we need to see how they tried to reconcile two discursive traditions that most modern commentators have viewed as essentially incompatible.

Conclusion

A post-modern constitutional history must move beyond the canonical texts that have shaped traditional accounts of the origins of the Bill of Rights. Challenging the canon not only requires introducing a new range of sources, it also necessitates reinterpreting traditional sources.

70. Adrienne Koch, ed., *Notes of Debates in the Federal Convention of 1787 Reported by James Madison* (Athens, Ohio: Ohio University Press, 1966), 488.

Rather than search for a single Anti-Federalist voice, it is important to consider a wider range of Anti-Federalist voices. Like the new constitutional history, post-modern constitutional history does not focus exclusively on formal legal thought and doctrine. It shares with the new constitutional history the belief that constitutionalism has shaped American society at all levels.[71]

This article has suggested a way of analyzing the structure of elite and popular constitutional discourse that moves beyond simple pluralism. It is necessary to explore further the role that different discourses played in both enabling and limiting various types of constitutional arguments. The purpose of restoring a voice to the inarticulate is not to champion their vision over that of established elites, but to demonstrate the way both variants of constitutionalism worked to include and exclude certain political possibilities. In the end, a post-modern constitutional history must reject all Whig narratives and anti-Whig narratives, whether they favor elites or non-elites. One immediate consequence of this approach is that it forces scholars to eschew the simple dichotomies embedded in traditional constitutional history: states' rights versus individual rights; "men of little faith" versus populist democrats; liberalism versus republicanism. A study of the discursive structure of Anti-Federalist rhetoric linked to the diverse communities of discourse within Anti-Federalism can provide a model for re-orienting the study of American constitutionalism during the Founding period. In a post-modern constitutional history, the neat and tidy narratives of an earlier generation must give way to a more conflicted, tension-filled account of our legal heritage.

---

71. On the culture of constitutionalism, see Hartog, "The Constitution of Aspiration and 'The Rights that Belong to Us All,' " *Journal of American History* 74 (1987): 1013–34.

[23]

Women's History Review, Volume 1, Number 3, 1993

Approaching the History of Rape and Sexual Violence: notes towards research

SHANI D'CRUZE
Crewe & Alsager College, United Kingdom

ABSTRACT This article seeks an historical interpretation of sexual violence against women and children through a discussion of cultures of masculinity. By means of an interdisciplinary review of the available literature it argues against historical explanations of sexual violence as deviance and supports perspectives which see sexual violence as an integral part of the maintenance of historically located patriarchal power relations. The argument draws upon Jackson's concept of 'sexual scripts' as providing neutralisations of violent male sexuality which mediate between culture, behaviour and consciousness. Legal institutions can be shown to share many such neutralisations either embodied within or through subversions of their own rules and procedures. Primary evidence focuses the discussion on working-class communities in later nineteenth-and early twentieth-century Lancashire, UK. Police and lower court records are employed to illustrate a prevailing culture of masculinity which targets (frequently sexual) violence onto women and children, which, to the extent that it occupies public space in the town, becomes the concern of local policing. Sources also show women using local police and courts to assert their own definitions of injury and employing informal strategies through social support networks to redress their grievances.

Research into sexual violence in the nineteenth century is not lightly undertaken. Both the author and readers of this paper inhabit a culture deeply implicated in sexual violence. The project is necessarily and unavoidably political. An attempt at dispassionate, discrete authorship runs the risk of becoming voyeuristic and exploitative. Research on sexual violence should be empowering, for those involved in its writing(s) and reading(s). It therefore demands methodologies devised as if to be similarly empowering to the women and children disclosed in the written sources, even where, as in the present case, those sources were generated by a formalised and patriarchal legal system.

This is, of course, a conceit. A document is a document, not a person. A historian interprets the evidence of the past, not the past itself.[1] Nevertheless, methodologies that read the fragmentary, partial and highly mediated sources against the grain of the overbearing power relations and seek women as actors and speakers as well as silenced victims, are both enabling in the present and pay respect to the past. They are also rigorous, thorough and careful. They can hold in creative tension the empathetic impulse (it has always been the same) the need for historical specificity (*something* must have changed). You cannot see the darns in the seamless hegemonic canopy without an awareness of the context(s) - historical, local, institutional - that gave rise to the source in question.

This paper expresses the preoccupations, chiefly about theory and methodology, of research in its early stages. It represents, I suppose, an intellectual base camp from which the larger and more testing explorations will proceed. It gleans from some of the available literature a conceptual toolkit of ideas and approaches and, thus enabled, tentatively applies these ideas in a preliminary venture into the primary sources. It enables some initial suggestions as to the social and cultural meanings of sexual violence, historically located in some working-class communities in later nineteenth- and early twentieth-century Lancashire. In particular it will suggest that a prevalent culture of masculinity in those communities can be associated with sexual violence and violence against women more generally.

Since Brownmiller's *Against our Will* (following Susan Griffin) established the feminist agenda, sexual violence and its history have been an important concern for the women's movement. Research on sexual violence in contemporary Western society has proliferated and established how very widespread an experience it is amongst women. Only in the last few years, however, have social historical studies of the subject begun to revise and refine Brownmiller's central premise, that rape is a phenomenon present throughout time and rooted (essentially) in an ever-present male project of subordinating and oppressing women. Her eclectic use of examples across a broad sweep of time has left her open to criticism from historians who seek to ground their explanations in historical specificity.[2] My own theoretical perspectives begin with the general feminist premise that sexuality is a crucial arena for the expression and contest of patriarchal power relations by gender and age, and violence is one means of appropriating and consolidating power within those relations.

The kinds of questions social historians seek to ask about sexual violence (what happened? to whom? how often?) are commonly interpreted within chronological parameters that comprehend a transition from medieval through industrial to contemporary society and a conceptual framework which addresses social and economic relations in some form. But such a line of enquiry is frequently frustrated by the nature and the scarcity of the sources. Consequently historical study of this topic (perhaps more than most others) is necessarily a discourse on and around the surviving evidences, not an unmediated description of 'what happened'. The scholarship that considers cultural representations of sexual violence, visually or through texts, provides many examples of this sort of approach.[3]

Anna Clark's recent study combines an analysis of power relations with both an appreciation of discourse and a sensitivity towards the experience of women in the past. Clark investigated sexual violence in the period 1770-1845, which was marked by the onset of industrialisation in England and long identified as important in the development of class relations. She considers sexual assault in the context of changing gender and class relations and argues for a changing function of sexual violence in the dynamics of men's power and women's resistance. Emerging middle-class dominance gave currency to ideologies that emphasised the preservation of women's chastity. Effectively this meant the restriction of women's sexuality to situations controlled by men, especially fathers and husbands. Women who lost chastity were 'fallen', and irrespective of external circumstances were blamed for their condition. This substituted the 'chivalric' role of the male protector for earlier 'libertine' views that had sanctioned the uncontrolled expression of male sexuality. Libertinism left women still as fair game but not necessarily morally responsible for the outcome.[4]

Clark argues that such changes curtailed women's ability to speak out about sex and sexual violence. Law courts effectively treated women as culpable through the mere fact of their bringing a case of rape. In domestic life, women were required to place themselves under the protection of husbands and fathers who were legally and traditionally entitled to underpin their patriarchal authority by actual or threatened violence. Clark is at pains to demonstrate numerous examples of women's resistance to such oppressions.

Clark makes effective use of a notorious murder of 1817. Mary Ashford, a young working-class woman, attended a dance at an inn and spent time under the stars with Abraham Thornton. Her drowned body was later found in a field, together with evidence of pursuit, struggle and violent intercourse. Thornton was tried for murder and acquitted. The subsequent media furore transformed Thornton into 'Thornville', an upper-class libertine, and Ashford into a pure and innocent heroine.[5]

Clark's emphasis on the gender dimension leaves the rise of the middle class and its association with the 'chivalric' view somewhat under-argued. But she does point out that working-class radicals were equally vociferous in their condemnation of upper-class libertines, making contact by gender across class and masking the sexual violence of working-class men. In 1817 both working- and middle-class political reformers would appreciate the condemnation of the upper class implicit in the polemic. The stereotype of the lascivious libertine embodied a middle-class critique of aristocratic sexual mores at an historical moment when such cultural distinctions could effectively underline developing class consciousness and support political opposition to a landed government characterised perhaps unjustly as unable to control popular disorder. 1817 was the year of the Blanketeers March, when the English middle class also feared working-class sedition and revolution.

Since Malthus, however, it was largely assumed that the seditious and impoverished populace were also sexually abusive and incontinent.[6] The polemic sought to point out to the middle class not only that 'their' women required protection but, more importantly, that middle-class women required protection from upper-class as well as lower-class men. Clark does not pursue in detail the implications of the potential similarities in behaviour between an alleged upper-class libertine and the unruly sexual disorder perceived by respectable segments of society in much working-class masculinity. Perhaps the libertine mode of masculinity had more historically specific applications in class terms than it had in terms of gender.

The extent of the change Clark detects from libertinism to chivalry has been questioned and one may also speculate as to the periodicity she indicates. She points out how libertinism remained in some areas of "masculine and elite culture".[7] Perhaps Clark has identified two views of male sexuality that have coexisted over a longer time scale, one or other having the ideological edge at any one time and place. I find difficulties also with Clark's generalising an internalisation of the need for protection to working- as well as middle-class women. A continuing complaint by nineteenth-century observers was the unruly, independent and allegedly promiscuous behaviour of working-class (young) women. For these women, protection could frequently be manifest as coercion or surveillance. Studies of nineteenth-century prostitution, for example, show punitive measures to control working-class women's sexuality and create the cultural stereotype of the 'magdalene' to counterpoise the 'prostitute' as well as the middle-class angel in the home.[8]

Returning to the Ashford case, Mary's transformation into an unsullied heroine is clearly necessary to counteract possible charges of unruly working-class female sexuality. I should like to consider a little further the 'gothicising' of Thornton (a bricklayer). In Clark's words:

> Polemicists portrayed him as "unnatural", "mad", a "monstrous beast completely different from normal men". As her staunch defender the Rev. Luke Booker thundered, "Mary Ashford was savagely siezed by a Sabine, and after experiencing the most brutal treatment, inhumanely immolated by her rapacious defiler!"[9]

The deviant rapist, the monster, the lurker in the bushes is a construction that has frequently been deployed as an explanation for rape. His apotheosis was perhaps reached in the person of Jack the Ripper. Judith Walkowitz's study of the Ripper murders of 1888, like Clark's study of the earlier period, considers gender and class.[10] There were also racial dimensions. The ripper was a Jew. 'Thornville' was a Sabine. In gender terms, the ideological utility of both Thornville and Jack was to encourage women to take male protection from this monstrous threat. In class terms, the Ripper, like Thornville, was a 'toff'. One way or another both of them got away with it. It could be argued that libertine Thornville was simply one variant on a broader monster theme. By 1888 the class dimensions were somewhat changed. Both middle- and upper-class men wanted to 'protect' the angels in their own homes. Some rushed to the East End, ostensibly to form chivalric vigilante patrols to 'protect' working-class women, but equally to indulge themselves in vicarious association with the Ripper and threaten violence to the fallen 'prostitutes' who lived and worked there.

The construction of the stranger/monster rapist depends on the notion that sexual violence is 'deviant'. One historian who discusses rape in terms of deviance is Roy Porter who explains sexual violence (particularly in the context of building patriarchally controlled states in Europe since the Early Modern period) as the socially disruptive acts of marginal men and thus not in the interests of patriarchal power maintenance. Marginal (in particular, young) men were "not yet absorbed into patriarchy, with its classic roles of husband and father; ... [who thus] ... lack the permanent erections of mature patriarchy – wealth, property, office, 'standing'".[11]

Setting aside the offensive linguistic presentation (when is a joke against patriarchs a reassertion of patriarchy?), Porter does raise an argument that needs to be considered. Jacques Rossiaud has uncovered 125 rape cases in Dijon between 1436 and 1486, 80% of which were collective attacks by 2-15 individuals. Some 85% of these Dijon rapists were 'young townsmen', many of them bachelors. This represents some one or two rapes per month, usually of unmarried or widowed women or wives with husbands not at home. The woman was generally kidnapped from her home, dragged out into the town and gang raped by these local *galants*.[12]

Does, however, Rossiaud's evidence support Porter's argument? Dijon rapists were youthful, but were they marginal? Rossiaud calculates that "one out of two city dwellers participated at least once in such an assault".[13] Can this proportion of the population be deemed marginal? Rossiaud does relate their behaviour to demographic patterns which encouraged older men to marry younger women, or to remarry swiftly if their wives died. Young men were in competition with older men for wives. To an extent these rapes were status competitions between older and younger men contested through violence done to women's bodies. It is very marked in Rossiaud's account, however, that the local patriarchs did not feel threatened by this violent disruption in the way that the Porter thesis would lead one to expect.

The town council took almost no action to control or suppress the activities of the *galants*. Rossiaud argues that "sexual violence was a normal and permanent aspect of urban life" and elsewhere, that the rapes "must have constituted a veritable rite of initiation or virilization for the neighbourhood bands".[14] As long as status channels existed for young men to inherit the privileges of their elders, the power conflicts between existing and aspiring patriarchs need not reach crisis point. The activities of the *galants* in fact helped support the patriarchal social order (which they would later come to control) by subordinating the women within it. Sexual violence did not subvert, it formed one aspect of the maintenance of patriarchal power.

Mary Ann Clawson's discussion of Early Modern confraternities is useful here.[15] She points out that the interests of patriarchy can operate across both class and age divisions. Youth confraternities were a way of channelling the potential disruptiveness of young men, who shared long-term interests with the patriarchs whose privileges they stood to inherit. The right of sexual access to women constituted part of such privilege, and one which could be distinguished from the property rights and status acquired through the full-time service of a wife. In short, it cannot be argued that Rossiaud's 'burgundy bums' were marginal.[16] There were too many of them. They were not engaged in powerless social protest, in fact they served the interests of patriarchy by maintaining a climate of fear which helped subordinate all women to the patriarchal social order. They did not challenge the social order, since they stood to inherit its privileges. This point can be reinforced by contrast through Ruggerio's study of renaissance Venice, where the only rapes treated seriously by the courts were those that did challenge the hierarchy of privilege – where commoners raped women or children 'belonging' to noble men. In this case, too, rape and the social and institutional reaction to it comprised part of the overall complex of power relations.[17]

A somewhat different way of accounting for sexual violence through deviance is advanced by Edward Shorter, who explains rape in Early Modern Europe as pent-up male sexual frustration occasioned by the late age of marriage.[18] According to Shorter most Early Modern men stayed (fairly) chaste. Deviants could not keep themselves under control. Rossiaud's evidence from pre-Reformation Dijon fundamentally undermines such arguments. Prostitution was openly practised. Most towns in this region ran public brothels, occasionally funded and administered by the town council. Local authorities licensed accredited prostitutes – the *femmes publiques*. Commercially run public baths and bawdy houses expanded the market for sex. Prostitutes catered for men of all ages, social and marital status, yet rape remained a common occurrence.

Rossiaud's study is particularly useful in illustrating how the nature and practice of masculine sexuality was part of an overall social and cultural identity. An acceptance of the social construction of sexuality jeopardises any attempt to explain sexual violence through 'sexual frustration", since that too is revealed as historically specific. David Lisak argues that explanations of rapists' motivations should be located in the sociocultural context of gender rather than sex.[19] However, the dominant discourse that has been identified as developing since the eighteenth century, understood (male) sexuality as unruly biological urges located in a body distinct from the rational, enlightened (male) mind. Sexuality was thus subversive and potentially uncontrollable leaving the male - for whom (as eventually encoded by Freud) adulthood meant the achievement of the discrete, controlled, independent self - with a real problem. Masculinity required control but also demanded the possession and deployment of a predatory sexuality defined as intrinsically uncontrollable. Psychologically based studies find the anger generated by this inherent contradiction turned aggressively against the objects of masculine sexuality - women.[20] By this (and related) argument(s), heterosexual masculine sexuality becomes necessarily implicated in violence.

The general association of male sexuality with violence is made by writers as different as Brownmiller and Porter, who both associate rape with the context of warfare.[21] Social anthropologist Peggy Reeves Sanday explains differential incidences of rape through understandings of culture, which combine considerations of symbol and myth as well as access to material resources. She argues that there is little rape where the power spheres of men and women are balanced. In rape-prone societies the sexual division of labour is marked and gender identities are strongly differentiated. The 'attainment' of masculinity by growing boys is associated with the need to demonstrate physicality and aggression often expressed in initiation rites at puberty to mark the separation of the boy from the mother.[22]

Linking cultural and psychological perspectives, Lisak associates "father-distant child rearing and the culture of violence" and draws on evidence of psychological studies that found an absent or hostile father a common factor in rapists' biographies. He argues that the suppression of feminine personality traits attributed as psychologically necessary for masculine development is made more difficult by father-absence and thus precipitates anger onto the mother. Her role is dictated by culturally determined child-rearing practices generally associated with relatively high levels of gender inequality - thus she is denied the cultural autonomy to challenge such practices. The growing boy's anger becomes generalised to all or other women and can provide the basis for motivations to sexual violence.[23]

Stevi Jackson has elaborated the concept of 'sexual scripts' that describe roles and situations which "provide the motivations for sexual conduct". Jackson describes the "complex process of learning" involving a "capacity to interpret and enact sexual scripts" which mediate between internal states and outside behaviour. The notion of scripts that can then interpret particular situations and sanction certain types of behaviour is a flexible one. Scripts exist in the plural, they can be changed. Scripts mean that it is available to one party to interpret a situation as one where sexual activity is appropriate, while the other party does not adhere to that particular script.[24] Scripts include moral prescriptions that define 'normal' behaviour and allow 'escape clauses' or neutralisations justifying behaviour in particular situations that may otherwise be seen as immoral. This does not necessarily mean that rape is defined in terms of sex, if scripts are available that define sex in terms of power. As well as neutralisations, scripts provide potential rapists with motivations:

> The battery of motivations in the rapist's armoury are continuously available to him. Once he has mobilised one or other or a combination of them, neutralising his guilt in advance, he is then morally free to act. There is no deterministic link between motives and action; neutralisation simply transforms a constant possibility into a specific probability.[25]

Hence, it is not certain 'types' of men who rape. The occurrence of sexual violence depends on the availability of scripts and the immediate and more general social environment, including the interaction of rapist and victim. The burden of Jackson's argument is that rape - sex with violence - is written into the sexual scripts far more widely socially available. Rape is therefore not deviant nor marginal. It is "simply an extreme manifestation of our culturally accepted patterns of male-female relationships ... an unofficial buttress of the *status quo*".[26] Jackson's comment sums up precisely the situation Rossiaud describes in pre-Reformation Dijon. The gang-rapists' conduct was seen as acceptable in that it was not challenged. An extension of the bucolic unruly activities of Clawson's confraternities, out for a little rough music.

Boys letting off steam. 'Laddish pranks'. Perhaps the kind of thing that was said about an incident in Burnley in 1924, when two young domestic servants out for a Sunday evening stroll were attacked by a gang of youths. Hilda Davies had her handbag stolen. The lads "also felt at Miss Dawson to see if she had anything. She shouted at them whereupon she was picked up and thrown over the wall". Was it perhaps all a joke when Jane Hunt was assaulted at Much Hoole in 1844? Apparently John Hunt (her husband?) and his friend Peter Entwistle got hold of her legs and tried to pull her to the ground. She escaped by calling for help and pulling the hair of her chief attacker, Entwistle. He ran off and "shouted cuckoo".

The joke continued to amuse over a century later. In the different social environment of the 1970s Ronald Barker thought it was a laugh when his mate "used to invite him (and his brother) to go and give it to 'one of the old bags' in Lumb Lane, one of Bradford's red-light districts. He [found] this more or less normal: its a prank. You kick instead of paying".[27] Only in that case the 'mate' was Peter Sutcliffe - later known as the Yorkshire Ripper.

Nicole Ward Jouve describes a misogynist aggressive culture of masculinity surrounding Peter Sutcliffe which provided a powerful neutralisation of his violence. That culture involved not only Sutcliffe's brothers and peers but also his father, interpreted by Ward Jouve as being absent or hostile in many ways. She attributes much of the inefficiency of the police enquiry to an implicit acquiescence by the authorities in many of the assumptions of this male, aggressive, misogynist culture. They, too, had read some of the same scripts. Incidentally, the police enquiry into the 1888 ripper murders was likewise dogged by missed opportunities and oversights. In a phrase quoted by Susan Edwards, cases of sexual violence against prostitutes constitute 'normal crimes'.[28]

Sutcliffe murdered and mutilated thirteen women and maimed seven others. He held them all to be 'prostitutes' (another neutralisation). The term was as loosely used here as it was in the nineteenth century debate around the Contagious Diseases Acts and the Edinburgh magdalene institutions.[29] Clark's argued transition from male libertinism to chivalry depended on the separation of the protected 'angel' from the policed 'prostitute'. Not all the women Sutcliffe attacked were offering sex for money, and closer investigation shows that those who were, employed this as just another financial strategy to support themselves and their dependants. It is the same tale that a roomful of impoverished London seamstresses told Henry Mayhew in 1849.[30] For working-class women, it seems that the connections between work, sexuality, the label 'prostitute' and the risk of male violence have persisted over time.

To incorporate such ideas into a research strategy means seeking evidence of a male culture of violence in an historically specific setting and to locate sexual violence in a context of violence against women more generally. In fact, the social historiography of the nineteenth century documents such comparable male behaviour usually defined as 'popular culture'. This is not to deny that women played any part in popular culture, but to argue that this culture was essentially gendered. It is, furthermore, not to argue that only working-class masculinity was associated with violence. The culture of the smoking room, the hunting field, the public school, the military academy, the medical school was likewise suffused with misogynist aggression.

There were some available outlets to discuss 'respectable' misogynist violence. Fictional bounders such as Arthur Huntington in Anne Bronte's novel *The Tenant of Wildfell Hall* were generally upper class and duly came to sticky ends. Celebrated cases - such as that of Caroline Norton in 1855 - stimulated debate. The voices of middle-class women such as Ellen Weeton were more muted. Her release from a violent husband came only at financial loss to herself and with punitive restrictions on her access to her own circle of friends and her young daughter. The husband and the attorney who drew up the marriage settlement and the deed of separation, both gained financially from the marriage. The attorney in question was Weeton's brother. Her telling of the events survives only through private correspondence.[31]

The wrongs done to Ellen Weeton and women in her social situation tended to be defined as private and as the outcome of deviance. Nevertheless, for class reasons working-class masculinity remained a persistently target of public criticism. A highly visible, unruly, aggressive, alcohol-fuelled culture increased middle-class certainty of the immorality of the poor from the late eighteenth century. Evangelical Christianity spurred on reform initiatives.[32] By targeting the delinquencies of the poor, polemicists were at the same time re-emphasising the polite domesticity of their own parlours, masking and thus to an extent enabling the sexual violence that took place there, and eventually forging a substantial consensus of middle- and upper-class 'gentility' against the unrespectable.

The remedy lay in imposing or cultivating some form of quasi-genteel domesticity.[33] Such reforms were specifically targeted at work shyness, drunk and disorderly behaviour or aggression in men and, as the prostitution debate makes clear, at apparent, pro-active sexuality in women. Also to the extent that this culture was made and employed by working-class men (for it had a real utility in a situation of exhausting, dangerous or debilitating physical work and incipient poverty), alcohol, violence, physicality, predatory sexuality and misogyny were inherent constituents of that brand of masculinity. When frequently this culture impinged on public space it became a preoccupation for local courts and police forces.

In Westhoughton, Lancashire (a mining and factory town) in May 1899, for example, two nineteen-year-old colliers and other young men were arrested for shouting, swearing and causing a disturbance by running a footrace in the street. Anthony Kelly had been imprisoned for 7 days a year earlier for non-payment of a 15 shilling fine for drunken and disorderly behaviour. He had been found swearing, shouting and 'making water on the footpath'. Similar cases appear elsewhere. In Littleborough, near Rochdale, the police records for 1877-81 show numerous instances of drunk and disorderly men, making a din in the highway, often with their coats off 'wanting to fight'. When William Taylor (alias Leggs), a collier, was taken in on 20 May 1877 for being drunk and urinating on the footpath it was noted that one Mary Franks was passing "and had to turn [her] head on one side".[34]

Women could be more directly targeted. Wives who sought to intervene and take their drunken husbands home could be assaulted themselves as was John Ramsden's wife in Westhoughton. They could be assaulted by their neighbours. As Fanny Nowell was returning to her factory work in Leyland after dinner on 20 January 1845 a drunken neighbour, John Beck, came out of his house and "struck and punched" her. A passer-by also saw him kick her. Even in instances not recognised by the court as sexual assault, there could be sexual implications to an attack. Alice Turner complained in 1843 that Henry Mayor had "got hold of me and abused me he got hold of me and was for pulling up my clothes and then struck me at the side of the head". When John Butterworth a miller and Richard Brigg a weaver were arrested in Littleborough in 1880 the policeman reported "I saw Butterworth and Rigg pulling each other about on the footpath getting hold of females & stopping them & causing people to leave the footpath ...". Butterworth and Rigg were fined 5 shillings apiece for obstruction. Incidents such as this take their place alongside indecent exposures, indecent assaults, an occasional case of rape and a large amount of domestic violence. Judging by the records, the policing of male violence in one or another form was a significant concern of local police and courts in the late nineteenth century.[35]

This was not the only pattern of working-class masculinity available. The 'improving artisan' eschewed drink, unruly pranks and sexual licence. Figures such as Francis Place combined a desire for an orderly, respectable home life with the acquisition of useful knowledge and political radicalism. David Vincent's discussion of working-class autobiographies gives ample testimony of this social persona, who probably stopped beating his wife, or according to Hammerton's reading of working-class dialect poetry, at least felt guilty about it. Nevertheless, Bailey's argument about the fragmented nature of working-class respectability means that these were not mutually exclusive choices and that individuals could become part of either cultural strand in their working, domestic or leisure identities.[36]

In brief, therefore, I have worked towards a conceptual framework that pays attention to patriarchy, power and social relations. Within this framework sexual violence is seen as a critical point of intersection and of separation of power relations by gender, class and age. Sexual violence is also located at one of the myriad thresholds between the public and the private. So often (*pace* Rossiaud) it happens between two people alone. Nevertheless it frequently reaches the historian's attention only because its evidence impacts on the publicly constituted (here the legal and police) sources.

Legal and criminal records form the basis of many of the better existing studies of rape and sexual violence. These records can generate long series of data which are amenable to both qualitative and quantitative analysis. The most serious drawback to this source is the comparatively few cases of rape and sexual violence that reach the courts. For example, indictments presented to the assize courts of Essex between 1559 and 1603 included 129 homicides, 110 highway robberies, 1460 simple or compound larcenies and 28 cases of rape. Hanawalt's investigation of 15,952 indictments in eight English courts between 1300 and 1348, found that 18% of these were homicides, 80% property crimes and only about 0.05% rapes. Nazife Bashar located only 274 cases of rape in English Assize records for the five home counties between 1558 and 1700, producing 45 guilty verdicts between them.[37] The proliferation of modern surveys that show high rates of women in survey populations who have experienced rape makes it no longer possible to consider the historical data as in any way reflecting the real incidence of sexual violence.

Liz Kelly interviewed 60 women in England in the mid-1980s, ten of whom were known to have been raped. During the course of her interview she found that in fact 30 had experienced rape, 56 sexual harassment and 42 had been subjected to some form of sexual assault. Betsy Stanko quotes data from rape crisis programmes in the USA and Britain which estimate that "as many as 75 per cent of rapes never come to the attention of the police". A survey of 1007 married and divorced women in England carried out in September 1989 shows that one in four of these women, aged between 18 and 54 had been raped. Fourteen per cent of women in this survey had been raped by husbands, 6% by acquaintances, 6% by boyfriends and only 2% by strangers. Four out of five raped wives reported that rape happened frequently. Of marital rapes, 44% were accompanied by actual or threatened violence.[38] If questions as to the historical incidence of sexual violence prove so difficult to answer, other ways of using such sources must be devised which can nevertheless yield a meaningful interpretation of sexual violence in the past.

Furthermore, since we can only understand sexual violence as an historical phenomenon through these sources (themselves the outcomes and evidences of the working out of power relations), there is a need to consider both institutions and discourses. The nineteenth-century arguments about female sexual passivity generated from, and supported by, medical and psychological discourses influenced legal practice. This represented a turnaround from Early Modern notions of more active female sexuality which had underpinned ideas of female sexual voraciousness and unruliness.[39] Women's credibility as witnesses in rape trials, however, was questioned from either side of this transition. If a women was thought to be sexually voracious rape was, of course, hardly likely. The corollary of sexual passivity, however, was that female sexuality needed to be awakened by male insistence. Hence 'no' meant 'yes' and rape was unlikely.

Legal definitions of rape and of sexual violence have themselves altered over time. Considering the definitions of rape alone, until at least the Early Modern Period (to *c.*1700) rape *raptus* meant abduction irrespective of intercourse (the theft of another man's property). Many cases, however, spoke in terms of *rapuit* meaning ravished. Codification of the law against sexual violence began with the Statutes of Westminster in 1275 and 1285, and established it as a serious crime with the possibility of a death penalty. This was abolished only in 1840. Lord Hale's legal definition established in the late seventeenth century effectively remained in force for over two centuries. Hale defined rape as vaginal penetration without consent but not necessarily involving emission.[40]

The high degree of credibility required from the raped woman, that she should be of previous 'good fame', should disclose the assault to a third party immediately, display some evidence of physical injury and be able to prove her efforts to resist, further narrowed the legal definitions. Much sexual violence as now understood fell outside such requirements. It has been a long standing tenet of English legal practice that varying degrees of physical force are compatible with securing a woman's consent to intercourse. Anna Clark quotes works of early nineteenth-century jurisprudence which state "contusions on various parts of the extremities and body ... are compatible with final consent on the part of the female" and again "it is to be recollected that many women will not consent without some force".[41] Because there were such serious doubts as to women's veracity in rape trials, those who did 'best' out of the courts were frequently very young, affluent, could be presented as 'innocent', were raped by strangers or were visibly physically injured. For other women the difficulty of proving rape or sexual violence in a court of law meant that seeing serious punishment meted out to the perpetrator was, and still is, not the usual occurence.[42]

Caroline Conley argues from her study of nineteenth-century magistrates' courts in England, that if an accused rapist had an ostensibly respectable background, particularly if he was middle or upper class, the courts sought to preserve his status in verdict and sentencing. Respectability was, in effect, not compromised by sexual misdemeanours, nor indeed by appearing in court on a charge of rape. A rapist lost respectability only if given severe punishment - imprisonment with hard labour - for his crime. In contrast a woman forfeited her respectability merely by the fact of having been raped. In many cases the court was simply not able to accept that the apparently normal chap before them or indeed "any man above the level of an animal" could be guilty of rape. Both the court and the accused had read the same script. Many rapists were therefore acquitted or given token punishment since their respectable status and demeanour could not be reconciled with the role of the (monster, deviant) rapist. In one case in 1872 the Lord Chief Justice refused to take any evidence, unable to accept that a respectable married man could rape his domestic servant, even though " ... the magistrates had set bail at £300 because of the serious injuries suffered by the victim". Conley provides many other instances of how courts at all levels subverted their own procedures and uncritically accepted the flimsiest evidence to the advantage of the accused man. Consequently she computes a conviction rate of 40% in rape trials as opposed to 85% for all other felonies.[43]

There is a polemical point here that the odds are always stacked so that women are disadvantaged. There is also a methodological point about the need to explain, as does Conley, exactly the discursive and institutional acrobatics required to produce that result in any particular historical moment. Finally there is a need to do somewhat more than to record women as victims. Conley has worked from newspaper accounts of trials which offer details of counsels', magistrates' or judges' remarks as well as the reported evidence. The original court and police records, though problematic in many ways and constructed for the purposes of the institution, do have other advantages.

It is possible to recover from police and petty sessions records for Lancashire from *c.* 1850, accounts of women who used the institutions to complain in public about violence including sexual violence inflicted on them and on their children, virtually irrespective of the institutional disadvantages they faced. Many of them of course failed, but what is perhaps most remarkable is that they tried at all to give public voice to their own definitions of injury. Emma Bamford prosecuted James Bamford for assault at Middleton in 1860. She complained, "A man pulled me about - got hold of me - tried to get me into the [*illegible*] - the def[endan]t tried to master me - he sd he wd keep me out all night if I wd not". E. Scott prosecuted John Heaney for indecent assault and said "Pris[oner] came into the house and took indecent liberties - put his hand up her clothes". Alice Dagger complained that Thomas Jolly "took me into the Petty, my arm is black by struggling with the def[endan]t".[44]

It is also possible to catch glimpses of informal strategies employed to gain support. Almost invariably (and unsurprisingly) the first call for help was to another woman. When Dinah Turner had been chased across the fields and assaulted by James Parr, a neighbour, it was to her sister Mary that she ran. Mary made sure she promptly made her complaint and eventually secured a conviction. When children were assaulted it generally fell to the mother to try and obtain redress as well as to support their child, whose pain was frequently manifest in their silence. It was a week - that is when next washing day came round - before Sarah Mills, a widow, discovered that her eleven-year-old daughter, Ada, had been raped.[45]

Sometimes the sources show a woman using informal support networks to remedy the injury and even to redress the grievance. Alice Wild was a live-in servant in an artisan household. She slept on the sofa in the kitchen and was repeatedly plagued by sexual advances late at night from the son of the household. After six days, and afraid to tell her mistress, she sought the help of a neighbour Sarah Ann Ashworth, a dyer's wife, who used her social connections to find Alice a new place at a blacksmiths and who spoke for her as a witness in court saying that "... the son had used her shamefully ...".[46]

The case of Elizabeth Hardman shows these mechanisms in somewhat more detail. Elizabeth was nine. Both her mother and father worked as pickers. Their lodger James Jackson was a collier. When the parents were out of the house on a Tuesday afternoon, 'Uncle Jim' ordered Elizabeth upstairs and raped her, injuring her to such an extent that her mother, Mary Hardman, thought the bleeding and discharge were due to venereal disease. Although she told her husband Jo, he remained the absent father and it was left to Mary to tackle James Jackson. Against his denials and threats ("... hold yr noise - Let it drop and say nought more ...") she extracted an admission and threw him out of the house. She also secured his agreement to pay for treatment for Elizabeth. Mary Hardman turned not to the doctor, but to a neighbour Elizabeth Tudor, who seems to have been a local healer. She originally quoted the high figure of 10 shillings to cure the child, but on seeing the extent of her injuries said the case was beyond her competence and sent Mary Hardman and Elizabeth to a doctor.[47]

The case was tried together with a second charge against Jackson for assaulting Elizabeth's friend Ann Fletcher. On one occasion he had also tried to lure her upstairs, but she would not go. Later he had contented himself with sitting the girl on his knee, with Elizabeth in the room, and putting "his hand up [her] petticoats". Although the second case failed, Jackson was committed to trial for the rape of Elizabeth Hardman.

The Hardman case indicates some of the neutralisations a rapist was able to apply to his conduct. Jackson was part of the family, 'Uncle Jim', almost a paternal figure. He was in the habit of being obeyed by little girls. When he ordered Elizabeth upstairs, or when he asked Ann Fletcher to get him change for a shilling, they did as he asked. The Tuesday afternoon of the rape was leisure time, and he had had a little to drink. The case also highlights the gender-divided role of parents. The father was absent throughout. He gave no testimony in court. The mother's role was crucial - she controlled household matters. Mary Hardman was also able to use her social support network for help and advice. Not only was Elizabeth Tudor involved, but it is hard to imagine that the incident would not have become common neighbourhood knowledge, and for the second case to be brought the consent and co-operation of Ann Fletcher's mother would have been necessary.

So what, in the end, can be salvaged from this telling of a child's pain and fear and her mother's courage? It is essential to retain an awareness that a document is just a document and a text is just a text even though historical knowledge of the institutional generation of such evidence provides a context in which its constructions and silences can be interpreted. A feminist commitment to making some sense of sexual violence can, however, be allied to a deployment of interdisciplinary academic perspectives which enable analysis of such behaviours in terms of power relations, partly worked out through discursive strategies of neutralisation.

Such sexual scripts seem to be particularly powerful because they form a component of more extensive cultures of masculinity. The precise attributes of such cultures are historically and socially specific and it is this specificity, along with the varied and non-determinist ways in which scripts mediate behaviour, consciousness and social relations, which enable women and children to emerge as more than passive victims. The primary sources indicate that adult women in particular had their own agendas and their own cultures, contesting and challenging dominant masculinities. The precise natures of such cultures for both men and women remain to be substantiated. The social and occupational bases of such communities will clearly colour working, domestic and leisure patterns and only comparative studies that relate the evidence of police and court records to the immediate historical context will provide more detailed explanations. Nevertheless, tentative though any conclusions must remain at this stage of research, it seems that despite a pervasive culture of misogynist violence, and despite legal institutions that shared some of the scripts that explained why it was all just a bit of harmless fun, or why she was asking for it anyway, working-class women and children were able, in the industrial towns of nineteenth-century Lancashire, to find voice to protest and to give support to each other in the endeavour.

Notes

[1] K. Jenkins (1991) *Rethinking History* (London:).

[2] S. Brownmiller (1975) *Against Our Will: men, women and rape* (London: Secker & Warburg Harmondsworth: Penguin, 1976); S. Griffin (1971) Rape: the all-American crime, *Ramparts,* 10; E. Shorter (1977) On writing the history of rape, *Signs*, 3, pp. 471-82; H. Hartmann & E. Ross (1978) Comment on 'On writing the history of rape', *Signs*, 3, pp. 931-935; R. R. Connell (1987) *Gender and Power: society, the person and sexual politics* (Oxford: Polity); J. Hanmer & M. Maynard (Eds) (1987) *Women, Violence and Social Control* (London: Macmillan).

[3] For example, S. Tomaselli & R. Porter (Eds) (1986) *Rape* (Oxford: Blackwell), contributions by Froma Zeitlin, Norman Bryson, Christopher Frayling; R. Thompson (1979) *Unfit for Modest Ears: a study of pornographic, obscene and bawdy works written or published in England in the second half of the seventeenth century* (London: Macmillan).

[4] A. Clark (1983) Rape or seduction? A controversy over sexual violence in the nineteenth century, in London Feminist History Group (Ed.) *The Sexual Dynamics of History*, pp. 13-27 (London: Pluto); A. Clark (1987) *Women's Silence, Men's Violence: sexual assault in England, 1770- 1845* (London: Pandora)

[5] Clark, Rape or seduction; Clark, *Women's Silence*, pp. 113-116, 124-126.

[6] E. P. Thompson (1963) *The Making of the English Working Class*, pp. 711-713, 723-34 (Harmondsworth: Penguin); D. G. Wright (1988)*Popular Radicalism: the working class experience, 1780-1850*, Ch. 4 (London: Longman); B. Hilton (1988) *The Age of Atonement: the influence of evangelicalism on social and economic thought, 1785-1865* (Oxford: Clarendon Press).

[7] R. Porter, Rape: does it have a historical meaning?, in Tomascelli & Porter, *Rape*, pp. 216-236; Clark, *Women's Silence* p. 129.

[8] J. Walkowitz (1980) *Prostitution and Victorian Society: women, class and the state* (Cambridge: Cambridge University Press); L. Mahood (1990) *The Magdalenes: prostitution in the nineteenth century* (London: Routledge); B. Littlewood & L. Mahood (1991) Prostitutes, magdalenes and wayward girls: dangerous sexualities of working class women in Victorian Scotland, *Gender and History*, 3, pp. 160-175.

[9] Clark, *Women's Silence*, p. 114.

[10] C. Frayling, The house that Jack built: some stereotypes of the rapist in the history of popular culture, in Tomaselli & Porter, *Rape*, pp. 174-215; J.R. Walkowitz (1982) Jack the Ripper and the myth of male violence, *Feminist Studies*, 8, pp. 542-573.

[11] Porter, *Rape*, p. 235.

[12] J. Rossiaud (1978) Prostitution, youth and society in the towns of southeastern France in the fifteenth century, in R. Foster & O. Ranum (Eds) *Deviants and the Abandoned in French Society*, pp. 1-46 (Baltimore: John Hopkins University Press).

[13] Ibid., p. 12.

[14] Ibid., pp. 8, 12.

[15] M. A. Clawson (1980) Early Modern fraternalism and the patriarchal family, *Feminist Studies*, 6, pp. 368-391; M. A. Clawson (1989) *Constructing Brotherhood: class, gender and fraternalism* (Princeton University Press).

[16] I am indebted to Jeffrey Richards for both the epithet and the introduction to Rossiaud's article.

[17] C. Ruggerio (1980) *The Boundaries of Eros: sex and sexuality in renaissance Venice*, Ch. 8 (Oxford: Oxford University Press).

[18] Shorter, On writing; Hartmann & Ross, Comment .

[19] D. Lisak (1991) Sexual aggression, masculinity and fathers, *Signs*, 16, pp. 238-262.

[20] V. J. Seidler (1991) Reason, desire, and male sexuality, in P. Caplan (Ed.) *The Cultural Construction of Masculinity*, pp. 82, 112 (London: Routledge); J. Weeks (1981) *Sex, Politics and Society: the regulation of sexuality since 1800* (London: Longman); N. Wood (1986) Foucault on the history of sexuality: an introduction, in V. Beechy & J. Donald (Eds) *Subjectivity and Social Relations* (Oxford: Oxford University Press).

[21] Brownmiller, *Against our Will*, Ch. 3; Porter, *Rape*.

[22] P. Reeves Sanday (1981) *Female Power and Male Dominance: on the origins of sexual inequality* (Cambridge: Cambridge University Press); P. Reeves Sanday, Rape and the silencing of the feminine, in Tomaselli & Porter, *Rape* , pp. 84-101; Lisak, Sexual aggression, p. 260.

[23] Lisak, Sexual aggression, p. 259; B. Whiting (1965) Sex, identity, conflict and physical violence: a comparative study, *American Anthropologist*, 67, pp. 123-140; see also M. Yaffe & E. C. Nelson (1982) *The Influence of Pornography on Behaviour* (New York: Academic Press).

[24] S. Jackson (1978) The social context of rape: sexual scripts and motivation, *Women's Studies International Quarterly*, 1, pp. 30, 29, 37.

[25] Ibid., p. 36.

[26] Ibid., p. 37.

[27] Burnley Police Sectional Occurrence Book, Lancashire Record Office (LRO), PLBu/13/1/1, 30 November 1924; Leyland and Amounderness Petty Sessions Justices Minute Book, LRO PSLel/1/4, 29 April 1844; N. Ward Jouve, *'The Streetcleaner': the Yorkshire Ripper case on trial*, p. 92 (London: Marion Boyars).

[28] Ward Jouve, *The Streetcleaner*, Ch. 6, 7.

[29] Walkowitz, *Prostitution*, Littlewood & Mahood, Prostitutes.

[30] E. P. Thompson & E. Yeo (Eds) (1973) *The Unknown Mayhew: selections from the 'Morning Chronicle', 1849-50*, pp. 137-217 (Harmondsworth: Penguin); Ward Jouve, *The Streetcleaner* , Ch. 12.

[31] As one commentator said of the Wakes in Lincolnshire in the early nineteenth century; "Wherever this sort of feast is yet kept up ... there is no little drunkenness among the men; and often dancing parties are attended with a rude familiarity towards the other sex near approaching licentiousness", Society of Antiquaries, Edward James Wilson Collection (Lincoln) Vol. xiii, MS p. 62, quoted in R. W. Malcolmson (1973) *Popular Recreations in English Society*, p. 77 (Cambridge: Cambridge University Press); see also J. M. Golby & A. W. Purdue, (1984) *The Civilization of the Crowd: popular culture in England, 1750-1900* (London: Batsford); James Walvin (1978) *Leisure and Society, 1830-1950* (London: Longman); E. Yeo & S. Yeo (Eds) (1981) *Popular Culture and Class Conflict, 1590-1914: explorations in the history of labour and leisure* (Brighton: Harvester); C. Hall (1986) The tale of Samuel and Jemima; gender and working class culture in early nineteenth century England, in T. Bennett, C. Mercer & Janet Woollacott (Eds) *Popular Culture and Social Relations* (Oxford: Oxford University Press); Anne Brontë , *The Tenant of Wildfell Hall* (Harmondsworth: Penguin, 1979); Caroline Norton (1979) A letter to the Queen, 1855, in P. Hollis (Ed.) *Women in Public, 1850-1900. Documents of the Victorian Women's Movement*, pp. 179-183 (London: George Allen & Unwin); E. Hall (Ed.) (1938) *Miss Weeton: the journal of a governess*, vol. 2, pp. 131-185 (Oxford: Clarendon Press).

[32] E. R. Norman (1976) *Church and Society in England, 1770-1970*, Ch. 2, 4 (Oxford: Clarendon Press); H. McLeod (1984) *Religion and the Working Class in Nineteenth Century Britain* (London: Macmillan); K. S. Inglis (1963) *Churches and the Working Classes in Victorian England* (London: Routledge); Hilton, *The Age of Atonement*.

[33] F. K. Prochaska (1980) *Women and Philanthropy in Nineteenth Century England* (Oxford: Oxford University Press).

[34] Westhoughton Police Sectional Occurrence Book, 1898-1908. LRO, PLA46/7, 9 May 1899; Ibid., 23 July 1898; Rochdale Divisional Police, Littleborough Sectional Occurrence Book, 1877-1881, LRO, QEV/17/4/21, for William Taylor, p. 7, 20 May 1877.

[35] Westhoughton Sectional Occurrence Book, 24 June 1899; Leyland and Amounderness Petty Sessions Justices Minute Book, PSLel/1/4, 20 January 1845, 18 September 1843; Littleborough Sectional Occurrence Book, p. 291, 15 March 1880.

[36] M. Thale (Ed.) (1972) *The Autobiography of Francis Place, 1771-1854* (Cambridge University Press); David Vincent (1981) *Bread, Knowledge and Freedom: a study of nineteenth century working class autobiography* (London: Methuen); G. Crossick (1978) *An Artisan Elite in Victorian Society: Kentish London, 1840-1880* (London: Croom Helm); A. James Hammerton (1991) The targets of rough music; respectability and domestic violence in Victorian England, *Gender and History*, 3, pp. 36-37; P. Bailey (1979) Will the real Bill Banks please stand up? Towards a role analysis of mid-Victorian respectability, *Journal of Social History*, 12, pp. 336-353.

[37] J. A. Sharpe (1984) *Crime in Early Modern England, 1550-1750*, p. 49 (London: Longman); B. Hanawalt (1979) *Crime and Conflict in English Communities, 1300-1348*, p. 66 (Cambridge: Harvard University Press); N. Bashar, Rape in England between 1550 and 1700, in London Feminist History Group, *The Sexual Dynamics of History*, pp. 34-35.

[38] L. Kelly (1988) *Surviving Sexual Violence*, p. 78 (Cambridge: Polity); E.A. Stanko (1985) *Intimate Intrusions: women's experience of male violence*, p. 37 (London: Routledge & Kegan Paul); *The Guardian*, 8 November 1990.

[39] L. Jordanova & P. Brown (1981) Oppressive dichotomies: the nature/culture debate, in *Women in Society. Interdisciplinary Essays*, pp. 224-241 (London: Cambridge Women's Studies Group Virago); B. Easlea (1981) *Science and Sexual Oppression: patriarchy's confrontation with women and nature* (London: Wiedenfeld); C. Smart (1992) Disruptive bodies and unruly sex: the regulation of reproduction and sexuality in the nineteenth century, in C. Smart (Ed.) *Regulating Womanhood: historical essays on marriage, motherhood and sexuality*, pp. 7-32 (London: Routledge); C. Dyhouse (1989) *Feminism and the Family in England, 1880-1939*, pp. 54-66, 166-185 (Oxford: Blackwell); Susan Kingsley Kent (1987) *Sex and Suffrage in Britain, 1860-1914*, Ch. 4 (Princeton University Press, 1987 London: Routledege, 1990); N. Z. Davis (1975) *Society and Culture in Early Modern Europe* (London: Duckworth);

A. McLaren (1984) *Reproductive Rituals: the perception of fertility in England from the sixteenth century to the nineteenth century* (London: Methuen).

[40] Bashar, Rape in England; J. M. Carter (1985) *Rape in Medieval England: an historical and sociological study* (New York: University Press of America); J. B. Post (1978) 'Ravishment of women and the statutes of Westminster', in J.H. Baker (Ed.) *Legal Records and the Historian*, pp. 150-160 (London: Royal Historical Society); B. Toner (1977) *The Facts of Rape* (London: Hutchinson); G. Geis (1978) Lord Hale, witches and rape, *British Journal of Law and Society*, 5, pp. 26-44.

[41] Toner, *The Facts*, pp. 95-96; Clark, Rape or seduction?, p. 17, quoting S. Farr 1815, *Elements of Medical Jurisprudence*, p. 45 (London) and T. R. Beck (1825) *Elements of Medical Jurisprudence*, pp. 55-57 (London).

[42] Post, Ravishment; Clark, *Women's Silence*; Bashar, Rape in England; Carter, *Rape in Medieval England*; C. Conley (1986) Rape and justice in Victorian England, *Victorian Studies*, 29, pp. 519-536; Stanko, *Intimate Intrusions*; S. Estrich (1987) *Real Rape* (Cambridge: Harvard University Press)

[43] Conley, Rape and Justice, pp. 523-524, 521. For judges' treatment of rape cases in contemporary British society, see K. Soothill (1990) Judges, the media and rape, *Journal of Law and Society*, 17, pp. 211-233; K. Soothill (1991) *Sex Crime in the News* (London: Routledge).

[44] Middleton and Tonge Petty Sessions Justices Minute Books, LRO, PSMi/1/1, 4 July 1860, 28 September 1859; Leyland and Amounderness Petty Sessions Justices Minute Books, LRO PSLel/1/4, 10 December 1942. For a similar argument about women's use of the courts to protest about domestic violence see, A. Clark, Humanity or justice? Wifebeating and the law in the eighteenth and nineteenth centuries, in Smart, *Regulating Womanhood*, pp. 187-206. See also N. Tomes (1978) A torrent of abuse: crime of violence between working-class men and women in London, 1840-75, *Journal of Social History*, 11, pp. 328-345.

[45] Middleton Petty Sessions, LRO, PSMi/1/1, 24 October 1860; Littleborough Police Sectional Occurrence Book, LRO, QEV/17/4/2, Monday 15 March 1880, p. 291.

[46] Middleton Petty Sessions, LRO, PSMi/1/1, 21 December 1859. On women's support networks, see E. Ross (1982) Survival networks: women's neighbourhood sharing in London before World War I, *History Workshop Journal*, pp. 4-27; E. Ross (1985) Fierce questions and taunts, *Feminist Studies*, 8, pp. 575-602; E. A. M. Roberts (1984) *A Woman's Place: an oral history of working-class women, 1890-1940* (Oxford: Basil Blackwell); R. Phillips (1980) Gender solidarities in late eighteenth-century urban France: the example of Rouen, *Histoire Sociale – Social History*, 13, pp. 325-337. J. Lambertz (1985) Sexual harrassment in the nineteenth century English cotton industry, *History Workshop Journal*, 19, pp. 29-61, shows women acting together to protect themselves from sexual harassment and assault.

[47] Middleton Petty Sessions, LRO, PSMi/1/1, 27 April 1861.

[24]

DISCUSSION

Christopher Tomlins

How who rides whom. Recent 'new' histories of American labour law and what they may signify

Since the early 1960s, 'new' has been the rage of American history. Genre after disciplinary genre has immersed itself in reconsideration and proclaimed itself transformed: thus the new political history, the new economic history, the new social, the new labour, and so forth.

Here I discuss examples of what some scholars have already begun to call 'the new American labor law history'.[1] I prefer to avoid this label. Though admittedly useful in distinguishing recent work from what has gone before, the label seems to me as likely to mislead as to clarify. First, although the common adjective suggests that some unity of purpose animates the many 'new' histories of the past thirty years, little commonality exists.[2] Second, to the extent that these recent investigations of labour law history constitute an identifiable genre of enquiry, its primary significance lies in how it offers a means of overcoming the chaos of new histories, not adding to it. Unfortunately, the exaggerated precision of 'new American labor law history' seems more likely to suggest that this is just another small group of academics staking out the boundaries of their arcane specialism; one more turf claim in the balkans of 1990s scholarship.

Labour law history's potential will be wasted if it is pursued simply as one more demarcated fragment of the professional canon seeking equal opportunity status. Its

[1] The books considered in detail in this essay are: K. Orren, *Belated Feudalism: Labor, the Law, and Liberal Development in the United States* (Cambridge and New York, 1991); R. J. Steinfeld, *The Invention of Free Labor: The Employment Relation in English and American Law and Culture, 1350–1870* (Chapel Hill, 1991); V. C. Hattam, *Labor Visions and State Power: The Origins of Business Unionism in the United States* (Princeton, 1993); and W. E. Forbath, *Law and the Shaping of the American Labor Movement* (Cambridge, Mass., 1991). For the label 'new American labor law history', see Wythe Holt, 'The new American labor law history', *Labor History*, xxv, 2 (Spring 1989), 275–93.

[2] G. Himmelfarb, 'Some reflections on the new history', *American Historical Review*, xciv, 3 (June 1989), 661–70.

utility lies in what it offers to historical enquiry at large: first, a site upon which the many interpretive and empirical arguments that currently constitute the pursuit of American social and labour history can be reconciled; and second, the most appropriate medium through which power and authority, and their politics, may be decisively reinserted into our investigations of what social relations mean. To justify these claims, let us consider briefly what 'newness' has meant in recent American history, and then discuss the histories of labour law now being written in light of the scholarly trajectories of the last quarter-century.

NEW HISTORIES

The first wave

At the outset, the 'new history' label spoke the unexceptionable impatience with received understandings that is the stuff of all intellectual enquiry, but also much more. It proclaimed that resort to certain methodologies – disciplined, positivist – would banish once and for all the erroneous conventional wisdoms that were the lame product of impressionistic narrative. Take Lee Benson's 1957 declaration of war on 'the impressionistic approach long dominant in American political historiography', his call for 'the attainment of genuinely objective historical interpretations of systematic, well-described, known data; that is, interpretations which can be described accurately as consistent with scientific procedures'.[3] In 1964, Robert W. Fogel's target was the malign influence of 'historicism' on economic history, in particular its premise 'that many, if not most, important issues in the economic history of societies are qualitative in nature and, therefore, not susceptible of quantitative analysis'.[4] For Fogel, as for Benson, unquantified statements in history were empirically unverifiable and therefore unscientific. Unscientific statements were unwarranted. As George G. S. Murphy put it in 1965, in 'all disciplines' debate on 'accepted means of establishing knowledge' had resulted in agreement on a single philosophy – scientific method.[5] To practise the new history thus meant transcending historical enquiry *per se* in favour of engagement in an epistemological consensus that was progressively reorganizing all knowledge-acquisition under one positivist regimen, whose ultimate end was the discovery and verification of the 'general laws of human behavior'.[6]

The second wave

As the reverberations of this first new history spread, critiques traced implications and outlined counter-moves in response. One of the most interesting of these – not least for its

[3] L. Benson, 'Research problems in American political historiography', quoted in D. Feller, 'Lee Benson and the *Concept of Jacksonian Democracy*', *Reviews in American History*, XX, 4 (December 1992), 591–601, at 591.

[4] R. W. Fogel, *Railroads and American Economic Growth: Essays in Econometric History* (Baltimore and London, 1964), 239.

[5] G. G. S. Murphy, 'The "new" history', *Explorations in Entrepreneurial History*, second series, II, 2 (Winter 1965), 132–46.

[6] Benson quoted in Feller, *op. cit.*, 599.

combativeness – was the famous polemic by Elizabeth Fox-Genovese and Eugene Genovese, "The political crisis of social history'.[7] The Genoveses excoriated the new history's 'wilful pretence at "value-free" analysis', its tilt toward positivism, and the resulting void in the analysis of social institutions where once had been history's prime mover, the politics and economics of class relations and class struggle. No less their target than right-liberal behaviourism, however, was what they represented as the characteristic 'left-liberal' response to it. Distinguishable though it might be in appearance and method, this second wave of newness seemed to the Genoveses more like an analogue of the first than an answer to it. Leftish scholars might not have signed on to the positivist quest for 'general behavioural laws' through econometrics and cliometrics, but they had made other concessions, surrendering to a more comforting set of behavioural disciplines, notably anthropology and ethnography, and choosing to reinterpret history's guts – social, political and economic relations – within new determining matrices of 'custom' and 'culture'. To the Genoveses, these were differences merely of style. Both wings of the new history were ensconced within the same infamous post-Marxist paradigm, obfuscators of society's underlying class structures of power and authority, collaborators in the same 'bourgeois swindle'. The proper subject of history was no more culture's webs than behaviour's 'laws'. It was 'the story of who rides whom and how'.[8]

The new labour history

The multiplying divisions of social history also eventually split the field of labour history. The appellation 'new labor history', dating from the late 1960s, had initially stood for 'new left' historians' revolt against the previous generation's New Deal-inspired history of unions and collective bargaining, and their attempts to found labour history instead on an examination of work, the workplace and working people. Because of American labour history's peculiar genealogy – the old labour history having been in large part a subfield of labour economics and industrial relations, with little of the passionate radicalism that people like the Tawneys and the Hammonds had infused into the tradition of English social and labour history – its original wisdoms had been established in a disciplinary environment that was already essentially positivist. Thus the first clear rupture in labour history was not the rebellion of positivist social scientism against narrative, as in the new political and economic history, but rather came somewhat later as an anti-positivist move against incumbent institutionalists. Animated at first by a raw desire to explore the world of the rank-and-file, this move later derived theoretical strength from neo-Marxist studies of the labour process and from the left fork of the new social history. But this rupture was followed during the 1980s by others occurring within the ranks of the 'new' labour historians, increasingly focused on the issues that had been identified by the Genoveses in 1976 – the extent to which the new turn should be followed if it led (as it increasingly did) away from informing and revising histories that could be organized on themes of class

[7] *Journal of Social History*, x, 2 (Winter 1976), 205–20.

[8] *ibid.*, 210–11, 214–15, 219.

formation and struggle and toward 'rival' claims of primacy for other fundamental categories of analysis – race and gender.[9]

By the late 1980s, this was the central issue in labour history's increasingly contentious debates: could practitioners agree on a primary site for, and primary engine of, social change? They could not. Increasingly, race and gender standpoints contested the centrality of the workplace and of class in interpretations of the formation of popular consciousness; historians showed little facility in dealing with this.[10] Meanwhile, neo-institutionalist scholars departed in an altogether different direction, reviving (in revised 'realist' garb) key aspects of the older liberal account of American labour history.[11] Labour historians' claim to be engaged on the development of a new explanatory synthesis for the course of American history sounded increasingly hollow. As David Montgomery put it in the course of a 1989 *Labor History* symposium on his book *The Fall of the House of Labor*,[12] calls for a synthesis 'seemed to assume that, even though we investigated a wide variety of topics, our ideas could be harmoniously blended'. In fact what the symposium had revealed was 'that we have no common theory of history'.[13]

Law and state in the new labour history

Recent explorations in the history of labour law have created a site upon which such problems in labour history may be remedied. Some of what labour law history promises is simply the potential to revise perspectives on the social and institutional phenomena which for a good part of the last century have been the stuff of orthodox labour history. For example, by bringing critical and historical analysis to the forms of knowledge or practice that, in legal convention, have constituted the realm of 'labour law' – collective bargaining relationships – labour law history has helped to alter radically our understandings of how and why these kinds of social relations get reflected in law, how their legal form is

[9] See generally C. L. Tomlins, '"Of the Old Time Entombed": the resurrection of the American working class and the emerging critique of American industrial relations', *Industrial Relations Law Journal*, x, 3 (1988), 426–44; A. Baron, 'Gender and labor history: learning from the past, looking to the future' in A. Baron (ed.), *Work Engendered: Toward a New History of American Labor* (Ithaca, 1991), 1–46; M. J. Buhle, 'Gender and labor history' in J.C. Moody and A. Kessler-Harris (eds), *Perspectives on American Labor History: The Problems of Synthesis* (DeKalb, 1989), 55–79.

[10] A. Kessler-Harris, 'A new agenda for American labor history: a gendered analysis and the question of class' in Moody and Kessler-Harris (eds), *ibid.*, 217–32, at 224–5.

[11] See, for example, H. J. Harris, 'The snares of liberalism? Politicians, bureaucrats and the shaping of federal labour relations policy in the United States, *c.* 1915–1947' in S. Tolliday and J. Zeitlin (eds), *Shop Floor Bargaining and the State* (Cambridge, 1985), 148–91.

[12] D. Montgomery, *The Fall of the House of Labor: The Workplace, the State, and American Labor Activism, 1865–1925* (Cambridge, 1987).

[13] D. Montgomery, 'Class, capitalism and contentment', assessing critiques by H. J. Harris, S. Jacoby, M. Kazin and R. Zieger, all in 'Symposium: the fall of the house of labor', *Labor History*, xxx, 1 (Winter 1989), 93–137. For other recent assessments of the state of the field, see M. Dubofsky, 'Lost in a fog: labor historians' unrequited search for a synthesis', *Labor History*, xxxii, 2 (Spring 1991), 295–300; J. C. Moody, 'Introduction' in Moody and Kessler-Harris (eds), *op. cit.*, ix–xix, at xiv.

determined, and what has been the nature of the interaction between legal form and social practice.[14]

As important, however, is labour law history's perspective on law. Like any form of knowledge, law is transitive, constructed in discourses whose rules of formation bear the imprint of social structure, and whose practices reproduce social structure in the knowledge – the 'facts' – constructed. Thus conceived, law may be regarded as a knowledge that records the play of social relations, but also dynamically reproduces them in the institutions and ideologies to which it gives effect. Exploration of its history is hence an exploration of the manner in which law reproduces the detail of people's lives by furnishing those lives with their 'facts'. Labour law history investigates the articulation of those facts in all the realms of social action that are fundamental to human existence – the social relations and, therefore, the power relations of people at work, and the social and power relations of labour's physical reproduction. It is a history of law's politics and ideology, of its modes of operation and transmission, of its constitutive capacities and of the relativity (the contingency) of those capacities. Its goal is a fully situated history of the meaning which law has assigned to the many and diverse social practices that constitute *labour* – in work, in production and in reproduction.

Below I discuss four recent examples of the genre of labour law history. Each illustrates a different dimension of the genre's practice of enquiry: *structure*, *meaning*, *consciousness* and *language*. No one dimension by itself supplies a sufficient or exclusive characterization of labour law history, nor do these four exhaust the repertoire of possibilities. Collectively, however, they help suggest the geometry of the site that current pursuits of labour law history are designing. Discussion of them indicates how labour law history can in turn bring the disparate and disunited elements of contemporary labour history into tighter analytic alignment.

First, though, a final preliminary. Labour law history is a development as much in the realm of legal history as of labour history. Let us therefore briefly consider what it owes to developments in that sphere.

The new legal history

American legal history was one of the very first areas of post-World War Two historical study to undergo the requisite transition to modernist newness. During the early 1950s, James Willard Hurst of the University of Wisconsin led a generation of legal scholars in a break-out from legal history's traditional 'internalist' focus on law as an autonomous box of doctrine, constructing in its stead a history that placed law firmly in a social and economic context and stressed its availability as a means for the realization of liberal-progressive

[14] These were the genre's initial concerns. See, for example, K. Klare, 'Labor law as ideology: toward a new historiography of collective bargaining law', *Industrial Relations Law Journal*, IV (1981), 450–82; J. B. Atleson, *Values and Assumptions in American Labor Law* (Amherst, 1983); C. L. Tomlins, *The State and the Unions: Labor Relations, Law, and the Organized Labor Movement in America, 1880–1960* (Cambridge, 1985).

social values.[15] Hurst himself, it has been claimed, was *sui generis*.[16] Whatever the truth of this, the 'school' he founded was clearly imprinted by the same empirical and behavioural methods that were making history over. 'From Wisconsin came a powerful, historically coherent view of law as a rational instrument that could be seized by the members of the dominant middle class to achieve consensual economic goals. The analytical image of law as a mirror of society, an image rooted in Parsonian functionalism, symbolized the substance and method of Wisconsin legal history.'[17]

The Hurstian paradigm has enjoyed considerable longevity in American legal history, and its externalist perspective and sympathy for positivist social science pervade both major syntheses of American legal history currently available, Lawrence Friedman's *A History of American Law* and Kermit Hall's *The Magic Mirror: Law in American History*. To Friedman, writing twenty years ago, social science was the means to detour around law's 'horrendous mass of detail', and he embraced it with enthusiasm, crafting history that treated American law 'not as a kingdom unto itself' but as a mirror of society. Sixteen years later, Hall took essentially the same track, albeit in a more deliberate, even wary manner that lacked Friedman's earlier exuberance.[18]

One reason for Hall's caution in reasserting the Wisconsin paradigm was the stirring in the interval between Friedman's book and his of 'critical legal history'.[19] Critical legal history comprehensively rejected both the Wisconsin school's 'pluralist materialist' instrumentalism and its invocation of social science as the appropriate means to study socio-legal phenomena.[20] In place of the functionalism of the mirror metaphor, critical legal historians began emphasizing law's relative autonomy, its doctrinal indeterminacy, its politics, its potentially constitutive role in the creation of both institutional and ideological outcomes and, not least, the complexities of its legitimating relationship to 'particular distributions of wealth and power'.[21] As a result, the stuff of law's old internalist history – concepts, meaning and doctrine – made a reappearance in legal historical practice; not, however, in the service of a conservative re-establishment of law's status as an autonomous metanarrative, but instead as a means of historicizing that metanarrative claim as relentlessly as, in its own way, the best of the Wisconsin school had historicized law's process. 'The result . . . is a growing body of historical studies that examines the

[15] R. W. Gordon, 'Introduction: J. Willard Hurst and the common law tradition in American legal historiography', *Law and Society Review*, x (1975), 9–55.

[16] A. Soifer, 'Reflections on the 40th anniversary of Hurst's growth of American law', *Law and Social Inquiry*, xvii, 1 (Winter 1992), 167–79.

[17] M. Grossberg, 'Social history update: "Fighting Faiths" and the challenges of legal history', *Journal of Social History*, xxv, 1 (1991), 191–201, at 191.

[18] L. M. Friedman, *A History of American Law* (New York, 1973), 10; K. L. Hall, *The Magic Mirror: Law in American History* (New York, 1989), 336. For assessments, see M. Grossberg, 'Legal history and social science: Friedman's *History of American Law*, the second time around', *Law and Social Inquiry*, xiii, 2 (Spring 1988), 359–83; C. L. Tomlins, 'A mirror crack'd? The rule of law in American history', *William and Mary Law Review*, xxxii, 2 (Winter 1991), 353–97.

[19] R. W. Gordon, 'Critical legal histories', *Stanford Law Review*, xxxvi, 1 (January 1984), 57–126.

[20] M. Tushnet, 'Perspectives on the development of American law: a critical review of Friedman's *A History of American Law*', *Wisconsin Law Review* (1977), 1 (1977), 83–109.

[21] Grossberg, 'Social history update', *op. cit.*, 194–5.

relationship between formal and informal law, depicts law as buried politics, and emphasizes the study of legal doctrines as ideological products.'[22]

The end of the beginning

While these critical stirrings in legal studies have given labour law history a good bit of its initial character, only one of the four authors whose work is considered below claims to be writing 'critical legal history' *per se*.[23] The story of labour law history's formation is as much one of a vacuum being filled from several different disciplinary directions simultaneously as it is the more conventional historiographer's description of successive influences encountered along a suspiciously linear developmental path.

That until recently there was a vacuum, however, is not to be doubted. Legal history before Hurst took little notice of labour. Nor was the new legal history of the Wisconsin school much more attentive. In his otherwise exhaustive study of the Wisconsin lumber industry in the nineteenth and early twentieth century, Hurst himself expressed merely casual interest in the subject.[24] For their part, labour historians overwhelmingly carried over a functionalist view of the legal order, which they derived either from old-style labour economics (if liberals) or orthodox Marxism (if radicals).[25] No doubt stories of similar blanks might be told in political science and sociology.

To the extent that the work of labour law historians thus far suggests a 'programme' it is one sympathetic in general terms to the agenda that the Genoveses articulated for social historians in 1976: that is, an explicit history of (as one might abbreviate it) 'who, whom and how'. But there is no sign in this of a rejection of the turn to culture. Nor should there be. Of all historians, they are perhaps best situated to retrieve the culture concept for causation by unearthing culture's politics. Precisely because of law's official role in the polity, Michael Grossberg has observed, legal history 'offers social historians a way of dealing with power and political authority, [the] issues that consistently bedevil them'.[26] Precisely because legal history's subject is a discourse that is irremediably political (whether one considers law as a modality of social action or as a set of institutions with 'official' transmission effects), legal historians are in a position to chart social relations, and the power relations implicated in those social relations, across multiple cultural dimensions without ever risking a loss of focus on the macro- and micro-politics of those relations' definition and distribution. It is this potential to address relations of production and reproduction across multiple fundamental forms of composition – of class *and* race *and* gender – while remaining all the time within the bounds of one strategy of historical enquiry that justifies the assertion of labour law history's promise as an academic 'site'.

[22] *ibid.*, 195.

[23] Steinfeld, *op. cit.*, vii.

[24] J. W. Hurst, *Law and Economic Growth: The Legal History of the Lumber Industry in Wisconsin, 1836–1915* (Madison, Wisconsin, 1964). See S. L. Harring and B. R. Strutt, 'Lumber, law and social change: the legal history of Willard Hurst' and J. W. Hurst, 'Response', both in *American Bar Foundation Research Journal*, Volume 1985, 1 (Winter 1985), 123–37, 138–44.

[25] Tomlins, '"Of the Old Time Entombed"', *op. cit.*, 428–9; C. L. Tomlins and A. J. King, 'Introduction: labor, law and history' in Tomlins and King (eds), *Labor Law in America: Historical and Critical Essays* (Baltimore, 1992), 2–3.

[26] Grossberg, 'Social history update', *op. cit.*, 196.

THE DIMENSIONS OF LABOUR LAW HISTORY

Structure

In *Belated Feudalism: Labor, the Law, and Liberal Development in the United States*, Karen Orren's founding image neatly summarizes the world of difference separating the labour law history of the last few years from the new legal history of the Wisconsin school. Writing of Hurst's seminal work, *Law and the Conditions of Freedom in the Nineteenth Century United States*, Orren notes how Hurst stressed nineteenth-century law's '"release of the energy", human and material, for industrial development'. From labour's perspective, however, the appropriate metaphor is one of constraint. 'Where Hurst sees a "flow" of resources, I see foundations, molds, fixed boundaries, barriers', with law as 'a great iron chain, twisting around and between individual enterprises and encircling the business system as a whole'.[27] The architectonic quality of the metaphors is very deliberate. Orren sees nineteenth-century labour law as a structure of ideas imprisoning American labour in a remote past, a metaphysical chain forged from feudal precedents that defined the performance of labour as a social relation of mastery and servitude. Her subject is both the chain itself and its eventual destruction, in the early twentieth century, at the hands of organized labour. In her analysis, that destruction signifies the expulsion of the last remnant of feudalism from modern society.

Basic to Orren's argument is her claim that the liberal state in America is of far more recent origin than the customary focus on its revolutionary 'founding' maintains. While the American Revolution and the Constitution confirmed liberalism's ascendancy as the dominant political ideology of market capitalism, remnants of feudalism continued to define some of the most essential elements of political and social life throughout the nineteenth century. Foremost among these was the law of master and servant – the foundation of the employment relationship, and as such the essential building block of America's developing market society.[28] Lines of English legal precedents and doctrines stretching back to the fourteenth and fifteenth centuries supplied American law's 'intellectual structure'.[29] At the end of the nineteenth century, master and servant law still stood dominant, the expression of a continuous unbroken line of Anglo-American legal regulation of labour stretching back more than six hundred years.

Against this backdrop, Orren casts the organized labour movement's epic struggles for collective bargaining in the fifty years after 1870 as a liberal rebellion aimed at replacing master and servant law's prescriptive structure of labour regulation with the social relations of voluntary action. As such, labour's rebellion was in its own right a decisive move in the distancing of modernity from feudalism. But labour's rebellion had wider implications, for the law's role in labour struggles helped draw attention to the other significant 'remnant' of feudalism embedded (and acknowledged) in the structure of the American state, namely the judiciary itself and its resort to the common law as an autonomous instrument of governance. By rebelling against master and servant law as a structure of labour regulation, the labour movement also created the conditions for a

[27] Orren, *op. cit.*, 79.
[28] *ibid.*, 68.
[29] *ibid.*, 121. See also 12, 68–71.

reordering of the judiciary's role in the American state and thus for a reordering of the structure of the American state itself. Not fulfilled until the 1930s, the promise of this institutional revolution was finally revealed in the New Deal's creation of a 'fully legislative polity' in America, and in the courts' acquiescence in that transformation. Fundamentally, labour's historical project was the creation of a truly liberal state, and it succeeded.

As all this should indicate, Orren conceives labour law history as a central element to the macro-structural and institutional history of the dawning of the modern world. Indeed, Orren considers anything conceived on less than a several-century sweep almost undeserving of the name history because by definition lacking in 'historical' perspective.[30] The desire to take a long view is not uncharacteristic of labour law historians, and it is welcome after so many years of labour/social history as micro-study. But the epic quality of Orren's account lends her commitment to *longue durée* argument a decidedly teleological character that skates over details in the interests of the larger development. For the sake of the contrast, Orren paints each side of the great divide of the 1890s – the 'before' and the 'after' – in primary colours. Take, for example, the central point of Orren's 'great chain of ideas' argument, her assertion of a seamless Anglo-American master and servant tradition. The point is established by an examination of the many English precedents used in nineteenth- and early twentieth-century American legal materials. These certainly underline that nineteenth-century American courts had resort to English law to govern the employment relationship. But it is less clear that seventeenth- and eighteenth-century courts did. Without that evidence, assertions of doctrinal continuity look shaky.[31] Similarly, once we get beyond the New Deal, are we really in a world of employment from which judicial defence of hierarchy has been banished?[32] In both instances, Orren sees historical development proceeding according to an iron logic that is resistant to ambiguity, contradiction or contingency.

The merit of Orren's account does not, however, lie in its details. Her particular achievement is that her account successfully establishes labour analytically at the centre of the study of the formation of the modern state. Whether one agrees with the contours of her account or not, one can be convinced by Orren's conceptualization of labour as the primary link between state, society and economy.[33] Labour is central because work, and authority over the process of performing work, is the basis for the organization of society and the institutions of government. Hence, legal regulation protective of the structures of authority constitutive of work is at the core of social and state organization. Hence, also, the organized labour movement's attempts to disrupt the structures of authority constitutive of work, and the law that protected those structures, had major implications for all social and governmental arrangements.

Orren's argument for the 'primacy' of labour in the processes of state formation echoes classic statements of eighteenth- and early nineteenth-century liberal political and economic theory, such as the labour theory of value. By exposing how institutional and doctrinal structures 'positioned' labour in the nineteenth century's political economy,

[30] *ibid.*, 30–1.

[31] For evidence of discontinuities on both sides of the Atlantic, see C. L. Tomlins, *Law, Labor and Ideology in the Early American Republic* (Cambridge, 1993).

[32] For an analysis of the expectations and obligations carried into the modern employment contract from master and servant law, see Atleson, *op. cit.*

[33] See, generally, Orren, *op. cit.*, 19–28.

however, Orren's historical analysis effectively denaturalizes the meaning of labour in those theories. In so doing (and in a way this is an odd outcome, for both in conception and in execution this is a profoundly whiggish book) Orren's history shows up the fundamental law-dependency, and thus the contingency, of labour's meaning. *Belated Feudalism*'s core concern is to demonstrate labour's centrality to the transformative creation of the modern state, but it also hints at the returns that may be gained from exploring how labour law doctrine situates labour in relation to other social, political and economic institutions.

Meanings

Conceiving labour law history as a history of contingent meanings, contending ideologies or discourses, and of the differrent ways these situate their subjects, is at best secondary to Orren's project. It is, however, central to Robert Steinfeld's. Thus, where Orren seeks to understand labour law primarily in terms of its relationship to the transformation of state structure, Steinfeld's *The Invention of Free Labor: The Employment Relation in English and American Law and Culture, 1350–1870* is more directly an examination of the shifting meanings that law imposes upon labour and the performers of labour, their modes of composition and their consequences. There are similarities. Like Orren, Steinfeld's subject is the birth of liberal modernity in the transition from feudalism. Like Orren, he sees this primarily in terms of succession – one meaning for labour succeeding another – rather than competition. Like Orren, too, he stresses the agency of working people as active participants in achieving the transformation he describes. On the other hand, Orren and Steinfeld disagree substantially on the timing of modernity's emergence, and hence on how to interpret it: whereas she postpones the decisive moments to the early twentieth century and associates them with structural changes in the state, for Steinfeld this is an early nineteenth-century development intimately associated with a revolution in concepts.

The Invention of Free Labor argues that the prevailing view of labour's place in American history is founded on a pervasive misunderstanding. By Steinfeld's reckoning, most historians have assumed the normativity of self-possession, or personal freedom, in employment. But such liberal-legal philosphical ideals are contingent and problematic creations of revolutions in political culture and popular imagination, not constant, metahistorical attributes of persons. The 'free' employment relation is not a norm at all, but the product of a major intellectual transformation played out over the course of the eighteenth century and not finally realized in legal discourse until the early years of the republic.

Neither in England nor in America, Steinfeld argues, does it make sense to think of labour freedom as a social norm at any time prior to the nineteenth century. In early modern England labour meant service, the alienation of rights over one's capacity to labour. Those rights, and the actual performance of labour, were defined by the (profoundly non-liberal) law of master and servant, whose most notable characteristic was denial, through the application of criminal restraints, that the labourer enjoyed freedom to depart service at will. The socio-legal bases of the master/servant relationship were various: *jurisdictional* right, as in the ancient vesting of magisterial authority over dependants in the head of a household; or *proprietorial* right, as in the claim of an employer to enjoy exclusive control of an employee's performance as an enforceable property right; or *community* right, as in the claim (manifested, for example, in wage and price assessment) that labour was a valuable resource crucial to the common welfare. But whatever the justification, law enforced unfreedom as a routine incident.

From this perspective, the colonial American innovation of voluntary indentured servitude – always recognized as 'unfree' labour by historians, but considered 'exceptional' – becomes simply one more variation on a universal theme of unfreedom. And, although somewhat freer in practice, Steinfeld concludes that wage labour in colonial America also fell within English master and servant law's constraints. Nor did the burgeoning conception of self-possession ('possessive individualism') make much difference, even when it began to stimulate a gradual reimagination of the individual in seventeenth- and eighteenth-century Anglo-American thought. Not until after the Revolution, animated in particular by burgeoning artisanal discussion of the meanings of citizenship, suffrage and slavery, did Americans for the first time begin to draw real legal-institutional distinctions between 'unfree' and 'free' labour. Free labour became synonymous with civic capacity, its mark the labourer's complete control over its disposal, conveniently summarized as mobility at will; traditional restraints came to be identified with those enjoying less than complete civic capacity. In this way freedom became the paradigm of labour, while continuing forms of unfreedom became associated with a series of increasingly distinct categories now located 'outside' labour law, peopled by those who did not possess characteristics (whiteness, adulthood and maleness) associated with freedom – apprenticeship, slavery (and later peonage), family (spousal/parental relations) and so forth. As for indentured servitude, it simply lost its conceptual moorings. It became impossible to conceive of voluntary servitude as anything other than a variation on slavery. The result was the disappearance of indentured servitude as a legal and social category.

Steinfeld insists that his is not a whiggish tale of change and progress. Free labour's invention did not put paid to relations of domination and subordination. It did, however, mean a fundamental change in the character of domination and subordination. After the conceptual revolution of the early nineteenth century, hierarchy in employment increasingly turned less on the direct possession of vested legal authority *per se* than on economic power. Elsewhere Steinfeld has argued that law is much more than 'a set of neutral background rules under which market actors are free to shape their relationships' with one another, for it is precisely law's distributions of power and meaning between and among actors that play the basic structuring role in their interactions.[34] But in his treatment here, law does in fact tend to retreat to the back of the stage. The nineteenth century's free labourer was to find compulsion relocated in the coercions of material need rather than of law.

As its title suggests, *The Invention of Free Labor* takes as an essential premise the artefactual quality of human institutions. Institutions have no inherent transhistorical attributes; rather, they are socially constituted. Law is one of the most potent mediums in which meanings are constituted because not only does it provide a reasonably precise language of constitution but also because it defends its meanings with sanctions. Indeed, in a very practical sense, establishing official meanings for social institutions and practices,

[34] R. J. Steinfeld, "The Philadelphia Cordwainers' case of 1806: the struggle over alternative legal constructions of a free market in labor' in Tomlins and King (eds), *op. cit.*, 20–43, particularly at 20–2.

and defending them, is precisely what law is for. But law is not a neutral in its construction of institutions for, notwithstanding its metanarrative claim to autonomy, law's own legitimacy relies to an important extent on its remaining consistent with the prevailing ideologies of its times.[35] The chaos of contingency hence yields to the congruence of rule. Indeed, in Steinfeld's hands, as in Orren's more structural account, this lends an almost tectonic quality to the shifts in *mentalité* that mark the passage of centuries.

Also like Orren's account, there is an air of inevitability about the story being told, which can lead the author to slide over inconvenient or conflicting details. For example, Steinfeld's, like Orren's, is an argument for Anglo-American continuity. He has to note, however, that what little is known about wage labour in the North American colonies would suggest that colonists were drawing explicit distinctions between free and unfree considerably earlier than he allows. Indeed, it may be a mistake to represent colonial labour law as a received element in an Anglo-American continuum, for available colonial sources contain explicit denials that English labour laws were ever authoritatively 'received'. This notwithstanding, Steinfeld remains committed to his early nineteenth-century sea-change, qualifying or excepting counter-evidence, or interpreting it out of existence.

Yet, as in Orren's case, *The Invention of Free Labor* is more fruitfully treated for what it is – an essay in interpretation and argument seeking to open up large questions for examination and analysis – than as an exhaustive attempt at resolution. Judged as such, the book succeeds as handsomely as Orren's, and in so doing again points up the wide potential reach of labour law history. Consider, for example, the proposition – for which here there is substantial support, both direct and indirect – that the law of master and servant be treated not as *ab initio* a form of law confined to employment relationships at all, but rather as the key modality of the regime of patriarchal magistracy that furnished late medieval/early modern state and society with its discourse of rule. Telling the history of master and servant law, then, becomes not an 'originist' telling of the foundations of the law of employment, but a telling of the common history of and relationships among a far wider array of productive and reproductive social institutions. Household, family, workshop, factory, farm, plantation; marriage, service, employment, apprenticeship, slavery, parenthood, filial relations – all may be united in the same history because all have in common historically shared legal conditions of existence as dimensions of exercise of or subjection to magistracy. In this way, labour law history enters a bid to become the history of society; not by allowing itself to dissolve into social history but rather by furnishing social history with a means of accessing in detail the incessant contest for power over production and reproduction that structures all social relations.

Consciousness

So far I have argued that recent scholarship illustrates labour law history's broad capacity to 'centre' labour in our understanding of Anglo-American social and political development, and that centring labour in this fashion offers wide-ranging analytical opportunities

[35] A. Woodiwiss, *Rights v. Conspiracy: A Sociological Essay on the History of Labour Law in the United States* (New York, 1990), 6–11.

once one recognizes the intimate historical relationship that exists in legal discourse between subjection to magistracy in employment and subjection to magistracy across the full range of productive and reproductive relationships that constitute society.[36] Without losing sight of these themes I want now to use another recent addition to the literature, Victoria C. Hattam's *Labor Visions and State Power: The Origins of Business Unionism in the United States*, to add a third dimension to my definition of labour law history's site – that of consciousness.

Labor Visions and State Power focuses on 'labour' in the traditional labour history sense of 'organized labour movement'. Charting labour movement development over the course of the nineteenth century, Hattam seeks a new perspective on the decisive organizational and political choices that organized labour made during the century's closing decade – the rejection of state-focused class politics in favour of 'business unionism' (characterized as a combination of 'antistatism and militance on the shopfloor').[37] What accounts for this marked contrast with the course of labour development elsewhere?[38] Hattam considers traditional 'exceptionalist' explanations – the alleged absence of an American radical tradition, the inhibiting effects of ethnic and racial diversity on political mobilization, the equally inhibiting effects of the established two-party system's entrenched loyalties, electoral laws and political machines – and finds them all wanting. The explanation, she argues, lies in the interaction between the unique bifurcated structure of the American state, particularly the enormous power granted to the judiciary, and the increasing salience in the labour movement of 'industrial' or 'wage-earner' class ideologies. Growing wage-earner consciousness after the Civil War put labour increasingly in conflict with a judiciary suspicious of its collectivist impulse. Labour found it could not win this fight because the judiciary's unique position in the state was secure from labour's attempts at political retaliation. Eventually, the organized labour movement foreswore securing power through the state and chose instead to concentrate on industrial militance: hence business unionism.[39]

Hattam's emphasis on the interaction of state structure and labour ideology makes her sensitive to subtleties that historians have missed. Courts policed working-class organization throughout the nineteenth century, but workers' relations with the courts changed over time. Rather than manifesting an objective logic of state structure or class antagonism, those relations were decisively mediated by ideology and culture. Historians have been too influenced by essentialist (materialist) conceptions of class, she argues, and have understated the salience of the ideational and cultural forms in which historical subjects express their own conceptions of difference or conflict, or by their silence register its absence.[40] Applying the lesson, Hattam's most basic finding is that labour's political culture in the post-Civil War period was fundamentally different from that of the

[36] For a more extended discussion of these possibilities, see C. L. Tomlins, 'Subordination, authority, law. Subjects in labor history', *International Labor and Working Class History* (forthcoming).

[37] Hattam, *op. cit.*, 26.

[38] Hattam relies on a contrast with English labour to point up American organized labour's antistatism; *ibid.*, 180–203.

[39] Where Orren sees labour's destiny as liberalism, Hattam assesses labour's successes against a more orthodox class agenda. Thus measured, she finds political defeat for labour at the end of the nineteenth century, not triumph.

[40] Hattam, *op. cit.*, 12.

antebellum years. This changes in consciousness explains the altered dynamics of labour's post-Civil War relationship with the state. Here, then, lie the 'origins' of business unionism.

The empirical spine of Hattam's argument is provided by a reassessment of the nineteenth century's labour conspiracy prosecutions. For most of the century, she argues, conspiracy prosecutions were the primary forum for interactions between the bifurcated state and American labour. This is not in itself a novel contention, but Hattam's emphasis on worker consciousness leads her to an original interpretation of the precise course taken by labour conspiracy prosecutions. Her most intriguing revision applies to the prosecutions of the antebellum period. Conventional accounts label them instances of class-conscious conflict, representing a biased judiciary's attack on a nascent trade union movement, but Hattam argues that the cases chart less class conflict than an ideological contest between differing conceptions of republican political economy (hierarchical, organic and centralized versus non-hierarchical, democratic and decentralized), a contest rooted firmly in late eighteenth-century political culture, not in the opening fissures of early industrialism. Rather than crush workers' organizations, courts sought to educate them in the ways of the dominant (organic) political economy. For their part, workers embraced organization hesitantly, thinking of it as an unpleasant and temporary necessity. Their ultimate vision throughout the antebellum period was a decentralized republican political economy of producers, not a collectivized economy of countervailing combinations.

After the Civil War, the character of action on both sides was dramatically different. Prosecutions were no longer educational, they were systematically punitive. For their part, rather than accept the courts' policing, labour organizations began to condemn it as an illegitimate abuse of judicial authority and campaigned for legislative intervention to curb the courts. Conspiracy was finally becoming the focus for disputation and political mobilization that labour historians had professed to see years earlier.

Hattam treats the altered post-Civil War history of conspiracy as a manifestation of an altered consciousness of class, itself reflecting a complex of changes in the course of class formation brought on by accelerating industrialism. But labour consciousness cannot simply be 'read off' from macro-social change. Rather, for Hattam, the history of the labour movement in the post-Civil War period is the history of a highly complex encounter between newer 'wage-earner' and the older 'producer' forms of class consciousness and she attempts to show how labour's different ideologies were manifested in different organizations and programmes. Organizations like the Knights of Labor that continued to see labour's future predominantly in terms supplied by the older 'producer' consciousness of anti-monopoly tended to follow strategies and articulate programmes that did not lead them into continual confrontation with state institutions. Organizations like the American Federation of Labor that manifested the newer wage-earner consciousness quickly found themselves in an antagonistic relationship with the state. At first they sought legislative guarantees for their right to organize free of judicial restraint, but the inability of those guarantees to contain the judiciary led them eventually to eschew politics altogether for voluntarist self-reliance. 'No one set of state–labor relations prevailed. Workers' response to the courts varied considerably both over time and across organizations.'[41] Consciousness

[41] *ibid.*, 16.

decisively mediated law's effectivity as a modality of rule impinging upon patterns of organization and class formation.

Aspects of *Labor Visions* can be questioned. Hattam creates interpretive room for her arguments by categorizing ideas or positions or interpretations according to starkly drawn oppositions or polarities. This can lead to caricature, not only of positions she wishes to criticize but also, ironically, of those she wishes to embrace. A particular contribution of her account of the antebellum period, for example, lies in its emphasis on the continuing salience of 'republican' rather than 'class' terms of debate to antebellum understandings of economic growth. But Hattam feels required, as it were by the logic of her argument, to go further and allege labour's willing acceptance of conspiracy prosecutions in the antebellum period. This is a claim as obtuse in its way as the romantic proletarianism that Hattam wishes to displace.

A second virtue of Hattam's account of the antebellum period is her insistence that historians revise their conceptualization of class so as to accord far greater weight to those whose behaviour and language they are interpreting: before drawing conclusions about the explanatory capacities of class, Hattam insists that one must seek to interpret historical circumstance in a manner consistent with the actors' own articulations of consciousness. At points, however, Hattam loses perspective on her own insight. Instead of historicizing class she substitutes an alternative essentialization of it by requiring that actors speak it in a particular form before its presence may be acknowledged. 'Class' and 'republican' languages become separated categorical systems. In her account of the post-war period, the contrast between organizational manifestations of 'producer' and 'trade union' consciousness also tends to rely on an explanatory strategy of sharp distinctions. Beginning at the level of competing 'narratives' or 'visions' of industrialization projected by labour leaders to mobilize working people, Hattam reads leadership ideology and formal programmes down into rank-and-file consciousness, local organizational behaviour and daily practice. This division of organizations and their members into internally uniform competing camps creates an overly dichotomized history of the labour movement and of labour consciousness.

A separate issue is suggested by the accounts we have already discussed. As Hattam acknowledges, her conclusions about class, consciousness, law, and the interaction of labour and state are based on the study of organizations and the law of organizations. The law of the employment relationship does not feature in her book. Yet this provided the conceptual foundation for much of what the courts had to say about labour throughout the nineteenth century. Karen Orren, for example, contends that in fact the ancient action of enticement, protecting the master's control of the workplace against third party interference, was the underlying wrong in all conspiracy and injunction proceedings against labour organizations.[42] Hattam's conclusions both as to the nature of labour's consciousness of law and the place furnished to labour in law do not allow for the way in which legal perceptions of labour were set by the terms of master/servant discourse, not a republican discourse at all but one of magistracy and subordination.

One may thus pick at the edges of Hattam's thesis. Yet its central conclusion – 'the historical contingency of the courts' power for shaping the American working class' – is of

[42] Orren, *op. cit.*, 122–35.

considerable significance for the project of labour law history. First, it helps counter what Fred Konefsky has described as the 'questionable' tendency of legal historians to 'elevate law to a central place in the cosmology of things'.[43] No less than its subjects, law occurs within a relational context the dynamics of which play a crucial part in establishing the terms of its effectivity in influencing behaviour and ideas. In Hattam's story, certain combinations of belief, action and institutional context gave courts (and law) strategic power to mould labour relations, others less so.[44]

Second, this same relational context reinforces human agency. Like Orren and Steinfeld, Hattam allows workers an important degree of agency, but does so in a way (through her stress on consciousness) that makes agency a subversive constant rather than a creature of particular 'strategic' moments of opportunity. Workers' relation to the state was neither invariant (that is, structurally determined), nor a simple reflection of underlying macro-processes of industrialization. Rather, it was 'mediated by different ideologies and acts of interpretation. Where class boundaries were drawn, which interests were pursued, and ultimately how workers related to the American legal system depended, to a considerable extent, on the different narratives labor leaders constructed of industrialization.'[45]

Language

It is liberating to argue that working life is at bottom materially indeterminate (or at least underdetermined), that outcomes are therefore open to different people's capacities to imagine and construct their own narratives of its 'facts', and that those narratives will inform the political and legal struggles through which ruling or 'hegemonic' accounts are confirmed or contested. But two questions appear. First, what are the conditions of a narrative's existence and of its admission to the realm of rule? Second, what is the nature of the ground upon which narratives compete? These are fundamental questions for labour law historians, particularly in light of the continuing popularity of Thompsonian formulations of the rule of law's capacity to furnish – institutionally and ideologically – 'a genuine forum' within which social conflicts might be fought out.[46] Our examination of them leads us to a final dimension of enquiry that helps define the genre, that of *language*.

The salience of language to labour law history is richly revealed in William E. Forbath's *Law and the Shaping of the American Labor Movement*. As in Hattam's case, the subject is the interrelationship between state power and organized labour. As attuned in his own way to the contingencies attending that relationship as she is, Forbath nevertheless comes to a more absolute conclusion. Law shapes. Its capacity to do so, moreover, is not constrained by consciousness, for consciousness is no less part of what it shapes than behaviour. In other words, law is more than an institutional process of 'regulation' in which courts moderate behaviour by the setting of metes and bounds; it is also an ideational process of colonization of other discourses. Law is the language of rule and all who would be heard on the subject end up using law's grammar.

[43] A. S. Konefsky, 'Law and culture in antebellum Boston', *Stanford Law Review*, XL, 4 (April 1988), 1119–59, at 1156.

[44] Hattam, *op. cit.*, 112–13.

[45] *ibid.*, 204.

[46] E. P. Thompson, *Whigs and Hunters: The Origin of the Black Act* (New York, 1977), 258–69.

Forbath's book is a second and deeper advance on territory reconnoitred in an earlier article, 'The ambiguities of free labor: labor and the law in the Gilded Age'.[47] There Forbath identified a distinctive constitutional discourse that, he argued, informed labour movement practices and attitudes throughout the post-Civil War years. Contrasting labour's solidaristic republicanism (free labour as 'the abolition of wage labor and the creation of a cooperative commonwealth')[48] with the liberal jurisprudence of the state and federal judiciary (free labour as individual freedom of contract), Forbath suggested that the existence of labour's constitutionalism indicated that law was open to multiple readings beyond the bounds of 'official' discourse, readings that were informed by, and that could in their turn inform, popular (in this case working-class) politics and culture.

Forbath's recovery of labour's alternative to *laissez-faire* constitutionalism was impressive. However, 'Ambiguities' was not without some of its own. After all, in the contest between these two 'deeply opposing visions of the future of the Constitution',[49] labour's jurisprudence not only lost and was forgotten, but when it had come to debate outside its own ranks it had been treated with ridicule. When the prime forums for legal debate and implementation – the courts – are structured to accord with the precepts of one party to debate (the courts' jurisconsular incumbents), the outcome of challenges to what the incumbent deems law from what it deems not-law seems close to a foregone conclusion. If law can be described as a field of competition between rival discourses, then, it is one in which professional juridical discourse enjoys a tremendous advantage. Its rules of formation are the rules of the game.

In *Law and the Shaping of the American Labor Movement*, Forbath appears to have arrived at some of these conclusions himself. Investigating the fate of the mutualistic discourse that he identified in his earlier work, Forbath finds that by the early twentieth century it had been all but crushed beneath the weight of a relentless judicial attack. Labour's attempts to implement its constitution through legislative protections intruding upon the employment contract were trumped by the courts, which mobilized their unique constitutional prerogative to determine what would and would not be 'law' in defence of their own individualistic discourse of freedom of contract. Attempts to legislate safeguards for organizing rights by securing anti-conspiracy and anti-injunction statutes met a similar fate.

Denied its own constitution, labour abandoned it to stand instead upon voluntarism – self-reliance. In Forbath's treatment it is the abdication of its earlier vision that is the essential meaning of labour's turn to voluntarism. Although represented by AFL President Samuel Gompers as a principled choice, voluntarism in fact meant a 'constricted voice'. It was a strategic choice made of 'necessity and grudging accommodation', keenly symbolizing the restricted range of options that law allowed.[50]

Law's hostility thus shaped the American labour movement instrumentally by crushing labour's earlier vision and by forcing it to adopt a strategy of organization and political action that denied it access to its most important strengths. And – in many ways the ultimate triumph – it shaped it discursively by robbing labour of its own language for

[47] *Wisconsin Law Review*, Volume 1985, 4 (1985), 767–817.

[48] *ibid.*, 769.

[49] *ibid.*, 817.

[50] Forbath, *Shaping*, *op. cit.*, 168.

protest and imposing law's own. Confronted by the unremitting pressure of court-designed 'semi-outlawry', the AFL progressively shed its nineteenth-century vocabulary of republican protest and state *action* for a law-inspired liberal-pluralist language of group rights and state *containment*. Ironically, says Forbath, it was 'the very intensity of judicial repression, combined with courts' broader institutional and ideological authority, [that] made the language of the law beckon as a framework within which to contend for relief'. Equally ironically, most courts then happily ignored labour's new rights talk, while archly sympathetic legal intellectuals dismissed it as altogether too naive – amateurish and gauche.[51]

Although Forbath finds law's influence on the labour movement to have been 'crucial and irreducible', he does specify some limits. Law, he tells us at the outset, is constitutive, not dictatorial. Embracing elements of social choice theory, Forbath argues that law 'shaped labor's strategic calculus' at crucial moments by freighting alternative courses of action with differential costs and benefits. Labour's choices, though always 'steered', were always rational. But rational actor models ignore law's ideology-effects. Law also steered labour's consciousness. So doing, law constrained labour's capacity to pursue modes of response arguably more effective than those imaginable within the terms supplied by liberal legalism's rights discourse, a constraint whose imprint remained into the New Deal years, and beyond.[52]

Forbath's closing observations return to the question of how to theorize law's effects, but offer a somewhat different slant. Revisiting 'Ambiguities', Forbath tells us here that law is open-ended and mutable, plural and open-textured, 'a tradition of discourse with divergent and critical strands'.[53] Readers may wonder whether the conclusion and the introduction are offering compatible formulations. Both, in any case, seem at variance with the intervening narrative, which tells a stark tale of labour's repression, defeat and colonization. Indeed, at its most crucial moment – labour's abandonment of solidaristic mutuality for voluntarism's collectivized individualism – this is not a story of steered choice at all. If voluntarism were labour's sign that it had abandoned its nineteenth-century vision under legal pressure, one might then expect to read of the beginnings of accommodation. But in Forbath's account law's assault continues unabated. Why should the AFL have persisted in its belief in voluntaristic activity when it seemed to make no difference, when, in fact, law's apparent hostility (its enthusiastic adherence to the labour injunction) actually grew? On the other hand, why – in light of that history – represent law as a discourse of multiple open-ended trajectories?

Shaping can be questioned in this way because Forbath refuses to conclude that law is bereft of emancipatory potential. 'Radical analyses of law and subaltern social consciousness cannot ignore the open-endedness and mutability of legal discourse. The language of law, like other languages about the social world, does not possess such immutable or intrinsic meanings that the mere act of speaking or thinking in it automatically binds the

[51] See, for example, Harvard Law School professor (and future Supreme Court justice) Felix Frankfurter on Andrew Furuseth's efforts to develop a 'labor' equity jurisprudence, which Forbath characterizes (accurately) as 'polite ridicule': *ibid.*, 167; F. Frankfurter and N. Greene, *The Labor Injunction* (New York, 1930), 207.

[52] Forbath, *Shaping*, *op. cit.*, ix–xiii.

[53] *ibid.*, 171.

speaker or thinker to a web of fixed associations, meanings, and values.'[54] Yet although that refusal leads Forbath to a conclusion that to a degree contests the history he has recounted, his reasons seem founded not on a faith in the ultimate morality of 'the rule of law' but on a much colder-eyed assessment of the ultimate necessity of grabbing for what scraps one can. For, like it or not, one cannot avoid law. Sober assessment of the circumstances under which opportunities might be prised out of it, not fulmination, must rule.[55]

Like the other works considered here, *Shaping* is as much an attempt to provoke as to conclude debate. The particular debate that Forbath wishes to start is an historically-aware policy debate, while the other authors may be more interested in interpretive issues. None, however, seeks closure. None of these works is an exposition of a well-worn paradigm, one more brick fashioned to fill a 'gap' in this or that pre-standing knowledge-wall. Each, instead, is bold, each to one degree or another is an experiment, each slices an original section through labour law for purposes of creating a history that demands our response.

This shared interest in opening debates is one of the field's strengths. It arises in large part from the attention that its exponents are giving to considering the issues of narrative and interpretation that they raise self-consciously, not as matters of fact or idiosyncratic opinion, but as matters of theory with consequences for contemporary action as well as perceptions of the past. Perhaps in this way, labour law history does after all have about it an element of family resemblance to the 'new' histories I surveyed at the outset – a willingness to be informed by its times, to look beyond history for ways of understanding what is found within it. But if that is the case, labour law history's newness bears little resemblance to the positivistic 'borrowing' and 'testing' of social science models that we encountered at the outset. The practice of labour law history is proving to be, rather, a means for the practice of social theory not on but in history, in a way that informs and transforms both. Labour law history gives its subjects a new presence among current concerns. That may turn out to be its most important contribution of all.

CONCLUSION: NOW WHAT?

At the conclusion of Forbath's narrative we find ourselves back on ground where Orren's *Belated Feudalism* also took us, considering the labour movement's place in the modern order, how it came about, and what it means. But what might look like a circular course has in fact been a spiral, for *Shaping* puts us off at a point distant from Orren's fully legislative polity. The New Deal state might have finally granted the associational liberties labour desired, but within the new order 'many of the old common law restraints on collective action' reasserted themselves, and have continued since to rule from the grave.[56] Indeed, one could hardly construct a starker contrast between two histories of the same subject, one study seeing twentieth-century liberal legalism as the fulfilment of labour's destiny, the other interpreting it as an imposition foreclosing a brighter, more solidaristic future.

[54] *ibid.*

[55] *ibid.*, 172–3.

[56] *ibid.*, 165–6.

To this extent, indeed, Orren and Forbath's differences over the meaning of American liberalism reproduce one of the classic polar battles of the 'old' and 'new' labour history.

The other accounts we have encountered here stand at intermediate points along the spiral between these two. Like Orren, Robert Steinfeld sees in liberalism the end point of a process of modernity's emergence from feudalism and recognizes labour's agency in that process, but Steinfeld tempers teleology with greater awareness of the ease with which asymmetries of power constructed in one discourse (the necessities of magistracy) can be reconstructed in another (the necessities of market proprietorship). Like Forbath, Victoria Hattam sees voluntarism as the outcome of a confrontation that labour did *not* win, but her stress on the relative autonomy of consciousness suggests that labour's imagination is not as deeply imprisoned within liberalism's narrative of industrialization as Forbath seems at times to suggest.

The variation here is in part a consequence of differences over how one interprets nineteenth-century American political history, in part how one understands what 'labour' should be in labour law history. As to the first, it suffices to say that readers of Orren and Steinfeld will not encounter republicanism during America's transition from feudalism, while readers of Hattam and Forbath most certainly will. This is a difference of fundamental importance. If one believes that during the nineteenth century republicanism represented an identifiable ideology that was distinct from liberalism and enjoyed considerable resonance among American working people, then an identification of liberalism as the labour movement's destiny (Orren) or as the embodiment, by default, of the full range of post-revolutionary possibility (Steinfeld) becomes problematic. Republicanism instead becomes a key to a distinct form of labour consciousness that is either an alternative to a wage earner consciousness (Hattam) or a constituent element of it (Forbath). To the extent that republicanism indeed lurks as a 'recessive radical strain'[57] in American political and legal discourse, its presence significantly disrupts the procession from feudalism to liberal (and, implicitly, social) democracy that defines 'modernity' and structures its conflicts.

The same split occurs on the second matter, how 'labour' is to be conceived as a subject. Orren and Steinfeld both understand labour in terms of work and employment. The labour law about which they write, principally, is the law of the employment relationship – the law of master and servant. Hattam and Forbath interpret labour to mean 'movement'. Hence they write primarily about the law of organization – conspiracy and the labour injunction – and about the place of law and legal institutions in the relationship between the state and the unions.

The latter focus is the more familiar and the more traditional. If labour law history is to perform the larger role that I have suggested for it, however, it must continue to move in the direction of the employment relation. Indeed, it must move beyond the employment relation to reconceive as 'labour' all relations in which production occurs and in which productive capacities are renewed. The overall goal of such a history should be to attempt a synthetic retheorization of labour as the primary object of struggle in American political economy and legal culture, and as the primary subject of the discourses defining that political economy and legal culture.

[57] *ibid.*, 172.

How to do this? I offer the following as one set of hypotheses: first, that all relations of production and reproduction are relations whose structures of power have been 'authorized' in some manner; second, that encountering and experiencing authority is the essence of what it means to 'labour', and therefore is the common factor in the lives of all people involved in relations of production and reproduction; and third, that law is society's most universal and compelling 'authorizing' discourse. Labour law history, then, becomes a history of law's authorization of power in social relations, a history of power authorized from specific standpoints – of class, gender and race – at specific productive and reproductive sites – the household, the family, the enterprise, the school, the state – and embodied in particular forms of situated experience.[58] It is a history of rivalry, for these standpoints and sites produce 'a teeming jungle of plural, contradictory orders, struggling for recognition',[59] whose multiplicity controverts orthodox legal discourse's metanarrative claim of law's objectively determinate content and consequent normative authority. But it is also a history of domination, for from those struggles emerges not anarchy but particular modalities of law that are chosen as agencies of rule.

Social history's greatest achievement in the last quarter-century has been its recovery of who and whom. But we still need to know much more about the constitution of their relationships, about the myriad 'ridings' that yoke who and whom together. Tracing the modalities of law will enable labour law history to tell us much about who *rides* whom. As important, however, it will also begin to tell us *how*.

American Bar Foundation, Chicago

[58] J. E. Grbich, 'The body in legal theory' in M. A. Fineman and N. S. Thomadsen (eds), *At the Boundaries of the Law: Feminism and Legal Theory* (New York, 1991), 61–72. The hypotheses adverted to in this paragraph are explored at much greater length in Tomlins, 'Subordination, authority, law', *op. cit.*

[59] R. W. Gordon, in 'An exchange on critical legal studies between Robert W. Gordon and William Nelson', *Law and History Review*, VI, 1 (1988), 139–209, at 181.

[25]

REVIEW ARTICLE

Writing 'Law and Society' Histories

David Sugarman*

W.R. Cornish and G. de N. Clark, **Law and Society in England, 1750–1950**, London: Sweet & Maxwell, 1989, xii + 690 pp, £42.00 hb, £29.50 pb.

Conceived over twenty years ago, this eagerly awaited text has been a long time in the making. While several draft papers were completed by Geoffrey Clark prior to his death in 1972, the vast bulk of the considerable material and writing that makes up this substantial book is the work of Bill Cornish. Without Cornish's assiduous commitment, this book would never have seen the light of day. Its appearance is undoubtedly an important event for modern legal history.

I

Law and Society in England, 1750–1950 (hereafter *Law and Society*) is a work of historical synthesis — much of it the finest of its kind to date — whose low-key presentation nonetheless demands our attention. Its ambition is dazzling: to explain the development of law and legal practice from 1750 to 1950 in the context of the surrounding political, economic and social climate.[1] This, then, is no antiquarian legal history but one whose aims are presentist and polemical. Its starting point is the continuing neglect of recent legal history within lawyers' legal history and legal education more generally. Thus, its title is itself a challenge, communicating a somewhat different vision of the enterprise than earlier, more conventional guides to legal history.

But the book aspires to more than the reorientation of legal history courses. Its ultimate *raison d'être* lies in its strong commitment to a liberal, contextual approach to legal education and scholarship. By treating law in a more systematically historical fashion than usual, the authors hope to contribute towards the broadening of legal education.[2] This recognises that legal history plays an important role in defining and legitimating the character of legal education and scholarship. From this perspective, legal history can and should be refashioned to take on the mantle of an all-purpose subversive, illuminating the connections between legal, socio-economic and political change, thereby enlarging and supplementing the study of law. Here, then, is a 690 page textbook that attempts to historicise in a contextual fashion those parts of the legal curriculum that other vehicles of liberalisation have not yet reached. In so far as the task can be undertaken, Cornish and Clark do it with a style and panache that can only be admired.

Notwithstanding its undoubted merits, this book also illustrates the considerable

*Professor of Law, Lancaster University.
I should like to thank Ronnie Warrington and Costas Douzinas for their helpful comments, Leonie Sugarman for her outstanding support and Bill Cornish for dealing with my questions with characteristic kindness.

1 p v.
2 p v.

pitfalls that await those bold spirits who venture to write general, 'law and society' type histories. For this reviewer at least, the authors' largely unspoken assumptions about the writing of history, and the means used to fulfil their laudable goals, obstructs to some degree what they purport to be doing. Thus, from time to time they accept highly questionable notions of the subject-matter of legal history, thereby unwittingly reproducing the values and conventions of the historiography and legal scholarship that they seek to transcend. Increasing the ratio of 'context' to 'law' and enlarging the references to the historical literature are undoubtedly useful; but they cannot of themselves achieve the larger ambitions of this text.

II

Law and Society takes the form of seven major survey essays covering the great institutions and developments of the English legal system (Criminal, Labour and Land Law, as well as Poverty and Education, Commerce and Industry, the Family and Accidents). It is prefaced by a wide-ranging introduction which explores 'the relation of law and the legal system to society in general, and to the economy and the organisation of politics.'[3] The chronology of the introduction, and several of the other essays, is divided into two periods: 1750 to 1875 and 1875 to 1950. In this way, the Judicature Acts 1873–75 serve as a convenient marker to separate the two halves of the narrative in most chapters.

The book draws together a wealth of materials from a multitude of different sources, legal as well as social, political and historical, and one of its excellent qualities is the way these coalesce to make what is often a readable if highly compressed and detailed story. The text is clear and engaging, and although there are occasional lapses, its crafting has obviously been a labour of love. It takes you along the many trails of English legal history in a manner that produces a most stimulating read. The occasional references to the literature of the period add to the pleasures of the text. Usually the main issues of concern are identified and the reasons for their importance stressed, so that it is known what to expect and why.

Most books on legal history select and organise their material around those institutions that are distinctively 'legal,' thereby replicating the core categories and assumptions of modern substantive law. Cornish and Clark largely break with this paradigm. Instead, their work is more functional and problem-orientated. It is organised around topics such as 'commerce and industry,' 'labour relations' and 'poverty and education.' Thus, alongside the usual fare, you also find an illuminating discussion of law reform in the context of poverty, poor relief, education, debt, public health and housing. Not all the chapters are of the same high quality. But at its best, as in the chapter on land, the history of legal doctrine is treated within a framework sensitive to issues such as urbanisation, the exploitation of land and the control of land use. Here, perhaps more than in the rest of the work, is a pioneering effort to bridge and unite the all too often separate fields of economic, urban, social and legal history.

This broader approach is related to another admirable feature of the book. While the increasing importance of legislation is only grudgingly acknowledged in much of lawyers' legal history, Cornish and Clark devote a great deal of attention to legislation and those areas transformed by statute.[4] These new directions are aided

3 p 1.
4 cf the critical comments in s VI below.

and abetted by the authors' search for clues far beyond the realms of legal doctrine and legal literature. What in Manchester[5] (and even more so, Atiyah[6]) was a welcome resort to the larger historical literature has in Cornish and Clark become a considerable appropriation of and reliance upon the literature of administrative, economic, social and political history on a scale that is probably unique in any general text on legal history. In this way, the book alerts law students and teachers to the pertinence of a wide-ranging body of historical literature still often neglected in more traditional legal studies.[7]

In summary, Cornish and Clark provide the best general textbook on modern legal history in England — one that is unlikely to be superseded for many years. It is vastly informative (one can only wonder at the sheer quantity of references and materials that are packed into its compass), stimulating and, above all, it firmly debunks the idea that legal history might be boring.

III

With so much erudition, not to mention hard work, it may seem ungrateful to ask for more, but Cornish and Clark aspire to set 'the history of substantive law and legal practice in the two centuries since industrialisation beside the surrounding politics and, even more, beside the economic and social conditions which gave the law its essential significance.'[8] To what extent do they accomplish this bold and admirable objective? Given that no book of this sort could be comprehensive and that significant selection was inevitable, the larger aims of the book stand or fall on the 'how' and 'why' of that selection; that is, its focus, its success in placing law and legal institutions within a satisfactory socio-economic and political context, and also the extent to which it sheds new light on the relationship between law, society, economy and politics.[9]

From this perspective, *Law and Society* is likely to disappoint many of its readers. As we have seen, the book covers a host of topics — politics, economy, ideas, education, class, property, contract, the courts and so on. Whilst all these have some relevance to and bearing on each other and on legal doctrine and institutions, the question of exactly *what* relevance often remains unaddressed. Why some topics and sources are included while others, seemingly more important to its general theme, are omitted — and why it tells the story of law and society one way rather than another — are left to the reader's imagination.

The reader might have expected some guidance from the lengthy first chapter to the volume, which is intended to 'lay a foundation for all that follows'[10] — perhaps a few concepts, some hints on how to understand changes in law, economy and society over time, and some signposting of the major historiographical and methodological debates, especially those that have dominated the field during the last 25 years. This chapter is the core of the book; and it seemingly accepts the

5 A.H. Manchester, *Modern Legal History* (London: Butterworths, 1980).

6 P.S. Atiyah, *The Rise and Fall of Freedom of Contract* (Oxford: Clarendon Press, 1979).

7 A separate Handbook is promised to provide further details on the primary and secondary sources for modern English legal history (p vii).

8 p v.

9 As Stuart Anderson put it, if a book of this sort is to avoid 'mere legal genealogy ... it cannot just catalogue legal ... change, it must also explain': 'The Lawyer as Historian' (1981) 44 MLR, pp 227–233.

10 p v.

need to address these sorts of questions. Thus, it professes to describe 'the relation of law and the legal system to society in general, and to the economy and the organisation of politics,'[11] and the connections between ideas, ideologies and socio-political and legal practices. Yet the sense of anticipation that this heady cocktail evokes is confounded by the time that one reaches the end of the chapter. Neither here nor in the rest of the book is there any sustained discussion of the relation between law, economy, society and politics. Similarly, the economic, cultural and political significance of law and lawyers receives scant attention. It is as if the authors believed that the facts speak for themselves. The minimal conceptual apparatus and the discussion of the historiography in this chapter are too limited and superficial to be really useful.

This can be illustrated if we consider one of the few general arguments in *Law and Society* -- what the book refers to as 'that most enticing of historical subjects'[12] — namely, the influence of ideas and ideology on legal and socio-economic change. This enthusiasm contrasts starkly with much of the more traditional lawyers' legal history, and is most welcome. Alas, the ensuing discussion is unduly confined. *Law and Society's* treatment of the relationship between ideas, ideologies and society takes two major forms. The first provides thumbnail histories of 'isms' such as individualism, utilitarianism, Evangelicalism and socialism, from which the authors briefly elaborate 'three recurrent dichotomies' which they claim encapsulate the leading ideas and ideologies of the period 1750–1950: what they term the distinctions between individualism and collectivism, between idealism and utilitarianism, and between a belief in the perfectibility of man and in his innate viciousness.[13] In fact, the bulk of the discussion here, and when the influence of ideas is considered in subsequent chapters of the book, concerns the authors' thesis that *laissez faire* and individualism were the dominant ideologies of Victorian England. The influence of *laissez faire* and individualism is one of the few fundamental themes of the book, and it probably constitutes its *leitmotif*. As the authors put it, 'We ourselves are of the view that "Laissez-faire" encapsulated an ideological attitude that for large numbers of people and those with real political influence, was a root position.'[14]

Now it is undoubtedly true that individualism and *laissez faire* were major features of nineteenth-century society; and it is a topic that has spawned an enormous and troubled literature. Nonetheless, for some time now historians have stressed the *ambiguities* of *laissez faire* and individualism. After all, the creation and preservation of a 'market economy' were in crucial respects sustained by the state: thus, one person's *laissez faire* was another's collectivism.[15] Moreover, during the last twenty-five years, a new history of political and economic thought has increasingly stressed that, both as an idea and as a practice, individualism and *laissez faire* were qualified in a host of ways.[16] In particular, alongside the values of individual initiative and self-help co-existed those of public responsibility, altruism, philanthropy, service and notions of the common good. Like the idea of individual self-

11 p 1.

12 p 1.

13 pp 60–61. For a persuasive criticism of the tendency to think of ideologies in terms of 'isms,' see J.B. Thompson's excellent study of *Ideology and Modern Culture* (Cambridge: Polity, 1990) pp 5–27.

14 p 64.

15 K. Polanyi, *The Great Transformation* (Boston: Beacon Press, 1944) pp 135–150; B. Supple, 'The State and the Industrial Revolution, 1700–1914' in C.M. Cipolla (ed), *The Fontana Economic History of Europe*, vol 3 (Glasgow: Fontana, 1973) pp 314–315.

16 A.J. Taylor, *Laissez-faire and State Intervention in Nineteenth-Century Britain* (London: Macmillan, 1972).

interest, these values had their roots in a rich body of eighteenth-century thought sustained in part by Continental notions of natural law, civic humanism and various religious creeds which, especially through the vehicle of the Scottish Enlightenment, had a significant influence on high Victorian culture. In short, this recent work has significantly challenged a historiographical tradition that treated eighteenth-century political and economic thought as the story of the rise of liberal individualism.[17]

This more complex notion of individualism parallels the work of social historians who have rejected the treatment of middle-class culture as Philistine, puritanical, atomistic and only interested in profit. Instead, social historians are stressing the manifold cultural institutions and practices of the middle classes, and the diversity of cultures within the middle and working classes.[18] For instance, the 'first generation of cotton masters in Lancashire was characterised by a striking variety of social and educational backgrounds, and every kind of religious and political avocation. They were as likely to be true-blue English Tories of the old school, port-drinking, fox-hunting, Anglican traditionalists as puritanical, Nonconformist, Liberal reformists . . . Success as an entrepreneur in the early textile industry clearly did not depend upon a particular kind of entrepreneurial mentality or "enterprise culture".'[19] Similarly, Victorian society exhibited what one historian has called a 'vast infrastructure of socialism' in the form of labour churches, the co-operative movement, socialist Sunday schools and clubs.[20] This approach rejects the notion that ideas, ideologies and practices are 'individualistic' or 'collectivist' in themselves. Instead, the extent to which ideas, ideologies and actions can be characterised as individualistic or collectivist will depend on the ways in which they were used and understood in specific historical contexts.[21] From these perspectives, the story told by *Law and Society* is less a story of a transformation from individualism to collectivism than of shifting strategies to deal with those factors that helped to remake society, such as the extension of the franchise and changes in ideas, changes that were powerfully accelerated by the Great War.

Similar problems, both evidential and conceptual, arise when, as in *Law and Society*, individualism is also elevated as the dominant ideology within the legal community. The supposed individualism of the common law mind is largely correct; but it is of limited value as an explanatory tool. This is because the notion is so indeterminate that it could often embrace very different value positions.[22] 'Indivi-

17 J.G.A. Pocock, *The Machiavellian Moment* (Princeton: Princeton UP, 1975), *Politics, Language and Time* (London: Methuen, 1972) and *Virtue, Commerce and History* (Cambridge: CUP, 1985); I. Hont and M. Ignatieff (eds), *Wealth and Virtue: The Shaping of Political Economy in the Scottish Enlightenment* (Cambridge: CUP, 1983); D. Winch, *Adam Smith's Politics* (Cambridge: CUP, 1978); B. Fontana, *Rethinking the Politics of Commercial Society* (Cambridge: CUP, 1985); J.W. Burrow, *Whigs and Liberals: Continuity and Change in English Political Thought* (Oxford: Clarendon Press, 1988); B. Hilton, *The Age of Atonement* (Oxford: Clarendon Press, 1988).

18 P. Joyce, *Work, Society and Politics* (London: Methuen, 1982); L. Davidoff and C. Hall, *Family Fortunes: Men and Women of the English Middle Class, 1780–1850* (London: Hutchinson, 1987); J. Woolf and J. Seed (eds), *The Culture of Capital* (Manchester: MUP, 1988); F.M.L. Thompson, *The Rise of Respectable Society: A Social History of Victorian Britain, 1830–1900* (London: Fontana, 1988).

19 J. Seed and J. Woolf, 'Introduction' in J. Woolf and J. Seed (eds), *ibid* pp 5–6.

20 R.J. Morris, 'Clubs, Societies and Associations' in F.M.L. Thompson (ed), *The Cambridge Social History of Britain, 1750–1950*, vol II (Cambridge: CUP, 1990) p 230.

21 D. Sugarman, 'Texts, Contexts and Interpretative Communities' in C. Joerges and D.M. Trubek (eds), *Critical Legal Thought: An Anglo-German Debate* (Baden-Baden: Nomos, 1989) pp 39–48.

22 S. Hedley, '"Superior Knowledge or Revelation': An Approach to Modern Legal History' (1987) 18 *Anglo-American L Rev*, pp 177–200. As Hedley shows, some of the recent work on the importance of freedom of contract within the legal community tends to underestimate the difficulties of ascertaining the values and beliefs of judges and lawyers, whose claims cannot be taken at face value. Moreover,

dualism' has become a shorthand which often obscures the complex interplay between personal, professional, religious, moral, economic and political factors. Why certain features of individualism prevailed over others in specific situations is something that has yet to be explained.

Moreover, it is surely too confining to limit the investigation of the common law mind largely to a commitment to *laissez faire*, precedent and, in the case of the Victorian judiciary, the 'desire to stand apart.'[23] In fact, the nature and scope of legal professionalism and the mindset of the legal community were more complex, contradictory and contested. Were lawyers independent of particular interests or dependent upon particular interests? Gentlemen with privileges and duties or men of business? Scientists or practitioners? Guardians of the public interest or of private interests? Aristocratic and anti-commercial or contractual and self-interested? Officers of the court or the hired hands of the client? The power and legitimacy of the profession depended, in part, upon how these contradictory images and discourses were synthesised and delineated, both within the profession and in its relation to society.[24] What were the presuppositions and conditions which caused lawyers to elevate social, moral and status concerns over immediate financial advantage (and *vice versa*) when determining the nature and parameters of their work? After all, barristers did not have to scorn the notion of a direct, contractual relationship with their clients; and solicitors need not have spurned accountancy, tax planning and so on, thereby creating a vacuum filled by accountants and banks.[25] The undoubted influence of *laissez faire* and individualism is no substitute for the greater historical specificity required in the analysis of such issues.

For broader and richer accounts of the common law mind, one will have to turn to Pocock's celebrated study of the insular, anti-historical and anti-intellectual discourses of the common law in the seventeenth century — a *mentalité* which, he claims, established the continuity and perfection of the common law (and of the English nation) by way of a quasi-religious or mystical process of law finding and application.[26] To this might be added Dawson's stress on the importance of the oral tradition of legal argumentation in England; and the work of Clanchy and Goodrich on the significance of the shift from oral to written communication for the power and authority of the legal community.[27] Finally, Arthurs' work on the

the conflation of legal thought with individualism is often grounded in the (unspoken) assumption that the legal community was more homogenous than was actually the case.

23 *Law and Society*, p 71.

24 D. Sugarman, 'Lawyers and Business in England, 1750–1914' in C. Wilton (ed), *'Without the Law': Lawyers and Business in Canada* (Toronto: Butterworths, 1991) pp 437–479.

25 D. Sugarman, *ibid*; A. Abbott, *The System of Professions* (Chicago: University of Chicago Press, 1988) pp 23–26, 202–205.

26 J.G.A. Pocock, *The Ancient Constitution and the Feudal Law* (Cambridge: CUP, 2nd ed, 1987) pp 255–305. There is now a growing body of research stressing the extent and importance of a knowledge of the civil law among judges and lawyers in early modern and modern England; and its influence on judicial decision making is beginning to be explored: see, for example, B. Levack, *The Civil Lawyers of England, 1603–1641* (Oxford: OUP, 1973); D.R. Coquilette, *The Civilian Writers of Doctors' Commons, London* (Berlin: Duncker & Humblot, 1988); and A.W.B. Simpson, 'Innovation in Nineteenth-Century Contract Law' (1975) 91 LQR, pp 247–262. *Law and Society* is silent on both the persistent and important influence of Continental ideas, and also the significance of England's role as the centre of a large imperial Empire for law and legal institutions. As a result, legal thought and practice appear even more parochial than was actually the case.

27 J.P. Dawson, *The Oracles of the Law* (Ann Arbor: University of Michigan Law School, 1968) pp 1–99; M.T. Clanchy, *From Memory to Written Record* (London: Edward Arnold, 1979); P. Goodrich, *Languages of Law* (London: Weidenfeld and Nicolson, 1990). See also W.T. Murphy, 'The Oldest Social Science?' (1991) 54 MLR, pp 182–215 and D. Sugarman, '"A Hatred of Disorder": Legal Science, Liberalism and Imperialism' in P. Fitzpatrick (ed), *Dangerous Supplements: Resistance and Renewal in Jurisprudence* (London: Pluto Press, 1991) pp 34–67.

dogma of 'legal centralism' in Victorian England clarifies that vein of the common law mind which assumes that only the courts and lawyers are the proper institutions for dealing with the law, with its corresponding tendency to deprecate or ignore other forms of ordering and organisation in society.[28]

Although there is no sustained discussion of the subject, it is clear that the authors treat law as separate from and secondary to society but determined by it. Thus, the book 'sets the history of . . . law . . . *beside* the *surrounding* politics and, even more, *beside* the economic and social conditions which gave the law its *essential* significance.'[29] Similarly, it explores legal history '*within* the economy and society which generated them.'[30] Now, this way of talking about law and society — with its separation of law and society, and its assumption that the major influences shaping law are located somewhere outside of and prior to law — has a long-standing pedigree. It is associated with liberal and leftist traditions of history writing. In recent years, however, it has been increasingly reproached throughout the human sciences. It has been challenged because law, society, culture and economy are not external to each other; they are part of a larger common complex. 'Economy,' 'property,' 'the family' and any other set of basic social practices are in crucial respects constituted, defined and therefore sustained by the law; and it is difficult to see the value of trying to describe and analyse those relations apart from law.[31] In short, by adopting a one-directional treatment of the relationship between law and society and rather unitary definitions of ideas, ideology and classes, the relationship between law and society becomes disengaged in ways that are at odds with the aims of the book.[32]

If there is little sustained effort devoted to explicating the relationship between law and society in the first chapter, there is often less in the later ones. Interesting and informative though they are, there is too little discussion of the connections between substantive law areas such as contract and company law and the contextual material summarised briefly in the first chapter — 'society and law,' 'economic growth and law,' 'politics and law,' 'ideologies and democracy' and so on. In substance, then, the form of the book is such that 'law' and 'society' are often detached from one another. The relevance, if any, of the contextual material in chapter one for the remainder of the book is never systematically explored.

28 H.W. Arthurs, *'Without the Law': Administrative Justice and Legal Pluralism in Nineteenth-Century England* (Toronto: University of Toronto Press, 1985).

29 p v, my emphasis.

30 p 1, my emphasis.

31 E.P. Thompson, *The Poverty of Theory* (London: Merlin, 1978) p 96. On the need for legal historians to escape from the confines of evolutionist and functionalist history writing, see D. Sugarman and G.R. Rubin, 'Towards a New History of Law and Material Society in England, 1750–1914' in G.R. Rubin and D. Sugarman (eds), *Law, Economy and Society, 1750–1914: Essays in the History of English Law* (Abingdon: Professional Books, 1984) esp pp 121–123; see also R.W. Gordon, 'Critical Legal Histories' (1984) 36 *Stanford LR*, pp 57–126.

32 cf the discussion of Hay's view that the effectivity of eighteenth-century criminal law depended upon a mixture of terror and gratitude. *Law and Society* argues that Hay's thesis only really holds if one regards the criminal justice system as 'mere superstructure' (p 567). In fact, Hay's argument cannot be dismissed as merely mistaken superstructuralism. His point was that the terror–mercy balance was not superstructural but essential to the maintenance of a propertied society which sought to rule without the continued need for a full-time police force, the direct enforcement of the army, infiltration by spies, etc: D. Hay *et al* (eds), *Albion's Fatal Tree* (London: Allen Lane, 1975) Ch 1.

IV

Writing a general textbook of the sort to which Cornish and Clark aspire is both exciting and daunting, especially at the moment. The last two decades have witnessed a remarkable renaissance in English legal history and it is the early modern and modern periods that have received most attention. This burgeoning interest in modern English legal history has been a cosmopolitan and interdisciplinary labour, involving many lawyers, historians and legal sociologists working and publishing in North America and Australasia as well as Britain. As the numbers of those working at the coalface has increased, so the boundaries of the subject have spread in almost every conceivable direction, and the number of publications, source materials, debates, questions and sub-fields mushroomed. The history of law in society has been transformed by this efflorescence.[33] Thus, today, perhaps more than ever, the writing of a general text on law in history encounters the inevitable 'difficulty presented by a moving target.'[34]

This expansion and transformation of research on law in history, and the fragmentation of historical writing that has accompanied it, mirrors what has been occurring on a somewhat larger scale within history generally, especially social history. Moreover, these changes have been qualitative as well as quantitative. The selectivity, omissions and interpretations of many long-standing unifying frameworks are no longer accepted. Revisionism is seemingly everywhere, and every historical sub-discipline has become something of a battlefield. Today, most historians have jettisoned the once dominant meta-narratives of history — the past as a journey to democracy or the past as a story of class struggle — and have opted instead for interpretative frameworks that are more particularistic, less teleological and which no longer reduce historians to mere gatherers of facts. For example, the traditional periodisation of the industrial revolution (1780–1850), the character of that revolution (a rapid shift towards large-scale factory production, urbanisation, secularisation, rationalisation and class conflict), and the treatment of the periods which both antedated it and succeeded it, have all been significantly rewritten. In contrast to the traditional story, a number of historians have emphasised the uneven, incomplete, contradictory and highly contingent nature of socio-economic change.[35] That some

33 D. Sugarman, 'Theory and Practice in Law and History' in B. Fryer *et al* (eds), *Law, State and Society* (London: Croom Helm, 1981) pp 70–106, and 'Taking Law and Lawyers Seriously' (forthcoming).

34 J. Burrow, *Whigs and Liberals* (Oxford: Clarendon Press, 1988) p ix, referring to the transformation of the historiography of eighteenth-century political thought.

35 M. Fores, 'The Myth of a British Revolution' (1981) *History* 66, pp 181–198; D. Cannadine, 'The Present and the Past in the English Industrial Revolution, 1880–1980' (1984) *P & P* 103, pp 131–172; E.A. Wrigley, 'The Process of Modernisation and the Industrial Revolution in England' (1972–73) *Jl Interdisciplinary Hist* iii, pp 249–260 and *Continuity, Chance and Change: The Character of the Industrial Revolution* (Cambridge: CUP, 1988); R. Samuel, 'The Workshop of the World: Steam Power and Hand Technology in Mid-Victorian England' (1977) *Hist Workshop* 3, pp 7–53; W.H. Sewell Jr, *Work and Revolution in France: The Language of Labor from the Old Regime to 1848* (Cambridge: CUP, 1980); C. Sabel and J. Zeitlin, 'Historical Alternatives to Mass Production' (1985) *P & P* 108, pp 133–176; C. Calhoun, *The Question of Class Struggle* (Chicago: Chicago UP, 1982); D. Washbrook, 'Progress and Problems: South Asian Economic and Social History, c 1720–1860' (1988) *Modern Asian Studs* 22, pp 5–40; W.M. Reddy, *Money and Liberty in Modern Europe: A Critique of Historical Understanding* (Cambridge: CUP, 1987); M. Berg, P. Hudson and M. Sonenscher (eds), *Manufacture in the Town and Country Before the Factory* (Cambridge: CUP, 1983); K. Tribe, *Genealogies of Capitalism* (London: Routledge, 1981). At more or less the same time as this body of work was developing within history, the writings of Foucault and other post-structuralists were using history writing to critique the so-called project of modernity and its associated notions of unitary histories of society: see, for example, D. Attridge *et al* (eds), *Post-Structuralism and the Question of History* (Cambridge: CUP, 1987).

institutions predominated over others did not necessarily reflect their moral or rational primacy.[36]

As the character and chronology of the nineteenth-century revolution in economy, politics, government and society have been subjected to revision and counter-revision, so the late seventeenth and eighteenth centuries, traditionally a mere prelude to 'the great transformation,'[37] are attracting much more attention. This valuable work has challenged in important respects the traditional characterisation of the eighteenth century (largely conflict-free, politically dominated by a tiny ruling elite and served by a small-scale and largely ineffective government administration). It has also posed important questions concerning the precise nature, extent and timespan of the changes in government, politics, economy and culture generally associated with the period 1780–1850.[38]

In criticising the old-style approaches to the period 1750–1950, historians have demonstrated that the traditional narratives are in some sense a construction or canon, without any secure legitimacy of themselves. The changes in history writing summarised above highlight the ways in which available alternatives and newly minted canons from hitherto marginalised perspectives — working class, feminist, black, Third World and so on — have been struggling to redefine the subject of early modern and modern history itself. This process of redefinition reflects and has sustained a greater critical awareness of the literary and rhetorical conventions of history and other factual and realist writing. But it has also loomed large as the basic assumptions, principles and methodologies of history writing and the status of historical knowledge have been questioned by, amongst others, Geertz, Habermas, Gadamer, Foucault and Derrida in ways which, despite their abstraction and jargon, are increasingly difficult to ignore.[39]

36 Sabel and Zeitlin, *op cit*.

37 K. Polanyi, *The Great Transformation*, *op cit*.

38 J.G.A. Pocock, *Virtue, Commerce and History* (Cambridge: CUP, 1985); N. McKendrick, J. Brewer and J.H. Plumb, *The Birth of a Consumer Society* (London: Europa, 1982); G. Holmes, *Augustan England: Professions, State and Society, 1680–1730* (London: Allen & Unwin, 1982); P. Langford, *A Polite and Commercial People: England 1727–1783* (Oxford: OUP, 1989); J. Brewer, *Party Politics and Popular Ideology at the Accession of George III* (Cambridge: CUP, 1976) and *The Sinews of Power: War, Money and the English State, 1688–1783* (New York: Alfred A. Knopf, 1989); P. Earle, *The Making of the English Middle Class: Business, Society and Family Life in London, 1660–1730* (London: Methuen, 1989). Cf J.C.D. Clark, *English Society* (Cambridge: CUP, 1985) and *Rebellion or Revolution* (Cambridge: CUP, 1986). See also two valuable essays by Joanna Innes, 'Jonathan Clark, Social History and England's Ancien Regime' (1987) *P & P*, 115, pp 165–200 and 'II Representative Histories: Recent Studies of Popular Politics and Political Culture in Eighteenth and Early Nineteenth-Century England' (1991) *Jr Hist Sociology* 4, pp 182–211.

39 J. Tully (ed), *Meaning and Context: Quentin Skinner and his Critics* (Cambridge: Polity, 1988); R. Porter and P. Burke (eds), *The Social History of Language* (Cambridge: CUP, 1987); P.J. Corfield (ed), *Language, History and Class* (Oxford: Blackwell, 1991); J.E. Toews, 'Intellectual History After the Linguistic Turn' (1989) *American Hist Rev* 94, pp 581–626; H.R. Veeser (ed), *The New Historicism* (New York: Routledge, 1989); D. Riley, *'Am I That Name?': Feminism and the Category of 'Women' in History* (London: Macmillan, 1988); G.S. Jones, *The Languages of Class: Studies in English Working Class History, 1832–1982* (Cambridge: CUP, 1983); D. LaCapra and S.L. Kaplan (eds), *Modern European Intellectual History: Reappraisals and New Perspectives* (Ithaca: Cornell UP, 1982); H. White, *The Content of Form: Narrative Discourse and Historical Representation* (Baltimore: Johns Hopkins Press, 1987); P. Ricoeur, *Time and Narrative* (Chicago: Chicago UP, 1984); M. Foucault, *The Order of Things: An Archaeology of the Human Sciences* (London: Tavistock, 1970), and 'Questions of Method' in G. Burchell *et al* (eds), *The Foucault Effect: Studies in Governmentality* (London: Harvester, 1991) pp 73–86; C. Geertz, *The Interpretation of Cultures* (New York: Basic Books, 1973) and *Local Knowledge* (New York: Basic Books, 1983); J. Clifford and G.E. Marcus (eds), *Writing Culture: The Poetics and Politics of Ethnography* (Berkeley: University of California Press, 1986); L. Hunt (ed), *The New Cultural History* (Berkeley: University of California Press, 1989); R. Chartier, *Cultural History* (Cambridge: Polity, 1988); P. Joyce, *Visions of the People: Industrial England and*

Fidelity to the sources remains a leading principle for historians, but it does not offer a way of interpreting them. Thus, Collingwood's famous aphorism that 'history is not contained in books and documents, it lives only as a present interest and pursuit, in the mind of the historian when he [sic] criticises and interprets those documents . . .'[40] has been taken up, enlarged and qualified in ways that have forced the historian as author, creator and interpreter to come out of the shadows. For the need to select not only which facts deserve attention but the interpretative framework which makes those facts coherent and meaningful requires the exercise of imagination. 'Ethnographic truths are thus inherently *partial* — committed and incomplete.'[41] The traditional exclusion of opinion in the name of objectivity and 'science,' and the pretence of authorial anonymity — whether in history or law — not only obscures the ways those knowledges are produced, but also makes it difficult to make allowances for their values when they are not declared. As the current controversy surrounding the character of the history curriculum in British schools (more dates, kings and queens; less on minorities and 'foreigners'?) underlines, history is a political battleground and also an important way in which we construct our national and individual identities.[42]

These new perspectives are not to every historian's taste. Indeed, it is difficult not to share the unease of many a historian when a few of the more *avant garde* proponents of 'newness' seem to abandon history's long-standing concern with agency, causation and context, or advocate that one history is as good as another.[43] Yet these new directions are too important to be ignored by those legal historians devoted to explicating the interface between law and society. This is not to suggest that every history book must labour the reader with long excursions on 'method' and 'theory.' On the other hand, it has become almost impossible simply to 'do' history. Legal history has to face the consequences of its own normative constructions; the lawyer's favourite phrase 'without responsibility' has no purchase here.

It is difficult to see how the authors of *Law and Society* can realise their larger goals if these problems and possibilities — especially in the light of the changed character of modern legal history, history generally and social theory alluded to above — are neither acknowledged nor self-consciously addressed, albeit in a preliminary fashion. For there are important choices to be explained concerning the nature, scope and subject-matter of the book — why 'this' rather than 'that' — which in turn shape its historical narrative. A little more openness or self-consciousness concerning these matters would undoubtedly enhance the book's cogency.[44]

---

the Question of Class, 1848–1914 (Cambridge: CUP, 1991) and 'History and Post-Modernism,' *P & P* (forthcoming); R. Young, *White Mythologies: Writing History and the West* (London: Routledge, 1990); D. Attridge *et al* (eds), *op cit*. The difficulty of understanding and recapturing the past has become an important juncture where history and literature meet, suggesting parallels between history and other types of writing: see, for example, Ricoeur, *op cit*, White, *op cit*, R. Barthes, 'History as Discourse' in M. Lane (ed), *Structuralism: A Reader* (London: Cape, 1970) pp 145–155; J. Barnes, *A History of the World in 10½ Chapters* (London: Cape, 1989); and S. Schama, *Dead Certainties* (Cambridge: Granta, 1991).

40 R.G. Collingwood, *The Idea of History* (Oxford: OUP, 1946) p 23.

41 J. Clifford, 'Introduction: Partial Truths' in J. Clifford and G.E. Marcus (eds), *op cit* p 7.

42 R. Samuel (ed), *Patriotism: The Making and Unmaking of British National Identity*, 3 vols (London: Routledge, 1989).

43 cf L. Stone's recent polemical note in *Past and Present*, addressed to those historians who 'wonder if history might be on the way to becoming an endangered species' (1991) *P & P* 131, pp 217–218.

44 See R. Smith, 'Does the History of Psychology have a Subject?' (1988) *Hist of Human Sciences* 1, 147–177, esp 148–152.

V

Law and Society is strangely silent about the authors' vantage point and how they construe what they study. It is a history book that treats the writing of history as though there were nothing more to it than the unproblematic stringing together of a narrative of what possibly happened. There is, for example, no elaboration of how they conceive the relationship between law and its context. While it is unusual for such issues to be tackled in traditional histories, one might expect a book concerned with challenging those histories to be more explicit and self-conscious about writing legal history. Indeed, its *raison d'être* implicitly recognises that the subject-matter of legal history is not unproblematical.[45] Yet this is contradicted by a rhetoric that minimises the role played by the authors in the construction of their text. Thus, the Preface modestly insists that 'it is only a work of survey and ordering.'[46] It then adds that, 'while the text seeks to point up the links between legal and related elements, it makes no attempt to supply a systematic account of political events or of economic and social change. It assumes that the reader has a working knowledge of such material.'[47] Here, the text, on the one hand, purports to explore 'the history of the legal institutions and doctrines within the economy and society which generated them'[48] but, on the other hand, negates this goal through its own self-imposed limitations. Moreover, the book avoids any substantial engagement with the debates concerning the relationship between law and society or the writing of history.[49] In these ways its 'objectivity' is textually constructed.

By pretending to be neutral, *Law and Society* inevitably masks assumptions far from neutral. By failing to explicate its way of 'doing' law and society history, the book is more vulnerable than the authors perhaps realise to the magnetic pull of those traditional notions of how best to undertake historical work which have proscribed and hindered the very 'law and society' histories that Cornish and Clark explicitly desire. In particular, there is the risk of slipping into a celebration of English ideas and institutions, an interpretation of history as human progress. Here, history becomes little more than a quest for the precursors of the present; and the present takes the form of a 'natural' reality. The period 1750 to 1950 is seen as a series of stages in the process of modernisation, or is measured against modern notions of rationality. From this perspective, change tends to be equated with progress, without attending to the way that change was resisted and negotiated. Our understanding of the 'otherness' of the past is thereby curtailed. The history of law and society becomes a mere sub-branch of the institutional history of the modern welfare state.[50]

Cornish and Clark are not unaware of the dangers of reading history through the proverbial wrong end of a telescope; indeed, they specifically advert to the problem. For example, in the course of the excellent discussion of the Strict Settlement they remark: 'On no subject is it easier to misperceive the earlier by the light of the later.'[51] Yet occasionally, that is precisely what is done.

45 Thus, the reference in the Preface that it seeks 'to remedy old neglects': p v.
46 p v — as if ordering and selection are neutral.
47 p v.
48 p 1.
49 See the references in n 39 above.
50 Thus echoing a long-standing tradition of English history writing, A.H. Manchester's pioneering *Modern Legal History* assures its readers at the very outset that, 'we can take considerable pride in both' the history of English law and its legal institutions: A.H. Manchester, *op cit* p v.
51 p 124.

It is the notion of increasing political freedom, something of great importance to the book, that best illustrates both its presentism and its partiality. The narrative here is one of gradual development towards a more or less satisfactory polity, where even the Public Order Act of 1936 can elicit the comment: 'From this time, police treatment of demonstrations became less noticeably partisan' — a statement which the book fails to vindicate.[52]

This tendency is most extensively displayed in the chapter on crime, policing and punishment.[53] The narrative of this chapter is organised around what the authors call the 'unquenchable flame' lit in the eighteenth century in favour of a new kind of punishment.[54] It is argued that, during the nineteenth century, the legal order became more civilised and humane. As crises arose so new laws were passed to solve them. The reader is left with the uneasy feeling that *Law and Society* has accepted the reformers' view of the world that, in the context of punishment, utilitarian and compensatory reactions to crime are good things. Perhaps they are; but the question is too full of doubt to admit any easy answer.

The problem of prison reform is one example of the spiral to which the endless efforts at reform leads: each new reform creates the conditions for its own counter reformation. Is the new regime of punishment significantly less implicated in social repression than the one it replaced? Within a utilitarian framework, punishment no doubt ought 'to fit the crime.' But what seems to have resulted is punishment almost as evil as the crimes which are supposed to be punished. All this testifies to the double-edged inheritance of the reform movement; that we cannot take its good intentions and 'reforms' at face value.

In an effort to counteract the implicit teleological bias of much of the older histories of crime, punishment and policing, a new revisionist historiography emerged in the mid-1970s. Here, the universal and liberating claims of the reformers are treated as paradoxical: irrespective of their good intentions, their humanitarian claims served, among other things, to justify a more thoroughgoing control of the individual. While some of this revisionism simplified a complex story, it nonetheless questioned the legitimacy of the reforms, exposing the extent and intrusiveness of the reformers' aspirations, in ways that have reinstated important questions of power and domination within the history of law and society. Moreover, it has enhanced our sense of the ways that 'crime' is a socially constructed category reflecting the particular anxieties and preoccupations of society at a specific point in time. This work suggests that we should pay closer attention to the role of law and legal institutions in the constitution of stereotypes and 'folk-devils' (like 'the criminal classes,' 'aliens,' and so on) whereby certain individuals become defined as a threat to society.[55]

Another valuable strand of the new revisionist histories is its increasing concern with the relation between changes in the criminal law, in particular the shift from a private system of prosecution brought by individuals to a public system of

52 p 616. Cf R. Reiner, *The Politics of the Police* (Brighton: Wheatsheaf, 1985).
53 Ch 8.
54 p 570.
55 M. Foucault, *Discipline and Punish* (New York: Pantheon, 1978); M. Ignatieff, *A Just Measure of Pain: The Penitentiary in the Industrial Revolution, 1750–1850* (London: Macmillan, 1978). For a critical assessment of the revisionist historiography, see M. Ignatieff, 'State, Civil Society and Total Institutions: A Critique of Recent Social Histories of Punishment' in D. Sugarman (ed), *Legality, Ideology and the State* (London: Academic Press, 1983) pp 183–211. See also M. Wiener, *Reconstructing the Criminal: Culture, Law and Policy in England, 1830–1914* (Cambridge: CUP, 1990). See also the discussion in s VI below.

prosecution dominated by the police, and the character of the English state. For example, it has been argued that changes in the ways that crime and criminals were understood sustained and were sustained by a new law and order state bureaucracy which were part of larger shifts in the nature and scope of state activity.[56]

What the new histories highlight is that the story of prison reform, followed by failure and new reforms, is a good example of the inadequacy of an implicit teleology. An insidious progressivism — that in some vague way things have changed for the better — has crept in, precisely because the book tries not to give itself any firm anchor point, any definitive or even provisional bias.

This reluctance makes it rather unsure of itself when trying to come to judgments on issues under discussion. Take the role of the Justices of the Peace, on which the authors rightly lay much stress. The book hovers between assessing JPs as goodies, baddies, indifferent mediocrities, ruthless servants of power, enlightened rulers and true servants of the community. Sometimes they appear as the right hands of the landed, only to reappear as the supporters of manufacturers and the middle classes. But the book also argues that JPs in the pre-1870 period '. . . *inevitably* reflected the values of the community rather than (sic) just those of the landed governors.'[57] No doubt they were some and all of these, but there is no way of deciding on the basis of what *Law and Society* tells us. The text sprays different viewpoints around the same phenomena, not because it is celebrating difference, but because it has not set itself any means for determining between different positions. Different ideas are set down, and the reader is left wondering what position is being advocated.

VI

At first blush, it may seem all too easy to highlight those topics that the authors have omitted. But on further reflection, such matters may aid our understanding of the book. For the selection or omission of certain topics *of itself* influences not only the definition of problems and specific conclusions, but also its more general interpretations. This is illustrated in the way that the state, state formation and regulation tend to be dealt with indirectly rather than head-on, while the history of constitutional and administrative law and the legislative process is omitted.[58]

56 V.A.C. Gatrell, 'The Decline of Theft and Violence in Victorian and Edwardian England' in V.A.C. Gatrell *et al* (eds), *Crime and the Law in Western Societies* (London: Europa, 1980) pp 238–337 and in F.M.L. Thompson (ed), *The Cambridge Social History of Britain, 1750–1950,* vol III (Cambridge: CUP, 1990); D. Hay and F. Snyder, 'Using the Criminal Law, 1750–1850: Policing, Private Prosecution and the State' in D. Hay and F. Snyder (eds), *Policing and Prosecution in Britain, 1750–1850* (Oxford: Clarendon Press, 1989) pp 3–54.

57 p 567 (emphasis added).

58 It is not that the state is totally absent, of course. It is there obliquely in the chapters on accidents, demonstrating the relation between private tort law and the state regulation of the workplace and, in the discussion of crime, the emergence of the welfare state and education. My point, however, is that given *Law and Society*'s goals, the book would be even more useful if it had addressed the relationship between state formation and legal change, including topics such as the distinctive character of the English state, the legislative process and the history of constitutional and administrative law. On the distinctiveness of the English state, and the issues that it suggests for legal historians, see G.E. Aylmer, 'The Peculiarities of the English State' (1990) *Jr Hist Sociology* 3, pp 201–220. Julian Hoppit, Joanna Innes and John Styles are currently completing research on eighteenth-century legislation which will illuminate the emergence of legislation and the legislative process: for a preliminary discussion, see J. Innes and J. Styles, 'The Crime Wave: Recent Writing on Crime and Criminal Justice in Eighteenth-Century England' (1986) *Jr Brit Studs* 25, pp 380–435, 420–430.

Thus, the many and varied efforts at 'the reformation of manners' and moral reform receive very little attention.[59] Yet, 'Drink and sex were the most popular pastimes of the working classes; possibly of all classes ... [and] law and government prescribed the ground rules ... .'[60] Zeal against drunkenness, public drinking, gambling, the popular press (especially when it was populist), popular sports and entertainments, blasphemy, prostitution, sexuality and obscenity, were just some of the many areas of life which justices, town councils, preachers and parliament sought to regulate, supervise or repress.[61] The great bulk of these efforts (none of which are treated in *Law and Society*) were directed at the working classes.

Let us take the examples of drunkenness and allied regulation of working class street life. Ordinary people encountered the state most frequently in the nineteenth century when they were drunk.[62]

> The penalties for being drunk in public were raised, reflecting the growing gravity with which the authorities regarded such lower-class behaviour: for London a fine of 40s (more than double a labourer's weekly wage), with the alternative of imprisonment, was introduced by the Metropolitan Police district in 1839 ... [The] appearance of uniformed police on the streets certainly led to [a] dramatic growth in the number of arrests and charges.[63]

The number of offences relating to drink and drunkenness comprised the single largest category of crimes. What we see here is a well-chronicled spiral. More policemen rather than any objective increase in the actual extent of drunkenness explains this increase in prosecutions.[64]

The second largest category of offences concerned the street life of the working classes:

> These were a mixed bag of offences: many were in effect created by the police themselves in exercising their virtually untrammelled discretion in applying ancient common law provisions against obstruction, nuisance, soliciting, loitering with intent to do a mischief, or suspicion of causing a breach of the peace; many more were created by municipal bye-laws against such things as street trading, street performers, street games and street betting; a few derived from general legislation ... Half or more of ordinary police work was concerned with street life ... The prevention or punishment of crime involving injury to persons or property was a minor part of their work.[65]

---

59 In so far as moral regulation is discussed, see p 33 (which alludes to moral regulation by church courts), and ch 6, which deals with poor relief and its alternatives.

60 F.M.L. Thompson, *The Rise of Respectable Society: A Social History of Victorian Britain, 1830–1900* (London: Fontana, 1988) p 307. This book and F.M.L. Thompson (ed), *The Cambridge Social History of Britain, 1750–1950, op cit*, illustrate the gulf between the subject-matter and conceptual assumptions of contemporary social history and those of *Law and Society*.

61 S. and B. Webb, *The History of Liquor Licensing in England* (London, 1903) Appendix, 'The Movement for the Reformation of Manners'; B. Harrison, *Drink and the Victorians* (London: Routledge, 1971); J.R. Walkowitz, *Prostitution and Victorian Society* (Cambridge: CUP, 1980); J. Weeks, *Sex, Politics and Society: The Regulation of Sexuality Since 1800* (London: Longman, 2nd ed, 1989); R. McGibbin, 'Working-Class Gambling in Britain, 1880–1939' (1979) *P & P* 82, pp 234–255; R.D. Storch, 'The Policeman as Domestic Missionary' (1976) *Journal of Social History*, pp 481–509, and 'The Plague of Blue Locusts: Police Reform and Popular Resistance in Northern England, 1840–57' (1975) *Int Rev of Social Hist* 20, pp 61–90; R.W. Malcolmson, *Popular Recreations in English Society, 1700–1850* (London: Hutchinson, 1973); L. Radzinowicz, *The History of English Criminal Law and its Administration Since 1750* (London: Stevens, 1986) vol 3, pp 141–207; J. Innes, 'Politics and Morals: The Reformation of Manners Movement in Later Eighteenth-Century England' in E. Hellmuth (ed), *The Transformation of Political Culture* (Oxford: OUP, 1990) pp 57–118.

62 S. and B. Webb, *op cit*; Harrison, *op cit*; F.M.L. Thompson, *op cit* p 329.

63 Thompson, *op cit*.

64 Thompson, *op cit* pp 329–330.

65 Thompson, *op cit* p 331.

The regulation of drunkenness and working-class street behaviour is but one instance of a wider phenomenon: namely, the role of the law in the construction of areas of social concern, scientific investigation and social reform, and the representation of 'the other' in society. For example, while London's expensive brothels were largely ignored by the police, police harassment of street prostitutes, especially during the operation of the Contagious Diseases Acts, resulted in substantial numbers of young and innocent working-class women being subject to intense police surveillance. 'In the same way that the "criminal class" became synonymous for the poorer sections of the working class, so "prostitute" became, in many instances, the noun to describe the women of this class.'[66] It is to this constitutive role of law, of law as a major political language, classifying and constructing the world, imposing order, defining hierarchy in the very marrow of society, which historians and social theorists concerned with the cultural and political significance of law are increasingly turning their attentions. This is not to claim that the law invariably changed behaviour. Heavy penalties did not deter drinking or prostitution, for instance. Moreover, while law and state might define the ground rules, it was not unusual for their actual operation to be left to local communities, religious and other voluntary associations and custom. This is to acknowledge the plurality of ordering and organisation in society and the ways in which the state had no monopoly here — which is another feature stressed in much of the new social history of law.[67] Law was not a top-down injunction but an arena of struggle whose impact was invariably subject to a process of continual negotiation and reconstruction, often involving a large section of the community.[68] This recognises the multiple ways in which the law was resisted, mediated and appropriated in practice, and the variety of institutions and non-institutions within and beyond the state legal order involved in shaping the meaning and effect of the law, and the competing meanings of 'the law' within any community.[69]

For example, from their very outset, the language and culture of popular radicalism were partly shaped by the conventions of the law and the narrative practices of legal argumentation. Here were alternative conceptions of law and politics — with their own notions of justice, constitutional propriety, civic responsibility and community — whose importance for the labour movement and party politics extended throughout the eighteenth and nineteenth centuries.[70] From this perspective, the 'public' or

66 C. Emsley, *Crime and Society in England, 1750–1900* (London: Longman, 1987) p 134.

67 J. Brewer and J. Styles (eds), *An Ungovernable People: The English and their Law in the Seventeenth and Eighteenth Centuries* (London: Hutchinson, 1980); D. Sugarman and G. Rubin, 'Towards a New History of Law and Material Society in England, 1750–1914' in G. Rubin and D. Sugarman (eds), *Law, Economy and Society: Essays in the History of English Law, 1750–1914* (Abingdon: Professional Books, 1984) pp 9–12, 31–36, 47–52; H.W. Arthurs, *'Without the Law': Administrative Justice and Legal Pluralism in Nineteenth-Century England* (Toronto: Toronto UP, 1985); H. Hartog, 'Pigs and Positivism' (1985) *Wisconsin L Rev*, pp 899–935; P. King, 'Gleaners, Farmers and the Failure of Legal Sanctions in England, 1750–1850' (1989) *P & P* 125, pp 116–150. See also A.L. Erickson's recent study of the tensions between the common law, equity, ecclesiastical and manorial law concerning the use of marriage settlements in early modern England. Erickson criticises historians of the strict settlement for concentrating on the common law and de-emphasising the other alternative legal regimes governing settlements which she claims were widely used by ordinary people: A.L. Erickson, 'Common Law versus Common Practice: The Use of Marriage Settlements in Early Modern England' (1990) *Ec Hist Rev*, 2nd ser, XLIII, pp 21–39.

68 J. Brewer and J. Styles (eds), *op cit*, and P. King, *op cit*.

69 In *Law and Society*, no attempt is made to ask what might be meant by 'law' in the context of the 200 year period chosen. The only concerted attempt to define the court process defines it exclusively in terms of the state legal order: thus, 'Courts are institutions developed by state authority to decide disputes on the complaint of one party and empowered by that authority to enforce their orders' (p 36).

70 J. Brewer in J. Brewer and J. Styles (eds), *op cit*; H. Cunningham, 'The Language of Patriotism'

'legal' sphere and the 'private' or the 'popular' sphere were not self-contained worlds, and some of the most exciting of the new legal history has been exploring the ways they were imbricated within each other.[71]

By largely neglecting the 'reformation of manners' movement, how the law was experienced by working people in their everyday lives, the role of law in forging political and social categories and identities, constituting and registering changing social attitudes and values, and the plurality of law and ordering, *Law and Society* cuts itself off from some of the best of the new histories of law in society, thereby reproducing the traditional divide between things 'legal' and 'non-legal.'

VII

Law and Society is a formidable, fascinating and frustrating work: formidable in its goals, learning and sheer hard work, fascinating in what it achieves, but also frustrating in the ways that, at least in some areas, its implicit theory misses its target so that law and society, legal history and history generally, remain estranged.[72] While it deepens the familiar picture, the picture itself remains largely traditional. Nonetheless, like the best history, even when one disagrees with its interpretations, *Law and Society* constantly informs and suggests, more especially by pulling together an array of historical subject-matter and references all too often kept apart within the disciplines of law and history.

In fairness to the authors, the foremost reasons for its limitations of focus may be largely pedagogical: namely, that *Law and Society* is conceived as a textbook, 'written primarily with the law student in mind' and, also, as the instrument for fostering more 'special courses devoted to the study of its period.'[73] Now, a general textbook embracing two hundred years of history cannot integrate in any detailed fashion political events and socio-economic change with law without taking on a size and complexity that abandons the very goals of the textbook form of literature. Certainly, the authors have done wonders to squeeze their work into less than 700 pages; and no doubt this helped the publishers to make it available in paperback from the outset — a decision that all students of modern legal history

(1981) *Hist Workshop* 12, pp 8–33; G.S. Jones, 'Rethinking Chartism' in his *Languages of Class* (Cambridge: CUP, 1983) pp 90–178; J. Epstein, 'Understanding the Cap of Liberty: Symbolic Practice and Social Conflict in Early Nineteenth-Century England' (1989) *P & P* 122, pp 75–118; R. McWilliams, 'The Titchborne Claimant and the People,' PhD, University of Sussex (1990).

71 See E.P. Thompson, 'A Grid of Inheritance: A Comment' in J. Goody *et al* (eds), *Family and Inheritance: Rural Society in Western Europe, 1200–1800* (Cambridge: CUP, 1976) pp 323–358. Several exemplary studies brilliantly illuminate the manifold ways in which ordinary people were involved in issues of law, justice, property, exchange and community in early modern France, Germany and Italy: C. Ginzburg, *The Cheese and the Worms: The Cosmos of a Sixteenth-Century Miller* (London: Routledge, 1982); D.W. Sabean, *Power in the Blood: Popular Culture and Village Discourse in Early Modern Germany* (Cambridge: CUP, 1984), and *Property, Production and Family in Neckarhausen, 1700–1870* (Cambridge: CUP, 1990); and M. Sonenscher, *The Hatters of Eighteenth-Century France* (Berkeley: University of California Press, 1987), and *Work and Wages: Natural Law, Politics and the Eighteenth-Century French Trades* (Cambridge: CUP, 1989). As regards nineteenth-century America, see W.E. Forbath's important and suggestive study, *Law and the Shaping of the American Labor Movement* (Cambridge: Harvard UP, 1991). This body of work is examined in my 'Taking Law and Lawyers Seriously' (forthcoming).

72 Perhaps part of the problem is that the book has been a long time in the making, and some of the discussion seems to focus on rather dated material. Similarly, with the form of the book: 'it has seemed broadly satisfactory to adhere to the breakdown of subject-matter and to more detailed sub-divisions within chapters which we settled upon long ago' (*Law and Society*, pp v–vi).

73 p v.

will warmly welcome. Yet the limitations of the textbook medium are also well known and, in recent years, law teachers have been choosing more adventurous forms of legal scholarship. The values of the student text — simplicity, brevity and comprehensiveness — may be inappropriate given the book's larger scholarly ambitions. And, as several commentators have emphasised, it is a form of literature which tends to encourage superficiality and orthodoxy and discourage the development of detailed or novel arguments and more reflexive forms of scholarship.[74] For example, the unremitting detail of the text would have been alleviated if the authors had illustrated their more general points by way of examples culled from everyday life. It is also a pity that no concluding chapter is provided to consolidate the main points of this vast panorama. In short, the book's intellectual goals might have been better served if it had been cast in the form of a collection of essays or case studies. Nonetheless, its lucid writing, its clear commitment to and enthusiasm for 'law and society' history and its unparalleled pointers to the vast secondary literature make it a valuable and much-needed addition to the 'law in context' movement and the effort to broaden legal education from within.

74 H.L.A. Hart, 'Dias and Hughes on Jurisprudence', (1958) IV *Jr Soc Pub Teachers of Law* pp 143–49; W.L. Twining, 'Is Your Textbook Really Necessary?', (1970) XI *Jr. Soc Pub Teachers of Law* pp 81–89; R. Smith, 'Does the History of Psychology Have a Subject?' *op. cit.*; D. Sugarman, 'A Hatred of Disorder' *op. cit.*

[Editor's Note: A further review of this book will appear in a later issue].

Name Index

* 9 7 8 0 8 1 4 7 8 0 3 2 9 *